Contents

Spark plug condition and bodywork repair colour pages between pages 32 and 33

Ford Escort Saloon Ghia model

Ford Orion GLX model

About this Manual

Its aim

The aim of this manual is to help you get the best value from your vehicle. It can do so in several ways. It can help you decide what work must be done (even should you choose to get it done by a garage), provide information on routine maintenance and servicing, and give a logical course of action and diagnosis when random faults occur. However, it is hoped that you will use the manual by tackling the work yourself. On simpler jobs it may even be quicker than booking the vehicle into a garage and going there twice, to leave and collect it. Perhaps most important, a lot of money can be saved by avoiding the costs a garage must charge to cover its labour and overheads.

The manual has drawings and descriptions to show the function of the various components so that their layout can be understood. Then the tasks are described and photographed in a clear step-by-step sequence.

Its arrangement

The manual is divided into Chapters, each covering a logical sub-division of the vehicle. The Chapters are each divided into Sections, numbered with single figures, eg 5; and the Sections into paragraphs (or sub-Sections), with decimal numbers following on from the Section they are in, eg 5.1, 5.2, 5.3 etc.

It is freely illustrated, especially in those parts where there is a detailed sequence of operations to be carried out. There are two forms of illustration: figures and photographs. The figures are numbered in sequence with decimal numbers, according to their position in the Chapter – eg Fig. 6.4 is the fourth drawing/illustration in Chapter 6. Photographs carry the same number (either individually or in related groups) as the Section or sub-Section to which they relate.

There is an alphabetical index at the back of the manual as well as a contents list at the front. Each Chapter is also preceded by its own individual contents list.

References to the 'left' or 'right' of the vehicle are in the sense of a person in the driver's seat, facing forward.

Unless otherwise stated, nuts and bolts are removed by turning anti-clockwise, and tightened by turning clockwise.

Vehicle manufacturers continually make changes to specifications and recommendations, and these, when notified, are incorporated into our manuals at the earliest opportunity.

We take great pride in the accuracy of information given in this manual, but vehicle manufacturers make alterations and design changes during the production run of a particular vehicle of which they do not inform us. No liability can be accepted by the authors or publishers for loss, damage or injury caused by any errors in, or omissions from, the information given.

Project vehicles

The main project vehicle used in the preparation of this manual, and appearing in many of the photographic sequences was a Ford Escort 1.6 GLX Saloon. Additional work was carried out and photographed on a 1.6 EFi version of the Escort GLX Estate and a 1.3 litre Escort Encore.

Introduction to the Ford Escort and Orion

The latest versions of the Ford Escort and Orion model range were introduced in September 1990. As with their predecessors, the Escort model range is extensive and includes a three and five-door Saloon, five-door Estate, soft top Cabriolet and Van versions, whilst the Orion is a traditional four-door Saloon with conventional rear luggage boot.

The power unit fitted is dependent on model. The options are basically revised versions of the engines fitted to the earlier Escort and Orion range, these being the 1.3 litre HCS overhead valve engine and the 1.4 or 1.6 litre CVH overhead camshaft engines. All engines have electronic engine management control to the ignition and fuel systems to provide greater efficiency and performance. The fuel system fitted is dependent on model and will be carburettor, CFi (central fuel injection) or on higher performance models, EFi (electronic fuel injection). A four or five-speed manual transmission, or a CTX automatic transmission option is fitted depending on model and all transmission types incorporate the differential unit to transfer drive direct to the front roadwheels.

Both the front and rear suspension assemblies have been redesigned to provide a high standard of roadholding and ride comfort. Disc front brakes and drum rear brakes are fitted to all models covered by this manual with Ford's anti-lock braking system (ABS) being fitted on some models.

As with earlier variants of the range, all models are designed with the emphasis on economical motoring, ease of maintenance and good performance.

Ford Escort Estate GLX model

Ford Escort Cabriolet model

General dimensions and weights

Dimensions

Overall length:
Escort Saloon	4036 mm
Escort Estate	4268 mm
Escort Van	4256 mm
Orion	4229 mm

Overall width:
Escort Saloon	1692 mm
Escort Estate and Orion	1690 mm
Escort Van	1688 mm

Overall height:
Escort Saloon and Orion	1378 to 1395 mm
Escort Estate	1394 to 1409 mm
Escort Van	1625 mm

Wheelbase:
Escort Saloon, Estate and Orion	2525 mm
Escort Van	2598 mm
Front track	1440 mm

Rear track:
With 7 inch drum brakes	1462 mm
With 8 inch drum brakes	1439 mm

Weights

Kerb weight:
Escort 3-door Saloon	901 to 1006 kg
Escort 5-door Saloon	921 to 1026 kg
Escort Estate	976 to 1041 kg
Escort Cabriolet	1117 kg
Orion	1006 to 1021 kg

Note: *The exact kerb weights are dependent on model and specification*

Maximum gross vehicle weight:
Escort 3-door Saloon	1350 to 1450 kg
Escort 5-door Saloon	1375 to 1475 kg
Escort Estate	1425 to 1525 kg
Escort Cabriolet	1525 kg
Orion	1425 to 1500 kg
Maximum roof rack load	75 kg

Maximum towing weight (braked trailer):
1.3 litre Escort Saloon and Orion	1140 kg
1.3 litre Escort Estate	1080 kg
1.4 litre Escort Saloon & Orion (carburettor models)	1160 kg
1.4 litre Escort Saloon & Orion (CFi models)	1200 kg
1.4 litre Escort Estate	1140 kg
1.6 litre Escort & Orion (all models)	1200 kg

Jacking, towing and wheel changing

To change a wheel, remove the spare wheel and the emergency jack supplied with the vehicle, apply the handbrake and chock the wheel diagonally opposite the one to be changed. On automatic transmission models, place the selector lever in P. Make sure that the vehicle is located on firm level ground and then slightly loosen the wheel nuts with the brace provided (where applicable remove the trim first). Locate the jack head in the jacking point nearest to the wheel to be changed and raise the jack using the other end of the brace. When the wheel is clear of the ground remove the nuts (and trim where applicable) and lift off the wheel. Fit the spare wheel and moderately tighten the nuts. Lower the vehicle and then tighten the nuts securely, to the specified torque setting (see Chapter 10 specifications). Refit the trim where applicable. With the spare wheel in position, remove the chock and stow the jack and tools (photo).

When jacking up the vehicle to carry out repair or maintenance tasks, a pillar or trolley type jack of suitable lifting capacity must be used and supplemented with axle stands positioned only beneath the appropriate points under the vehicle. The accompanying illustration of the underside of the vehicle indicates the jacking and support points under the vehicle (according to type). On Saloon and Estate models,

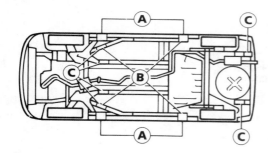

Underside view of the vehicle showing the jacking point locations – all models except van

A   Jacking points for emergency jack supplied with vehicle
B   Jack points for workshop hoist
C   Additional support points
Trolley jacks to be positioned under points B and C only

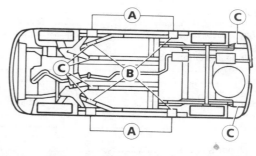

Underside view of the vehicle showing the jacking point locations – Van model

A   Jacking points for emergency jack supplied with vehicle
B   Jack points for workshop hoist
C   Additional support points
Trolley jacks to be positioned under points B and C only

Vehicle emergency jack location in the spare wheel well

Front towing eye

Rear towing eye

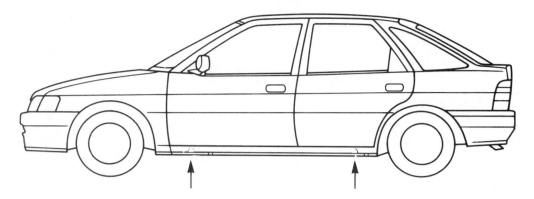

Side view of Escort Saloon showing emergency jack point locations

Emergency jack supplied with vehicle is located as shown

note that the vehicle must never be jacked up at the rear under the axle beam.

The maximum kerb weight of the vehicle must not be exceeded when jacking and supporting the vehicle. Do not under any circumstances jack up the rear of the vehicle under the rear axle. Never work under, around or near a raised vehicle unless it is adequately supported in at least two places with axle stands.

The vehicle may be towed for breakdown recovery purposes only

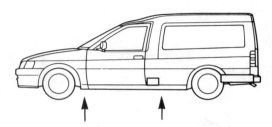

Side view of Van showing emergency jack point locations

using the towing eyes positioned at the front and rear of the vehicle (photos). These eyes are intended for towing loads only and must not be used for lifting the vehicle either directly or indirectly.

Models fitted with a catalytic converter must not be tow (or push) started. It should also be noted that fuel injection models have an automatic choke that operates in conjunction with the starter motor and therefore unless the engine is already warmed up to its normal operating temperature, it will not be possible to start the engine by towing.

If the vehicle is equipped with automatic transmission the selector lever must be positioned in the N position, the towing speed must not exceed 30 mph (50 kph) and the towing distance must not exceed 30 miles (50 km).

Before towing the vehicle, it is most important that the ignition key is set at the II position to ensure that the steering is unlocked and that the various switches (indicators and lights) are functional. It should also be noted that the brake servo action will not be operating with the engine switched off and therefore an allowance will need to be made for reduced braking efficiency.

Buying spare parts and vehicle identification numbers

Buying spare parts

Spare parts are available from many sources; for example, Ford garages, other garages and accessory shops, and motor factors. Our advice regarding spare part sources is as follows.

Officially appointed Ford garages – This is the best source for parts which are peculiar to your vehicle and are not generally available (eg complete cylinder heads, internal gearbox components, badges, interior trim etc). It is also the only place at which you should buy parts if the vehicle is still under warranty. To be sure of obtaining the correct parts, it will be necessary to give the storeman the vehicle identification number, and if possible, take the old parts along for positive identification. Many parts are available under a factory exchange scheme – any parts returned should always be clean. It obviously makes good sense to go straight to the specialists on your vehicle for this type of part, as they are best equipped to supply you.

Other garages and accessory shops – These are often very good places to buy the materials and components required for the maintenance of your vehicle (eg oil filters, spark plugs, bulbs, drivebelts, oils and greases, touch-up paint, filler paste, etc). They also sell general accessories, usually have convenient opening hours, charge lower prices and can often be found not far from home.

Motor factors – Good factors will stock all the more important components which wear out comparatively quickly (eg exhaust systems, brake pads, seals and hydraulic parts, clutch components, bearing shells, pistons, valves etc). Motor factors will often provide new or reconditioned components on a part exchange basis – this can save a considerable amount of money.

Vehicle identification numbers

Modifications are a continuing and unpublicised process in vehicle manufacture, quite apart from major model changes. Spare parts manuals and lists are compiled upon a numerical basis, the individual vehicle identification numbers being essential to correct identification of the component concerned.

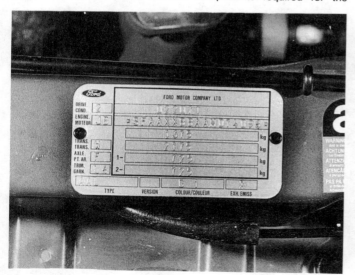

Vehicle identification plate

Chassis number etched into the floor to right-hand side of the driver's seat.

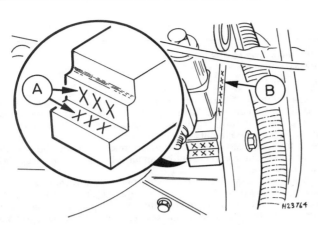

HCS engine identification numbers location

A   Engine code (side or upper face)
B   Serial number

When ordering spare parts, always give as much information as possible. Quote the vehicle model, year of manufacture, body and engine numbers as appropriate.

The *vehicle identification plate* is located on the top of the front crossmember in the engine compartment (photo).

The *chassis number* is located in the same position and is also located in a recess in the floor to the right-hand side of the driver's seat, access being gained after lifting the aperture cover (photo).

CVH engine identification number location is on (A) the right-hand side or (B) the left-hand side according to model and equipment

The *body number and paint code numbers* are located on the vehicle identification plate.

The *engine number* location is dependent on the engine type. On the HCS (OHV) engine, it is stamped on the front left-hand side of the cylinder block towards the transmission (facing the radiator). On the CVH (OHC) type engine the location of the engine number is dependent on the equipment fitted, but is on the exhaust side of the engine and is either towards the timing case end or the transmission end.

Safety first!

However enthusiastic you may be about getting on with the job in hand, do take the time to ensure that your safety is not put at risk. A moment's lack of attention can result in an accident, as can failure to observe certain elementary precautions. There will always be new ways of having accidents, and the following points do not pretend to be a comprehensive list of all dangers; they are intended rather to make you aware of the risks and to encourage a safety-conscious approach to all work you carry out on your vehicle.

Essential DOs and DON'Ts

DON'T rely on a single jack when working underneath the vehicle. Always use reliable additional means of support, such as axle stands, securely placed under a structural part of the vehicle that you know will not give way.

DON'T attempt to loosen or tighten high-torque nuts (eg wheel hub nuts) while the vehicle is on a jack; it may be pulled off.

DON'T start the engine without first ascertaining that the transmission is in neutral (or 'Park' where applicable) and the handbrake applied.

DON'T suddenly remove the filler cap from a hot cooling system – cover it with a cloth and release the pressure gradually first, or you may get scalded by escaping coolant.

DON'T attempt to drain oil, automatic transmission fluid, or coolant until you are sure it has cooled sufficiently to avoid scalding you.

DON'T grasp any part of the engine, exhaust or catalytic converter without first ascertaining that it is sufficiently cool to avoid burning you.

DON'T allow brake fluid or antifreeze to contact vehicle paintwork.

DON'T syphon toxic liquids such as fuel, brake fluid or antifreeze by mouth, or allow them to remain on your skin.

DON'T inhale dust – it may be injurious to health (see *Asbestos* below).

DON'T allow any spilt oil or grease to remain on the floor – wipe it up straight away, before someone slips on it.

DON'T use ill-fitting spanners or other tools which may slip and cause injury.

DON'T attempt to lift a heavy component which may be beyond your capability – get assistance.

DON'T rush to finish a job, or take unverified short cuts.

DON'T allow children or animals in or around an unattended vehicle.

DON'T park vehicles with catalytic converters over combustible materials such as dry grass, oily rags, etc, if the engine has recently been run. Catalytic converters reach extremely high temperatures and any such materials in close proximity may ignite.

DON'T run vehicles equipped with catalytic converters without the exhaust system heat shields fitted.

DO wear eye protection when using power tools such as an electric drill, sander, bench grinder etc, and when working under the vehicle.

DO use a barrier cream on your hands prior to undertaking dirty jobs – it will protect your skin from infection as well as making the dirt easier to remove afterwards; but make sure your hands aren't left slippery. Note that long term contact with used engine oil can be a health hazard.

DO keep loose clothing (cuffs, tie etc) and long hair well out of the way of moving mechanical parts.

DO remove rings, wristwatch etc, before working on the vehicle – especially the electrical system.

DO ensure that any lifting tackle or jacking equipment used has a safe working load rating adequate for the job, and is used precisely as recommended by the manufacturer.

DO keep your work area tidy – it is only too easy to fall over articles left lying around.

DO get someone to check periodically that all is well when working alone on the vehicle.

DO carry out work in a logical sequence and check that everything is correctly assembled and tightened afterwards.

DO remember that your vehicle's safety affects that of yourself and others. If in doubt on any point, get specialist advice.

IF, in spite of following these precautions, you are unfortunate enough to injure yourself, seek medical attention as soon as possible.

Asbestos

Certain friction, insulating, sealing, and other products – such as brake linings, brake bands, clutch linings, gaskets, etc – contain asbestos. *Extreme care must be taken to avoid inhalation of dust from such products since it is hazardous to health.* If in doubt, assume that they *do* contain asbestos.

Fire

Remember at all times that petrol is highly flammable. Never smoke, or have any kind of naked flame around, when working on the vehicle. But the risk does not end there – a spark caused by an electrical short-circuit, by two metal surfaces contacting each other, by careless use of tools, or even by static electricity built up in your body under certain conditions, can ignite petrol vapour, which in a confined space is highly explosive.

Whenever possible disconnect the battery earth terminal before working on any part of the fuel or electrical system, and never risk spilling fuel on to a hot engine or exhaust. Catalytic converters run at extremely high temperatures, and consequently can be an additional fire hazard. Observe the precautions outlined elsewhere in this Section.

It is recommended that a fire extinguisher of a type suitable for fuel and electrical fires is kept handy in the garage or workplace at all times. Never try to extinguish a fuel or electrical fire with water.

Note: *Any reference to a 'torch' appearing in this manual should always be taken to mean a hand-held battery-operated electric lamp or flashlight. It does NOT mean a welding/gas torch or blowlamp.*

Fumes

Certain fumes are highly toxic and can quickly cause unconsciousness and even death if inhaled to any extent, especially if inhalation takes place through a lighted cigarette or pipe. Petrol vapour comes into this category, as do the vapours from certain solvents such as trichloroethylene. Any draining or pouring of such volatile fluids should be done in a well ventilated area.

When using cleaning fluids and solvents, read the instructions carefully. Never use materials from unmarked containers – they may give off poisonous vapours.

Never run the engine of a motor vehicle in an enclosed space such as a garage. Exhaust fumes contain carbon monoxide which is extremely poisonous; if you need to run the engine, always do so in the open air or at least have the rear of the vehicle outside the workplace. Although vehicles fitted with catalytic converters have greatly reduced toxic exhaust emissions, the above precautions should still be observed.

If you are fortunate enough to have the use of an inspection pit, never drain or pour petrol, and never run the engine, while the vehicle is standing over it; the fumes, being heavier than air, will concentrate in the pit with possibly lethal results. Where a catalytic converter is fitted, extra care will be needed against burns when working in the area of the converter unit. It operates at very high temperatures and will take longer to cool off than the rest of the exhaust system.

The battery

Batteries which are sealed for life require special precautions which are normally outlined on a label attached to the battery. Such precautions are primarily related to situations involving battery charging and jump starting from another vehicle.

Do not cause a spark or position a naked light in close proximity to the battery. It will normally be giving off a certain amount of hydrogen gas, which is highly explosive.

Whenever possible disconnect the battery earth terminal before working on the fuel or electrical systems.

If possible, loosen the filler plugs or cover when charging the battery from an external source. Do not charge at an excessive rate or the battery may burst. Special care should be taken with the use of high charge-rate boost chargers to prevent the battery from overheating.

Take care when topping up and when carrying the battery. The acid electrolyte, even when diluted, is very corrosive and should not be allowed to contact clothing, eyes or skin.

Always wear eye protection when cleaning the battery to prevent the caustic deposits from entering your eyes.

Mains electricity and electrical equipment

When using an electric power tool, inspection light, diagnostic equipment etc, which works from the mains, always ensure that the appliance is correctly connected to its plug and that, where necessary, it is properly earthed. Do not use such appliances in damp conditions and, again, beware of creating a spark or applying excessive heat in the vicinity of fuel or fuel vapour. Also ensure that the appliances meet the relevant national safety standards.

Ignition HT voltage

A severe electric shock can result from touching certain parts of the ignition system, such as the HT leads, when the engine is running or being cranked, particularly if components are damp or the insulation is defective. Where an electronic ignition system is fitted, the HT voltage is much higher and could prove fatal, especially to wearers of cardiac pacemakers.

Jacking and vehicle support

The jack provided with the vehicle is designed primarily for emergency wheel changing, and its use for servicing and overhaul work on the vehicle is best avoided. Instead, a more substantial workshop jack (trolley jack or similar) should be used. Whichever type is employed, it is essential that additional safety support is provided by means of axle stands designed for this purpose. Never use makeshift means such as wooden blocks or piles of house bricks, as these can easily topple or, in the case of bricks, disintegrate under the weight of the vehicle. Further information on the correct positioning of the jack and axle stands is provided in the *Jacking, towing and wheel changing* Section.

If removal of the wheels is not required, the use of drive-on ramps is recommended. Caution should be exercised to ensure that they are correctly aligned with the wheels, and that the vehicle is not driven too far along them so that it promptly falls off the other ends or tips the ramps.

General repair procedures

Whenever servicing, repair or overhaul work is carried out on the car or its components, it is necessary to observe the following procedures and instructions. This will assist in carrying out the operation efficiently and to a professional standard of workmanship.

Joint mating faces and gaskets

When separating components at their mating faces, never insert screwdrivers or similar implements into the joint between the faces in order to prise them apart. This can cause severe damage which results in oil leaks, coolant leaks, etc, upon reassembly. Separation is best achieved by tapping along the joint with a soft-faced hammer in order to break the seal. However, note that this method may not be suitable where dowels are used for component location.

Where a gasket is used between the mating faces of two components, ensure that it is renewed on reassembly and fit it dry unless otherwise stated in the repair procedure. Make sure that the mating faces are clean and dry with all traces of old gasket removed. When cleaning a joint face, use a tool which is not likely to score or damage the face, and remove any burrs or nicks with an oilstone or fine file.

Make sure that tapped holes are cleaned with a pipe cleaner and keep them free of jointing compound, if this is being used, unless specifically instructed otherwise.

Ensure that all orifices, channels or pipes are clear and blow through them, preferably using compressed air.

Oil seals

Oil seals can be removed by levering them out with a wide flat-bladed screwdriver or similar implement. Alternatively, a number of self-tapping screws may be screwed into the seal and these used as a purchase for pliers or some similar device in order to pull the seal free.

Whenever an oil seal is removed from its working location, either individually or as part of an assembly, it should be renewed.

The very fine sealing lip of the seal is easily damaged and will not seal if the surface it contacts is not completely clean and free from scratches, nicks or grooves. If the original sealing surface of the component cannot be restored, and the manufacturer has not made provision for slight relocation of the seal relative to the sealing surface, the component should be renewed.

Protect the lips of the seal from any surface which may damage them in the course of fitting. Use tape or a conical sleeve where possible. Lubricate the seal lips with oil before fitting and, on dual-lipped seals, fill the space between the lips with grease.

Unless otherwise stated, oil seals must be fitted with their sealing lips toward the lubricant to be sealed.

Use a tubular drift or block of wood of the appropriate size to install the seal and, if the seal housing is shouldered, drive the seal down to the shoulder. If the seal housing is unshouldered, the seal should be fitted with its face flush with the housing top face (unless otherwise instructed).

Screw threads and fastenings

Seized nuts, bolts and screws are quite a common occurrence where corrosion has set in, and the use of penetrating oil or releasing fluid will often overcome this problem if the offending item is soaked for a while before attempting to release it. The use of an impact driver may also provide a means of releasing such stubborn fastening devices when used in conjunction with the appropriate screwdriver bit or socket. If none of these methods works, it may be necessary to resort to the careful application of heat, or the use of a hacksaw or nut splitter device.

Studs are usually removed by locking two nuts together on the threaded part and then using a spanner on the lower nut to unscrew the stud. Studs or bolts which have broken off below the surface of the component in which they are mounted can sometimes be removed using a proprietary stud extractor. Always ensure that a blind tapped hole is completely free from oil, grease, water or other fluid before installing the bolt or stud. Failure to do this could cause the housing to crack due to the hydraulic action of the bolt or stud as it is screwed in.

When tightening a castellated nut to accept a split pin, tighten the nut to the specified torque, where applicable, and then tighten further to the next split pin hole. Never slacken the nut to align the split pin hole unless stated in the repair procedure.

When checking or retightening a nut or bolt to a specified torque setting, slacken the nut or bolt by a quarter of a turn, and then retighten to the specified setting. However, this should not be attempted where angular tightening has been used.

For some screw fastenings, notably cylinder head bolts or nuts, torque wrench settings are no longer specified for the latter stages of tightening, 'angle-tightening' being specified instead. Typically, a fairly low torque wrench setting will be applied to the bolts/nuts in the correct sequence, followed by one or more stages of tightening through specified angles.

Locknuts, locktabs and washers

Any fastening which will rotate against a component or housing in the course of tightening should normally have a washer between it and the relevant component or housing.

Spring or split washers should always be renewed when they are used to lock a critical component such as a big-end bearing retaining bolt or nut. Locktabs which are folded over to retain a nut or bolt should always be renewed.

Self-locking nuts can be re-used in non-critical areas, providing resistance can be felt when the locking portion passes over the bolt or stud thread. However, it should be noted that self-locking stiffnuts tend to lose their effectiveness after long periods of use, and in such cases should be renewed as a matter of course.

Split pins must always be replaced with new ones of the correct size for the hole.

When thread-locking compound is found on the threads of a fastener which is to be re-used, it should be cleaned off with a wire brush and solvent, and fresh compound applied on reassembly.

Special tools

Some repair procedures in this manual entail the use of special tools such as a press, two or three-legged pullers, spring compressors etc. Wherever possible, suitable readily available alternatives to the manufacturer's special tools are described and are shown in use. In some instances, where no alternative is possible, it has been necessary to resort to the use of a manufacturer's tool and this has been done for reasons of safety as well as the efficient completion of the repair operation. Unless you are highly skilled and have a thorough understanding of the procedures described, never attempt to bypass the use of any special tool when the procedure described specifies its use. Not only is there a very great risk of personal injury, but expensive damage could be caused to the components involved.

Environmental considerations

When disposing of used engine oil, brake fluid, antifreeze etc, give due consideration to any detrimental environmental effects. Do not, for instance, pour any of the above liquids down drains into the general sewage system or onto the ground to soak away. Many local council refuse tips provide a facility for waste oil disposal as do some garages. If none of these facilities are available, consult your local Environmental Health Department for further advice.

With the universal tightening-up of legislation regarding the emission of environmentally harmful substances from motor vehicles, most current vehicles have tamperproof devices fitted to the main adjustment points of the fuel system. These devices are primarily designed to prevent unqualified persons from adjusting the fuel/air mixture with the chance of a consequent increase in toxic emissions. If such devices are encountered during servicing or overhaul, they should, wherever possible, be renewed or refitted in accordance with the vehicle manufacturer's requirements or current legislation.

Tools and working facilities

Introduction

A selection of good tools is a fundamental requirement for anyone contemplating the maintenance and repair of a motor vehicle. For the owner who does not possess any, their purchase will prove a considerable expense, offsetting some of the savings made by doing-it-yourself. However, provided that the tools purchased meet the relevant national safety standards and are of good quality, they will last for many years and prove an extremely worthwhile investment.

To help the average owner to decide which tools are needed to carry out the various tasks detailed in this manual, we have compiled three lists of tools under the following headings: *Maintenance and minor repair, Repair and overhaul,* and *Special.* Newcomers to practical mechanics should start off with the *Maintenance and minor repair* tool kit and confine themselves to the simpler jobs around the vehicle. Then, as confidence and experience grow, more difficult tasks can be undertaken, with extra tools being purchased as, and when, they are needed. In this way, a *Maintenance and minor repair* tool kit can be built up into a *Repair and overhaul* tool kit over a considerable period of time without any major cash outlays. The experienced do-it-yourselfer will have a tool kit good enough for most repair and overhaul procedures and will add tools from the *Special* category when it is felt that the expense is justified by the amount of use to which these tools will be put.

Maintenance and minor repair tool kit

The tools given in this list should be considered as a minimum requirement if routine maintenance, servicing and minor repair operations are to be undertaken. We recommend the purchase of combination spanners (ring one end, open-ended the other); although more expensive than open-ended ones, they do give the advantages of both types of spanner.

Combination spanners:
  Metric – 8, 9, 10, 11, 12, 13, 14, 15, 17 & 19 mm
Adjustable spanner – 35 mm jaw (approx)
Engine sump/gearbox/rear axle drain plug key (where applicable)
Spark plug spanner (with rubber insert)
Spark plug gap adjustment tool

Set of feeler gauges
Brake adjuster spanner (where applicable)
Brake bleed nipple spanner
Screwdrivers:
  Flat blade – approx 100 mm long x 6 mm dia
  Cross blade – approx 100 mm long x 6 mm dia
Combination pliers
Hacksaw (junior)
Tyre pump
Tyre pressure gauge
Grease gun (where applicable)
Oil can
Oil filter removal tool
Fine emery cloth
Wire brush (small)
Funnel (medium size)

Repair and overhaul tool kit

These tools are virtually essential for anyone undertaking any major repairs to a motor vehicle, and are additional to those given in the *Maintenance and minor repair* list. Included in this list is a comprehensive set of sockets. Although these are expensive, they will be found invaluable as they are so versatile – particularly if various drives are included in the set. We recommend the ½ in square-drive type, as this can be used with most proprietary torque wrenches. If you cannot afford a socket set, even bought piecemeal, then inexpensive tubular box spanners are a useful alternative.

The tools in this list will occasionally need to be supplemented by tools from the Special list.

Sockets (or box spanners) to cover range in previous list
Reversible ratchet drive (for use with sockets) (photo)
Extension piece, 250 mm (for use with sockets)
Universal joint (for use with sockets)
Torque wrench (for use with sockets)
Self-locking grips
Ball pein hammer
Soft-faced mallet (plastic/aluminium or rubber)

Sockets and reversible ratchet drive

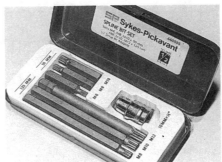

Spline bit set

Spline key set

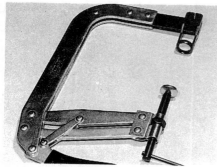

Valve spring compressor

Piston ring compressor

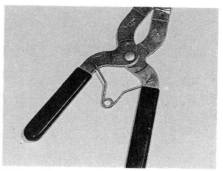

Piston ring removal/installation tool

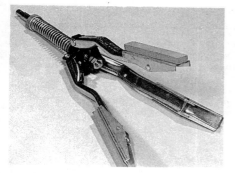

Cylinder bore hone

Three-legged hub and bearing puller

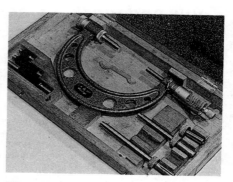

Micrometer set

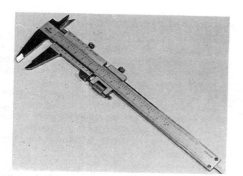

Vernier calipers

Dial test indicator and magnetic stand

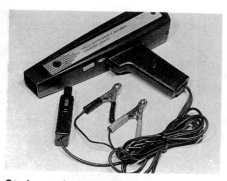

Stroboscopic timing light

Cylinder compression gauge

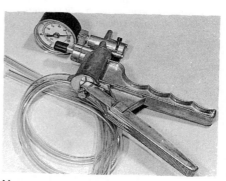

Vacuum pump and gauge

Screwdrivers:
> Flat blade – long & sturdy, short (chubby), and narrow (electricians) types
> Cross blade – long & sturdy, and short (chubby) types

Pliers:
> Long-nosed
> Side cutters (electricians)
> Circlip (internal and external)

Cold chisel – 25 mm
Scriber
Scraper
Centre punch
Pin punch
Hacksaw
Brake hose clamp
Brake bleeding kit
Selection of twist drills
Steel rule/straight-edge
Allen keys (inc. splined/Torx type) (photos)
Selection of files
Wire brush
Axle-stands
Jack (strong trolley or hydraulic type)
Light with extension lead

Special tools

The tools in this list are those which are not used regularly, are expensive to buy, or which need to be used in accordance with their manufacturer's instructions. Unless relatively difficult mechanical jobs are undertaken frequently, it will not be economic to buy many of these tools. Where this is the case, you could consider clubbing together with friends (or joining a motorists' club) to make a joint purchase, or borrowing the tools against a deposit from a local garage or tool hire specialist. It is worth noting that many of the larger DIY superstores now carry a large range of special tools for hire at modest rates.

The following list contains only those tools and instruments freely available to the public, and not those special tools produced by the vehicle manufacturer specifically for its dealer network. You will find occasional references to these manufacturer's special tools in the text of this manual. Generally, an alternative method of doing the job without the vehicle manufacturer's special tool is given. However, sometimes there is no alternative to using them. Where this is the case and the relevant tool cannot be bought or borrowed, you will have to entrust the work to a franchised garage.

> Valve spring compressor (photo)
> Valve grinding tool
> Piston ring compressor (photo)
> Piston ring removal/installation tool (photo)
> Cylinder bore hone (photo)
> Balljoint separator
> Coil spring compressors (where applicable)
> Two/three-legged hub and bearing puller (photo)
> Impact screwdriver
> Micrometer and/or vernier calipers (photos)
> Dial test indicator (photo)
> Stroboscopic timing light (photo)
> Dwell angle meter/tachometer
> Universal electrical multi-meter
> Cylinder compression gauge (photo)
> Hand-operated vacuum pump and gauge (photo)
> Clutch plate alignment set (photo)
> Brake shoe steady spring cup removal tool (photo)
> Bush and bearing removal/installation set (photo)
> Stud extractors (photo)
> Tap and die set (photo)
> Lifting tackle
> Trolley jack

Buying tools

For practically all tools, a tool factor is the best source since he will have a very comprehensive range compared with the average garage or

Clutch plate alignment set

Brake shoe steady spring cup removal tool

Bush and bearing removal/installation set

Stud extractor set

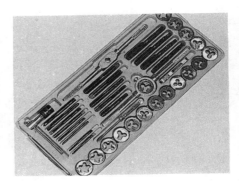

Tap and die set

accessory shop. Having said that, accessory shops often offer excellent quality tools at discount prices, so it pays to shop around.

Remember, you don't have to buy the most expensive items on the shelf but it is always advisable to steer clear of the very cheap tools. There are plenty of good tools around at reasonable prices, but always aim to purchase items which meet the relevant national safety standards. If in doubt, ask the proprietor or manager of the shop for advice before making a purchase.

Care and maintenance of tools

Having purchased a reasonable tool kit, it is necessary to keep the tools in a clean and serviceable condition. After use, always wipe off any dirt, grease and metal particles using a clean, dry cloth, before putting the tools away. Never leave them lying around after they have been used. A simple tool rack on the garage or workshop wall for items such as screwdrivers and pliers is a good idea. Store all normal spanners and sockets in a metal box. Any measuring instruments, gauges, meters, etc, must be carefully stored where they cannot be damaged or become rusty.

Take a little care when tools are used. Hammer heads inevitably become marked and screwdrivers lose the keen edge on their blades from time to time. A little timely attention with emery cloth or a file will soon restore items like this to a good serviceable finish.

Working facilities

Not to be forgotten when discussing tools is the workshop itself. If anything more than routine maintenance is to be carried out, some form of suitable working area becomes essential.

It is appreciated that many an owner mechanic is forced by circumstances to remove an engine or similar item without the benefit of a garage or workshop. Having done this, any repairs should always be done under the cover of a roof.

Wherever possible, any dismantling should be done on a clean, flat workbench or table at a suitable working height.

Any workbench needs a vice; one with a jaw opening of 100 mm (4 in) is suitable for most jobs. As mentioned previously, some clean dry storage space is also required for tools, as well as for any lubricants, cleaning fluids, touch-up paints and so on, which become necessary.

Another item which may be required, and which has a much more general usage, is an electric drill with a chuck capacity of at least 8 mm ($\frac{5}{16}$ in). This, together with a good range of twist drills, is virtually essential for fitting accessories.

Last, but not least, always keep a supply of old newspapers and clean, lint-free rags available, and try to keep any working area as clean as possible.

Spanner jaw gap and bolt size comparison table

Jaw gap – in (mm)	Spanner size	Bolt size
0.197 (5.00)	5 mm	M 2.5
0.216 (5.50)	5.5 mm	M 3
0.218 (5.53)	$\frac{7}{32}$ in AF	
0.236 (6.00)	6 mm	M 3.5
0.250 (6.35)	$\frac{1}{4}$ in AF	
0.275 (7.00)	7 mm	M 4
0.281 (7.14)	$\frac{9}{32}$ in AF	
0.312 (7.92)	$\frac{5}{16}$ in AF	
0.315 (8.00)	8 mm	M 5
0.343 (8.71)	$\frac{11}{32}$ in AF	
0.375 (9.52)	$\frac{3}{8}$ in AF	
0.394 (10.00)	10 mm	M 6
0.406 (10.32)	$\frac{13}{32}$ in AF	
0.433 (11.00)	11 mm	M 7
0.437 (11.09)	$\frac{7}{16}$ in AF	$\frac{1}{4}$ in SAE
0.468 (11.88)	$\frac{15}{32}$ in AF	
0.500 (12.70)	$\frac{1}{2}$ in AF	$\frac{5}{16}$ in SAE
0.512 (13.00)	13 mm	M8
0.562 (14.27)	$\frac{9}{16}$ in AF	$\frac{3}{8}$ in SAE
0.593 (15.06)	$\frac{19}{32}$ in AF	
0.625 (15.87)	$\frac{5}{8}$ in AF	$\frac{7}{16}$ in SAE
0.669 (17.00)	17 mm	M 10
0.687 (17.44)	$\frac{11}{16}$ in AF	
0.709 (19.00)	19 mm	M 12
0.750 (19.05)	$\frac{3}{4}$ in AF	$\frac{1}{2}$ in SAE
0.781 (19.83)	$\frac{25}{32}$ in AF	
0.812 (20.62)	$\frac{13}{16}$ in AF	
0.866 (22.00)	22 mm	M 14
0.875 (22.25)	$\frac{7}{8}$ in AF	$\frac{9}{16}$ in SAE
0.937 (23.79)	$\frac{15}{16}$ in AF	$\frac{5}{8}$ in SAE
0.945 (24.00)	24 mm	M 16
0.968 (24.58)	$\frac{31}{32}$ in AF	
1.000 (25.40)	1 in AF	$\frac{11}{16}$ in SAE
1.062 (26.97)	1 $\frac{1}{16}$ in AF	$\frac{3}{4}$ in SAE
1.063 (27.00)	27 mm	M 18
1.125 (28.57)	1 $\frac{1}{8}$ in AF	
1.182 (30.00)	30 mm	M 20
1.187 (30.14)	1 $\frac{3}{16}$ in AF	
1.250 (31.75)	1 $\frac{1}{4}$ in AF	$\frac{7}{8}$ in SAE
1.260 (32.00)	32 mm	M 22
1.312 (33.32)	1 $\frac{5}{16}$ in AF	
1.375 (34.92)	1 $\frac{3}{8}$ in AF	
1.418 (36.00)	36 mm	M 24
1.437 (36.49)	1 $\frac{7}{16}$ in AF	1 in SAE
1.500 (38.10)	1 $\frac{1}{2}$ in AF	
1.615 (41.00)	41 mm	M 27

Booster battery (jump) starting

When jump starting a car using a booster battery, observe the following precautions.

(a) Before connecting the booster battery, make sure that the ignition is switched off.

(b) Ensure that all electrical equipment (lights, heater, wipers etc) is switched off.

(c) Make sure that the booster battery is the same voltage as the discharged one in the vehicle.

(d) If the battery is being jump started from the battery in another vehicle, the two vehicles MUST NOT TOUCH each other.

(e) Make sure that the transmission is in Neutral (manual gearbox) or Park (automatic transmission).

Connect one jump lead between the positive (+) terminals of the two batteries. Connect the other jump lead first to the negative (−) terminal of the booster battery, and then to a good earthing point on the vehicle to be started, such as a bolt or bracket on the engine block, at least 45 cm (18 in) from the battery if possible. Do not connect the earth lead direct to the earth lead terminal of the flat battery. Make sure that the jump leads will not come into contact with the fan, drivebelts or other moving parts of the engine.

Start the engine using the booster battery, then with the engine running at idle speed, disconnect the jump leads in the reverse order of connection.

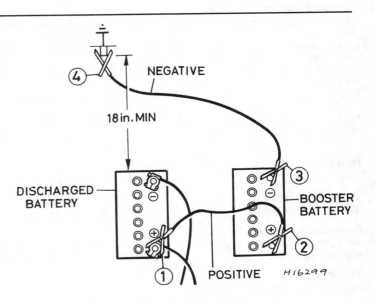

Jump start lead connections for negative earth vehicles – connect leads in order shown

Conversion factors

Length (distance)

Inches (in)	X	25.4	= Millimetres (mm)	X	0.0394	= Inches (in)
Feet (ft)	X	0.305	= Metres (m)	X	3.281	= Feet (ft)
Miles	X	1.609	= Kilometres (km)	X	0.621	= Miles

Volume (capacity)

Cubic inches (cu in; in^3)	X	16.387	= Cubic centimetres (cc; cm^3)	X	0.061	= Cubic inches (cu in; in^3)
Imperial pints (Imp pt)	X	0.568	= Litres (l)	X	1.76	= Imperial pints (Imp pt)
Imperial quarts (Imp qt)	X	1.137	= Litres (l)	X	0.88	= Imperial quarts (Imp qt)
Imperial quarts (Imp qt)	X	1.201	= US quarts (US qt)	X	0.833	= Imperial quarts (Imp qt)
US quarts (US qt)	X	0.946	= Litres (l)	X	1.057	= US quarts (US qt)
Imperial gallons (Imp gal)	X	4.546	= Litres (l)	X	0.22	= Imperial gallons (Imp gal)
Imperial gallons (Imp gal)	X	1.201	= US gallons (US gal)	X	0.833	= Imperial gallons (Imp gal)
US gallons (US gal)	X	3.785	= Litres (l)	X	0.264	= US gallons (US gal)

Mass (weight)

Ounces (oz)	X	28.35	= Grams (g)	X	0.035	= Ounces (oz)
Pounds (lb)	X	0.454	= Kilograms (kg)	X	2.205	= Pounds (lb)

Force

Ounces-force (ozf; oz)	X	0.278	= Newtons (N)	X	3.6	= Ounces-force (ozf; oz)
Pounds-force (lbf; lb)	X	4.448	= Newtons (N)	X	0.225	= Pounds-force (lbf; lb)
Newtons (N)	X	0.1	= Kilograms-force (kgf; kg)	X	9.81	= Newtons (N)

Pressure

Pounds-force per square inch (psi; lbf/in^2; lb/in^2)	X	0.070	= Kilograms-force per square centimetre (kgf/cm^2; kg/cm^2)	X	14.223	= Pounds-force per square inch (psi; lbf/in^2; lb/in^2)
Pounds-force per square inch (psi; lbf/in^2; lb/in^2)	X	0.068	= Atmospheres (atm)	X	14.696	= Pounds-force per square inch (psi; lbf/in^2; lb/in^2)
Pounds-force per square inch (psi; lbf/in^2; lb/in^2)	X	0.069	= Bars	X	14.5	= Pounds-force per square inch (psi; lbf/in^2; lb/in^2)
Pounds-force per square inch (psi; lbf/in^2; lb/in^2)	X	6.895	= Kilopascals (kPa)	X	0.145	= Pounds-force per square inch (psi; lbf/in^2; lb/in^2)
Kilopascals (kPa)	X	0.01	= Kilograms-force per square centimetre (kgf/cm^2; kg/cm^2)	X	98.1	= Kilopascals (kPa)
Millibar (mbar)	X	100	= Pascals (Pa)	X	0.01	= Millibar (mbar)
Millibar (mbar)	X	0.0145	= Pounds-force per square inch (psi; lbf/in^2; lb/in^2)	X	68.947	= Millibar (mbar)
Millibar (mbar)	X	0.75	= Millimetres of mercury (mmHg)	X	1.333	= Millibar (mbar)
Millibar (mbar)	X	0.401	= Inches of water (inH$_2$O)	X	2.491	= Millibar (mbar)
Millimetres of mercury (mmHg)	X	0.535	= Inches of water (inH$_2$O)	X	1.868	= Millimetres of mercury (mmHg)
Inches of water (inH$_2$O)	X	0.036	= Pounds-force per square inch (psi; lbf/in^2; lb/in^2)	X	27.68	= Inches of water (inH$_2$O)

Torque (moment of force)

Pounds-force inches (lbf in; lb in)	X	1.152	= Kilograms-force centimetre (kgf cm; kg cm)	X	0.868	= Pounds-force inches (lbf in; lb in)
Pounds-force inches (lbf in; lb in)	X	0.113	= Newton metres (Nm)	X	8.85	= Pounds-force inches (lbf in; lb in)
Pounds-force inches (lbf in; lb in)	X	0.083	= Pounds-force feet (lbf ft; lb ft)	X	12	= Pounds-force inches (lbf in; lb in)
Pounds-force feet (lbf ft; lb ft)	X	0.138	= Kilograms-force metres (kgf m; kg m)	X	7.233	= Pounds-force feet (lbf ft; lb ft)
Pounds-force feet (lbf ft; lb ft)	X	1.356	= Newton metres (Nm)	X	0.738	= Pounds-force feet (lbf ft; lb ft)
Newton metres (Nm)	X	0.102	= Kilograms-force metres (kgf m; kg m)	X	9.804	= Newton metres (Nm)

Power

Horsepower (hp)	X	745.7	= Watts (W)	X	0.0013	= Horsepower (hp)

Velocity (speed)

Miles per hour (miles/hr; mph)	X	1.609	= Kilometres per hour (km/hr; kph)	X	0.621	= Miles per hour (miles/hr; mph)

Fuel consumption

Miles per gallon, Imperial (mpg)	X	0.354	= Kilometres per litre (km/l)	X	2.825	= Miles per gallon, Imperial (mpg)
Miles per gallon, US (mpg)	X	0.425	= Kilometres per litre (km/l)	X	2.352	= Miles per gallon, US (mpg)

Temperature

Degrees Fahrenheit = (°C x 1.8) + 32

Degrees Celsius (Degrees Centigrade; °C) = (°F – 32) x 0.56

* It is common practice to convert from miles per gallon (mpg) to litres/100 kilometres (l/100km), where mpg (Imperial) x l/100 km = 282 and mpg (US) x l/100 km = 235

Fault diagnosis

Contents

Introduction

The vehicle owner who does his or her own maintenance according to the recommended service schedules should not have to use this Section of the manual very often. Modern component reliability is such that, provided those items subject to wear or deterioration are inspected or renewed at the specified intervals, sudden failure is comparatively rare. Faults do not usually just happen as a result of sudden failure, but develop over a period of time. Major mechanical failures in particular are usually preceded by characteristic symptoms over hundreds or even thousands of miles. Those components which do occasionally fail without warning are often small and easily carried in the vehicle.

With any fault finding, the first step is to decide where to begin investigations. Sometimes this is obvious, but on other occasions a little detective work will be necessary. The owner who makes half a dozen haphazard adjustments or replacements may be successful in curing a fault (or its symptoms), but will be none the wiser if the fault recurs and

ultimately may have spent more time and money than was necessary. A calm and logical approach will be found to be more satisfactory in the long run. Always take into account any warning signs or abnormalities that may have been noticed in the period preceding the fault – power loss, high or low gauge readings, unusual smells, etc – and remember that failure of components such as fuses or spark plugs may only be pointers to some underlying fault.

The items which follow provide an easy reference guide to the more common problems which may occur during the operation of the vehicle. These problems and their possible causes are grouped under headings denoting various components or systems, such as Engine, Cooling system, etc. The Chapter and/or Section which deals with the problem is also shown in brackets. Whatever the fault, certain basic principles apply. These are as follows:

Verify the fault. This is simply a matter of being sure that you know what the symptoms are before starting work. This is particularly important if you are investigating a fault for someone else who may not have described it very accurately.

Don't overlook the obvious. For example, if the vehicle won't start, is there petrol in the tank? (Don't take anyone else's word on this particular point, and don't trust the fuel gauge either!) If an electrical fault is indicated, look for loose or broken wires before digging out the test gear.

Cure the disease, not the symptom. Substituting a flat battery with a fully charged one will get you off the hard shoulder, but if the underlying cause is not attended to, the new battery will go the same way. Similarly, changing oil-fouled spark plugs for a new set will get you moving again, but remember that the reason for the fouling (if it wasn't simply an incorrect grade of plug) will have to be established and corrected.

Don't take anything for granted. Particularly, don't forget that a 'new' component may itself be defective (especially if it's been rattling around in the boot for months), and don't leave components out of a fault diagnosis sequence just because they are new or recently fitted. When you do finally diagnose a difficult fault, you'll probably realise that all the evidence was there from the start.

Realise your limits. The diagnostic and repair scope for the average DIY mechanic with basic tools and test facilities is fairly limited when it comes to diagnosing and repairing certain components of the vehicle. This particularly applies to the fuel and ignition systems which are now managed by a common electronic control unit (ECU). Unless a component is obviously defective or components are freely available for testing by substitution, the aid of a Ford dealer or suitable specialist will be necessary. Do not attempt to improvise test meter checks. The incorrect application of test probes between some component connector pins can cause irreparable damage to the internal circuitry of some components in the engine management system.

1 Engine

Engine fails to rotate when attempting to start

- Battery terminal connections loose or corroded (Chapter 12).
- Battery discharged or faulty (Chapter 12).
- Broken, loose or disconnected wiring in the starting circuit (Chapter 12).
- Defective starter solenoid or switch (Chapter 12).
- Defective starter motor (Chapter 12).
- Starter pinion or flywheel ring gear teeth loose or broken (Chapter 12).
- Engine earth strap broken or disconnected (Chapter 12).
- Automatic transmission not in Park/Neutral position, starter inhibitor switch faulty or incorrect selector adjustment (Chapter 7).

Engine rotates but will not start

- Fuel tank empty.
- Battery discharged (engine rotates slowly) (Chapter 12).
- Battery terminal connections loose or corroded (Chapter 12).
- Ignition components damp or damaged (Chapters 1 and 5).
- Broken, loose or disconnected wiring in the ignition circuit (Chapters 1 and 5).
- Worn, faulty or incorrectly gapped spark plugs (Chapter 1).
- Choke mechanism sticking, incorrectly adjusted, or faulty (Chapter 4).
- Major mechanical failure (eg camshaft drive) (Chapter 2).
- Defective fuel pump relay or blown fuse – fuel injection system (Chapter 12).
- Defective fuel pressure regulator – fuel injection system (Chapter 4).
- Defective idle speed control valve (1.6 EFi models).
- Defective fuel injectors (fuel injection system (Chapter 4).
- Engine management system faulty (Chapter 5).

Engine difficult to start when cold

- Battery discharged (Chapter 12).
- Battery terminal connections loose or corroded (Chapter 12).
- Worn, faulty or incorrectly gapped spark plugs (Chapter 1).
- Choke mechanism sticking, incorrectly adjusted, or faulty (Chapter 4).

- Other ignition system fault (Chapters 1 and 5).
- Low cylinder compressions (Chapter 2).
- Engine management system fault (Chapter 5).

Engine difficult to start when hot

- Air filter element dirty or clogged (Chapter 1).
- Choke mechanism sticking, incorrectly adjusted, or faulty (Chapter 4).
- Carburettor float chamber flooding or fuel percolation (Chapter 4).
- Low cylinder compressions (Chapter 2).
- Engine management system fault (Chapter 5).

Starter motor noisy or excessively rough in engagement

- Starter pinion or flywheel ring gear teeth loose or broken (Chapter 12).
- Starter motor mounting bolts loose or missing (Chapter 12).
- Starter motor internal components worn or damaged (Chapter 12).

Engine starts but stops immediately

- Insufficient fuel reaching carburettor or fuel injector(s) (Chapter 4).
- Loose or faulty electrical connections in the ignition circuit (Chapters 1 and 5).
- Vacuum leak in the fuel system, induction system and/or the associated system hoses (Chapter 4).
- Blocked carburettor jet(s) or internal passages (Chapter 4).

Engine idles erratically

- Incorrectly adjusted idle speed and/or mixture settings – carburettor models (Chapter 1).
- Air filter element clogged (Chapter 1).
- Vacuum leak in the fuel system, induction system or associated hoses (Chapter 4).
- Defective idle speed control valve – 1.6 EFi models (Chapter 4).
- Defective fuel pressure regulator – fuel injection models (Chapter 4).
- Leak in MAP sensor vacuum hose – fuel injection system (Chapter 4).
- Base idle speed or fuel mixture incorrectly set – 1.6 EFi models (Chapter 4).
- Throttle plate control motor defective – CFi system (Chapter 4).
- Worn, faulty or incorrectly gapped spark plugs (Chapter 1).
- Incorrectly adjusted valve clearances (Chapter 2).
- Uneven or low cylinder compressions (Chapter 2).
- Camshaft lobes worn (Chapter 2).
- Timing belt incorrectly tensioned (Chapter 2).
- Engine management system fault (Chapter 5).

Engine misfires at idle speed

- Worn, faulty or incorrectly gapped spark plugs (Chapter 1).
- Faulty spark plug HT leads (Chapter 1).
- Incorrectly adjusted idle mixture settings – carburettor models (Chapter 1).
- Vacuum leak at the fuel system, induction system or associated hoses (Chapter 4).
- Incorrectly adjusted valve clearances (Chapter 2).
- Uneven or low cylinder compressions (Chapter 2).
- Disconnected, leaking or perished crankcase ventilation hoses (Chapter 4).

Engine misfires throughout the driving speed range

- Blocked carburettor jet(s) or internal passages (Chapter 4).
- Carburettor worn or incorrectly adjusted (Chapters 1 and 4).
- Fuel filter choked (Chapter 1).
- Fuel pump faulty or delivery pressure low (Chapter 4).
- Fuel tank vent blocked or fuel pipes restricted (Chapter 4).
- Vacuum leak at the carburettor, inlet manifold or associated hoses (Chapter 4).
- Worn, faulty or incorrectly gapped spark plugs (Chapter 1).
- Faulty spark plug HT leads (Chapter 1).
- Faulty ignition coil (Chapter 5).
- Uneven or low cylinder compressions (Chapter 2).

Engine hesitates on acceleration

- Worn, faulty or incorrectly gapped spark plugs (Chapter 1).
- Carburettor accelerator pump faulty (Chapter 4).
- Blocked carburettor jets or internal passages (Chapter 4).
- Vacuum leak in the fuel system, induction system or associated hoses (Chapter 4).
- Carburettor worn or incorrectly adjusted (Chapters 1 and 4).

Engine stalls

- Incorrectly adjusted idle speed and/or mixture settings (Chapter 1).
- Blocked carburettor jet(s) or internal passages (Chapter 4).
- Vacuum leak at the carburettor, inlet manifold or associated hoses (Chapter 4).
- Fuel filter choked (Chapter 1).
- Fuel pump faulty or delivery pressure low (Chapter 4).
- Fuel tank vent blocked or fuel pipes restricted (Chapter 4).

Engine lacks power

- Carburettor worn or incorrectly adjusted (Chapter 1).
- Timing belt incorrectly fitted or tensioned (Chapter 2).
- Fuel filter choked (Chapter 1).
- Fuel pump faulty or delivery pressure low (Chapter 4).
- Uneven or low cylinder compressions (Chapter 2).
- Worn, faulty or incorrectly gapped spark plugs (Chapter 1).
- Vacuum leak in the fuel system, induction system or associated hoses (Chapter 4).
- Limited operation system (LOS) activated – fuel injection system (Chapter 4).
- Brakes binding (Chapter 1).
- Clutch slipping (Chapter 6).
- Automatic transmission fluid level incorrect (Chapter 1).
- Engine management system fault (Chapter 5

Engine backfires

- Timing belt incorrectly fitted or tensioned (Chapter 2).
- Carburettor worn or incorrectly adjusted (Chapter 1).
- Vacuum leak in the fuel system, induction system or associated hoses (Chapter 4).
- Engine management system fault (Chapter 5).

Oil pressure warning light illuminated with engine running

- Low oil level or incorrect grade (Chapter 1).
- Faulty oil pressure transmitter (sender) unit (Chapter 2).
- Worn engine bearings and/or oil pump (Chapter 2).
- High engine operating temperature (Chapter 2).
- Oil pressure relief valve defective (Chapter 2).
- Oil pick-up strainer clogged (Chapter 2).

Engine runs-on after switching off

- Idle speed excessively high (Chapter 1).
- Faulty anti-run-on solenoid (Chapter 4).
- Excessive carbon build-up in engine (Chapter 2).
- High engine operating temperature (Chapters 2 and 3).

Engine noises

Pre-ignition (pinking) or knocking during acceleration or under load

- Ignition timing incorrect (Chapter 1).
- Incorrect grade of fuel (Chapter 4).
- Vacuum leak at the carburettor, inlet manifold or associated hoses (Chapter 4).
- Excessive carbon build-up in engine (Chapter 2).
- Worn or damaged ignition system component (Chapter 5).
- Carburettor worn or incorrectly adjusted (Chapter 4).

Whistling or wheezing noises

- Leak in fuel induction system (Chapter 4).
- Leaking exhaust manifold gasket or pipe to manifold joint (Chapter 4).
- Leaking vacuum hose (Chapters 4, 5 and 9).
- Blowing cylinder head gasket (Chapter 2).

Tapping or rattling noises

- Incorrect valve clearances (Chapter 2).
- Worn valve gear or camshaft (Chapter 2).
- Ancillary component fault (water pump, alternator etc) (Chapters 3 and 12).

Knocking or thumping noises

- Worn big-end bearings (regular heavy knocking, perhaps less under load) (Chapter 2).
- Worn main bearings (rumbling and knocking, perhaps worsening under load) (Chapter 2).
- Piston slap (most noticeable when cold) (Chapter 2).
- Ancillary component fault (alternator, water pump etc) (Chapters 3 and 12).

2   Cooling system

Overheating

- Insufficient coolant in system (Chapter 1).
- Thermostat faulty (Chapter 3).
- Radiator core blocked or grille restricted (Chapter 3).
- Electric cooling fan or thermoswitch faulty (Chapter 3).
- Pressure cap faulty (Chapter 3).
- Water pump drivebelt worn, or incorrectly adjusted (Chapter 1).
- Inaccurate temperature gauge sender unit (Chapter 3).
- Air lock in cooling system (Chapter 3).

Overcooling

- Thermostat faulty (Chapter 3).
- Inaccurate temperature gauge sender unit (Chapter 3).

External coolant leakage

- Deteriorated or damaged hoses or hose clips (Chapter 1).
- Radiator core or heater matrix leaking (Chapter 3).
- Pressure cap faulty (Chapter 3).
- Water pump seal leaking (Chapter 3).
- Boiling due to overheating (Chapter 3).
- Core plug leaking (Chapter 2).

Internal coolant leakage

- Leaking cylinder head gasket (Chapter 2).
- Cracked cylinder head or cylinder bore (Chapter 2).

Corrosion

- Infrequent draining and flushing (Chapter 1).
- Incorrect antifreeze mixture or inappropriate type (Chapter 1).

3   Fuel and exhaust system

Excessive fuel consumption

- Air filter element dirty or clogged (Chapter 1).
- Carburettor worn or incorrectly adjusted (Chapters 1 and 4).
- Choke cable incorrectly adjusted or choke sticking (Chapter 4).
- Tyres underinflated (Chapter 1).

Fuel leakage and/or fuel odour

- Damaged or corroded fuel tank, pipes or connections (Chapter 1).
- Carburettor float chamber flooding (Chapter 4).

Excessive noise or fumes from exhaust system

- Leaking exhaust system or manifold joints (Chapter 1).
- Leaking, corroded or damaged silencers or pipe (Chapter 1).
- Broken mountings causing body or suspension contact (Chapter 1).

4   Clutch

Pedal travels to floor – no pressure or very little resistance

- Broken clutch cable (Chapter 6).
- Incorrect clutch adjustment (Chapter 6).
- Faulty clutch pedal self-adjust mechanism (Chapter 6).
- Broken clutch release bearing or fork (Chapter 6).
- Broken diaphragm spring in clutch pressure plate (Chapter 6).

Clutch fails to disengage (unable to select gears)

- Incorrect clutch adjustment (Chapter 6).
- Faulty clutch pedal self-adjust mechanism (Chapter 6).
- Clutch disc sticking on gearbox input shaft splines (Chapter 6).
- Clutch disc sticking to flywheel or pressure plate (Chapter 6).
- Faulty pressure plate assembly (Chapter 6).
- Gearbox input shaft seized in crankshaft spigot bearing (Chapter 2).
- Clutch release mechanism worn or incorrectly assembled (Chapter 6).

Clutch slips (engine speed increases with no increase in vehicle speed)

- Incorrect clutch adjustment (Chapter 6).
- Faulty clutch pedal self-adjust mechanism (Chapter 6).
- Clutch disc linings excessively worn (Chapter 6).
- Clutch disc linings contaminated with oil or grease (Chapter 6).
- Faulty pressure plate or weak diaphragm spring (Chapter 6).

Judder as clutch is engaged

- Clutch disc linings contaminated with oil or grease (Chapter 6).
- Clutch disc linings excessively worn (Chapter 6).
- Clutch cable sticking or frayed (Chapter 6).
- Faulty or distorted pressure plate or diaphragm spring (Chapter 6).
- Worn or loose engine or gearbox mountings (Chapter 2).
- Clutch disc hub or gearbox input shaft splines worn (Chapter 6).

Noise when depressing or releasing clutch pedal

- Worn clutch release bearing (Chapter 6).
- Worn or dry clutch pedal bushes (Chapter 6).
- Faulty pressure plate assembly (Chapter 6).
- Pressure plate diaphragm spring broken (Chapter 6).
- Broken clutch disc cushioning springs (Chapter 6).

5   Manual gearbox

Noisy in neutral with engine running

- Input shaft bearings worn (noise apparent with clutch pedal released but not when depressed) (Chapter 7).*
- Clutch release bearing worn (noise apparent with clutch pedal depressed, possibly less when released) (Chapter 6).

Noisy in one particular gear

- Worn, damaged or chipped gear teeth (Chapter 7).*

Difficulty engaging gears

- Clutch fault (Chapter 6).
- Worn or damaged gear linkage (Chapter 7).
- Incorrectly adjusted gear linkage (Chapter 7).
- Worn synchroniser units (Chapter 7).*

Jumps out of gear

- Worn or damaged gear linkage (Chapter 7).
- Incorrectly adjusted gear linkage (Chapter 7).
- Worn synchroniser units (Chapter 7).*
- Worn selector forks (Chapter 7).*

Vibration

- Lack of oil (Chapter 1).
- Worn bearings (Chapter 7).*

Lubricant leaks

- Leaking differential output oil seal (Chapter 7).
- Leaking housing joint (Chapter 7).*
- Leaking input shaft oil seal (Chapter 7).*

Although the corrective action necessary to remedy the symptoms described is beyond the scope of the home mechanic, the above information should be helpful in isolating the cause of the condition so that the owner can communicate clearly with a professional mechanic.

6   Automatic transmission

Note: *Due to the complexity of the automatic transmission, it is difficult for the home mechanic to properly diagnose and service this unit. For problems other than the following, the vehicle should be taken to a Ford dealer or automatic transmission specialist.*

Fluid leakage

- Automatic transmission fluid is usually deep red in colour. Fluid leaks should not be confused with engine oil which can easily be blown onto the transmission by airflow.
- To determine the source of a leak, first remove all built-up dirt and grime from the transmission housing and surrounding areas using a degreasing agent or by steam cleaning. Drive the vehicle at low speed so airflow will not blow the leak far from its source. Raise and support the vehicle and determine where the leak is coming from. Common areas of leakage are.

  (a) Oil pan (Chapters 1 and 7).
  (b) Dipstick tube (Chapters 1 and 7).
  (c) Transmission to oil cooler fluid pipes/unions Chapter 7).

Transmission fluid brown or has burned smell

- Transmission fluid level low or fluid in need of renewal (Chapter 1).

General gear selection problems

- Chapter 7, Part B, deals with checking and adjusting the selector linkage on automatic transmissions. Common problems which may be attributed to a poorly adjusted linkage are.

  (a) Engine starting in gears other than Park or Neutral.
  (b) Indicator on gear selector lever pointing to a gear other than the one actually being used.
  (c) Vehicle moves when in Park or Neutral.
  (d) Poor gearshift quality or erratic gear changes.

- Refer to Chapter 7, Part B for the selector linkage adjustment procedure.

Transmission will not downshift (kickdown) with accelerator fully depressed

- Low transmission fluid level (Chapter 1).
- Incorrect selector mechanism adjustment (Chapter 7, Part B).

Engine will not start in any gear, or starts in gears other than Park or Neutral

- Faulty starter inhibitor switch (Chapter 12).
- Incorrect selector mechanism adjustment (Chapter 7, Part B).

Transmission slips, shifts roughly, is noisy or has no drive in forward or reverse gears

- There are many probable causes for the above problems, but the home mechanic should be concerned with only one possibility – fluid level. Before taking the vehicle to a dealer or transmission specialist, check the fluid level and condition of the fluid as described in Chapter 1. Correct the fluid level as necessary or change the fluid and filter if needed. If the problem persists, professional help will be necessary.

7 Driveshafts

Clicking or knocking noise on turns (at slow speed on full lock)

- Lack of constant velocity joint lubricant (Chapter 8).
- Worn outer constant velocity joint (Chapter 8).

Vibration when accelerating or decelerating

- Worn inner constant velocity joint (Chapter 8).
- Bent or distorted driveshaft (Chapter 8).

8 Braking system

Note: *Before assuming that a brake problem exists, make sure that the tyres are in good condition and correctly inflated, the front wheel alignment is correct and the vehicle is not loaded with weight in an unequal manner. Apart from checking the condition of all pipe and hose connections, any faults occurring on the Anti-lock braking system should be referred to a Ford dealer for diagnosis.*

Vehicle pulls to one side under braking

- Worn, defective, damaged or contaminated front or rear brake pads/shoes on one side (Chapter 1).
- Seized or partially seized front or rear brake caliper/wheel cylinder piston (Chapter 9).
- A mixture of brake pad/shoe lining materials fitted between sides (Chapter 1).
- Brake caliper mounting bolts loose (Chapter 9).
- Rear brake backplate mounting bolts loose (Chapter 9).
- Worn or damaged steering or suspension components (Chapter 10).

Noise (grinding or high-pitched squeal) when brakes applied

- Brake pad or shoe friction lining material worn down to metal backing (Chapter 1).
- Excessive corrosion of brake disc or drum (especially if the vehicle has been standing for some time) (Chapter 1).
- Foreign object (stone chipping etc) trapped between brake disc and splash shield (Chapter 1).

Excessive brake pedal travel

- Inoperative rear brake self-adjust mechanism (Chapter 1).
- Faulty master cylinder (Chapter 9).
- Air in hydraulic system (Chapter 9).

Brake pedal feels spongy when depressed

- Air in hydraulic system (Chapter 9).
- Deteriorated flexible rubber brake hoses (Chapter 9).
- Master cylinder mounting nuts loose (Chapter 9).
- Faulty master cylinder (Chapter 9).

Excessive brake pedal effort required to stop vehicle

- Faulty vacuum servo unit (Chapter 9).
- Disconnected, damaged or insecure brake servo vacuum hose (Chapter 9).
- Primary or secondary hydraulic circuit failure (Chapter 9).
- Seized brake caliper or wheel cylinder piston(s) (Chapter 9).
- Brake pads or brake shoes incorrectly fitted (Chapter 1).
- Incorrect grade of brake pads or brake shoes fitted (Chapter 1).
- Brake pads or brake shoe linings contaminated (Chapter 1).

Judder felt through brake pedal or steering wheel when braking

- Excessive run-out or distortion of front discs or rear drums (Chapter 9).
- Brake pad or brake shoe linings worn (Chapter 1).

- Brake caliper or rear brake backplate mounting bolts loose (Chapter 9).
- Wear in suspension, steering components or mountings (Chapter 10).

Brakes binding

- Seized brake caliper or wheel cylinder piston(s) (Chapter 9).
- Incorrectly adjusted handbrake mechanism or linkage (Chapter 1).
- Faulty master cylinder (Chapter 9).

Rear wheels locking under normal braking

- Rear brake shoe linings contaminated (Chapter 1).
- Faulty brake pressure compensators in the rear wheel cylinders (Chapter 9).

9 Suspension and steering systems

Note: *Before diagnosing suspension or steering faults, be sure that the trouble is not due to incorrect tyre pressures, mixtures of tyre types or binding brakes.*

Vehicle pulls to one side

- Defective tyre (Chapter 1).
- Excessive wear in suspension or steering components (Chapter 10).
- Incorrect front wheel alignment (Chapter 10).
- Accident damage to steering or suspension components (Chapter 10).

Wheel wobble and vibration

- Front roadwheels out of balance (vibration felt mainly through the steering wheel) (Chapter 10).
- Rear roadwheels out of balance (vibration felt throughout the vehicle) (Chapter 10).
- Roadwheels damaged or distorted (Chapter 10).
- Faulty or damaged tyre (Chapter 10).
- Worn steering or suspension joints, bushes or components (Chapter 10).
- Wheel nuts loose (Chapter 10).

Excessive pitching and/or rolling around corners or during braking

- Defective shock absorbers (Chapter 10).
- Broken or weak coil spring and/or suspension component (Chapter 10).
- Worn or damaged anti-roll bar or mountings (Chapter 10).

Wandering or general instability

- Incorrect front wheel alignment (Chapter 10).
- Worn steering or suspension joints, bushes or components (Chapter 10).
- Roadwheels out of balance (Chapter 10).
- Faulty or damaged tyre (Chapter 1).
- Wheel bolts loose (Chapter 10).
- Defective shock absorbers (Chapter 10).

Excessively stiff steering

- Lack of steering gear lubricant (Chapter 10).
- Seized tie-rod end balljoint or suspension balljoint (Chapter 10).
- Broken or incorrectly adjusted power-assisted steering pump drivebelt (Chapter 1).
- Incorrect front wheel alignment (Chapter 10).
- Steering rack or column bent or damaged (Chapter 10).

Excessive play in steering

- Worn steering column universal joint(s) or intermediate coupling (Chapter 10).
- Worn steering track-rod end balljoints (Chapter 10).
- Worn rack and pinion steering gear (Chapter 10).
- Worn steering or suspension joints, bushes or components (Chapter 10).

Lack of power assistance

- Broken or incorrectly adjusted power-assisted steering pump drivebelt (Chapter 1).
- Incorrect power-assisted steering fluid level (Chapter 1).
- Restriction in power-assisted steering fluid hoses (Chapter 10).
- Faulty power-assisted steering pump (Chapter 10).
- Faulty rack and pinion steering gear (Chapter 10).

Tyre wear excessive

Tyres worn on inside or outside edges
- Tyres underinflated (wear on both edges) (Chapter 1).
- Incorrect camber or castor angles (wear on one edge only) (Chapter 10).
- Worn steering or suspension joints, bushes or components (Chapter 10).
- Excessively hard cornering.
- Accident damage.

Tyre treads exhibit feathered edges
- Incorrect toe setting (Chapter 10).

Tyres worn in centre of tread
- Tyres overinflated (Chapter 1).

Tyres worn on inside and outside edges
- Tyres underinflated (Chapter 1).

Tyres worn unevenly
- Tyres out of balance (Chapter 1).
- Excessive wheel or tyre run-out (Chapter 1).
- Worn shock absorbers (Chapter 10).
- Faulty tyre (Chapter 1).

10   Electrical system

Note: *For problems associated with the starting system, refer to the faults listed under the 'Engine' heading earlier in this Section.*

Battery will not hold a charge for more than a few days

- Battery defective internally (Chapter 12).
- Battery electrolyte level low (Chapter 1).
- Battery terminal connections loose or corroded (Chapter 12).
- Alternator drivebelt worn or incorrectly adjusted (Chapter 1).
- Alternator not charging at correct output (Chapter 12).
- Alternator or voltage regulator faulty (Chapter 12).
- Short-circuit causing continual battery drain (Chapter 12).

Ignition warning light remains illuminated with engine running

- Alternator drivebelt broken, worn, or incorrectly adjusted (Chapter 1).
- Alternator brushes worn, sticking, or dirty (Chapter 12).
- Alternator brush springs weak or broken (Chapter 12).
- Internal fault in alternator or voltage regulator (Chapter 12).
- Broken, disconnected, or loose wiring in charging circuit (Chapter 12).

Ignition warning light fails to come on

- Warning light bulb blown (Chapter 12).
- Broken, disconnected, or loose wiring in warning light circuit (Chapter 12).
- Alternator faulty (Chapter 12).

Lights inoperative

- Bulb blown (Chapter 12).
- Corrosion of bulb or bulbholder contacts (Chapter 12).
- Blown fuse (Chapter 12).
- Faulty relay (Chapter 12).
- Broken, loose, or disconnected wiring (Chapter 12).
- Faulty switch (Chapter 12).

Instrument readings inaccurate or erratic

Instrument readings increase with engine speed
- Faulty voltage regulator (Chapter 12).

Fuel or temperature gauge give no reading
- Faulty gauge sender unit (Chapters 3 or 4).
- Wiring open-circuit (Chapter 12).
- Faulty gauge (Chapter 12).

Fuel or temperature gauges give continuous maximum reading
- Faulty gauge sender unit (Chapter 3 or 4).
- Wiring short-circuit (Chapter 12).
- Faulty gauge (Chapter 12).

Horn inoperative or unsatisfactory in operation

Horn operates all the time
- Horn push either earthed or stuck down (Chapter 12).
- Horn cable to horn push earthed (Chapter 12).

Horn fails to operate
- Blown fuse (Chapter 12).
- Cable or cable connections loose, broken or disconnected (Chapter 12).
- Faulty horn (Chapter 12).

Horn emits intermittent or unsatisfactory sound
- Cable connections loose (Chapter 12).
- Horn mountings loose (Chapter 12).
- Faulty horn (Chapter 12).

Windscreen/tailgate wipers inoperative or unsatisfactory in operation

Wipers fail to operate or operate very slowly
- Wiper blades stuck to screen, or linkage seized or binding (Chapter 12).
- Blown fuse (Chapter 12).
- Cable or cable connections loose, broken or disconnected (Chapter 12).
- Faulty relay (Chapter 12).
- Faulty wiper motor (Chapter 12).

Wiper blades sweep over too large or too small an area of the glass
- Wiper arms incorrectly positioned on spindles (Chapter 1).
- Excessive wear of wiper linkage (Chapter 12).
- Wiper motor or linkage mountings loose or insecure (Chapter 12).

Wiper blades fail to clean the glass effectively
- Wiper blade rubbers worn or perished (Chapter 1).
- Wiper arm tension springs broken or arm pivots seized (Chapter 1).
- Insufficient windscreen washer additive to adequately remove road dirt film (Chapter 1).

Windscreen/tailgate washers inoperative or unsatisfactory in operation

One or more washer jets inoperative
- Blocked washer jet (Chapter 12).
- Disconnected, punctured, kinked or restricted fluid hose (Chapter 12).
- Insufficient fluid in washer reservoir (Chapter 1).

Washer pump fails to operate
- Broken or disconnected wiring or connections (Chapter 12).
- Blown fuse (Chapter 12).
- Faulty washer switch (Chapter 12).
- Faulty washer pump (Chapter 12).

Washer pump runs for some time before fluid is emitted from jets
- Faulty one-way valve in fluid supply hose (Chapter 12).

Electric windows inoperative or unsatisfactory in operation

Window glass will only move in one direction
- Faulty switch (Chapter 12).

Window glass slow to move
- Incorrectly adjusted door glass guide channels (Chapter 11).
- Regulator seized or damaged, or in need of lubrication (Chapter 11).
- Door internal components or trim fouling regulator (Chapter 11).
- Faulty motor (Chapter 11).

Window glass fails to move
- Incorrectly adjusted door glass guide channels (Chapter 11).
- Blown fuse (Chapter 12).
- Faulty relay (Chapter 12).
- Broken or disconnected wiring or connections (Chapter 12).
- Faulty motor (Chapter 12).

Central locking system inoperative or unsatisfactory in operation

Complete system failure
- Blown fuse (Chapter 12).
- Faulty relay (Chapter 12).
- Broken or disconnected wiring or connections (Chapter 12).

Latch locks but will not unlock, or unlocks but will not lock
- Faulty master switch (Chapter 12).
- Broken or disconnected latch operating rods or levers (Chapter 11).
- Faulty relay (Chapter 12).

One solenoid/motor fails to operate
- Broken or disconnected wiring or connections (Chapter 12).
- Faulty solenoid/motor (Chapter 12).
- Broken, binding or disconnected latch operating rods or levers (Chapter 11).
- Fault in door latch (Chapter 11).

MOT test checks

Introduction

Motor vehicle testing has been compulsory in Great Britain since 1960 when the Motor Vehicle (Tests) Regulations were first introduced. At that time testing was only applicable to vehicles ten years old or older, and the test itself only covered lighting equipment, braking systems and steering gear. Current vehicle testing is far more extensive and, in the case of private cars, is now an annual inspection commencing three years after the date of first registration.

This Section is intended as a guide to getting your car through the MOT test. It lists all the relevant testable items, how to check them yourself, and what is likely to cause the vehicle to fail. Obviously it will not be possible to examine the vehicle to the same standard as the professional MOT tester who will be highly experienced in this work and will have all the necessary equipment available. However, working through the following checks will provide a good indication as to the condition of the vehicle and will enable you to identify any problem areas before submitting the vehicle for the test. Where a component is found to need repair or renewal, a cross reference is given to the relevant Chapter in the manual where further information and the appropriate repair procedures will be found.

The following checks have been sub-divided into three categories as follows.

(a) Checks carried out from the driver's seat.
(b) Checks carried out with the car on the ground.
(c) Checks carried out with the car raised and with the wheels free to rotate.

In most cases the help of an assistant will be necessary to carry out these checks thoroughly.

Checks carried out from the driver's seat

Handbrake (Chapters 1 and 9)

Test the operation of the handbrake by pulling on the lever until the handbrake is in the normal fully-applied position. Ensure that the travel of the lever (the number of clicks of the ratchet) is not excessive before full resistance of the braking mechanism is felt. If so this would indicate incorrect adjustment of the rear brakes or incorrectly adjusted handbrake cables. With the handbrake fully applied, tap the lever sideways and make sure that it does not release which would indicate wear in the ratchet and pawl. Release the handbrake and move the lever from side to side to check for excessive wear in the pivot bearing. Check the security of the lever mountings and make sure that there is no corrosion of any part of the body structure within 30 cm (12 in) of the lever mounting. If the lever mountings cannot be readily seen from inside the vehicle, carry out this check later when working underneath.

Footbrake (Chapters 1 and 9)

Check that the brake pedal is sound without visible defects such as excessive wear of the pivot bushes or broken or damaged pedal pad. Check also for signs of fluid leaks on the pedal, floor or carpets which would indicate failed seals in the brake master cylinder. Depress the brake pedal slowly at first, then rapidly until sustained pressure can be held. Maintain this pressure and check that the pedal does not creep down to the floor which would again indicate problems with the master cylinder. Release the pedal, wait a few seconds then depress it once until firm resistance is felt. Check that this resistance occurs near the top of the pedal travel. If the pedal travels nearly to the floor before firm resistance is felt, this would indicate incorrect brake adjustment resulting in 'insufficient reserve travel' of the footbrake. If firm resistance cannot be felt, ie the pedal feels spongy, this would indicate that air is present in the hydraulic system which will necessitate complete bleeding of the system. Check that the servo unit is operating correctly by depressing the brake pedal several times to exhaust the vacuum. Keep the pedal depressed and start the engine. As soon as the engine starts, the brake pedal resistance will be felt to alter. If this is not the case, there may be a leak from the brake servo vacuum hose, or the servo unit itself may be faulty.

Steering wheel and column (Chapter 10)

Examine the steering wheel for fractures or looseness of the hub, spokes or rim. Move the steering wheel from side to side and then up and down, in relation to the steering column. Check that the steering wheel is not loose on the column, indicating wear in the column splines or a loose steering wheel retaining nut. Continue moving the steering wheel as before, but also turn it slightly from left to right. Check that there is no abnormal movement of the steering wheel, indicating excessive wear in the column upper support bearing, universal joint(s) or flexible coupling.

Electrical equipment (Chapter 12)

Switch on the ignition and operate the horn. The horn must operate and produce a clear sound audible to other road users. Note that a gong, siren or two-tone horn fitted as an alternative to the manufacturer's original equipment is not acceptable.

Check the operation of the windscreen washers and wipers. The washers must operate with adequate flow and pressure and with the jets adjusted so that the liquid strikes the windscreen near the top of the glass.

Operate the windscreen wipers in conjunction with the washers and check that the blades cover their designed sweep of the windscreen without smearing. The blades must effectively clean the glass so that the driver has an adequate view of the road ahead and to the front nearside and offside of the vehicle. If the screen smears or does not clean adequately, it is advisable to renew the wiper blades before the MOT test.

Depress the footbrake with the ignition switched on and have your assistant check that both rear stop lights operate, and are extinguished when the footbrake is released. If one stop light fails to operate it is likely that a bulb has blown or there is a poor electrical contact at, or near the bulbholder. If both stop lights fail to operate, check for a blown fuse, faulty stop light switch or possibly two blown bulbs. If the lights stay on when the brake pedal is released, it is possible that the switch is at fault.

Seat belts (Chapter 11)

Note: The following checks are applicable to the seat belts provided for the driver's seat and front passenger's seat. Both seat belts must be of a type that will restrain the upper part of the body; lap belts are not acceptable.

Check the security of all seat belt mountings

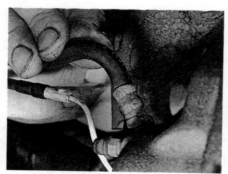

Check the flexible brake hoses for cracks and damage

Examine the steering rack rubber gaiters for condition and security

Shake the roadwheel vigorously to check for excess play in the wheel bearings and suspension components

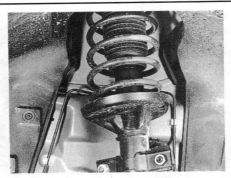

Inspect the front (shown) and where applicable, the rear suspension strut units

Check the condition of the shock absorber mountings and bushes (arrowed)

Carefully examine the seat belt webbing for cuts or any signs of serious fraying or deterioration. If the seat belt is of the retractable type, pull the belt all the way out and examine the full extent of the webbing.

Fasten and unfasten the belt ensuring that the locking mechanism holds securely and releases properly when intended. If the belt is of the retractable type, check also that the retracting mechanism operates correctly when the belt is released.

Check the security of all seat belt mountings and attachments which are accessible, without removing any trim or other components, from inside the car (photo). Any serious corrosion, fracture or distortion of the body structure within 30 cm (12 in) of any mounting point will cause the vehicle to fail. Certain anchorages will not be accessible, or even visible from inside the car and in this instance further checks should be carried out later, when working underneath. If any part of the seat belt mechanism is attached to the front seat, then the seat mountings are treated as anchorages and must also comply as above.

Checks carried out with the car on the ground

Electrical equipment (Chapter 12)

Switch on the side lights and check that both front and rear side lights are illuminated and that the lenses and reflectors are secure and undamaged. This is particularly important at the rear where a cracked or damaged lens would allow a white light to show to the rear, which is unacceptable. It is also worth noting that any lens that is excessively dirty, either inside or out, such that the light intensity is reduced, could also constitute a fail.

Switch on the headlamps and check that both dipped beam and main beam units are operating correctly and at the same light intensity. If either headlamp shows signs of dimness, this is usually attributable to a poor earth connection or severely corroded internal reflector. Inspect the headlamp lenses for cracks or stone damage. Any damage to the headlamp lens will normally constitute a fail, but this is very much down to the tester's discretion. Bear in mind that with all light units they must operate correctly when first switched on. It is not acceptable to tap a light unit to make it operate.

The headlamps must be aligned so as not to dazzle other road users when switched to dipped beam. This can only be accurately checked using optical beam setting equipment so if you have any doubts about the headlamp alignment, it is advisable to have this professionally checked and if necessary reset, before the MOT test.

With the ignition switched on, operate the direction indicators and check that they show a white or amber light to the front and red or amber light to the rear, that they flash at the rate of between one and two flashes per second and that the 'tell-tale' on the instrument panel also functions. Examine the lenses for cracks or damage as described previously.

Footbrake (Chapters 1 and 9)

From within the engine compartment examine the brake pipes for signs of leaks, corrosion, insecurity, chafing or other damage and check the master cylinder and servo unit for leaks, security of their mountings or excessive corrosion in the vicinity of the mountings.

Turn the steering as necessary so that the right-hand front brake flexible hose can be examined. Inspect the hose carefully for any sign of cracks or deterioration of the rubber. This will be most noticeable if the hose is bent in half and is particularly common where the rubber portion enters the metal end fitting (photo). Turn the steering onto full left then full right lock and ensure that the hose does not contact the wheel, tyre, or any part of the steering or suspension mechanism. While your assistant depresses the brake pedal firmly, check the hose for any bulges or fluid leaks under pressure. Now repeat these checks on the left-hand front hose. Should any damage or deterioration be noticed, renew the hose.

Steering mechanism and suspension (Chapters 1 and 10)

Have your assistant turn the steering wheel from side to side slightly, up to the point where the steering gear just begins to transmit this movement to the roadwheels. Check for excessive free play between the steering wheel and the steering gear which would indicate wear in the steering column joints, wear or insecurity of the steering column to steering gear coupling, or insecurity, incorrect adjustment, or wear in the steering gear itself. Generally speaking, free play greater than 1.3 cm (0.5 in) for vehicles with rack and pinion type steering or 7.6 cm (3.0 in) for vehicles with steering box mechanisms should be considered excessive.

Have your assistant turn the steering wheel more vigorously in each direction up to the point where the roadwheels just begin to turn. As this is done, carry out a complete examination of all the steering joints, linkages, fittings and attachments. Any component that shows signs of wear, damage, distortion, or insecurity should be renewed or attended to accordingly. On vehicles equipped with power steering also check that the power steering pump is secure, that the pump drivebelt is in satisfactory condition and correctly adjusted, that there are no fluid leaks or damaged hoses, and that the system operates correctly. Additional checks can be carried out later with the vehicle raised when there will be greater working clearance underneath.

Check that the vehicle is standing level and at approximately the correct ride height. Ensure that there is sufficient clearance between the suspension components and the bump stops to allow full suspension travel over bumps.

Shock absorbers (Chapter 10)

Depress each corner of the car in turn and then release it. If the shock absorbers are in good condition the corner of the car will rise and then settle in its normal position. If there is no noticeable damping effect from the shock absorber, and the car continues to rise and fall, then the shock absorber is defective.

Exhaust system (Chapter 1)

Start the engine and with your assistant holding a rag over the tailpipe, check the entire system for leaks which will appear as a rhythmic fluffing or hissing sound at the source of the leak. Check the effectiveness of the silencer by ensuring that the noise produced is of a level to be expected from a vehicle of similar type. Providing that the system is structurally sound, it is acceptable to cure a leak using a proprietary exhaust system repair kit or similar method.

Checks carried out with the car raised and with the wheels free to rotate

Jack up the front and rear of the car and securely support it on axle stands positioned at suitable load bearing points under the vehicle structure. Position the stands clear of the suspension assemblies and ensure that the wheels are clear of the ground and that the steering can be turned onto full right and left lock.

Steering mechanism (Chapters 1 and 10)

Examine the steering rack rubber gaiters for signs of splits, lubricant leakage or insecurity of the retaining clips (photo). If power steering is fitted, check for signs of deterioration, damage, chafing or leakage of the fluid hoses, pipes or connections. Also check for excessive stiffness or binding of the steering, a missing split pin or locking device or any severe corrosion of the body structure within 30 cm (12 in) of any steering component attachment point.

Have your assistant turn the steering onto full left then full right lock. Check that the steering turns smoothly without undue tightness or roughness and that no part of the steering mechanism, including a wheel or tyre, fouls any brake flexible or rigid hose or pipe, or any part of the body structure.

Front and rear suspension and wheel bearings (Chapters 1 and 10)

Starting at the front right-hand side of the vehicle, grasp the roadwheel at the 3 o'clock and 9 o'clock positions and shake it vigorously. Check for any free play at the wheel bearings, suspension ball joints, or suspension mountings, pivots and attachments. Check also for any serious deterioration of the rubber or metal casing of any mounting bushes, or any distortion, deformation or severe corrosion of any components. Look for missing split pins, tab washers or other locking devices on any mounting or attachment, or any severe corrosion of the vehicle structure within 30 cm (12 in) of any suspension component attachment point. If any excess free play is suspected at a component pivot point, this can be confirmed by using a large screwdriver or similar tool and levering between the mounting and the component attachment. This will confirm whether the wear is in the pivot bush, its retaining bolt or in the mounting itself (the bolt holes can often become elongated). Now grasp the wheel at the 12 o'clock and 6 o'clock positions, shake it vigorously and repeat the previous inspection (photo). Rotate the wheel and check for roughness or tightness of the front wheel bearing such that imminent failure of the bearing is indicated. Carry out all the above checks at the other front wheel and then at both rear wheels. Note, however, that the condition of the rear wheel bearings is not actually part of the MOT test, but if they are at all suspect, it is likely that this will be brought to the owner's attention at the time of the test.

Roadsprings and shock absorbers (Chapters 1 and 10)

On vehicles with strut type suspension units, examine the strut assembly for signs of fluid leakage, corrosion or severe pitting of the piston rod or damage to the casing (photo). Check also for security of the mounting points.

If coil springs are fitted check that the spring ends locate correctly in their spring seats, that there is no severe corrosion of the spring and that it is not cracked, broken or in any way damaged.

If the vehicle is fitted with leaf springs, check that all leaves are intact, that the axle is securely attached to each spring and that there is no wear or deterioration of the spring eye mountings, bushes, and shackles.

The same general checks apply to vehicles fitted with other suspension types, such as torsion bars, hydraulic displacer units etc. In all cases ensure that all mountings and attachments are secure, that there are no signs of excessive wear, corrosion, cracking, deformation or damage to any component or bush, and that there are no fluid leaks or damaged hoses or pipes (hydraulic types).

Inspect the shock absorbers for signs of fluid leakage, excessive wear of the mounting bushes or attachments or damage to the body of the unit (photo).

Driveshafts (front-wheel drive vehicles) (Chapter 1)

With the steering turned onto full lock, rotate each front wheel in turn and inspect the constant velocity joint gaiters for splits or damage (photo). Also check the gaiter is securely attached to its respective housings by clips or other methods of retention.

Continue turning the wheel and check that each driveshaft is straight with no sign of damage.

Braking system (Chapter 1)

If possible, without dismantling, check for wear of the brake pads and the condition of the discs. Ensure that the friction lining material has not worn excessively and that the discs are not fractured, pitted, scored or worn excessively.

Carefully examine all the rigid brake pipes underneath the car and the flexible hoses at the rear. Look for signs of excessive corrosion,

Inspect the constant velocity joint gaiters (arrowed) for splits or damage

chafing or insecurity of the pipes and for signs of bulging under pressure, chafing, splits or deterioration of the flexible hoses.

Look for signs of hydraulic fluid leaks at the brake calipers or on the brake backplates indicating failed hydraulic seals in the components concerned.

Slowly spin each wheel while your assistant depresses the footbrake then releases it. Ensure that each brake is operating and that the wheel is free to rotate when the pedal is released.

Examine the handbrake mechanism and check for signs of frayed or broken cables, excessive corrosion or wear or insecurity of the linkage. Have your assistant operate the handbrake while you check that the mechanism works on each relevant wheel and releases fully without binding.

Exhaust system (Chapter 1)

Starting at the front, examine the exhaust system over its entire length checking for any damaged, broken or missing mountings, security of the pipe retaining clamps and condition of the system with regard to rust and corrosion.

Wheels and tyres (Chapter 1)

Carefully examine each tyre in turn on both the inner and outer walls and over the whole of the tread area and check for signs of cuts, tears, lumps, bulges, separation of the tread and exposure of the ply or cord due to wear or other damage. Check also that the tyre bead is correctly seated on the wheel rim and that the tyre valve is sound and properly seated. Spin the wheel and check that it is not excessively distorted or damaged particularly at the bead rim. Check that the tyres are of the correct size for the car and that they are of the same size and type on each axle. They should also be inflated to the specified pressures.

Using a suitable gauge check the tyre tread depth. The current legal requirement states that the tread pattern must be visible over the whole tread area and must be of a minimum depth of 1.6 mm over at least three-quarters of the tread width. It is acceptable for some wear of the inside or outside edges of the tyre to be apparent but this wear must be in one even circumferential band and the tread must be visible. Any excessive wear of this nature may indicate incorrect front wheel alignment which should be checked before the tyre becomes excessively worn. See Chapters 1 and 10 for further information on tyre wear patterns and front wheel alignment.

Body corrosion

Check the condition of the entire vehicle structure for signs of corrosion in any load bearing areas. For the purpose of the MOT test all chassis box sections, side sills, subframes, crossmembers, pillars, suspension, steering, braking system and seat belt mountings and anchorages should all be considered as load bearing areas. As a general guide, any corrosion which has seriously reduced the metal thickness of a load bearing area to weaken it, is likely to cause the vehicle to fail. Should corrosion of this nature be encountered, professional repairs are likely to be needed.

Chapter 1 Routine maintenance and servicing

Contents

Lubricants, fluids and capacities
Maintenance schedule
Maintenance procedures

Specifications

Engine
Oil filter	Champion C104

Engine codes:
1.3 litre carburettor non-catalyst (15.04)	JBD
1.4 litre carburettor non-catalyst (NEEC 5th)	FUH
1.4 litre CFi with catalyst (83 US)	F6F
1.6 litre carburettor non-catalyst (15.04)	LUK
1.6 litre EFi non-catalyst (15.04)	LJE
1.6 litre EFi with catalyst (83 US)	LJF

Cooling system
Expansion tank pressure cap rating	1.2 bars

Antifreeze mixture (by volume)

	Antifreeze	Water
Protection to – 25°	40%	60%
Protection to – 40°C	50%	50%

Fuel and exhaust systems
Air filter element:
1.3 litre engine	Champion W153
1.4 litre engine	Champion W226
1.6 litre engine, code LUK	Champion W226
1.6 litre engine, codes LJE & LJF	Champion U502
Fuel filter (1.6 litre engine, codes LJE & LJF)	Champion L204

Idle speed (with engine cooling fan on):
1.3 litre engine	750 ± 50 rpm
1.4 litre engine, code FUH	800 ± 50 rpm
1.4 litre engine, code F6F	900 ± 50 rpm
1.6 litre engine, code LUK	800 ± 50 rpm
1.6 litre engine, code LJE	900 ± 50 rpm
1.6 litre engine, code LJF	900 ± 25 rpm

Idle mixture (CO) content:
1.3 litre engine	1.0 ± 0.5%
1.4 litre engine, code FUH	1.0 ± 0.5%
1.4 litre engine, code F6F	Not adjustable
1.6 litre engine, code LUK	1.5 ± 0.5%
1.6 litre engine, code LJE	0.8 ± 0.25%
1.6 litre engine, code LJF	Not adjustable
Minimum fuel octane requirement	95 RON unleaded

Ignition system – general
Firing order:

1.3 litre engine .... 1 – 2 – 4 – 3
1.4 & 1.6 litre engines .... 1 – 3 – 4 – 2
No 1 cylinder location.. Crankshaft pulley end
Ignition timing .... Non-adjustable, computer-controlled
Spark plugs:

1.3 litre engine .... Champion RS9YCC or RS9YC
1.4 litre engine, code FUH... Champion RC7YCC or RC7YC
1.4 litre engine, code F6F .... Champion RC7YCC or RC7YC4
1.6 litre engine, code LUK .... Champion RC7YCC or RC7YC
1.6 litre engine, codes LJE & LJF .... Champion RC6YC or C6YCC
Electrode gap:

1.3 litre engine .... 1.0 mm
1.4 litre engine, code FUH... 0.8 mm
1.4 litre engine, code F6F .... 1.0 mm
1.6 litre engine, codes LUK & LJE .... 0.8 mm
1.6 litre engine, code LJF .... 1.0 mm
Ignition HT leads:

1.3 litre engine .... Champion type not available
1.4 & 1.6 litre engines .... Champion CLS 9

Braking system
Minimum front brake disc pad thickness............................ 1.5 mm
Minimum rear brake shoe lining thickness .... 1.0 mm

Suspension and steering
Power-assisted steering pump drivebelt deflection – refer to alternator drivebelt deflection
Tyre pressures – refer to Specifications in Chapter 10

Electrical system
Alternator drivebelt deflection (see text – Section 10):

All models... 4 mm
Alternator drivebelt tension:

1.3 litre engine with new drivebelt................................ 350 to 450 N
1.3 litre engine with used drivebelt............................... 250 to 350 N
1.4 and 1.6 litre engine with new drivebelt .... 400 to 500 N
1.4 and 1.6 litre engine with used drivebelt .... 300 to 400 N
Wiper blade type:

Windscreen .... Champion X-5103
Tailgate/rear window... Champion X-5103

Torque wrench settings

	Nm	lbf ft
Engine oil drain plug	21 to 28	15 to 20
Spark plugs:		
1.3 litre engine	14 to 20	12 to 15
1.4 and 1.6 litre engines	17 to 33	13 to 24
Manual transmission filler/level plug	23 to 30	17 to 22
Wheel nuts	70 to 100	52 to 74

Are your plugs trying to tell you something?

Normal.
Grey-brown deposits, lightly coated core nose. Plugs ideally suited to engine, and engine in good condition.

Heavy Deposits.
A build up of crusty deposits, light-grey sandy colour in appearance.
Fault: Often caused by worn valve guides, excessive use of upper cylinder lubricant, or idling for long periods.

Lead Glazing.
Plug insulator firing tip appears yellow or green/yellow and shiny in appearance.
Fault: Often caused by incorrect carburation, excessive idling followed by sharp acceleration. Also check ignition timing.

Carbon fouling.
Dry, black, sooty deposits.
Fault: over-rich fuel mixture.
Check: carburettor mixture settings, float level, choke operation, air filter.

Oil fouling.
Wet, oily deposits. Fault: worn bores/piston rings or valve guides; sometimes occurs (temporarily) during running-in period.

Overheating.
Electrodes have glazed appearance, core nose very white – few deposits. Fault: plug overheating. Check: plug value, ignition timing, fuel octane rating (too low) and fuel mixture (too weak).

Electrode damage.
Electrodes burned away; core nose has burned, glazed appearance. Fault: pre-ignition. Check: for correct heat range and as for 'overheating'.

Split core nose.
(May appear initially as a crack). Fault: detonation or wrong gap-setting technique. Check: ignition timing, cooling system, fuel mixture (too weak).

WHY DOUBLE COPPER IS BETTER FOR YOUR ENGINE.

Unique Trapezoidal Copper Cored Earth Electrode

50% Larger Spark Area

Copper Cored Centre Electrode

Champion Double Copper plugs are the first in the world to have copper core in both centre _and_ earth electrode. This innovative design means that they run cooler by up to 100°C – giving greater efficiency and longer life. These double copper cores transfer heat away from the tip of the plug faster and more efficiently. Therefore, Double Copper runs at cooler temperatures than conventional plugs giving improved acceleration response and high speed performance with no fear of pre-ignition.

Champion Double Copper plugs also feature a unique trapezoidal earth electrode giving a 50% increase in spark area. This, together with the double copper cores, offers greatly reduced electrode wear, so the spark stays stronger for longer.

 FASTER COLD STARTING

 FOR UNLEADED OR LEADED FUEL

 ELECTRODES UP TO 100°C COOLER

 BETTER ACCELERATION RESPONSE

 LOWER EMISSIONS

50% BIGGER SPARK AREA

 THE LONGER LIFE PLUG

Plug Tips/Hot and Cold.
Spark plugs must operate within well-defined temperature limits to avoid cold fouling at one extreme and overheating at the other.
Champion and the car manufacturers work out the best plugs for an engine to give optimum performance under all conditions, from freezing cold starts to sustained high speed motorway cruising.
Plugs are often referred to as hot or cold. With Champion, the higher the number on its body, the hotter the plug, and the lower the number the cooler the plug.

Plug Cleaning
Modern plug design and materials mean that Champion no longer recommends periodic plug cleaning. Certainly don't clean your plugs with a wire brush as this can cause metal conductive paths across the nose of the insulator so impairing its performance and resulting in loss of acceleration and reduced m.p.g.
However, if plugs are removed, always carefully clean the area where the plug seats in the cylinder head as grit and dirt can sometimes cause gas leakage.
Also wipe any traces of oil or grease from plug leads as this may lead to arcing.

CHAMPION

DOUBLE COPPER

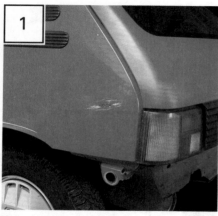

This photographic sequence shows the steps taken to repair the dent and paintwork damage shown above. In general, the procedure for repairing a hole will be similar; where there are substantial differences, the procedure is clearly described and shown in a separate photograph.

First remove any trim around the dent, then hammer out the dent where access is possible. This will minimise filling. Here, after the large dent has been hammered out, the damaged area is being made slightly concave.

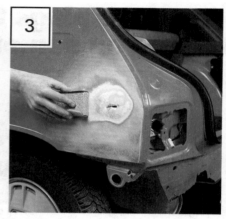

Next, remove all paint from the damaged area by rubbing with coarse abrasive paper or using a power drill fitted with a wire brush or abrasive pad. 'Feather' the edge of the boundary with good paintwork using a finer grade of abrasive paper.

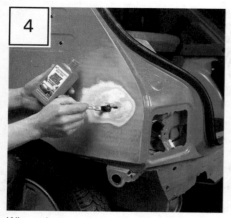

Where there are holes or other damage, the sheet metal should be cut away before proceeding further. The damaged area and any signs of rust should be treated with Turtle Wax Hi-Tech Rust Eater, which will also inhibit further rust formation.

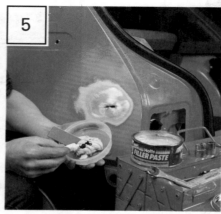

For a large dent or hole mix Holts Body Plus Resin and Hardener according to the manufacturer's instructions and apply around the edge of the repair. Press Glass Fibre Matting over the repair area and leave for 20-30 minutes to harden. Then ...

... brush more Holts Body Plus Resin and Hardener onto the matting and leave to harden. Repeat the sequence with two or three layers of matting, checking that the final layer is lower than the surrounding area. Apply Holts Body Plus Filler Paste as shown in Step 5B.

For a medium dent, mix Holts Body Plus Filler Paste and Hardener according to the manufacturer's instructions and apply it with a flexible applicator. Apply thin layers of filler at 20-minute intervals, until the filler surface is slightly proud of the surrounding bodywork.

For small dents and scratches use Holts No Mix Filler Paste straight from the tube. Apply it according to the instructions in thin layers, using the spatula provided. It will harden in minutes if applied outdoors and may then be used as its own knifing putty.

Use a plane or file for initial shaping. Then, using progressively finer grades of wet-and-dry paper, wrapped round a sanding block, and copious amounts of clean water, rub down the filler until glass smooth. 'Feather' the edges of adjoining paintwork.

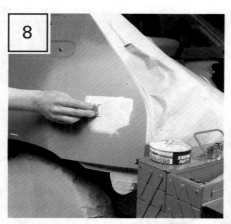

7 Protect adjoining areas before spraying the whole repair area and at least one inch of the surrounding sound paintwork with Holts Dupli-Color primer.

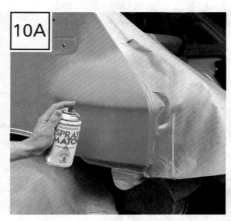

8 Fill any imperfections in the filler surface with a small amount of Holts Body Plus Knifing Putty. Using plenty of clean water, rub down the surface with a fine grade wet-and-dry paper – 400 grade is recommended – until it is really smooth.

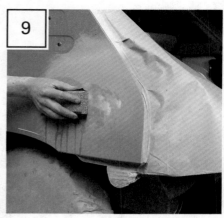

9 Carefully fill any remaining imperfections with knifing putty before applying the last coat of primer. Then rub down the surface with Holts Body Plus Rubbing Compound to ensure a really smooth surface.

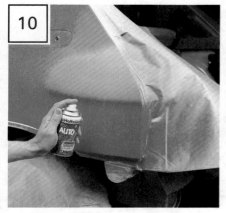

10 Protect surrounding areas from overspray before applying the topcoat in several thin layers. Agitate Holts Dupli-Color aerosol thoroughly. Start at the repair centre, spraying outwards with a side-to-side motion.

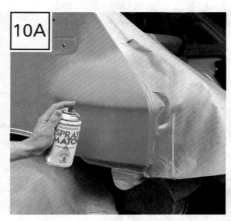

10A If the exact colour is not available off the shelf, local Holts Professional Spraymatch Centres will custom fill an aerosol to match perfectly.

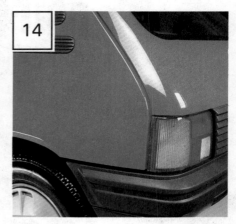

10B To identify whether a lacquer finish is required, rub a painted unrepaired part of the body with wax and a clean cloth.

11 If *no* traces of paint appear on the cloth, spray Holts Dupli-Color clear lacquer over the repaired area to achieve the correct gloss level.

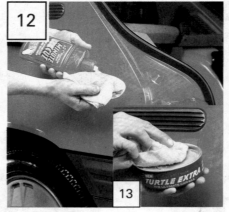

12 The paint will take about two weeks to harden fully. After this time it can be 'cut' with a mild cutting compound such as Turtle Wax Minute Cut prior to polishing with a final coating of Turtle Wax Extra.

13

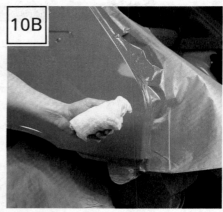

14 When carrying out bodywork repairs, remember that the quality of the finished job is proportional to the time and effort expended.

HAYNES No1 for DIY

Haynes publish a wide variety of books besides the world famous range of *Haynes Owners Workshop Manuals*. They cover all sorts of DIY jobs. Specialist books such as the *Improve and Modify* series and the *Purchase and DIY Restoration Guides* give you all the information you require to carry out everything from minor modifications to complete restoration on a number of popular cars. In addition there are the publications dealing with specific tasks, such as the *Car Bodywork Repair Manual* and the *In-Car Entertainment Manual*. The *Household DIY* series gives clear step-by-step instructions on how to repair everyday household objects ranging from toasters to washing machines.

Whether it is under the bonnet or around the home there is a Haynes Manual that can help you save money. Available from motor accessory stores and bookshops or direct from the publisher.

Lubricants, fluids and capacities

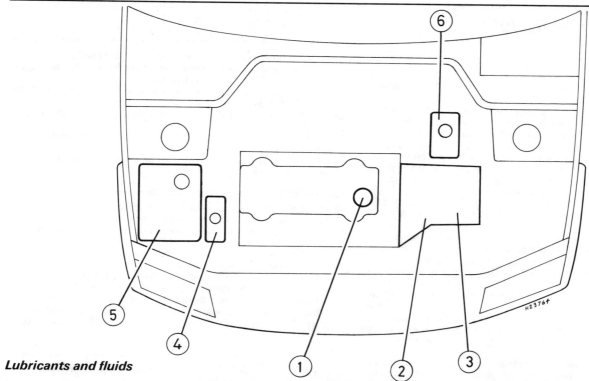

Lubricants and fluids

Component or system	Lubricant type/specification	Duckhams recommendation
1 Engine	Multigrade engine oil, viscosity range SAE 10W/30 to 20W/50, to API SG	Duckhams QXR, Hypergrade, or 10W/40 Motor Oil
2 Manual gearbox	SAE 80 high pressure gear oil	Duckhams Hypoid 80
3 Automatic transmission	Fluid to Ford specification ESP-M2C 166- H	Duckhams Uni-Matic or D-Matic
4 Power-assisted steering	Fluid to Ford specification ESP-M2C 166- H	Duckhams Uni-Matic or D-Matic
5 Cooling system	Ethylene-glycol based antifreeze, suitable for use in mixed-metal systems (Ford specification ESD-M97B-49-A)	Duckhams Universal Antifreeze and Summer Coolant
6 Brake hydraulic fluid	Super DOT 4 Hydraulic fluid to Ford specification ESD-M6C57-A	Duckhams Universal Brake and Clutch Fluid
Wheel hub bearing grease (front and rear)	To Ford specification SAM-1C-9111A	Duckhams LB10 or LBM10

Capacities

Engine oil
Capacity (excluding filter):
HCS (OHV) engine .... 3.25 litres
CVH (OHC) engine .... 3.50 litres
Difference between MAX and MIN dipstick marks:
All engines .... 1.0 litre

Cooling system (including heater)
1.3 HCS engine .... 7.1 litres
1.4 CVH engine .... 7.6 litres
1.6 CVH engine .... 7.8 litres

Fuel tank .... 55.0 litres

Manual gearbox (including differential)
Four-speed .... 2.8 litres
Five-speed .... 3.1 litres

Automatic transmission
Total capacity – less oil cooler .... 3.5 litres
Total capacity – with oil cooler .... 3.6 litres

Washer system reservoir
Excluding headlamp washer system .... 4.0 litres
Including headlamp washer system............................... 8.0 litres

Maintenance schedule

Introduction

This Chapter is designed to help the DIY owner maintain the Ford Escort/Orion with the goals of maximum economy, safety, reliability and performance in mind.

On the following pages is a master maintenance schedule, listing the servicing requirements, and the intervals at which they should be carried out as recommended by the manufacturers. The operations are listed in the order in which the work can be most conveniently undertaken. For example, all the operations that are performed from within the engine compartment are grouped together, as are all those that require the car to be raised and supported for access to the suspension and underbody. Alongside each operation in the schedule is a reference which directs the reader to the Sections in this Chapter covering maintenance procedures or to other Chapters in the Manual, where the operations are described and illustrated in greater detail. Specifications for all the maintenance operations, together with a list of lubricants, fluids and capacities are provided at the beginning of this Chapter. Refer to the accompanying photographs of the engine compartment and the underbody of the vehicle for the locations of the various components.

Servicing your vehicle in accordance with the mileage/time maintenance schedule and step-by-step procedures will result in a planned maintenance programme that should produce a long and reliable service life. Bear in mind that it is a comprehensive plan, so maintaining some items but not others at the specified intervals will not produce the same results.

The first step in this maintenance programme is to prepare yourself before the actual work begins. Read through all the procedures to be undertaken then obtain all the parts, lubricants and any additional tools needed.

Every 250 miles (400 km) or weekly

Operations internal and external

Check, and if necessary adjust, the tyre pressures (Section 8)

Operations in the engine compartment

Check the engine oil level (Section 1)
Check the engine coolant level (Section 2)
Check the screen washer fluid level (Section 10)
Check the battery electrolyte level where a low-maintenance or regular-maintenance type battery has replaced a maintenance-free type battery (Section 10)

Every 6000 miles (10 000 km) or 12 months, whichever comes first

In addition to all the items listed above, carry out the following:

Operations internal and external

Check tightness of the roadwheel nuts (Section 8)
Visually examine the tyres for tread depth, and wear or damage (Section 8)
Check the operation of the lights, indicators, horn(s), instruments and windscreen washer system(s) (Section 10)
Check the operation of the heating/air conditioning system (Section 2)
Check operation and condition of the seat belts (Section 9)

Operations with the vehicle raised and supported

Renew the engine oil (Section 1)
Renew the oil filter (Section 1)
Check the front brake disc pads for wear (Section 7)

Check the rear brake linings for excessive wear (Section 7)
Visually examine the brake lines and hoses for security and signs deterioration and/or damage (Section 7)
Visually examine the underbody, wheel arches and body panels for damage (Section 9)
Check the exhaust system for condition, leakage and security (Section 3)
Check the driveshafts and rubber gaiters for damage and leakage (Section 6)
Check for excessive wear and security of the suspension front lower arm balljoints (Section 8)

Operations in the engine compartment

Check for oil and coolant leaks (Sections 1 and 2)
Check the idle speed and CO content (Section 3)
Check idle fuel mixture adjustment on carburettor models only (Section 3)*
Check base idle speed on 1.6 EFi models only (Section 3)*
Check the brake fluid level (Section 7)
Check the automatic transmission fluid level (Section 5)
Check, and if necessary renew, the spark plugs (Section 4)
Check the operation of and lubricate the bonnet catch (Section 9)
*At first 6000 miles (10 000 km) service on carburettor and fuel injected engines, then every 12 000 miles (20 000 km) thereafter on carburettor engines only)

Every 12 000 miles (20 000 km) or 24 months, whichever comes first

The operations are the same as for the 6000 mile (10 000 km) service but with the following amendments:

Operations with the vehicle raised and supported

Check the manual transmission oil level (Section 5)

Operations in the engine compartment

Check and if required, adjust the valve clearances – HCS engine (Chapter 2)
Renew the spark plugs (Section 4)
Check the power-assisted steering fluid level (Section 8)
Check the condition and tension of all drivebelts (Section 10)
Where applicable, check the air conditioning system hoses and connections and the freon level (Section 2)

Every 24 000 miles (40 000 km) or 48 months, whichever comes first

The operations are the same as for the 6000 mile (10 000 km) service but with the following amendments:

Operations internal and external

Check and if necessary adjust the front wheel alignment (Chapter 10)

Operations with the vehicle raised and supported

Renew the fuel filter – fuel injection models (Section 3)*
Renew the automatic transmission fluid (Section 5)
Adjust the handbrake (Section 7)

Operations in the engine compartment

Check the condition of the oil filler cap – HCS engine (Section 1)
Renew the air filter element (Section 3)
Check the air cleaner temperature control (Section 3)
Renew the crankcase emission adaptor – HCS engine and CVH carburettor and CFi engines (Section 3)

Renew the crankcase emission pad – EFi engine (Section 3)
Starting at 48 000 miles (84 000 km) and every 48 000 miles (84 000 km) thereafter.

Every 36 000 miles (60 000 km)

Operations in the engine compartment
Renew the timing belt – CVH engine (Chapter 2)

Operations external
Check the front wheel alignment (Chapter 10)

Every 36 months

Operations with the vehicle raised and supported
Renew the brake hydraulic fluid (Section 7)

Every 48 months

Operations in the engine compartment
Drain, flush and refill the cooling system, and renew the antifreeze (Section 2)

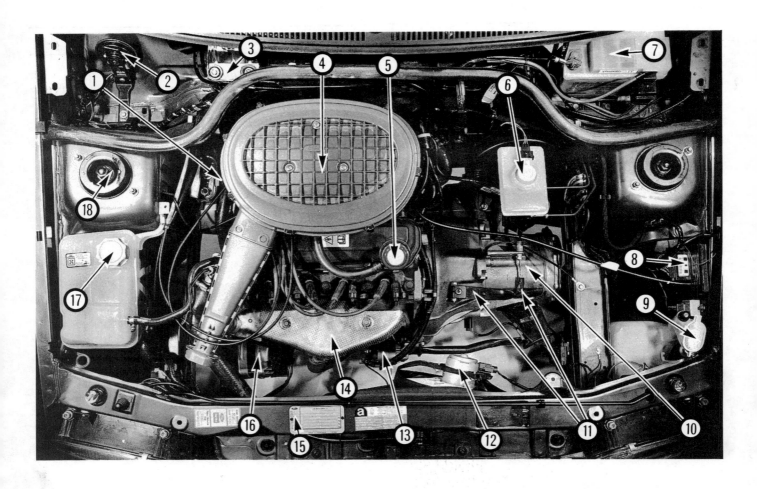

Engine compartment component locations – 1.3 litre HCS (OHV) engine

1   Oil level dipstick location
2   Anti-theft alarm horn
3   Windscreen wiper motor
4   Air cleaner
5   Engine oil filler cap
6   Brake master cylinder
    reservoir

7   Battery
8   Engine management
    control module
9   Washer fluid reservoir
10 Transmission

11 Clutch operating lever and
    cable
12 Cooling fan
13 Starter motor
14 Exhaust heat shield/air
    deflector

15 Vehicle identification plate
    (VIN)
16 Alternator
17 Coolant expansion tank
18 Suspension upper
    mounting

Engine compartment component locations – 1.6 litre CVH (OHC) carburettor engine

1   Oil level dipstick location
2   Anti-theft alarm horn
3   Windscreen wiper motor
4   Air cleaner
5   Engine oil filler cap
6   Brake master cylinder
    reservoir

7   Battery
8   Ignition coil
9   Engine management
    control module
10 Washer fluid reservoir
11 Transmission

12 Clutch cable
13 Cooling fan
14 Starter motor
15 Exhaust heat shield/air
    deflector
16 Vehicle identification plate
    (VIN)

17 Intake air temperature
    control valve
18 Coolant expansion tank
19 Suspension upper
    mounting

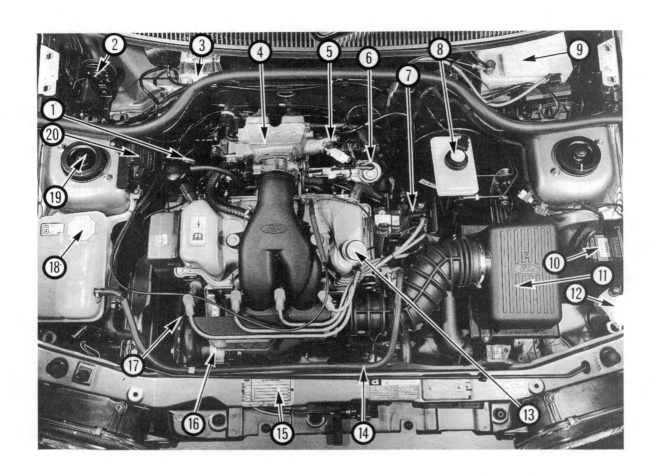

Engine compartment component locations – 1.6 litre CVH (OHC) EFi engine

1 Oil level dipstick location	6 Fuel pressure regulator	11 Air cleaner housing	16 Alternator
2 Anti-theft alarm horn	7 Ignition coil	12 Washer fluid reservoir	17 Alternator drivebelt
3 Windscreen wiper motor	8 Brake master cylinder	13 Engine oil filler cap	18 Coolant expansion tank
4 Throttle body	reservoir	14 Cooling fan	19 Suspension upper
5 Air charge temperature	9 Battery	15 Vehicle identification plate	mounting
sensor	10 EDIS control module	(VIN)	20 MAP sensor

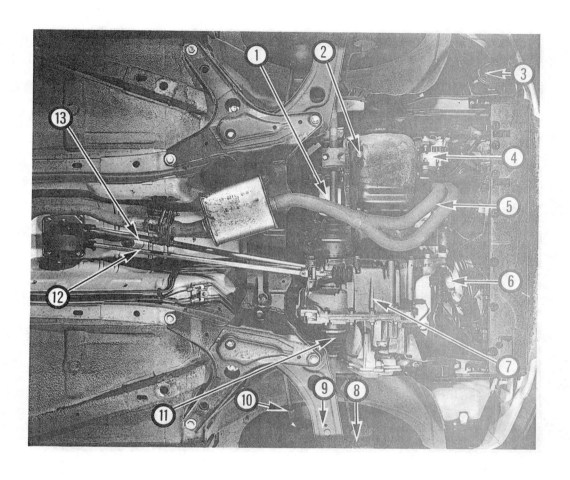

Underside view at front end showing component locations on the 1.3 litre HCS (OHV) engined model

1	Engine oil filter	5	Exhaust downpipe	8	Brake caliper	11	Driveshaft
2	Engine oil drain plug	6	Cooling fan	9	Lower suspension arm	12	Gearshift rod
3	Horn	7	Transmission	10	Track rod	13	Stabiliser rod (transmission)
4	Alternator						

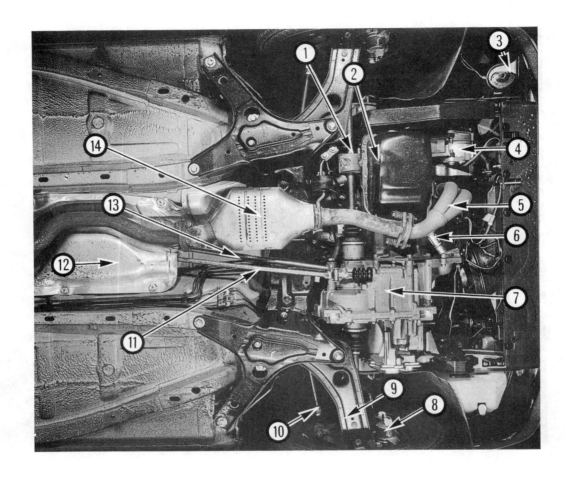

Underside view at front end showing component locations on the 1.6 litre CVH (OHC) EFi-engined model

1 Driveshaft	5 Exhaust downpipe	9 Lower suspension arm	12 Heatshield
2 Engine oil drain plug	6 HEGO sensor	10 Track rod	13 Stabiliser rod (transmission)
3 Horn	7 Transmission	11 Gearshift rod	14 Catalytic converter
4 Alternator	8 Brake caliper		

Underside view at rear end showing component locations on the 1.3 litre HCS (OHV) engined model

1 Fuel filler pipe	3 Fuel tank	5 Rear axle beam	7 Exhaust system
2 Handbrake cable adjuster	4 Suspension mounting	6 Exhaust rear silencer	support/insulator

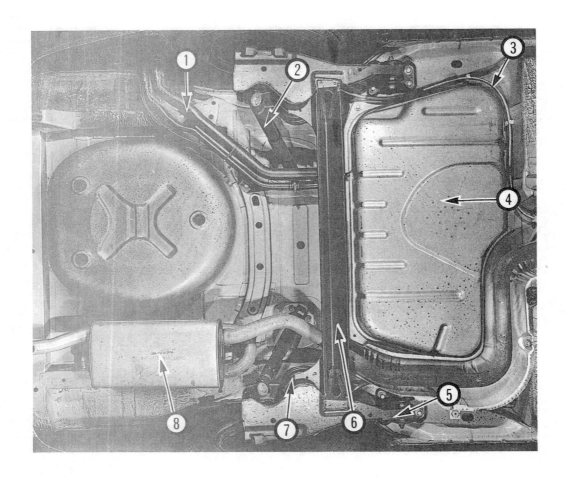

Underside view at rear end showing component locations on the 1.6 litre CVH (OHC) EFi-engine model

1 Fuel filler pipe	3 Handbrake cable	5 Suspension mounting	7 Rear coil spring
2 Shock absorber	4 Fuel tank	6 Rear axle beam	8 Exhaust system *rear silencer*

Maintenance procedures

1 Engine

Engine oil level check

1   The engine oil level is checked with a dipstick that extends through a tube and into the sump at the bottom of the engine. The dipstick is located towards the rear right-hand side of the engine.

2   The oil level should be checked with the vehicle standing on level ground and before it is driven, or at least 5 minutes after the engine has been switched off. If the oil is checked immediately after driving the vehicle, some of the oil will remain in the upper engine components and oil galleries, resulting in an inaccurate reading on the dipstick.

3   Withdraw the dipstick from the tube and wipe all the oil from its end with a clean rag or paper towel. Insert the clean dipstick back into the tube as far as it will go, then withdraw it once more. Check that the oil level is between the upper (MAX) and lower (MIN) marks/notches on the dipstick. If the level is at (or below) the lower (MIN) mark/notch, pull free or unscrew the oil filler cap (according to type) on the top of the valve cover and add fresh oil of the correct grade until the level is on the upper (MAX) mark/notch, but take care not to overfill (photos). Note that the difference between the minimum and maximum marks/notches on the dipstick corresponds to 1 litre.

4   Always maintain the level between the two dipstick marks/notches. If the level is allowed to fall below the lower mark/notch, oil starvation may result which could lead to severe engine damage. If the engine is overfilled by adding too much oil, this may result in oil fouled spark plugs, oil leaks or oil seal failures.

5   An oil can spout or funnel may help to reduce spillage when adding oil to the engine. Always use the correct grade and type of oil as shown in *Lubricants, fluids and capacities*.

Engine oil and filter renewal

6   Frequent oil and filter changes are the most important preventative maintenance procedures that can be undertaken by the DIY owner. As engine oil ages, it becomes diluted and contaminated, which leads to premature engine wear.

7   Before starting this procedure, gather together all the necessary tools and materials (photo). Also make sure that you have plenty of clean rags and newspapers handy to mop up any spills. Ideally, the engine oil should be warm as it will drain better and more built-up sludge will be removed with it. Take care, however, not to touch the exhaust or any other hot parts of the engine when working under the vehicle. To avoid any possibility of scalding, and to protect yourself from possible skin irritants and other harmful contaminants in used engine oils, it is advisable to wear rubber gloves when carrying out this work. Access to the underside of the vehicle will be greatly improved if it can be raised on a lift, driven onto ramps or jacked up and supported on axle stands. Whichever method is chosen, the sump drain plug should be at the lowest point to enable the oil to drain fully. This requires the vehicle to be as level as possible since the drain plug is located in the centre of the sump.

8   Position a suitable container (of sufficient capacity) beneath the drain plug. Clean the drain plug and the area around it, then slacken it half a turn (photo). If possible, try to keep the plug pressed into the sump while unscrewing it by hand the last couple of turns. As the plug releases from the threads, move it away sharply so the stream of oil issuing from the sump runs into the container, not up your sleeve.

9   Allow some time for the old oil to drain, noting that it may be necessary to reposition the container as the oil flow slows to a trickle.

10   After all the oil has drained, wipe off the drain plug with a clean rag and renew its sealing washer. Clean the area around the drain plug opening then refit and tighten the plug to the specified torque setting.

11   If applicable at this service, move the oil drain container into position under the oil filter. On HCS engines the filter is located on the inlet manifold side of the cylinder block, whilst on CVH engines it is located on the exhaust manifold side of the cylinder block.

12   Using an oil filter removal tool, slacken the filter initially (photo).

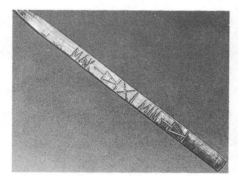

1.3A Engine oil dipstick MAXimum and MINimum level markings

1.3B Topping up the engine oil level (1.3 HCS engine)

1.3C Topping up the engine oil level (1.6 CVH engine)

1.7 Tools required for engine oil and filter renewal

1.8 Engine oil drain plug in the sump (HCS engine)

1.12 Oil filter removal using a strap wrench (CVH engine)

1.14A Engine oil filter (HCS engine)

1.14B Engine oil filter (CVH engine)

Loosely wrap some rags around the oil filter, then unscrew it and immediately position it with its open end uppermost to prevent further spillage of oil. Remove the oil filter from the engine keeping it upright. Withdraw the oil container and holding the filter over it, invert the filter and empty its oil into the container.

13   Use a clean rag to remove all oil, dirt and sludge from the filter sealing area on the engine. Check the old filter to make sure that its rubber sealing ring has not stuck to the engine. If it has, carefully remove it.

14   Apply a light coating of clean oil to the new sealing ring on the new filter then screw it into position on the engine (photos). Tighten the filter by hand only – do not use any tools. Initially tighten the filter to the point where its seal is just in contact with the mating face on the engine, then further tighten it by three quarters of one turn to secure. Wipe clean the exterior of the oil filter.

15   Remove all tools from under the vehicle then if applicable, lower the vehicle to the ground.

16   Unscrew the oil filler cap on the valve cover and fill the engine with the specified quantity and grade of oil, as described earlier in this Section. Pour the oil in slowly otherwise it may overflow from the top of the valve cover. Check that the oil level is up to the maximum mark on the dipstick.

17   Start the engine and run it for a few minutes while checking for leaks around the oil filter seal and the sump drain plug.

18   Switch off the engine and wait a few minutes for the oil to settle in the sump once more. With the new oil circulated and the filter now completely full, recheck the level on the dipstick and add more oil if necessary.

19   Dispose of the used engine oil safely with reference to *Tools and working facilities* in the preliminary Sections of this Manual.

Oil filler cap check – HCS engine

20   Remove and inspect the cap to ensure that it is in good condition and not blocked up with sludge. Clean it if necessary by brushing the inner mesh filter with petrol and blowing through with light pressure from an air line. Renew the cap if it is badly congested.

General engine checks

21   Visually inspect the engine joint faces, gaskets and seals for any signs of water or oil leaks. Pay particular attention to the areas around the cylinder head gasket joint, valve cover joint, sump joint, and oil filter. Bear in mind that over a period of time some very slight seepage from these areas is to be expected but what you are really looking for is any indication of a serious leak. Should a leak be found, renew the offending gasket or oil seal by referring to the appropriate Chapters in this Manual.

22   Also check the security and condition of all the engine related pipes and hoses. Ensure that all cable ties or securing clips are in place and in good condition. Clips which are broken or missing can lead to chafing of the hoses, pipes or wiring which could cause more serious problems in the future.

2   Cooling, heating and ventilation systems

Coolant level check

Warning: *DO NOT attempt to remove the expansion tank pressure cap when the engine is hot, as there is a very great risk of scalding.*

1   All models are equipped with a pressurised cooling system. A translucent expansion (de-gas) tank is located on the right-hand side of the engine compartment. As engine temperature increases, the coolant expands and travels through the hose to the expansion tank. As the engine cools, the coolant is automatically drawn back into the system to maintain the correct level.

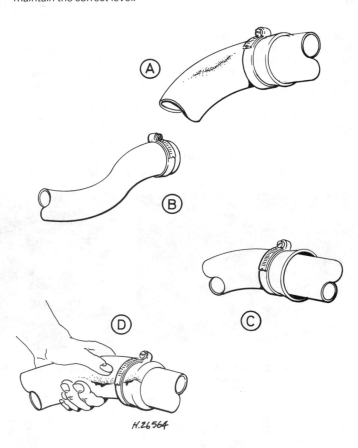

H.26564

Fig. 1.1 Coolant hose inspection (Sec 2)

A   Check hose for chafed or burned areas; these may lead to sudden and costly failure

B   A soft hose indicates inside deterioration, leading to contamination of the cooling system and clogging of the radiator

C   A hardened hose can fail at any time; tightening the clamps will not seal the joint or prevent leaks

D   A swollen hose or one with oil-soaked ends indicates contamination from oil or grease. Cracks and breaks can be easily seen by squeezing the hose

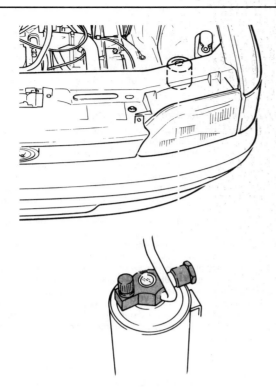

Fig. 1.2 Air conditioning system refrigerant reservoir and level sight glass (arrowed) (Sec 2)

2   The coolant level in the expansion tank should be checked regularly. The level in the tank varies with the temperature of the engine. When the engine is cold, the coolant level should be up to the maximum (MAX) level mark on the side of the tank (photo). When the engine is hot, the level will be slightly above the mark.

3   If topping up is necessary, wait until the engine is cold, then slowly unscrew the pressure cap on the expansion tank. Allow any remaining pressure to escape then fully unscrew the cap. If the coolant level needs topping up when the engine is hot, wait for a period of ten minutes, then place a cloth over the pressure cap, initially loosen off the pressure cap by one turn only to allow the system pressure to escape. Once the pressure is released, the cap can be removed and the coolant level topped up.

4   Add a mixture of water and antifreeze (see below) through the expansion tank filler neck until the coolant is up to the maximum (MAX) level mark. It should be noted that if water only is added, the mixture strength of the antifreeze will be diluted and its effectiveness reduced (photo). Refit and tighten the pressure cap. Where the engine is still hot, it is advisable to add hot coolant to prevent the possibility of internal engine damage caused by sudden contraction.

5   The addition of coolant should only be necessary at very infrequent intervals. If frequent topping up is required, it is likely there is a leak in

the system. Check the radiator, all hoses and joint faces for any sign of staining or actual wetness, and rectify as necessary. If no leaks can be found, it is advisable to have the pressure cap and the entire system pressure-tested by a dealer or suitably equipped garage as this will often show up a small leak not previously visible.

Coolant draining

Warning: *Wait until the engine is cold before starting this procedure. Do not allow antifreeze to come in contact with your skin or painted surfaces of the vehicle. Rinse off spills immediately with plenty of water.*

6   If the engine is cold, unscrew and remove the pressure cap from the expansion tank. If it is not possible to wait until the engine is completely cold, wait for a period of ten minutes then place a cloth over the pressure cap of the expansion tank and slowly unscrew the cap one full turn. Wait until all pressure has escaped, then remove the cap.

7   Place a suitable container beneath the radiator drain plug which is located in the rear face, near the base of the left-hand end tank (photo).

8   Loosen the plug and allow the coolant to drain into the container.

9   Both engine types also have a cylinder block drain plug, the removal of which ensures full draining of coolant from the engine. The engine drain plug is located next to the rear core plug on the exhaust manifold side of the cylinder block.

10   If the system needs to be flushed after draining, refer to the following paragraphs, otherwise tighten the drain plug in the radiator.

System flushing

11   With time the cooling system may gradually lose its efficiency if the radiator matrix becomes choked with rust and scale deposits. If this is the case, the system must be flushed as follows. First drain the coolant as already described.

12   Loosen the retaining clips and disconnect the top and bottom hoses from the radiator. Insert a garden hose in the radiator top hose connection stub and allow the water to circulate through the radiator until it runs clear from the bottom outlet.

13   To flush the engine and the remainder of the system, remove the thermostat as described in Chapter 3, then insert the garden hose into the thermostat coolant passage in the cylinder head and allow the water (under low pressure) to circulate through the engine until it runs clear from the bottom hose.

14   In severe cases of contamination the radiator should be reverse-flushed. To do this, first remove it from the vehicle as described in Chapter 3, invert it and insert a hose in the bottom outlet. Continue flushing until clear water runs from the top hose outlet.

15   If, after a reasonable period, the water still does not run clear, the radiator should be flushed with a good proprietary cleaning system such as Holts Radflush or Holts Speedflush. The regular renewal of corrosion inhibiting antifreeze should prevent severe contamination of the system. Note that as the radiator is of aluminium it is important not to use caustic soda or alkaline compounds to clean it.

Coolant filling

16   Tighten the radiator drain plug and where applicable, refit the cylinder block drain plug. If the cooling system was flushed through, refit the thermostat and reconnect the cooling system hoses.

17   Slowly pour the appropriate mixture of water and antifreeze into

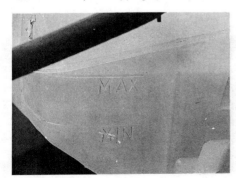

2.2 Coolant reservoir MAXimum and MINimum level marks

2.4 Topping up the coolant level with specified anti-freeze mixture

2.7 Radiator drain plug location (arrowed)

the expansion tank. Continue to fill the expansion tank until the coolant is at the maximum level.

18   Start the engine and run it at 1500 rpm (a fast idle speed) for approximately 4 minutes. Keep the expansion tank topped up to the maximum level during this period.

19   Refit the pressure cap to the expansion tank and run the engine at 1500 rpm for a few minutes until the electric cooling fan cuts in. During this period the coolant will circulate around the engine and any remaining air will be purged to the expansion tank.

20   Switch off the engine and allow it to cool, then check the coolant level as described earlier and top up if necessary.

Antifreeze mixture

21   The antifreeze should always be renewed at the specified intervals. This is necessary not only to maintain the antifreeze properties, but also to prevent corrosion which would otherwise occur as the corrosion inhibitors become progressively less effective.

22   Always use an ethylene-glycol based antifreeze which is suitable for use in mixed metal cooling systems. The percentage quantity of antifreeze and levels of protection afforded are indicated in the Specifications.

23   Before adding antifreeze the cooling system should be completely drained, preferably flushed, and all hoses checked for condition and security.

24   After filling with the correct water/antifreeze mixture, a label should be attached to the radiator or expansion tank stating the type and concentration of antifreeze used and the date installed. Any subsequent topping up should be made with the same type and concentration of antifreeze.

25   Do not use engine antifreeze in the screen washer system, as it will cause damage to the vehicle paintwork. A screen wash such as Turtle Wax High Tech Screen Wash should be added to the washer system in the recommended quantities.

General cooling system checks

26   The engine should be cold for the cooling system checks, so perform the following procedure before driving the vehicle or after the engine has been switched off for at least three hours.

27   Remove the expansion tank filler cap (see above) and clean it thoroughly inside and out with a rag. Also clean the filler neck on the expansion tank. The presence of rust or corrosion in the filler neck indicates that the coolant should be changed. The coolant inside the expansion tank should be relatively clean and transparent. If it is rust-coloured, drain and flush the system and refill with a fresh coolant mixture.

28   Carefully check the radiator hoses and heater hoses along their entire length. Renew any hose which is cracked, swollen or deteriorated. Cracks will show up better if the hose is squeezed. Pay close attention to the hose clips that secure the hoses to the cooling system components. Hose clips can pinch and puncture hoses, resulting in cooling system leaks. If wire type hose clips are used, it may be a good idea to replace them with screw-type clips.

29   Inspect all the cooling system components (hoses, joint faces etc) for leaks. A leak in the cooling system will usually show up as white or rust-coloured deposits on the area adjoining the leak. Where any problems of this nature are found on system components, renew the component or gasket with reference to Chapter 3.

30   Undo the retaining screws along the top face of the front grille panel, lift the panel clear to allow access to inspect the front face of the radiator. Clean the front of the radiator with a soft brush to remove all insects, leaves etc, imbedded in the radiator fins. Be extremely careful not to damage the radiator fins or cut your fingers on them. Refit the grille.

Heating/air conditioning system check

31   Check that the heating system and, where fitted, the air conditioning system operates correctly. Inspect the system hoses for any signs of leaks, which if present, must be renewed without delay. If any air conditioning hoses are in need of replacement, entrust the task to a Ford dealer or air conditioning specialist.

32   During the winter period it is advisable to run the air conditioning system occasionally in order to ensure correct functioning of the compressor.

33   The refrigerant (freon) level in the air conditioning system must be checked at the specified intervals by examining it through the sight glass in the top face of the refrigerant reservoir. The reservoir is located in the front left-hand corner of the engine compartment. When making the check the ambient air temperature should be at least 18°C. Start the engine, allow it to run at idle speed and then switch on the air conditioning system. Set the blower switch to the recirculating air position '3'. Check that the fluid stream viewed through the reservoir sight glass is clear of bubbles after a period of about 10 seconds, if not, consult your Ford dealer or an air conditioning specialist and have the system checked further.

3   Fuel and exhaust systems

Warning: *Certain procedures in this Section require the removal of fuel lines and connections which may result in some fuel spillage. Before carrying out any operation on the fuel system refer to the precautions given in Safety first! at the beginning of this Manual and follow them implicitly. Petrol is a highly dangerous and volatile liquid and the precautions necessary when handling it cannot be overstressed.*

Air cleaner filter element renewal

1   The air cleaner element must be renewed at the specified intervals or more frequently where the vehicle is used regularly in dusty or dirty environments.

2   To renew the element, undo the retaining screws and/or release the cover securing clips according to type, then lift the cover from the air cleaner body (photos).

3   Remove the filter element from inside the air cleaner body.

4   The manufacturers also specify renewal of the crankcase emission adaptor (or in the case of the CVH engine fitted with the EFi system, the crankcase emission pad) at the same time as the air filter element is renewed.

5   Clean the inside of the air cleaner body and fit a new filter element and crankcase emission adaptor pad (as applicable). Do not attempt to clean the element for re-use, it must be renewed.

6   Refit the top cover and secure with the retaining clips and screws.

3.2A On non-EFi models, undo the air filter cover retaining screws ...

3.2B ... and release the clips to ...

3.2C ... withdraw the filter cover and the element

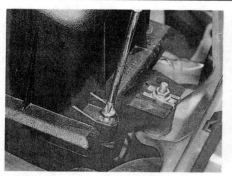

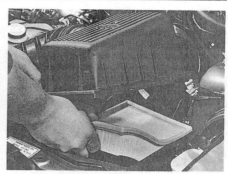

3.2D On EFi models, undo the air filter cover screws ...

3.2E ... and release the clips to ...

3.2F ... withdraw the cover and lift out the element

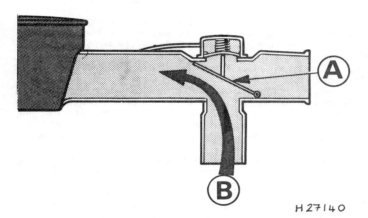

Fig. 1.3 Air cleaner temperature control valve location in the intake duct showing the valve (A) in the open position allowing warm airflow from the exhaust manifold (B) (Sec 3)

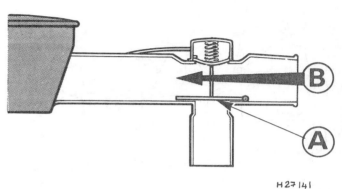

Fig. 1.4 Air cleaner temperature control valve (A) in the closed position allowing cool airflow (B) (Sec 3)

Air cleaner temperature control system check (Carburettor fuel system)

7   In order for the engine to operate efficiently, the temperature of the air entering the inlet system must be controlled within certain limits.

8   The air cleaner has two sources of air, one direct from the outside of the engine compartment, and the other from a shroud on the exhaust manifold. A wax-controlled thermostatic valve controls a flap inside the air cleaner inlet. When the ambient air temperature is below the predetermined level the flap directs air from the exhaust manifold shroud, and as the temperature of the incoming air rises the flap opens to admit more air from outside the vehicle until eventually it is fully open.

9   This check must be made when the engine is cold. Detach and remove the air cleaner inlet trunking.

10   Examine the position of the check valve within the duct. When the air temperature around the valve is below 28°C, the valve must be open to allow hot air to enter the filter (see Fig. 1.3).

11   Refit the inlet duct. Start the engine and run it until it reaches its normal operating temperature, then stop the engine, remove the intake duct and check that the valve has closed off the air passage from the exhaust and opened the main (cool) air intake (see Fig. 1.4). If the flap does not operate correctly check that it is not seized. Apart from this there is no adjustment possible and the unit should be renewed if faulty. Refit the air intake duct to complete.

Fuel filter renewal (CFi and EFi systems)

12   An in-line fuel filter is provided in the fuel pump outlet line. To remove it, raise and support the vehicle at the front on axle stands.

13   Locate a suitable container beneath the filter, then loosen off the fuel supply line retaining clip and allow the pressure in the system to be released.

Fig. 1.5 Fan sensor multi-plug with temporary wire connected (Sec 3)

14   Release the supply and outlet hose clips and detach the hoses from the filter unit.

15   Unscrew the filter clamp bolt and withdraw the filter, taking care not to spill any fuel remaining in it.

16   Fit the new filter making sure that the fuel direction arrows on the body are pointing away from the fuel pump side (photo). Depending on the type of filter fitted, if crimped type clips were used to secure the hoses, these should be replaced with worm-drive alternatives.

17   When the filter is fitted and the hoses reconnected, turn the ignition on and off five times to activate the pump, then check the fuel filter and hose connections for any sign of fuel leaks before lowering the vehicle to the ground.

3.16 Fuel filter showing direction of flow arrow (EFi model)

3.26 Mixture adjustment (carburettor models)

3.33 Base idle speed adjusting screw (arrowed) in the throttle housing (EFi model)

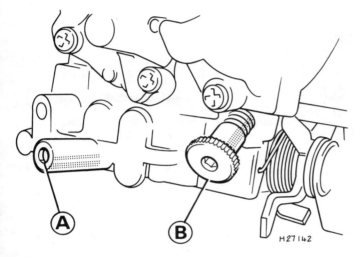

Fig. 1.6 Carburettor idle mixture adjustment screw (A) and idle speed screw (B) (Sec 3)

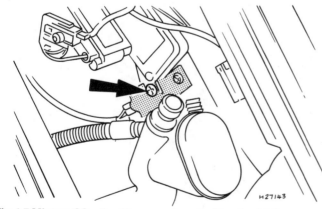

Fig. 1.7 Mixture CO adjusting screw (arrowed) on the 1.6 litre EFi engine (Sec 3)

Idle speed and CO content adjustment (Carburettor models)

18   Before carrying out the following checks and if necessary adjustments, ensure that the spark plugs are in good condition and correctly gapped (see Sec 4). To carry out the checks/adjustments, an accurate tachometer and an exhaust gas analyzer (CO meter) will be required.

19   Make sure that all electrical components are switched off during the following procedures.

20   Connect a tachometer to the engine in accordance with the manufacturer's instructions and insert the probe of an exhaust gas analyzer (CO meter) into the exhaust tailpipe. As previously mentioned,

these items are essential in obtaining an accurate setting. If they are not available, an approximate check/adjustment can be made as a temporary measure providing they are further checked out as soon as is possible using a tachometer and a CO meter.

21   Run the engine at a fast idle speed until it reaches its normal operating temperature and the cooling fan cuts-in. Turn the engine off then disconnect the cooling fan lead at the sensor in-line connector. Now connect a temporary wire to the fan sensor multi-plug, as shown in Fig. 1.5, to enable the fan to operate continuously during the following checks and adjustments (if required). Take care to keep clear of the fan during the following operations when working in the engine compartment.

22   Where fitted, disconnect the throttle kicker vacuum pipe and plug the end. To identify the throttle kicker unit, refer to photo 18.1A in Chapter 4.

23   Check that the vehicle lighting and other electrical loadings (apart from the fan) are switched off, restart the engine, then increase the engine speed to 3000 rpm for 30 seconds and repeat this at three minute intervals during the check/adjustment procedures. This will ensure that any excess fuel is cleared from the inlet manifold.

24   Ensure that the throttle is fully released, allow the meters to stabilise for a period of 3 to 5 seconds then check the idle speed against that specified. If adjustment is necessary, turn the idle speed screw until the engine is idling at the specified speed. Any checks and adjustments must be completed within 30 seconds of the meters stabilising.

25   If adjustment to the mixture is required, the tamperproof cap will need to be removed from the carburettor to gain access to the mixture screw. To do this, first unclip the fuel trap from the side of the air cleaner unit, then remove the air cleaner unit ensuring that the crankcase ventilation trap remains connected. Prise free the tamperproof cap (with the aid of a thin-bladed screwdriver), then with the vacuum and emission control pipes connected to it, relocate the air cleaner unit temporarily into position.

26   Turn the mixture adjustment screw clockwise to weaken the mixture or anti-clockwise to richen it until the CO reading is as given in the Specifications (photo). If a CO meter is not being used, weaken the mixture as described, then enrich the mixture until the maximum engine speed is obtained, consistent with even running.

27   If necessary, re-adjust the idling speed then check the CO reading again. Repeat as necessary until both the idling speed and CO reading are correct.

28   Where required by law, fit a new tamperproof cap to the mixture adjustment screw.

29   Disconnect the tachometer and the CO meter, refit the air cleaner unit and reconnect the fan sensor lead multi-plug to complete.

Base idle speed adjustment (1.6 litre EFi models)

30   Proceed as described in paragraphs 18 to 20 inclusive (for carburettor models), then continue as follows.

31   Run the engine at a fast idle speed until it reaches its normal operating temperature and the cooling fan cuts into operation, then check the CO content of the exhaust and compare it against the specified reading. If the CO content reading is incorrect it can be adjusted by prising free the tamperproof cap for access to the CO adjustment screw then turning the screw in the required direction to suit.

32   Check the base idle speed by first disconnecting the multi-plug from the idle speed control valve. Increase the engine speed to 2000 rpm and holding it at that speed for 30 seconds, fully release the throttle and check if the base idle speed registered is as specified in Chapter 4.

33   If adjustment is necessary, prise free the tamperproof plug using a suitable small screwdriver to gain access to the base idle adjustment screw in the throttle body. Turn the screw in the required direction to adjust the base idle speed to the specified amount. Turning the screw anti-clockwise increases the idle speed (photo).

34   Repeat the procedure outlined in paragraph 32 to recheck and further adjust the base idle speed if required, then fit a new tamperproof plug into position.

35   Reconnect the idle speed control valve multi-plug, and check that the engine speed briefly rises to about 900 rpm, then drops down to the specified normal idle speed.

36   On completion, disconnect the tachometer and the CO meter, but continue running the engine at idle speed for a period of about five minutes to enable the engine management module to relearn its values before switching it off.

General fuel system checks

37   The fuel system components and fixings should be periodically inspected for condition and security. If the smell of petrol is noticed while driving or after the vehicle has been parked, the system should be thoroughly inspected immediately.

38   The fuel system is most easily checked with the vehicle raised on a hoist or suitably supported on axle stands so the components underneath are readily visible and accessible.

39   Remove the fuel tank filler cap and check it for damage. Check that the seal surfaces of the cap and the filler neck are clean and in good condition. Renew the cap if necessary.

40   With the vehicle raised, inspect the fuel tank and filler neck for punctures, cracks and other damage. The connection between the filler neck and tank is especially critical. Sometimes a filler neck or connecting hose will leak due to loose retaining clamps or a general deterioration of its condition.

41   Carefully check all rubber hoses and metal fuel lines leading away from the fuel tank. Check for loose connections, deteriorated hoses, crimped lines and other damage. Pay particular attention the vent pipes and hoses which often loop up around the filler neck and can become blocked or crimped. Follow the lines to the front of the vehicle, carefully inspecting them all the way. Renew damaged sections as necessary.

42   From within the engine compartment, check the security of all fuel hose attachments and inspect the fuel hoses and vacuum hoses for kinks, chafing and deterioration.

43   Check the operation of the throttle linkage and lubricate the linkage components with a few drops of light oil.

Exhaust system check

44   With the engine cold (at least an hour after the vehicle has been driven), check the complete exhaust system from the engine to the end of the tailpipe. Ideally the inspection should be carried out with the vehicle on a hoist to permit unrestricted access, but if a hoist is not available raise and support the vehicle safely on axle stands.

45   Check the exhaust pipes and connections for evidence of leaks, severe corrosion and damage. Make sure that all brackets and mountings are in good condition and tight. Leakage at any of the joints or in other parts of the system will usually show up as a black sooty stain in the vicinity of the leak. Holts Flexiwrap and Holts Gun Gum exhaust repair systems can be used for effective repairs to exhaust pipes and silencer boxes, including ends and bends. Holts Flexiwrap is an MOT approved permanent exhaust repair. Holts Firegum is suitable for the assembly of all exhaust system joints except for the joints forward of the catalytic converter unit (where applicable). In this instance it is important that **no** sealant is applied.

46   Rattles and other noises can often be traced to the exhaust system, especially the brackets and mountings. Inspect the condition of the mountings and insulators (photo). Try to move the pipes and silencers. If the components can come into contact with the body or suspension parts, secure the system with new mountings or if possible, separate the joints and twist the pipes as necessary to provide additional clearance.

47   Run the engine at idling speed then temporarily place a cloth rag over the rear end of the exhaust pipe and listen for any escape of exhaust gases that would indicate any leaks in the system.

3.46 Inspect the condition of the exhaust system mountings and insulators

48   On completion lower the vehicle to the ground.

49   The inside of the exhaust tailpipe can be an indication of the running condition of the engine. The exhaust deposits here are an indication of the engine's state-of-tune. If the pipe is black and sooty, the engine is in need of a tune-up, including a thorough fuel system inspection and adjustment.

Pulse air system

50   Where fitted, unclip and remove the lid from the pulse air system reservoir (see Chapter 4). Remove the element and clean it by soaking it in petrol, then dry it. Wipe clean the inside surfaces of the reservoir.

51   Soak the element in clean engine oil and insert it into position in the reservoir, then refit the lid. Ensure that the lid clips firmly into position.

4   Ignition system

Warning: *Voltages produced by an electronic ignition system are considerably higher than those produced by conventional systems. Extreme care must be taken when working on the system with the ignition switched on. Persons with surgically-implanted cardiac pacemaker devices should keep well clear of the ignition circuits, components and test equipment.*

Spark plug check and renewal

1   The correct functioning of the spark plugs is vital for the correct running and efficiency of the engine. It is essential that the plugs fitted are appropriate for the engine, the suitable type being specified at the beginning of this Chapter. If the correct type of plug is used and the engine is in good condition, the spark plugs should not need attention between scheduled renewal intervals, except for adjustment of their gaps. Spark plug cleaning is rarely necessary and should not be attempted unless specialised equipment is available as damage can easily be caused to the firing ends.

2   To remove the plugs, first open the bonnet then clean and inspect the HT leads to see if they are numerically marked for positional identification. If they are not numbered, mark the HT leads one to four to correspond to the appropriate cylinder number (number one cylinder is at the crankshaft pulley end of the engine). Pull the HT leads from the plugs by gripping the end fitting, not the lead, otherwise the lead connection may be fractured.

3   It is advisable to remove any dirt from the spark plug recesses using a clean brush, vacuum cleaner or compressed air before removing the plugs. This will prevent any dirt dropping into the cylinders.

4   Unscrew the plugs using a spark plug spanner, suitable box spanner or a deep socket and extension bar (photo). Keep the socket in

4.4A Tools required for removing, adjusting and refitting the spark plugs

4.4B Spark plug removal using the correct type box socket

4.10A Measuring the spark plug electrode gap using a feeler gauge

4.10B Measuring the spark plug electrode gap using a special gauge

4.11 Adjusting spark plug electrode gap using special tool

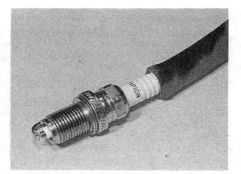

4.13A Use a short length of rubber hose to facilitate insertion of the spark plugs

alignment with the spark plug, otherwise if it is forcibly moved to either side, the ceramic top of the spark plug may be broken off. As each plug is removed, examine it as follows.

5   Examination of the spark plugs will give a good indication of the condition of the engine. If the insulator nose of the spark plug is clean and white, with no deposits, this is indicative of a weak mixture or too hot a plug (a hot plug transfers heat away from the electrode slowly, a cold plug transfers heat away quickly).

6   If the tip and insulator nose are covered with hard black-looking deposits, then this is indicative that the mixture is too rich. Should the plug be black and oily, then it is likely that the engine is fairly worn, as well as the mixture being too rich.

7   If the insulator nose is covered with light tan to greyish brown deposits, then the mixture is correct and it is likely that the engine is in good condition.

8   If the spark plug has only completed 6000 miles (10 000 km) in accordance with the routine maintenance schedule, it should still be serviceable until the 12 000 mile (20 000 km) service when it is renewed. However, it is recommended that it is re-gapped in order to maintain peak engine efficiency and to allow for the 0.025 mm normal increase in gap which occurs approximately every 1000 miles. If, due to engine condition, the spark plug is not serviceable, it should be renewed.

9   The spark plug gap is of considerable importance as, if it is too large or too small, the size of the spark and its efficiency will be seriously impaired. For the best results the spark plug gap should be set in accordance with the Specifications at the beginning of this Chapter.

10   To set it, measure the gap with a feeler gauge, and then bend open, or close, the outer plug electrode until the correct gap is achieved (photos). The centre electrode should never be bent, as this may crack the insulator and cause plug failure.

11   Special spark plug electrode gap adjusting tools are available from most motor accessory shops (photo).

12   Before fitting the spark plugs check that the threaded connector sleeves are tight and that the plug exterior surfaces and threads are clean.

13   It is very often difficult to insert spark plugs into their holes without cross-threading them. To avoid this possibility, fit a short length of 5/16 inch internal diameter rubber hose over the end of the spark plug. The flexible hose acts as a universal joint to help align the plug with the plug hole. Should the plug begin to cross-thread, the hose will slip on the spark plug, preventing thread damage to the aluminium cylinder head. Remove the rubber hose and tighten the plug to the specified torque using the spark plug socket and a torque wrench (photos). Refit the remaining spark plugs in the same manner.

14   Clean and inspect the HT leads as described below prior to reconnecting them in their correct order.

HT leads check and renewal

15   The spark plug HT leads should be checked whenever new spark plugs are installed in the engine.

16   Ensure that the leads are numbered before removing them to avoid confusion when refitting. Pull one HT lead from its plug by gripping the end fitting, not the lead, otherwise the lead connection may be fractured.

17   Check inside the end fitting for signs of corrosion, which will look like a white crusty powder. Push the end fitting back onto the spark plug ensuring that it is a tight fit on the plug. If it isn't, remove the lead again and use pliers to carefully crimp the metal connector inside the end fitting until it fits securely on the end of the spark plug.

18   Using a clean rag, wipe the entire length of the lead to remove any built-up dirt and grease. Once the lead is clean, check for burns, cracks and other damage. Do not bend the lead excessively or pull the lead lengthwise – the conductor inside might break.

19   Compress the lead to ignition coil retaining clips and disconnect the other end of the lead from its location in the ignition coil. The coil is similar in appearance to a conventional ignition distributor and is mounted on the rear end face of the cylinder head. Again, detach the lead by gripping it on the end fitting. Check for corrosion and a tight fit in the same manner as the spark plug end. If an ohmmeter is available,

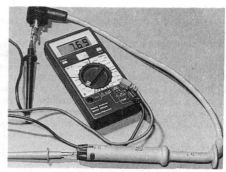

4.13B Tightening a spark plug to the specified torque wrench setting

4.19A Disconnecting an HT lead from the ignition coil (CVH engine)

4.19B Check HT leads for continuity as shown

check the HT leads for continuity (by connecting the meter between the spark plug end and the coil end of the lead) (photos). Refit the lead securely on completion.
20   Check the remaining HT leads one at a time, in the same way.
21   If new HT leads are required, purchase a set suitable for your specific vehicle and engine.
22   Even with the ignition system in first class condition, some engines may still occasionally experience poor starting attributable to damp ignition components. To disperse moisture, Holts Wet Start can be very effective. Holts Damp Start should be used for providing a sealing coat to exclude moisture from the ignition system, and in extreme difficulty, Holts Cold Start will help to start a car when only a very poor spark occurs.

5   Manual gearbox and automatic transmission

Manual gearbox oil level check

1   Position the vehicle over an inspection pit, on vehicle ramps, or jack it up, but make sure that it is level.
2   Unscrew the filler plug from the front-facing side of the gearbox (photo).
3   The oil level is correct when it is level with or no more than 10 mm below the bottom edge of the filler hole. A suitable length of wire rod bent to suit can be inserted and used as a dipstick to assess the level of the oil below the filler hole.
4   Where necessary top up the level using the correct grade of oil then refit and tighten the filler plug (photo).
5   If the gearbox requires frequent topping up, check it for leakage especially around the driveshaft oil seals and repair as necessary.

Automatic transmission fluid level check

6   Check the fluid level when the car has been recently used and the fluid is hot.
7   Position the vehicle on level ground then apply the handbrake and move the selector lever through the various positions three times finally positioning it in P.
8   Allow the engine to run for a minute, then with the engine still idling, withdraw the dipstick from the transmission housing, wipe it on a clean cloth, insert it again then withdraw it once more and read off the level. Ideally the level should be in the centre of the mark on the dipstick. The fluid must never be allowed to fall below the bottom of the mark otherwise there is a risk of damaging the transmission. The transmission must never be overfilled so that the level is above the top of the mark otherwise there is a risk of overheating.
9   If topping-up is necessary, turn the engine off then add a quantity of the specified fluid to the transmission through the dipstick tube. Use a funnel with a fine mesh screen to avoid spillage and to ensure that any foreign matter is trapped.
10   After topping-up recheck the level again, as described above, refit the dipstick and switch off the engine.

Automatic transmission fluid renewal

11   The automatic transmission fluid should only be changed when the transmission is cold.
12   Position the vehicle over an inspection pit, on vehicle ramps, or jack it up, but make sure that it is level.
13   Place a suitable container beneath the drain plug on the transmission sump pan. Remove the dipstick to speed up the draining operation.
14   Unscrew the drain plug in the transmission sump pan and allow the fluid to drain into the container.

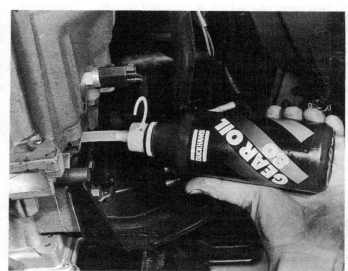

5.2 Unscrewing the manual transmission oil filler/level plug

5.4 Topping up the oil level in the manual transmission

6.1A Check the condition of the outer ...

15   When all the fluid has drained (this may take quite some time) clean the drain plug then refit it together with a new seal and tighten it securely.

16   Place a funnel with a fine mesh screen in the dipstick tube and fill the transmission with the specified type of fluid. Depending on the extent to which the fluid was allowed to drain, the maximum amount of fluid required when filling the transmission will be approximately 4.2 litres, but due to fluid remaining in the system, it is most unlikely to require all of this amount. Add about half this amount and then run the engine up to its normal operating temperature and check the level on the dipstick. When the level approaches the maximum mark, proceed as detailed in paragraphs 8 and 9 to check the level and complete the final topping up as described.

6   Driveshafts

Driveshaft rubber gaiter and CV joint check

1   With the vehicle raised and securely supported on axle stands, turn the steering onto full lock then slowly rotate the roadwheel. Inspect the condition of the outer constant velocity (CV) joint rubber gaiters while squeezing the gaiters to open out the folds. Check for signs of cracking, splits or deterioration of the rubber which may allow the escape of grease and lead to the ingress of water and grit into the joint. Also check the security and condition of the retaining clips. Repeat these checks on the inner CV joints. If any damage or deterioration is found, the gaiters should be renewed as described in Chapter 8 (photos).

2   At the same time check the general condition of the outer CV joints themselves by first holding the driveshaft and attempting to rotate the wheels. Repeat this check on the inner joints by holding the inner joint yoke and attempting to rotate the driveshaft.

3   Any appreciable movement in the CV joint indicates wear in the joint, wear in the driveshaft splines or a loose driveshaft retaining nut.

6.1B ... and inner driveshaft CV joint gaiters

7   Braking system

Hydraulic fluid level check

1   The brake fluid reservoir is located on the top of the brake master cylinder which is attached to the front of the vacuum servo unit. The maximum and minimum marks are indicated on the side of the translucent reservoir and the fluid level should be maintained between these marks at all times.

2   The brake fluid inside the reservoir is readily visible. With the car on level ground the level should normally be just below the MAXimum mark but at least above the MINimum (Danger) mark.

3   Progressive wear of the brake pads and brake shoe linings causes the level of the brake fluid to gradually fall, so that when the brake pads are renewed, the original level of the fluid is restored. It is not therefore necessary to top up the level to compensate for this minimal drop, however the level must never be allowed to fall below the minimum mark.

4   If topping-up is necessary, first wipe the area around the filler cap with a clean rag before removing the cap. When adding fluid, pour it carefully into the reservoir to avoid spilling it on surrounding painted surfaces. Be sure to use only the specified hydraulic fluid since mixing different types of fluid can cause damage to the system (photo). See *Lubricants, fluids and capacities* at the beginning of this Chapter.

Warning: *Brake hydraulic fluid can harm your eyes and damage painted surfaces, so use extreme caution when handling and pouring it. Do not use fluid that has been standing open for some time as it absorbs moisture from the air. Excess moisture can cause a dangerous loss of braking effectiveness.*

5   When adding fluid it is a good idea to inspect the reservoir for contamination. The system should be drained and refilled if deposits, dirt particles or contamination are seen in the fluid.

6   After filling the reservoir to the correct level, make sure that the cap is refitted securely to avoid leaks and the entry of foreign matter.

7   If the reservoir requires repeated replenishing to maintain the

7.4 Topping up the fluid level in the brake master cylinder reservoir

correct level, this is an indication of an hydraulic leak somewhere in the system which should be investigated immediately.

Hydraulic fluid renewal

8   The procedure is similar to that for the bleeding of the hydraulic system as described in Chapter 9, except that the brake fluid reservoir should be emptied by syphoning, using a clean poultry baster or similar before starting, and allowance should be made for the old fluid to be removed from the circuit when bleeding a section of the circuit.

Front brake disc pad wear check

9   Apply the handbrake, then jack up the front of the vehicle and support it on axle stands.
10   For better access to the front brake calipers, remove both front wheels.
11   The thickness of the pad linings can be assessed by viewing them through the window in the caliper housing. If the pads are worn down to (or beyond) the specified thickness, they must be renewed as described in Chapter 9.

Rear brake shoe lining wear check

12   Raise and support the vehicle at the rear on axle stands. Chock the front roadwheels.
13   Working from underneath at the rear, prise free and remove the small inspection plug from the inner face of the backplate of each rear brake unit, then with the aid of a torch, look through the inspection hole and inspect the brake lining at that point to assess for excessive wear. Although this method allows for an initial inspection to be made, if the linings appear to have worn down to or beyond the minimum specified thickness, the rear brake drums and shoe assemblies will need to be removed for an accurate assessment and if necessary, the shoes renewed. This procedure is described in Chapter 9.
14   Check that each brake shoe lining thickness (including the shoe) is not less than the thickness given in the Specifications.
15   If any one lining thickness is less than the minimum amount, renew all the rear brake shoes as described in Chapter 9.

Hydraulic pipes and hoses inspection

16   Check for signs of leakage at the pipe unions, then examine the flexible hoses for signs of cracking, chafing and fraying.
17   The brake pipes should be examined carefully for signs of dents, corrosion or other damage. Corrosion should be scraped off, and if the depth of pitting is significant, the pipes renewed. This is particularly likely in those areas underneath the vehicle body where the pipes are exposed and unprotected.
18   Renew any defective brake pipes and/or hoses as described in Chapter 9.

Handbrake check and adjustment

19   Chock the front roadwheels and fully release the handbrake.
20   Raise the vehicle at the rear and support it on axle stands.
21   Check that the handbrake cables are correctly routed and secured by the retaining clips at the appropriate points under the vehicle.
22   The handbrake is checked for adjustment by measuring the amount of movement possible in the handbrake adjuster plungers. These are located on the inside face of each rear brake backplate (photo). The total movement of the two plungers combined should be between 0.5 and 2.0 mm. If the movement measured is outside of this tolerance, the handbrake is in need of adjustment. Adjustment is made altering the position of the in-line cable adjuster sleeve. This is shown in photo 19.4 in Chapter 9.
23   When adjustment to the handbrake is necessary, a new adjustment sleeve locking pin will be required and this must therefore be obtained before making the adjustment.
24   To adjust the handbrake, first ensure that it is fully released, then firmly apply the footbrake a few times to ensure that the rear brake adjustment is taken up by the automatic adjusters. Extract the locking pin from the adjuster sleeve, then turn the sleeve to set the combined movement of the plungers within the tolerance range specified (0.5 to 2.0 mm). Turn the locking nut by hand as tight as is possible (two clicks) against the adjustment sleeve. Now grip the locknut with a suitable wrench and turn it a further two clicks (maximum).
25   Secure the adjustment by inserting the new lock pin.

7.22 Handbrake adjustment plunger

26   Check that the operation of the handbrake is satisfactory, then lower the vehicle to the ground, apply the handbrake and remove the chocks from the front wheels.

8 Suspension and steering

Front suspension and steering check

1   Raise the front of the vehicle and securely support it on axle stands.
2   Visually inspect the balljoint dust covers and the steering rack and pinion gaiters for splits, chafing or deterioration (photos). Any wear of these components will cause loss of lubricant together with dirt and water entry, resulting in rapid deterioration of the balljoints or steering gear.
3   On vehicles equipped with power-assisted steering, check the fluid hoses for chafing or deterioration and the pipe and hose unions for fluid leaks. Also check for signs of fluid leakage under pressure from the steering gear rubber gaiters which would indicate failed fluid seals within the steering gear.
4   Grasp the roadwheel at the 12 o'clock and 6 o'clock positions and try to rock it. Very slight free play may be felt, but if the movement is appreciable further investigation is necessary to determine the source. Continue rocking the wheel while an assistant depresses the footbrake. If the movement is now eliminated or significantly reduced, it is likely that the hub bearings are at fault. If the free play is still evident with the

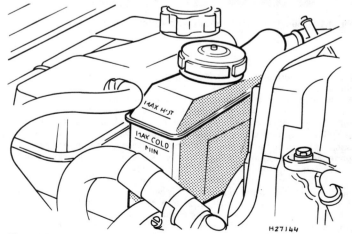

Fig. 1.8 Power-assisted steering fluid reservoir showing MAXimum and MINimum level marks (Sec 8)

Condition	Probable cause	Corrective action	Condition	Probable cause	Corrective action
Shoulder wear	• Underinflation (wear on both sides) • Incorrect wheel camber (wear on one side) • Hard cornering	• Check and adjust pressure • Repair or renew suspension parts • Reduce speed	**Feathered edge** **Toe wear**	• Incorrect toe setting	• Adjust front wheel alignment
Centre wear	• Overinflation	• Measure and adjust pressure	**Uneven wear**	• Incorrect camber or castor • Malfunctioning suspension • Unbalanced wheel • Out-of-round brake disc/drum	• Repair or renew suspension parts • Repair or renew suspension parts • Balance tyres • Machine or renew disc/drum

Fig. 1.9 Tyre wear patterns and causes (Sec 8)

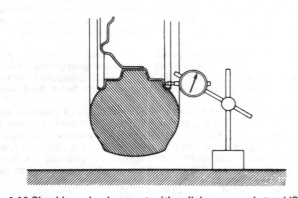

Fig. 1.10 Checking wheel run-out with a dial gauge and stand (Sec 8)

footbrake depressed, then there is wear in the suspension joints or mountings.

5   Now grasp the wheel at the 9 o'clock and 3 o'clock positions and try to rock it as before. Any movement felt now may again be caused by wear in the hub bearings or the steering track rod balljoints. If the outer balljoint is worn the visual movement will be obvious. If the inner joint is suspect it can be felt by placing a hand over the rack and pinion rubber gaiter and gripping the track rod. If the wheel is now rocked, movement will be felt at the inner joint if wear has taken place.

6   Using a large screwdriver or flat bar check for wear in the suspension mounting bushes by levering between the relevant suspension component and its attachment point. Some movement is to be expected as the mountings are made of rubber, but excessive wear should be obvious. Also check the condition of any visible rubber bushes, looking for splits, cracks or contamination of the rubber.

7   With the car standing on its wheels, have an assistant turn the steering wheel back and forth about an eighth of a turn each way. There should be very little, if any, lost movement between the steering wheel and roadwheels. If this is not the case, closely observe the joints and mountings previously described, but in addition check the steering column universal joints for wear and also check the rack and pinion steering gear itself.

Power-assisted steering fluid level check

8   The power steering fluid reservoir is located on the right-hand side of the engine compartment, inboard of the coolant expansion tank.

9   For the fluid level to be checked, the front wheels must be pointing straight ahead and the engine should be stopped. The vehicle must be positioned on level ground.

10   Refer to Fig. 1.8 and check that the fluid is on the maximum level mark.

11   Before removing the filler cap use a clean rag to wipe the cap and the surrounding area to prevent any foreign matter from entering the reservoir. Unscrew and remove the filler cap.

12   Top up if necessary with the specified grade of automatic transmission fluid. Be careful not to introduce dirt into the system, and do not overfill. Frequent topping up indicates a leak which should be investigated.

Power-assisted steering drivebelt check, adjustment and renewal

13   Refer to Section 10 of this Chapter; the procedure is included in the alternator drivebelt adjustment.

Wheel and tyre maintenance and tyre pressure checks

14   The original tyres on this vehicle are equipped with tread wear indicator (TWI) bands which will appear when the tread depth reaches approximately 1.6 mm. Most tyres have a mark around the tyre at regular intervals to indicate the location of the tread wear indicators, the mark being TWI, an arrow or the tyre manufacturer's symbol. Tread wear can also be monitored with a simple inexpensive device known as

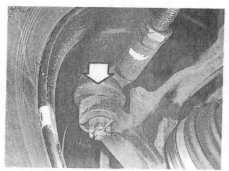

8.2A Check the condition of the track rod balljoint seal (arrowed)

8.2B Check the condition of the lower arm balljoint seal (arrowed)

8.2C Check the condition of the steering rack gaiters

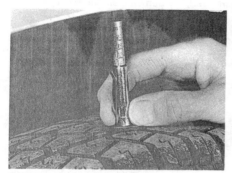

8.14 Tyre tread depth check

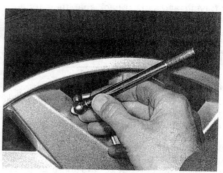

8.16 Check the tyre pressures using a reliable gauge

a tread depth indicator gauge (photo).

15   Wheels and tyres should give no real problems in use provided that a close eye is kept on them with regard to excessive wear or damage. To this end, the following points should be noted.

16   Ensure that tyre pressures are checked regularly and maintained correctly. Checking should be carried out with the tyres cold and not immediately after the vehicle has been in use. If the pressures are checked with the tyres hot, an apparently high reading will be obtained owing to heat expansion. Under no circumstances should an attempt be made to reduce the pressures to the quoted cold reading in this instance, or effective under-inflation will result. Most garage forecourts have a pressure line which combines a gauge to check, and where necessary adjust the tyre pressures, but they usually vary in accuracy due to general misuse and abuse. It therefore pays to carry a good quality tyre pressure gauge in the vehicle to make the regular checks required and ensure pressure accuracy (photo).

17   Note any abnormal tread wear with reference to Fig. 1.9. Tread pattern irregularities such as feathering, flat spots and more wear on one side than the other are indications of front wheel alignment and/or balance problems. If any of these conditions are noted, they should be rectified as soon as possible.

18   Under-inflation will cause overheating of the tyre owing to excessive flexing of the casing, and the tread will not sit correctly on the road surface. This will cause a consequent loss of adhesion and excessive wear, not to mention the danger of sudden tyre failure due to heat build-up.

19   Over-inflation will cause rapid wear of the centre part of the tyre tread coupled with reduced adhesion, harder ride, and the danger of shock damage occurring in the tyre casing.

20   Regularly check the tyres for damage in the form of cuts or bulges, especially in the sidewalls. Remove any nails or stones embedded in the tread before they penetrate the tyre to cause deflation. If removal of a nail reveals that the tyre has been punctured, refit the nail so that its point of penetration is marked. Then immediately change the wheel and have the tyre repaired by a tyre dealer. Do not drive on a tyre in such a condition. In many cases a puncture can be simply repaired by the use of an inner tube of the correct size and type, although make sure that the item which caused the puncture is removed first. If in any doubt as to

the possible consequences of any damage found, consult your local tyre dealer for advice.

21   Periodically remove the wheels and clean any dirt or mud from the inside and outside surfaces. Examine the wheel rims for signs of rusting, corrosion or other damage. Light alloy wheels are easily damaged by 'kerbing' whilst parking, and similarly steel wheels may become dented or buckled. Renewal of the wheel is very often the only course of remedial action possible. Ensure that the wheel retaining nuts are tightened to the specified torque wrench setting.

22   The balance of each wheel and tyre assembly should be maintained to avoid excessive wear, not only to the tyres but also to the steering and suspension components. Wheel imbalance is normally signified by vibration through the vehicle's bodyshell, although in many cases it is particularly noticeable through the steering wheel. Conversely, it should be noted that wear or damage in suspension or steering components may cause excessive tyre wear. Out-of-round or out-of-true tyres, damaged wheels and wheel bearing wear/maladjustment also fall into this category. Balancing will not usually cure vibration caused by such wear.

23   Wheel balancing may be carried out with the wheel either on or off the vehicle. If balanced on the vehicle, ensure that the wheel-to-hub relationship is marked in some way prior to subsequent wheel removal so that it may be refitted in its original position.

24   General tyre wear is influenced to a large degree by driving style – harsh braking and acceleration or fast cornering will all produce more rapid tyre wear. Interchanging of tyres may result in more even wear, however it is worth bearing in mind that if this is completely effective, the added expense is incurred of replacing simultaneously a complete set of tyres, which may prove financially restrictive for many owners.

25   Front tyres may wear unevenly as a result of wheel misalignment. The front wheels should always be correctly aligned according to the settings specified by the vehicle manufacturer.

26   Legal restrictions apply to many aspects of tyre fitting and usage and in the UK this information is contained in the Motor Vehicle Construction and Use Regulations. It is suggested that a copy of these regulations is obtained from your local police if in doubt as to current legal requirements with regard to tyre type and condition, minimum tread depth, etc.

9 Bodywork

Underbody and general body check

1   With the vehicle raised and supported on axle stands or over an inspection pit, thoroughly inspect the underbody and wheel arches for signs of damage and corrosion. In particular examine the bottom of the side sills and concealed areas where mud can collect. Where corrosion and rust is evident, press and tap firmly on the panel with a screwdriver and check for serious corrosion which will necessitate repairs. If the panel is not seriously corroded, clean away the rust and apply a new coating of underseal. Refer to Chapter 11 for more details of body repairs.

2   Check that the doors, bonnet and tailgate/bootlid close securely. Lubricate the hinges, the striker plates and the bonnet catch.

3   Check all external body panels for damage and rectify where necessary.

4   Check the seat belts for satisfactory operation and condition. Inspect the webbing for fraying and cuts. Check that they retract smoothly and without binding into their reels.

10   Electrical system

Battery check and maintenance

Caution: *Before carrying out any work on the vehicle battery, read through the precautions given in Safety first! at the beginning of this Manual. If the battery is to be disconnected, reference must also be made to Section 4 in Chapter 12 for special notes and precautions on disconnecting and reconnecting the battery leads.*

1   Inspect the condition of the battery cables and the tightness of their clamps to ensure good electrical connections. Check the entire length of each cable for cracks and frayed conductors.

2   If corrosion (visible as white, fluffy deposits) is evident, remove the cables from the battery terminals, clean them with a small wire brush then refit them. Corrosion can be kept to a minimum by applying a layer of petroleum jelly to the clamps and terminals after they are reconnected.

3   Make sure that the battery tray is in good condition and the battery retaining clamp is secure.

4   Corrosion on the tray, retaining clamp and the battery itself can be removed with a solution of water and baking soda. Thoroughly rinse all cleaned areas with plain water, but take care not to soak adjacent electrical components (cover them with a plastic sheet as a precaution).

5   Any metal parts of the vehicle damaged by corrosion should be covered with a zinc-based primer, then painted.

6   Further information on the battery including testing and recharging it will be found in Chapter 12. Information on jump-starting the vehicle using a second (booster) battery, is described at the beginning of this Manual.

Alternator drivebelt check, adjustment and renewal

7   The alternator drivebelt is located on the front right-hand side of the engine. Due to its function and material composition, the belt is prone to failure after a period of time and should therefore be inspected and adjusted periodically.

8   The belt configuration depends on the engine fitted and on whether the model is equipped with power-assisted steering or air conditioning.

9   Since the drivebelt is located close to the right-hand side of the engine compartment, it is possible to gain better access by raising the front of the vehicle and supporting it on axle stands to allow access from the underside. Where required, unbolt and remove the drivebelt guard to allow access to the drivebelt.

10   With the engine switched off, inspect the full length of the alternator drivebelt for cracks and separation of the belt plies. It will be necessary to progressively turn the engine over in order to allow those sections of the belt around the pulleys to run clear so that the complete belt is inspected thoroughly. Twist the belt between the pulleys so that both sides can be viewed. Also check for fraying, and glazing which gives the belt a shiny appearance. Check the pulleys for nicks, cracks, distortion and corrosion which if present will necessitate renewal of the belt.

11   The tension of the belt is checked by pushing on it at a point midway between the pulleys (photo). Ford technicians use a special

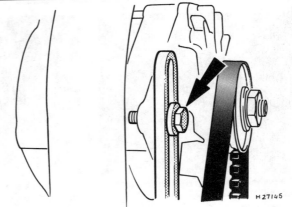

Fig. 1.11 Alternator upper mounting/sliding arm adjuster bolt (arrowed) – V-belt with sliding arm type adjuster (Sec 10)

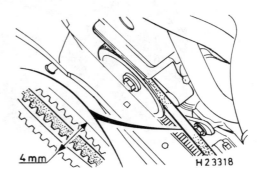

Fig. 1.12 Adjusting alternator drivebelt tension – V-belt with sliding arm type adjuster (Sec 10)

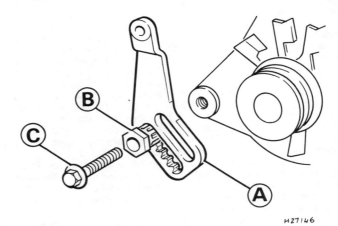

Fig. 1.13 Alternator drivebelt adjuster – rack and pinion type (Sec 10)

A   Adjuster arm   C   Central bolt
B   Pinion nut

spring-tensioned tool which is set to apply a force to the belt and the deflection then measured. The force applied is dependent on model and is given in the Specifications. An alternative arrangement can be made by using a straight-edge, steel rule and spring balance. Hold the straight-edge across the two pulleys, then position the steel rule on the belt, apply the force with the spring balance, and measure the deflection.

12   If adjustment is necessary proceed as follows according to belt type.

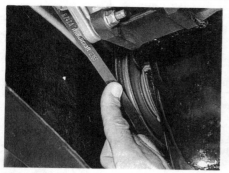

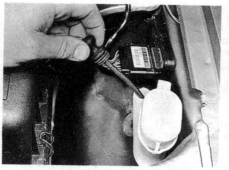

10.11 Checking the tension of the alternator drivebelt

10.22 Checking the level of fluid in the washer fluid reservoir

10.32 Windscreen wiper arm retaining nut

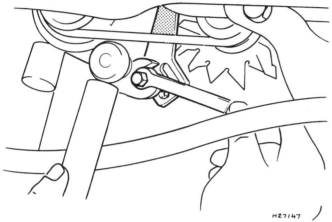

Fig. 1.14 Alternator drivebelt tensioning method – rack and pinion type adjuster (Sec 10)

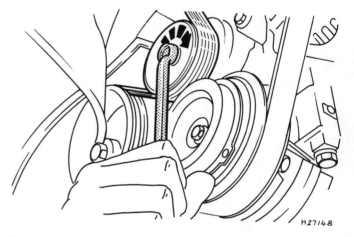

Fig. 1.15 Automatic drivebelt adjustment – flat 'polyvee' type (Sec 10)

Turn the adjuster clockwise to release the tension from the belt

Flat 'polyvee' type drivebelt

13   Where this type of drivebelt is fitted, the adjuster is an automatic type and no adjustment is necessary after it is set (on fitting the drivebelt).

V-belt with sliding arm type adjuster

14   Loosen off the alternator mounting and drivebelt adjustment bolts, pivot the alternator as required to provide the correct drive belt tension, then retighten the bolts to secure.

V-belt with rack and pinion type adjuster

15   Loosen off the alternator mounting bolts and the adjusting arm centre bolt. Turn the pinion nut as required to take up the tension of the drivebelt and holding it at the required setting, tighten the central bolt securely to lock the adjuster arm and set the tension.
16   Tighten the alternator mounting bolts (front first) securely.
17   Run the engine for about five minutes, then recheck the tension.
18   To renew a drivebelt, slacken the belt tension fully as described above, according to engine type. On the flat 'polyvee' type drivebelt, turn the belt adjuster in a clockwise direction to release the tension from the drivebelt. Slip the belt off the pulleys then fit the new belt ensuring that it is routed correctly. With the belt in position, adjust the tension as previously described. On the polyvee type drivebelt, releasing the tensioner nut will cause the tension to be taken up automatically.

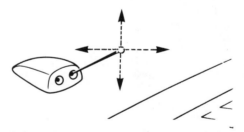

Fig. 1.16 Adjust washer jets with pin in direction required (Sec 10)

Lights, indicators, horn(s) and instruments

19   Check that the operation of all external lights and indicators (front and rear) is satisfactory.
20   Check for satisfactory operation of the instrument panel, its illumination and warning lights, the switches and their function lights.
21   Check the horn(s) for satisfactory operation.

Windscreen/tailgate washer fluid and jets

22   Check the level of windscreen/washer fluid in the reservoir. The

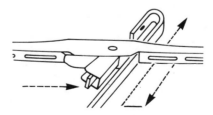

Fig. 1.17 Windscreen wiper blade removal from the arm (Sec 10)

reservoir is located at the front left-hand corner of the engine compartment and supplies washer fluid to both the windscreen, headlamp glass and tailgate/rear window. To check the fluid level, press the cover in and withdraw the dipstick (photo).
23   To top up the fluid level, remove the cover from the washer

reservoir and add the required amount of washer fluid. Use a screen wash such as Turtle Wax High Tech Screen Wash in the recommended quantities.

24   Check that the washer jets direct the fluid onto the upper part of the windscreen/tailgate/rear window/headlamp and if necessary adjust the small sphere on the jet with a pin.

Windscreen/tailgate wiper blades and arms check and renewal

Wiper blades

25   The wiper blades should be renewed when they have deteriorated, cracked, or no longer clean the windscreen or rear window/tailgate glass effectively.

26   Lift the wiper arm and blade away from the glass.

27   Release the catch on the arm, turn the blade through 90° and withdraw the blade from the arm fork.

28   Insert the new blade into the arm, making sure that it locates securely.

Wiper arms

29   Check the wiper arms for worn hinges and weak springs, and renew as necessary.

30   Lift the hinged cover for access to the retaining nut.

31   Make sure that the wiper is in its rest position, and note this position for correct refitting. If necessary, switch the wipers on and off in order to allow them to return to the 'park' position.

32   Unscrew the retaining nut and pull the arm from the spindle (photo). If necessary use a screwdriver to prise off the arm, being careful not to damage the paintwork. On the tailgate/rear window wiper it will help if the arm is moved to its fully-raised position before removing it from the spindle.

33   Fit the new arm using a reversal of the removal procedure.

Chapter 2 Engine

Contents

Specifications

General

Type	Four-cylinder in-line, overhead valve, water cooled
Designation	HCS
Bore	73.96 mm
Stroke	75.48 mm
Capacity	1297 cc
Firing order	1–2–4–3 (No 1 cylinder at timing cover end)
Direction of crankshaft rotation	Clockwise
Compression ratio	9.5 : 1
Compression pressure (at starter motor speed)	13 to 16 bars

Cylinder block

Material	Cast iron
Cylinder bore diameter:	
Standard 1	73.94 to 73.95 mm
Standard 2	73.50 to 73.96 mm
Standard 3	73.96 to 73.97 mm
Standard 4	73.97 to 73.98 mm
Oversize 0.5 mm	74.50 to 74.51 mm
Oversize 1.0 mm	75.00 to 75.01 mm

Crankshaft

Number of main bearings	5
Main bearing journal diameter:	
Standard	56.990 to 57.000 mm
0.254 mm undersize	56.726 to 56.746 mm
0.508 mm undersize	56.472 to 56.492 mm
0.762 mm undersize	56.218 to 56.238 mm
Main bearing running clearance	0.009 to 0.056 mm
Big-end bearing running clearance	0.006 to 0.060 mm
Crankpin (big-end) journal diameter:	
Standard	40.99 to 41.01 mm
0.254 mm undersize	40.74 to 40.76 mm
0.508 mm undersize	40.49 to 40.51 mm
0.762 mm undersize	40.24 to 40.26 mm
Big-end bearing running clearance	0.009 to 0.056 mm
Crankshaft endfloat	0.075 to 0.285 mm
Thrust washer thickness:	
Standard	2.80 to 2.85 mm
Oversize	2.99 to 3.04 mm

Pistons and piston rings

Piston ring end gap:	
Compression rings	0.25 to 0.45 mm
Oil control ring	0.20 to 0.40 mm
Ring gap position:	
Top	Offset 180° from oil control ring gap
2nd	Offset 90° from oil control ring gap
Oil control	Aligned with gudgeon pin

Gudgeon pins

Length	63.3 to 64.6 mm
Outside diameter:	
White	18.026 to 18.029 mm
Red	18.029 to 18.032 mm
Blue	18.032 to 18.035 mm
Yellow	18.035 to 18.038 mm
Interference fit in connecting rod (at 21°C)	0.016 to 0.048 mm
Clearance in piston (at 21°C)	0.008 to 0.014 mm
Piston-to-bore clearance	0.015 to 0.050 mm

Connecting rods

Endfloat	0.100 to 0.250 mm

Cylinder head

Material	Cast iron
Maximum acceptable gasket face distortion measured over full length	0.15 mm
Valve seat angle (inlet and exhaust)	45°
Valve seat width (inlet and exhaust)	1.18 to 1.75 mm*

The inlet and exhaust valves have special inserts which cannot be recut using conventional tools.

Camshaft

Drive	Chain
Number of bearings	3
Camshaft endfloat	0.02 to 0.19 mm

Valves

Head diameter:	
Inlet	34.40 to 34.60 mm
Exhaust	28.90 to 29.10 mm
Valve length:	
Inlet	103.7 to 104.4 mm
Exhaust	104.2 to 104.7 mm
Stem diameter (standard)	7.0 mm
Valve clearance (cold):	
Inlet	0.20 mm
Exhaust	0.30 to 0.35 mm
Valve spring free length	41.0 mm

Lubrication system

System pressure:	
Idling	0.60 bar
At 2000 rpm	1.50 bar
Oil pump type	Rotor

Lubrication system (continued)
Oil pump clearances:

Outer rotor-to-body	0.14 to 0.26 mm
Inner rotor-to-outer rotor	0.051 to 0.127 mm
Rotor endfloat	0.025 to 0.06 mm

Torque wrench settings

	Nm	lbf ft
Camshaft thrust plate bolts	4 to 5	3 to 4
Camshaft sprocket bolt	16 to 20	12 to 14
Crankshaft pulley bolt	110 to 120	81 to 88
Rocker assembly pedestal bolts	40 to 46	30 to 34
Flywheel bolts – see text	64 to 70	47 to 51
Exhaust manifold	21 to 25	15 to 18
Inlet manifold	16 to 20	12 to 15
Main bearing cap	88 to 102	65 to 72
Big-end bearing cap bolts (renew):		
Stage 1	4	3
Stage 2	Further quarter turn (90°)	Further quarter turn (90°)
Sump:		
Stage 1	6 to 8	4 to 6
Stage 2	8 to 11	6 to 8
Stage 3 (with engine warm)	8 to 11	6 to 8
Oil drain plug	21 to 28	15 to 20
Oil pressure switch	13 to 15	10 to 11
Cylinder head bolts (may be re-used once only):		
Stage 1	30	22
Stage 2	Further quarter turn (90°)	Further quarter turn (90°)
Stage 3	Further quarter turn (90°)	Further quarter turn (90°)
Timing chain tensioner	7 to 9	5 to 6
Front (timing) cover	7 to 10	5 to 7
Crankshaft rear oil seal cover	16 to 20	12 to 14
Rocker cover bolts	4 to 5	3 to 4
Oil pump	16 to 20	12 to 14
Oil pump cover	8 to 12	6 to 9
Oil pressure warning light switch	13 to 15	10 to 11
Engine mountings:		
Mounting to cylinder block bracket	102 to 138	75 to 102
Mounting bracket to cylinder block	58 to 79	43 to 58
Brace to engine mounting	58 to 79	43 to 58
Suspension strut top mounting bracket	70 to 79	51 to 71

Part B: CVH (OHC) engines

General

Type	Four-cylinder in-line, overhead camshaft, water cooled
Designation	CVH
Bore:	
1.4 litre	77.42 mm
1.6 litre	79.96 mm
Stroke:	
1.4 litre	74.30 mm
1.6 litre	79.52 mm
Capacity:	
1.4 litre	1392 cc
1.6 litre	1596 cc
Firing order	1–3–4–2 (No 1 cylinder at timing case end)
Direction of crankshaft rotation	Clockwise
Compression ratio:	
1.4 litre	8.5:1
1.6 litre 2V engine	9.5:1
1.6 litre EFi engine	9.75:1
Compression pressure (at starter motor speed)	12 to 14 bars

Cylinder block

Material	Cast iron
Cylinder bore diameter:	
1.4 litre (production):	
Standard classes 1 to 4	77.22 to 77.26 mm
Oversize classes A to C	77.51 to 77.54 mm
1.4 litre (service):	
Standard	77.254 to 77.255 mm
0.29 mm oversize	77.525 to 77.535 mm
0.50 mm oversize	77.745 to 77.755 mm

Cylinder block (continued)
Cylinder bore diameter:
- 1.6 litre (production):
  - Standard classes 1 to 4 .... 79.94 to 79.98 mm
  - Oversize classes A, B and C .... 80.23 to 80.26 mm
- 1.6 litre (service):
  - Standard .... 79.965 to 79.975 mm
  - 0.29 mm oversize .... 80.245 to 80.255 mm
  - 0.50 mm oversize .... 80.465 to 80.475 mm

Main bearing shell inside diameter (fitted):
- Standard .... 58.011 to 58.038 mm
- 0.25 mm undersize .... 57.761 to 57.788 mm
- 0.50 mm undersize .... 57.511 to 57.538 mm
- 0.75 mm undersize .... 57.261 to 57.288 mm

Crankshaft
Number of main bearings 5

Main bearing journal diameter:
- Standard .... 57.98 to 58.00 mm
- 0.25 mm undersize .... 57.73 to 57.75 mm
- 0.50 mm undersize .... 57.48 to 57.50 mm
- 0.75 mm undersize .... 57.23 to 57.25 mm

Main bearing running clearance .... 0.011 to 0.058 mm

Semi-circular thrust washer thickness:
- Standard .... 2.301 to 2.351 mm
- Oversize .... 2.491 to 2.541 mm

Crankshaft endfloat .... 0.09 to 0.30 mm

Crankpin (big-end) journal diameter:
- Standard .... 47.89 to 47.91 mm
- 0.25 mm undersize .... 47.64 to 47.66 mm
- 0.50 mm undersize .... 47.39 to 47.41 mm
- 0.75 mm undersize .... 47.14 to 47.16 mm
- 1.00 mm undersize .... 46.89 to 46.91 mm

Big-end bearing running clearance .... 0.006 to 0.060 mm

Pistons and piston rings
Piston ring end gaps:
- Compression rings .... 0.30 to 0.50 mm
- Oil control rings on 1.4 litre 2V and CFi and 1.6 litre 2V .... 0.40 to 1.40 mm
- Oil control rings on 1.6 EFi .... 0.25 to 0.40 mm

Piston diameter – 1.4 litre (production):
- Standard classes 1 to 4 .... 77.190 to 77.230 mm
- Oversize classes A to C .... 77.480 to 77.510 mm

Piston diameter – 1.4 litre (service):
- Standard .... 77.210 to 77.235 mm
- 0.29 mm oversize .... 77.490 to 77.515 mm
- 0.50 mm oversize .... 77.710 to 77.735 mm

Piston diameter – 1.6 litre non-EFi (production):
- Standard classes 1 to 4 .... 79.910 to 79.950 mm
- Oversize classes A to C .... 80.200 to 80.230 mm

Piston diameter – 1.6 litre non EFi (service):
- Standard .... 79.930 to 79.955 mm
- 0.29 mm oversize .... 80.210 to 80.235 mm
- 0.50 mm oversize .... 80.430 to 80.455 mm

Piston diameter – 1.6 litre EFi (production):
- Standard classes 1 to 4 .... 79.915 to 79.955 mm
- Oversize classes A to C .... 80.205 to 80.235 mm

Piston diameter – 1.6 litre EFi (service):
- Standard .... 79.935 to 79.955 mm
- 0.29 mm oversize .... 80.215 to 80.235 mm
- 0.50 mm oversize .... 80.435 to 80.455 mm

Piston to bore clearance (production):
- All except 1.6 EFi .... 0.020 to 0.040 mm
- 1.6 EFi .... 0.015 to 0.035 mm

Piston to bore clearance (service):
- All except 1.6 EFi .... 0.010 to 0.045 mm
- 1.6 EFi .... 0.010 to 0.040 mm

Gudgeon pins
Length:
- 1.4 litre .... 63.000 to 63.800 mm
- 1.6 litre (non EFi) .... 66.200 to 67.000 mm
- 1.6 litre EFi .... 63.000 to 63.800 mm

Gudgeon pins (continued)

Outside diameter:	
White	20.622 to 20.625 mm
Red	20.625 to 20.628 mm
Blue	20.628 to 20.631 mm
Yellow	20.631 to 20.634 mm
Clearance in piston	0.005 to 0.011 mm
Interference in connecting rod	0.013 to 0.045 mm

Connecting rods

Big-end bearing shell inside diameter (fitted):	
Standard	47.916 to 47.950 mm
0.25 mm undersize	47.666 to 47.450 mm
0.50 mm undersize	47.416 to 47.450 mm
1.00 mm undersize	46.916 to 46.950 mm
Clearance between big-end bearing shell and big-end journal	0.006 to 0.060 mm

Cylinder head

Material	Aluminium
Combustion chamber volume:	
1.4 litre	38.88 to 41.88 cc
1.6 litre non EFi	47.36 to 50.36 cc
1.6 litre EFi	53.36 to 55.38 cc
Maximum acceptable gasket face distortion:	
Measured over distance of 26 mm	0.04 mm
Measured over distance of 156 mm	0.08 mm
Measured over full length	0.15 mm
Maximum depth when skimming cylinder head mating surface:	0.30 mm
Minimum combustion chamber depth after skimming:	
1.4 litre	17.40 mm
1.6 litre	19.10 mm
Camshaft bearing bore diameters in cylinder head (standard):	
Bearing 1	44.783 to 44.808 mm
Bearing 2	45.033 to 45.058 mm
Bearing 3	45.283 to 45.308 mm
Bearing 4	45.533 to 45.558 mm
Bearing 5	45.783 to 45.808 mm
Camshaft bearing bore diameters in cylinder head (oversize):	
Bearing 1	45.188 to 45.163 mm
Bearing 2	45.438 to 45.413 mm
Bearing 3	45.668 to 45.663 mm
Bearing 4	45.983 to 45.913 mm
Bearing 5	46.188 to 46.163 mm
Valve tappet bore diameter (standard)	22.235 to 22.265 mm
Valve tappet bore diameter (oversize)	22.489 to 22.519 mm
Valve seat angle	44°30' to 45°30'
Valve seat width	1.75 to 2.32 mm
Upper seat correction angle:	
Inlet	15°
Exhaust	15°(*)
Lower seat correction angle:	
Inlet	77°
Exhaust	70°(*)
Lower seat cutter correction angle:	
Inlet	75°
Exhaust	70°(*)

The cylinder head has valve seat rings on the exhaust side. These valve seats cannot be recut with conventional tools.

Valves

Operation	Hydraulic tappets and rocker arms
Head diameter:	
Inlet – 1.4 litre	39.90 to 40.10 mm
Inlet – 1.6 litre	41.90 to 42.10 mm
Exhaust – 1.4 litre	33.90 to 34.10 mm
Exhaust – 1.6 litre	36.90 to 37.10 mm
Valve stem diameter – standard:	
Inlet	8.025 to 8.043 mm
Exhaust	7.999 to 8.017 mm
Valve stem diameter – 0.2 mm oversize:	
Inlet	8.225 to 8.243 mm
Exhaust	8.199 to 8.217 mm
Valve stem diameter – 0.4 mm oversize:	
Inlet	8.425 to 8.443 mm
Exhaust	8.399 to 8.417 mm

Valves (continued)

Valve stem to guide clearance:	
Inlet	0.020 to 0.063 mm
Exhaust	0.046 to 0.089 mm
Valve spring free length – 1.4 and 1.6 (non-EFi) engines:	
Blue/blue	47.20 mm
White/blue	45.40 mm
Valve spring free length – 1.6 EFi engine:	
Red/red	46.90 mm
Green/green	48.30 mm
Valve timing (1 mm of cam lift: all rocker arms fitted except the one being checked):	
1.4 litre:	
Inlet valve opens	15°ATDC
Inlet valve closes	30°ABDC
Exhaust valve opens	28°BBDC
Exhaust valve closes	13°BTDC
1.6 litre (non-EFi):	
Inlet valve opens	4°ATDC
Inlet valve closes	32°ABDC
Exhaust valve opens	38°BBDC
Exhaust valve closes	10°BTDC
1.6 litre EFi:	
Inlet valve opens	4°ATDC
Inlet valve closes	30°ATDC
Exhaust valve opens	44°BBDC
Exhaust valve closes	10°BTDC
Inlet and exhaust valve lift:	
1.4 litre	9.3 to 9.7 mm
1.6 litre (non EFi)	9.5 to 9.9 mm
1.6 litre EFi	10.3 to 10.7 mm

Camshaft

Drive method	Toothed belt
Number of bearings	5
Cam lift (inlet and exhaust):	
1.4 litre	4.79 mm
1.6 litre non EFi	6.09 mm
1.6 litre EFi	6.57 mm
Camshaft endfloat	0.05 to 0.15 mm

Lubrication system

System pressure:	
Minimum pressure at idle speed	1.0 bar
Minimum pressure at 2000 rpm	2.8 bars
Oil pressure relief valve opening pressure	4.7 to 6.0 bars
Oil pressure warning light actuating pressure	0.3 to 0.5 bars
Oil pump type	Rotor
Oil pump clearances:	
Outer rotor-to-body	0.060 to 0.190 mm
Inner to outer rotor	0.05 to 0.18 mm
Rotor endfloat (relative to mating face)	0.014 to 0.100 mm

Torque wrench settings

	Nm	lbf ft
Main bearing caps	90 to 100	66 to 74
Big-end bearing caps – see text	30 to 36	22 to 26
Oil pump	8 to 11	6 to 8
Oil pump cover	8 to 12	6 to 8
Oil pump intake to cylinder block	17 to 23	12 to 17
Oil pump intake to pump	8 to 12	6 to 8
Oil cooler threaded sleeve to cylinder block	55 to 60	40 to 44
Rear oil seal carrier	8 to 11	6 to 8
Crankshaft position sensor	4 to 5	3 to 3.7
Flywheel – see text	82 to 92	60 to 68
Cylinder head bolts – see text:		
Stage 1	24 to 40	18 to 30
Stage 2	40 to 60	30 to 44
Stage 3	Angle tighten further 90°	
Stage 4	Angle tighten further 90° (no further tightening required)	
Crankshaft pulley bolt	100 to 115	74 to 85
Camshaft thrust plate	9 to 13	7 to 10
Camshaft toothed belt sprocket – see text	54 to 59	40 to 44
Timing belt tensioner	16 to 20	12 to 15
Rocker studs to cylinder head	18 to 23	13 to 17

Torque wrench settings (continued)

	Nm	lbf ft
Rocker arms	25 to 29	18 to 21
Rocker cover	6 to 8	4 to 6
Timing belt cover	9 to 11	7 to 8
Oil pressure switch	18 to 22	13 to 16
Oil drain plug	21 to 28	15 to 21
Engine/transmission mountings:		
Mounting to cylinder block bracket	102 to 138	75 to 101
Mounting bracket to cylinder block	76 to 104	56 to 76
Brace to front axle crossmember	58 to 79	43 to 58
Brace to engine mounting	58 to 79	43 to 58
Suspension strut top mounting nuts	70 to 97	52 to 71
Transmission mountings:		
Rear left-hand bracket to mounting	58 to 79	43 to 58
Front left-hand bracket to mounting	58 to 79	43 to 58
Rear left-hand bracket to transmission	41 to 58	30 to 43
Brace to front engine transmission/mounting bracket	41 to 58	30 to 43
Cylinder block/transmission case stiffener (1.6 litre)	40 to 50	30 to 37
Gearshift stabiliser to transmission	50 to 60	37 to 44
Shift rod to transmission selector shaft	14 to 17	10 to 12

Part A: HCS engine – in-car engine repair procedures

1 General information

How to use this Chapter

This part of Chapter 2 describes those repair operations that can be reasonably undertaken with the 1.3 litre HCS (OHV) engine in the vehicle. Similar information concerning the 1.4 and 1.6 litre CVH (OHC) engines will be found in Part B of this Chapter.

Part C of this Chapter covers information concerning engine removal/refitting and overhaul procedures of the cylinder block and cylinder head for both engine types. Reference to the contents list at the start of the Chapter will indicate the appropriate Part and the Section(s)

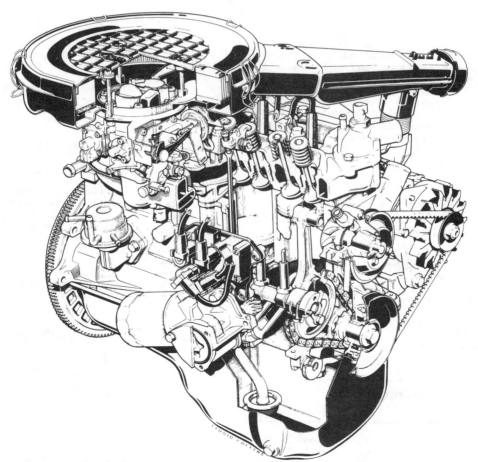

Fig. 2.1 Cutaway view of the HCS engine (Sec 1)

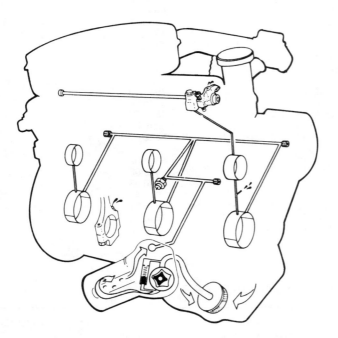

Fig. 2.2 HCS engine lubrication circuit (Sec 1)

to refer to for the information concerned on the various operations according to engine type.

Engine description (HCS type)

The engine is an overhead valve, water-cooled, four cylinder in-line design, designated HCS. It is mounted transversely at the front of the vehicle together with the transmission to form a combined power unit.

The crankshaft is supported in five shell type main bearings. The connecting rod big-end bearings are also split shell type and are attached to the pistons by interference fit gudgeon pins. Each piston is fitted with two compression rings and one oil control ring.

The camshaft, which runs on bearings within the cylinder block is chain driven from the crankshaft and operates the valves via pushrods and rocker arms. The valves are each closed by a single valve spring and operate in guides integral in the cylinder head.

The oil pump is mounted externally on the crankcase, incorporates a full-flow oil filter and is driven by a skew gear on the camshaft. The fuel pump is also driven from the camshaft, via an eccentric lobe.

Repair operations possible with the engine in the vehicle

The following repair operations can be undertaken with the engine in the vehicle.

(a) Cylinder head – removal and refitting.
(b) Valve clearances – adjustment.
(c) Rocker shaft assembly – removal and refitting.
(d) Crankshaft front oil seal – renewal.
(e) Oil filter renewal.
(f) Oil pump – removal and refitting.
(g) Sump – removal and refitting.
(h) Piston/connecting rod assemblies – removal and refitting.
(i) Engine/transmission mountings – removal and refitting.

2 Compression test – description and interpretation

1   A compression check will tell you what mechanical condition the top end of the engine is in. Specifically it can tell you if the compression is down due to leakage caused by worn piston rings, defective valves and seats or a blown head gasket.

2   A compression gauge will be required to make the check and these are readily available from most motoring accessory shops.
3   When making the check, the engine must be at its normal operating temperature and the battery must be fully-charged.
4   The spark plugs will need to be removed but prior to unscrewing them, clean the area around them using compressed air if available (otherwise a small brush or even a bicycle pump will do), to prevent the possibility of any dirt entering the cylinders.
5   Remove all of the spark plugs from the engine (refer to Chapter 1).
6   Disconnect the 3-pin plug from the DIS ignition coil (under the inlet manifold on the HCS engine).
7   Fit the compression gauge into the No 1 spark plug hole.
8   Arrange for an assistant to hold the accelerator pedal fully depressed to the floor while at the same time cranking the engine over several times on the starter motor. Observe the compression gauge reading. The compression will build up fairly quickly in a healthy engine. Low compression on the first stroke, followed by gradually increasing pressure on successive strokes indicates worn piston rings. A low compression on the first stroke which does not rise on successive strokes, indicates leaking valves or a blown head gasket (a cracked cylinder head could also be the cause). Deposits on the underside of the valve heads can also cause low compression. Record the highest gauge reading obtained, then repeat the procedure for the remaining cylinders and compare the readings with the specified compression pressures given at the start of this Chapter.
9   Add some engine oil (about three squirts from a plunger type oil can) to each cylinder through the spark plug holes and then repeat the test.
10   If the compression increases after the oil is added it is indicative that the piston rings are definitely worn. If the compression does not increase significantly, the leakage is occurring at the valves or the head gasket. Leakage past the valves may be caused by burned valve seats and/or faces or warped, cracked or bent valves.
11   If two adjacent cylinders have equally low compressions, it is most likely that the head gasket has blown between them. The appearance of coolant in the combustion chambers or crankcase would verify this condition.
12   If one cylinder is about 20 per cent lower than the other, and the engine has a slightly rough idle, a worn lobe on the camshaft could be the cause.
13   If the compression is unusually high, the combustion chambers are most likely coated with carbon deposits and are in need of decarbonising.
14   On completion of the checks, refit the spark plugs and reconnect the HT leads and the DIS ignition coil plug.

3 Top Dead Centre (TDC) for number one piston – locating

1   Top dead centre (TDC) is the highest point of the cylinder that each piston reaches as the crankshaft turns. Each piston reaches its TDC position at the end of its compression stroke and then again at the end of its exhaust stroke. For the purpose of engine timing, the TDC at the end of the compression stroke for the number 1 piston is used. On all engines covered by this manual, the number 1 cylinder is at the crankshaft pulley end of the engine. Proceed as follows.
2   Ensure that the ignition is switched off. Disconnect the HT leads from the spark plugs, then unscrew and remove the plugs having removed all loose dirt from around their seals beforehand.

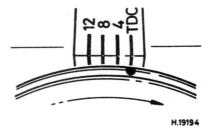

H.19194

Fig. 2.3 Timing index marks on the crankshaft pulley and timing cover (Sec 3)

4.5 Adjusting the valve clearances

3 Turn the engine over by hand (spanner on the crankshaft pulley) to the point where the timing mark on the crankshaft pulley aligns with the TDC (0) mark on the timing cover. As the pulley mark nears the timing mark, the number one piston is simultaneously approaching the top of its cylinder. To ensure that it is on its compression stroke, place a finger over the number one cylinder plug hole and feel to ensure that air pressure exits from the cylinder as the piston reaches the top of its stroke.

4 A further check to ensure that the piston is on its compression stroke can be made by first removing the air cleaner unit (Chapter 4), then unbolting and removing the rocker cover to allow the movement of the valves and rockers to be observed.

5 With the TDC timing marks of the crankshaft pulley and timing cover in alignment, rock the crankshaft back and forth a few degrees each side of this position and observe the action of the valves and rockers to the number one cylinder. When the number one piston is at the TDC firing position, the inlet and exhaust valve of the number one cylinder will be fully closed but the corresponding valves of the number four cylinder will be seen to rock open and closed.

6 If the inlet and exhaust valves of the number one cylinder are seen to rock whilst those of number four cylinder are shut, the timing is 180° out and the crankshaft will need to be turned one full rotation to bring the number one piston up to the top of its cylinder on the compression stroke.

7 Once the number 1 cylinder has been positioned at TDC on the compression stroke, TDC for any of the other cylinders can then be located by rotating the crankshaft clockwise (in its normal direction of rotation), 180° at a time and following the firing order (see Specifications).

4 Valve clearances – checking and adjustment

1 This operation must be carried out with the engine cold. The air cleaner unit (see Chapter 4 for details), the engine rocker cover and the spark plugs must first be removed. As the plugs and their HT leads are removed, note their order of fitting so that they may be refitted in their original locations.

2 Using a ring spanner or socket on the crankshaft on the crankshaft pulley bolt, turn the crankshaft in a clockwise direction until the No 1 piston is at TDC position on its compression stroke. This can be verified by checking the that the pulley and the timing cover marks are in alignment, also that the valves of the No 4 cylinder are rocking so that the smallest movement of the crankshaft will cause one No 4 rocker to move up, the other down.

3 Starting from the thermostat end of the cylinder head, the valves are identified as follows.

Valve No.	Cylinder No.
1 – Exhaust	1
2 – Inlet	1
3 – Exhaust	2
4 – Inlet	2
5 – Inlet	3
6 – Exhaust	3
7 – Inlet	4
8 – Exhaust	4

4 Adjust the valve clearances by following the sequence given in the following table. Turn the crankshaft pulley 180° (half a turn) after adjusting each pair of valve clearances.

Valves rocking	Valves to adjust
7 and 8	1 (exhaust), 2 (inlet)
5 and 6	3 (exhaust), 4 (inlet)
1 and 2	8 (exhaust), 7 (inlet)
3 and 4	6 (exhaust), 5 (inlet)

5 The clearances for the inlet and exhaust valves differ (see specifications). Use a feeler gauge of the appropriate thickness to check each clearance between the end of the valve stem and the rocker arm (photo). The gauge should be an interference sliding fit (not slack, but not tight) between the valve and rocker arm. Where adjustment is necessary, turn the adjuster bolt as required with a ring spanner to set the clearance at that specified. The adjuster bolts are of stiff thread type and require no locking nut.

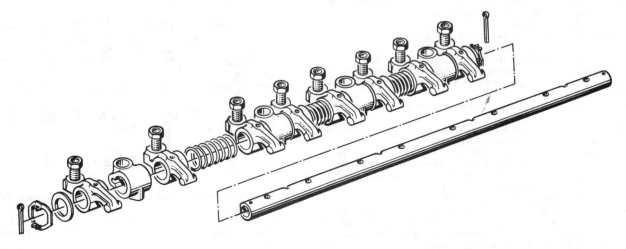

Fig. 2.4 Rocker shaft and associated components (Sec 5)

6   Refit the rocker cover and tighten its retaining bolts to the specified torque setting in a uniform manner.

7   Refit the spark plugs and reconnect the HT leads.

8   Refit the air cleaner unit as described in Chapter 4.

5   Cylinder head rocker gear – removal, inspection and refitting

Removal

1   Remove the air cleaner unit as described in Chapter 4.

2   Detach the HT leads from the spark plugs. Pull on the connector of each lead (not the lead) and note the order of fitting.

3   Unscrew the four retaining bolts and lift the rocker cover clear of the cylinder head.

4   Unscrew the four retaining bolts and lift the rocker gear unit from the cylinder head. As the unit is withdrawn, ensure that the respective pushrods remain seated in their respective positions in the engine. If the pushrods are to be removed, keep them in the correct order of fitting by inserting them in a piece of card and numbering them 1 to 8 from the thermostat end of the cylinder head.

Inspection

5   To dismantle the rocker shaft unit, extract the split pin from one end of the shaft, then withdraw the spring and plain washers from the shaft.

6   Slide off the rocker arms, the support pedestals and coil springs from the shaft, but take care to keep them in their original order of fitting (photo).

7   Clean the respective components and inspect them for signs of excessive wear or damage. Check that the oil lubrication holes in the shaft are clean.

8   Check the rocker shaft and arm pads which bear on the valve stem end faces for wear and scoring and check each rocker arm on the shaft for excessive wear. Renew any components as necessary.

Refitting

9   Apply clean engine oil to the rocker shaft prior to reassembling.

10   Reassemble in the reverse order of dismantling. Make sure that the 'flat' on the rear end of the rocker shaft is to the same side as the rocker arm adjusting screws (closest to the thermostat end of the cylinder head when fitted). This is essential for the correct lubrication of the cylinder head components (photo).

6   Cylinder head – removal and refitting

Removal

1   If the engine is still in the vehicle, first carry out the following preliminary operations described in paragraphs 2 to 13 inclusive. If the engine has been removed, commence at paragraph 14.

2   Disconnect the battery earth lead.

3   Refer to Chapter 4 and remove the air cleaner unit.

4   Refer to Chapter 1 and drain the cooling system.

5   Disconnect the hoses from the thermostat housing.

6   Disconnect the heater (coolant) hoses from the inlet manifold.

7   Disconnect the accelerator and choke cables from the carburettor (see Chapter 4 for details).

8   Disconnect the fuel and vacuum hoses from the carburettor and inlet manifold.

9   Disconnect the HT leads from the spark plugs and the support bracket. Unscrew and remove the spark plugs.

10   Disconnect the electrical leads from the temperature gauge sender, radiator cooling fan, the engine coolant temperature sender (beneath the inlet manifold), the radio earth lead on the inlet manifold and the anti-run-on (dieselling) valve at the carburettor.

11   Remove the engine oil filler cap and breather hose.

12   Raise the vehicle at the front end and support it on axle stands.

13   Undo the three retaining nuts and disconnect the exhaust downpipe from the manifold. Remove the flange gasket. (Note that both the gasket and the joint self locking nuts must be renewed.) To prevent the exhaust system from being strained, tie the downpipe up using

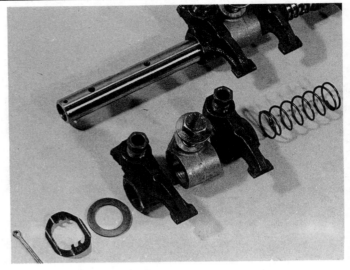

5.6 Partially dismantled rocker shaft

5.10 Flat on the rocker shaft (arrowed) to same side as rocker arm adjusting screws

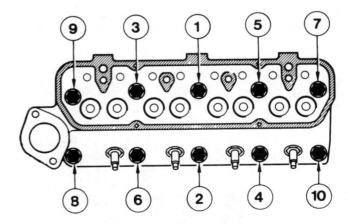

Fig. 2.5 Cylinder head retaining bolt tightening sequence (Sec 6)

strong wire or a length of cord to support it. Lower the vehicle.

14   Unscrew the four retaining bolts and remove the rocker cover and its gasket.

15   Undo the four retaining bolts and lift clear the rocker gear

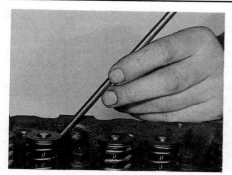

6.16A Withdraw the pushrods ...

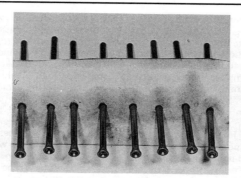

6.16B ... and locate them in a card as shown to keep them in order of fitting

6.21A Cylinder head gasket direction of fitting mark

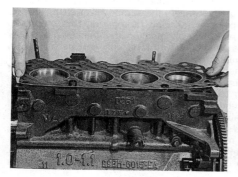

6.21B Cylinder head gasket in position on the top face of the cylinder block

6.23A Tightening the cylinder head bolts (stage one)

6.23B Cylinder head bolt tightening (stages 2 and 3) using an angle gauge

assembly from the cylinder head.

16   Lift out the respective pushrods. Keep them in order of fitting by inserting them in a piece of card and numbering them 1 to 8 from the thermostat end of the cylinder head (photos).

17   Progressively unscrew and loosen off the cylinder head retaining bolts in the reverse sequence to that shown for tightening in Fig. 2.5. When they are all loosened off, remove the bolts, then lift clear the cylinder head and remove the gasket. Whilst the gasket must always be renewed, it should be noted that the cylinder head retaining bolts may be re-used, but once only. They should be marked accordingly with a punch or paint mark. If there is any doubt as to how many times the bolts have been used, they must be renewed.

18   To dismantle/overhaul the cylinder head, refer to Sections 38, 39 and 40 in Part C of this Chapter. It is normal for the cylinder head to be decarbonised and the valves to be reground whenever the head is removed.

Refitting

19   Prior to refitting the cylinder head, clean all carbon deposits, dirt

and any traces of the old cylinder head gasket from the mating faces of both the head and the cylinder block. Do not allow any dirt to drop into the cylinder bores, oil passages or waterways, if it does remove it. Clean the threads of the cylinder head bolts or fit new ones (as applicable) and clean out the bolt holes in the block. In extreme cases, note that screwing a bolt into an oil filled hole can cause the block to fracture due to hydraulic pressure.

20   If there is any doubt as to the condition of the exhaust and inlet manifold gaskets, the manifolds must be removed and the gaskets renewed, but ensure that the mating faces are clean before fitting new gaskets.

21   Check that the new cylinder head gasket is the same type as the original and the top (or OBEN) marking is facing up. Locate the new cylinder head gasket onto the top face of the cylinder block and over the dowels. Ensure that it is correctly aligned with the coolant passages and oilways (photos).

22   Lower the cylinder head carefully into position, then insert the retaining bolts and hand tighten them.

23   Tightening of the cylinder head bolts must done in three stages

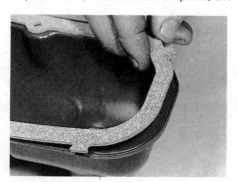

6.29A Engage tags of rocker cover gasket into the cut-outs in the cover

6.29B Refitting the rocker cover

and in the sequence shown in Fig. 2.5. First tighten all of the bolts in the sequence shown to the stage one torque setting. When all of the bolts are tightened to the stage one setting, further tighten each bolt (in sequence) through the specified angle of rotation. When the second stage tightening is completed on all of the bolts, further tighten them to the stage three angle setting (in sequence) to complete. Where possible, use an angular torque setting gauge attachment tool for accurate tightening of stages two and three (photos).

24   Lubricate with clean engine oil and then insert the respective pushrods into their original locations in the engine.

25   Refit the rocker shaft assembly. As it is fitted, ensure that the rocker adjuster screws engage with their corresponding pushrods.

26   Refit the rocker shaft retaining bolts, hand tighten them and then tighten them to the specified torque wrench setting. As they are tightened, some of the rocker arms will apply pressure to the ends of the valve stems and some of the rocker pedestals will not initially be in contact with the cylinder head but these should pull down as the bolts are tightened to their specified torque. If for any reason they do not, avoid the temptation to overtighten in order to pull them into position, but loosen off the bolts and check the cause of the problem. It may be that the rocker adjuster screws require loosening off in order to allow the assembly to be tightened down as required.

27   Adjust the valve clearances as described in Section 4.

28   Refit the spark plugs and tighten them to the specified torque (Chapter 1).

29   Fit a new gasket to the rocker cover then refit the rocker cover into position (photos). Tighten the cover retaining bolts to the specified torque wrench setting.

30   The remainder of the refitting procedure is a reversal of the removal process. Tighten all fastenings to their specified torque setting (where given). Refer to the appropriate Section in Chapter 4 for details on reconnecting the accelerator and choke cables. Ensure that all coolant, fuel, vacuum and electrical connections are securely made.

31   On completion, top up the engine oil and coolant levels. When the engine is restarted, check for any sign of fuel, oil and/or coolant leakages from the various cylinder head joints.

7 Crankshaft pulley – removal and refitting

Removal

1   Disconnect the battery earth lead.

2   Raise and support the vehicle at the front end on axle stands.

3   Undo the three retaining bolts and remove the plastic cover from the underside of the alternator drivebelt.

4   Loosen off the crankshaft pulley retaining bolt. To prevent the crankshaft from turning, engage 1st or reverse gear and chock the front roadwheels. Alternatively, unbolt and remove the clutch housing cover plate and jam the starter ring gear on the flywheel.

5   Loosen off the alternator mounting/adjuster bolts then pivot the alternator to slacken off the tension from the drivebelt and disengage the belt from the crankshaft pulley.

6   Unscrew and remove the crankshaft pulley bolt and withdraw the pulley from the front end of the crankshaft. If it does not pull off by hand, lever it free using a pair of suitable levers positioned diagonally opposite each other behind the pulley.

7   If required, the crankshaft front oil seal can be renewed at this stage as described in Section 13.

Refitting

8   Refitting is a reversal of the removal procedure. When the pulley is refitted, tighten the retaining bolt to the specified torque setting. Relocate the drivebelt over the pulley and adjust the tension as described in Chapter 1.

9   Refit the plastic cover and lower the vehicle to complete.

8 Timing chain cover – removal and refitting

Removal

1   Remove the crankshaft pulley as described in the previous Section.

2   A combined timing cover and water pump gasket is fitted during production and if this is still in position, it will be necessary to drain the cooling system and remove the water pump as described in Chapter 3. If the water pump and/or the timing cover have been removed at any time, the single gasket used originally will have been replaced by an individual item; in which case the water pump can remain in position.

3   Unscrew the retaining bolts and carefully prise free the timing chain cover. Note that two of the retaining bolts also secure the sump at the front end. Remove the engine front face to cover gasket. If the sump-to-timing cover gasket is damaged during the removal of the cover, it will be necessary to drain and remove the sump in order to renew the gasket, in which case refer to Section 10 for details.

4   Clean the mating faces of the timing chain cover and the engine.

5   If necessary, renew the crankshaft front oil seal in the timing cover prior to refitting the cover (see Section 13).

Refitting

6   Before refitting the cover into position, clean the contact faces at the point where the timing cover meets the sump gasket each side and smear the faces at this point with sealant; it is important that a good seal is made at this point. As previously mentioned, if the sump gasket is damaged on either side at the front, it must be renewed (see Section 10) prior to refitting the timing cover.

7   Lightly lubricate the front end of the crankshaft and the radial lip of the timing cover oil seal (already installed in the cover). Using a new gasket, fit the timing chain cover, centring it with the aid of the crankshaft pulley – lubricate the seal contact surfaces beforehand (photo). Where applicable, leave out the timing bolt which also secures the water pump at this stage.

8   Where applicable, refit the water pump as described in Chapter 3.

9   Refit the crankshaft pulley as described in the previous Section. Refer to Chapter 1 for details on refitting and adjusting the alternator drivebelt.

9 Timing chain, sprockets and tensioner – removal, inspection and refitting

Removal

1   Disconnect the battery earth lead.

2   Remove the timing chain cover as described in the previous Section.

3   Refer to Section 10 for details and remove the sump.

4   Note its orientation and remove the oil slinger from the front face of the crankshaft (photo).

5   Retract the chain tensioner cam back against its spring pressure

8.7 Fitting the timing cover. Crankshaft pulley used as aid to centring

9.4 Oil slinger removal from crankshaft

9.5 Chain tensioner arm removal from the pivot pin. Note tensioner retaining bolts (arrowed)

9.14A Fit the timing chain to the crankshaft and camshaft sprockets ...

9.14B ... and check that the timing marks on the sprockets are in alignment

9.15 Bend locktabs against the camshaft retaining bolt heads to secure

then slide the chain tensioner arm from its pivot pin on the front main bearing cap (photo).

6   Unbolt and remove the chain tensioner.

7   Bend back the lockplate tabs from the camshaft sprocket bolts then unscrew and remove the bolts.

8   Withdraw the sprocket complete with the timing chain.

Inspection

9   Examine the teeth on the timing sprockets for any signs of excessive wear or damage.

10   The timing chain should always be renewed if a major engine overhaul is to be made. Slack links and pins are indicative of a worn chain. Unless the chain is known to be relatively new, it should be renewed.

11   Examine the rubber cushion on the tensioner spring leaf. If grooved or deteriorated it must be renewed.

Refitting

12   Commence reassembly by bolting the timing chain tensioner into position. Check that the face of the tensioner cam is parallel with the face of the cylinder block, ideally using a dial gauge. The maximum permissible error between the two measuring points is 0.2 mm. Release and turn the timing chain tensioner as required to achieve this (if necessary). Refer to the specifications for the tightening torque details.

13   Turn the crankshaft so that the timing mark on its sprocket is directly in line with the centre of the camshaft sprocket mounting flange.

14   Engage the camshaft sprocket with the timing chain and then engage the chain around the teeth of the crankshaft sprocket. Push the camshaft sprocket onto its mounting flange and check that the sprocket retaining bolt holes are in alignment. Also check that the timing marks of both sprockets face each other. If required, turn the camshaft/sprocket as required to achieve this. It may also be necessary to remove the camshaft from the chain in order to reposition it in the required location in the chain to align the timing marks. This is a 'trial and error' procedure which must be continued until the exact alignment of the bolt holes and also that of the timing marks is made (photos).

15   Insert and tighten the camshaft sprocket retaining bolts to the specified torque wrench setting. Bend up the tabs of the new lockplate to secure (photo).

16   Retract the timing chain tensioner cam and then slide the tensioner arm onto its pivot pin. Release the cam so that it bears on the arm.

17   Refit the oil slinger to the front of the crankshaft sprocket so that its convex side faces the sprocket.

18   Refit the timing case as described in the previous Section.

19   Refit the sump as described in Section 10. Top up the engine oil level as described in Chapter 1.

20   Reconnect the battery as described in Chapter 12.

21   When the engine is restarted check for any sign of oil or coolant leaks from the sump and water pump (if disturbed).

10 Sump – removal and refitting

Removal

1   Disconnect the battery earth lead.

2   Refer to Chapter 1 and drain the engine oil. Refit the sump drain plug.

3   Undo the three retaining nuts and detach the exhaust downpipe from the manifold flange. Note that the flange gasket will require renewal on reassembly. Allowing sufficient clearance for sump removal, tie the exhaust downpipe up with a suitable length of wire or cord to prevent the system straining the insulators.

4   Note the connections and then detach the starter motor wiring and the battery warning light lead.

5   Undo the two retaining bolts and remove the clutch housing cover plate.

6   Undo the eighteen bolts securing the sump to the base of the engine crankcase, then prise free and lower the sump. If the sump is stuck tight to the engine, cut around the flange gasket with a sharp knife then lightly tap and prise it free. Keep the sump upright as it is lowered to prevent spillage of any remaining oil in it. Also be prepared for oil drips from the crankcase when the sump is removed.

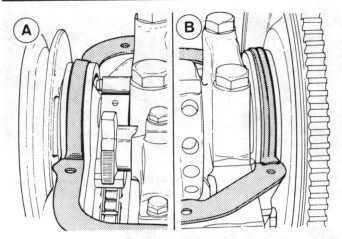

Fig. 2.6 Sump gasket fitting details at the timing cover end (A) and the flywheel end (B) (Sec 10)

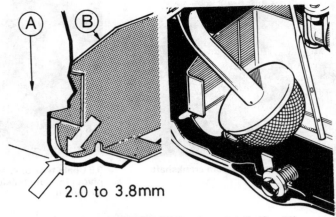

Fig. 2.7 Sump (A) and oil baffle (B) clearance details (Sec 10)

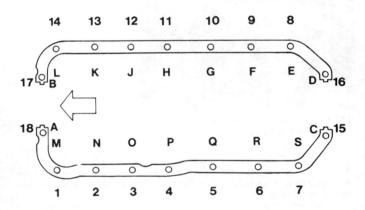

Fig. 2.8 Sump bolt tightening sequence – arrow indicates crankshaft pulley end of engine (Sec 10)

Refer to the Specifications for torque values
Stage 1 – tighten in alphabetical order
Stage 2 – tighten in numerical order
Stage 3 – tighten in alphabetical order

7   Remove any dirt and old gasket from the contact faces of the sump and crankcase and wash the sump out thoroughly before refitting. Check that the mating faces of the sump are not distorted. Check that the oil pick-up strainer is clear, cleaning it if necessary.

Refitting

8   Remove the old gaskets from the timing cover end and flywheel end and clean their location faces. Apply a dab of sealing compound to the mating faces where the ends of each cork half gasket are to be fitted (see Fig. 2.6). Stick the new cork gaskets into position on the block face using clean thick grease to retain them, then locate the new rubber gaskets into their slots in the timing cover and rear oil seal carrier. The lugs of the cork gasket halves fit under the cut-outs in the rubber gaskets (photo).
9   Before offering up the sump, check that the gap between the sump and the oil baffle is between 2.0 and 3.8 mm (see Fig. 2.7). Do not use a dented or damaged sump as the indicated dimension is important for correct engine lubrication.
10   Fit the sump into position and locate the retaining bolts. Initially tighten them all finger-tight, then further tighten them in the sequence shown in Fig. 2.8 to the three stage torque wrench setting specified.
11   Refit the lower plate to the front face of the clutch housing.
12   Reconnect the starter motor and battery warning light wiring.

10.8 Lugs of cork gasket halves to fit under the cut-outs in the rubber gaskets

13   Check that the mating faces are clean, locate a new gasket and reconnect the exhaust downpipe to the manifold using new self-locking nuts tightened securely.
14   Check that the oil drain plug is fitted and tightened to the specified torque, then lower the vehicle to the ground.
15   Top up the oil level in the sump as described in Chapter 1, (taking care not to over-fill).
16   Reconnect the battery, start the engine and run it up to its normal operating temperature is reached. Check that no oil leaks are evident around the sump joint.

11   Oil pump – removal and refitting

Removal

1   The oil pump is externally mounted on the rear facing side of the crankcase.
2   Raise and support the vehicle at the front end on axle stands, allowing sufficient working clearance underneath.
3   Unscrew and remove the oil filter cartridge. It should unscrew by hand but will probably be tight and require the aid of a strap wrench to loosen it off. Catch any oil spillage in a suitable container.
4   Undo the three retaining bolts and withdraw the oil pump from the engine (photo).

11.4 Unscrewing the oil pump retaining bolts

11.7 Refitting the oil pump. Note the new gasket

5   Clean all traces of the old gasket from the mating surfaces of the pump and engine.

Refitting

6   If the original oil pump has been dismantled and reassembled and is to be re-used or a new pump unit is to be fitted, it must first be primed

with engine oil prior to fitting. To do this, turn its driveshaft and simultaneously inject clean engine oil into it.
7   Locate a new gasket into position on the pump mounting flange, insert the pump and engaging the drive gear as it is fitted. Fit and tighten the retaining bolts to the specified torque wrench setting (photo).
8   Fit a new oil filter into position on the oil pump body as described in Chapter 1.
9   Lower the vehicle to the ground and top up the engine oil level to replenish that lost during the previous operations.

12   Oil pump – dismantling, inspection and reassembly

Dismantling

1   To inspect the oil pump components for excessive wear, undo the retaining bolts and remove the cover plate from the pump body. Remove the O-ring seal from the cover face (photo).
2   Wipe the exterior of the pump housing clean.

Inspection

3   Noting their orientation, extract and clean the rotors and the inner body of the pump housing. Inspect them for signs of severe scoring or excessive wear, which if evident will necessitate renewal of the pump unit.
4   Using a feeler gauge set, check the clearances between the pump body and the outer rotor, the inner-to-outer rotor clearance and the amount of rotor endfloat (photos).

12.1 Extract the O-ring from the groove in the oil pump

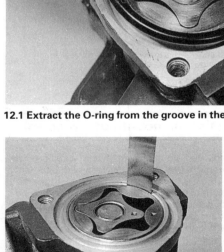

12.4A Checking the outer body-to-rotor clearance

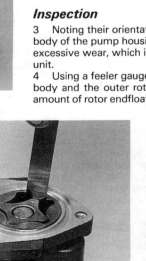

12.4B Checking the inner rotor to outer rotor clearance

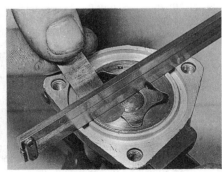

12.4C Checking the rotor endfloat

5   Check the drive gear for signs of excessive wear or damage.
6   If the clearances measured are outside the specified maximum clearances and/or the drivegear is in poor condition, the pump unit must be renewed.

Reassembly

7   Refit the rotors into the pump (in their original orientation), lubricate the rotors and the new O-ring seal with clean engine oil and refit the cover. Tighten the retaining bolts to the specified torque wrench setting.

13   Crankshaft oil seals – renewal

Front oil seal

1   Disconnect the battery earth lead.
2   Raise the vehicle at the front end and support it on axle stands.
3   Refer to Section 7 for details and remove the crankshaft pulley.
4   Using a suitable claw tool extract the oil seal from the timing cover, but take care not to damage the seal housing. As it is removed, note the fitted orientation of the seal in the housing.
5   Clean the oil seal housing in the timing case, lubricate the sealing lips of the new seal and the crankshaft stub with clean engine oil.
6   Locate the new seal into position so that it is squarely located on the crankshaft stub and in the housing, and is correctly orientated. Drift it initially into position by fitting a temporary distance piece against the seal, then draw it fully home by refitting the crankshaft pulley and retaining bolt.
7   When the seal is fully fitted, remove the crankshaft pulley bolt, pulley and distance piece.
8   Lightly lubricate the rubbing surface of the pulley, then refit the pulley as described in Section 7.
9   Refit and adjust the alternator drivebelt as described in Chapter 1, then lower the vehicle to complete.

Rear oil seal

10   With the engine or transmission removed from the vehicle for access, remove the clutch unit as described in Chapter 6.
11   Jam the teeth of the starter ring gear on the flywheel to prevent the flywheel from turning, then unscrew and remove the flywheel retaining bolts. Lift the flywheel from the rear end face of the crankshaft.
12   Using a suitably clawed tool, lever the seal from the rear seal housing (taking care not to damage the housing). As it is removed, note the fitted orientation of the seal.
13   Clean the seal housing, the crankshaft rear flange face and the flywheel mating surface.
14   One of two possible methods may be used to insert the new oil seal, depending on the tools available.
15   If Ford service tool No 21-011 is available, lubricate the crankshaft flange and the oil seal inner lip with clean engine oil. Position the seal onto the service tool (ensuring correct orientation), then press the seal into its housing.
16   If the service tool is not available, remove the engine sump (Section 10), then unscrew the Torx head bolts retaining the rear seal housing in position and remove the seal from the rear face of the cylinder block. New gaskets will be required for both the seal housing and the sump when refitting. Clean the seal housing seat and the mating surfaces of the sump and the crankcase. To fit the seal squarely into its housing without damaging either component, place a flat block of wood across the seal, then carefully tap the seal into position in the housing. Do not allow the seal to tilt as it is being fitted. Lubricate the crankshaft flange and the oil seal inner lip with clean engine oil, then with a new gasket located on the seal housing/crankcase face, fit the housing into position. Take care not to damage the seal lips as it is passed over the crankshaft rear flange (photos). Centralise the seal on the shaft, then insert and tighten the housing retaining bolts to the specified torque setting. Refit the sump with reference to Section 10.
17   Check that the crankshaft rear flange and the flywheel mating faces are clean, then refit the flywheel by reversing its removal method. Lightly oil the flywheel retaining bolts as they are fitted and tighten them in a progressive sequence to the specified torque setting.
18   Refit the clutch unit as described in Chapter 6.

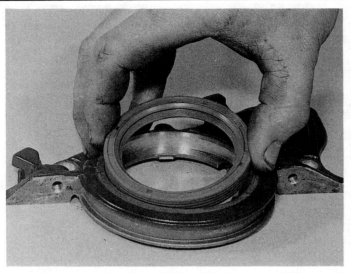

13.16A Positioning the crankshaft rear oil seal in its housing

13.16B Fitting the rear oil seal housing with a new gasket in position on the rear face of the cylinder block

14   Engine/transmission mountings – renewal

1   The engine mountings can be removed if the weight of the engine/transmission is supported by one of the following alternative methods.
2   Either support the weight of the assembly from underneath using a jack and a suitable piece of wood inter-spaced between the jack saddle and the sump (to prevent damage), or from above by attaching a hoist to the engine. A third method is to use a suitable support bar with end pieces which will engage in the water channel each side of the bonnet lid aperture. Using an adjustable hook and chain connected to the engine, the weight of the engine and transmission can then be taken from the mountings.
3   Once the weight of the engine and transmission is suitably supported, any of the mountings can be unbolted and removed. The engine mounting and its brace can be removed together once the brace is unbolted from the front axle crossmember. As they are disconnected and removed, note the location and orientation of the fixings and any associated fittings.

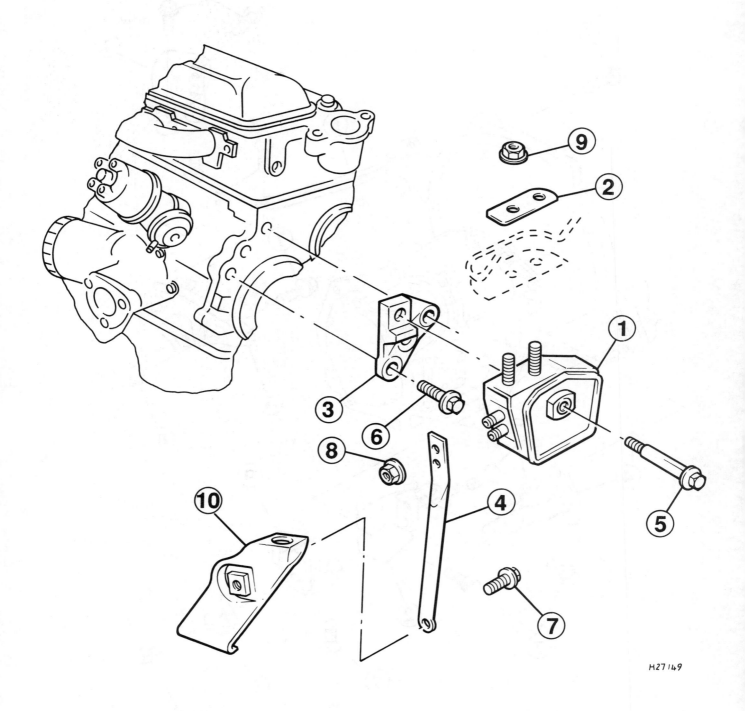

Fig. 2.9 Right-hand engine mounting components – HCS engine (Sec 14)

1 Insulator
2 Reinforcement plate
3 Mounting bracket
4 Support
5 Bolt and washer
6 Bolt
7 Bolt
8 Self-lock nut
9 Self-lock nut
10 Insulator

H27149

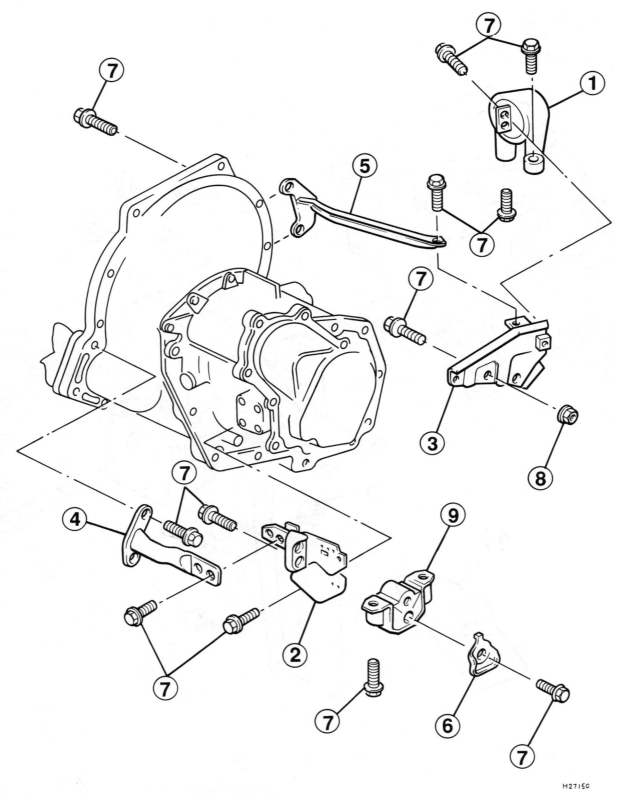

Fig. 2.10 Manual transmission mounting components (Sec 14)

1	Engine support insulator	4	Support stay	6	Retainer	8	Self-lock nut
2	Mounting bracket	5	Support stay	7	Bolt and washer	9	Engine support bracket
3	Bracket						

Fig. 2.11 Right-hand engine mounting components – CVH engine (Sec 14)

1 Insulator
2 Reinforcement plate
3 Engine mounting bracket
4 Support stay
5 Bolt and washer
6 Self-lock nut
7 Engine support insulator

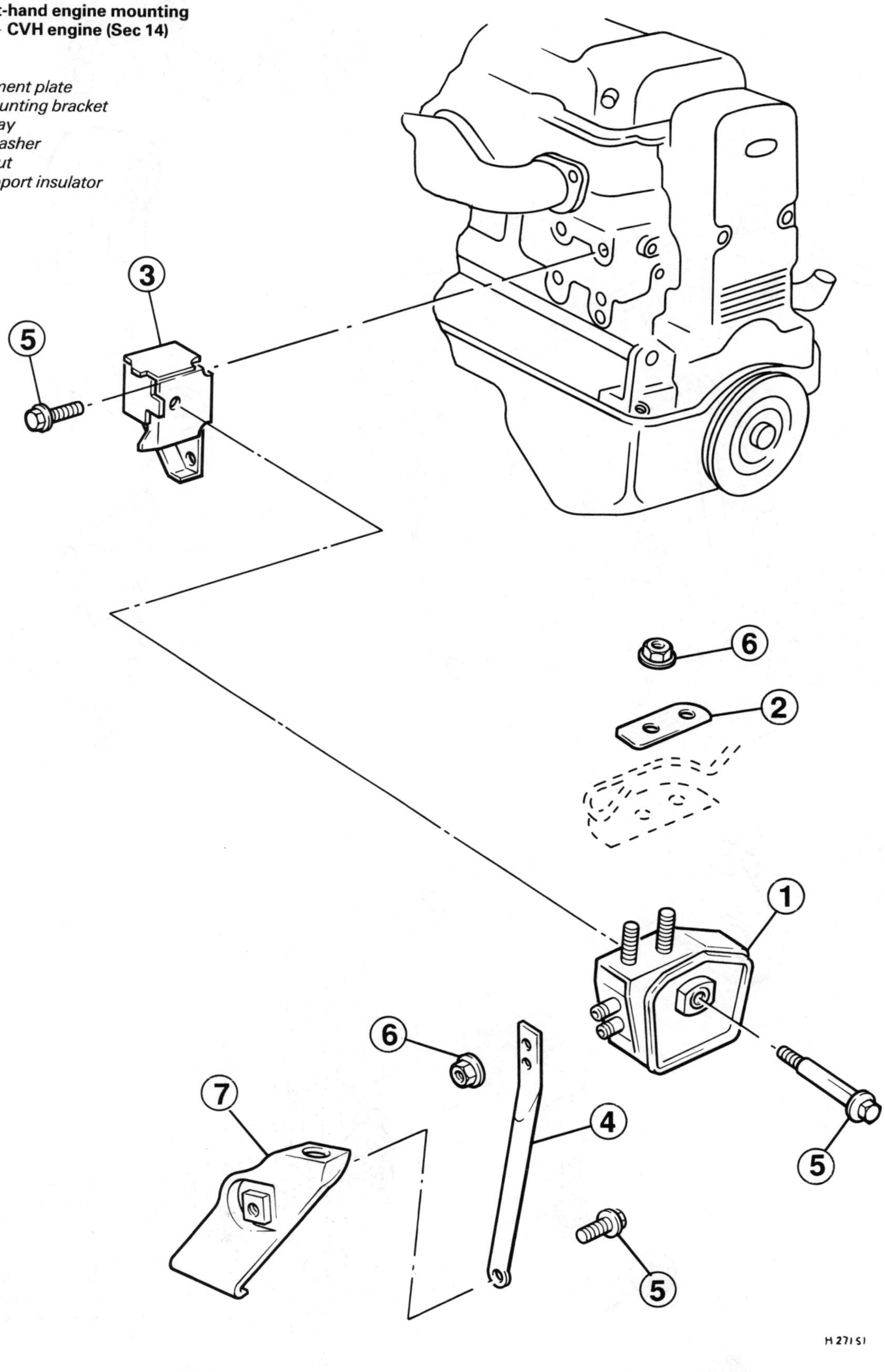

H 271 S1

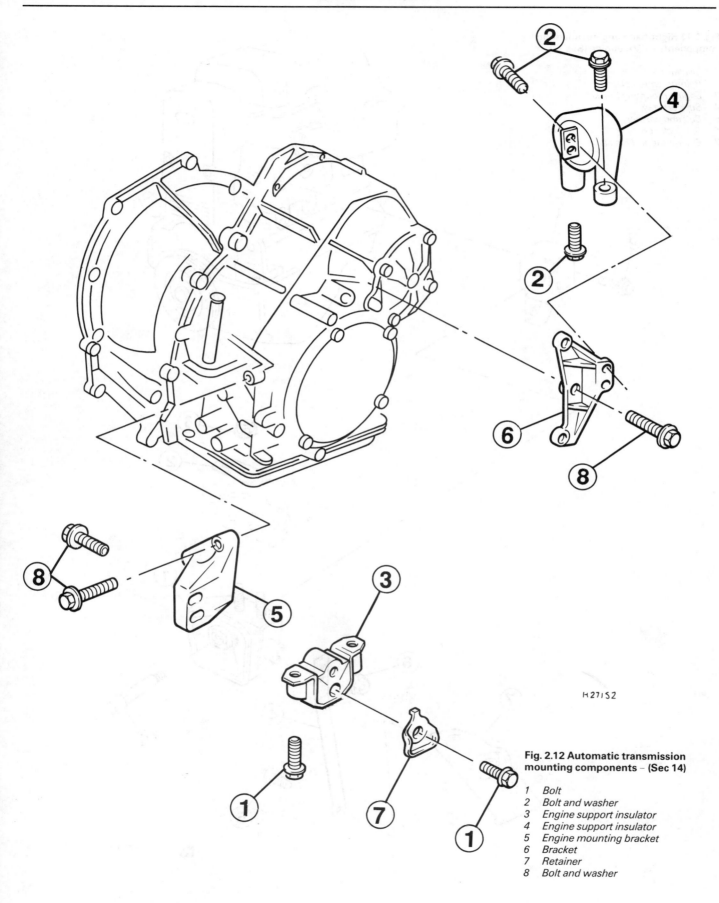

H 271 S2

Fig. 2.12 Automatic transmission mounting components – (Sec 14)

1   Bolt
2   Bolt and washer
3   Engine support insulator
4   Engine support insulator
5   Engine mounting bracket
6   Bracket
7   Retainer
8   Bolt and washer

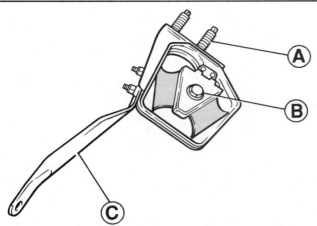

Fig. 2.13 Engine mounting and brace (Sec 14)

H27153

A   *Fixture to front apron*   C   *Brace*
B   *Engine mounting bolt*

4   If on removal the mountings are found to be cracked, distorted or in generally poor condition, they must be renewed.
5   Refitting of all mountings is a reversal of the removal procedure. Ensure that the original sequence of washers and associated fittings are correctly located.
6   Do not fully tighten the mounting fixings until all of the mountings are in position. Check that the mounting rubbers do not twist or distort as the mounting bolts and nuts are tightened to their specified torque wrench settings.

15   Flywheel – removal, inspection and refitting

Refitting

1   Remove the clutch unit as described in Chapter 6.
2   Unscrew the six retaining bolts and remove the flywheel from the rear end flange of the crankshaft. A tool similar to that shown in photo 15.5 can be fitted to prevent the flywheel/crankshaft from rotating as the bolts are removed and later refitted. If on removal the retaining bolts are found to be in poor condition (stretched threads etc) they must be renewed.

15.5 Tightening the flywheel retaining bolts to the specified torque. Note the tool engaging with the ring gear teeth to jam the flywheel/crankshaft from rotating

Inspection

3   Inspect the starter ring gear on the flywheel for any broken or excessively worn teeth. If evident, the ring gear must be renewed, but due to the removal and refitting method required, this is a task best entrusted to a Ford dealer or a competent garage.
4   The clutch friction surface on the flywheel must be carefully inspected for grooving and any hairline cracks (caused by overheating). If these conditions are evident, it may be possible to have the flywheel surface ground to renovate it providing that the balance is not upset. Regrinding is a task for an automotive engineer. If surface grinding is not possible, the flywheel must be renewed.

Refitting .

5   Check that the mating faces of the flywheel and the crankshaft are clean before refitting. Lubricate the threads of the retaining bolts with engine oil before they are screwed into position. Locate the flywheel onto the crankshaft and insert the bolts. Hand tighten them initially, then tighten them in a progressive sequence to the specified torque wrench setting (photo).
6   Refit the clutch unit as described in Chapter 6.

Part B: CVH engine – in-car engine repair procedures

16   General information

How to use this Chapter

This part of Chapter 2 is devoted to in-vehicle repair procedures for the 1.4 and 1.6 litre CVH (OHC) engines. Similar information covering the 1.3 litre HCS (OHV) engine will be found in Part A of this Chapter. All procedures concerning engine removal and refitting and engine block/cylinder head overhaul procedures is covered in Part C of this Chapter.
Most of the operations included in this part of the Chapter are based on the assumption that the engine is still installed in the vehicle. Therefore, if this information is being used during a complete engine overhaul, with the engine already removed, many of the steps here will not apply.

Engine description

The 1.4 and 1.6 litre CVH (Compound Valve angle, Hemispherical combustion chambers) engines are of four cylinder, in-line, overhead camshaft type, mounted transversely together with the transmission at the front of the vehicle.
The crankshaft is supported in five split-shell type main bearings within the cast iron crankcase. The connecting rod big-end bearings are split-shell type and the pistons are attached by interference fit gudgeon pins. Each piston has two compression rings and one oil control ring.
The cylinder head is of light alloy construction and supports the camshaft in five bearings. Camshaft drive is by a toothed composite rubber belt which is driven by a sprocket on the front end of the crankshaft. The camshaft has an offset dog at the rear end which engages with and drives the DIS ignition coil unit. The toothed drivebelt

closes, the oil passes through a port in the body of the cam follower, through four grooves in the plunger and into the cylinder feed chamber. From the chamber, the oil flows to a ball type non-return valve and into the pressure chamber. The tension of the coil spring causes the plunger to press against the valve and so eliminate any free play. As the cam lifts the follower, the oil pressure in the pressure chamber is increased and the non-return valve closes off the port feed chamber. This in turn provides a rigid link between the cam follower, the cylinder and the plunger. These then rise as a unit to open the valve. The cam follower-to-cylinder clearance allows the specified quantity of oil to pass from the pressure chamber, oil only being allowed past the cylinder bore when the pressure is high during the moment of the valve opening. When the valve closes, the escape of oil will produce a small clearance and no pressure will exist in the pressure chamber. The feed chamber oil then flows through the non-return valve and into the pressure chamber so that the cam follower cylinder can be raised by the pressure of the coil spring, eliminating free play until the valve is operated again.

As wear occurs between the rocker arm and the valve stem, the quantity of oil that flows into the pressure chamber will be slightly more than the quantity lost during the expansion cycle of the cam follower. Conversely, when the cam follower is compressed by the expansion of the valve, a slightly smaller quantity of oil will flow into the pressure chamber than was lost.

A rotor type oil pump is mounted on the timing cover end of the engine and is driven by a gear on the front end of the crankshaft. A full-flow type oil filter is fitted and is mounted on the side of the crankcase.

Repair operations possible with the engine in the vehicle

The following operations can be undertaken with the engine in the vehicle.

(a) *Timing belt renewal.*
(b) *Camshaft oil seal – renewal.*
(c) *Camshaft – removal and refitting.*
(d) *Cylinder head – removal and refitting.*
(e) *Crankshaft front oil seal – renewal.*
(f) *Sump – removal and refitting.*
(g) *Pistons/connecting rods – removal and refitting.*
(h) *Engine/transmission mountings – removal and refitting.*

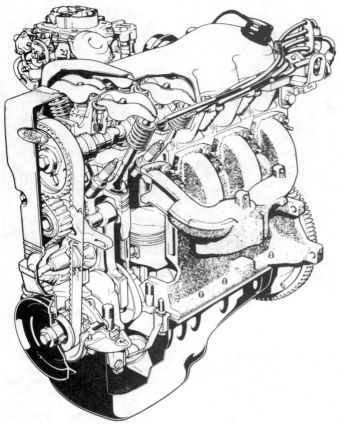

Fig. 2.14 Cutaway view of the CVH engine (Sec 16)

also drives the water pump, which is mounted on the timing belt end of the engine.

Hydraulic cam followers operate the rocker arms and valves. The cam followers are operated by pressurised engine oil. When a valve

Fig. 2.15 Sectional views showing operation of the hydraulic tappets (Sec 16)

A   *Valve closed*
B   *Valve open*
C   *Plunger*
D   *Cylinder*
E   *Feed chamber*
F   *Non-return valve*
G   *Coil spring*
H   *Pressure chamber*
J   *Body*

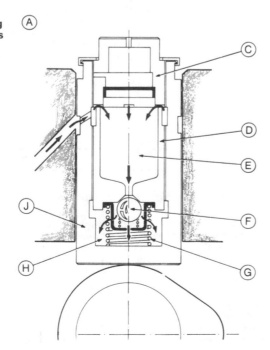
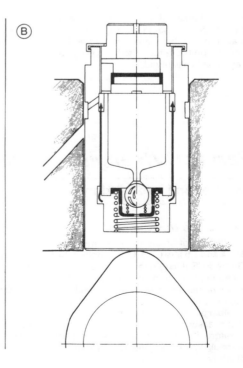

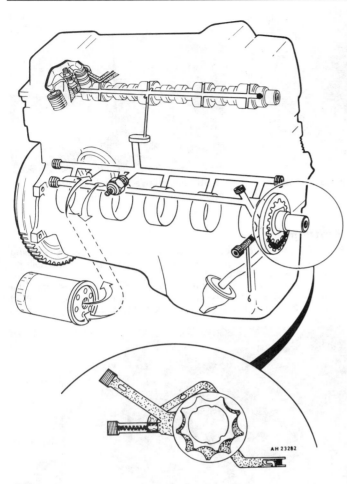

Fig. 2.16 CVH engine lubrication circuit (Sec 16)

18.6A Crankshaft pulley notch (arrowed) aligned with the TDC (0) mark on the timing cover

18.6B Camshaft sprocket timing mark aligned with the TDC mark on the front face of the cylinder head

17 Compression test – description and interpretation

Refer to Section 2 in Part A of this Chapter.

18 Top Dead Centre (TDC) for number one piston – locating

1   Top dead centre (TDC) is the highest point of the cylinder that each piston reaches as the crankshaft turns. Each piston reaches its TDC position at the end of its compression stroke and then again at the end of its exhaust stroke. for the purpose of engine timing, the TDC at the end of the compression stroke is used. On all engines covered in this Section of the manual, the number one cylinder is at the timing case end of the engine. Proceed as follows.
2   Disconnect the battery earth lead.
3   Undo the two retaining bolts and remove the upper timing cover.
4   Raise the vehicle at the front end and support it on axle stands.
5   Undo the retaining bolts and remove the cover from the underside of the crankshaft drivebelt pulley.
6   Fit a spanner onto the crankshaft pulley bolt and turn the crankshaft in its normal direction of travel to the point where the crankshaft pulley timing notch is aligned with the TDC index timing mark on the timing cover. Although the crankshaft is now in top dead centre alignment, with piston numbers one and four at the top of their stroke, the number

one piston may not be on its compression stroke. This is confirmed when the timing index pointer of the camshaft sprocket is exactly aligned with the TDC mark on the front face of the cylinder head (photos).
7   With the engine set at number one piston on TDC, refit the drivebelt pulley cover, lower the vehicle and refit the upper timing cover.
8   Reconnect the battery. Note that when the engine is restarted on EFi models, it must be run as described in Section 4 of Chapter 12 to allow the engine management module to relearn its values.

19 Cylinder head rocker cover – removal and refitting

Removal

1   Disconnect the battery earth lead.
2   On 1.4 litre engines, refer to Chapter 4 for details and remove the air cleaner unit. Disconnect the crankcase ventilation hose from the rocker cover.

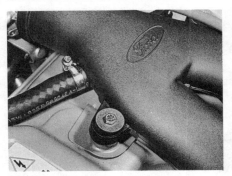

19.3 Air intake duct to rocker cover attachment bolt (EFi engine)

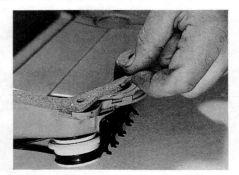

19.9A Fitting a new gasket to the rocker cover

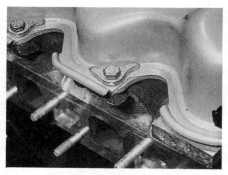

19.9B Rocker cover retaining bolts and plate washers

3   On 1.6 litre engines, disconnect the HT leads from the spark plugs then detach them from the air intake duct and the rocker cover. Position them out of the way. Loosen off the retaining clips and detach the air intake hose and the breather hose from the air intake duct and the crankcase breather hose from the rocker cover. Undo the two retaining bolts and remove the air intake duct (manifold) from the top of the rocker cover (photo).
4   Undo the two bolts retaining the upper half of the timing cover and remove it.
5   Refer to Chapter 4 for details and disconnect the accelerator cable from the throttle housing and the adjuster bracket above the rocker cover. Position the cable out of the way.
6   Where applicable, refer to Chapter 4 for details and disconnect the choke cable from the carburettor.
7   Unscrew and remove the rocker cover retaining bolts and washers, then lift the cover from the cylinder head. Note that the rocker cover gasket will need renewal on refitting.

Refitting

8   Before refitting the rocker cover, clean the mating surfaces of both the cylinder head and the cover.
9   Locate the new gasket and then refit the rocker cover in the reverse order of removal. Fit the cover retaining bolts and washers. Ensure that the grooves in the plate washers are facing upwards as they are fitted (photos). Tighten the cover retaining bolts to the specified torque wrench setting. Refer to Chapter 4 for details on reconnecting the accelerator cable and choke cable (as applicable).
10   On completion, reconnect the battery earth lead. On restarting the engine on 1.6 EFi models, proceed as described in Section 4 of Chapter 12 so that the engine management module can relearn its values.

20   Crankshaft pulley – removal and refitting

Removal

1   Disconnect the battery earth lead.
2   Raise the vehicle at the front end and support it on axle stands.
3   Unbolt and remove the cover from the underside of the crankshaft pulley.
4   Loosen off the alternator mounting and adjuster fixings, pivot the alternator inwards to release the tension on the drivebelt, then release the belt from the crankshaft pulley.
5   If timing drivebelt renewal is also intended, set the engine at TDC as described in Section 18 before removing the crankshaft pulley and retaining bolt.
6   To prevent the crankshaft from turning as the pulley bolt is loosened off, remove the starter motor as described in Chapter 12 and then jam the starter ring gear on the periphery of the flywheel/driveplate using a suitable lever (photo).
7   Unscrew and remove the crankshaft pulley retaining bolt and its washer. Withdraw the pulley from the front end of the crankshaft (photo). If necessary, lever it free using a pair of diagonally opposed levers positioned behind the pulley.

Refitting

8   Refit in the reverse order of removal. Tighten the pulley retaining bolt to the specified torque setting and refer to Chapter 1 for details on adjusting the alternator drivebelt.
9   On completion, reconnect the battery earth lead. On restarting the engine on 1.6 EFi models, proceed as described in Section 4 of Chapter 12 so that the engine management module can relearn its values.

20.6 Using a suitable bar to lock the flywheel ring gear

20.7 Crankshaft pulley removal

21.2 Upper timing cover removal

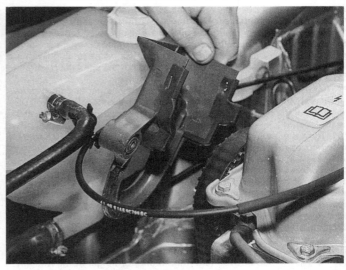

21.4 Lower timing cover removal

21 Timing belt covers – removal and refitting

Removal

1 Disconnect the battery earth lead.
2 Undo the two retaining bolts and remove the upper timing cover (photo).
3 Refer to the previous Section for details and remove the crankshaft pulley.
4 Unscrew the two bolts securing the lower timing cover and remove it (photo).

Refitting

5 Refit in the reverse order of removal. Tighten the cover retaining bolts to the specified torque wrench setting.
6 On completion, reconnect the battery earth lead. When restarting the engine on 1.6 EFi models, proceed as described in Section 4 of Chapter 12 so that the engine management module can relearn its values.

22 Timing belt and tensioner – removal, refitting and adjustment

Removal

1 Referring to the previous Sections for details, remove the rocker cover, the crankshaft pulley and the lower timing cover.

2 Check that the crankshaft is set with the number one piston at TDC (on its compression stroke) before proceeding. If necessary, refer to Section 18 for further details.
3 To check the drivebelt for correct adjustment, proceed as described in paragraph 13 below. To remove the drivebelt, proceed as follows.
4 Loosen off the two bolts securing the drivebelt tensioner and then using a large screwdriver, prise the tensioner to one side to loosen off the drivebelt tension. Secure the tensioner in this position by retightening the bolts (photo).
5 If the original drivebelt is to be refitted, mark it for direction of travel and also the exact tooth engagement positions on all sprockets. Slip the drivebelt from the camshaft, water pump and crankshaft sprockets (photo). Whilst the drivebelt is removed, avoid any excessive movement of the sprockets otherwise the piston crowns and valves may come into contact and be damaged.
6 If required, withdraw the crankshaft sprocket. If it is a tight fit on the crankshaft, a puller or two suitably large screwdrivers can be used to release its grip. Withdraw the thrust washer and the Woodruff key from the crankshaft.

Refitting

7 If previously removed, fit the thrust washer, Woodruff key and crankshaft sprocket onto the crankshaft. Before refitting the belt, check that the crankshaft is still at the TDC position with the small projection on the belt sprocket front flange aligned with the TDC mark on the oil pump housing (photo). Also ensure that the camshaft sprocket is set with its TDC pointer aligned with the corresponding timing mark on the cylinder head. If necessary, adjust the sprockets slightly. As previously mentioned, avoid any excessive movement of the sprockets whilst the belt is removed.
8 Engage the timing belt teeth with the teeth of the crankshaft

22.4 Timing belt tensioner retaining bolts (arrowed)

22.5 Timing belt removal

22.7 Sprocket and oil pump housing TDC marks in alignment

sprocket and then pull the belt vertically upright on its right-hand run. Keep it taught and engage it with the teeth of the camshaft sprocket. If the original belt is being refitted, check that the belt direction of travel is correct and realign the belt to sprocket marks made during removal to ensure that the exact original engagement positions are retained. When the belt is fully fitted on the sprockets, check that the sprocket positions have not altered.

9   Carefully manoeuvre the belt around the tensioner and engage its teeth with the water pump sprocket, again ensuring that the TDC positions of the crankshaft and camshaft are not disturbed as the belt is finally located.

10   Refit the lower timing cover and tighten its retaining bolts to the specified torque setting. Refit the crankshaft pulley and tighten its retaining bolt to the specified torque setting.

11   To take up belt slack, loosen off the tensioner and move it towards the front of the car to apply an initial tension to the belt. Secure the tensioner in this position, then remove the flywheel ring gear locking device.

12   Rotate the crankshaft through two full revolutions in (the normal direction of travel), returning to the TDC position (camshaft sprocket to cylinder head). Check that the crankshaft pulley notch is aligned with the TDC (0) mark on the lower half of the timing cover.

13   Grasp the belt between the thumb and forefinger at the midway point between the crankshaft and camshaft sprockets on the right-hand side. The belt tension is correct when it should just be possible to twist the belt through 90° at this point (photo). To adjust the belt, loosen off the tensioner retaining bolts then move the tensioner as required using a suitable screwdriver as a lever, then retighten the retaining bolts. Rotate the crankshaft to settle the belt, then recheck the tension. It may take two or three attempts to get the tension correct. On completion, tighten the tensioner bolts to the specified torque wrench setting.

14   It should be noted that this setting is approximate and the belt tension should be rechecked by a Ford dealer with the special tensioner setting tool at the earliest opportunity.

15   Refit the starter motor (refer to Chapter 12).

16   Refit the rocker cover and the upper timing cover. Check that the mating surfaces of the rocker cover and cylinder block face are clean and use a gasket where necessary. Tighten the retaining bolts of each cover to the respective torque settings.

17   Refit the alternator drivebelt, adjust its tension as described in Chapter 1, then refit the crankshaft pulley cover.

18   Refit the air cleaner and the air intake ducting.

19   On completion, reconnect the battery earth lead. When restarting the engine on 1.6 EFi models, proceed as described in Section 4 of Chapter 12 so that the engine management module can relearn its values.

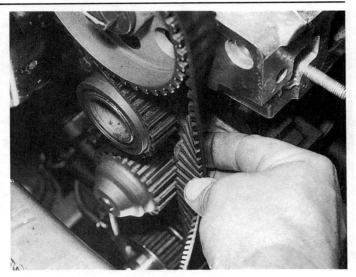

22.13 Checking the tension of the timing belt

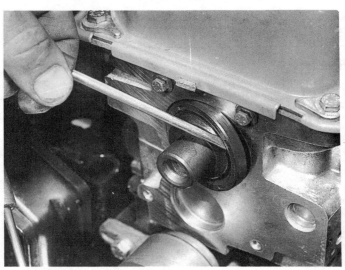

23.4 Camshaft front oil seal removal

23 Camshaft oil seal – renewal

1   Disconnect the battery earth lead.

2   Refer to the previous Section for details, remove the upper timing cover, set the engine at TDC, then loosen off the timing belt tensioner and disengage the timing belt from the camshaft sprocket.

3   Pass a bar through one of the holes in the camshaft sprocket to prevent the camshaft from rotating, then unscrew and remove the sprocket retaining bolt. Note that this bolt **must be renewed** when refitting the camshaft sprocket. Remove the sprocket and note the Woodruff key fitted to the camshaft.

4   The oil seal is now accessible for removal. Note its direction of fitting, then using a suitable screwdriver or a tool with a hooked end to lever and extract the seal from its housing (but take care not to damage the housing with the tool) (photo).

5   Check that the housing is clean before fitting the new seal. Lubricate the lips of the seal and the running faces of the camshaft with clean engine oil, then carefully locate the seal over the camshaft and drive it squarely into position using a suitable tube or a socket (photo). An alternative method of fitting is to draw it squarely into position using the old sprocket bolt and a suitable distance piece.

6   With the seal fully inserted in its housing, remove the bolt and distance piece (if used), install the Woodruff key, then fit the camshaft sprocket into position and fit the **new** retaining bolt. The threads of the bolt should be smeared with a sealing compound prior to fitting. Locate the timing belt onto the camshaft sprocket then tighten the retaining bolt to the specified torque wrench setting (photos).

7   Adjust the tension of the timing belt as described in the previous Section then refit the upper timing cover.

8   On completion, reconnect the battery earth lead. When restarting the engine on 1.6 EFi models, proceed as described in Section 4 of Chapter 12 so that the engine management module can relearn its values.

24 Camshaft, rocker arms and tappets – removal, inspection and refitting

Removal

1   Disconnect the battery earth lead.

2   Refer to the appropriate earlier Sections in this Chapter and remove the timing belt upper cover and the rocker cover.

3   On carburettor models, refer to Chapter 4 and remove the fuel pump.

4   Detach, unbolt and remove the ignition coil, its support bracket and the interference capacitor from the end of the cylinder head as described in Chapter 5.

5   Undo the retaining nuts and remove the guides, rocker arms and spacer plates (photos). Keep the respective components in their original order of fitting by marking them with a piece of numbered tape or by using a suitable sub-divided box.

23.5 Using a socket to tap the camshaft oil seal into place

23.6A Refit the camshaft sprocket ...

23.6B ... and tighten the retaining bolt to the specified torque whilst retaining the sprocket as shown

24.5A Undo the rocker arm retaining nut ...

24.5B ... withdraw the guide ...

24.5C ... followed by the rocker arm ...

24.5D ... and spacer plate

24.6A Removing an hydraulic tappet

24.6B Store tappets in clearly-marked container filled with oil to prevent oil loss

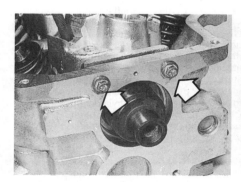

24.11A Undo the two retaining bolts (arrowed) ...

24.11B ... and lift out the camshaft thrust plate

24.12A Pierce the centre of the blanking plug ...

24.12B ... and lever it out of the cylinder head

24.13 Withdraw the camshaft from the cylinder head

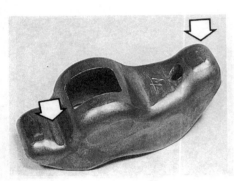

24.20 Inspect the rocker arm contact points indicated for excessive wear

24.23 Driving a new blanking plug into position

24.27 Lubricate the rocker arm assemblies as they are refitted

6   Withdraw the hydraulic tappets, again keeping them in their original fitted sequence (photos).

7   Unbolt and remove the cover from the crankshaft pulley, then with a spanner engaged on the crankshaft pulley bolt, turn the crankshaft over to set the engine on TDC. Refer to Section 18 for further details.

8   With the engine set at TDC, loosen off the timing belt tensioner retaining bolts and slacken off the tension from the belt. Disengage the timing belt from the camshaft sprocket.

9   Pass a suitable bar or rod through the holes in the camshaft sprocket to lock it and then unscrew and remove the sprocket retaining bolt. Note that the bolt **must be renewed** when refitting. Withdraw the camshaft sprocket and note its Woodruff key.

10   Extract the camshaft oil seal as described in Section 23.

11   Before removing the camshaft and its thrust plate, check and take note of the amount of camshaft endfloat using a dial gauge or feeler gauges. With the camshaft endfloat measured and noted, unscrew the two retaining bolts and then extract the camshaft thrust plate from its pocket at the front end of the cylinder head (photos).

12   At the rear end of the cylinder head, pierce the camshaft blanking plug with a suitable tool and then lever it out of its aperture (photos).

13   Withdraw the camshaft from the cylinder head at the rear (ignition coil) end (photo). Take care not to damage the bearings in the cylinder head as the shaft is withdrawn.

Inspection

14   Clean and inspect the various components removed for signs of excessive wear.

15   Examine the camshaft bearing journals and lobes for damage or wear. If evident, a new camshaft must be fitted or one that has been renovated by a company specialising in exchange components.

16   Compare the previously measured camshaft endfloat with that specified. If the endfloat is outside of the specified tolerance, the thrust plate must be renewed.

17   The camshaft bearing bore diameters in the cylinder head should be measured and checked against the tolerances specified. A suitable measuring gauge will be required for this but if not available, check for excessive movement between the camshaft journals and the bearings.

If the bearings are found to be unacceptably worn, a new cylinder head is the only answer as the bearings are machined direct in the head.

18   It is seldom that the hydraulic tappets are badly worn in the cylinder head bores but again, if the bores are found to be worn beyond an acceptable level, the cylinder head must be renewed.

19   If the contact surface of the cam lobes show signs of depression or grooving, note that they cannot be renovated by grinding as the hardened surface will be removed and the overall length of the tappet(s) will be reduced. The self-adjustment point of the tappet will be exceeded as a result, so that the valve adjustment will be affected and they will then be noisy in operation. Therefore, renewal of the tappet is the only remedy in this case.

20   Inspect the rocker arm contact surfaces for excessive wear and renew if necessary (photo).

Refitting

21   Refitting the camshaft and its associated components is a reversal of the removal procedure but note the following special points.

22   Lubricate the camshaft bearings, the camshaft and the thrust plate with clean engine oil prior to fitting them. As the camshaft is inserted, take care not to damage the bearings in the cylinder head. Refer to the specifications for the thrust plate retaining bolts torque. When the thrust plate bolts are tightened, make a final check to ensure that the camshaft endfloat is as specified.

23   A new front oil seal must be fitted after the camshaft has been installed (see previous Section for details). It will also be necessary to insert a new blanking plug into the rear end of the cylinder head. Drive it squarely into position so that it is flush with the head (photo).

24   Refit the camshaft sprocket and fit a **new** retaining bolt with its threads smeared with sealing compound. Tighten the bolt to the specified torque setting.

25   Refit and tension the timing belt as described in Section 22.

26   Lubricate the hydraulic tappets with hypoid oil before refitting them into their original locations in the cylinder head.

27   Lubricate and refit the rocker arms and guides in their original sequence, use new nuts and tighten them to the specified torque setting (photo). It is essential before each rocker arm is installed and its

nut tightened, that the respective cam follower is positioned at its lowest point (in contact with the cam base circle). Turn the cam (using the crankshaft pulley bolt) as necessary to achieve this.

28   Use a new rocker cover gasket and to ensure that a good seal is made, check that its location groove is clear of oil, grease or any portions of old gasket. When in position, tighten the cover retaining bolts to the specified torque setting. Ensure that the cover bolt plate washers are correctly orientated with their grooves facing upwards.

29   Refit the remaining components with reference to the relevant Sections in this, or the appropriate Chapters elsewhere in the manual.

30   On completion, reconnect the battery earth lead. When restarting the engine on 1.6 EFi models, proceed as described in Section 4 of Chapter 12 so that the engine management module can relearn its values.

25   Cylinder head – removal and refitting

Removal

1   Disconnect the battery earth lead.
2   Drain the cooling system as described in Chapter 1.
3   Refer to Section 19 and disconnect/remove the items described in paragraphs 2 to 7 inclusive.
4   Loosen off the retaining clips and disconnect the upper coolant hose, the expansion tank hose and the heater hose from the thermostat housing. Also disconnect the heater hose from the inlet manifold.
5   On models fitted with central fuel injection (CFi), disconnect the heated coolant hose from the injector unit.
6   On models fitted with electronic fuel injection (EFi), disconnect the coolant hose from the injector intermediate flange and at the thermostat housing.
7   On 1.6 EFi equipped models, disconnect the following.

   (a)   The MAP sensor vacuum hose from the inlet manifold upper section.
   (b)   The carbon canister solenoid valve vacuum hose from the inlet manifold upper section.
   (c)   Disconnect the oil trap vacuum hose at the 'T' piece connector.
   (d)   The brake servo vacuum hose from the inlet manifold upper section by pressing in the clamp ring and simultaneously pulling the hose free from the connection.

8   Disconnect the following fuel supply/return hoses. Remember that the fuel system is pressurised and care must be taken when loosening off the connections. Observe all safety precautions for handling fuel (read *Safety first!*) and catch any fuel spillage in a cloth. Plug the hoses and connections to prevent further spillage and the possible ingress of dirt.

   (a)   On carburettor (non CFi) equipped models, disconnect the fuel supply hose from the pump and the return hose from the carburettor.
   (b)   On CFi models, pull free and detach the fuel return hose from the injection unit and the supply hose at the connector.
   (c)   On 1.6 EFi models, detach the fuel supply hose from the fuel rail. Disconnect the return line from the fuel pressure regulator.

9   On CFi models, disconnect the brake servo vacuum hose from the inlet manifold, the MAP sensor vacuum hose from the sensor and the carbon canister connecting hose at the injection unit.
10   Note their connections and routings and disconnect the following wiring connectors or multi-plugs from the following items.

   (a)   Temperature gauge sender unit.
   (b)   DIS ignition coil.
   (c)   Coolant temperature sensor.
   (d)   Cooling fan temperature sensor.
   (e)   Carburettor (where applicable).
   (f)   Radio earth lead.
   (g)   Road speed sensor (where applicable).
   (h)   Engine wiring loom (where necessary).
   (i)   Intake air temperature sensor (where applicable).

11   On CFi models, detach the throttle adjuster motor, throttle position sensor and injector lead plugs.

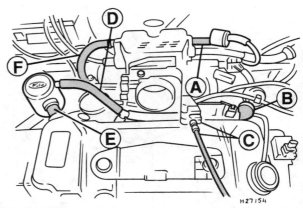

Fig. 2.17 Vacuum hoses and throttle cable connections on the EFi engine (Sec 25)

A   *Hose to MAP sensor*
B   *Crankcase ventilation breather hose*
C   *Throttle cable and clip*
D   *Oil trap hose and T-piece connector*
E   *Hose to oil trap*
F   *Hose to carbon canister solenoid valve*

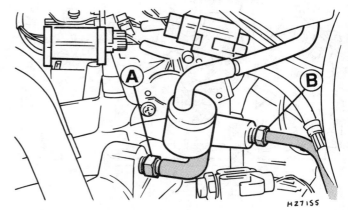

Fig. 2.18 Vacuum hose to the MAP sensor (A) and the brake servo unit (B) on the CFi engine (Sec 25)

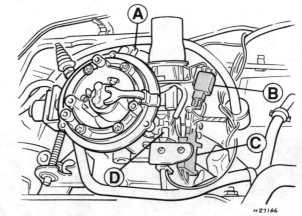

Fig. 2.19 Wiring connections to be detached on the 1.4 litre CFi engine (Sec 25)

A   *Coolant temperature sensor*
B   *Throttle adjuster motor*
C   *Throttle position sensor*
D   *Injector*

12   Where still attached, disconnect the HT leads from the DIS ignition coil and the spark plugs.
13   Unscrew the two retaining bolts and remove the timing belt upper cover.

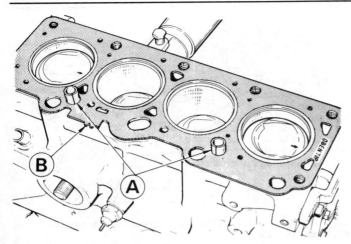

Fig. 2.20 Cylinder head location dowels (A) and gasket identity teeth (B) (Sec 25)

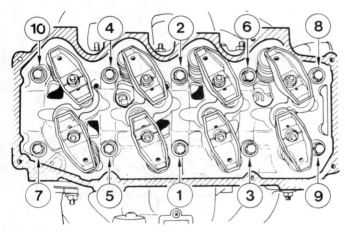

Fig. 2.21 Cylinder head retaining bolt tightening sequence (Sec 25)

14   Loosen off the timing belt tensioner retaining bolts and move the tensioner to release the tension from the drivebelt. Support the belt and lift it clear of the camshaft sprocket.
15   Raise the vehicle at the front end and support it on axle stands.
16   Unscrew the retaining nuts and detach the exhaust downpipe from the manifold. Remove the gasket and tie the downpipe up to support it; note that a new gasket must be fitted on reassembly. Where applicable, disconnect the pulse air supply hose from the check valve and noting their connections (to ensure correct reassembly), the

appropriate system vacuum hoses at the PVS (three port vacuum switch) under the inlet manifold.
17   Before it is released and removed, the cylinder head must first have cooled down to room temperature (about 20°C).
18   Unscrew the cylinder head retaining bolts progressively in the reverse order to that shown for tightening in Fig. 2.21. It is important to note that the cylinder head bolts must only be used once and therefore when they are removed, the bolts must be discarded and new bolts obtained for refitting the cylinder head.
19   Remove the cylinder head complete with its manifolds. If necessary, grip the manifolds and rock it free from the location dowels on the top face of the cylinder block. Do not attempt to tap it sideways or lever between the head and the block top face.
20   Remove the cylinder head gasket. This must always be renewed and it is essential that the correct type, suitable to the engine, is obtained. Save the old gasket and when ordering the new replacement, show it to the supplier so that the identification marks (teeth) enable him to provide you with the correct gasket type. Compare the old with the new to make sure you have the correct gasket type before fitting it.

Refitting

21   Before refitting the cylinder head, the mating surfaces of both the head and the cylinder block must be perfectly clean and the locating dowels must be in position. Clean the retaining bolt holes of oil. In extreme cases it is possible for oil and coolant left in the bolt holes to crack the head due to the hydraulic effect when the bolts are inserted.
22   To prevent the possibility of the valves and pistons coming into contact as the head is fitted, turn the crankshaft over to position the No 1 piston approximately 20 mm below its TDC position in the bore (photo).
23   Locate the cylinder head gasket into position on the top face of the cylinder block, locating it over the dowels. Ensure that the gasket is fitted the correct way up as indicated by its OBEN-TOP marking (photos).
24   Lower the cylinder head into position ensuring that it fits over the locating dowels, then insert the **new** retaining bolts (photos). Hand tighten the bolts initially, then tighten them in the order shown in Fig. 2.21 in the four stages to the specified torque setting. After the first two stages, mark the bolt heads with a dab of quick drying paint so that the paint spots all face the same direction. Now tighten the bolts (Stage 3) through a further 90°(quarter turn), followed by a further 90° (Stage 4). At each stage, tighten the bolts only in the sequence shown before moving on to the next stage. If all the bolts have been tightened equally, all of the paint spots should be facing the same direction. *The bolts must not be re-torqued.*
25   Rotate the camshaft toothed belt pulley and position it so that its TDC index mark pointer is in alignment with the TDC index spot mark on the front end face of the cylinder head (see photo 18.6B).
26   Now turn the crankshaft pulley and position its TDC index mark (notch) in alignment with the TDC (0) indicator on the front face of the timing case, taking the shortest route (not visa-versa) (see photo 18.6A).
27   Refit the timing belt over the camshaft sprocket and then tension the drivebelt as described in Section 22.
28   The remainder of the refitting procedures are a reversal of the removal. Refer to the appropriate Sections both in this Chapter and 3 and 4 for specific details when reconnecting the engine, cooling system and fuel system components.

25.22 Position the number 1 piston 20 mm down the bore

25.23A Fit the cylinder head gasket as marked (TOP) ...

25.23B ... and locate it over the dowels

25.24A Lower the cylinder head into position

25.24B Insert the new cylinder head bolts

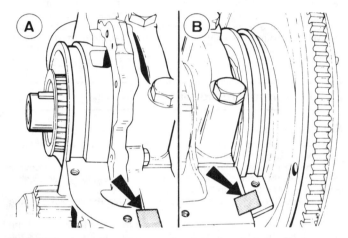

Fig. 2.22 Apply sealing compound at the points indicated before refitting the sump (Sec 26)

A *Crankcase-to-oil pump housing*

B *Crankcase-to-rear oil seal carrier*

29 On completion, check that the engine oil level is correct and refill the cooling system as described in Chapter 1.
30 Check that all wiring connections are securely and correctly made. Before restarting the engine, refer to Section 52 for special details concerning the check and restart procedures after a major overhaul. When restarting the engine on 1.6 EFi models, reference must also be made to Section 4 of Chapter 12 for special restart procedures to enable the engine management module to relearn its values.

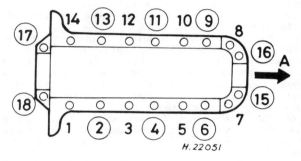

Fig. 2.23 Sump bolt tightening sequence (Sec 26)

A indicates crankshaft pulley end of engine

26 Sump – removal and refitting

Removal

1 Disconnect the battery earth lead.
2 Drain the oil from the engine as described in Chapter 1.
3 Check that the handbrake is fully applied, then raise the vehicle at the front end and support it on axle stands.
4 On models fitted with a controlled catalytic converter, pull free the HEGO sensor lead multi-plug and disconnect it. *If the engine has been recently run, take particular care against burning when working in the area of the catalytic converter.*
5 Undo the retaining nuts and detach the exhaust downpipe from the manifold (noting that the flange gasket must be renewed when reconnecting). Where applicable, also detach the downpipe at the rear of the catalytic converter and release it from the front mounting.
6 On 1.6 litre engines, undo the retaining bolts and remove the

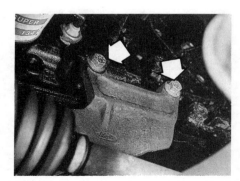

26.6A Auxiliary bracing bracket to engine bolts (oil filter side) – 1.6 litre only

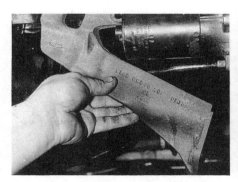

26.6B Auxiliary bracing bracket removal from the starter motor side of the engine – 1.6 litre only

26.7 Removing the clutch cover plate

26.8 Removing the sump from the engine

26.11 Applying sealant to the oil pump-to-crankcase joint

engine-to-transmission auxiliary bracing brackets (photos).

7   Undo the retaining bolts and remove the clutch cover plate from the front face of the bellhousing (photo).

8   Unscrew the sump retaining bolts in progressive sequence and remove them. Support and lower the sump pan taking care not to spill any oil remaining in it as it is removed (photo). If the sump is stuck to the base of the crankcase, prise it free using a screwdriver but take care not to damage the sump flange face. If it is really stuck in position, check first that all of the bolts are removed, then cut around the sump gasket with a sharp knife to help in easing free the joint.

9   After the sump is removed, further oil will almost certainly continue to drip down from within the crankcase, some old newspapers positioned underneath will soak up the spillage whilst the sump is removed.

10   Clean the sump of old oil and sludge using paraffin or a suitable engine cleaner solution. Clean any traces of old gasket and sealer from the mating faces of the sump and the crankcase.

Refitting

11   Smear a suitable sealing compound onto the junctions of the crankcase-to-oil seal carrier at the rear and the crankcase-to-oil pump housing at the front on each side (photo).

12   Insert a new rubber seal in the groove in the rear oil seal carrier and the oil pump case. As an aid to correct sump alignment when refitting it, screw ten M6 studs into the cylinder block in the circled number positions shown in Fig. 2.23.

13   Fit a new gasket over the studs. Fit the sump into position ensuring that the spacing pimples sit in the gasket, then insert bolts into the available holes and finger tighten them only at this stage. Now remove the studs and fit the remaining bolts, again finger-tight.

14   Tighten the sump bolts in a progressive, numerical sequence shown in Fig. 2.23 to the specified torque wrench setting.

15   Fit the oil drain plug with a new seal and tighten it to the specified torque wrench setting.

16   Refit the clutch cover plate.

17   Reconnect the exhaust downpipe according to type as described in Chapter 4.

18   On completion, lower the vehicle and reconnect the battery as described in Chapter 12. When restarting the engine on 1.6 EFi models, reference must also be made to Section 4 of Chapter 12 for special re-start procedures to enable the engine management module to re-learn its values.

27   Oil pump – removal and refitting

Removal

1   Detach the battery earth lead and remove the alternator drivebelt as described in Chapter 1.

2   Remove the crankshaft pulley (Section 20), the timing belt covers (Section 21), the timing belt, crankshaft sprocket and thrust washer (Section 22), and the sump (Section 26).

3   Unscrew the retaining nut/bolts and remove the oil pick-up pipe (photo).

4   Unbolt and withdraw the oil pump unit from the front face of the engine. Clean the oil pump for inspection. Refer to Section 28 for the inspection procedures. The oil seal in the oil pump housing should always be renewed (Section 29).

Refitting

5   Before refitting the oil pump and the associated fittings, clean off the respective mating faces. A new oil pump gasket must be obtained as well as the seals and gaskets for the other associated components to be refitted.

6   When refitting the oil pump, precautionary measures must be taken to avoid the possibility of damaging the new oil pump oil seal as it is engaged over the shoulder and onto its journal on the crankshaft. Extract the Woodruff key from the groove in the crankshaft, then cut a plastic shim which will furl over and protrude beyond the shoulder of the seal journal on the crankshaft. This will allow the seal to ride over the step and avoid damaging the seal lip as it is pushed into position on the crankshaft.

27.3 Removing the oil intake pipe

27.7 Prime the oil pump prior to fitting

27.8A Refit the oil pump

27.8B With the oil pump refitted, remove the protective shim (arrowed)

27.10 Locating the Woodruff key into the groove in the crankshaft

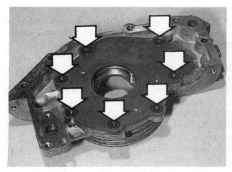

28.2 Oil pump cover plate retaining screws (arrowed)

28.3A Outer rotor to oil pump body clearance check

28.3B Outer to inner rotor clearance check

7   If a new oil pump is being fitted or the old pump is to be re-used after cleaning and inspection, first prime the pump by squirting clean engine oil into it and simultaneously rotating the drive gear a few times (photo).

8   Align the pump gear flats with those on the crankshaft, then fit the oil pump. Check that the sump mating faces of the oil pump and the base of the crankcase are flush each side, then tighten the retaining bolts to the specified torque setting. Remove the protective shim (photos).

9   Refit the oil pick-up tube to the oil pump using a new gasket. Refer to the specifications for the tightening torque details.

10   Unwind and remove the insulation tape from the crankshaft. Slide the thrust washer onto the front end of the crankshaft then insert the Woodruff key into position in the groove in the crankshaft (photo). The key must be located with its flat edge parallel with the line of the crankshaft to ensure that the crankshaft sprocket slides fully into position as it is being refitted.

11   Refit the crankshaft sprocket, the timing belt, timing cover and crankshaft drivebelt pulley (as described in the appropriate earlier Sections of this Chapter). Refit and adjust the alternator drivebelt as described in Chapter 1.

12   On completion, lower the vehicle and reconnect the battery as described in Chapter 12. When restarting the engine on 1.6 EFi models, reference must also be made to Section 4 of Chapter 12 for special re-start procedures to enable the engine management module to re-learn its values.

28 Oil pump – dismantling, inspection and reassembly

1   The oil pump fitted is a low friction rotor type driven from the front end of the crankshaft. Where a high mileage engine is being reconditioned, it is recommended that a new oil pump is fitted.

2   To inspect the rotor assembly in the pump unit, undo the retaining screws and remove the cover plate (photo). Remove the O-ring seal.

3   Clean the rotors and the inside of the pump housing, then visually

28.3C Rotor endfloat check

28.4 Inner and outer rotor matchmarks

29.5 Crankshaft front oil seal (arrowed)

29.19 Rear oil seal removal

29.20 Rear oil seal installation

inspect the various components for signs of excessive wear and scoring (photos). Check the pump components for wear using feeler gauges in the same manner as that described for the HCS (OHV) engine in Section 12 in Part A of this Chapter, but refer to the accompanying photographs and the Specifications for the allowable oil pump tolerances applicable in the CVH engine Specifications.

4   When reassembling the pump unit, ensure that the inner (driving) and outer (driven) rotors are located with the corresponding indented matchmarks facing the same way (photo).

29 Crankshaft oil seals – renewal

Front oil seal

1   Disconnect the battery earth lead.
2   Raise the vehicle at the front and support it on axle stands.
3   Remove the alternator drivebelt as described in Chapter 1.
4   Remove the crankshaft pulley (Section 20), the timing covers (Section 21), the timing belt and crankshaft sprocket, Woodruff key and thrust washer (Section 22).
5   The oil seal is now accessible for removal from the front face of the oil seal housing (photo). To withdraw the seal a suitably hooked tool will be required, but if possible use Ford special tool No 21-096. Take care not to damage the oil seal housing during removal. As it is removed, note the fitted orientation of the seal in its housing.
6   Clean the oil seal housing and the crankshaft stub, then lubricate the lips of the new seal and the crankshaft front stub with clean engine oil.
7   The oil seal should be drawn into position using the Ford special tool No 21-093A, but failing this, use a tube of suitable diameter, the crankshaft pulley bolt and washers. *Do not hammer the seal into position.* To protect the seal lips as it is fitted onto the crankshaft, cut a thin sheet of plastic to suit and furl it round the front of the crankshaft, over the seal journal shoulder.
8   When the seal is fully fitted, remove the special tool (or fabricated tool) and withdraw the plastic protector shim. Check that the crankshaft is still at the TDC position and refit the Woodruff key, thrust washer and sprocket. Refit and tension the timing belt then refit the timing cover and crankshaft pulley as described in the appropriate Sections earlier in this Chapter.
9   Refit and adjust the alternator drivebelt as described in Chapter 1.
10   On completion, lower the vehicle and reconnect the battery as described in Chapter 12.
11   When re-starting the engine on 1.6 EFi models, reference must also be made to Section 4 of Chapter 12 for special re-start procedures to enable the engine management module to re-learn its values.

Rear oil seal

12   With the engine or transmission removed from the vehicle for access, remove the clutch unit as described in Chapter 6.
13   Jam the starter ring gear teeth of the flywheel (or driveplate) to prevent the crankshaft from turning, then unscrew and remove the flywheel (or driveplate) retaining bolts. Remove the flywheel (or driveplate) from the rear end face of the crankshaft. Note that **new** flywheel/driveplate bolts will be required during reassembly.

14   If available, use Ford special tool No 21-151 or a suitable clawed tool to extract the seal from its housing. If the seal housing is removed from the rear face of the engine, the seal can be removed as described in paragraph 19. As it is removed, note the direction of fitting and take care not to damage the seal housing as the seal is extracted.
15   Clean the seal housing, the crankshaft rear flange face and the flywheel/driveplate mating surfaces.
16   One of two possible methods may be used to insert the new oil seal, depending on the tools available.
17   If Ford special service tool No 21-095 is available, lubricate the seal lips of the seal and its running face on the crankshaft with clean engine oil. Position the seal (correctly orientated) into the special tool, then draw the seal into the housing using two flywheel/driveplate securing bolts so that the seal is against the stop.
18   If the correct Ford service tool is not available, it will be necessary to remove the oil seal carrier housing. To do this first drain and remove the sump as described in Section 26, then unscrew the seal housing retaining bolts and remove the housing from the rear face of the crankcase.
19   Drive the old seal from the housing by carefully tapping it from its aperture using a suitable punch as shown (photo). As it is removed, note the direction of fitting and take care not to damage the seal housing as the seal is extracted.
20   New gaskets will be required for the seal housing and sump during reassembly. Clean the mating faces of the seal housing, the crankcase and sump. Insert the new seal squarely into its housing and to avoid damaging the seal or the housing, place a flat piece of wood across the face of the seal and carefully tap the seal into position in the housing. Do not allow the seal to tilt in the housing as it is being fitted (photo).
21   Refer to Section 49 in Part C of this Chapter for details on refitting the oil seal housing.
22   Refit the sump with reference to Section 26.
23   Check that the mating faces of the crankshaft and flywheel/driveplate are clean, then refit the flywheel/driveplate using **new** bolts as described in Section 31.
24   Refit the clutch unit as described in Chapter 6.

30 Engine/transmission mountings – renewal

The procedure for renewing the engine mountings on the CVH series engine are much the same as those described for the HCS series in Part A of this Chapter, therefore refer to Section 14 in that Part for details.

31 Flywheel/driveplate – removal, inspection and refitting

Removal

1   Access to the flywheel (manual transmission) or driveplate (automatic transmission) is gained by first removing the transmission

31.2 Flywheel retaining bolts

(Chapter 7) and then on manual transmission models, removing the clutch unit (Chapter 6).

2 Unscrew and remove the six flywheel/driveplate retaining bolts and carefully withdraw the flywheel/driveplate from the rear face of the crankshaft (photo). Note that the retaining bolts must be renewed.

Inspection

3 The inspection procedures for the flywheel/driveplate are the same as those described for the HCS engine type in Part A, Section 15 of this Chapter but note that the grinding procedures do not apply to the driveplate (which cannot be reground).

Refitting

4 Check that the mating faces of the flywheel/driveplate and crankshaft are clean before refitting.
5 Smear the **new** retaining bolt threads with sealant. Place the flywheel/driveplate into position on the rear end face of the crankshaft. Check that all of the bolt holes in the flywheel/driveplate are in exact alignment with the corresponding bolt holes in the crankshaft, then insert the bolts and tighten them in a progressive sequence to the specified torque wrench setting.
6 Refit the clutch (manual transmission models) as described in Chapter 6.
7 Refit the transmission (according to type) as described in Chapter 7.

Part C: Engine removal and general engine overhaul procedures

32 General information

Included in this part of Chapter 2 are details of removing the engine/transmission from the vehicle, and its general overhaul procedures for the cylinder head, cylinder block/crankcase and associated engine components.

The information ranges from advice concerning preparation for an overhaul and the purchase of replacement parts, to detailed step-by-step procedures covering removal, inspection, renovation and refitting of the internal engine components.

After Section 35 or 36 (as applicable), all instructions are based on the assumption that the engine has been removed from the vehicle. For information concerning in-vehicle engine repair, as well as the removal and refitting of the external components necessary for the overhaul, refer to Part A (HCS engine) or Part B (CVH engine) of this Chapter and to Section 35 or 36 in this part. Ignore any preliminary dismantling operations that are no longer applicable once the engine has been removed from the vehicle.

All specifications relating to engine overhaul are detailed at the start of this Chapter.

33 Engine overhaul – general information

It is not always possible to determine when, or if, an engine should be completely overhauled, as a number of factors must be considered.

High mileage is not necessarily an indication that an overhaul is required, while low mileage does not preclude the need for an overhaul. The frequency of servicing is probably the most important consideration. An engine which has had regular oil and filter changes, as well as other required maintenance, will most likely give many thousands of miles of reliable service. Conversely, a neglected engine may require an overhaul very early in its life.

Excessive oil consumption may simply be caused by worn valve stem seals but it may also indicate that piston rings, valve seals and/or valve guides may well be in need of attention. Make sure that oil leaks are not responsible before deciding that the rings, valves and/or guides are badly worn. Perform a cylinder compression check (Section 2) to determine the general condition of the engine and the possible extent of any work required.

Check the oil pressure with a gauge fitted in place of the oil pressure sender unit, and compare it with the specified pressure requirement. If the pressure is considerably lower than that specified, it may be that the pressure relief valve is stuck, but failing this the most probable cause will be excessively worn big-end and/or main bearings.

An engine overhaul involves restoring the internal parts to the specifications of a new engine. During an overhaul, the pistons and rings are renewed and the cylinder bores are reconditioned. New main bearings and connecting rod bearings are generally fitted and if necessary, the crankshaft may be reground to restore the bearing journals. The cylinder head valves are usually serviced at this time as they will almost certainly require attention to restore them to a serviceable condition. While the engine is being overhauled, other components such as the starter motor and alternator can be checked and if necessary, overhauled as well. The end result should be an as new engine that will give many trouble-free miles.

Note: *Critical cooling system components such as hoses, drivebelts, thermostat and water pump MUST be renewed when an engine is overhauled. The radiator should be carefully checked to ensure that it is not clogged or leaking. It is a good idea to renew the oil pump whenever the engine is overhauled.*

Before beginning an engine overhaul, read through the entire procedure to familiarise yourself with the scope and requirements of the job. Overhauling an engine is not difficult if you follow all of the instructions carefully, have the necessary tools and equipment and pay close attention to all specifications: it can however be time-consuming (but time well spent). Plan on the vehicle being off the road for a minimum period of two weeks, especially if parts must be taken to an engineering workshop for repair or reconditioning. Check on the availability of parts and make sure that any special tools that will be required are obtained in advance. Most work can be undertaken with standard hand tools, although a number of precision measuring tools are required for the inspection of certain parts to assess if they are worn beyond an acceptable level and require renovation or renewal. Often the engineering works will undertake the inspection of parts and offer advice concerning reconditioning and renewal.

Note: *Always wait until the engine has been completely disassembled and all components, especially the engine block have been inspected before finally deciding what service repair operations are to be performed by an engineering works. Since the condition of the cylinder block will be the major factor to consider when determining whether to overhaul the* original engine or to obtain a reconditioned unit, do not purchase parts or have any overhaul work undertaken on any components until after the block has been thoroughly inspected.

As a general rule, time is the primary cost of an overhaul, so it does not pay to fit worn or substandard parts.

As a final note, to ensure maximum life and minimum trouble from a reconditioned engine, everything must be assembled with care and in a spotlessly clean environment.

34   Engine removal – methods and precautions

If you have decided that an engine must be removed for overhaul or major repair work, certain preliminary steps must be taken.

Locating a suitable place to work is extremely important. Adequate work space, along with storage space for the vehicle will be needed. If a workshop or garage is not available, at the very least, a level, firm and flat work area will suffice.

Cleaning the engine compartment and the engine before commencing the removal procedures will help keep tools clean and organised.

An engine hoist and a support beam or tripod will also be required. Make sure that the equipment to be used is rated in excess of the combined weight of the engine and transmission. Safety is of a primary importance when considering the possible hazards involved in removing the engine from the vehicle.

If the engine is to be removed by a novice, an assistant should be at hand. Advice and aid from someone more experienced would also be helpful. There are instances where one person cannot simultaneously perform all of the operations required when removing the engine from the vehicle.

Plan the operation ahead of the actual removal to ensure that all of the tools and equipment required are obtained. Some of the equipment necessary to remove and subsequently install the engine (apart from the items already mentioned) include a heavy duty floor jack, some axle stands, a complete set of spanners, sockets and general tools as described in the front of this manual. A heavy duty engine/transmission trolley will be most beneficial to transport the unit to the point of dismantling once it is removed from the engine compartment. Where any equipment is to be hired, plan in advance to perform all possible operations beforehand. This will save money and time. In addition to tools, plenty of rags and cleaning solvent for mopping up spilled oil, coolant and fuel will also be essential.

Plan for the estimated period the vehicle is expected to be out of use. Where engineering works will be required to perform some of the more specialised work which cannot be accomplished by the home mechanic, they should be consulted beforehand to estimate the time they require to complete any possible renovation work to be performed. An estimate of their costs should also be obtained at the same time in order to assess the feasibility of any repair costs against those in obtaining a service replacement.

Always be extremely careful when removing and refitting the engine. Serious injury can result from careless actions. Plan ahead, take your time and a job of this nature, although major, can be successfully accomplished.

Note that in the case of the CVH engine, although it may be possible to remove the engine on its own (leaving the transmission in position), it is not considered practical due to the restricted space allowed to disengage the engine from the transmission.

35   Engine – removal and refitting (HCS engine)

Removal

1   Disconnect the battery earth lead.
2   Refer to Chapter 3 for details and drain the engine coolant.
3   Refer to Chapter 1 for details and drain the engine oil. Refit the drain plug to the sump on completion to prevent the leakage of any remaining oil in the engine.
4   Refer to Chapter 11 for details and remove the bonnet. Position it out of the way in a safe place where it will not get damaged.

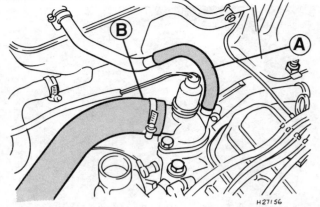

Fig. 2.24 Disconnect the overflow hose (A) and the top hose (B) from the thermostat (Sec 35)

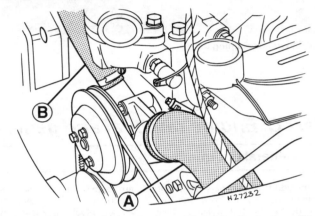

Fig. 2.25 Disconnect the bottom hose (A) and the heater hose (B) from the water pump (Sec 35)

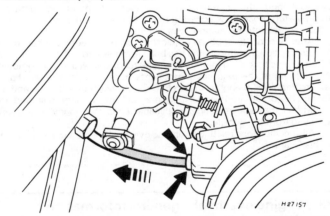

Fig. 2.26 Detach the servo vacuum hose from the manifold (Sec 35)

5   Refer to Chapter 4 for details and remove the air cleaner unit.
6   Release the retaining clips and detach the coolant hoses from the thermostat housing, the bottom hose from the radiator to the water pump, the heater hoses at the bulkhead connection and, where applicable, at the inlet manifold. Allow for coolant spillage as the hoses are detached, note their routing and position them out of the way.
7   Disconnect the fuel trap vacuum hose from the inlet manifold.
8   Disconnect the brake servo unit vacuum hose from the inlet manifold by pushing the hose retainer in towards the manifold and simultaneously pulling free the hose.
9   Refer to Chapter 4 for details and detach the accelerator cable and the choke cable from the carburettor.
10   Compress the quick release couplings at the sides and detach the fuel supply hose (red clip) and return hose (white clip) from the fuel pump unit. Allow for fuel spillage as the hoses are disconnected and

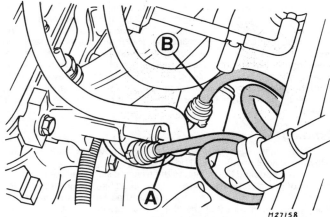

Fig. 2.27 Fuel supply (A) and return (B) hose connections at the fuel pump (Sec 35)

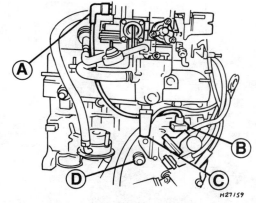

Fig. 2.28 Wiring connections to the HCS engine (Sec 35)

A   Idle cut-off valve
B   DIS ignition coil
C   Engine coolant temperature sensor (ECT)
D   Oil pressure switch

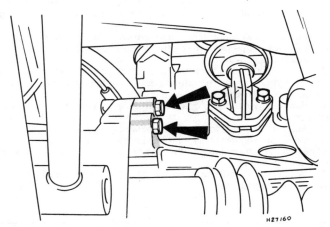

Fig. 2.29 Engine-to-transmission flange attachment bolts – HCS engine (Sec 35)

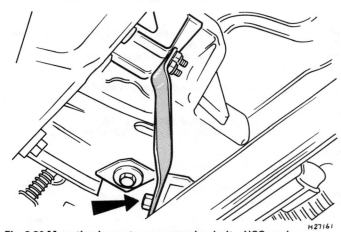

Fig. 2.30 Mounting brace-to-crossmember bolt – HCS engine (Sec 35)

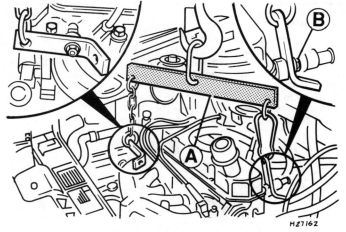

Fig. 2.31 Engine lifter and attachment points (A) and M8 x 35 bolt location (B) – HCS engine (Sec 35)

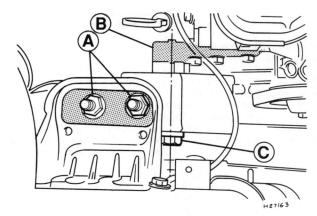

Fig. 2.32 Detach the engine mounting fixing at the points indicated (Sec 35)

A   Front apron panel bracket nuts
B   Mounting bracket
C   Bolt-to-engine bracket

35.11 Engine speed/crankshaft position sensor and multi-plug

plug the exposed ends to prevent further spillage and the ingress of dirt. Position the hoses out of the way.

11   Note their locations and disconnect the wiring connectors from the following (photo).

   (a)   *Coolant temperature gauge sender unit (on the coolant connector).*
   (b)   *The oil pressure switch.*
   (c)   *The radio earth lead (on the inlet manifold).*
   (d)   *The cooling fan thermo-switch (on the thermostat housing cover).*
   (e)   *The DIS ignition coil.*
   (f)   *The crankshaft position sensor (CPS).*
   (g)   *The ECT engine coolant temperature sensor (on the engine/transmission flange).*
   (h)   *The idle cut-off valve (on the carburettor).*

12   Raise the vehicle at the front end and support it on axle stands.
13   Unscrew the three retaining nuts and detach the exhaust downpipe from the exhaust manifold. Remove the seal from the joint flange.
14   Refer to Chapter 12 for details and remove the starter motor.
15   Undo the two retaining bolts and remove the clutch lower cover plate.
16   Unscrew the retaining bolt and detach the gearshift stabiliser from the transmission.
17   Unscrew and remove the engine/transmission flange attachment bolts shown in Fig. 2.29 and also the bolt fitted from the front, securing the earth lead (from the underside).
18   Unscrew and remove the single bolt (shown in Fig. 2.30) securing the engine mounting brace to the crossmember.
19   Check that the appropriate underside attachments are disconnected and out of the way, then lower the vehicle to the ground.
20   Unbolt and remove the heat shield from the exhaust manifold.
21   Attach a suitable hoist to the engine. It is possible to fabricate lift eyes to connect the hoist to the engine, but make sure that they are strong enough and connect them to the inlet and exhaust manifold at diagonally opposite ends of the engine.
22   With the hoist securely connected, take the weight of the engine, then unscrew the two retaining nuts to detach the engine mounting from the apron panel and the single bolt to disconnect it at the mounting bracket.
23   Locate a jack under the transmission and raise it to take the weight of the transmission.
24   Unscrew and remove the remaining engine to transmission retaining bolts on the upper flange.
25   Check around the engine to ensure that all of the relevant fixings and attachments are disconnected and out of the way for the removal.
26   Enlist the aid of an assistant, then move the engine forwards and away from the transmission whilst simultaneously raising the transmission. When the engine is separated from the transmission,

carefully guide it up and out of the engine compartment. Do not allow the weight of the engine to hang on the transmission input shaft at any point during the removal (or refitting) of the engine. When the engine sump is clear of the vehicle, swing the power unit out of the way and lower it onto a trolley (if available) and transport it to the place of cleaning and inspection. Unless a mobile hoist is being used, it will be necessary to move the vehicle rearwards and out of the way in order to allow the engine to be lowered for removal. In this instance, ensure that the weight of the transmission is well supported as the vehicle is moved.

Refitting

27   Refitting is in general, a reversal of the removal procedure, but the following special points should be noted.
28   Before coupling the engine to the transmission, smear a moderate amount of grease onto the transmission input shaft splines (refer to the specifications in Chapter 6 for the grease type), and if the clutch has been removed, ensure that the clutch disc (driven hub) is centralised and disconnect the clutch cable from the release lever on the transmission casing.
29   Tighten all fixings to their recommended torque wrench settings.
30   Check that the mating faces are clean and fit a new exhaust downpipe-to-manifold gasket and self locking nuts when reconnecting this joint.
31   Ensure that all wiring connections are correctly and securely made.
32   Remove the plugs from the fuel lines before reconnecting them correctly and securely.
33   Reconnect and adjust the accelerator and choke cables as described in Chapter 4. The refitting details for the air cleaner unit are also given in that Chapter.
34   Renew any coolant hoses (and/or retaining clips) that are not in good condition.
35   Refer to Chapter 6 for details on reconnecting the clutch cable.
36   When the engine is fully refitted, check that the various hoses are connected and then top up the engine oil and coolant levels as described in Chapter 1.
37   When engine refitting is completed, refer to Section 52 for the engine start up procedures.

36   Engine (and transmission) – removal and refitting (CVH engines)

Removal

1   Disconnect the battery earth lead.
2   Refer to Chapter 1 for details and drain the engine coolant.
3   Refer to Chapter 1 for details and drain the engine oil. Refit the drain plug to the sump on completion to prevent any remaining oil from draining off.
4   Refer to Chapter 11 for details and remove the bonnet. Store it in a safe area where it will not get damaged.
5   Refer to Chapter 4 for details and remove the air cleaner unit. On EFi

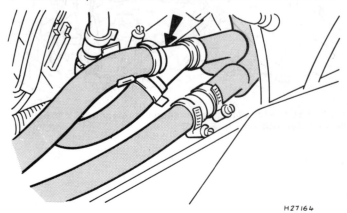

Fig. 2.33 Heater coolant hoses and Y-connector on EFi models (Sec 36)

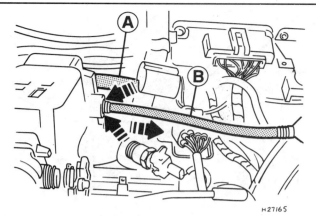

Fig. 2.34 Vacuum hose to MAP sensor (A) and brake servo (B) – CVH engines (Sec 36)

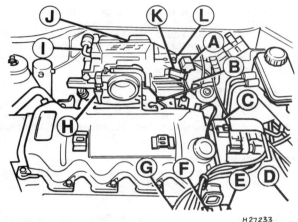

Fig. 2.36 Engine and associated component wiring plug connections – CVH engines (Sec 36)

A	Main wiring loom	G	Engine speed/crankshaft
B	Speed sender unit		position sensor (CPS)
C	DIS ignition coil	H	Throttle position sensor
D	Reversing light switch		(TPS)
E	Cooling fan temperature	I	Idle speed control valve
	sensor	J	Coolant temperature
F	Temperature gauge		sensor
	sender	K	Air charge temperature
			sensor
		L	Oil pressure switch

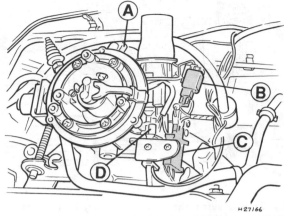

Fig. 2.35 Wiring connections to the CFi unit on the 1.4 litre engine (Sec 36)

A	Coolant temperature	C	Throttle position sensor
	sensor	D	Injector
B	Throttle adjustment motor		

in the system lines is under pressure and care must be taken to catch the release of fuel in a cloth when the fuel lines are detached. Plug the exposed ends of the hoses and connections to prevent the ingress of dirt and further fuel spillage. Position the hoses out of the way.

10   Press the clamp ring inwards and simultaneously pull free the brake servo hose from the inlet manifold. Position it out of the way.

11   On CFi and EFi models, detach the vacuum hose from the MAP sensor and also the hose between the carbon canister and the fuel injection unit.

12   Note their connections and routings and detach the following wiring connections, according to model (photos).

(a)   Coolant temperature sender unit (to the gauge).
(b)   Oil pressure switch.
(c)   DIS ignition coil unit.
(d)   Coolant temperature sensor.
(e)   Cooling fan temperature sensor.
(f)   Carburettor.
(g)   Earth lead (radio).
(h)   Reversing light switch (from transmission).
(i)   Engine speed/crankshaft position sensor (CPS).
(j)   Earth leads from the transmission and engine.

Additional items specific to CFi models only.

(a)   Intake air temperature sensor.
(b)   Road speed sensor.
(c)   Throttle adjustment motor.
(d)   Throttle position sensor.
(e)   Injector harness connector.

Additional items specific to EFi models only.

(a)   Idle speed control valve.
(b)   Throttle position sensor (TPS).
(c)   Air charge temperature sensor.
(d)   Speed sender unit (adjacent to the speedometer cable connection on the transmission).
(e)   Injector harness connector.

13   Unscrew the retaining bolt and detach the bracket locating the wiring and coolant hoses above the transmission.

14   Disconnect the speedometer drive cable from the transmission.

15   On manual transmission models, disconnect the clutch cable from the release lever at the transmission (see Chapter 6 for details). Position the cable out of the way.

16   Unscrew the two retaining bolts and detach the engine/transmission mounting from the mounting bracket (photo).

17   Raise and support the vehicle at the front end on axle stands. Allow sufficient clearance under the vehicle to withdraw the engine and transmission units from under the front end.

18   Where applicable, release the multi-plug from the bracket and

models, disconnect and remove the air intake duct between the manifold and the air cleaner unit. Remove the air cleaner cover and the element from the air cleaner housing.

6   Release the retaining clips and detach the coolant top hose, the heater hose and the radiator overflow hose from the thermostat housing. Disconnect coolant hose from the inlet manifold and the bottom hose from the water pump and/or the radiator (photos). On CFi models, also disconnect the coolant hose from the injection unit and on EFi models, detach the heater hose Y-connector. Allow for coolant spillage as the hoses are detached, note their routing and position them out of the way.

7   Refer to Chapter 4 for details and disconnect the accelerator cable from the throttle linkage and support/adjuster bracket. Where applicable, also disconnect the choke cable. Position the cable(s) out of the way.

8   On carburettor models, disconnect the fuel supply hose from the fuel pump and the return hose from the carburettor.

9   On CFi models, detach the fuel hose at the injector/pressure regulator unit and the return line by compressing the couplings whilst pulling the hoses free from their connections. On EFi models, unscrew the union nut to detach the fuel line from the fuel rail and release the retaining clip to detach the return pipe from the pressure regulator. Fuel

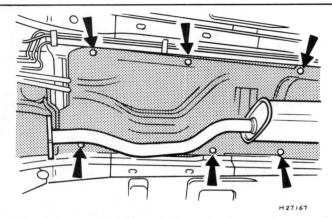

Fig. 2.37 Exhaust system heat shield showing the securing nut and bolt locations – CVH engines (Sec 36)

Fig. 2.38 Manual transmission shift rod clamp bolt (A), stabiliser-to-transmission bolt (B) and washer (C) (Sec 36)

disconnect the wiring connector from the HEGO sensor in the exhaust downpipe (photo).

19   Undo the three retaining bolts, detach the exhaust downpipe from the manifold and collect the gasket from the flange joint. Now disconnect the exhaust downpipe from the rest of the system and remove it from the vehicle (photo). Where applicable, disconnect the pulse air supply hose from the check valve and noting their connections (to ensure correct reassembly), detach the appropriate system vacuum hoses at the PVS (three point vacuum switch) under the inlet manifold.

20   Where fitted, undo the four retaining nuts and two bolts securing the front part of the exhaust heat shield to the floor, then remove the heat shield.

21   Note their connections and detach the wiring from the starter motor and the alternator. Detach the battery warning light lead and disconnect the alternator lead cable tie from the crossmember. Unbolt and remove the starter motor.

22   On manual transmission models, engage fourth gear to assist in correct adjustment of the gearchange during reassembly. If it is likely that the gear lever will be moved from this position before refitting, mark the relative position of the transmission shift rod and the selector shaft before separating them. Undo the clamp bolt and then pull free and detach the shift rod from the selector shaft.

Manual transmission models

23   Unscrew the retaining bolt and detach the shift rod stabiliser from the transmission. As it is detached, note the washer located between the stabiliser and the transmission. Tie the stabiliser and the shift rod up out of the way.

Automatic transmission models

24   Unclip and detach the wiring connector from the starter inhibitor switch (on the transmission housing).

36.6A Coolant hose connections to the thermostat (arrowed)

36.6B Bottom hose connection to the radiator (arrowed)

36.12A Coolant temperature sender unit

36.12B Oil pressure switch

36.12C Engine speed/crankshaft position sensor (CPS)

36.16 Engine/transmission mounting bracket bolts (arrowed)

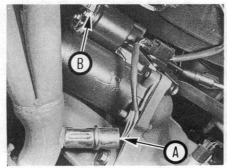

36.18 View showing wiring connections to the HEGO sensor (A) and starter motor (B)

36.19 Exhaust downpipe to manifold connecting flange and securing bolts

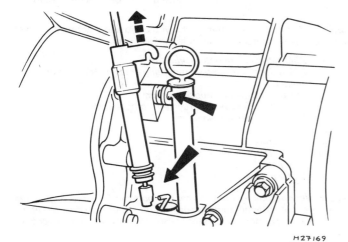

Fig. 2.39 Detach the cam plate cable from the cam plate link (automatic transmission) (Sec 36)

Fig. 2.40 Automatic transmission oil cooler pipe connections (Sec 36)

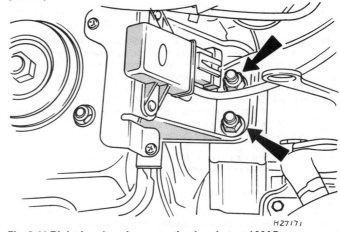

Fig. 2.41 Right-hand engine mounting bracket and MAP sensor on the EFi engine (Sec 36)

25   Referring to Chapter 4 for details, unhook the cam plate cable from the carburettor or fuel injection unit (as applicable) at the transmission end of the cable. Undo the retaining bolt and detach the cable sheath bracket from the transmission. Detach the cam plate operating cable from the link.

26   Undo the two nuts from the selector cable bracket which connect it to the lever on the selector shaft, disconnect the yoke from the lever on the selector shaft and the cable from the lever.

27   Unscrew the union nuts and disconnect the oil cooler feed and return pipes from the transmission. Allow for a certain amount of spillage and plug the connections to prevent the ingress of dirt.

All models

28   Note the direction of fitting, unscrew the retaining nut and withdraw the Torx type clamp bolt securing the lower suspension arm to the spindle carrier on each side.

29   Refer to Chapter 10 for details and detach the right-hand steering track rod from the spindle carrier.

30   Insert a suitable lever between the right-hand driveshaft inner joint and the transmission housing and prise free the driveshaft from the transmission; be prepared for oil spillage from the transmission case through the vacated driveshaft aperture. As it is being prised free, simultaneously pull the roadwheel (spindle and shaft) outwards on that side to enable the shaft inboard end to separate from the transmission. Once it is free, suspend and support the driveshaft from the steering gear to prevent unnecessary strain being placed on the driveshaft joints. The outer joint must not be angled in excess of 45°, the inner joint no more than 20°. Refer to Chapter 8 for further details if necessary.

31   Insert a suitable plastic plug (or if available, an old driveshaft joint), into the transmission driveshaft aperture to immobilise the gears of the differential unit.

32   Proceed as described above in paragraphs 29 and 31 and disconnect the left-hand driveshaft from the transmission but suspend

the driveshaft from the track rod on that side to support it.

33   Unscrew the retaining bolts and remove the brace between the transmission left front mounting bracket and the transmission flange (photo).

34   Connect a suitable lift hoist and sling to the engine, connecting to the lift eyes (photo). When securely connected, take the weight of the engine/transmission unit so that the tension is relieved from the mountings.

35   Unscrew the two retaining bolts and detach the transmission front mounting from the side member.

36   Unscrew the three retaining bolts and remove the camshaft drive belt cover.

37   Unscrew the two retaining nuts and detach the right-hand engine

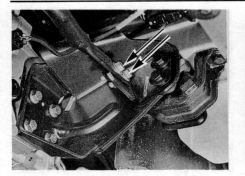

36.33 Brace retaining bolts (arrowed) to the front left-hand side transmission mounting bracket

36.34 Showing engine lift bar and eye attachment point (arrowed)

36.40 Engine/transmission unit being removed from under the front of the vehicle. Note the use of a crawler board

mounting from the suspension strut mounting. On EFi engines, remove the MAP sensor.

38　The engine/transmission unit should now be ready for removal from the vehicle. Check that all of the associated connections and fittings are disconnected from the engine and transmission and positioned out of the way.

39　Enlist the aid of an assistant to help steady and guide the power unit down through the engine compartment as it is removed. If available, position a suitable engine trolley or crawler board under the engine/transmission so that when lowered, the power unit can be withdrawn from the front end of the vehicle and moved to the area where it is to be cleaned and dismantled. On automatic transmission models, particular care must be taken not to damage the transmission oil pan during the removal and subsequent refitting process.

40　Carefully lower the engine and transmission unit, ensuring that no fittings become snagged. Detach the hoist and remove the power unit from under the vehicle (photo).

41　To separate the engine from the transmission, refer to Chapter 7.

Refitting

42　Refitting is a reversal of removal, however note the following additional points.

(a)　Refer to the applicable Chapters and Sections as for removal.
(b)　Fit new spring clips to the grooves in the inboard end of the right and left-hand driveshafts. Lubricate the splines with transmission oil prior to fitting.
(c)　Renew the exhaust flange gasket when reconnecting the exhaust. Ensure that all wires are routed clear of the exhaust system and, on catalytic converter models, ensure that the heat shields are securely and correctly fitted.
(d)　Ensure that all earth lead connections are clean and securely made.
(e)　Tighten all nuts and bolts to the specified torque.
(f)　Refill the engine and transmission with oil with reference to Chapter 1.
(g)　Refill the cooling system with reference to Chapter 1.

43　When engine and transmission refitting is complete, refer to the procedures described in Section 52 before restarting the engine.

37　Engine overhaul – dismantling sequence

1　The engine dismantling and reassembly tasks are made easier if the engine is mounted on a portable engine stand. These stands can be hired from a tool hire shop. Before mounting the engine on a stand, the flywheel/driveplate must first be removed to enable the engine-to-stand fixing bolts to be fitted.

2　If a stand is not available, it is possible to dismantle the engine with it suitably supported on a strong workbench or on the floor. Be careful not to tip or drop the engine when working without a stand.

3　If a reconditioned engine is to be fitted, all external components of the original engine must be removed in order to transfer them to the

replacement unit (just as they will if you are doing a complete engine rebuild). These components include the following.

(a)　Alternator and mounting brackets.
(b)　DIS ignition coil unit (and mounting bracket), HT leads and spark plugs.
(c)　The thermostat and housing cover.
(d)　Carburettor/fuel injection system components.
(e)　Inlet and exhaust manifolds.
(f)　Oil filter.
(g)　Fuel pump.
(h)　Engine mountings.
(i)　Flywheel/driveplate.
(j)　Water pump.

Note: *When removing the external components from the engine, pay close attention to details that may be helpful or important during refitting. Note the fitting positions of gaskets, seals, washers, bolts and other small items.*

4　If you are obtaining a short motor (which consists of the engine cylinder block, crankshaft, pistons and connecting rods all assembled), the cylinder head, sump, oil pump and timing chain/belt will have to be removed also.

5　If a complete overhaul is planned, the engine can be dismantled and the internal components removed in the following order.

(a)　Inlet and exhaust manifolds.
(b)　Timing chain/belt, tensioner and sprockets.
(c)　Cylinder head.
(d)　Flywheel/driveplate.
(e)　Sump.
(f)　Oil pump.
(g)　Pistons (with connecting rods).
(h)　Crankshaft.
(i)　Camshaft and tappets (HCS engine).

6　Before starting the dismantling and overhaul procedures, make sure that you have all of the correct tools for the jobs to be tackled. Refer to the introductory pages at the start of this manual for further information.

38　Cylinder head – dismantling

HCS (OHV) engine

1　Unscrew and remove the five retaining bolts and lift off the inlet manifold (complete with carburettor). Remove the inlet manifold-to-cylinder head gasket.

2　Unscrew and remove the eight retaining nuts and lift off the exhaust manifold from the cylinder head. Remove the exhaust manifold-to-cylinder head gasket.

3　Unscrew and remove the temperature gauge sender unit.

4　To remove the valve springs and valves from the cylinder head a standard valve spring compressor will be required. Fit the spring compressor to the first valve and spring to be removed. Assuming that all of the valves and springs are to be removed, start by compressing the No 1 valve (nearest the timing cover end) spring (photo). Take care not

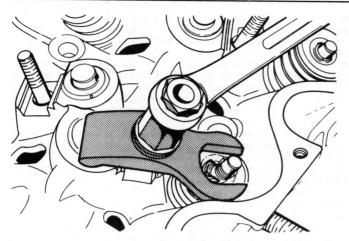

Fig. 2.42 Compressing a valve spring using a fork type compressor – CVH engines (Sec 38)

to damage the valve stem with the compressor and do not over-compress the spring or the valve stem may bend. When tightening the compressor, it may be found that the spring retainer does not release and the collets are then difficult to remove. In this instance, remove the compressor then press a piece of tube (or a socket of suitable diameter) so that it does not interfere with the removal of the collets, against the retainer's outer rim. Tap the tube (or socket) with a hammer to unsettle the components.

5   Refit the compressor and wind it in to enable the collets to be extracted (photo).

6   Loosen off the compressor and remove the retainer and spring. Withdraw the valve from the cylinder head (photos).

7   Prise up and remove the valve stem seal (photo).

8   Repeat the removal procedure with each of the remaining seven valve assemblies in turn. As they are removed, keep the individual valves in their respective order of fitting by placing them in a piece of card which has holes punched in it numbered 1 to 8 (from the timing cover end) and group their springs, collets and retainers in a similar manner. Alternatively, place each assembly in a separately labelled bag (photo).

CVH (OHC) engines

9   Remove the camshaft, rocker arms and tappets as described in Section 24 in Part B of this Chapter.

10   Valve removal should commence with No 1 valve (nearest the timing belt end). As they are removed, keep the valves and their associated components in the originally installed order by placing them in a piece of card which has holes punched in it, numbered 1 to 8. Alternatively, place each assembly in a separately labelled bag (see photo 38.8)

11   Compress the valve spring of the number 1 valve using a suitable valve compressor. A conventional valve spring compressor will be ideal, but if preferred a forked tool (Part No 21-097) can be purchased or fabricated. The tool engages on the rocker stud, and a nut and distance piece are used to compress it and the valve spring (see Fig. 2.42).

12   Compress the valve spring (and upper retainer) just enough to enable the split collets to be released from the groove in the top of the valve stem, then separate and extract the split collets from the valve. Do not compress the spring any further than is necessary or the valve stem may bend. If the valve spring retainer does not release from the collets as the spring is compressed, remove the compressor and position a piece of suitable tube over the end of the retainer so that it does not impinge on the collets. Place a small block of wood under the valve head (with the head resting face down on the workbench) then tap the end of the tube with a hammer. Now refit the compressor tool and compress the valve spring. The collets should release.

13   Extract the split collets, then slowly unscrew, release and remove the compressor.

14   Withdraw the upper retainer and the valve spring from the valve stem, then remove the valve from the underside of the cylinder head.

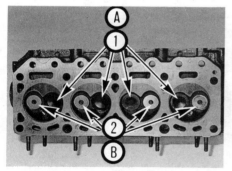

38.4 Underside view of the cylinder head and valves

A *Inlet side*
B *Exhaust side*
1 *Inlet valves*
2 *Exhaust valves*

38.5 Compress the valve spring to remove the collets

38.6A Remove the valve spring retainer and spring ...

38.6B ... followed by the valve

38.7 Prise off the valve stem oil seal

38.8 Use a labelled plastic bag to store and identify valve components

Use a suitable screwdriver to prise free and remove the valve stem oil seal from the guide.

15 Remove the lower retainer.

16 Repeat the preceding operation and remove the remaining valves.

39 Cylinder head and valve assemblies – inspection and renovation

Cylinder head

1 With the cylinder head removed and dismantled, the carbon deposits should be cleaned from the combustion chambers using a suitable scraper and a rotary wire brush fitted to an electric drill. Take care not to damage the surfaces of the cylinder head, valves and valve seats. Note that the valve seats cannot be re-worked using conventional tools (photo).

2 Check the valves and guides for excessive wear by inserting each valve in turn into its guide in the cylinder head so that approximately one third enters the valve and rock it from side-to-side. If there is any more than a barely perceptible movement, the guides will have to be reamed (working from the valve seat end) and oversize stem valves fitted. This work is best entrusted to a Ford dealer.

3 Examine the valve seats. Normally the seats do not deteriorate but the valve heads are more likely to burn away and in this instance they can be refaced by grinding-in as described below. If the valve seats are cracked or need recutting, consult a Ford dealer or an automotive engineering workshop as the valve seats cannot be re-cut using conventional tools.

4 Check the cylinder head mating surfaces for distortion using a straightedge (metal rule or similar) (photo). Any distortion beyond the specified amount must be rectified by surface grinding – again a task to be entrusted to a Ford dealer or automotive engineer.

Valves

5 If it was found that the valve stems and guides were worn beyond an acceptable amount and the guides have had to be reamed out, new oversize valves will have to be fitted (photo). The old valves will also need renewal if their stems are found to be distorted. These can be checked by rolling the stems on a perfectly flat surface so that any distortion will become apparent.

6 Whether the original valves are to be re-used or new valves fitted, their contact faces and the seats in the cylinder head will need to be refaced or 'ground-in' to ensure a good seal when the valves are closed. Where the original valves are concerned, ensure that the sealing face and the valve head of each valve is clean of old carbon deposit before starting to regrind it.

7 Before starting to grind in the valves, support the cylinder head so that there is sufficient clearance underneath for the valve stem to project without being obstructed.

8 Take the first valve and apply a little 'coarse' grinding paste to the bevelled edge of the valve head. A drop or two of paraffin applied to the contact faces will speed up the grinding process, but take care not to allow any of the grinding paste to come into contact with the valve stem. Lubricate the valve stem and guide with engine oil, then insert the valve into its guide and apply the suction grinding tool to its head. Now grind the valve seat by rotating the grinding tool back and forth between the palms of the hands so that as it progresses, the gritty action felt at the start is felt to become smoother. Lift the tool a little and continue the grinding action until the action is smoothed out, then lift the tool and apply some 'fine' paste to the valve and repeat the process (photo). When the process with the fine paste is completed, lift the valve and wipe both it and the seat in the cylinder head clean of paste. Examination of the seat and valve contact face should show an even matt silver band on both components. If it is found that the facings still have black spots or an uneven seal band, further grinding is required to acquire the necessary finish.

9 When the valve is ground to a satisfactory finish, remove it from the cylinder head and thoroughly wash away all traces of the grinding paste from the valve and cylinder head using petrol.

10 Repeat the operation on the remaining valves, but take care not to mix up their fitting sequence.

Valve components

11 Check that the free length of each valve spring is as specified and

39.1 Combustion chamber and valve seats (arrowed)

39.4 Checking the cylinder head gasket surface for distortion

39.5 Measuring a valve stem diameter

39.8 Grinding in a valve

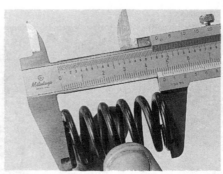

39.11 Measuring a valve spring free length

renew them if necessary (photo). Only renew the springs as a set, not individually.

12 Examine the collets and retainers for any signs of damage or distortion and renew as necessary.

13 The valve stem seals must always be renewed as a matter of course whenever the cylinder head is overhauled.

14 When overhauling the cylinder head, the rocker gear assembly should also be inspected and renovated as necessary. Inspection of the rocker gear assembly is dealt with in Section 5 for HCS engines and Section 24 for CVH engines.

40 Cylinder head – reassembly

1 Before reassembling the cylinder head, first ensure that it is perfectly clean and no traces of grinding paste are left in the head or on the valves and guides.

2 Commence reassembly of the cylinder head by lubricating the valve stems and guides with clean engine oil.

HCS (OHV) engine

3 Insert the first valve into its guide. Wipe the oil from the top of the valve stem then wind some insulation tape over the split collet location groove to protect the new valve stem seal as it is fitted over the valve and into position. As the seal is fitted, support the valve to prevent it from falling out and push the seal down the valve and locate it flush to the valve guide. Press the seal down firmly and evenly using a suitable diameter tube or socket and take care not to distort the seal as it is located. Check that the seal spring is correctly located to ensure that it seals correctly, then remove the tape from the valve stem (photos).

4 Locate the valve spring and its retainer over the valve stem and engage the valve spring compressor. Compress the spring and retainer just enough to allow the split collets to be inserted in the location groove in the valve stem, noting that a little grease applied to the collet groove

40.3A Tape the end of the valve stem before fitting the valve stem seal

40.3B Press the seal into position using a suitable socket

40.7 Fit the lower retainer

40.8 Locate the seal and tap it into position over the guide

40.9 Insert the valve

40.10A Fit the spring ...

40.10B ... and the retainer

40.11 Insert the split collets into the groove in the valve stem

41.5 Checking the camshaft endfloat

41.7 Withdrawing the camshaft from the front of the engine

41.8 Tappet withdrawal using a valve grinding tool suction cup

will help retain them in position. Holding the collets in position, slowly release and remove the valve spring compressor.

5   Repeat the operation on the remaining valves, ensuring that each valve is fitted in its appropriate location.

6   On completion, support the cylinder head on a suitable piece of wood and lightly strike the end of each valve stem in turn with a plastic- or copper-faced hammer to fractionally open the valve and seat the valve components.

CVH (OHC) engines

7   Working on one valve at a time, fit the lower retainer into position (photo).

8   Check for correct orientation, then fit the new oil seal into position over the guide. Drive or press the seal squarely into place using a suitable tube or socket (photo).

9   To protect the seal lips from being damaged by the collet grooves in the valve stem as it is passed through the seal, wipe any oil from the stem at the top and mask the split collet groove on the stem with insulating tape. Lubricate the lips of the valve stem seal and insert the valve (photo).

10   Remove the tape from the grooved section of the valve stem, then locate the spring and the upper retainer over the valve (photos).

11   Locate the valve spring compressor into position and compress the spring and cup down the valve stem so that the collet's groove is exposed above the upper retainer. Lightly grease the collet's groove in the stem, (to retain the collets in position) then locate the split collets into the groove in the stem. Slowly release and remove the valve spring compressor. As the compressor is released, ensure that the collets remain fully seated in the groove and the upper retainer rides up over them to secure them in position (photo).

12   Repeat the above operations on the remaining valves, ensuring that each valve assembly is returned to its original position, or where new valves have been fitted, onto the seat on which it was ground to.

13   When all of the valves have been fitted, support the cylinder head on a wooden block and using a plastic or copper-faced hammer, lightly tap the end of each valve stem in turn to seat the respective valve assemblies.

14   Refit the camshaft, tappets and rocker arms to the cylinder head as described in Section 24.

41   Camshaft and tappets – removal, inspection and refitting (HCS engine)

Removal

1   Remove the cylinder head as described in Section 6.

2   Remove the timing chain and the camshaft sprocket as described in Section 9.

3   Refer to Section 10 and remove the engine sump.

4   Invert the engine so that it is supported on its cylinder head face (on a clean work area). This is necessary to make all of the tappets slide to the top of their stroke, thus allowing the camshaft to be withdrawn. Rotate the camshaft through a full turn to ensure that all of the tappets

slide up their bores, clear of the camshaft.

5   Before removing the camshaft, check its endfloat using a dial gauge mounted on the front face of the engine or feeler gauges. Pull the camshaft fully towards the front (timing case) end of the engine, insert feeler gauges between the camshaft sprocket flange and the camshaft thrust plate to assess the endfloat clearance (photo). The camshaft endfloat must be as specified.

6   Undo the two retaining bolts and remove the camshaft thrust plate.

7   Carefully withdraw the camshaft from the front end of the engine (photo).

8   Extract each tappet in turn and keep them in order of fitting by inserting them in a card with eight holes in it numbered 1 to 8 (from the timing case end of the engine). A valve grinding tool will be found to be useful for the removal of tappets (photo).

Inspection

9   Examine the camshaft bearing journals and lobes for damage or excessive wear. If evident, the camshaft must be renewed.

10   Examine the camshaft bearing internal diameters for signs of damage or excessive wear. If evident, the bearings must be renewed by a Ford dealer.

11   If not carried out on removal, check the camshaft endfloat as described in paragraph 5. If the endfloat exceeds the specified tolerance, renew the thrust plate.

12   It is seldom that the tappets wear excessively in their bores but it is likely that after a high mileage, the cam lobe contact surfaces will show signs of depression or grooving.

13   Where this condition is evident, renew the tappets. Grinding out the grooves and wear marks will reduce the thickness of the surface hardening and accelerate further wear.

41.17 Refitting the camshaft thrust plate

Refitting

14   To refit the tappets and the camshaft, it is essential that the crankcase is inverted.

15   Lubricate their bores and the tappets. Insert each tappet fully into its original bore in the cylinder block.

16   Lubricate the camshaft bearings, camshaft and thrust plate, then insert the camshaft into the crankcase from the timing case end.

17   Fit the thrust plate and tighten the retaining bolts to the specified torque setting (photo). Check that the camshaft is able to freely rotate and that the endfloat is as specified.

42   Piston/connecting rod assemblies – removal

1   Remove the cylinder head as described in Section 6 for HCS engines, or Section 25 for CVH engines.

2   Remove the sump as described in Section 10 for HCS engines or Section 26 for CVH engines.

3   On HCS engines check that the connecting rod big-end caps have adjacent matching numbers facing towards the camshaft side of the engine. On CVH engines, check that the connecting rods have identification numbers – these should be found on the exhaust side of the big-ends. Number 1 assembly is at the timing case end of the engine. If any markings are missing or are indistinct, make some of your own with quick drying paint (see Fig. 2.43).

4   Unscrew the retaining bolts and remove each big-end cap in turn. Note that new big-end retaining bolts will be required during reassembly. If the bearing shells are likely to be used again, tape them to their respective caps for safekeeping.

5   Before removing any of the piston and connecting rod assemblies, inspect the extent of any wear ridge at the top of the bores. If the ridge in each bore is well pronounced, it should be removed with a scraper or if available, a ridge removal tool, before the piston and rod assemblies are pushed up out of the bores. The piston rings may otherwise snag under the ridge and as well as preventing the piston from being removed, may in extreme circumstances cause the rings to break.

6   Remove each piston/rod assembly from its bore by pushing it up from the connecting rod end and pulling it out from the top. Take care not to score the side of the bore with the connecting rod big-end as it passes up through the block.

7   As each piston/connecting rod is removed, temporarily reconnect the appropriate big-end cap to its rod to ensure that the bearing shells do not fall out and get mixed up.

43   Crankshaft – removal

1   Remove the following items with reference to the appropriate Sections in Part A (HCS engine) or Part B (CVH engines) of this Chapter.

(a)   Cylinder head.
(b)   Timing cover and chain/belt.
(c)   Sump.
(d)   Piston and connecting rods. (Can be left in position in the block if the big-end caps are removed and the piston/rods are all pushed up to the top of the their bores).
(e)   Flywheel/driveplate.
(f)   Crankshaft oil seal housing (CVH engines).

HCS (OHC) engine

2   Check that the three main bearing caps have marks to indicate their respective fitted positions in the block. They also have arrow marks pointing towards the timing case end of the engine to indicate correct orientation.

3   Unscrew the retaining bolts and remove the main bearing caps. Remove the oil intake pipe for access to the bolt of the number 2 bearing. If the caps are reluctant to separate from the block face, lightly tap them free using a plastic- or copper-faced hammer. If the bearing shells are likely to be used again, keep them with their bearing caps for safekeeping. However, unless the engine is known to be of low mileage, it is recommended that they be renewed.

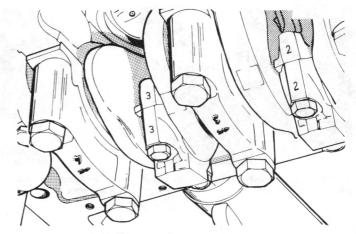

Fig. 2.43 Connecting rod big-end bearing cap and main bearing cap markings – HCS engine (Sec 42)

4   Lift the crankshaft out from the crankcase, then extract the upper bearing shells and side thrust washers. Keep them with their respective caps for correct repositioning if they are to be used again.

5   Remove the crankshaft oil seals from the timing cover and the rear oil seal housing.

CVH (OHC) engines

6   Check that each main bearing cap is numerically marked for positional identification. Each cap should also have an arrow marking to indicate its direction of fitting (arrow points to the timing case end).

7   Unscrew the retaining bolts and remove the main bearing caps. As they are removed, keep each bearing shell with its cap (in case they are to be used again). Note that the bearing shells in the main bearing caps are plain (no groove). It is recommended that the shells be renewed, unless the engine is known to be of low mileage.

8   Lift out the crankshaft from the crankcase.

9   Remove each bearing shell in turn from the crankcase and keep them in order of fitting. Note that the upper shell halves are grooved. Also remove the semi-circular thrust washer from each side of the central main bearing web and keep them in their order of fitting.

44   Cylinder block/crankcase – cleaning and inspection

Cleaning

1   Prior to cleaning, remove all external components and senders. On the HCS engine, make sure that the camshaft and tappets are removed before carrying out thorough cleaning of the block (see Section 41). On the CVH engine, remove the engine ventilation cap from the recess in the rear corner of the cylinder block and if still fitted, undo the retaining screw and withdraw the engine speed sensor from the bellhousing face.

2   Ideally the cylinder block/crankcase should be thoroughly cleaned internally and externally using a steam cleaner and then blown dry using compressed air. Although such facilities are not generally available to the home mechanic (or some garages), the alternative method using a proprietary engine cleaner can be just as effective if a little more time consuming.

3   Clean out the oilways using a length of wire or by applying compressed air through the passages.

Warning: *Wear eye protection when using compressed air!*

The coolant passages are best cleaned through by applying a cold water jet from a hose. For complete cleaning, the core plugs should be removed. Drill a small hole in them, then insert a self-tapping screw and pull out the plugs using a pair of grips or a slide-hammer.

4   Scrape all traces of gasket from the cylinder block, taking care not to damage the head and sump mating faces.

45.2 Removing a piston ring with the aid of a feeler gauge blade

45.5 Measuring piston ring-to-groove clearance

45.6 Checking piston ring end gap

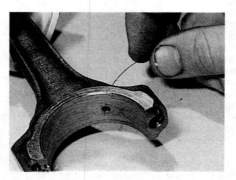

45.7 Measuring a piston diameter

45.10 Check that the oilway in the base of the connecting rod is clear – CVH engines

Inspection

5   Examine the crankcase and block for stripped threads in the bolt holes. If evident, threads inserts can normally be fitted.

6   Cracks in the casting may be repaired by welding or stitching but both methods are extremely specialised processes and must only be entrusted to an acknowledged expert. Where such treatment is required, get a fixed quote first if possible as it is not normally a cheap process.

7   After coating the mating surfaces of the new core plugs with suitable sealant refit them in the cylinder block. Make sure that they are driven in straight and seated properly or leakage could result. Special tools are available for this purpose, but a large socket, with an outside diameter that will just slip into the core plug will work just as well.

8   If the engine is not going to be reassembled right away, lubricate the cylinder bores with clean engine oil then position the engine in a safe place and cover it with a large plastic bag to keep it clean and prevent it rusting.

45   Piston/connecting rod assemblies – inspection

1   The connecting rod gudgeon pin is an interference fit in the piston bosses. To check for wear between the pin and the small-end eye, support the connecting rod in a vice (but take care not to distort it) and rock the piston on the pin axis line. If any wear is present, the gudgeon pin will need renewal. Special heating and installing equipment is required to remove (and refit) the piston and connecting rod assemblies and where this necessary, it will therefore have to be entrusted to a Ford dealer or a specialist automotive engineer. Note that the connecting rods may carry a letter indicating their weight category: all rods in one engine must be of the same weight category.

2   The removal of the piston rings is, however, within the scope of the home mechanic. Although the modern piston ring is relatively malleable compared with earlier types, care must be taken not to snap them when expanding the rings during their removal from and refitting to the piston ring grooves. If a ring expanding tool is not available, grip the open ends of the ring to be removed and carefully prise them open just enough to enable the ring inside diameter to clear the piston outside diameter. As the ring is moved up over the piston, take care not to score the piston with the inside corners of the ring ends (photo). To assist in removing the lower compression and the oil control ring up and over the vacated grooves of the other rings, slide two or three feeler blades down between the ring and the piston at equidistant points, then slide the ring up over the piston.

3   Care must be taken when handling the rings as they have sharp edges when worn and can easily cut the fingers. As each ring is removed from its piston, keep it in order and orientation of fitting both for inspection purposes and particularly if there is a possibility of the rings being re-used (to ensure correct relocation to their original grooves).

4   When the rings are removed from the pistons, clean the pistons for inspection. The carbon deposits in the ring grooves can be cleaned out using a suitable scraper. The broken end of an old piston ring or hacksaw blade can be ground to suit for this purpose, but take care not to damage the ring lands (walls) in the groove or undercut the groove depths.

5   Examine the pistons for excessive scoring, damage and/or wear. With the ring grooves cleaned out, the rings can be reverse-inserted into their respective grooves to check for excessive wear in the grooves (photo). The top compression grooves are the ones most likely to have worn beyond an acceptable level and this is normally apparent by tapered (rather than parallel) ring lands. Where worn grooves are found, they will need to be machined parallel and oversize rings fitted to suit. This is again a task to be entrusted to a specialist engine reconditioner.

6   The piston rings should be individually pushed squarely down their respective bores (about one third down) and their ring end gaps checked to ensure that they are as specified (photo). Where the gaps are found to be too small they can be opened out by carefully grinding their ends back to suit. This applies to new rings as well as the originals and is

46.2 Using a penny to check the crankshaft journals for scoring

46.4 Measuring the diameter of a crankshaft journal

46.12 Measuring a crankshaft journal running clearance using Plastigage

particularly important when the cylinders have been rebored and/or new pistons and rings are to be fitted. When fitting new piston rings to old pistons (and even with new pistons), check that the rings are not tight in their grooves.

7   Before fitting the piston rings to their pistons, each piston should be inserted into its bore and the piston-to-bore clearance checked using feeler gauges. This applies even when new pistons are to be fitted. The clearance must be as specified. If the clearance is too small, the piston will overheat and seize up. Use a micrometer as shown to check a piston for excessive wear (photo).

8   If the engine has not been rebored, the cylinder bores should be roughened (honed) with a honing tool in a diagonally horizontal manner (to assist the new piston ring to bed in) prior to refitting the pistons.

9   Note that each piston is marked for fitting direction by an arrow mark on the crown and/or a dimple in the side face near the gudgeon pin, both of which face to the front when fitted. If new pistons of the original size are being fitted, it is important to check that they are of the correct diameter to suit the bore.

10   On CVH engines, pass a thin gauge wire through the lubrication hole in the base of the rod to ensure that the oilway is clear (photo).

46 Crankshaft – inspection

1   Clean the crankshaft and dry it with compressed air if available.

Warning: *Wear eye protection when using compressed air!*

Be sure to clean the oil holes with a pipe cleaner or similar probe.

2   Check the main and big-end bearing journals for uneven wear, scoring, pitting and cracking. Rub a penny across each journal several times (photo). If a journal picks up copper from the penny, it is too rough and must be reground.

3   Remove any burrs from the crankshaft oil holes with a stone, file or scraper.

4   Using a micrometer, measure the diameter of the main and connecting rod journals and compare the results with the Specifications at the beginning of this Chapter (photo). By measuring the diameter at a number of points around each journal's circumference, you will be able to determine whether or not the journal is out-of-round. Take the measurement at each end of the journal, near the webs, to determine if the journal is tapered. If any of the measurements vary by more than 0.0254 mm, the crankshaft will have to be reground and undersize bearings fitted.

5   The main bearing running clearance can be measured in either of two ways. One method is to fit the main bearing caps to the cylinder block, with bearing shells in place. With the cap retaining bolts tightened to the specified torque, measure the internal diameter of each assembled pair of bearing shells using a vernier dial indicator or internal micrometer. If the diameter of each corresponding crankshaft journal is measured and then subtracted from the bearing internal diameter, the result will be the main bearing running clearance.

6   The second method is to use an American product known as Plastigage (type PG1). This consists of a fine thread of perfectly round plastic which is compressed between the bearing cap and each crankshaft journal in turn. When the cap is removed, the plastic is deformed and can be measured with a special card gauge supplied with the kit. The running clearance is determined from this gauge. Plastigage is sometimes difficult to obtain in this country but enquiries at one of the larger specialist chains of quality motor factors should produce the name of a stockist in your area. The procedure for using Plastigage is as follows.

7   With the upper main bearing shells in place, carefully lay the crankshaft in position. Do not use any lubricant; the crankshaft journals and bearing shells must be perfectly clean and dry. Position the crankshaft in the crankcase so that the normal TDC point of the first journal to be checked, is at the BDC position in the crankcase for the best access.

8   Cut a length of the Plastigage (slightly shorter than the width of the main bearings) and place the Plastigage strip across the width of the crankshaft journal at its TDC point.

9   With the bearing shell in position in the appropriate cap, fit the cap over its journal, ensuring correct orientation (arrow mark pointing towards the front of the engine). Take care not to disturb the Plastigage. Tighten the bearing cap retaining bolts to the specified torque. Note that if the oil intake pipe is still fitted on the 1.3 litre engine, it will need to be removed in order to allow the access for the number two main bearing bolt to be tightened.

10   Do not rotate the crankshaft at any time once the bearing cap is fitted.

11   Remove the bolts and carefully lift off the main bearing cap, again taking care not to disturb the Plastigage or rotate the crankshaft. If any of the bearing caps are difficult to remove, tap them from side-to-side with a soft-faced mallet.

12   Compare the width of the crushed Plastigage on the journal to the scale printed on the Plastigage envelope to obtain the main bearing running clearance (photo). Note the journal number and the main bearing running clearance measured.

13   Repeat this procedure with the each of the other main bearings in turn, each bearing being measured individually.

14   If the clearance is not as specified, and the bearing shells and/or the crankshaft main bearing journals are worn beyond an acceptable amount, they will need to be reground or renewed (as applicable). Before deciding that different size shells are needed, make sure that no dirt or oil was trapped between the bearing shells and the caps or block when the clearance was measured. If the Plastigage was wider at one end than at the other, the journal may be tapered.

15   Carefully scrape away all traces of the Plastigage material from the crankshaft and bearing shells using a fingernail or other object to prevent scoring the shells.

16   To measure the big-end bearing running clearance, the same general procedures apply as those described for the crankshaft main bearing journals above. If the Plastigage method is being used, ensure that the crankpin journal and the big-end bearing shells are clean and dry. Engage the connecting rod and shell with the crankpin, lay the Plastigage strip on the crankpin, then fit the other shell and bearing cap (in its previously noted position), tightening the nuts to the specified torque wrench setting. *Do not rotate the crankshaft during this operation.* Remove the cap and check the running clearance by measuring the Plastigage as previously described.

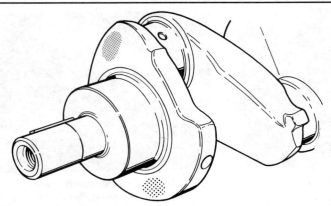

Fig. 2.44 Paint identification markings for the main and big-end bearing journals (Sec 47)

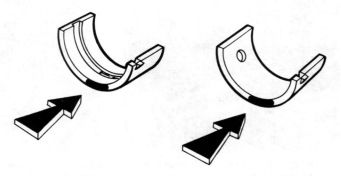

Fig. 2.45 Bearing shell colour code markings (arrowed). Note that the lower half shell is a plain bearing (Sec 47)

17   Check the oil seal journals as applicable at each end of the crankshaft for wear and damage. If the seal has worn an excessive groove in the journal, consult an engine overhaul specialist who will be able to advise whether a repair is possible or whether a new crankshaft is necessary.

47   Main and big-end bearings – inspection

1   Even though the main and big-end bearings should be renewed during the engine overhaul, the old bearings should be retained for close examination, as they may reveal valuable information about the condition of the engine. Where applicable, the size identification mark for undersize bearing shells is stamped on the back metal and this information should be given to the supplier of the new shells. 'Standard' main and big-end bearing shells are classified according to tolerance; they either carry no paint mark on the side or they carry a yellow mark. Bearing shells fitted to an undersize crankshaft or an oversize cylinder block have the relevant identification mark on their rear face. Except for service main and big-end bearings shells for 0.5 and 0.75 mm undersize crankshaft journals, the production repair size shells are marked with a green or black identification mark on their outer edge.
2   Bearing failure occurs because of lack of lubrication, the presence of dirt or other foreign particles, overloading the engine, and corrosion. Regardless of the cause of bearing failure, it must be corrected before the engine is reassembled to prevent it from happening again.
3   When examining the bearings, remove them from the engine block, the main bearing caps, the connecting rods and the rod caps and lay them out on a clean surface in the same general position as their location in the engine. This will enable you to match any bearing problems with the corresponding crankshaft journal.
4   Dirt and other foreign particles get into the engine in a variety of ways. It may be left in the engine during assembly, or it may pass through filters or the crankcase ventilation system. It may get into the oil, and from there into the bearings. Metal chips from machining operations and normal engine wear are often present. Abrasives are sometimes left in engine components after reconditioning, especially when parts are not thoroughly cleaned using the proper cleaning methods. Whatever the source, these foreign objects often end up embedded in the soft bearing material and are easily recognized. Large particles will not embed in the bearing and will score or gouge the bearing and journal. The best prevention for this cause of bearing failure is to clean all parts thoroughly and keep everything spotlessly clean during engine assembly. Frequent and regular engine oil and filter changes are also recommended.
5   Lack of lubrication (or lubrication breakdown) has a number of interrelated causes. Excessive heat (which thins the oil), overloading (which squeezes the oil from the bearing face) and oil leakage (from excessive bearing clearances, worn oil pump or high engine speeds) all contribute to lubrication breakdown. Blocked oil passages, which usually are the result of misaligned oil holes in a bearing shell, will also oil starve a bearing and destroy it. When lack of lubrication is the cause of bearing failure, the bearing material is wiped or extruded from the steel backing of the bearing. Temperatures may increase to the point where the steel backing turns blue from overheating.

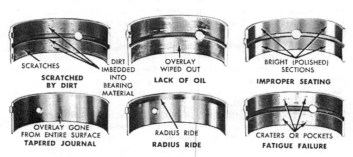

Fig. 2.46 Typical bearing failures (Sec 47)

6   Driving habits can have a definite effect on bearing life. Full throttle, low speed operation (labouring the engine) puts very high loads on bearings, which tends to squeeze out the oil film. These loads cause the bearings to flex, which produces fine cracks in the bearing face (fatigue failure). Eventually the bearing material will loosen in pieces and tear away from the steel backing. Short trip driving leads to corrosion of bearings because insufficient engine heat is produced to drive off the condensed water and corrosive gases. These products collect in the engine oil, forming acid and sludge. As the oil is carried to the engine bearings, the acid attacks and corrodes the bearing material.
7   Incorrect bearing installation during engine assembly will lead to bearing failure as well. Tight fitting bearings leave insufficient bearing oil clearance and will result in oil starvation. Dirt or foreign particles trapped behind a bearing shell result in high spots on the bearing which lead to failure.

48   Engine overhaul – reassembly sequence

1   Before reassembly begins ensure that all new parts have been obtained and that all necessary tools are available. Read through the entire procedure to familiarise yourself with the work involved, and to ensure that all items necessary for reassembly of the engine are at hand. In addition to all normal tools and materials, it is recommended that Loctite 275 setting sealer or Hylomar PL32M sealants be used where applicable during engine reassembly. These are recommended by and obtained from Ford dealers.
2   In order to save time and avoid problems, engine reassembly can be carried out in the following order (as applicable).

   (a)   *Engine ventilation cap – CVH engines.*
   (b)   *Tappets and camshaft.*
   (c)   *Crankshaft and main bearings.*
   (d)   *Pistons and connecting rods.*
   (e)   *Oil pump.*
   (f)   *Sump.*
   (g)   *Flywheel/driveplate.*
   (h)   *Cylinder head.*
   (i)   *Timing sprockets and chain/belt.*
   (j)   *Engine external components.*

49.3 Crankshaft lowered into position (HCS engine)

3   Ensure that everything is clean prior to reassembly. As mentioned previously, dirt and metal particles can quickly destroy bearings and result in major engine damage. Use clean engine oil to lubricate during reassembly.

49   Crankshaft – refitting and endfloat check

Note: *Where the crankshaft, its main bearing journals and/or bearing shells have been renovated and/or renewed, it is advisable to recheck the main bearing running clearances as described in Section 46 before final refitting of the crankshaft.*

HCS (OHV) engine

1   Wipe clean the main bearing shell seats in the crankcase, then insert the respective upper shells (dry) into position in the crankcase. Note that the upper shells have grooves in them (the lower shells are plain and have a wider location lug). Where the old main bearings are being refitted, ensure that they are located in their original positions.
2   Smear the crankshaft side thrust washers with grease, then fit them into position in the crankcase so that their oil grooves are facing outwards (away from the central web).
3   Now lubricate the main bearing journals and bearings with clean engine oil and lower the crankshaft into position in the crankcase (photo).
4   Fit the lower shells into their respective bearing caps, lubricate the shells with clean engine oil and then fit them into position in the crankcase. As they are fitted, ensure that they are correctly located in numerical order and also are correctly orientated with the arrow mark on each cap facing to the front.
5   Insert the main bearing cap retaining bolts and tighten them to their specified torque wrench setting. Note that if the oil intake pipe is fitted, it will need to be removed in order to allow access to the number two main bearing bolt.
6   Now check the crankshaft endfloat. A dial gauge should be used if available, but feeler gauges will suffice if inserted between the thrust washer-to-crankshaft machined face (the procedures being the same as those shown for the CVH engine type in photos 49.16A and B). Move the crankshaft fully in one direction and then the other and check the endfloat. If it is not as specified, the thrust washers will need to be replaced with suitable alternatives from the various oversizes available.
7   To refit the oil intake pipe, first clean the joint area, then coat the area indicated in Fig. 2.48 with the specified activator. Wait for a period of ten minutes then smear the shaded area with the specified adhesive and immediately press the intake pipe into position in the crankcase.
8   If removed, fit the Woodruff key fully into its groove at the front of the crankshaft, then slide the crankshaft sprocket over the key and onto

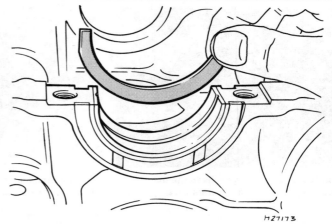

Fig. 2.47 Fit the side thrust washers into position with their oil groove faces outwards (Sec 49)

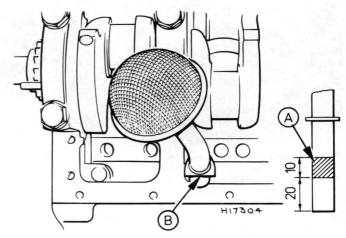

Fig. 2.48 Oil intake pipe refitting details – HCS engine (Sec 49)

A   Area of sealant application – dimensions in mm
B   Edge must be parallel with engine longitudinal axis

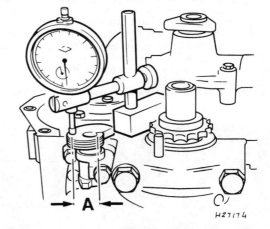

Fig. 2.49 Checking the chain tensioner cam for parallel between the measuring points indicated – HCS engine (Sec 49)

A   20 mm

the shaft. Use the drivebelt pulley, washer and retaining bolt to press the sprocket into position, then remove the bolt, washer and the pulley.
9   Locate the timing chain tensioner into position on the front face of the cylinder block, ensuring that the tensioner cam face is parallel to the block face. Use a dial gauge to measure between the points indicated in

49.10 Fit the bearing shells to the main bearing housings in the crankcase

49.11 Fit the crankcase ventilation cap and its retaining spring

49.13 Lower the crankshaft into position in the crankcase

49.15A Locate the main bearing caps ensuring correct orientation as indicated by the arrows and numbers

49.15B Crankshaft and all main bearings refitted

49.16A Crankshaft endfloat check using a dial gauge

Fig. 2.49 and ensure that the maximum deviation between the two points does not exceed 0.2 mm.

CVH (OHC) engines

10   Wipe clean the main bearing shell seats in the crankcase, then insert the respective upper shells (dry) into position in the crankcase. Note that with the exception of the front main bearing, the upper shells have grooves in them (the lower half bearings are plain). The upper and lower front shells are narrower in section and both have an oil groove in them. Where the old main bearings are being refitted, ensure that they are located in their original positions (photo).
11   Relocate the crankcase ventilation cap and its retaining spring into position in the crankcase (photo).
12   Smear the crankshaft side thrust washers with grease, then fit

them into position in the crankcase so that their oil grooves are facing outwards (away from the central web as shown in Fig. 2.47).
13   Now lubricate the main bearing journals and bearings with clean engine oil and lower the crankshaft into position in the crankcase (photo).
14   Fit the lower shells into their respective bearing caps, lubricate the shells with clean engine oil and then fit them into position in the crankcase. As they are fitted, ensure that they are correctly located in numerical order and are correctly orientated with the arrow mark on each cap to the front.
15   Insert the main bearing cap retaining bolts and tighten them to their specified torque wrench setting (photos).
16   Now check the crankshaft endfloat. A dial gauge should be used if available, but feeler gauges will suffice if inserted between the thrust washer-to-crankshaft machined face. Move the crankshaft fully in one

49.16B Crankshaft endfloat check using a feeler gauge

49.17A Using a plastic shim to protect the lips of the rear oil seal as it is fitted onto the rear flange of the crankshaft (CVH engine)

49.17B Check that the sump mating faces of the seal housing and the base of the crankcase are parallel using a rule (arrow) when tightening the rear oil seal housing retaining bolts (CVH engine)

direction and then the other and check the endfloat. If not as specified, the thrust washers will need to be replaced with suitable alternatives from the various oversizes available (photos).

17   With the new rear oil seal fitted in its housing, lubricate the running surface on the crankshaft and the oil seal lip with clean engine oil, locate a new gasket onto the rear face of the crankcase and refit the oil seal housing and seal. To avoid damaging the lips of the seal as it is passed over the end of the crankshaft, locate a thin plastic shim, cut to size, over the rear flange of the crankshaft so that it protrudes and press the seal over the shim. With the seal in position, withdraw the shim. Centralise the seal on the shaft, check that the housing to sump flange faces are flush to the sump face on the base of the crankcase, then insert and tighten the housing retaining bolts to the specified torque (photos).

18   Refit the oil pump unit as described in Section 27.

50 Piston rings – refitting

1   Install the new piston rings by fitting them over the top of the piston. If a ring expander is not available, use feeler gauges (as during removal) to assist in guiding the rings down over the ring lands and into their appropriate grooves. If the original rings are to be refitted, ensure that they are fitted to their original positions in their respective pistons.

2   Start by fitting the oil control scraper ring to each piston in turn and note that the garter spring of each oil control ring must be fitted so that its ends abut, but do not overlap.

3   When fitting the second (intermediate) compression rings, ensure that the 'TOP' or manufacturer's mark is uppermost.

4   Finally, when fitting the top compression rings it should be noted that they are molybdenum coated and extra care must be taken to avoid damaging their coatings when handling them.

5   On the HCS engine, when all of the rings are fitted to each piston, arrange them so that the gaps are positioned as specified in the Specifications.

6   On the CVH engine, when all of the rings are fitted to each piston, arrange them so that the gaps are spaced at 120° intervals and with no gaps positioned above the gudgeon pin hole.

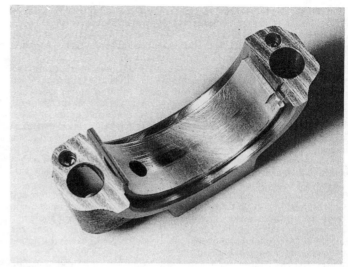

51.2 Fit the big-end bearing shell in the cap with the bearing tongue in the cap groove

51 Piston/connecting rod assemblies – refitting and big-end bearing running clearance check

1   Clean the backs of the big-end bearing shells and the recesses in the connecting rods and big-end caps. If new shells are being fitted, ensure

51.5A Locate the ring compressor over the piston then fit the piston and connecting rod into the appropriate cylinder bore ...

51.5B ... ensuring that the arrow mark on the piston crown points to the timing end of the engine

51.6A Connecting rod and big-end cap markings

51.6B Big-end cap bolts are Torx type on some models

51.6C Angle-tighten the big-end bolts using the correct tool (HCS only) ...

51.6D ... or a fabricated type as shown (HCS only)

that all traces of the protective grease are cleaned off using paraffin. Wipe the shells and connecting rods dry with a lint-free cloth.

2   Press the big-end bearing shells into the connecting rods and caps in their correct positions. Make sure that the location tabs are engaged with the cut-outs in the connecting rods (photo).

3   Where the crankshaft big-end journals have been reground and new big-end bearing shells are being fitted, it is advisable to recheck each big-end running clearance before finally refitting the piston and connecting rod assemblies into the cylinder block. This procedure is described in Section 50. Having checked the running clearance of all the crankpin journals and taken any corrective action necessary, clean off all traces of Plastigage from the bearing shells and crankpin and continue reassembly.

4   Commence the refitting by lubricating the No 1 piston and piston rings with clean engine oil. Check that the gaps are positioned as described in Section 50.

5   Fit a ring compressor to No 1 piston then insert the piston and connecting rod into No 1 cylinder. With No 1 crankpin at its lowest point, drive the piston carefully into the cylinder with the wooden handle of a hammer and at the same time guide the connecting rod onto the crankpin. Make sure that the arrow on the piston crown faces the timing case end of the engine (photos).

6   Fit the No 1 big-end bearing cap to the connecting rod, ensuring correct orientation (number-on-rod and number-on-cap in alignment) and engagement of the two dowels. Fit and tighten the **new** retaining bolts to the specified torque setting. On HCS engines, the bolts are then further angle-tightened as specified using the correct angle tightening tool if it is available, but if not, fabricate a card template and mark the appropriate angle markings on it (photos).

7   Check that the connecting rod big-end bearing endfloat is as specified, then rotate the crankshaft to ensure that it is free and not binding before moving on to fit the next piston/connecting rod assembly.

8   Repeat the foregoing procedures on the remaining piston/connecting rod assemblies.

52   Engine – initial start-up after overhaul

1   With the engine refitted in the vehicle, double-check the engine oil, transmission and coolant levels. Also double-check that all wiring connections are securely and correctly made. When reconnecting the battery earth lead, refer to the information in Section 4 of Chapter 12 concerning engine restarting procedures on EFi models.

2   With the fuel supply hose disconnected and clamped or plugged to prevent the engine from starting, crank the engine over on the starter until the oil pressure light goes out.

3   Reconnect the fuel supply hose.

4   Start the engine, noting that this may take a little longer than usual whilst fuel is pumped through to the engine.

5   While the engine is idling, check for fuel, water and oil leaks. Don't be alarmed if there are some odd smells and smoke from parts getting hot and burning off oil deposits.

6   Keep the engine idling until hot water is felt circulating through the top hose, and where applicable, the auto-choke feed and return hoses, then switch it off. If one or the other of the coolant hoses to the auto-choke unit fails to warm up they probably have an air lock and require bleeding. Bleed them by carefully loosening off the appropriate hose clip and ease the hose a fraction from its connection. As soon as coolant is seen to flow from it, reconnect the hose and retighten its retaining clip. Take care against scalding when bleeding any part of the cooling system by wearing gloves or wrapping a rag around the end of the hose being bled.

7   After a few minutes, recheck the oil and water levels and top up as necessary.

8   There is no requirement to re-tighten the cylinder head bolts after an initial 'running-in' mileage has been completed.

9   If new pistons, rings or crankshaft bearings have been fitted, the engine must be run-in for the first 500 miles (800 km). Do not operate the engine at full throttle or allow it to labour in any gear during this period. It is recommended that the oil and filter be changed at the end of this period.

Chapter 3
Cooling, heating and air conditioning systems

Contents

Specifications

System type .... Pressurized, pump assisted thermo-syphon with front mounted radiator and thermo-electric cooling fan

Pressure cap rating
All models .... 1.2 bar

Radiator
Type.. Aluminium crossflow core (corrugated fin on tube), with plastic side tanks. Oil cooler in left-hand tank on automatic transmission models

Thermostat
Type.. Wax
Opening temperature.. 85 to 95°C
Fully open temperature .... 99 to 105°C

Water pump
Type.. Centrifugal, belt driven
Drivebelt tension:
    HCS (OHV) engine .... 4 mm deflection at longest belt run between pulleys
    CVH (OHC) engine .... Pump driven by timing belt. Refer to Chapter 2 for tensioning details

Anti-freeze
Type/specification.. Ethylene-glycol based anti-freeze, suitable for use in mixed-metal systems. Ford specification ESD-M97B-49-A (Duckhams Universal Antifreeze and Summer Coolant)
Recommended concentration .... 45% by volume

Torque wrench settings	Nm	lbf ft
Thermostat housing	7 to 10	5 to 7
Water pump pulley	9 to 11	6 to 8
Water pump retaining bolts	7 to 11	5 to 7

Torque wrench settings (continued)

	Nm	lbf ft
Cooling fan motor-to-shroud	9 to 12	7 to 9
Cooling fan shroud-to-radiator	3 to 5	2 to 3
Heater housing to body	7 to 11	5 to 8
Air conditioning system components:		
Condenser to side member	7 to 9	5 to 6
Shroud to radiator	3 to 5	2 to 3.5
Dehydrator to radiator bracket	5 to 8	4 to 8
High pressure switch to dehydrator	12 to 15	9 to 11
Expansion valve to evaporator	4 to 5	3.0 to 3.5
Air conditioner housing to cowl panel	6 to 8	5 to 6
Low and high pressure lines to compressor	20 to 26	15 to 19
Low pressure liquid line to expansion valve	5.7 to 7.8	4 to 6
Dehydrator connecting line to condensor	14 to 19	11 to 14
Lines to dehydrator	14 to 19	11 to 14
Compressor to bracket	20 to 27	15 to 20
Compressor driveplate to compressor	11 to 16	8 to 12

1 General information

The cooling system is of the pressurised type consisting of a belt-driven pump, aluminium crossflow radiator, expansion tank, electric cooling fan and a thermostat. The system functions as follows. Cold coolant in the bottom of the radiator passes through the bottom hose to the water pump where it is pumped around the cylinder block and head passages. After cooling the cylinder bores, combustion surfaces and valve seats, the coolant reaches the underside of the thermostat, which is initially closed. The coolant passes through the heater and inlet manifold and is returned to the water pump.

When the engine is cold the coolant circulates through the cylinder block, cylinder head, heater and inlet manifold. When the coolant reaches a predetermined temperature, the thermostat opens and the coolant then passes through the top hose to the radiator. As the coolant circulates through the radiator it is cooled by the inrush of air when the car is in forward motion. Airflow is supplemented by the action of the electric cooling fan when necessary. Upon reaching the bottom of the radiator, the coolant is now cooled and the cycle is repeated.

When the engine is at normal operating temperature the coolant expands and some of it is displaced into the expansion tank. This coolant collects in the tank and is returned to the radiator when the system cools.

The electric cooling fan, mounted behind the radiator, is controlled by a thermostatic switch located in the thermostat housing. At a predetermined coolant temperature the switch contacts close, thus actuating the fan. The layout of the air conditioning system is shown in Fig. 3.15.

It is important to observe the following special precautions when dealing with any part of the air conditioning system, its associated components and any items which necessitate disconnection of the system.

(a) If for any reason the system must be disconnected, entrust this task to your Ford dealer or a refrigeration engineer.
(b) It is essential that the system be professionally discharged prior to welding in the vicinity of the system, before having the vehicle oven-dried at a temperature exceeding 110°C after repainting and before disconnecting any part of the system.
(c) The refrigeration circuit contains a liquid refrigerant (Freon) and it is therefore dangerous to disconnect any part of the system without specialised knowledge and equipment.
(d) The refrigerant must not be allowed to come in contact with a naked flame otherwise a poisonous gas will be created. Do not allow the fluid to come in contact with the skin or eyes.

2 Electric cooling fan assembly – testing, removal and refitting

Testing

1 Detach the wiring multi-plug from the thermostatic switch in the thermostat housing, then using a suitable piece of wire, bridge the two connections within the plug. Switch the ignition on and check if the cooling fan operates. If the fan operates, the thermostatic switch is at fault and requires renewal as described in the following Section. Remove the bridging wire from the plug and reconnect the wiring connector to complete the test. If, however, the fan fails to operate, either the switch or the fan motor are at fault and require renewal. The fan can be further checked by connecting it directly to the battery. To remove the fan assembly, proceed as follows for standard system models or refer to Section 17 for the removal and refitting details for air conditioned models.

2.3A Detach the cooling fan motor wiring connector ...

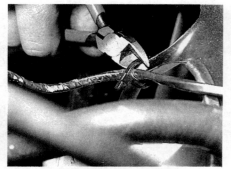

2.3B ... and release the wiring from the shroud/motor support arm ...

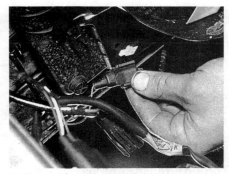

2.3C ... and from the locating clip

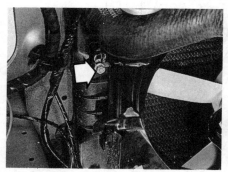

2.4 Cooling fan shroud-to-radiator bolt (arrowed)

2.5 Withdrawing the cooling fan shroud and motor from under the vehicle

2.6 Fan motor-to-shroud nuts

Removal

2   Disconnect the battery earth lead.
3   Detach the wiring multi-plug from the fan motor and then unclip and remove the wiring from the retaining clips on the shroud. Also where applicable, disconnect the coolant heater hose from the location clips on the cooling fan shroud (photos).
4   Unscrew and loosen off the two bolts (one each side) securing the cooling fan shroud to the radiator (photo).
5   Lift the fan unit complete with its shroud so that the shroud is clear of the securing bolts, then lower and remove the assembly from underneath the vehicle (photo). Take care not to damage the core of the radiator as the fan assembly is withdrawn.
6   If required, the fan motor can be detached from the shroud by unscrewing the three retaining nuts (photo).

Refitting

7   Refitting is a reversal of the removal procedure. Tighten the shroud to radiator bolts and the fan to shroud nuts to the specified torque setting. Ensure that the wiring connection is cleanly and securely made and locate the loom in the retaining clips.

3   Electric cooling fan thermostatic switch – testing, removal and refitting

Testing

1   The electric cooling fan thermostatic switch is located in the thermostat housing (photo). If it develops a fault it is most likely to fail open-circuit. This will result in the fan motor remaining stationary even though the coolant temperature exceeds the switch-on point. The coolant may even reach boiling point.
2   To test for a faulty thermostatic switch, proceed as described in paragraph 1 of the previous Section.

Removal

3   To remove the switch, disconnect the battery negative terminal and drain the cooling system, as described in Chapter 1.
4   Disconnect the wiring multi-plug from the thermostatic switch and then unscrew the switch from the thermostat housing. Remove the sealing washer.

Refitting

5   Refitting is a reversal of removal, but fit a new sealing washer and tighten the switch securely. Refill the cooling system as described in Chapter 1.

4   Temperature gauge sender unit – removal and refitting

Removal

1   Unscrew the expansion tank filler cap. If the engine is hot, place a

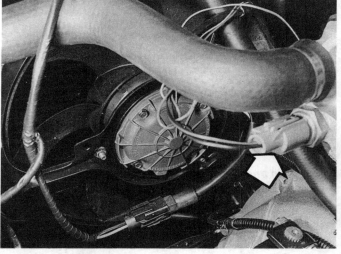

3.1 Cooling fan thermostatic switch location (arrowed) in the thermostat housing (CVH engine)

cloth over the cap and unscrew it slowly, allowing all the pressure to escape before removing the cap completely.
2   Place a suitable container beneath the radiator drain plug outlet. Unscrew the plug and drain approximately 1 litre of the coolant. Retighten the drain plug.
3   Disconnect the wire from the sender unit (located in the coolant connecter/cylinder head).
4   Unscrew the sender unit from its location.

Refitting

5   Refitting is a reversal of removal, but tighten the unit securely. Top up the cooling system with reference to Chapter 1.

5   Radiator – removal, inspection, cleaning and refitting

Removal

1   Disconnect the battery leads.
2   Drain the cooling system as described in Chapter 1.
3   Remove the cooling fan assembly as described in Section 2.
4   Raise and support the vehicle at the front end on axle stands.
5   Loosen off their retaining clips and detach the top, bottom and expansion hoses from the radiator (photos).
6   Where applicable, disconnect the automatic transmission fluid cooling pipes from the radiator. As they are disconnected, allow for fluid loss, plug the fluid hoses and connections to prevent further loss of fluid and the ingress of dirt into the system. If air conditioning is fitted, remove the splash shield (see paragraph 8), then undo the three

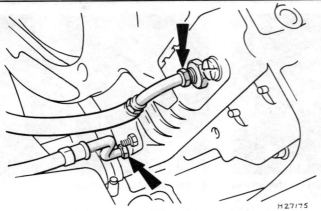

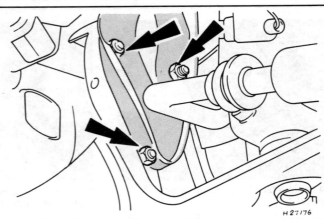

Fig. 3.1 Automatic transmission fluid cooling pipe connections to the radiator – arrowed (Sec 5)

Fig. 3.2 Air conditioner condenser retaining nuts – arrowed (Sec 5)

retaining nuts and detach the air conditioning condenser from the side of the radiator side deflector.

7   Unscrew the two retaining bolts on each side of the radiator (underneath the radiator), then supporting it, lower the radiator clear of the locating lugs at the top and carefully withdraw it from underneath the front end of the vehicle (photo).

8   Detach the rubber mounts, the side deflectors and the bottom mounting from the radiator. If required, the splash shield can be removed from the radiator by undoing the six retaining screws or drilling out the pop rivets and extracting the retaining clips (according to type) (photos).

Inspection and cleaning

9   Radiator repair is best left to a specialist, but minor leaks may be

sealed using a radiator sealant such as Holts Radweld. Extensive damage should be repaired by a specialist or the unit exchanged for a new or reconditioned radiator. Clear the radiator matrix of flies and small leaves with a soft brush, or by hosing, flushing the radiator thoroughly with clean water. If after a reasonable period, the water still does not run clear, the radiator should be flushed with a good proprietary cleaning system such as Holts Radflush or Holts Speed flush.

Refitting

10   Refitting is a reversal of removal, but check the mounting bushes and if necessary renew them. If the splash shield was detached from the base of the radiator, refit it using new pop rivets or retaining clips according to type (photo). Refill the cooling system with reference to Chapter 1. On automatic transmission models check, and if necessary

5.5A Detach the top hose ...

5.5B ... the bottom hose and expansion hose from the radiator

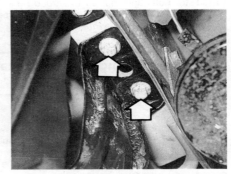

5.7 Radiator retaining bolts (arrowed)

5.8A Radiator mounting rubber

5.8B Drilling out a radiator-to-splash shield rivet

5.10 Pop riveting the anti-splash shield to the radiator

top up, the automatic transmission fluid level.

11   When reconnecting the battery earth lead, refer to Section 4 in Chapter 12 for special notes concerning engine restarting procedures on EFi models.

6   Thermostat – removal, testing and refitting

Removal

1   Drain the cooling system so that the coolant level is below the thermostat location (see Chapter 1).

2   Loosen the clip/s and disconnect the hose(s) from the thermostat housing (photos).

3   Disconnect the thermostatic switch wire multi-plug from the thermostat housing.

4   Unscrew the retaining bolts and remove the thermostat housing (photo).

5   Remove the gasket from the mating face of the thermostat housing, then using suitable pliers, compress the thermostat retaining clip and remove it from the housing. Extract the thermostat from the housing (noting its direction of fitting) and where applicable, remove the O-ring seal (photos).

Testing

6   To test whether the unit is serviceable, suspend it on a string in a saucepan of cold water, together with a thermometer. Heat the water and note the temperature at which the thermostat begins to open. Continue heating the water until the thermostat is fully open and then remove it from the water.

7   The temperature at which the thermostat should start to open is stamped on the upper face of the unit. If the thermostat does not start to

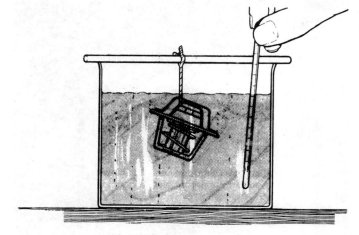

Fig. 3.3 Testing the thermostat (Sec 6)

open at the specified temperature, or does not fully open in boiling water or fully close when removed from the water, then it must be discarded and a new one fitted.

Refitting

8   Refitting is a reversal of removal. Renew the O-ring seal and the housing gasket (photo).

9   Top up the cooling system with reference to Chapter 1.

6.2A Detaching the expansion tank top hose from the thermostat housing on the HCS engine. Thermostatic switch is also shown (arrowed)

6.2B Detaching the heater hose from the thermostat housing (CVH engine)

6.4 Removing the thermostat housing (CVH engine)

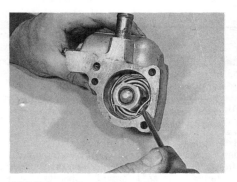

6.5A Release the retaining clip ...

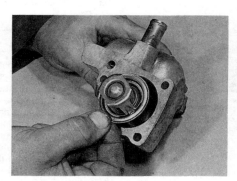

6.5B ... extract the thermostat ...

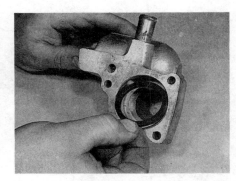

6.5C ... and where applicable, remove the O-ring seal

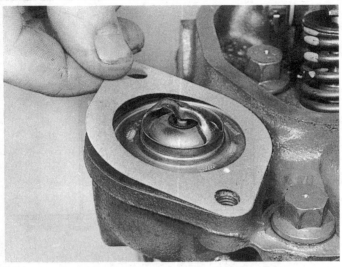

6.7 Use a new gasket when refitting the thermostat housing

7 Water pump (HCS engine) – removal and refitting

Removal

1   Disconnect the battery earth lead.
2   Drain the cooling system as described in Chapter 1.
3   Loosen off the alternator mounting and adjustment fastenings, then pivot the alternator in towards the engine to slacken off the drivebelt tension, and release the drivebelt from the water pump pulley.
4   Unscrew and remove the retaining bolts and remove the drivebelt pulley from the water pump. Use a suitable strap wrench to prevent the pulley from rotating when unscrewing its retaining bolts.
5   Loosen off the coolant hose securing clips and disconnect the hoses from the water pump.
6   Unscrew the retaining bolts and withdraw the water pump from the engine.

Refitting

7   Clean all traces of gasket from the engine and the water pump mating faces. Ensure that the mating faces are clean and dry. Note that the water pump gasket fitted during production is integral with the timing cover gasket and this will need to be cut away using a sharp knife, keeping as close to the timing cover as possible.

7.9 Refitting the water pump to the HCS engine. Note the new gasket

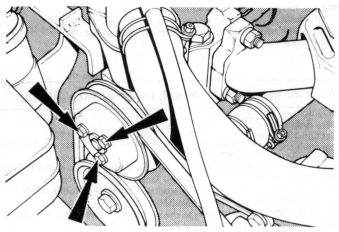

Fig. 3.4 Water pump pulley retaining bolts on the HCS engine (Sec 7)

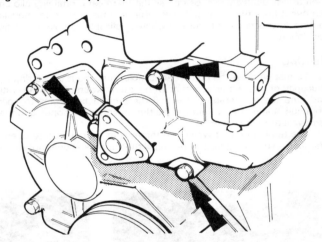

Fig. 3.5 Water pump retaining bolts on the HCS engine (Sec 7)

8   No provision is made for the repair of the water pump and therefore if it is noisy or defective in any way, it must be renewed.
9   Refitting is a reversal of the removal procedure. Use a new gasket, lightly smeared with jointing compound, and tighten the retaining bolts to the specified torque setting (photo).
10   Refit and adjust the drivebelt tension as described in Chapter 1.
11   Refill the cooling system as described in Chapter 1.
12   Reconnect the battery earth lead.

8 Water pump (CVH engine) – removal and refitting

Removal

1   Disconnect the battery earth lead.
2   Drain the engine coolant as described in 1.
3   Loosen off the alternator mounting/adjustment bolts and move the alternator in towards the engine to slacken off the drivebelt tension. Remove the alternator drivebelt.
4   Fit a suitable spanner onto the crankshaft pulley bolt and turn the engine over by hand (in a clockwise direction) to align the TDC markings of the timing cover and the indent in the crankshaft pulley.
5   The crankshaft pulley and retaining bolt must now be removed. To prevent the crankshaft from moving from the TDC position as the bolt is unscrewed, remove the starter motor as described in Chapter 12 and jam the starter ring gear on the flywheel/driveplate with a suitable tool.
6   Unscrew and remove the crankshaft pulley bolt and withdraw the pulley from the front end of the crankshaft.

8.10 Detach the coolant hose from the water pump

8.11 Removing the water pump from the CVH engine

7 Unscrew the retaining bolts and remove the timing case upper and lower half covers.
8 Apply a dab of quick drying paint to mark the relative fitted positions of the timing belt teeth and the sprockets so that the belt can be refitted in its original position on reassembly.
9 Loosen off the timing belt tensioner retaining bolts, then slide the tensioner sideways to slacken off the timing belt tension. Slip the timing belt from the sprockets.
10 Loosen off the coolant hose retaining clip and detach the coolant hose from the water pump (photo).
11 Unscrew and remove the four bolts securing the water pump to the front end face of the cylinder block and then withdraw the pump unit from the vehicle (photo).

Refitting

12 Clean the engine water pump mating faces. Ensure that the mating faces are clean and dry.
13 No provision is made for the repair of the water pump and therefore if it is noisy or defective in any way, it must be renewed.
14 Refitting is a reversal of the removal procedure. Tighten the retaining bolts to the specified torque and ensure that the coolant hose connection to the water pump is securely made.
15 Refit the timing belt and tension it as described in Chapter 2 before refitting the timing covers and the crankshaft pulley.
16 Remove the tool used to jam the crankshaft (in the starter ring gear), then refit the starter motor as described in Chapter 12.
17 Top up the cooling system as described in Chapter 1 and check for any signs of leaks.
18 When reconnecting the battery earth lead, refer to Section 4 in Chapter 12 for special notes concerning engine restarting procedures on EFi models.

9 Expansion tank – removal and refitting

Removal

1 Partially drain the cooling system so that the coolant level drops below the expansion tank. Refer to Chapter 1 for details.
2 Before disconnecting the coolant hoses from the expansion tank, it is advisable to clamp them just short of their connections to the expansion tank to prevent spillage of coolant and the ingress of air when they are detached.
3 Loosen off the coolant hose clips at the expansion tank and detach the hoses from it. If they are not clamped, secure them in a manner so that their ends are raised to minimise coolant spillage.
4 Unscrew the two retaining screws and remove the expansion tank from the inner wing panel.

Refitting

5 Refit in the reverse order of removal. Top up the cooling system as described in Chapter 1.

10 Heater unit and matrix – removal and refitting

Removal

1 Disconnect the battery earth lead.
2 Drain the cooling system as described in Chapter 1. Ensure that the heater controls are positioned on the hot setting as the system is drained.
3 Undo the retaining clips and detach the heater coolant supply and return hoses at their bulkhead connections.
4 A small amount of coolant (about half-a-litre), will have remained in the heater matrix after draining. In order to prevent the possibility of the coolant spilling onto the carpets during the removal of the heater, it is advisable to blow through one of the connections to eject the remaining coolant out through the other vacant connection.
5 Undo the two retaining screws and detach the heater matrix cover plate and gasket from the bulkhead.
6 Refer to Chapter 12 for details and remove the radio/cassette unit from the facia.

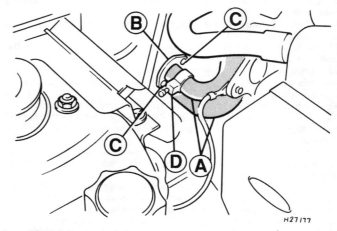

Fig. 3.6 Coolant heater hose connections to heater at bulkhead (Sec 10)

A   Coolant hoses   C   Screws
B   Cover plate   D   Clip

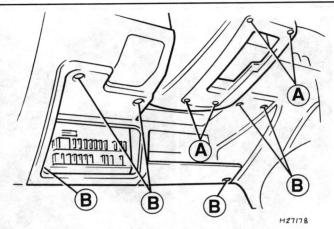

Fig. 3.7 Retaining screw locations of the lower steering column shroud (A) and lower facia (B) – left-hand drive version shown (Sec 10)

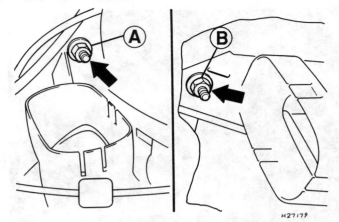

Fig. 3.8 Left-hand (A) and right-hand (B) heater housing securing nuts – arrowed (Sec 10)

20   To remove the heater matrix (radiator) from the heater unit, undo the two retaining bolts and carefully withdraw it.

Refitting

21   Refitting is a reversal of the removal procedure. When fitting the heater unit into position, engage the lugs of its flange with the support bracket on the cowl panel and guide the matrix into position through the opening in the bulkhead.

22   Check that all wiring and coolant hose and air duct connections are securely made. Tighten the retaining nuts to the specified torque.

23   On completion, slowly refill the cooling system as described in Chapter 1.

24   When reconnecting the battery earth lead, refer to Section 4 in Chapter 12 for special notes concerning engine restarting procedures on EFi models.

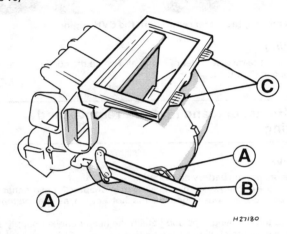

Fig. 3.9 Heater unit showing matrix retaining screws (A), matrix (B) and unit locating lugs (C) (Sec 10)

7   Undo the two retaining screws and remove the stowage unit from under the radio/cassette aperture.

8   Peel back the front door weather strip (seal) from the 'A' pillar adjacent to the facia. Undo the retaining screw and remove the 'A' pillar trim. Repeat the procedure on the opposite side.

9   Undo the two retaining screws and remove the upper steering column shroud.

10   Undo the four retaining screws and remove the lower steering column shroud.

11   Refer to Fig. 3.7 and undo the facia retaining screws from the positions indicated.

12   Undo the single retaining screw and withdraw the column switches from the steering column. As they are withdrawn, disconnect the wiring multi-plugs.

13   Refer to Chapter 11 for details and remove the centre console.

14   Pull free the covers from the right- and left-hand heater control levers, then unclip and disconnect the cables from their connections on the heater unit each side.

15   Prise free the cover from each of the three facia securing bolt apertures on the top face of the facia unit, also the cover from the radio/cassette recess.

16   Unscrew and remove the ten Torx type retaining bolts and pull the facia unit rearwards to partially withdraw it, taking care not to stretch the wiring harnesses under the facia (see Chapter 11).

17   Pull free the footwell air vent from the heater housing connection.

18   Pull free the air ducts from the heater housing connections (two each side and two in the centre).

19   Undo the two retaining nuts and disconnect the heater housing from the cowl panel by withdrawing it downwards and removing it from the side.

11   Heater blower unit – removal and refitting

Removal

1   Disconnect the battery earth lead.

2   On carburettor and CFi-engined models, refer to Chapter 4 for details and remove the air cleaner unit.

3   Peel back the seal strip from the top edge of the bulkhead.

4   Cut the ties and detach the hose and wiring loom from the bulkhead.

5   Undo the six retaining bolts and remove the cover from the air chamber (see Fig. 3.10).

6   Release the heater blower cover from its guides and remove it.

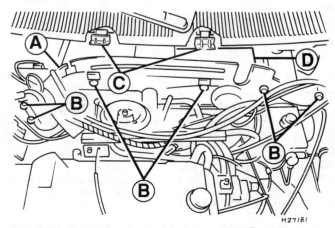

Fig. 3.10 Air chamber and associate components (Sec 11)

A Bulkhead cover   C Blower cover guides
B Cover retaining bolts   D Blower cover

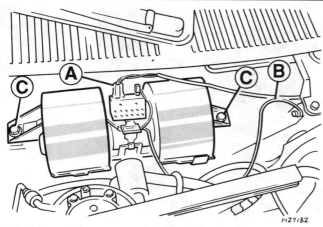

Fig. 3.11 Heater blower motor unit (Sec 11)

A   *Resistor multi-plug*   C   *Blower unit securing nuts*
B   *Earth lead*

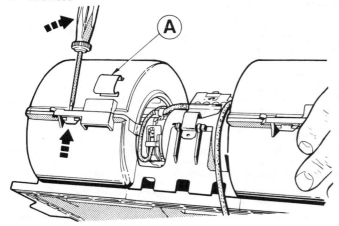

Fig. 3.12 Heater blower unit locking clip (A) removal (Sec 11)

7   Disconnect the wires from the blower motor then undo the two retaining nuts and withdraw the blower motor from the air chamber.
8   To remove the motor from its housing, pull free the lock clips and release the securing lugs using a pin punch. Detach the connector from the blower resistor unit, bend the retaining tabs up and then separate the motor (with resistor) from the retainer. Remove the motor from the housing.

Refitting

9   Refitting is a reversal of the removal procedure. When reassembling the blower motor housing covers, ensure that the locating lugs are fully engaged.

10   When reconnecting the battery earth lead, refer to Section 4 in Chapter 12 for special notes concerning engine restarting procedures on EFi models.

12   Heater resistor unit – removal and refitting

Removal

1   Disconnect the battery earth lead.
2   Refer to the previous Section and proceed as described in paragraphs 2 to 5 inclusive.
3   Detach the wiring connector and the multi-plug from the resistor unit. Bend up the securing tabs and withdraw the resistor unit from the heater motor assembly.

Refitting

4   Refit in the reverse order of removal. Ensure that the resistor retaining tabs are fully engaged and secure.
5   When reconnecting the battery earth lead, refer to Section 4 in Chapter 12 for special notes concerning engine restarting procedures on the EFi model.

13   Heater control panel – removal and refitting

Removal

1   Disconnect the battery earth lead.
2   Undo the two retaining screws from its upper edge and withdraw the instrument panel surround.
3   Carefully prise free the three heater/fresh air and blower switch control knobs, then loosen off the central vent retaining screws and partially withdraw the panel just enough to allow access to the wiring connectors on the inside face of the panel.
4   Where applicable, disconnect the wiring multi-plugs from the heated rear window and rear fog lamp switches, then remove the central vent unit.
5   Pull free the covers, then disconnect the control cables from each side of the heater unit. The right-hand side cable operates the temperature control valve and the left-hand cable operates the air distribution valve (photo).
6   Undo the two screws securing the heater control panel to the facia. Withdraw the panel from the facia just enough to allow the heater blower switch wiring plug to be detached, then fully withdraw the control panel and feed the control cables through the facia aperture (photos).

Refitting

7   Refit in the reverse order of removal. Ensure that the control cables are correctly re-routed (with no tight bends). Check that the cables and the wiring connectors are securely refitted.

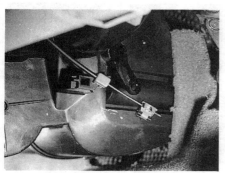

13.5 Heater temperature control cable connection on the right-hand side of the heater unit

13.6A Control panel retaining screws (arrowed)

13.6B Control panel removal

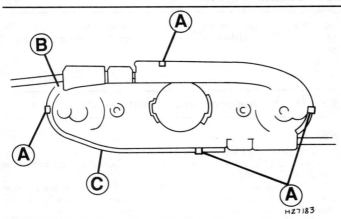

Fig. 3.13 Heater control unit retaining tabs (A), cover (B) and baseplate (C) (Sec 14)

8 When reconnecting the battery earth lead, refer to Section 4 in Chapter 12 for special notes concerning engine restarting procedures concerning EFi models.

14 Heater control cables – removal and refitting

Removal

1 Remove the control panel as described in the previous Section.
2 Referring to Fig. 3.13, bend the retaining tabs straight and then detach the cover from the baseplate to open the heater control unit.
3 Cut the cable retaining clips free, then release the cables from the toothed guide strips to remove them. Note that the retaining clips will need to be renewed during reassembly.

Refitting

4 Refitting is a reversal of the removal procedure.When reconnecting the battery earth lead, refer to Section 4 in Chapter 12 for special notes concerning engine restarting procedures concerning EFi models.

15 Face level air vent (right- and left-hand) – removal and refitting

Removal

1 Disconnect the battery earth lead.

Right-hand side vent

2 Undo the two retaining screws from its upper edge and withdraw the instrument panel surround.

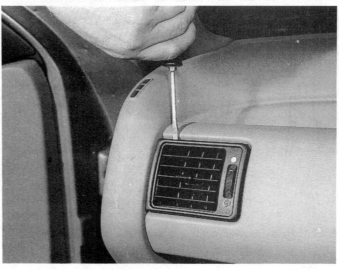

15.4 Prising free the left-hand side vent

3 Undo the two retaining screws and withdraw the face level vent from the facia. Where applicable, detach the wiring connectors from the switches in the panel.

Left-hand side vent

4 Open the glovebox lid, then unscrew the vent retaining screw from the underside of the box roof (directly under the vent). Carefully prise free and remove the vent (photo).

Refitting

5 Refit in the reverse order of removal. When reconnecting the battery earth lead, refer to Section 4 in Chapter 12 for special notes concerning engine restarting procedures on EFi models.

16 Face level air vent (centre) – removal and refitting

Removal

1 Disconnect the battery earth lead.
2 Undo the two retaining screws from its upper edge and withdraw the instrument panel surround.
3 Carefully prise free the three heater/fresh air and blower switch control knobs, then loosen off the central vent retaining screws and partially withdraw the panel (photos).
4 Where applicable, disconnect the wiring multi-plugs from the heated rear window and rear fog lamp switches, then remove the central vent unit.

16.3A Prise free the control knobs ...

16.3B ... undo the retaining screws ...

16.3C ... and partially withdraw the central vent/control panel

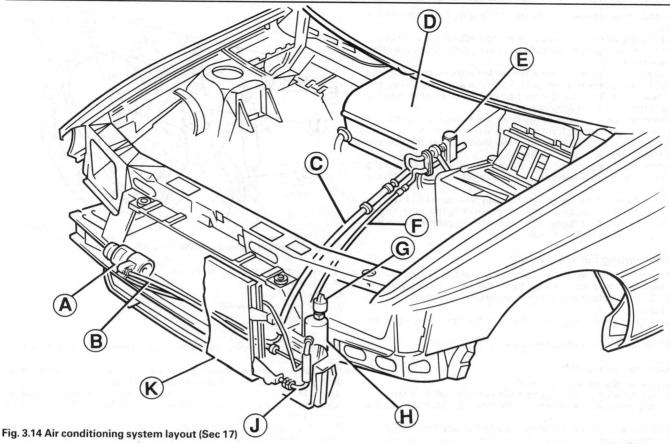

Fig. 3.14 Air conditioning system layout (Sec 17)

A   Condenser
B   Compressor-to-condenser
    pipe

C   Compressor-to-expansion
    valve
D   Evaporator and blower
E   Expansion valve

F   Expansion
    valve-to-dehydrator pipe
G   High pressure switch
H   Dehydrator

J   Dehydrator-to-condenser
    pipe
K   Condenser

H27184

Refitting

5   Refit in the reverse order of removal. Ensure that the wiring multi-plugs are securely reconnected.
6   When reconnecting the battery earth lead, refer to Section 4 in Chapter 12 for special notes concerning engine restarting procedures on EFi models.

17   Air conditioning system components – removal and refitting

Warning: *The system should be professionally discharged before carrying out any of the following work. Cap or plug the pipe lines as soon as they are disconnected to prevent the entry of moisture. Refer to the precautions given in Section 1 before proceeding.*

Electric cooling fan motor

1   Disconnect the battery earth lead.
2   Detach the wiring multi-plugs from the air conditioning fan motor and the motor resistor. Cut free the cable ties securing the wires to the bracket.
3   Working from above, unscrew the left-hand retaining nut from the fan motor support frame. Raise and support the vehicle, then working from underneath, unscrew and remove the right-hand retaining nut from the support frame.
4   Undo the four retaining bolts and detach the transmission brace from the bearer and transmission flange.
5   Remove the starter motor (Chapter 12).
6   Detach and remove the exhaust downpipe (Chapter 4).
7   Lift the support frame and fan motor from the mounting each side

and withdraw it from underneath the vehicle. If required, undo the three retaining nuts and detach the fan unit from the support frame.
8   Refit in the reverse order of removal. Tighten all fastenings to their specified torque wrench settings, ensure that all wiring connections are securely made and, where applicable, relocate the wiring using new cable ties.
9   When reconnecting the battery earth lead, refer to Section 4 in Chapter 12 for special notes concerning engine restarting procedures on EFi models.

De-ice switch

10   Disconnect the battery earth lead.

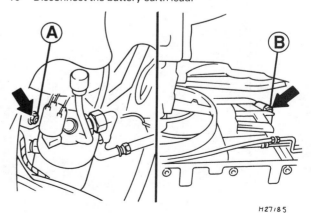

Fig. 3.15 Left-hand (A) and right-hand (B) fan motor support frame retaining nuts – arrowed (Sec 17)

H27185

11   On carburettor engine models, refer to Chapter 4 and remove the air cleaner unit.
12   Pull free the air chamber seal from the top edge of the bulkhead.
13   Unclip the wiring from the bulkhead cover, cutting free the cable ties where necessary.
14   Disconnect the air conditioning line gasket securing plate from the bulkhead, then unscrew and remove the six retaining bolts and detach the bulkhead cover from the air chamber. Pull the evaporator housing cover from the guides and withdraw it.
15   Detach the two vacuum hoses from the vacuum reservoir and detach the wiring multi-plug from the vacuum motor switch.
16   Undo the single retaining screw and then remove the vacuum reservoir from the evaporator housing.
17   Detach the wiring multi-plug from the de-ice switch, extract the switch sensor from the evaporator and disconnect the switch from the housing.
18   Refit in the reverse order of removal. Use new cable ties to secure the wiring to the bulkhead cover. When reconnecting the battery earth lead, refer to Section 4 in Chapter 12 for special notes concerning engine restarting procedures for EFi models.

Air conditioning control switch

19   The switch is located in the main heating and ventilation control panel. Remove the control panel from the facia as described in Section 13, then unclip the air conditioning/blower motor switch from the control unit.
20   Disconnect the wiring multi-plug and the light lead from the switch.
21   Refit in the reverse order of removal.

Vacuum motor switch

22   Disconnect the battery earth lead.
23   Detach the wiring multi-plug from the vacuum motor switch, then undo the two retaining screws and remove the switch from the vacuum reservoir.
24   Refit in the reverse order of removal but ensure that the seal is seated correctly. When reconnecting the battery earth lead, refer to Section 4 in Chapter 12 for special notes concerning engine restarting procedures on EFi models.

Air duct operation vacuum motor

25   Disconnect the battery earth lead.
26   On carburettor engine models, refer to Chapter 4 for details and remove the air cleaner unit.
27   Peel back the air chamber seal and remove it from the top of the bulkhead.
28   Unclip and detach the wiring from the bulkhead cover, cutting free any cable ties as necessary.
29   Undo the three retaining bolts and detach the air conditioning line plate and gasket from the bulkhead.
30   Undo the six securing bolts and withdraw the bulkhead cover from the air chamber.
31   Pull free and remove the evaporator housing cover from the guides.

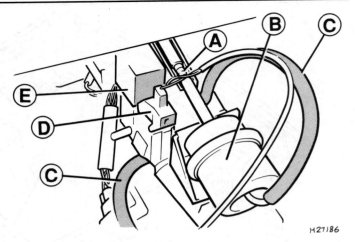

Fig. 3.16 Vacuum motor assembly (Sec 17)

A   Vacuum motor link clamp screw
B   Vacuum motor
C   Vacuum hoses
D   Vacuum motor switch
E   De-ice switch

32   Undo the clamping screw and detach the vacuum motor link (see Fig. 3.16).
33   Unscrew the two retaining nuts and withdraw the vacuum motor. As it is withdrawn, detach the vacuum hose from it.
34   Refit in the reverse order of the removal. Ensure that the vacuum hose and wiring connections are securely made. Renew the cable ties to relocate the wiring to the bulkhead cover.
35   When reconnecting the battery earth lead, refer to Section 4 in Chapter 12 for special notes concerning engine restarting procedures on EFi models.

Vacuum reservoir

36   Proceed as described in paragraphs 25 to 31 inclusive above, then continue as follows.
37   Detach the two vacuum hoses from the vacuum reservoir. Detach the wiring multi-plug from the vacuum motor switch, then undo the retaining screw and remove the vacuum reservoir from the evaporator housing.
38   Undo the two retaining screws and remove the vacuum motor switch from the reservoir.
39   Refit in the reverse order of the removal. Ensure that the vacuum hose and wiring connections are securely made. Renew the cable ties to relocate the wiring to the bulkhead cover.
40   When reconnecting the battery earth lead, refer to Section 4 in Chapter 12 for special notes concerning engine restarting procedures on EFi models.

Chapter 4
Fuel, exhaust and emission control systems

Contents

Specifications

Part A: Carburettor system
Fuel grade
Fuel octane requirement .... 95 RON unleaded

Fuel pump
Type.. Mechanical, operated by an eccentric on the camshaft
Delivery pressure .... 0.24 to 0.38 bar

Carburettor (general)
Type.. Twin choke, downdraught
Application/identification:
    1.3 HCS engine .... Weber 2V TLDM
    1.4 and 1.6 CVH engine .... Weber 2V TLD
Choke type .... Manual or automatic

Weber TLDM
Fast idle speed .... 2500 rpm
Float height .... 28 to 30 mm
Throttle kicker operating speed (automatic transmission) .... 1800 to 2000 rpm

	Primary	Secondary
Venturi diameter	19	20
Main jet	90	122
Emulsion jet	F113	F75
Air correction jet	185	130

Weber TLD
Float height:
    1.4 litre .... 31.0 ± 0.5 mm
    1.6 litre (non-air conditioned) .... 31.0 ± 0.5 mm
    1.6 litre (with air conditioning) .... 29.0 ± 0.5 mm
Choke pull down (maximum):
    1.4 litre .... 3.1 ± 0.5 mm
    1.6 litre .... 4.5 ± 0.5 mm
Choke fast idle (on kickdown step):
    1.4 litre .... 1900 ± 50 rpm
    1.6 litre (with manual steering) .... 1750 ± 50 rpm
    1.6 litre (with power steering) .... Module controlled

	Primary	Secondary
Venturi diameter:		
1.4 litre	20	22
1.6 litre	21	23
Main jet:		
1.4 litre	107	140
1.6 litre (non air conditioned)	115	140
1.6 litre (with air conditioning)	115	127
Emulsion tube	F105	F57
Air correction jet:		
1.4 litre	195	170
1.6 litre (non air conditioned)	180	150
1.6 litre (with air conditioning)	185	125

Throttle kicker speed:
    1.4 litre .... 1400 rpm
    1.6 litre .... 1300 rpm

Torque wrench settings

	Nm	lbf ft
Fuel pump	16 to 20	11 to 14
Inlet manifold	16 to 20	11 to 14
Exhaust manifold	21 to 25	16 to 18
Exhaust manifold heat shield	14 to 19	10 to 14
Exhaust system 'U'bolt clamps	35 to 40	26 to 30
Exhaust pipe to manifold	35 to 40	25 to 29

Part B: Fuel injection systems
Application/identification:
    1.4 litre .... Weber EEC IV Central Fuel injection (CFi)
    1.6 litre LJE engine .... Electronic Fuel injection (EFi)
    1.6 litre LJF engine... Electronic Fuel injection (EFi), with regulated catalytic converter

Weber EEC IV CFi system
Basic idle speed .... 750 ± 50 rpm
Fuel pump type .... Ford or Bosch 'in-tank', electronic roller cell
Output pressure (minimum) .... 3 bars at 12 volts
Pressure regulator type... Diaphragm
Regulated pressure .... 1 bar

Weber EEC IV EFi system
Basic idle speed (idle speed control valve detached)................................... 750 ± 50 rpm
Injectors .... Weber, electronically operated
Fuel pump .... Ford electric, 'in-tank'
Output pressure (minimum) .... 3 bars at 12 volts
Pressure regulator .... Weber

Weber EEC IV EFi system (continued)

Control pressure:

Engine running	2.3 to 2.5 bars	
Engine stopped	3.0 ± 0.1 bars	

Torque wrench settings

	Nm	lbf ft
Weber CFi system:		
CFi unit (to manifold)..	12 to 15	9 to 11
Air charge temperature sensor	20 to 25	15 to 18
Inlet manifold..	16 to 20	12 to 14
Exhaust manifold...	14 to 17	10 to 12
Exhaust heat shield	14 to 19	10 to 14
Exhaust pipe to manifold...	35 to 40	26 to 29
HEGO sensor	50 to 70	37 to 52
Weber EFi system:		
Idle speed control valve unit.......................................	3.5 to 5.0	2.6 to 3.6
Fuel pressure regulator	8 to 12	6 to 8
Fuel rail bolts...	21 to 25	16 to 18
Air charge temperature sensor	20 to 25	15 to 18
Fuel filter unions...	14 to 20	11 to 14
Inlet manifold	16 to 20	12 to 14
Inlet manifold upper to lower section nuts	16 to 20	12 to 14
Exhaust manifold...	14 to 17	10 to 12
Exhaust pipe to manifold...	35 to 40	26 to 29
Exhaust heat shield	14 to 19	10 to 14
Exhaust system 'U'bolt clamps....................................	35 to 40	26 to 29

Part A: Carburettor system

1 General description and precautions

General description

The fuel system on all models with carburettor induction comprises a rear-mounted fuel tank, a mechanical diaphragm fuel pump, a carburettor and an air cleaner.

The fuel tank is mounted at the rear, under the floor pan behind the rear seats. The tank has a 'ventilation to atmosphere system' through a combined roll-over/anti-trickle fill valve assembly, located in the left-hand rear wheel arch. A filler neck sensing pipe, integral with the fuel tank filler pipe will shut off the fuel pump filler gun when the predetermined maximum level of fuel is reached in the tank, so preventing spillage and wastage. A conventional fuel level sender unit is mounted in the top face of the fuel tank.

One of two fuel pump types will be fitted, depending on the engine type. On HCS (OHV) engines, the fuel pump is operated by a pivoting rocker arm; one end rests on an eccentric lobe on the engine camshaft and the other end is attached to the fuel pump diaphragm. The pump fitted to the CVH (OHC) engine is operated by a separate pushrod, one end rests on an eccentric lobe on the engine camshaft and the other rests on the pump actuating rod which operates the diaphragm. Both types of mechanical pump incorporate a nylon filter and are of the sealed unit type (they cannot be serviced or overhauled).

A twin venturi Weber carburettor is fitted, further details being given in Section 12 or 18 of this Chapter.

The air cleaner unit incorporates a 'waxstat' controlled air intake, supplying either hot air from a heat box mounted around the exhaust manifold, or cool air from a duct in the front of the vehicle.

Precautions

Warning: *Many of the procedures in this manual entail disconnecting the fuel pipes and connections which usually results in fuel spillage. Before carrying out any operation on the fuel system, first refer to the precautions given in Safety First! at the start of this manual and follow them implicitly. Petrol is a highly volatile and dangerous liquid and the precautions necessary when handling it cannot be overstressed.*

Reference must also be made to Chapter 5, Section 2 for precautionary notes concerning the ignition system, to Chapter 12, Section 2 for general notes concerning the electrical system, and any further safety-related text contained within the appropriate Section, before working on the vehicle. When disconnecting the automatic choke or other coolant hoses, ensure that the cooling system is not pressurised (refer to Chapter 2). *Do not work on or near a hot cooling system.*

Certain adjustment points in the fuel system are protected by tamperproof caps, plugs or seals. In some territories, it is an offence to drive a vehicle with broken or missing tamperproof seals. Before disturbing a tamperproof seal, first check that no local or national laws will be broken by doing so, and fit a new tamperproof seal after adjustment is complete, where required by law. Do not break tamperproof seals on any vehicle whilst it is still under warranty.

When working on fuel system components, scrupulous cleanliness must be observed and care must be taken not to introduce any foreign matter into the fuel lines or components. Carburettors in particular are delicate instruments and care must be taken not to disturb any components unnecessarily. Before attempting work on a carburettor, ensure that the relevant spares are available; it should be noted that a complete strip down of a carburettor is unlikely to cure a fault which is not immediately obvious, without introducing new problems. If persistent problems occur, it is recommended that the services of a Ford dealer or a carburettor specialist is sought. Most dealers will be able to provide carburettor rejetting and servicing facilities. Where necessary, it may be possible to purchase a reconditioned carburettor.

2 Air cleaner unit – removal and refitting

Note: *Air cleaner element renewal and air cleaner temperature control system checks are described in Chapter 1.*

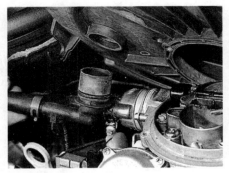

2.4A Disconnecting the oil separator/crankcase ventilation hose from the air cleaner (CVH engine)

2.4B Disconnecting the vacuum hose from the inlet manifold (CVH engine)

2.4C Disconnecting the ACT connector (CVH engine)

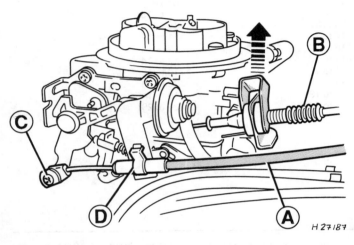

Fig. 4.1 Cable connections to the carburettor on the HCS engine (Sec 3)

A   *Choke cable*
B   *Accelerator cable*
C   *Choke cable inner cable connection*
D   *Choke cable support bracket connection*

3.2 Disconnecting the accelerator cable from the pedal

3.4 Accelerator inner (A) and outer (B) cable connection to the CVH (carburettor) engine

Removal

1   Disconnect the battery earth lead.
2   On CVH engine models, pull free and release the accelerator cable from the locating clip on the side of the air cleaner unit.
3   Undo the three retaining bolts and partially lift the air cleaner unit from the carburettor so that the hose and wiring connections to the underside of the air cleaner body are accessible.
4   Note their connections and routings, then detach the wiring and hoses from the underside of the air cleaner unit. On the CVH engine also disconnect the vacuum hose from the inlet manifold (photos).
5   Lift the air cleaner unit clear from the carburettor.
6   If required, the air charge temperature (ACT) sensor can be unscrewed and removed from the base of the air cleaner unit.

Refitting

7   Refit in the reverse order of removal. Renew any hoses that are perished or cracked and ensure that all fittings are securely and correctly reconnected.

3   Accelerator cable (manual transmission) – removal, refitting and adjustment

Removal

1   Disconnect the battery earth lead.
2   Working inside the vehicle, disconnect the cable from the top of the accelerator pedal, release the grommet and pull the cable free from the pedal (photo). Withdraw the cable through the engine side of the bulkhead.
3   Refer to Section 2 and remove the air cleaner unit.
4   Detach the inner cable from the carburettor linkage (photo).
5   Prise free the retaining clip, detach the outer cable from the support bracket and remove the cable.

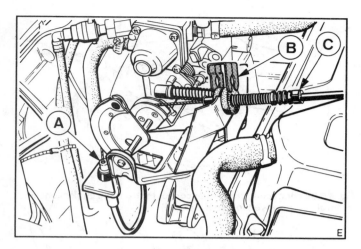

Fig. 4.2 Cam plate cable connections to the carburettor – CTX automatic transmission models (Sec 4)

A Cam plate cable
B Clip
C Cable adjuster sleeve

Refitting and adjustment

6 To refit the cable, feed the inner cable through the bulkhead and reconnect the inner cable to the accelerator pedal.
7 Locate the grommet in the bulkhead, then push the outer cable into it to secure it in the bulkhead.
8 Lubricate the cable grommet at the carburettor end with a mild soapy solution, then reconnect the cable to the carburettor. Locate the outer cable by pulling it towards the rocker cover.
9 Have an assistant depress the accelerator pedal fully and hold it in this position. The outer cable should be seen to move in its grommet. Refit the securing clip to the bracket, then release the accelerator pedal.
10 Depress the accelerator pedal then release it and check that the throttle opens and shuts fully. Further adjust if necessary before refitting the air cleaner unit and reconnecting the battery.

4 Accelerator (cam plate) cable (CTX automatic transmission) – adjustment

1 The cable from the accelerator pedal leads to a cam plate linkage mechanism bolted to the transmission. This mechanism actuates the transmission throttle valve via a throttle valve cable and also cam plate cable connected between the cam plate and the accelerator linkage at the carburettor.
2 As all three cables have to be adjusted at the same time and access to the Ford special tool is required, it is recommended that a Ford dealer be entrusted with the cable adjustments and/or renewal.
3 Where required, the cam cable can be detached and adjusted at the carburettor end as follows
4 First refer to Section 2 and remove the air cleaner unit.
5 Manually open the accelerator linkage to release the tension on the inner cable and release it from the accelerator quadrant.
6 Note the set position of the outer cable in its adjustment/location bracket, then prise up and release the securing clip to detach the cable and adjuster sleeve from the bracket.
7 Reconnection of the cable to the carburettor is a reversal of the above procedure. Ensure that the cable is correctly positioned in the location/adjuster bracket as noted during removal. Prior to refitting the air cleaner unit, check that the cam cable operates in a satisfactory manner and the throttle fully opens and closes.
8 If the cable is in need of adjustment, release the cable by pressing the orange (or red) button on the cable auto adjuster mechanism. As the cable is released, it will be heard to click.
9 Adjust the cable by moving the rear of the cable cam and turning the throttle to the fully open position. The cable will automatically adjust as

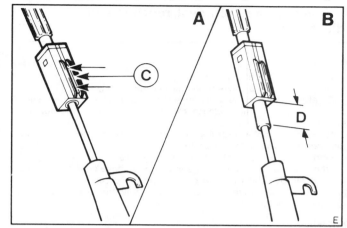

Fig. 4.3 Cam plate cable release showing cable taut (A) and released (B). Also shown are the release button (C) and 20 mm pre-adjustment/10 mm post-adjustment minimum protrusion (D) (Sec 4)

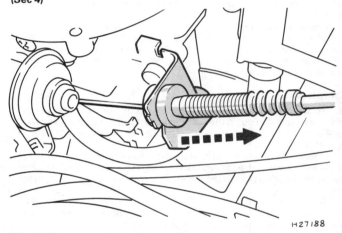

Fig. 4.4 Outer cam plate cable position in support/adjustment bracket prior to adjusting (Sec 4)

required and the adjuster will be heard to click as it makes the adjustment.
10 Release the cable cam then remove the clip from the cable. Pull the outer cable in the direction of the rocker cover to position it as shown in Fig. 4.4. Lubricate the location grommet with a soapy solution to assist.
11 Have an assistant to fully depress the accelerator cable, then refit the clip to the grommet. Release the pedal then actuate the throttle to ensure that it fully opens and closes.
12 Refit the air cleaner as described in Section 2 and reconnect the battery earth lead.

5 Accelerator pedal – removal and refitting

Removal

1 Disconnect the battery earth lead.
2 Peel back the carpet and insulation from the driver's footwell to allow access to the accelerator pedal.
3 Detach the accelerator cable from the pedal (see Sec 3 or 4), then release the circlip from the pivot shaft and remove the accelerator pedal.

Refitting

4 Refit in the reverse order of removal. On completion, check the action of the pedal and the cable to ensure that the throttle has full unrestricted movement and fully returns when released.
5 Reconnect the battery earth lead.

6   Choke cable – removal, refitting and adjustment

Removal

1   Disconnect the battery earth lead.
2   Refer to Section 2 and remove the air cleaner unit.
3   Carefully prise free the choke inner cable from its linkage connection on the carburettor, then release the outer cable from the support bracket.
4   Release the choke control knob from the cable by depressing the retaining pin on the underside of the knob.
5   Undo the choke control-to-trim retaining collar.
6   Undo and remove the screw securing the choke control recessed trim and remove the trim and cable control. Detach the 'choke on' warning light lead from the control, then withdraw the choke cable from the facia trim (passing it through the bulkhead).

Refitting

7   To refit the cable, first pass it through the bulkhead and trim panel, then refit the retaining collar and attach the wiring connector. Fit the trim recess to the main trim panel and tighten the retaining screw to secure. Push the knob into position on the choke cable control so that it is felt to lock into engagement.
8   Reconnect the inner choke cable to the carburettor linkage.
9   Pull the choke control knob fully out (to the full on position). Return to the carburettor end and move the choke lever by hand to its full on position and hold there whilst simultaneously reconnecting the outer cable to its support bracket.

Adjustment

10   To check that the choke cable is correctly adjusted, the control knob must be pulled out in the full on position and the choke lever, (A in Fig. 4.6) must be in contact with its stop (B). Adjust as required if necessary.
11   Press the choke knob fully in (to the off position), then check that the choke linkage at the carburettor has fully returned to its off position and the choke valve plate in the carburettor is at a right angle (90°) to the venturi.
12   Refit the air cleaner.
13   Reconnect the battery, turn the ignition on, operate the choke and check that the choke warning light operates correctly.

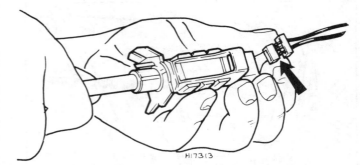

Fig. 4.5 Disconnecting the wiring connector from the choke control (control unit removed for clarity) (Sec 6)

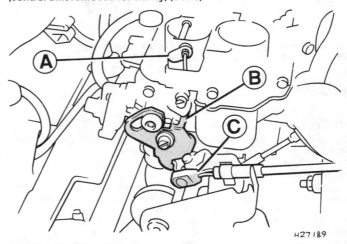

Fig. 4.6 Choke cable adjustment (Sec 6)

A   Choke lever   C   Cable in 'full on' position
B   Full choke stop

7   Fuel pump – testing, removal and refitting

Note: *Refer to the precautionary notes in Section 1 before proceeding.*

Testing

1   Access to the fuel pump on HCS (OHV) engine models is best gained from underneath the vehicle (photos). Raise and support it on axle stands at the front end.
2   The fuel pump may be tested by disconnecting the fuel feed pipe from the carburettor and placing its open end in a suitable container.
3   Detach the multi-plug from the DIS ignition coil, or the LT lead from the negative terminal of the ignition coil to prevent the engine from firing.
4   Actuate the starter motor. If the fuel pump is in good working order, regular well-defined spurts of fuel should eject from the open end of the disconnected fuel pipe.
5   If this does not occur, and there is fuel in the tank, the pump is defective and must be renewed. The fuel pump is a sealed unit and cannot be repaired.

7.1A Underside view of the fuel pump fitted to an HCS (OHV) engine

7.1B Fuel pump location on the CVH (OHC) engine

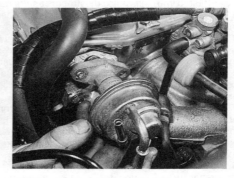

7.10 Fuel pump removal from the CVH engine

Removal

6   Two types of mechanical fuel pump are fitted, the application depending on the engine type. Some models may also be fitted with a fuel vapour separator and if this is removed, its pipes should be labelled to avoid the possibility of confusion and incorrect attachment on refitting.
7   To remove the fuel pump, first disconnect the battery earth lead.
8   Where applicable, remove the air cleaner to improve access to the fuel pump (see Sec 2).
9   Disconnect the fuel pipes from the fuel pump, noting their respective connections for refitting. Plug the hoses to prevent the ingress of dirt and fuel spillage.
10   Unscrew and remove the retaining bolts or nuts (as applicable) and remove the fuel pump (photo).
11   Recover the gasket/spacer and if required, withdraw the pump operating pushrod (CVH engine only) (photo).
12   Thoroughly clean the mating faces on the pump and engine.

Refitting

13   Refit in the reverse order of removal. Be sure to use a new gasket and tighten the securing bolts/nuts to the specified torque wrench setting. Ensure that the hoses are correctly and securely reconnected. If they were originally secured with crimped type hose clips, discard them and fit screw clamp type clips.
14   When the engine is restarted, check the pump connections for any signs of fuel leaks.

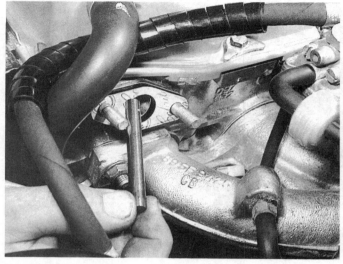

7.11 Withdrawing the fuel pump pushrod from the CVH engine

8   Fuel tank – removal, inspection and refitting

Note: *Refer to the precautionary notes in Section 1 before proceeding.*

Removal

1   Run the fuel level as low as possible prior to removing the tank.
2   Disconnect the battery earth lead.
3   Remove the fuel filler cap then syphon or pump out the remaining fuel from the fuel tank (there is no drain plug). The fuel must be emptied into a suitable container for storage.
4   Raise and support the vehicle on axle stands at the rear.
5   Disconnect the fuel filler pipe from the fuel tank (photo). Drain any remaining fuel into the container for safe storage and plug the hose and tank connections. Disconnect the handbrake cable locating strap from the fuel filler pipe on the tank.
6   Disconnect the filler neck pipe sensing hose from the rear of the tank (photo).
7   Support the underside of the fuel tank to hold it in position, then remove the four retaining bolts from the positions indicated in Fig. 4.7 (photo).
8   Partially lower the fuel tank and detach the ventilation tube from the tank top surface. Also disconnect the fuel tank sender unit wiring multi-plug and hoses.
9   Slowly lower the tank and as it is withdrawn detach the filler pipe.

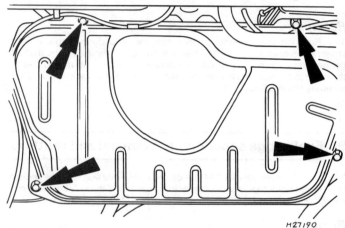

Fig. 4.7 Fuel tank retaining bolt locations (arrowed) (Sec 8)

Inspection

10   Whilst removed, the fuel tank can be inspected for damage or corrosion. Removal of the sender unit (see Sec 9) will allow a partial inspection of the interior. If the tank is contaminated with sediment or water, swill it out with clean petrol. Do not under any circumstances undertake any repairs on a leaking or damaged fuel tank – this must be entrusted to a specialist. The only alternative is to renew the fuel tank.
11   Check the condition of the filler pipe seal in the fuel tank and renew it if necessary.

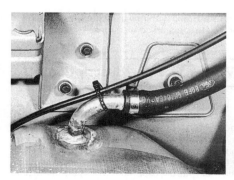

8.5 Fuel filler pipe connection to the fuel tank. Note the handbrake cable locating strap

8.6 Fuel tank sensing hose-to-pipe connection (arrowed)

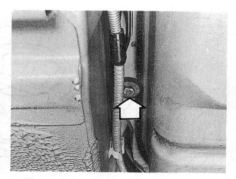

8.7 Fuel tank securing bolt at the front edge

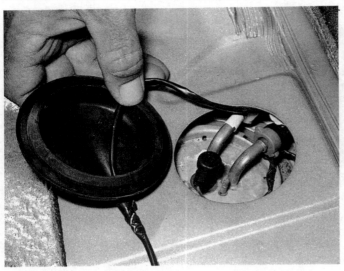

9.1 Fuel level sender unit and connections – carburettor model

10.3 Roll-over valve location on fuel filler pipe

Refitting

12   Refitting is a reversal of the removal procedure. Apply a light smear of grease to the filler pipe seal to ease fitting. Ensure that all connections are securely fitted. If evidence of contamination was found, do not return any previously removed fuel to the tank unless it is carefully filtered first.

9   Fuel gauge sender unit – removal and refitting

Note: *Ford Special tool 23-014 is required to remove and refit the sender unit. Unless this tool is available or a similar tool can be fabricated, the sender removal and refitting must be entrusted to a Ford dealer.*

Removal

1   The fuel tank sender unit is located in the top of the tank and access to the sender unit connections can be made by first removing the rear seat, then prising free the rubber grommet from the floor pan (photo).
2   Engage the special tool into the sender unit then carefully turn the sender unit and release it from the tank.

Refitting

3   Refit the sender unit in the reverse order of removal. Be sure to fit a new seal and lubricate it with a smear of grease to prevent it from distorting when fitting the sender unit.

H27191

Fig. 4.8 Sender unit removal from the fuel tank using special tool No 23-014 (Sec 9)

10   Roll-over valve – removal and refitting

Removal

1   Detach the battery earth lead.
2   Raise and support the vehicle at the rear on axle stands. Remove the rear wheel on the fuel filler cap side to improve the access under the wheel arch.
3   Undo the retaining screw, withdraw the roll-over valve from the filler pipe, detach the vent hoses and remove the valve (photo).

Refitting

4   Refit in the reverse order of removal.

11   Fuel tank filler pipe – removal and refitting

Note: *Refer to the precautionary notes in Section 1 before proceeding.*

Removal

1   Refer to Section 8 and remove the fuel tank.
2   Detach the roll-over valve clamp and undo the filler pipe securing screws and then lower the pipe from the vehicle.

Refitting

3   Refit in the reverse order of removal. Lubricate the filler pipe seal to ease assembly prior to fitting. When reconnecting the quick fit connectors, ensure that they are pushed fully onto the pipe (up the bead).
4   When the fuel tank is refitted, refill with fuel and check for any signs of leaks from the filler pipe and associated connections.

12   Carburettor (Weber TLDM) – description

The carburettor is of twin venturi, downdraught type, featuring a fixed size main jet system, adjustable idle system, a mechanically-operated accelerator pump and a vacuum-operated power valve. A manually-operated cold start choke is fitted and a throttle kicker is utilized on some models.
In order to comply with emission control regulations and maintain good fuel consumption, the main jets are calibrated to suit the 1/4 to 3/4 throttle range. The power valve is therefore only used to supply additional fuel during full throttle conditions.
The accelerator pump is fitted to ensure a smooth transmission from the idle circuit to the main jet system. As the accelerator pedal is

Fig. 4.9 Exploded view of the Weber TLDM carburettor (Sec 12)

A   Anti-dieselling (fuel cut-off) valve
B   Emulsion tubes
C   Air correction jets
D   Choke pull-down diaphragm unit
E   Manual choke linkage
F   Needle valve
G   Float
H   Fast idle adjustment screw
J   Idle speed adjustment screw
K   Fuel mixture adjustment screw
L   Throttle plates
M   Power valve unit
N   Accelerator pump unit
P   Throttle kicker (where fitted)
Q   Upper body gasket
R   Main jets

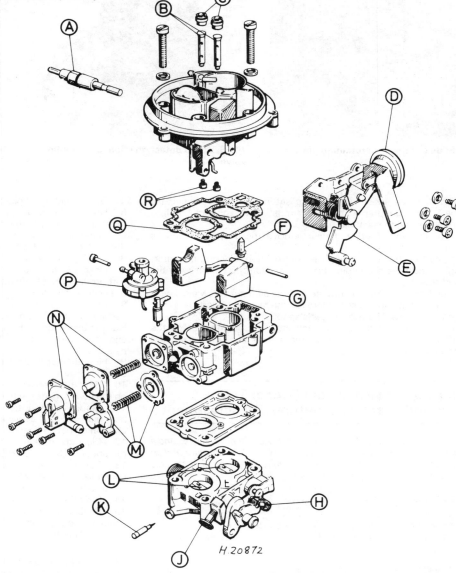

depressed, a linkage moves the diaphragm within the accelerator pump and a small quantity of fuel is injected into the venturi, to prevent a momentary weak mixture and resultant engine hesitation.

The manually operated choke features a vacuum operated pull-down mechanism which controls the single choke plate under certain vacuum conditions.

The throttle kicker (where fitted) functions with the ACT sensor and acts as an idle speed compensator, which operates when required under certain operating conditions.

An anti-dieselling (fuel cut-off) valve is fitted to prevent the possibility of the engine running on after the ignition is switched off.

Adjustment procedures are described in Chapter 1, but it is important to note that accurate adjustments can only be made using the necessary equipment.

13 Carburettor (Weber TLDM) – fast idle adjustment

Note: *Before carrying out any carburettor adjustments, ensure that the spark plug gaps are set as specified and that all electrical and vacuum connections are secure. To carry out checks and adjustments, an accurate tachometer and an exhaust gas analyzer (CO meter) will be required.*

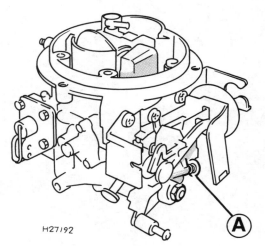

Fig. 4.10 Fast idle adjuster screw location (A) in the Weber TLDM carburettor (Sec 13)

14.6A Slide out the float retaining pin ...

14.6B ... then detach the float and needle valve

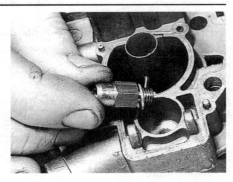

14.7 Remove the needle valve housing and its washer

1   Check the idle speed and mixture settings are as specified (as described in Chapter 1). These must be correct before checking/adjusting the fast idle speed.
2   Switch the engine off and then remove the air cleaner unit as described in Section 2.
3   Actuate the choke by pulling the control knob fully out, then start the engine and note the engine fast idle speed. Compare it with the specified speed.
4   If adjustment is required, turn the fast idle adjuster screw clockwise to decrease, or anti-clockwise to increase, the fast idle speed.
5   Recheck the fast idle and basic idle speeds.
6   On completion of the adjustment, stop the engine, detach the tachometer and CO meter, reconnect the radiator cooling fan lead and refit the air cleaner.

14   Needle valve and float (Weber TLDM carburettor) – removal, refitting and adjustment

Note: *Refer to Section 1 before proceeding. Note that new gaskets and a washer (seal) will be required when reassembling. A tachometer and an exhaust gas analyzer (CO meter) will also be required to check the idle speed and mixture settings on completion.*

Removal and refitting

1   Disconnect the battery earth lead.
2   Remove the air cleaner unit as described in Section 2.
3   Clean the exterior of the carburettor, then disconnect the fuel supply hose.

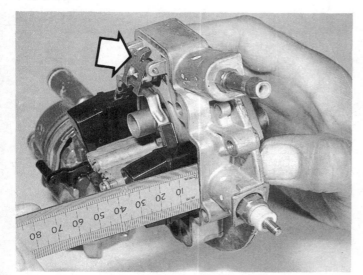

14.17 Measuring the float level adjustment (TLD carburettor shown) – adjustment tag arrowed

4   Disconnect the choke control cable.
5   Undo and remove the six retaining screws (four of which are Torx type) and carefully lift the carburettor upper body clear.
6   Invert and support the upper body of the carburettor for access to the float and pivot. Lightly tap out the float pivot pin then withdraw the float, taking care not to distort the arms of the float (photos).
7   Unscrew the needle valve housing and extract it from the carburettor upper body (photo). Collect the washer from the threads of the needle valve housing.
8   Clean and inspect the components for signs of damage or wear, particularly the pivot holes in the float arm. Check the float for signs of leakage by shaking it to see if it contains fuel. Clean the float chamber and jets (refer to Sec 17 for details). Renew any components as necessary.
9   Fit a new washer over the needle valve housing threads and then carefully screw the valve unit into position in the upper body.
10   Refit the needle valve, float and retaining pin, ensuring that the tag on the float engages with the ball and clip of the needle valve.
11   Before refitting the upper body to the carburettor, check and if necessary adjust the float level as described in paragraphs 16 to 18. Also check the float and needle valve for free movement.
12   Clean the gasket contact faces, then locate a new gasket and refit the upper body to the carburettor.
13   Reconnect the fuel supply hose and the choke cable. Adjust the choke cable as described in Section 6. If the fuel hose was originally secured with a crimped type clip, discard it and fit a screw clamp type.
14   Refit the air cleaner unit as described in Section 2.
15   Reconnect the battery earth lead, then restart the engine and check the idle speed and mixture settings and adjust if necessary as described in Chapter 1.

Float level adjustment

16   With the carburettor upper body removed as described in paragraphs 1 to 5 inclusive, proceed as follows.
17   Support the carburettor upper body vertically, ensuring that the needle valve is shut off. Locate the new upper body gasket to the carburettor upper body, then measure the distance between the gasket and the step on the float (photo).
18   If the measurement is not as specified, adjust the setting by carefully bending the tag on the float as required, then recheck.
19   Refitting should be carried out in accordance with paragraphs 12 to 15 inclusive.

15   Throttle kicker unit (Weber TLDM carburettor) – removal, refitting and adjustment

Note: *A tachometer and exhaust gas analyzer (CO meter) will be required to check and make any adjustment necessary.*

Removal and refitting

1   Disconnect the battery earth lead.

2   Disconnect the ACT multi-plug.
3   Refer to Section 2 and remove the air cleaner unit.
4   Detach the vacuum hose from the kicker unit. Undo the two retaining screws, detach the linkage and remove the kicker unit.
5   Refitting the kicker unit is a reversal of the removal procedure. If the unit is to be checked for adjustment, loosely locate the air cleaner unit, reconnect the ACT plug and the battery earth lead, then proceed as follows.

Adjustment

6   Start and run the engine up to its normal operating temperature (at which point the cooling fan will start to operate) then switch the engine off.
7   Loosen off the air cleaner (if not already loose), and detach the wiring connector of the cooling fan thermostatic switch. Bridge the terminals in the connector with a suitable piece of wire to actuate the cooling fan and keep it running. Start the engine and run it at 3000 rpm for 30 seconds to stabilise it, then release the throttle and check (and if necessary adjust) the idle speed and mixture setting as described in Chapter 1. Stop the engine.
8   Remove the air cleaner unit, then detach the vacuum hose between the throttle kicker and the inlet manifold at source (but not the vacuum supply to the ignition module). Connect a new length of vacuum hose direct between the manifold and the kicker unit.
9   Restart the engine and check the engine speed. The throttle kicker should increase the engine speed above its normal idle. Check the speed registered against the specified throttle kicker operating speed.
10   If required, the throttle kicker speed can be adjusted by prising free the tamperproof plug (A in Fig. 4.11) and the adjustment screw turned as necessary.
11   When the adjustment is complete, stop the engine, fit a new tamperproof plug, disconnect the temporary vacuum hose (between the manifold and the kicker unit) and reconnect the original hose (between the carburettor and the kicker unit).
12   Reconnect the cooling fan thermostatic switch plug, refit and secure the air cleaner unit and disconnect the tachometer and CO meter to complete.

16   Carburettor (Weber TLDM) – removal and refitting

Note: *Refer to the precautionary notes in Section 1 before proceeding. Note that new gaskets will be required on refitting and a tachometer and an exhaust gas analyzer will be required on completion.*

Removal

1   Disconnect the battery earth lead.
2   Remove the air cleaner unit as described in Section 2.
3   Disconnect the accelerator cable from the carburettor (Section 3 or 4 according to type).
4   Disconnect the choke cable from the carburettor (Section 6).
5   Disconnect the fuel hose from the carburettor and plug its end to

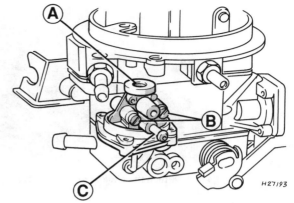

Fig. 4.11 Throttle kicker unit showing adjustment point (A), unit retaining screws (B) and vacuum take-off (C) (Sec 15)

prevent fuel spillage and the ingress of dirt. If a crimped type hose clip is fitted, cut it free but take care not to damage the hose. Crimped clips must be discarded and replaced with screw clamp type clips during refitting.
6   Disconnect the wiring from the anti-dieselling (fuel cut-off) valve.
7   Unscrew and remove the four carburettor-to-manifold retaining Torx head screws then carefully lift the carburettor from the manifold.

Refitting

8   Clean the carburettor and manifold gasket mating faces.
9   Refit in the reverse order of removal. Fit a new gasket and tighten the retaining screws securely. Ensure that the fuel supply hose connection to the carburettor is securely fitted and a new screw clamp retaining clip fitted to replace the original crimped type clip (where applicable).
10   Reconnect the accelerator cable and adjust it as described in Section 3 or 4 as applicable.
11   Reconnect the choke cable and adjust it as described in Section 6.
12   Refer to Section 2 and refit the air cleaner.
13   When the battery is reconnected, start the engine and check the idle speed and mixture settings as described in Chapter 1.

17   Carburettor (Weber TLDM) – dismantling, cleaning, inspection and reassembly

Note: *Check parts availability before dismantling. If possible, obtain an overhaul kit containing all the relevant gaskets, seals, etc, required for reassembly prior to dismantling the carburettor.*

Dismantling

1   With the carburettor removed from the vehicle, prepare a clean, flat work surface prior to commencing dismantling. The following procedures may be used for partial or complete dismantling as required.

17.3A Undo the retaining screws ...

17.3B ... and remove the carburettor upper body

17.5 Extracting the anti-dieselling (fuel cut-off) valve

17.6A Detach the choke plate operating link ...

17.6B ... and undo the three retaining screws (arrowed) to detach the mechanism

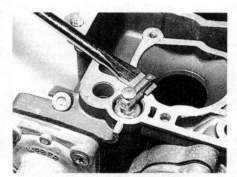

17.11 Carefully prise out the accelerator pump discharge tube assembly

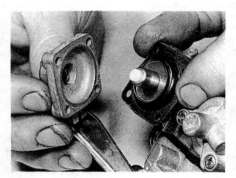

17.12A Remove the cover from the accelerator pump cover ...

17.12B ... followed by the diaphragm ...

17.12C ... and the return spring and valve unit

17.13A Undo the power valve assembly securing screws ...

17.13B ... then detach the cover, return spring and diaphragm

2   Clean the exterior of the carburettor, then unscrew and remove the anti-dieselling (fuel cut-off) valve from the upper body, but ensure that the seal washer is removed together with the valve.
3   Undo the two retaining screws and lift the upper carburettor body from the lower section (photos).
4   Remove the float and needle valve unit from the carburettor upper body as described in Section 14.
5   Unscrew and remove the anti-dieselling (fuel cut-off) valve (photo).
6   Undo the three screws securing the choke mechanism and detach it (photos).
7   Unscrew and remove the two air correction jets from the underside of the upper body. Note the size and location of each to ensure correct refitting.
8   Invert the upper body so that the emulsion tubes can fall out of their apertures (above the air correction jets). Remove the emulsion tubes from their locations, again having noted the size and location of each.
9   Unscrew and remove the main jets, again having noted their fitted positions.
10   Dismantle the carburettor lower (main) body as follows.

11   Prise free the accelerator pump discharge tube, but take care not to damage it or the carburettor body (photo).
12   Undo the four screws securing the accelerator pump unit and remove the cover followed by the diaphragm and return spring. The valve unit should come out on the end of the return spring (photos). Check that the valve is complete and with its O-ring seal (where applicable).
13   Undo the three retaining screws and remove the power valve unit. Remove the cover and return spring followed by the diaphragm (photos).
14   Where fitted, undo the retaining screws and remove the throttle kicker unit from the lower (main) body.
15   Prise free and remove the tamperproof seal, then unscrew and remove the fuel mixture screw (photo).
16   Undo the retaining screws and remove the throttle housing from the carburettor main body (photo).

Cleaning and inspection

17   Wash the carburettor components, drillings and passages with

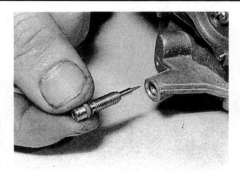

17.15 Unscrew and remove the fuel mixture screw

17.16 Separating the throttle housing from the carburettor main body

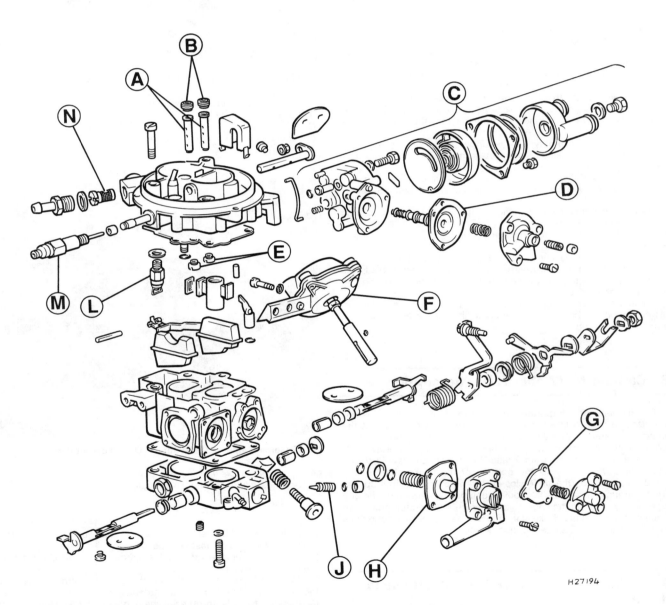

Fig. 4.12 Exploded view of the Weber TLD type carburettor as fitted to the 1.6 litre engine (Sec 18)

A   Emulsion tubes
B   Air correction jets
C   Automatic choke unit
D   Choke pull-down
    diaphragm

E   Main jets
F   Secondary barrel
    diaphragm

G   Power valve diaphragm
H   Accelerator pump
    diaphragm
J   Mixture screw

L   Needle valve
M   Anti dieselling (fuel cut-off)
    valve
N   Fuel supply filter

clean petrol then blow them dry using a low pressure air line. A high pressure air line must not be applied to the accelerator pump discharge assembly or the pump supply valve as they each contain a rubber Vernay valve and these can easily be damaged under high pressure. *Never use a piece of wire for cleaning purposes.*

18   Examine all of the carburettor components for signs of damage or wear, paying particular attention to the diaphragms, throttle spindle and plates, needle valve and mixture screw; the power valve jet is adjacent to the primary main jet. Renew all diaphragms, sealing washers and gaskets as a matter of course.

Reassembly

19   Refit the throttle housing to the carburettor main body (fitting a new gasket), and secure with its retaining screws.

20   Refit the fuel mixture screw. Make an initial adjustment by screwing it fully in (but do not overtighten or screw it onto its seat), then unscrew it two full turns.

21   Where fitted, reassemble the throttle kicker, ensuring that its diaphragm lies flat and that the relative position of the operating link to the kicker cover is correct.

22   Fit the power valve unit and ensure that its diaphragm lies flat and the vacuum gallery aligns with the diaphragm and housing.

23   Refit the accelerator pump unit. Take care not to damage the valve as it is inserted and check that the O-ring seal is correctly located on the end of the valve. Check that the valve is not trapped by the spring.

24   Refit the accelerator pump discharge jet. Take care not to damage the valve and/or the O-ring seal and ensure that they are correctly located.

25   Commence reassembly of the upper body by inserting the emulsion tubes and the air correction jets into their respective ports (as noted during removal).

26   Screw the anti-dieselling (fuel cut-off) valve into position. Ensure that the aluminium washer is fitted and take care not to overtighten the valve.

27   Refit the needle valve and the float unit and adjust the float setting as described in Section 14.

28   Refit the choke control mechanism and secure with its three retaining screws.

29   Locate a new gasket onto the mating face, then refit the carburettor upper body to the main body. As they are reassembled, take care not to snag the float on the carburettor main body. Fit and tighten the retaining screws to secure.

30   With the carburettor reassembled, refit it to the vehicle and adjust it as described in Chapter 1. Where applicable, check and adjust the throttle kicker setting.

18   Carburettor (Weber TLD) – description

1   This carburettor incorporates many of the features of the TLDM type fitted to the 1.3 litre model. The main differences are that the secondary venturi (barrel) is vacuum-operated, and that a coolant-heated automatic choke control system is fitted (photos).

2   The choke system is fully automatic. When the engine is cold, the bi-metal spring which controls the position of the choke plate is fully wound up and holds the plate closed. As the engine warms up, the bi-metal spring is heated by the coolant and begins to unwind, thereby progressively opening the choke plate. A vacuum operated pull-down mechanism controls the choke plate under certain operating conditions and an internal fast idle system is incorporated.

19   Carburettor (Weber TLD) – fast idle speed adjustment

Note: *Before carrying out any carburettor adjustments, ensure that the spark plug gaps are set as specified and that all electrical and vacuum connections are secure. To carry out checks and adjustments, an accurate tachometer and an exhaust gas analyzer (CO meter) will be required.*

1   Check that the idle speed and mixture settings are as specified (as

18.1A General view of the Weber TLD type carburettor

A   *Throttle kicker unit (not fitted on all models)*
B   *Accelerator pump*
C   *Power valve*
D   *Choke diaphragm (automatic choke)*

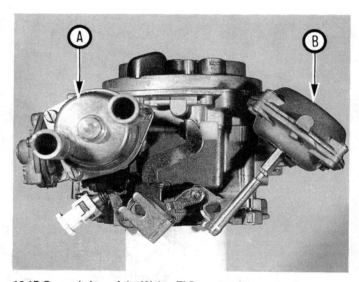

18.1B General view of the Weber TLD type carburettor

A   *Automatic choke housing*
B   *Secondary barrel vacuum diaphragm*

described in Chapter 1). These must be correct before checking/adjusting the fast idle speed.

2   Switch the engine off and then remove the air cleaner unit as described in Section 2.

3   With the engine at its normal operating temperature and a tachometer connected in accordance with the manufacturer's instructions, hold the throttle linkage partly open, then close the choke plate until the fast idle adjustment screw aligns with the 4th step on the fast idle cam (Fig. 4.13). Release the throttle linkage so that the fast idle speed adjustment screw rests on the cam. Release the choke plate. The linkage will hold it in the fast idle speed setting position.

4   Without touching the accelerator pedal, start the engine and record the fast idle speed achieved. If adjustment is required, turn the fast idle speed adjuster screw until the specified fast idle speed is obtained.

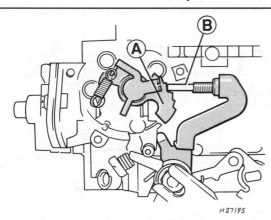

Fig. 4.13 Fast idle adjustment on the TLD carburettor showing the adjuster screw (B) on 4th step of the fast idle cam (A). Note that the housing is removed for clarity (Sec 19)

5   When the throttle linkage is opened, the choke plate should return to its fully open position. If this does not happen, either the engine is not at its normal operating temperature or the automatic choke mechanism is faulty.

6   Switch off the engine and disconnect the tachometer. Refit the air cleaner unit.

20   Needle valve and float (Weber TLD carburettor) – removal, refitting and adjustment

1   Refer to Section 14 and proceed as described except for the following difference.

2   In paragraph 4, ignore the instruction to detach the choke cable (an automatic choke is fitted to the TLD type carburettor). Instead, clamp the coolant supply and return hoses which lead to the automatic choke unit to minimise coolant loss and ensure that the cooling system is not pressurised (see Chapter 3). Identify, then detach both of the coolant hoses at the automatic choke housing (photo). Catch any coolant spillage in a suitable container.

3   On completion, reconnect the hoses to the auto-choke unit and remove the clamps from the hoses. Check and top up the coolant level on completion (see Chapter 1).

21   Automatic choke (Weber TLD carburettor) – adjustment

1   Disconnect the battery earth lead.

2   Remove the air cleaner as described in Section 2.

3   Disconnect the coolant hoses to the choke unit as described in paragraph 2 of the previous Section.

4   Note the position of the choke coil housing alignment marks, then undo the three retaining screws and withdraw the automatic choke bi-metal coil housing.

5   Remove the inner heat shield. To check and if necessary adjust the maximum vacuum choke plate pull-down, secure the choke plate lever in the closed position by fitting a rubber band, open the throttle to allow the choke plate to fully close then release the throttle.

6   Using a screwdriver as shown in Fig. 4.16, push the diaphragm open to its stop and measure the clearance between the lower edge of the choke plate and the venturi using a twist drill or other suitable gauge rod. Where the clearance is outside that specified, remove the plug from the diaphragm housing and turn the adjuster screw (now exposed) in the required direction.

7   Fit a new diaphragm housing plug and remove the rubber band.

8   Refit the heat shield so that its slotted hole engages over the choke housing peg.

20.2 Coolant hose connections to the auto-choke unit on the TLD type carburettor

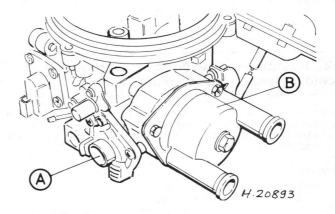

Fig. 4.14 Automatic choke unit on the Weber TLD type carburettor showing the pull-down diaphragm housing (A) and the choke bi-metal spring housing (B) (Sec 21)

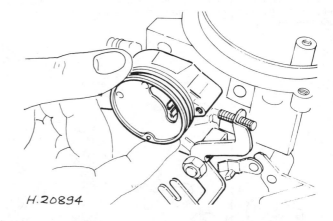

Fig. 4.15 Removing the inner heat shield from the automatic choke housing (Sec 21)

9   Refit the bi-metal coil housing by first connecting the bi-metal spring to the choke lever (ensuring correct engagement), locate the housing and hand tighten the three retaining screws. Rotate the housing to align the index line on the housing with the dot mark on the choke main body (see Fig. 4.17), then retighten the retaining screws.

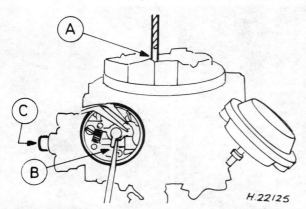

Fig. 4.16 Choke plate pull-down adjustment on the Weber TLD carburettor (Sec 21)

A   *Twist drill*
B   *Diaphragm held full open*
C   *Adjuster screw*

10   Reconnect the coolant hoses with reference to paragraph 3 in the previous Section.
11   Refit the air cleaner unit as described in Section 3.

22   Automatic choke (Weber TLD carburettor) – removal, inspection and refitting

Note: *Refer to the precautionary notes in Section 1 before proceeding. A new carburettor upper body gasket will be required when reassembling and on completion, a tachometer will be required to check the fast idle speed adjustment.*

Removal

1   Disconnect the battery earth lead.
2   Remove the air filter unit as described in Section 2.
3   To prevent excess coolant loss, clamp the coolant supply and return hoses to the automatic choke unit and ensure that the cooling system is not pressurised (see Chapter 3). Identify, then detach both of the coolant hoses at the automatic choke housing. Catch any coolant spillage in a suitable container.
4   Detach the fuel pipe and the anti-dieselling (fuel cut-off) valve. A crimped type hose clip must be replaced with a screw clamp type clip during reassembly.

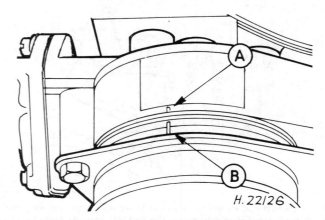

Fig. 4.17 Index marks on the automatic choke housing (B) and body (A) to be in alignment (Sec 21)

5   Unscrew and remove the retaining screws (two conventional and four Torx type) then lift the carburettor upper body clear and remove it.
6   Note the position of the choke housing alignment marks, then undo the three retaining screws and remove the choke bi-metal coil unit. Remove the internal heat shield.
7   To remove the automatic choke unit, undo the three retaining screws and detach the choke link from the operating lever.
8   Undo the three retaining screws to remove the vacuum diaphragm unit.
9   If dismantling the choke mechanism any further, note the component fitment as an aid to reassembly but do not detach the choke spindle.

Inspection

10   Clean and inspect all components for wear, damage and/or distortion. Pay particular attention to the condition of the vacuum (pull-down) diaphragm and the choke housing O-ring. Renew any items that are defective (or suspect).

Refitting

11   Reassemble the automatic choke mechanism making references to the notes taken during dismantling and to Fig. 4.18. Note that no lubricants must be used.
12   Refit the vacuum unit, making reference to the notes taken during dismantling. Ensure that the diaphragm is lying flat before tightening the housing retaining screws.
13   Locate the O-ring (ensuring that it is correctly seated), then

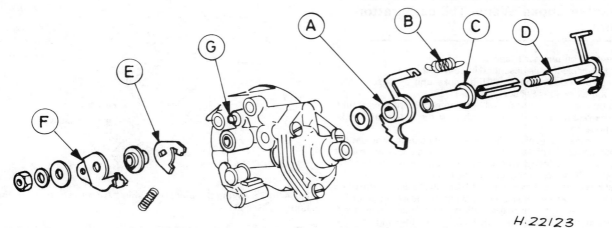

Fig. 4.18 Automatic choke unit and associated components on the Weber TLD carburettor (Sec 22)

A   *Operating link/fast idle cam*
B   *Fast idle cam return spring*
C   *Spindle*
D   *Connecting rod and lever assembly*
E   *Pull-down link*
F   *Actuating lever*
G   *Automatic choke housing*

reconnect the choke link. Refit the automatic choke unit and secure with the retaining screws. Check and adjust the maximum vacuum choke plate pull-down as described in the previous Section (paragraphs 5 and 6).

14   Refit the inner heat shield ensuring that the location peg is securely engaged in its notch.

15   Refit the automatic choke housing and the bi-metal spring unit as described in the previous Section (paragraph 9).

16   Refit the carburettor upper body unit ensuring that a new gasket is used and that the mating surfaces are clean. Fit the retaining screws to secure.

17   Reconnect the fuel hose to the carburettor, using new screw type hose clips to secure (in place of the crimped type where necessary).

18   Reconnect the anti-dieselling (fuel cut-off) valve.

19   Reconnect the coolant hoses to the automatic choke unit, then check and if necessary, top up the cooling system as described in Chapter 1.

20   Reconnect the battery earth lead, then check and adjust the fast idle speed as described in Section 19.

21   Refit the air cleaner unit (Sec 2).

23 Carburettor (Weber TLD) – removal and refitting

Note: *Refer to the precautionary notes in Section 1 before proceeding. Note that a new gasket will be required when refitting the carburettor. When the carburettor is refitted, a tachometer and an exhaust gas analyzer will be required to check the idle speed and fuel mixture settings.*

Removal

1   Disconnect the battery earth lead.

2   Remove the air cleaner unit as described in Section 2.

3   Release any pressure remaining in the cooling system (see Chapter 3) and then detach the two coolant hoses from the automatic

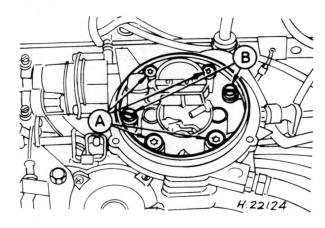

Fig. 4.19 Weber TLD carburettor showing the four Torx type retaining screws (A). The two conventional screws (B) secure the upper and lower carburettor body sections together (Sec 23)

choke unit. Catch coolant spillage in a suitable container. Identify each hose for subsequent refitting then plug their ends or position them as high as possible to prevent coolant leakage.

4   Disconnect the accelerator cable from the linkage at the carburettor as described in Sec 3 or 4 (as appropriate).

5   Detach the electrical lead from the anti-dieselling (fuel cut-off) solenoid (photo). Where applicable, also detach the idle speed control motor multi-plug and the throttle position sensor wiring multi-plug.

6   Detach the fuel feed hose at the carburettor (photo). As it is detached, plug the end of the hose to prevent excessive fuel spillage and the ingress of dirt. Where a crimped type hose clip is fitted, cut it free taking care not to damage the hose; a new screw clamp type clip will need to be obtained to replace the crimped clip during reassembly.

7   Disconnect the relevant vacuum pipes from the carburettor (photo).

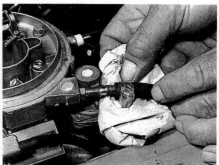

23.4 Disconnecting the lead from the anti-dieselling (fuel-cut off) valve

23.5 Disconnecting the fuel line at the carburettor

23.6 Disconnecting the vacuum hose from the secondary barrel diaphragm unit

23.7A Undo the retaining screws ...

23.7B ... and lift the carburettor from the manifold

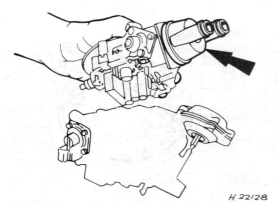

Fig. 4.20 Removing the Weber TLD carburettor upper body (Sec 24)

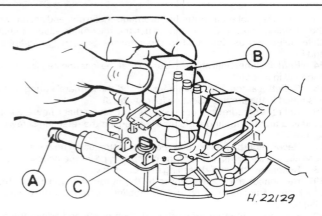

Fig. 4.21 Float and needle valve removal on the Weber TLD carburettor (Sec 24)

A   Fuel feed connection   C   Needle valve
B   Float

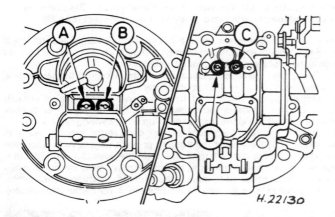

Fig. 4.22 Jet arrangement in the upper body of the Weber TLD carburettor (Sec 24)

A   Primary air correction jet   C   Secondary main jet
B   Secondary air correction   D   Primary main jet
    jet

As they are detached, label them to ensure correct reassembly.
8   Unscrew and remove the four Torx type retaining screws and carefully lift clear the carburettor from the inlet manifold (photos). Remove the gasket.

Refitting

9   Clean the carburettor and the inlet manifold mating faces.
10   Refit the carburettor in the reverse order of removal, ensuring that a new gasket is fitted. Tighten the retaining screws to the specified torque wrench setting.
11   If they are perished or were damaged during removal, renew the fuel and/or vacuum hoses.
12   Reconnect the automatic choke unit hoses and then check/top up the cooling system if required as described in Chapter 1.
13   Finally, check the idle speed and fuel mixture settings and adjust if necessary as described in Chapter 1.

24   Carburettor (Weber TLD) – dismantling, cleaning/inspection and reassembly

1   Proceed as described in Section 17 for the TLDM carburettor but refer to the appropriate illustrations for the TLD type carburettor (Figs. 4.20 to 4.22). The following differences should also be observed.

(a)   When refitting the adjuster screw, make the initial adjustment by screwing it fully into position (without overtightening it), then unscrewing it by three full turns.
(b)   Refer to Section 20 to adjust the needle valve and float.
(c)   When the carburettor is reassembled and refitted, check and adjust it as described in Chapter 1.

Part B: Fuel injection systems

25   General description and precautions

Two completely different types of fuel injection systems are available on the 1.4 and 1.6 litre engines. Both come under the overall control of the EEC-IV engine management system. The ignition sub-system is described and dealt with in Chapter 5.

In both systems the fuel is supplied from the rear-mounted fuel tank by an integral electric fuel pump (and combined fuel level sender unit). The fuel is passed through an in-line filter within the engine compartment, then to the fuel injection unit. The fuel is maintained at the required operating pressure by a pressure regulator unit.

A three way regulated catalytic converter (with HEGO sensor) is fitted into the exhaust system on some 1.4 and 1.6 litre fuel injected engine models, and where this is the case the system is designed to comply with the '83 US Emission Regulation level.

An inertia fuel cut-off switch is fitted to all fuel injection models to ensure that the fuel supply to the engine is switched off in the event of an accident or similar impact.

1.4 CFi models

The CFi unit is a relatively simple device when compared with a conventional carburettor. Fuel is injected by a single solenoid valve (fuel injector) which is mounted centrally on top of the unit. It is this feature which gives the system CFi (or Central Fuel Injection) its name.

The injector is energised by an electrical signal sent from the EEC-IV engine management module. When energised, the injector pintle is lifted from its seat and atomized fuel is delivered into the inlet manifold under pressure. The electrical signals take two forms of current. A high

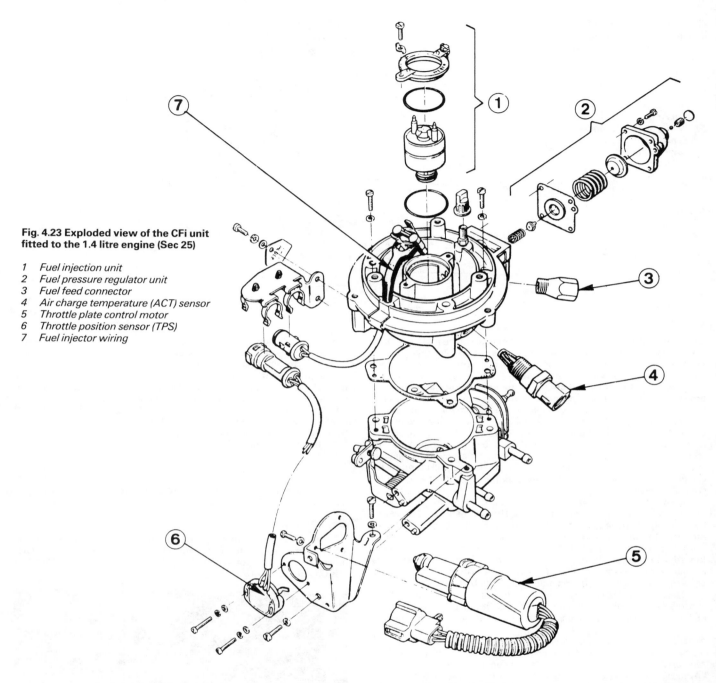

Fig. 4.23 Exploded view of the CFi unit fitted to the 1.4 litre engine (Sec 25)

1 Fuel injection unit
2 Fuel pressure regulator unit
3 Fuel feed connector
4 Air charge temperature (ACT) sensor
5 Throttle plate control motor
6 Throttle position sensor (TPS)
7 Fuel injector wiring

current to open the injector and a low current to hold it open for the duration required. At idle speed the injector is pulsed at every other intake stroke rather than with every stroke as during normal operation.

The air-to-fuel mixture ratio is regulated by values obtained from the distributor (engine speed), engine coolant temperature (ECT) sensor, manifold absolute pressure (MAP) sensor, air charge sensor (ACT), idle tracking switch, heated exhaust gas oxygen (HEGO) sensor and the throttle position sensor (TPS). No adjustments to the fuel mixture are possible.

The throttle position sensor enables the EEC-IV engine management module to compute both throttle position and its rate of charge. Extra fuel can then be provided for acceleration when the throttle is suddenly opened. Throttle position information, together with the idle tracking switch, provide the engine management module with the closed throttle position information.

The throttle plate control motor (mounted on the side of the CFi unit) regulates the idle speed by reacting to the signals sent by the engine

management module. The signals are calculated by the values and information provided from the ECT sensor, the idle tracking switch and the throttle position sensor. When closed throttle positions are sensed, the management module enters the idle speed mode or dashpot mode (according to engine speed). Any engine speed fluctuations when the idle speed mode is engaged are controlled by the management module to provide a constant idle speed.

To prevent the engine from running on (or dieselling) when it is switched off, the engine management module sends a signal to the throttle plate control motor to fully close the throttle plate and return it to its preset position ready for restarting. When the ignition is switched on to restart the engine, the motor repositions the throttle plate to the position required in accordance to the conditions.

1.6 litre EFi models

Fuel is supplied under pressure from the fuel pump to the fuel

Fig. 4.24 General view of the fuel injection system arrangement on the 1.6 litre EFi model (Sec 25)

1   Throttle housing
2   Upper inlet manifold section
3   Wiring loom connector
4   Air charge temperature (ACT) sensor
5   Wiring harness ducting
6   Fuel distributor rail
7   Lower section of inlet manifold
8   Cylinder head
9   Fuel injector
10 Fuel pressure regulator
11 Vacuum hose
12 Air filter trunking

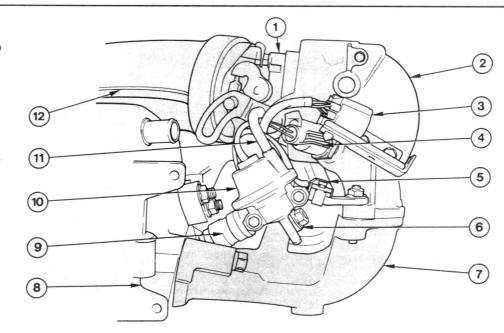

distributor rail mounted on top of the inlet manifold. The fuel rail acts as a pressurised fuel reservoir for the fuel injectors and retains them in their positions in the inlet manifold tracks. The electro-mechanical injectors have only 'on' or 'off' positions, the volume of fuel being injected to meet the engine operating conditions being determined by the amount of time that the injectors are opened. The volume of fuel required for one power stroke is determined by the engine management module and is divided by two equal amounts. The first half of the required volume is injected into the static air ahead of the inlet valve one complete engine revolution before the inlet valve is due to open. After one further revolution, the inlet valve opens and the required fuel volume is injected into the air flow being drawn into the cylinder. The fuel will therefore be consistently injected to two inlet valves simultaneously at a particular crankshaft position.

The volume of air drawn into the engine is governed by the air filter unit and other variable operating factors. These variables are assessed by the engine management unit and the corresponding signals are produced to actuate the injectors accordingly.

The engine base idle speed can be adjusted (if required), by turning the adjuster screw (covered by a tamperproof cap) in the throttle housing. Provision for adjusting the fuel mixture is made by the mixture screw in the potentiometer unit mounted on the bulkhead.

If the engine management module develops a fault or one of the sensors fails, a 'limited operation strategy' (LOS) feature is actuated to enable the vehicle to be driven, but at reduced power and efficiency.

Note: *It is important to note that the engine management module on EFi models incorporates a self test facility known as KAM (Keep Alive Memory), the function of which is to assist Ford mechanics in identifying any system faults which may occur. If the battery is disconnected at any time, the KAM values will be lost and it will be necessary to follow the procedures outlined in Section 4 of Chapter 12 to restore the KAM values.*

Fuel injection system precautions

Refer to the precautions outlined in Section 1 of this Chapter (for the carburettor variants), but note that on fuel injection models the system is pressurised and therefore additional care must be taken when disconnecting the fuel lines and hoses. When disconnecting a fuel line union, loosen the union slowly to allow the pressure to be progressively released from the joint rather than quickly causing fuel to spray from the joint. Have a clean cloth at hand to wrap around the joint and soak up any escaping fuel. After use, dispose of the rag safely.

Catalytic converter precautions

On models fitted with a catalytic converter, it should be noted that the converter operates at an extremely high temperature. Ensure that

the underbody heat shields are securely and correctly fitted and if it is removed, take care not to knock or damage the converter. It is also important to note that catalytic converter models must only run on unleaded petrol. If the tank is accidentally filled with leaded fuel at any time, it must be drained and refilled with unleaded fuel before the vehicle is used. If the vehicle is used with leaded fuel at any time, permanent damage to the catalytic converter (and the HEGO sensor) may be caused. Damage to the catalytic converter can also be caused by running the vehicle when the engine oil level is too high (beyond the MAX mark on the dipstick).

26 Air cleaner unit – removal and refitting

CFi system

1   The removal and refitting procedures for the air cleaner unit on 1.4 litre CFi engines is basically similar to that described for the air filter unit on CVH carburettor-engined models. Refer to Section 2 in Part A of this Chapter for details.

26.2 General view of the air filter (A) and air duct (B) fitted to the 1.6 litre EFi engine

EFi system

2   Undo the retaining nut at the front, then loosen off the air duct to filter housing clip screw and detach the air duct from the housing (photo).

3   Unscrew and remove the two retaining nuts on the underside of the housing (that secure it to the location studs).

4   Disconnect the hose at the base of the unit (to the inlet manifold) and lift the air cleaner unit clear.

5   Refit in the reverse order of removal. Ensure that the air hose and duct are securely located.

27 Accelerator cable – removal, refitting and adjustment

Removal

1   Fold back the carpet and insulation in the driver's footwell to gain access to the accelerator pedal.

2   Detach the accelerator cable from the pedal.

3   Working at the throttle housing end of the cable. Pivot the throttle quadrant by hand to release the tension from the cable, then detach the inner cable nipple from the throttle lever (photo).

4   Detach the outer cable from the adjuster/support bracket, then remove the cable (photo).

Refitting and adjustment

5   Refit in the reverse order of removal. When the cable is reconnected at each end, actuate the accelerator and check that the throttle fully opens and shuts without binding. Ensure that there is a small amount of slack in the inner cable when the throttle is fully released. If adjustment is required, release the outer cable retaining clip from the cable at the adjustment/support bracket, slide the cable through the adjuster grommet to the point required, then refit the retaining clip to secure it in the set position.

27.3 Disconnecting the accelerator inner cable from the throttle quadrant

27.4 Accelerator outer cable location at the adjuster/support bracket

28 Accelerator pedal – removal and refitting

Refer to Section 5 in Part A of this Chapter, although on EFi models refer to Section 4 of Chapter 12 when reconnecting the battery.

29 Fuel pump/sender unit – removal and refitting

1   A combined fuel pump and level sender unit are located in the top face of the fuel tank (photo). The combined unit can only be detached and withdrawn from the tank after the tank is released and lowered from under the vehicle. Refer to Section 8 and remove the fuel tank, then proceed as follows.

2   With the fuel tank removed, the pump/sender unit can be unscrewed and lifted from it. The pump/sender unit should only be unscrewed using the Ford special tool number 23-026. If this tool is not readily available, it may be possible to loosen off the pump/sender unit using a suitable lever engaged in the tabs to ease it free, but take care not to damage the tabs and/or the fuel pipes and wiring connectors.

3   Withdraw the unit upwards from the tank and detach the seal ring. The seal ring must be renewed whenever the pump/sender unit is withdrawn from the tank.

29.1 Combined fuel level sender/pump unit and connections – fuel injection model

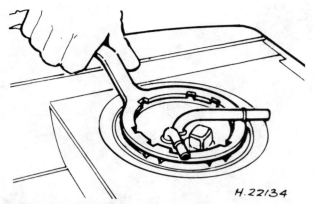

Fig. 4.25 Fuel pump/sender unit removal from the fuel tank using Ford special tool 23-026 (Sec 29)

4   Refit in the reverse order of removal. Lightly coat the new unit seal ring with grease to ease fitting and ensure that the seal is not distorted as the unit is fitted into position. Insert the unit so that the lug of the unit is in engagement with the slot in the tank aperture, then turn the unit to lock and secure.

30   Fuel tank – removal and refitting

Refer to Section 8 in Part A of this Chapter and proceed as described.

31   Fuel injection system components – testing

Note: *If a fault develops in the fuel injection system, the following basic checks can be made, but only after ascertaining that the ignition system is in good working condition. Unless the problem is known to emanate from a particular item in the system, the following basic checks should be made in the order given. If the basic checks fail to identify any faults, have the system checked out by a Ford dealer or fuel injection specialist.*

Fuel pump

1   To check that the fuel pump is working, switch on the ignition and listen to hear if the pump is heard to operate. The pump should be heard to operate for about one second then automatically stop. The pump is located in the top of the fuel tank and is best heard through the filler pipe aperture (cap removed) or with the rear seat tilted forward and the rubber plug prised free from the access aperture in the floor (to the right-of-centre).

2   If the pump does not appear to operate at all, check that the wiring connection to the top of the pump/sender unit is securely attached. If this is in order, check the position of the inertia (fuel cut-off) switch located behind the front footwell kick panel on the driver's side. If the switch has been de-activated, turn the ignition key to the 'O' position, then inspect the injection system for any sign of leaks. If leaks are found, they must be rectified. The inertia switch can be reset by turning the ignition key to the 'II' position for a few moments then turn the key to the 'I' position. The switch should be reset and the pump be heard to operate.

3   If the pump still fails to operate, check the condition of the fuel pump relay and fuse. Renew either (or both) if necessary.

Fuel supply at the CFi unit

4   Refer to Section 2 in Part A and remove the air cleaner unit

5   Disconnect the multi-plug connector from the HT coil (to prevent the engine from starting).

6   Get an assistant to turn the engine over on the starter motor whilst you look down through the top of the CFi unit and check that fuel is seen to be delivered into the central venturi.

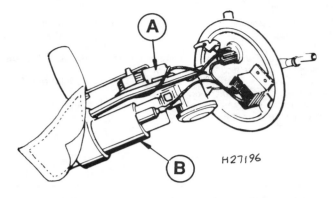

Fig. 4.26 In-tank fuel pump (B) and sender unit (A) (Sec 29)

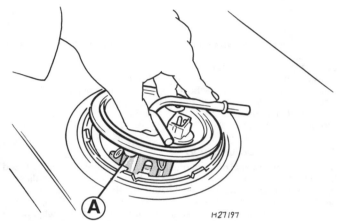

Fig. 4.27 Fuel pump/sender unit refitment to the tank showing position of the locating lug (A) (Sec 29)

Fig. 4.28 Check the points indicated for induction leaks (CFi system) (Sec 31)

7   If the fuel supply is seen to be acceptable but the engine refused to start, it may be that the catalytic converter is blocked or damaged. To check, detach the catalytic converter from the exhaust system (see Part C in this Chapter) and try to start the engine. If the engine starts, the catalytic converter is proved to at fault and must be renewed.

Throttle plate control motor (CFi system models)

8   Open the bonnet, start the engine and check for any signs of induction leaks at the points indicated in Fig. 4.28. Inspect the position of the throttle plate control motor by getting an assistant to start the engine then turn the ignition key off. The motor should be seen to retract and then extend so that it is ready for the next engine restart. The throttle plate control motor can be individually checked for operation by connecting up a 12 volt battery supply direct to the motor multi-plug as

Fig. 4.29 Throttle plate control motor check on the CFi system. Inset shows test connections to multi-plug (Sec 31)

shown in Fig. 4.29. Depending on the polarity, the motor should extend or retract. Changing the polarity should reverse the action.

Limited operation strategy (LOS) system (EFi system models)

9   The function of this system is to provide a basic back-up fuel supply to enable the vehicle to continue in use (at a reduced performance) should a fault develop in the engine management system or the associated sensors. To check if the system has been activated, switch on the ignition and listen to the operation of the fuel pump. It should operate for a period of one second, then automatically stop. If it continues to operate, the LOS system is activated and it will therefore be necessary to have the engine management system and sensors checked and any fault rectified. This task requires the use of specialised equipment and knowledge and must therefore be entrusted to a Ford garage.

Engine and fuel system wiring, vacuum and fuel line connections

10   Check and inspect all engine management and fuel injection system wiring connections, vacuum hoses and fuel line connections for condition and security. Renew any that are found to be in poor or suspect condition.

32   Fuel injection system components (1.4 litre CFi system) – removal and refitting

Note: *Before proceeding with any of the following operations, the precautions outlined in Section 25 must be noted and adhered to. In addition to this, the battery must be disconnected in most instances for the removal of the various items of the system.*

Fuel injector

1   Disconnect the battery earth lead.
2   Remove the air cleaner unit as described in Section 2 Part A.
3   Slowly loosen off the fuel feed pipe to the CFi unit to allow the system pressure to be released. Catch any fuel spillage in a clean cloth.
4   Release the injector feed wiring multi-plug and detach it from the injector (pulling on the plug – not the wire) (photo).
5   Bend over the locking tabs retaining the injector screws then undo and remove the screws. Withdraw the injector retaining collar, then carefully withdraw the injector unit from the CFi unit (noting its orientation) followed by its seal (photos).
6   Refit in the reverse order of removal. Always use new seals in the CFi unit and the retaining collar and lightly lubricate them with clean engine oil prior to assembly. Take care not to damage the seals as they are fitted and as the injector is fitted, check that the location peg correctly engages.

Fuel pressure regulator

7   Refer to paragraphs 24 to 32 in this Section and remove the CFi unit from the vehicle.
8   Unscrew and remove the four regulator unit retaining screws and

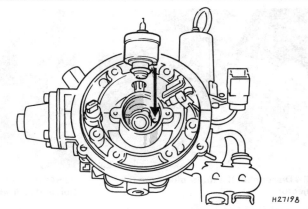

Fig. 4.30 Showing position of the injector location peg (Sec 32)

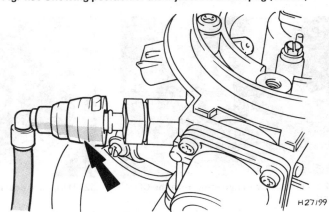

Fig. 4.31 Loosen off the fuel feed pipe indicated to release the pressure in the system (Sec 32)

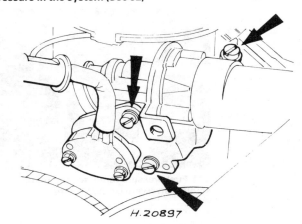

Fig. 4.32 Throttle plate control motor retaining screws (arrowed) (Sec 32)

remove the regulator unit (photo). As they are removed, note the fitting positions and the orientation of the unit components. **Do not** (unless absolutely necessary) attempt to prise out the plug or adjust the screw in the centre of the housing (if no plug fitted), as this will alter the system pressure.
9   Examine the components and renew any that are defective or suspect.
10   To refit, position the regulator unit on its side, Then insert the small spring, the valve, diaphragm (ensuring that it seats correctly), large spring, cup and then the regulator cover. Insert and tighten the retaining screws, but take care not to overtighten them or the cover will be distorted.
11   Carefully place the ball into position on the spring cup and ensure that it seats correctly.

32.4 Disconnect the multi-plug from the injector

32.5A Remove the injector retaining collar bolt and locktab ...

32.5B ... and remove the injector retaining collar

32.5C Withdraw the injector from the CFi unit

32.5D Injector seal location in the CFi unit

32.5E Withdrawing the seal from the injector retaining collar

32.8 Fuel pressure regulator and retaining screws (arrowed) (shown *in situ*)

32.17 Throttle position sensor retaining screws (arrowed) (throttle plate motor removed)

12   If removed, fit the central Allen type adjuster screw, hand tighten it and then unscrew it (from the hand-tight position) three full turns to make a provisional adjustment.

13   Refit the CFi unit in accordance with paragraphs 33 to 35 in this Section, but note that further checks for fuel leaks must be made with the engine running. The fuel system pressure must be checked by a Ford dealer or other suitable specialist at the earliest opportunity.

Throttle position sensor

14   Disconnect the battery earth lead.
15   Refer to Section 2 Part A and remove the air cleaner unit.
16   Release the throttle position sensor wiring multi-plug.
17   Unscrew and remove the throttle position sensor retaining screws and remove the sensor (photo).
18   Refit in the reverse order of removal. When refitting the sensor unit, ensure that the actuating arm is correctly located.

Air charge temperature sensor

19   Disconnect the battery earth lead.
20   Refer to Section 2 Part A and remove the air cleaner unit.
21   Disconnect the wiring plug from the air charge sensor unit (pulling on the plug, not the wire).
22   Unscrew and remove the sensor unit from the CFi unit.
23   Refit in the reverse order of removal. Tighten the sensor to the specified torque wrench setting.

Fuel injection unit

24   Disconnect the battery earth lead.
25   Refer to Section 2 Part A and remove the air cleaner unit.
26   Position a suitable drain tray under the coolant hose connections to the CFi unit, then detach the hoses from the unit. Plug or clamp the hoses to prevent further coolant spillage whilst the hoses are detached.
27   Slowly loosen off the fuel feed pipe union at the CFi unit to release

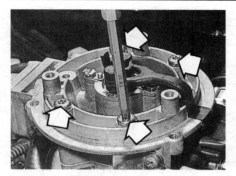

32.32 CFi unit retaining screws (arrowed)

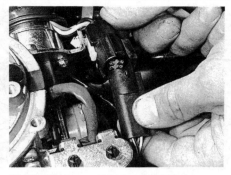

32.38A Disconnecting the throttle plate control motor multi-plug

32.38B Releasing the throttle position sensor multi-plug from the retaining clip

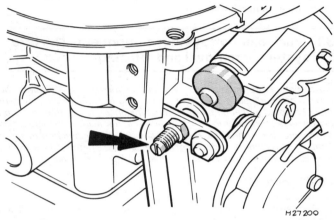

Fig. 4.33 Idle speed motor adjustment screw (Sec 32)

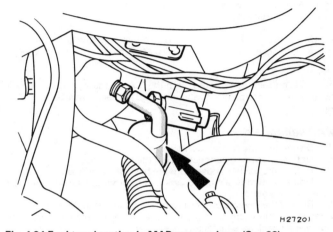

Fig. 4.34 Fuel trap location in MAP vacuum hose (Sec 32)

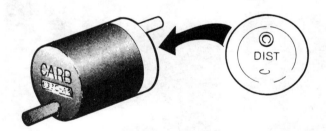

Fig. 4.35 Fuel trap orientation markings (Sec 32)

the pressure from the system, then detach the feed pipe.

28   Disconnect the fuel return pipe from the CFi unit.

29   Refer to Section 27 and disconnect the accelerator cable from the CFi unit.

30   Disconnect the air charge temperature sensor, throttle plate control motor and throttle position sensor wiring multi-plug connectors.

31   Disconnect the vacuum hose from the CFi unit.

32   Unscrew and remove the four retaining screws and remove the CFi unit from the inlet manifold (photo). Remove the gasket.

33   Clean the CFi unit and the inlet manifold mating faces.

34   Refit in the reverse order of removal. Tighten the retaining bolts to the specified torque wrench setting. Check and top up the cooling system as required (Chapter 1).

35   When the CFi unit is refitted, turn the ignition on and off at least five times and check for leaks.

Throttle plate control motor

36   Disconnect the battery earth lead.

37   Refer to Section 2 Part A and remove the air cleaner unit.

38   Detach the wiring multi-plugs from the throttle position sensor,

the throttle plate control motor and the retaining clips on the bracket (photos).

39   Undo and remove the motor support bracket screws and remove the bracket complete with the motor from the CFi injection unit.

40   Undo the motor retaining screws and remove it from the support bracket.

41   Refit in the reverse order of removal, but note the following.

(a)   When refitting the motor and its support bracket to the injector unit, the throttle position sensor must locate on the accelerator linkage and the bracket must align with the pegs.

(b)   When the wiring multi-plugs are reconnected, blank off the air cleaner vacuum connection on the inlet manifold, reconnect the battery and then restart the engine.

(c)   Run the engine until it reaches its normal operating temperature, then connect up a tachometer in accordance with the manufacturer's instructions and check the idle speed against that specified. If adjustment is required, remove the tamperproof cap, loosen off the locknut and then turn the screw to set the idle speed to that specified. Retighten the locknut and fit a new tamperproof cap.

(d)   Disconnect the tachometer, unplug the vacuum connection at the inlet manifold, then refit the air cleaner unit. On completion, the idle speed should be checked by a Ford garage or fuel injection specialist who has the required equipment to engage with the EEC-IV engine management module for accurate idle speed setting operations.

Fuel trap

42   A fuel trap is fitted to the MAP vacuum sensor hose at the position indicated in Fig. 4.34.

43   To remove the fuel trap, first disconnect the battery earth lead, then noting its orientation, disconnect the vacuum hoses from the fuel trap and withdraw it.

44   Refit in the reverse order of removal. It is important to ensure that

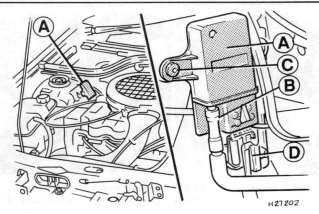

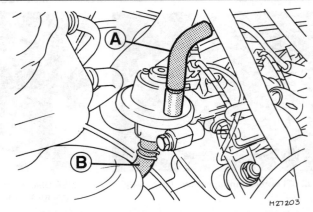

Fig. 4.36 Manifold Absolute Pressure sensor location and connections (Sec 32)

A	MAP sensor	C Retaining screw(s)
B	Vacuum hose	D Multi-plug

Fig. 4.37 Fuel pressure regulator showing vacuum pipe (A) and return pipe connections (B) (Sec 33)

the trap is correctly orientated, with the 'CARB' mark on one end face towards the inlet manifold, and the 'DIST' mark towards the MAP sensor.

MAP sensor

45   Disconnect the battery earth lead.
46   Detach the wiring connector from the MAP sensor.
47   Detach the vacuum hose from the base of the sensor.
48   Undo the two retaining screws and remove the sensor unit from the inner wing panel.
49   Refit in the reverse order of removal. Ensure that the vacuum and wiring connections are correctly made, then on completion, restart the engine and check for satisfactory operation.

33 Fuel injection system components (1.6 litre EFi system) – removal and refitting

Note: *Before proceeding with any of the following operations, the precautions outlined in Section 25 concerning the fuel injection system must be noted and adhered to. In most instances, the battery must be disconnected for the removal of the various items included in this Section and where this is the case, reference should subsequently be made to Chapter 12, Section 4 for details of reconnecting the battery and allowing the EEC-IV engine management module to relearn its values.*

Fuel injectors

1   Disconnect the battery earth lead.
2   Loosen off the retaining clip and detach the warm air hose duct from the exhaust manifold (photo).

33.2 Disconnecting the warm air duct from the exhaust manifold

33.6 Throttle body retaining screws (lower screws are hidden)

33.8A Disconnect the wiring connector from each injector ...

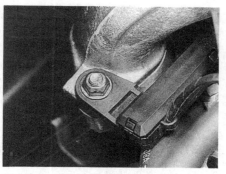

33.8B ... unbolt the wiring harness ...

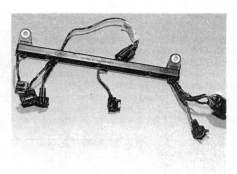

33.8C ... and remove the injector wiring harness

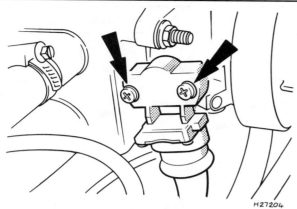

Fig. 4.38 Throttle position sensor (TPS) securing screws (Sec 33)

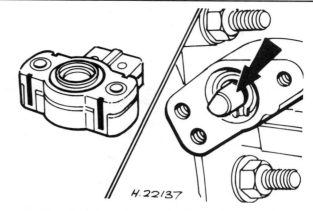

Fig. 4.39 Align throttle position sensor 'D' section on shaft when refitting (Sec 33)

3   Disconnect the ignition HT lead connectors from the spark plugs and release the leads from their locating grooves in the air intake duct. Position them out of the way.
4   Unscrew the retaining nuts and the bolt and detach the throttle cable support bracket at the throttle body.
5   Disconnect the wiring connector from the throttle position sensor.
6   Unscrew the four retaining bolts and remove the throttle body and its mating face gasket (photo).
7   Disconnect the wiring multi-plug from the engine coolant temperature sensor (ECT) and the air charge sensor (ACT).
8   Disconnect the wiring connectors from the injectors, then undo the two retaining bolts and detach the wiring harness from the fuel rail (photos).
9   Loosen off the fuel supply pipe at the fuel rail. Loosen it slowly to allow the pressure in the system to be released and catch any fuel

spillage in a clean cloth. Plug the rail and pipe to prevent further fuel spillage and the possible ingress of dirt.
10   Disconnect the fuel return and vacuum pipes from the regulator, and catch any spillage in a clean cloth.
11   Unscrew the fuel rail securing bolts and carefully withdraw the rail (complete with injectors) from the engine (photos).
12   Detach the fuel injectors from the fuel rail and then remove the upper and lower seal from each injector. All seals must be renewed (even if only one injector is to be renewed).
13   Prior to refitting the injectors, ensure that all mating surfaces are perfectly clean (photo). Lubricate the new injector seals with clean engine oil to ease their assembly to the injectors.
14   Refitting is a reversal of the removal procedure. Refer to the specifications at the start of this Chapter for the tightening torques. When refitting the fuel distributor rail, ensure that the injectors are

33.11A Remove the injector rail retaining bolts ...

33.11B ... release each injector ...

33.11C ... and withdraw the fuel rail and injectors

33.13 Fuel injector with new seals fitted

33.21 Idle speed control valve and wiring connector

correctly located. Ensure that the mating surfaces of the throttle housing are perfectly clean before assembling.

15   On completion, restart the engine and check the various fuel connections for any signs of leaks.

Fuel pressure regulator

16   Position a drain tray beneath the regulator to catch fuel spillage, then slowly loosen off the fuel return pipe securing clip and detach the pipe from the regulator.

17   Pull free the vacuum pipe from the regulator connector.

18   Unscrew the two retaining bolts and remove the regulator unit. Remove the old sealing ring for renewal.

19   Refit in the reverse order of removal. Lubricate the new seal ring with clean engine oil to ease assembly. When the regulator is refitted and the fuel and vacuum lines are reconnected, turn the ignition on and off five times (without cranking the engine) and check for any sign of fuel leaks before restarting the engine.

Idle speed control valve

20   Disconnect the battery earth lead.

21   Detach the wiring multi-plug connector from the idle speed control valve (photo).

22   Undo the four retaining screws and remove the idle speed control valve.

23   Refitting is a reversal of the removal procedure. Ensure that the mating faces of the valve and inlet manifold are clean before reassembling.

24   When the valve is refitted, restart the engine and check that there are no induction leaks. Run the engine until its normal operating temperature is reached and check that the idle speed is stable. Stop the engine, connect up a tachometer in accordance with the maker's instructions, then restart the engine and check that the idle speed is as specified with all electrical items (lights, heater blower motor, etc) switched off, then on. The idle speed should remain the same. Switch off the electrical items and turn the engine off and detach the tachometer to complete the test.

Throttle position sensor

25   Disconnect the battery earth lead.

26   Detach the wiring multi-plug from the throttle position sensor, then undo the two retaining screws and remove the sensor unit from the throttle housing.

27   Refit in the reverse order of removal. As it is fitted, engage the 'D' drive of the spindle shaft (with the moulded side toward the manifold). Take care not to turn the centre of the sensor unit beyond its normal operating arc.

28   On completion, restart the engine and check for satisfactory operation.

Air charge temperature sensor

29   Disconnect the battery earth lead.

30   Detach the wiring connector from the sensor unit, then unscrew and remove the sensor unit from the inlet manifold (refer to Fig. 4.24 for location).

31   Clean the threads of both the sensor and the manifold before refitting.

32   Smear the threads of the sensor with a suitable thread sealant, then refit it in the reverse order of removal.

Throttle housing

33   Proceed as described in paragraphs 1 to 4 at the start of this Section.

34   Disconnect the vacuum hoses from the inlet manifold and the pressure regulator.

35   Detach the wiring connections from the idle speed control valve, the temperature sensor and the harness connector.

36   Disconnect the fuel return hose from the pressure regulator unit.

37   Unscrew the throttle housing to manifold retaining nuts and unbolt the throttle housing support bracket bolts. Remove the throttle housing and gasket.

38   Refit in the reverse order of removal. Check that the mating faces are clean and fit a new gasket.

34   Fuel cut-off switch – removal and refitting

Removal

1   Disconnect the battery earth lead.

2   Undo the retaining screws and remove the driver's footwell kick panel (photo).

3   Undo the retaining screws and withdraw the cut-off (inertia) switch unit from the body (photo). As it is withdrawn, disconnect the wiring connector to the switch.

Refitting

4   Reconnect the wiring connector to the switch, ensuring that it is felt to snap securely into position.

5   Relocate the switch and refit the screws to secure it.

6   Reset the switch by pushing the top button down, then refit the side kick panel.

7   Reconnect the battery and restart the engine to ensure that the switch has reset.

34.2 Remove the side kick panel for access to ...

34.3 ... the fuel cut-off switch

Part C: Manifolds, exhaust and emission control systems

35 Exhaust system – general

The exhaust system fitted during production is of two-piece construction whilst those available in service are three-piece. A twin downpipe from the manifold is fitted to all models. The system is supported to the underside of the vehicle by rubber insulators.

A three-way regulated catalytic converter is fitted to the exhaust system on some 1.4 and 1.6 litre fuel injection models and is located at the rear end of the exhaust manifold downpipe. The catalytic converter operates at very high temperatures (above 320°C) and this must be considered when working in the area adjacent to it in order to avoid burns. The converter unit is a relatively fragile device and must not be dropped or knocked as it is easily damaged.

Various emission control features are built into all models covered, the type and extent of the system used being dependent on engine type and model. Refer to Section 39 for further details.

Holts Flexiwrap and Holts Gun Gum exhaust repair systems can be used for effective repairs to exhaust pipes and silencer boxes, including ends and bends. Holts Flexiwrap is an MOT approved permanent exhaust repair. Holts Firegum is suitable for the assembly of all exhaust system joints (except those joints forward of the catalytic converter).

36 Inlet manifold – general

Note: *Refer to the precautions in Section 1 or 25 (as applicable) before starting any work. Where removal is intended, an accurate tachometer will be required to check the idle speed once the unit is refitted to the vehicle. An exhaust gas analyzer (CO meter) will also be required to check the fuel mixture.*

1   A single-piece cast aluminium inlet manifold is used on all models except the 1.6 EFi model, which has a two-piece manifold comprising an upper and lower section bolted together.
2   On all models the inlet manifold is secured to the cylinder head by bolts and/or nuts and washers (as applicable).
3   Where the manifold is to be removed, first remove the carburettor and its associated fittings or the fuel injectors (with fuel rail) and associated fittings (as applicable). Refer to the appropriate Section(s) in Part A or B in this Chapter for the relevant details. On the fuel injection engines, the upper manifold is removed complete with the throttle housing. Note the position of any brackets, electrical and vacuum connections which are also secured to or by the manifold and/or its fixings as they are disconnected to ensure correct reassembly (photo).
4   When the manifold is removed, clean all traces of the old gasket from the mating surfaces of the manifold and the cylinder head. New gasket(s) must be used when refitting (photos).
5   An inlet manifold heater unit is housed in the base of the manifold on the 1.4 CFi models and if required it can be removed by extracting the circlip and withdrawing the unit from the manifold. Refitting of the heater unit is a reversal of the removal procedure.
6   Refer to the Specifications at the start of this Chapter for the various torque wrench setting requirements. When refitting is complete on EFi models, reconnect the battery and restart the engine in the manner described in Section 4 of Chapter 12 to allow the engine management module to re-learn its values.

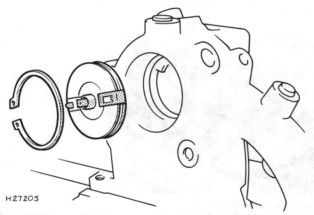

Fig. 4.40 Inlet manifold heater and retaining clip (1.4 litre CFi engine) (Sec 36)

37 Exhaust manifold – general

Note: *Never work on or near a hot exhaust system and in particular, the catalytic converter (where fitted).*

1   The exhaust manifold is secured to the cylinder head by studs and nuts and is similarly attached to the exhaust downpipe. An airbox/heatshield is bolted to the manifold to direct exhaust heated air into the air intake system during the engine warm up period. Access to the exhaust manifold retaining nuts is gained by first removing the airbox/heatshield (photos).
2   With the airbox/heatshield withdrawn, the removal and refitting of the exhaust manifold is a straightforward task requiring no special tools. Highly corroded retaining stud threads should be cleaned using a wire brush and treated with some penetrating oil prior to unscrewing the nuts to ease their removal (photo). Where applicable, disconnect the pulse air supply pipes from the manifold.
3   During removal and refitting, access from underneath the vehicle at

36.3 Inlet manifold retaining bolt also securing the engine lift eye and an earth lead

36.4A Inlet manifold and fittings (1.6 litre carburettor engine)

36.4B Inlet manifold refitting. Note the new gasket (arrowed)

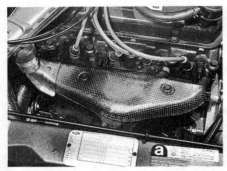

37.1A Exhaust manifold airbox/heatshield on the 1.3 litre (HCS) engine

37.1B Airbox/heatshield removal from the 1.6 litre (CVH) carburettor engine

37.1C Airbox/heatshield removal from the 1.6 litre (CVH) EFi engine

37.2 Exhaust manifold removal from the 1.6 litre (CVH) carburettor engine

37.3 Exhaust manifold-to-downpipe flange and securing nuts are accessible from underneath the vehicle

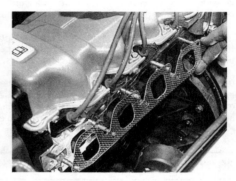

37.5A Fit a new exhaust manifold gasket ...

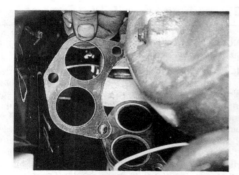

37.5B ... and manifold-to-downpipe gasket ...

37.6 Refit the exhaust manifold (1.6 litre EFi engine shown)

the front end will be required to detach the exhaust downpipe from the manifold. Raise the vehicle and support it on axle stands at the required height before working underneath (photo).

4   On models fitted with a catalytic converter unit, a HEGO sensor is fitted in the exhaust downpipe and the wiring to it should not be stretched. When the downpipe is detached from the manifold it should be tied up and supported to prevent possible damage to the system retaining straps. If necessary, disconnect the wire from the HEGO sensor to prevent it being stretched and damaged.

5   When the exhaust manifold is removed, clean all traces of the old gasket from the mating surfaces of the cylinder head, manifold and downpipe flange. Renew the gaskets as a matter of course (photos).

6   Refit the manifold in the reverse order of removal. Tighten the retaining bolts to their specified torque wrench settings (photo). Ensure that all adjacent wiring and hoses are clear of the exhaust system and manifold and on completion check the system joints for any signs of

leaks. If the battery earth lead was disconnected, refer to Section 4 in Chapter 12 when reconnecting for special procedures applicable to EFi engined models.

38   Exhaust system – renewal

Note: *Do not work on or near a hot exhaust system and in particular, the catalytic converter (where fitted). The catalytic converter operates at an extremely high temperature. Ensure that the underbody heat shields are securely and correctly fitted and if it is removed, take care not to knock or damage the converter.*

1   Due to the sectional design of the exhaust system, it is possible to

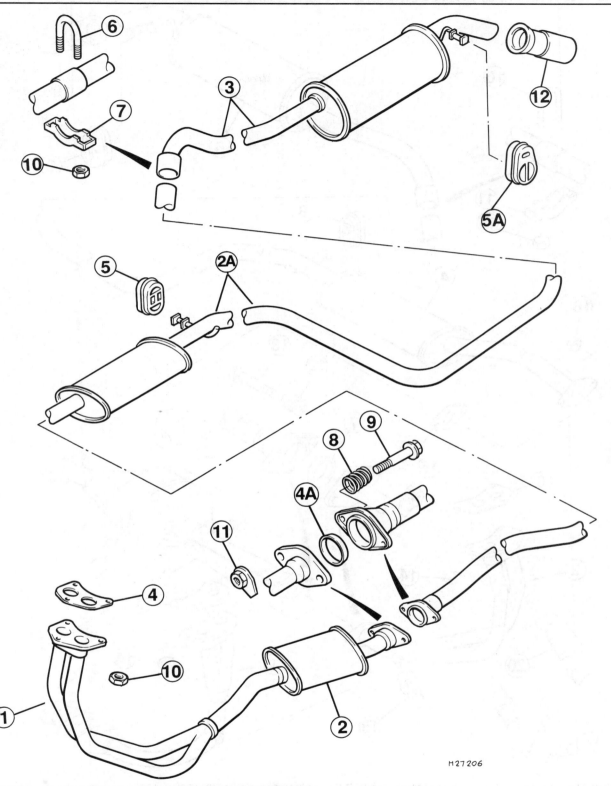

Fig. 4.41 Exhaust system fitted to carburettor engined models (Sec 38)

1	Front downpipe	4	Gasket	7	Clamp	11	Nut
2	Front muffler section	4A	Joint	8	Spring	12	Rear muffler outlet trim (1.4
2A	Centre section	5	Rubber insulator	9	Bolt		and 1.6 engines only)
3	Rear muffler section	6	U-bolt	10	Self-lock nut		

H27206

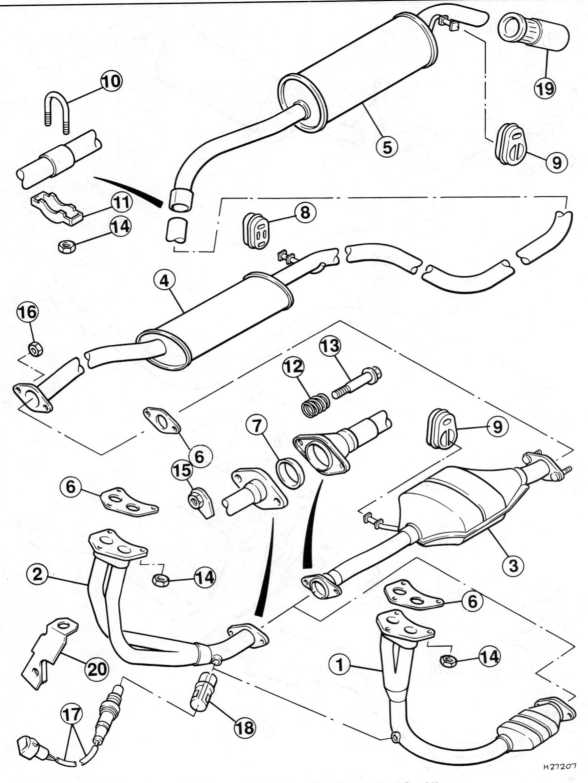

Fig. 4.42 Exhaust system fitted to the 1.4 litre CFi engine model (1.6 litre EFi system similar) (Sec 38)

1	Front downpipe (manual transmission)	5	Rear muffler (1.6 litre EFi tailpipe differs)	10	U-bolt	16	Nut
2	Front downpipe (CTX transmission)	6	Gasket	11	Clamp	17	HEGO sensor
		7	Joint	12	Spring	18	Heat shield
3	Catalyst unit	8	Rubber insulator	13	Bolt	19	Rear muffler outlet trim
4	Front muffler	9	Rubber insulator	14	Self-lock nut	20	Bracket
				15	Nut		

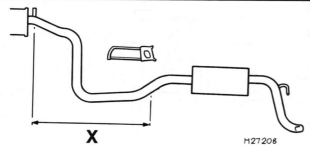

Fig. 4.43 Cut at points indicated (according to model) when renewing the rear muffler (Sec 38)

X = 720 mm (all models except Van)
X = 914 mm (Van models)

renew a damaged or corroded section rather than the complete system if required. If renewing the complete system, two categories have to be considered, a two-piece production system or a three-piece service replacement system.

2   On the production fitted system, the downpipe assembly and the rear silencer can be renewed independently as required. The catalytic converter (where fitted) may also be renewed if necessary (photo). The remaining centre section of the system, comprising the main pipe run, front silencer and resonator box (as applicable), cannot be renewed separately. In this instance, service replacement sections including the rear silencer must be fitted.

3   On a service replacement system, all sections can be renewed independently as required.

4   Although certain exhaust section removal and refitting operations are possible without the need to remove the whole of the system, there are instances where this will be necessary. It should also be noted that it is easier to work on the system with it removed completely from the vehicle.

5   Unless suitable ramps or a vehicle inspection pit is available, the vehicle will need to be raised and supported on axle stands to allow access to work on the system. Allow the exhaust system to cool off before inspecting and/or working on it. This is particularly important on models with a catalytic converter.

6   To remove the complete system, undo the retaining nuts and detach the downpipe from the exhaust manifold. Where a catalytic converter is fitted, disconnect the wiring connector from the HEGO sensor. Unhook and release the system from the rubber insulators to lower the system and withdraw it from under the vehicle (photo). During removal, take care not to damage the catalytic converter (where fitted).

7   If renewing the rear muffler section on a production system, refer to Fig. 4.43 and using a hacksaw, cut it free at an angle of 90° to the pipe and at the appropriate dimensions from the centre support towards the rear.

8   If renewing the rear muffler section on a service replacement system, undo the retaining nuts to release the 'U' clamp, then separate the rear section.

9   If renewing a catalytic converter, support the converter unit and undo the retaining flange bolts at its front and rear flange connections, unhook it from the support insulator then remove the unit from the system. If the old catalytic converter is to be refitted, take care not to knock the converter unit during removal as it is easily damaged (photos).

10   Clean all system mating flanges and joints prior to reassembly. Check that the insulators are in good condition and renew any where necessary. If renewing an insulator strap on a catalytic converter exhaust system, it is essential that the correct high temperature resistant type is fitted (photo).

11   When refitting the exhaust system, use new gaskets/seals where/as applicable and refer to the specifications for the torque wrench settings (photo). A suitable exhaust sealant such as Holts Firegum can be applied to the joints to ensure a leak-free system (but not to the forward joint of a catalytic converter).

12   When the exhaust system is refitted, check to ensure that the insulator mountings are not distorted and that the system is clear of adjacent components. Where applicable, check that the wiring connection to the HEGO sensor is secure and that the wire is routed clear of the downpipe.

38.2 Catalytic converter

38.6 Typical exhaust system support and insulator

38.9A Catalytic converter-to-downpipe flange joint. Note location of the HEGO sensor (arrowed)

38.9B Catalytic converter-to-rear exhaust system flange joint

38.10 Catalytic support strap and special heatproof insulator

38.11 Fitting a new exhaust flange joint seal

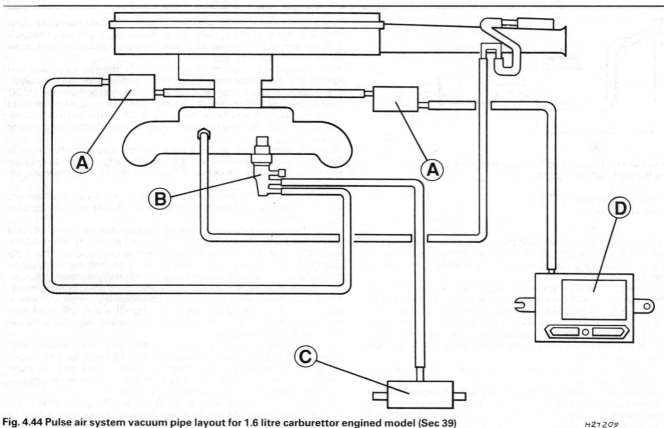

Fig. 4.44 Pulse air system vacuum pipe layout for 1.6 litre carburettor engined model (Sec 39)　　H27209

| A | Fuel traps | B | Ported vacuum switch (PVS) | C | Vacuum operated air valve | D | ESC Hybrid H2 module |

13　Before lowering the vehicle, start the engine and check the system for any signs of leaks.

14　It should be noted that where a new catalytic converter unit has been fitted, it is normal for an unpleasant odour caused by the chemical hydrogen sulphide (a smell similar to that of rotten eggs) to be given off for an initial period.

39　Emission control systems

Fuel and exhaust emission control

1　The vehicles covered in this manual are fitted with differing emission control level systems depending on type, all of which operate in conjunction with the engine management system.

2　The 1.3 litre (HCS) engine models and the 1.4 and 1.6 litre (CVH) engine carburettor models are fitted with a 15.04 and NEEC 5th emission level system.

3　The 1.4 litre (CVH) CFi engine models are fitted with an 83 US emission level system (with catalytic converter).

4　The 1.6 litre (CVH) EFi engine model is fitted with a 15.04 emission level (with no catalytic converter) or an 83 US emission level (with catalytic converter).

5　On carburettor engine models, the control module is mounted on the left-hand inner wing panel within the engine compartment. On both the 1.4 CFi and 1.6 EFi engine models, the fuel and emission control systems are controlled by the EEC IV module which is located behind the front passenger side kick panel.

6　The engine management system fitted is specific to the vehicle type and its fuel/emission control features. With all system types, data is supplied from various sensors to the engine management module which enable it to provide the maximum engine operating efficiency under all operating conditions whilst minimising the harmful exhaust emissions. The emission control system is divided into three categories: fuel evaporative emission control, crankcase emission control and exhaust emission control. Dependent on the engine and transmission type, and the emission control regulations, various control measures are used.

Fuel evaporative emission control

7　The function of the fuel evaporative emission control (EVAP) system is to control the vaporous hydrocarbon emissions from the fuel tank. Emission control regulations in the UK are less stringent than in certain other countries and fuel evaporative emission control systems are limited on vehicles meeting 15.04 regulations. Carburettor float chambers are vented internally, whilst fuel tanks vent to atmosphere through a combined roll-over/anti-trickle-fill valve.

8　On 1.4 and 1.6 litre models built to meet the 83 US emission regulation, the fuel tank vents through a combined roll-over/anti-trickle-fill valve to a carbon canister in the engine compartment. With this system, when the engine is switched off, fuel vapours from the tank are transferred to the canister (at which point the canister purge solenoid is closed). When the engine is restarted, the purge solenoid opens, and the vapours are directed into the engine inlet manifold to be burnt off during the normal combustion process. A restrictor prevents excess fuel vapour being directed to the inlet manifold.

Crankcase emission control

9　On HCS engines, a closed circuit crankcase ventilation system is used ensuring that blow-by gases from the crankcase together with oil vapour are directed into the induction system and burnt off in the combustion process.

10　The system consists of a vented oil filler cap (with an integral mesh filter) and a hose connecting it to a connector on the underside of the air filter housing. A further hose leads from the adaptor/filter to the inlet manifold. Under conditions of idle and part load, the emission gases are directed into the inlet manifold and dispensed with in the combustion

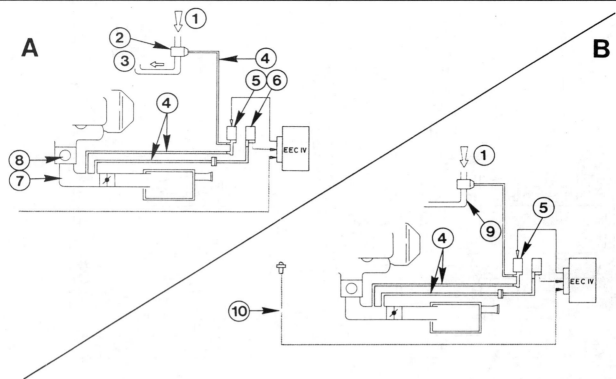

Fig. 4.45 Pulse air system layout and operating modes on 1.4 litre CFi engined models (Sec 39)

A	Open loop mode (system operational)	1	Fresh air (from pulse air cleaner/filter)	4	Vacuum	8	CFi unit
B	Closed loop mode (system non-operational)	2	Air control valve (open)	5	Pulse air control solenoid	9	Air control valve (closed)
		3	Fresh air to exhaust port	6	MAP sensor	10	HEGO sensor signal
				7	Inlet manifold		

process. Additional air is supplied through two small orifices next to the mushroom valve in the air filter housing, the object of which is to prevent high vacuum build-up. Under full load conditions, when the inlet manifold vacuum is weak, the mushroom valve in the filter housing opens and the emissions are directed through the filter housing into the engine induction system and thence into the combustion chambers. This arrangement eliminates any fuel mixture control problems.

11   On the CVH engine models, a closed circuit type crankcase ventilation system is used, the function of which is basically the same as that described for the HCS engine type, but the breather hose connects direct to the rocker cover. The oil filler cap incorporates a separate filter in certain applications (photo).

Exhaust emission control

12   The exhaust emission control systems employed across the range of models vary in complexity and application. On carburettor engine models, various vacuum control valves are integrated into the fuel system and these together with the associated sensors working in conjunction with the management module, assist to control engine operation and minimise exhaust emissions.

13   A **Pulse Air System** is used on 1.4 litre CFi and some versions of the 1.4 and 1.6 litre carburettor engine models. The system supplies fresh air into the respective exhaust ports during the warm-up stage, its function being to reduce the time taken for the catalyst to reach its normal operating temperature thus reducing the CO and HC content in the exhaust emission. The main components of the system are a vacuum-operated air control valve and a pulse air control solenoid (1.4 litre CFi) or check valve (carburettor engines).

14   On the 1.4 litre CFi engine model, the pulse air system operates in conjunction with and is controlled by the EEC IV management system, whilst on the carburettor model, the system is controlled by a three port vacuum switch (PVS) incorporating a coolant temperature sensor which is mounted on the underside of the inlet manifold. The pulse air valve ensures that the air only flows in one direction. When an exhaust valve

opens, the resultant high exhaust gas pressure causes the pulse air valve to close. When an exhaust valve closes, the resultant vacuum caused in the exhaust manifold opens the pulse air valve and fresh air is supplied into the exhaust gas flow system.

15   A **Catalytic Converter** is fitted to some models to reduce the harmful exhaust gas emissions. As the exhaust gases pass through the

39.11 Crankcase ventilation system filter on the 1.6 litre (CVH) engine

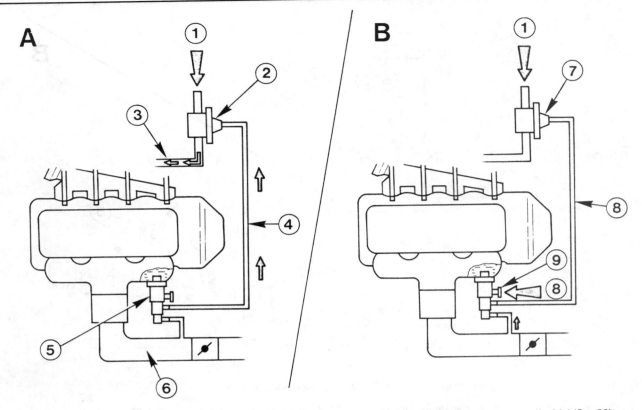

Fig. 4.46 Pulse air system layout and operating modes on 1.4 and 1.6 litre carburettor engined models (where applicable) (Sec 39)

A   Pulse air system operational (coolant temperature below 70°C)

B   Pulse air system non-operational (coolant temperature above 70°C)

1   Fresh air (from pulse air cleaner/filter)

2   Air control valve (open)
3   Fresh air to exhaust port
4   Vacuum
5   Ported vacuum switch

6   Inlet manifold
7   Air control valve (closed)
8   Atmospheric pressure
9   Filter

converter unit, they are cleaned by a honeycomb structure which has a porous ceramic substrate and an alumina-based washcoat. For the catalytic converter to operate efficiently it is essential that the air-to-fuel ratio in the engine is correctly controlled. A Heated Exhaust Gas Oxygen (HEGO) sensor unit is located in the exhaust downpipe forward of the catalytic converter and its function is to measure the mixture ratio of the exhaust gases and transmit its readings to the engine management module. This in turn can then adjust the fuel/air mixture ratio accordingly.

40   Emission control system components – removal and refitting

Catalytic converter

1   Refer to Section 38 and proceed as described. Allow the cooling system to completely cool off if the vehicle has been recently used before proceeding.

HEGO sensor

2   Detach the battery earth lead.
3   Raise and support the vehicle at the front end on axle stands to allow access to the underside of the exhaust system at the front end. Allow the exhaust system to completely cool off before proceeding if the vehicle has been recently used.
4   Detach the HEGO sensor wiring multi-plug connector (photo).
5   Withdraw the HEGO sensor heat shield.
6   Unscrew and remove the HEGO sensor, together with its seal ring from the exhaust downpipe but take care not to touch the tip of the HEGO sensor.

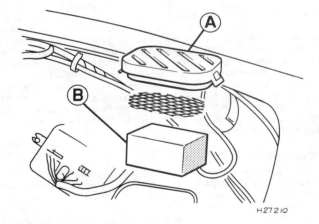

Fig. 4.47 Pulse air system air cleaner unit (Sec 40)

A   Reservoir lid   *B   Filter element*

7   Before refitting the sensor, clean its threads and those in the exhaust downpipe. Fit a new seal to the sensor then screw it into position and tighten it to the specified torque wrench setting.
8   Refit the heat shield and reconnect the wiring multi-plug. The multi-plug lock tabs must be felt to snap into engagement as the plug is reconnected.
9   Before lowering the vehicle from the axle stands, reconnect the battery and start the engine and check around the sensor for any sign of leaks.

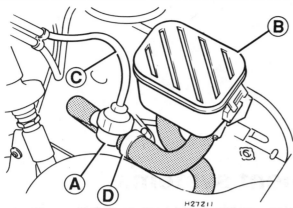

Fig. 4.48 Vacuum operated air valve and connections (Sec 40)

A	Vacuum air valve unit	C	Vacuum hose
B	Pulse air reservoir	D	Air hose securing clip

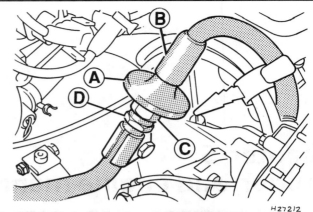

Fig. 4.49 Pulse air check valve connections (Sec 40)

A	Check valve	C	Air valve nut
B	Air hose	D	Tube nut

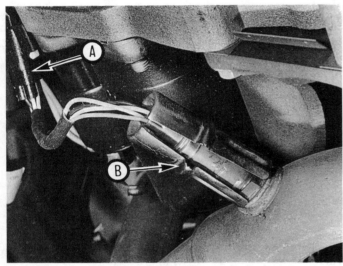

40.4 HEGO sensor showing multi-plug (A) and heat shield (B)

40.11 EVAP system carbon canister and connections viewed from above (coolant expansion reservoir removed) – 1.6 litre EFi model

A Carbon canister
B Canister purge solenoid
C Canister securing bolt
D Canister vapour pipe

Carbon canister (where fitted)

10 Disconnect the battery earth lead.
11 The canister is located in the forward section of the right-hand wheel arch (beneath the coolant expansion reservoir). Access to the top of the unit is made by removing the coolant expansion reservoir (photo). Access to the underside of the unit is gained by raising the vehicle at the front and removing the roadwheel on the right-hand side. Ensure that the vehicle is securely supported on axle stands before working under the wheel arch.
12 Disconnect the hose from the unit and plug it to prevent the ingress of dirt.
13 Undo the retaining screws and withdraw the unit from under the wheel arch.
14 Refit in the reverse order of removal. Unplug the hose before reconnecting it and ensure that it is clean and securely connected.

Pulse air delivery tubing

15 Disconnect the battery earth lead.
16 Remove the air cleaner unit (Section 2).
17 Disconnect the air hose from the air valve.
18 Unbolt and detach the air tube from its fixing to the transmission.
19 Loosen off the four nuts securing the air delivery tubes to the exhaust manifold, then carefully withdraw the delivery tubes as a unit. Do not apply undue force to the tubes as they are detached.
20 Refit in the reverse order of removal.

Pulse air filter and reservoir

21 Detach the lid from the filter body and lift out the filter element

from the reservoir. If required, the reservoir can be removed by detaching the air hoses from the base of the unit and withdrawing the unit from the vehicle.
22 Refit in the reverse order of removal.

Vacuum operated air valve

23 Disconnect the battery earth lead.
24 Detach the two vacuum hoses from the valve.
25 Loosen off the air hose clamp and detach the air hose from the valve.
26 Detach the remaining air hose. Note the orientation of the valve and remove it from the vehicle.
27 When refitting the valve, ensure that it is fitted the correct way round. Refitting is otherwise a reversal of the removal procedure.

Pulse air check valve

28 Disconnect the battery earth lead.
29 Detach the air hoses from the check valve.
30 Hold the lower tube nut at the base of the valve firm with a suitable spanner and unscrew the valve using a spanner fitted on the upper nut.
31 Refit in the reverse order of removal. Ensure that the valve is correctly positioned before fully tightening the tube nut against the valve nut.

Chapter 5
Ignition and engine management systems

Contents

Specifications

System type	High output, fully electronic, distributorless ignition system (DIS or EDIS), with specific module control according to engine type
Output (minimum)...	37 kilovolt (open circuit condition)
Primary resistance..	0.5 ± 0.05 ohms
Firing order:	
1.3 HCS engine	1–2–4–3
1.4 and 1.6 CVH engines	1–3–4–2
Location of number 1 cylinder	Crankshaft pulley end
HT lead resistance (maximum per lead)	30 000 ohms

Torque wrench settings	Nm	lbf ft
Spark plugs:		
1.3 HCS engine (taper seat)	14 to 20	12 to 15
1.4 and 1.6 CVH engine (flat seat)	17 to 33	13 to 24
DIS ignition coil mounting bracket-to-engine	9 to 12	7 to 9
DIS ignition coil-to-mounting bracket	5 to 7	4 to 5

1 General information

1   The ignition system is responsible for igniting the air/fuel mixture in each cylinder at the correct moment in relation to the engine speed and load.

2   Low tension (LT) voltage from the battery is passed to the ignition coil where it is converted to high tension (HT) voltage. The high tension voltage is powerful enough to jump the spark plug electrode gap many times a second under high compression pressure, providing that the system is in good condition.

3   A Distributorless Ignition System (DIS) is used on all carburettor engined models, or EDIS on all fuel injection engined models, in which the main functions of the conventional distributor are replaced by a computerised module and a coil unit. The coil unit combines a double ended pair of coils and each time a coil receives an ignition signal, two sparks are produced, at each end of the secondary windings. One spark goes to a cylinder on compression stroke and the other goes to the corresponding cylinder on its exhaust stroke. The first will give the correct power stroke, but the second spark will have no effect, occurring as it does during exhaust conditions.

4   The engine speed and crankshaft position are indicated by a variable reluctance type sensor (CPS) which is axially mounted in an aperture in the rear flange of the cylinder block. The sensor is positioned in close proximity to the front face of the flywheel which has 36-1 indent indexes. These enable the sensor to detect the 'toothed' pattern in the flywheel and transmit the crankshaft speed and position signals to the

1.4 Front face of the flywheel showing the indents with single large indent arrowed

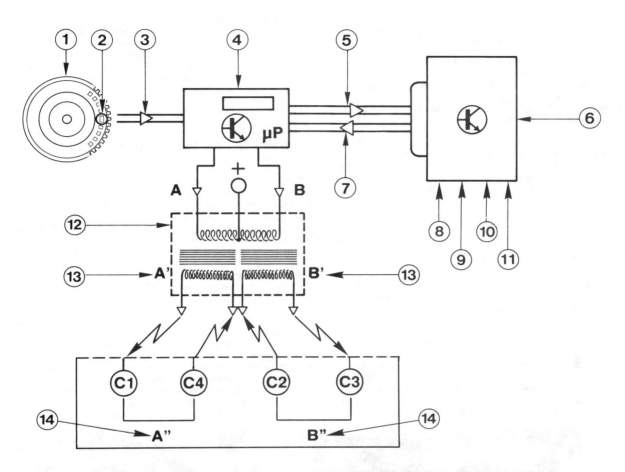

Fig. 5.1 Distributorless ignition system (EDIS) as fitted to the 1.4 litre (CFi) and 1.6 litre (EFi) CVH engine models (Sec 1)

A   Ignition circuit A
B   Ignition circuit B
C1 Cylinder No 1
C2 Cylinder No 2
C3 Cylinder No 3
C4 Cylinder No 4
1   Flywheel

2   Crankshaft speed/position sensor
3   Reference signal (to EDIS module)
4   EDIS module
5   Profile ignition pulse (PIP) signal

6   EEC IV module
7   Spark advance word signal (SAW)
8   Inlet manifold pressure signal
9   Coolant temperature signal

10 Throttle position signal
11 Octane adjust
12 DIS coil
13 Coil A and B
14 Trigger pulse for cylinder (pair)

management module (photo). The module is mounted on the left-hand inner wing (apron) panel. The system type and the module fitted depend on the engine size and fuel system arrangement. They are categorised as follows.

5   1.3 HCS engine: This system is controlled by a UESC module (on 15.04 emission level models) or a UPAC type module (on NEEC 5th emission level models). Input readings from an inlet manifold sensor (incorporated in the module), a crankshaft position/speed sensor and an engine coolant sensor enable the exact ignition timing to be processed in accordance with the operating conditions. An air (intake) charge temperature sensor is also fitted on models complying with the NEEC 5th emission control regulations, the function of which is to enable the module to regulate the fuel/air mixture for improved control of exhaust emissions.

6   1.4 and 1.6 CVH carburettor engine: The engine management module fitted on these engine variants is dependent on the emission level requirement. On 1.4 and 1.6 litre models required to meet the less stringent 15.04 Emission Level, and the 1.4 litre model required to comply with the more demanding NEEC 5th Emission Level, an Electronic Spark Control Polymide (ESCP) module is fitted. The 1.6 litre engine required to meet the NEEC 5th Emission Control standard is

fitted with an Electronic Spark Control (ESC) Hybrid H2 module. This latter model also incorporates a catalytic converter in the exhaust system and a pulse air sensor in the air intake system. On all types, input readings from an inlet manifold sensor (incorporated in the module), a crankshaft position/speed sensor and an engine coolant sensor enable the exact ignition timing to be processed in accordance with the operating conditions. An air (intake) charge temperature sensor is also fitted on 1.6 litre models complying with the NEEC 5th emission control regulations, the function of which is to enable the module to regulate the fuel/air mixture for improved control of exhaust emission. The 1.6 litre models fitted with the CTX (automatic) transmission, power steering and/or air conditioning, are fitted with an ESC P3 module which provides an electronic idle speed control.

7   1.4 CVH engine with CFi and 1.6 CVH engine with EFi: The engine management module on these models operates in conjunction with an EDIS 4 module, in which the signal indicated by the engine speed/position sensor is transmitted to the EDIS module. This converts the input information to a square wave form signal, known as PIP (Profile Ignition Pick-up), and this is in turn then transmitted to the main module. This information, together with data received from other sensors (engine coolant temperature sensor, air charge temperature sensor, manifold absolute pressure sensor and throttle position sensor) is processed and enables the module to provide the engine with the optimum ignition timing.

8 Due to the sophisticated nature of the electronic ignition system the following precautions must be observed to prevent damage to the components and reduce risk of personal injury.

   (a) *Ensure that the ignition is switched off before disconnecting any of the ignition wiring.*
   (b) *Ensure that the ignition is switched off before connecting or disconnecting any ignition test equipment.*
   (c) *Do not allow an HT lead to short out or spark against the computer control unit body.*

Warning: *The voltages produced by the electronic ignition system are considerably higher than those produced by conventional systems. Extreme care must be taken when working on the system with the ignition switched on. Persons with surgically-implanted cardiac pacemaker devices should keep well clear of the ignition circuits, components and test equipment.*

2 Ignition system – testing

There are two main symptoms indicating faults in the ignition system. Either the engine will not start (or fire), or the engine is difficult to start and misfires. Apart from checking the condition and serviceability of the ignition HT leads, connectors and the spark plugs, the only other item that can be easily checked out is that the engine and engine management earth leads and their connections are clean and secure.

In damp climatic conditions, the HT leads may be effected by moisture. To disperse moisture, Holts Wet Start can be very effective. Holts damp start should be used for providing a sealing coat to exclude moisture from the ignition system, and in extreme difficulty, Holts Cold Start will help to start the engine when only a weak spark occurs.

There is very little that can be tested using conventional methods on the electronic ignition circuits because they are integrated into the engine management system. Substitution of individual components in the system concerned is one method of finding and curing a fault but this could prove an expensive method. It is therefore strongly recommended that fault diagnosis of the ignition/engine management system be entrusted to a Ford dealer with the required diagnostic testing equipment. Such equipment can quickly, safely and accurately diagnose any faults in the system, whereas unauthorised tampering can easily do more harm than good.

3 Coil – removal and refitting

Removal

1 Disconnect the battery earth lead.
2 The location of the ignition coil is dependent on the engine type. On the 1.3 litre HCS engine, the coil is mounted on the side of the cylinder block, beneath the inlet manifold. On 1.4 and 1.6 litre CVH engines, the coil is more accessible, being located on a mounting bracket bolted to the rear end of the cylinder head. The coil removal for each type is otherwise the same. First compress the retaining clip and detach the wiring multi-plug from the ignition coil unit (photo).
3 The coil can be removed with the HT leads left attached, in which case disconnect the leads from their respective spark plugs and from the location clips in the rocker cover or air intake duct (as applicable). If preferred, the HT leads can be disconnected from the coil. First check that both the ignition HT leads and their fitted positions are clearly marked numerically to ensure correct refitting. Spot mark them accordingly if necessary using quick drying paint.
4 If disconnecting the leads from the spark plugs, pull them free by gripping on the connector, not the lead. To detach the leads from the ignition coil, compress the retaining arms of each lead connector at the coil and detach each lead in turn (photo).
5 Unscrew the three Torx type retaining screws and remove the coil

3.2 Disconnecting the multi-plug from the ignition coil (CVH engine shown)

3.4 Disconnecting an HT lead from the ignition coil (CVH engine)

3.5A Unbolting the ignition coil from the HCS engine

3.5B Removing the ignition coil from the CVH engine (leaving the HT leads attached)

3.6A Detach the wiring connector from the capacitor (where fitted) ...

3.6B ... and undo the three coil mounting bracket bolts – arrowed (CVH engine)

4.2 Disconnecting the wiring connector from the engine speed/position sensor (on the HCS engine)

unit from its mounting on the end of the engine (photos).

6   If required, the coil mounting bracket can be removed from the rear end of the cylinder head on the CVH engine. Where a capacitor is mounted on top of the bracket disconnect its lead connector, then unscrew and remove the three coil bracket retaining bolts and withdraw the mounting bracket (photos).

Refitting

7   Refit in the reverse order of removal. Ensure that the HT leads are correctly and cleanly reconnected. Check that the lugs of the retaining arms on the coil end connectors fully engage to secure each HT lead to the coil.

8   Reconnect the battery and restart the engine. On EFi models, follow the engine restart procedure in Section 4 of Chapter 12 to allow the engine management module to relearn its values.

4   Engine speed/position sensor – removal and refitting

Removal

1   Disconnect the battery earth lead.

2   Compress the retaining clip and pull free the wiring multi-plug connector from the speed sensor unit, but take care to pull on the connector, not the lead (photo).

3   Undo the retaining Torx type screw and withdraw the engine speed/position sensor from its location in the bellhousing flange of the cylinder block (photo).

Refitting

4   Refit in the reverse order of removal, but ensure that the sensor is fully inserted into its aperture. On completion, reconnect the battery and restart the engine. On EFi models follow the restart procedure described in Section 4 of Chapter 12 to allow the engine management module to relearn its values.

5   Engine management control module (carburettor models) – removal and refitting

Removal

1   Disconnect the battery earth lead.

2   Detach the vacuum hose from the module.

3   According to type, either compress the lock tab securing the wiring

4.3 Engine speed/position sensor shown removed from engine

5.3 Engine management control module and wiring connection on the 1.6 litre carburettor engine model

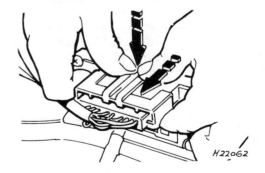

Fig. 5.2 Disconnecting the wiring connector from the UESC/UPAC type module on a 1.3 litre engine (Sec 5)

multi-plug in position, or where applicable, undo the retaining bolt, then withdraw the plug from the module (photo).

4   Undo the retaining screws and remove the module from the inner wing apron panel.

Refitting

5   Refit in the reverse order of removal. On completion, reconnect the battery and restart the engine.

6.2 EDIS control module and wiring connection on the 1.6 litre EFi model

7.2 Engine management control module location on the 1.6 litre EFi model

3   Undo the two retaining screws and remove the module from the inner wing panel.

Refitting

4   Refit in the reverse order of removal. On completion, reconnect the battery and restart the engine. On EFi models follow the procedure described in Section 4 of Chapter 12 to allow the engine management module to relearn its values.

7.3 Engine management control module removal on the 1.6 litre EFi model

6   EDIS control module (CFi and EFi engine models) – removal and refitting

Removal

1   Disconnect the battery earth lead.
2   Disconnect the wiring multi-plug from the module, pulling on the plug, not the wire (photo).

7   Engine management control module (CFi and EFi models) – removal and refitting

Removal

1   Disconnect the battery earth lead.
2   Working inside the vehicle, remove the side kick panel from the front passenger's footwell to gain access to the management module (photo).
3   Release the module from its retaining bracket, then unscrew the retaining bolt and remove the wiring multi-plug from the module (photo).

Refitting

4   Refit in the reverse order of removal. On completion, reconnect the battery and restart the engine. On EFi models follow the restart procedure described in Section 4 of Chapter 12 to allow the engine management module to relearn its values.

Chapter 6 Clutch

Contents

Specifications

Type .... Single dry plate with diaphragm spring. Operated by self adjusting cable

Clutch disc (driven plate)
Diameter:
    1.3 and 1.4 litre .... 190 mm
    1.6 litre .... 220 mm
Lining thickness .... 3.20 mm (nominal)
Input shaft and release bearing guide sleeve grease .... To Ford specification ESD-MIC220-A (refer to a Ford dealer)

Torque wrench settings

	Nm	lbf ft
Pressure plate to flywheel	25 to 34	18 to 25
Clutch release lever to lever shaft	21 to 28	16 to 21
Clutch housing cover plate	34 to 46	25 to 34

1 General information

All manual transmission models are equipped with a cable-operated single dry plate diaphragm spring clutch assembly. The unit consists of a steel cover (dowelled and bolted to the rear face of the flywheel), the pressure plate and diaphragm spring.

The clutch disc is free to slide along the splines of the gearbox input shaft and is held in position between the flywheel and the pressure plate by the pressure of the diaphragm spring. Friction lining material is riveted to the clutch disc (driven plate) which has a spring cushioned hub to absorb transmission shocks and help ensure a smooth take-up of the drive.

The clutch is actuated by a cable, controlled by the clutch pedal. The clutch release mechanism consists of a release arm and bearing which are in permanent contact with the fingers of the diaphragm spring. Depressing the clutch pedal actuates the release arm by means of the cable. The arm pushes the release bearing against the diaphragm fingers, so moving the centre of the diaphragm spring inwards. As the centre of the spring is pushed in, the outside of the spring pivots out, so moving the pressure plate backwards and disengaging its grip on the clutch disc.

When the pedal is released, the diaphragm spring forces the pressure plate back into contact with the friction linings on the clutch disc. The disc is now firmly held between the pressure plate and the flywheel, thus transmitting engine power to the gearbox.

Wear of the friction material on the clutch disc is automatically compensated for by a self-adjusting mechanism attached to the clutch pedal. The mechanism consists of a toothed segment, a notched pawl and a tension spring. One end of the clutch cable is attached to the segment which is free to pivot on the pedal, but is kept in tension by the spring. As the pedal is depressed the pawl contacts the segment thus locking it and allowing the pedal to pull the cable and operate the clutch. As the pedal is released the tension spring causes the segment to move free of the pawl and rotate slightly, thus taking up any free play that may exist in the cable.

2 Clutch cable – removal and refitting

Removal

1 Disengage the clutch cable from the release lever by gripping the inner cable with pliers and pulling it forwards to disengage the cable nipple from the release lever. Take care not to damage the cable if it is to

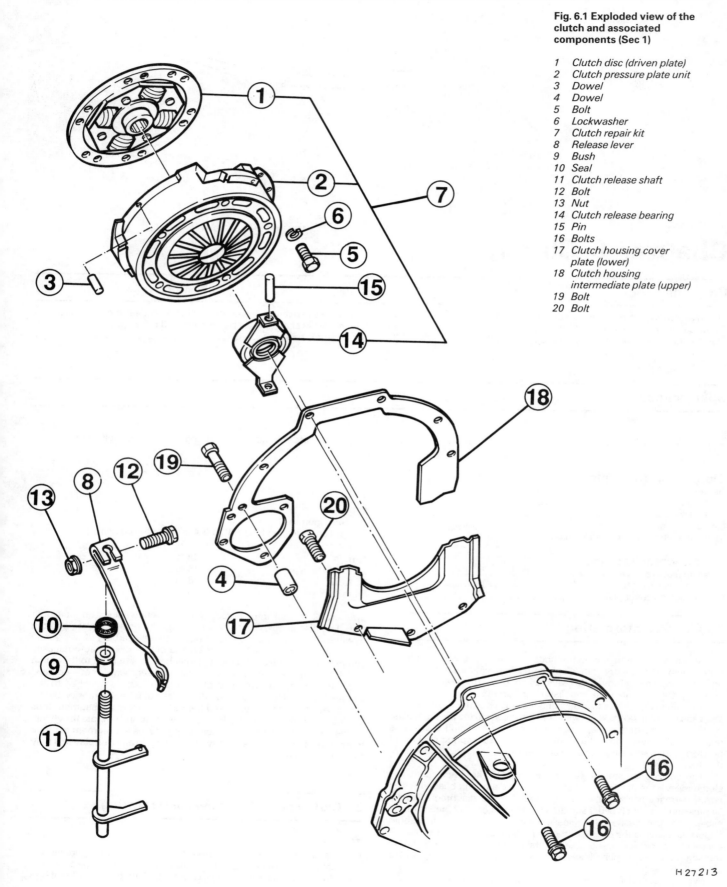

Fig. 6.1 Exploded view of the clutch and associated components (Sec 1)

1   Clutch disc (driven plate)
2   Clutch pressure plate unit
3   Dowel
4   Dowel
5   Bolt
6   Lockwasher
7   Clutch repair kit
8   Release lever
9   Bush
10 Seal
11 Clutch release shaft
12 Bolt
13 Nut
14 Clutch release bearing
15 Pin
16 Bolts
17 Clutch housing cover plate (lower)
18 Clutch housing intermediate plate (upper)
19 Bolt
20 Bolt

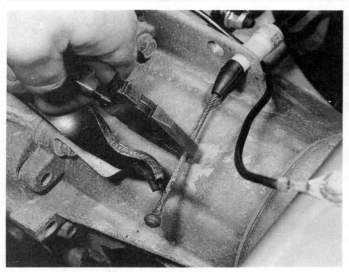

2.1A Disengage the clutch cable from the lever ...

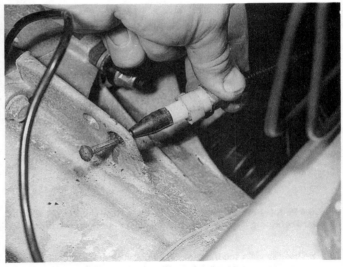

2.1B ... and withdraw the cable through the locating lug

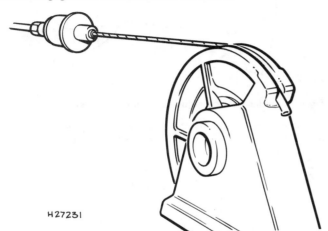

Fig. 6.2 Clutch cable connection at the pedal end (Sec 2)

be re-used. Disengage the outer cable from the support lug on top of the bellhousing (photos).

2   Working from the driver's footwell, unhook the segment tension spring from its pedal location.

3   Release the cable from the pedal segment so that it may be withdrawn through the engine compartment.

4   Pull the cable through the aperture in the bulkhead and withdraw it from the engine compartment.

Refitting

5   To refit the cable, thread it through from the engine compartment and fit the inner cable over the segment, engaging the nipple to secure it. Reconnect the tension spring.

6   Reconnect the cable at the transmission end by passing it through the support lug on the top of the transmission and engaging it with the release lever. On completion, operate the clutch and check it for satisfactory operation.

3   Clutch pedal – removal and refitting

Removal

1   Disconnect the battery negative terminal.

2   Disconnect the clutch cable at the transmission end by slipping the cable nipple out of the release fork and disengaging the outer cable from the bracket on the bellhousing.

3   Referring to Chapter 12 for details, detach the fusebox and the relay

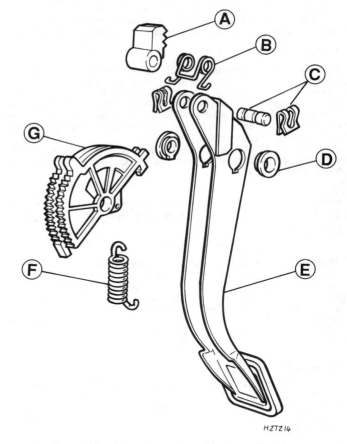

Fig. 6.3 Clutch pedal and associated components (Sec 3)

A   Pawl
B   Pawl tension spring
C   Pedal connecting rod and clip
D   Pedal/shaft bushes
E   Clutch pedal
F   Toothed segment tension spring
G   Toothed segment

multi-plugs, then position the fusebox unit out of the way to allow access to the clutch pedal.

4   Release the clutch cable from the pedal (see Sec 2).

5   Release the brake light switch in a clockwise direction and extract it from the pedal bracket.

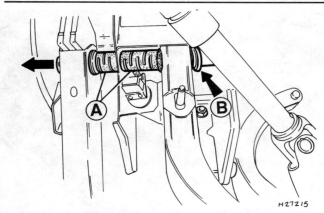

Fig. 6.4 Pedal shaft removal showing the spacer sleeves (A) and the inboard retaining clip (B) – left-hand drive version shown (Sec 3)

6   Release the clip securing the brake pedal connecting rod.
7   Release the retaining clip from the end of the pedal shaft, then slide the shaft through (away from the steering column) and remove the brake pedal, the spacer sleeves and the clutch pedal.
8   The pedal can now be dismantled as necessary by prising out the bushes, the tension spring or the adjustment mechanism as required.

Refitting

9   Refitting is a reversal of the removal procedure. Lubricate the pedal shaft using a suitable 'dry' lubricant. When fitting the shaft bushes, ensure that they are correctly located. Do not refit the toothed segment tension spring into position until after the pedal is fitted onto the shaft. The pawl and its tension spring must be fitted so that the pawl is bearing on the toothed segment. Pull the spring into position using a suitable length of temporarily attached wire.
10   On completion, operate the clutch pedal to ensure satisfactory operation of the clutch. Also check that the brake stop light switch is functioning correctly.

4   Clutch assembly – removal, inspection and refitting

Warning: *Dust created by clutch wear and deposited on the clutch components may contain asbestos which is a health hazard. DO NOT blow it out with compressed air or inhale any of it. DO NOT use petrol or petroleum-based solvents to clean off the dust. Brake system cleaner or methylated spirit should be used to flush the dust into a suitable receptacle. After the clutch components are wiped clean with rags, dispose of the contaminated rags and cleaner in a sealed, marked container.*

Removal

1   Access to the clutch may be gained in one of two ways. Either the engine/transmission unit can be removed, as described in Chapter 2, and the transmission separated from the engine, or the engine may be left in the car and the transmission unit removed independently, as described in Chapter 7.
2   Having separated the transmission from the engine, unscrew and remove the six clutch cover retaining bolts, working in a diagonal sequence and slackening the bolts only a few turns at a time. Hold the flywheel stationary by positioning a screwdriver over the front location dowel on the cylinder block and engaging it with the starter ring gear.
3   Ease the clutch cover off its locating dowels and be prepared to catch the clutch disc which will drop out as the cover is removed. Note which way round the disc is fitted (photo).

Inspection

4   With the clutch assembly removed, clean off all traces of asbestos dust using a dry cloth. This is best done outside or in a well-ventilated area; asbestos dust is harmful, and must not be inhaled.
5   Examine the linings of the clutch disc for wear and loose rivets, and

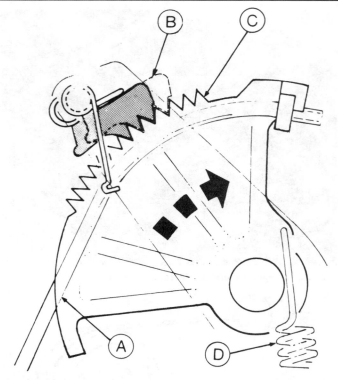

Fig. 6.5 Clutch cable self-adjusting mechanism (Sec 3)

A   Clutch cable   C   Toothed segment
B   Pawl   D   Tension spring

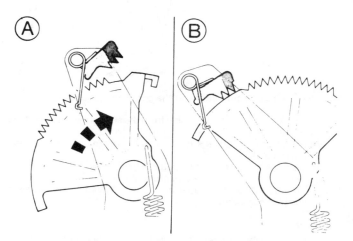

Fig. 6.6 Positioning of the clutch self-adjuster mechanism prior to refitting the pedal (Sec 3)

A   Lift pawl and turn the   B   Pawl bearing on the
    segment   smooth section of the
                                  segment

the disc rim for distortion, cracks, broken torsion springs and worn splines. The surface of the friction linings may be highly glazed, but as long as the friction material pattern can be clearly seen this is satisfactory. If there is any sign of oil contamination, indicated by a continuous, or patchy, shiny black discoloration, the disc must be renewed and the source of the contamination traced and rectified. This will be either a leaking crankshaft oil seal or gearbox input shaft oil seal, or both. The renewal procedure for the former is given in Chapter 2, however renewal of the gearbox input shaft oil seal should be entrusted to a Ford dealer as it involves dismantling the gearbox and the renewal

4.3 Removing the clutch cover and disc from the flywheel

4.9 Clutch disc (driven plate) orientation mark

4.12 Centralising the clutch unit

4.16 With the clutch unit centralised, tighten the clutch cover retaining bolts to the specified torque wrench setting

of the clutch release bearing guide tube using a press. The disc must also be renewed if the lining thickness has worn down to, or just above, the level of the rivet heads.

6   Check the machined faces of the flywheel and pressure plate. If either is grooved, or heavily scored, renewal is necessary. The pressure plate must also be renewed if any cracks are apparent, or if the diaphragm spring is damaged or its pressure suspect.

7   With the gearbox removed it is advisable to check the condition of the release bearing, as described in Section 5.

Refitting

8   It is important that no oil or grease is allowed to come into contact with the friction material of the clutch disc or the pressure plate and flywheel faces. To ensure this, it is advisable to refit the clutch assembly with clean hands and to wipe down the pressure plate and flywheel faces with a clean dry rag before assembly begins.

9   Begin reassembly by placing the clutch disc against the flywheel, ensuring that it is correctly orientated. It may be marked 'flywheel side', but if not, position it with the word 'schwungradseite' stamped in the disc face towards the flywheel (photo).

10   Place the clutch cover over the dowels, refit the retaining bolts and tighten them finger-tight so that the clutch disc is gripped, but can still be moved.

11   The clutch disc must now be centralised so that, when the engine and transmission are mated, the splines of the gearbox input shaft will pass through the splines in the centre of the clutch disc hub.

12   Centralisation can be carried out by inserting a round bar through the hole in the centre of the clutch disc, so that the end of the bar rests in the innermost hole in the rear end of the crankshaft (photo).

13   Using the support bearing as a fulcrum, move the bar sideways or up and down to move the clutch disc in whichever direction is necessary to achieve centralisation.

14   Centralisation can then be checked by removing the bar and viewing the clutch disc hub in relation to the support bearing. When the support bearing appears exactly in the centre of the clutch disc hub, the position is correct.

15   An alternative and more accurate method of centralisation is to use a commercially available clutch aligning tool obtainable from most accessory shops (see *Tools and working facilities* at the beginning of this Manual).

16   Once the clutch is centralised, progressively tighten the cover bolts in a diagonal sequence to the torque setting given in the Specifications (photo).

17   Ensure that the input shaft splines, driven plate (clutch disc) splines and release bearing guide sleeve are clean. Apply a thin smear of the special grease given in the Specifications to the entire surface of the input shaft splines and the release bearing guide sleeve. *Only the specified grease should be used because other lubricants can cause problems after a short time in service. Do not apply any more grease than stated otherwise the excess will inevitably find its way onto the friction linings when the vehicle is in use.*

18   The transmission can now be refitted to the engine by referring to the relevant Chapter of this Manual.

5 Clutch release bearing – removal, inspection and refitting

Removal

1   To gain access to the release bearing it is necessary to separate the engine and transmission either by removing the transmission unit individually, or by removing both units as an assembly and separating

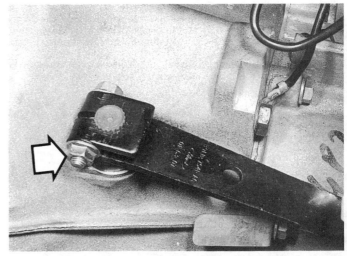

5.2 Clutch release lever-to-shaft connection with clamp bolt and nut (arrowed)

5.3 Withdrawing the clutch release bearing from the release fork

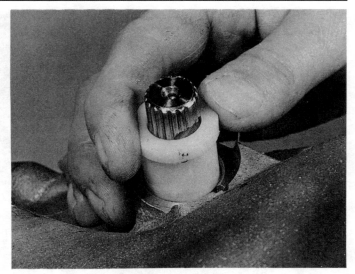

6.3 Removing the nylon bush from the release shaft

Inspection

4   Check the bearing for smoothness of operation and renew it if there is any sign of harshness or roughness as the bearing is spun.

Refitting

5   Refit the bearing in the reverse order of removal. Ensure that the clutch release lever and shaft are reassembled as marked during removal and tighten the retaining bolt to the specified torque wrench setting.

6.4 Removing the clutch release shaft

them after removal. Depending on the method chosen, the appropriate procedures will be found in Chapter 2 or Chapter 7.

2   With the transmission removed from the engine, undo the clamp bolt securing the clutch lever to the release shaft. Mark the relative position of the shaft to the lever, then withdraw the lever from the shaft (photo).

3   Draw the release bearing from its guide sleeve and unhook it from the locating pin on the upper release shaft fork (photo).

6   Clutch release shaft and bush – removal and refitting

Removal

1   Remove the clutch release bearing as described in the previous Section.

2   Remove the protective cap from around the top of the release shaft splines to allow access to the bush.

3   Extract the bush by gently levering it from the housing using a pair of screwdrivers, then lift it out over the splines of the input shaft (photo).

4   With the bush removed, the release shaft can be withdrawn (if required) by lifting it from its lower bearing bore, manoeuvring it sideways and withdrawing it downwards (photo).

Refitting

5   Refit in the reverse order of removal. Slide the bush over the shaft and locate it so that it is flush in the upper housing, then fit the protective cap.

6   Refit the release bearing as described in the previous Section.

Chapter 7 Transmission

Contents

Specifications

Part A: Manual transmission

Type .... Four or five speeds and reverse. Synchromesh on all forward gears. Final drive integral with main gearbox

Gear ratios

Four-speed transmission:
    1st 3.15:1
    2nd.. 1.19:1
    3rd... 1.28:1
    4th... 0.95:1
    Reverse 3.77:1

Five-speed transmission – 1.3 and 1.4 litre carburettor engined models:
    1st 3.15:1
    2nd.. 1.91:1
    3rd... 1.28:1
    4th... 0.95:1
    5th... 0.75:1
Reverse 3.62:1

Five-speed transmission – 1.4 litre fuel injection engined models:
    1st 3.58:1
    2nd.. 2.04:1
    3rd... 1.32:1
    4th... 0.95:1
    5th... 0.76:1
    Reverse 3.62:1

1.6 litre engine:
    1st 3.15:1
    2nd.. 1.91:1
    3rd... 1.28:1
    4th... 0.95:1
    5th... 0.76:1
    Reverse 3.62:1

Final drive ratios

1.3 litre engine.. 3.84:1
1.4 litre carburettor engine... 3.82:1
1.4 litre fuel injection engine.. 4.06:1
1.6 litre engine.. 3.82:1

Torque wrench settings

	Nm	lbf ft
Oil filler level plug	23 to 30	17 to 22
Reversing light switch	16 to 20	12 to 15
Engine-to-transmission bolts	35 to 45	26 to 33
Clutch housing cover plate bolts	34 to 46	25 to 34
Engine/transmission housing braces (1.6 litre)	40 to 50	30 to 37
Engine transmission rear left-hand mounting bracket-to-transmission...	41 to 58	30 to 43
Engine/transmission rear left-hand mounting bracket-to-rubber mounting	58 to 79	43 to 58
Engine/transmission front left-hand mounting bracket-to-rubber mounting	58 to 79	43 to 58
Engine/transmission front left-hand mounting bracket brace	41 to 58	30 to 43
Gearshift stabiliser rod-to-transmission	50 to 60	37 to 44
Gearshift rod to transmission selector shaft	14 to 17	10 to 12
Selector gate to housing	18 to 23	13 to 17
Small housing section-to-large housing retaining bolts	12 to 14	9 to 10
Gearshift housing-to-floor	6 to 8	5 to 6
Gearshift gaiter-to-body	2	1.4
Gearshift stabiliser rod-to-housing	5 to 7	3.7 to 5.1

Part B: Automatic transmission

Type .... Automatic, continuously variable over full speed range

Final drive ratio 3.842:1

Torque wrench settings

	Nm	lbf ft
Transmission fluid cooling pipes-to-oil cooler	18 to 22	13 to 16
Transmission fluid cooling pipe connections to transmission housing....	24 to 31	18 to 23
Transmission fluid cooling pipe connections at transmission	22 to 26	16 to 19
Starter inhibitor switch	10 to 14	7 to 10
Transmission-to-engine flange bolts	27 to 50	20 to 37
Torsional vibration damper to flywheel	24 to 33	18 to 24
Lower engine adaptor plate (clutch housing cover)	7.5 to 10	5 to 7
Selector lever housing to floor	8.5 to 11.5	6 to 8
Selector cable bracket to transmission housing	34 to 46	25 to 34
Selector lever rod-to-lever guide	20 to 25	15 to 18
Transmission housing front bracket	41 to 58	30 to 43
Front bracket to mounting	58 to 79	43 to 58
Front mounting to side member	58 to 79	43 to 58
Rear bracket to mounting	58 to 79	43 to 58
Rear bracket to transmission mounting	58 to 79	43 to 58
Rear mounting to chassis crossmember	58 to 79	43 to 58

Part A: Manual gearbox

1 General information

1 The manual transmission is either of four- or five-speed constant mesh type with one reverse gear. Baulk ring synchromesh gear engagement is used on all the forward gears.

2 Both the gearbox and the differential unit are housed in a two-section light alloy housing which is bolted to the transversely-mounted engine (photo). The five-speed transmission has fifth gear and its synchromesh unit contained in a housing attached to the side of the main transmission case.

3 The transmission is lubricated independently of the engine, the capacity differing according to the gearbox type (see *Lubricants, fluids and capacities* in Chapter 1). The gearbox and differential both share the same lubricating oil. Torque from the gearbox output shaft is transmitted to the crownwheel (which is bolted to the differential unit) and then from the differential gears to the driveshafts.

4 Gearshift is by means of a floor-mounted gear lever which is connected by a remote control housing and gearshift rod to the gearbox selector shaft.

1.2 Manual transmission unit coupled to the HCS (OHV) engine

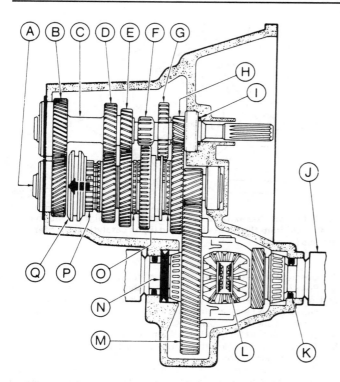

Fig. 7.1 Sectional view of the four-speed transmission (Sec 1)

A	Mainshaft	K	Oil seal
B	4th gear	L	Driveshaft snap ring
C	Input shaft		engaged in differential
D	3rd gear	M	Final drive gear
E	2nd gear		(crownwheel)
F	Reverse gear	N	Diaphragm springs
G	Reverse idler gear	O	1st/2nd synchro with
H	1st gear		reverse gear
I	Input shaft oil seal	P	3rd/4th synchro
J	Driveshaft inner CV joint	Q	3rd/4th synchro ring (4th
			gear engaged)

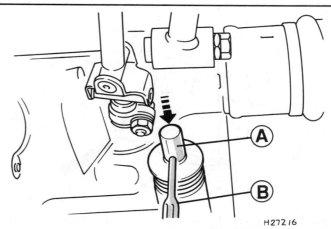

Fig. 7.2 Gearchange linkage/mechanism adjustment (Sec 2)

A   Selector shaft   B   Rod or punch

2   Gearchange linkage/mechanism – adjustment

1   Apply the handbrake then jack up the front of the vehicle and support it on axle stands.
2   On four-speed models, move the gear lever fully into the 2nd gear engagement position. On five-speed models, move the gear lever fully into the 4th gear engagement position.
3   Working from underneath the vehicle, loosen off the gearshift rod-to-gear selector shaft clamp bolt and disengage the shift rod from the transmission selector shaft (photos). Slide the selector shaft back and forth to find its central position, then turn the selector shaft to the right and left to find the central position in the transversal plane. Hold the selector shaft in the centralised position, then insert a suitable rod (or punch) into the hole in the selector shaft in the transmission and move it as far forwards as possible (see Fig. 7.2).
4   Insert the fabricated 'lock pin' adjustment tool (from the left-hand side) and secure it in position with a sturdy elastic band or similar as shown in Fig. 7.3.
5   Check that the selector shaft coupling surfaces are free of grease, then reconnect the gearshift rod onto the transmission selector shaft and secure it by tightening the clamp bolt to the specified torque setting.

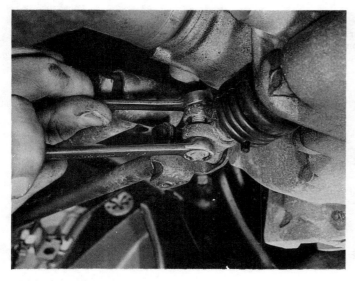

2.3A Loosen off the clamp bolt ...

2.3B ... and disengage the gearshift rod from the selector shaft

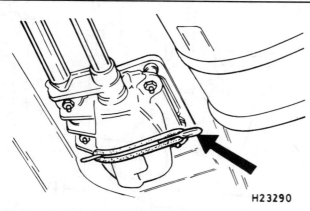

Fig. 7.3 Gear lever locked in position by fabricated tool with elastic band to secure it (Sec 2)

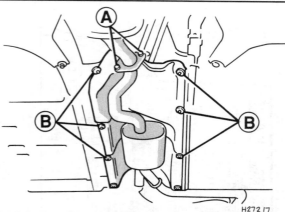

Fig. 7.4 Detach the exhaust system at the front joint (A) and the heatshield from the points indicated (B) on catalytic converter models (Sec 3)

6   Extract the locking pin, then check the gear lever movement for the satisfactory engagement of all gears, selecting each gear in turn to confirm that the mechanism has been correctly reset. Further minor adjustment may be required.
7   With the adjustment correctly made, lower the vehicle to complete.

3   Gearchange linkage/mechanism – removal and refitting

Removal

1   Working inside the car, first engage second gear (four-speed transmission) or fourth gear (five-speed transmission). This will provide the correct re-engagement and adjustment for the gearchange mechanism during reassembly.

2   Unscrew and remove the gear lever knob.
3   Prise free and release the gear lever boot from the centre console and remove it upwards from the gear lever. If required, the gear lever-to-selector unit can be prised free and withdrawn to inspect the selector balljoint from above (photos).
4   Loosen off the four gear lever retaining nuts (photo).
5   Apply the handbrake, then jack up the front of the vehicle and support it on axle stands.
6   Working beneath the vehicle, release the flexible exhaust pipe mountings and disconnect the exhaust system from the downpipe. On catalytic converter models, also detach the heat shield from the underside of the floor pan to allow access to the underside of the gear lever for its removal. When detaching the exhaust system refer to Chapter 4 for details.
7   Mark the relative fitted positions of the selector shaft and gearshift

3.3A Disengage the gear lever-to-console boot for access to the unit retaining nuts

3.3B Remove the lever gaiter to inspect the gear lever balljoint from above

3.4 Four gear lever retaining nuts (arrowed)

3.8A Unscrewing the stabiliser-to-transmission bolt. Note washer (arrowed)

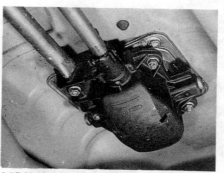

3.8B Underside view of the gear lever unit

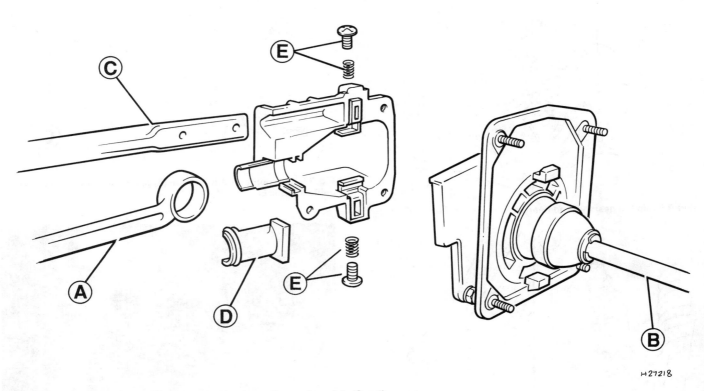

Fig. 7.5 Exploded view of the gear lever mechanism – 5-speed models (Sec 4)

A   Gearshift rod   C   Stabiliser rod   D   Guide bushes   E   Screws and springs
B   Gear lever

rod, then undo the clamp bolt and separate the shaft from the rod.
8   Unscrew and remove the gearshift rod stabiliser retaining bolt (photos). Note the position of the washer as the bolt is withdrawn. Support the gear lever assembly from underneath and have an assistant unscrew and remove the four gear lever retaining nuts within the vehicle, then lower and withdraw the gearchange mechanism from underneath the vehicle.

Refitting

9   Refitting is a reversal of removal, but lubricate the pivot points with grease. Before lowering the vehicle from the axle stands, check and if necessary adjust the gearchange linkage as described in Section 2.

4 Gearchange mechanism – dismantling, overhaul and reassembly

Dismantling

1   On four-speed models, extract the circlip and remove the rubber spring and spring cup from the gear lever. Turn the damping plate slightly, release the half-shells (using a screwdriver) then separate the damper plate from the gearchange mechanism. Undo the four retaining bolts and detach the cover from the gearchange gate.
2   On five-speed models, extract the circlip shown in photo 3.3B and remove the rubber spring and spring carrier from the gear lever. Undo the retaining screw on each side and remove the lateral locating guides and springs. Undo the four retaining bolts and nuts, then separate the gear lever casing halves to remove the gear lever, gearshift rod and the lateral locating guides.

Overhaul

3   Clean and inspect the various component parts of the gearchange mechanism. Renew any components which show signs of excessive wear or damage.
4   In addition to checking the gearchange mechanism itself, also ensure that the stabiliser rod bush is in good condition. If the bush is in poor condition, it can cause engine and transmission noises to be transmitted to the interior of the vehicle. If renewing the bush, note the position of the voids and take care not to distort or damage the new bush as it is drawn into position.

Reassembly

5   Reassemble the gearchange mechanism in the reverse order of

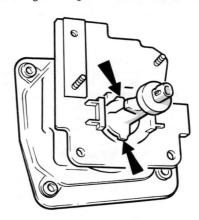

Fig. 7.6 Location lugs of gear lever must seat in upper housing slots (Sec 4)

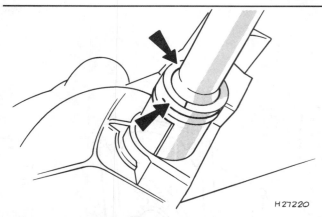

Fig. 7.7 Clip the gearshift rod bearing into place to secure (Sec 4)

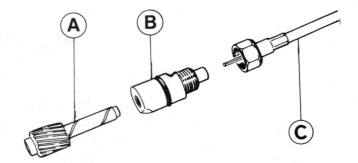

Fig. 7.8 Speedometer drive pinion (A) pinion bearing (B) and drive cable (C) (Sec 5)

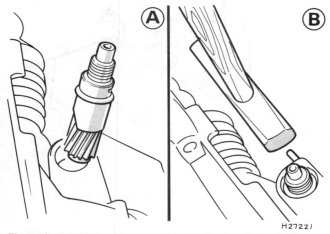

Fig. 7.9 Insert the speedometer drive pinion/bearing unit (A) and secure with a new retaining pin (Sec 5)

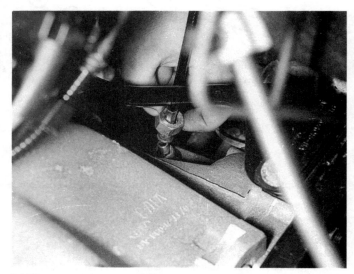

5.2 Disconnecting the speedometer cable from the pinion

dismantling. Ensure that the gear lever locating lugs engage in the slots in the upper half of the mechanism casing before clipping the gearshift rod bearing into position.

6   When fitting the circlip to secure the rubber spring and spring carrier, the gap of the clip must be at the front or to the rear so that it engages with the two lateral notches in the lever.

5   Speedometer drive pinion and/or cable – removal and refitting

Removal

1   Disconnect the battery earth lead.

2   Undo the retaining nut and withdraw the speedometer cable from its drive pinion in the top face of the transmission (photo).

3   To remove the cable, detach and withdraw the instrument cluster sufficiently to detach the speedometer cable from the rear of the cluster (refer to Chapter 12 for details). The cable can then be released from its retaining clips and grommets and withdrawn through the bulkhead from the engine compartment side (photo).

4   To remove the drive pinion from the transmission, grip the retaining pin with self-locking grips or pliers and withdraw it from the drive pinion housing. Pull the drive pinion out of its housing, but take care not to tilt it because the pinion and bearing are not secured and can easily be separated if the pinion is snagged.

Refitting

5   When refitting the pinion to the transmission, fit a new O-ring seal and lubricate it with a smear of grease. Lubricate the pinion shaft with

5.3 Withdrawing the speedometer cable through the bulkhead

engine oil. Ensure that the pinion is fully engaged, then drive the retaining pin into position so that it is felt to contact its stop and protrudes by approximately 5 mm.

6   Refit in the reverse order of removal. When refitting the cable, ensure that the bulkhead grommet seats securely and where applicable

6.8 Levering out an old driveshaft oil seal

6.10 Driving a new driveshaft oil seal into position using a suitable socket

the tape mark on the cable is positioned at the grommet.
7   On completion, reconnect the battery earth lead. On EFi models, restart the engine and run it as described in Section 4 of Chapter 12 to allow the engine management system to relearn its values.

6   Differential output oil seal – renewal

1   Apply the handbrake then jack up the front of the vehicle and support it on axle stands. Remove the roadwheel on the appropriate side.
2   Unscrew the nut securing the steering track rod end to the steering arm, then use a balljoint removal tool to separate the balljoint taper.
3   Unscrew the retaining nut and then withdraw the through-bolt (noting its direction of fitting) from the spindle carrier to lower suspension arm balljoint. Disconnect the balljoint from the spindle carrier by levering it downwards, but take care not to damage the rubber gaiter or the joint. If necessary, prise open the clamp on the spindle carrier to allow the joint to be separated from it.
4   Position a suitable container beneath the inboard end of the driveshaft and the transmission to catch any oil spillage as the driveshaft is withdrawn from the transmission.
5   Using a suitable lever, carefully prise free and withdraw the driveshaft from the transmission. Insert the lever between the transmission casing reinforcement rib and the shaft inner joint to avoid damaging the transmission casing (see photo 2.8 in Chapter 8). As the driveshaft is being prised free, have an assistant simultaneously pull the suspension unit outwards on that side to assist its withdrawal. When separated from the transmission, tie the driveshaft up using a length of strong cord or wire to prevent it hanging free. Note that the CV joint at the transmission end must not be allowed to be bent beyond an angle of 17°. The outboard CV joint has a stop and must not be angled beyond this point. Take care not to damage the driveshaft gaiters.
6   The snap ring in the groove at the inboard end of the driveshaft splines must be renewed before the driveshaft is refitted. Prise free and remove the old snap ring.
7   Wipe clean the old oil seal, note its orientation and measure its fitted depth below the casing edge. This is necessary to determine the correct fitted position of the new oil seal if the special Ford fitting tool (16-018) is not being used.
8   Remove the old oil seal by first using a small drift to tap the outer edge of the seal inwards so that the opposite edge of the seal tilts out of the casing. Use a screwdriver to carefully lever the old seal from the housing (photo). Alternatively, a pair of pliers can be used to pull the oil seal out of the casing. Take care not to damage the splines of the differential side gear or the oil seal housing.

9   Wipe clean the oil seal seating in the casing.
10   Carefully locate the new oil seal squarely into the casing. If possible, use the special Ford tool (16-018) to drive the new seal into position to the required fitted depth. If the tool is not available, use a piece of metal tube or a socket of the required diameter and tap the oil seal into position to its correct depth as previously noted (photo).
11   Fit the new snap ring into its groove at the inboard end of driveshaft and smear the splines of the driveshaft and the lips of the new oil seal with grease.
12   Have an assistant initially pull the roadwheel hub outwards to allow the inboard end of the driveshaft to be guided into position, then engage the driveshaft with the splines of the differential gear. Push the driveshaft squarely into position to the point where the snap ring is felt to snap into engagement with the differential side gear.
13   Reconnect the lower suspension arm balljoint to the spindle carrier unit. As the retaining bolt is fitted, ensure that it engages with the groove of the ballstud and also ensure that the bolt is fitted in the direction noted during its removal. Tighten the retaining nut to the specified torque (see Chapter 10).
14   Clean the track rod arm balljoint taper and the steering arm, then refit the balljoint to the arm and tighten the nut to the specified torque (see Chapter 10).
15   Top up the gearbox oil level with the correct quantity and grade of oil with reference to Chapter 1.
16   Refit the roadwheel and lower the vehicle to the ground.

7   Reversing lamp switch – removal and refitting

Removal

1   Apply the handbrake, then jack up the front of the vehicle and support it on axle stands.
2   Disconnect the wiring from the reversing lamp switch (photo).
3   Unscrew the switch from the side of the transmission and remove the washer.

Refitting

4   Clean the location in the gearbox and the threads of the switch.
5   Insert the switch together with a new washer and tighten it to the specified torque wrench setting.
6   Reconnect the wiring.

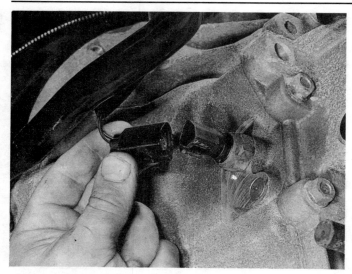

7.2 Disconnecting the reversing light switch lead

7   Check and if required, top up the gearbox oil level with the correct quantity and grade of oil with reference to Chapter 1.
8   Lower the vehicle to the ground.

8   Manual gearbox – removal and refitting

Note: *This Section describes the removal of the gearbox leaving the engine in position in the car, however if an adequate hoist is available it may be easier to remove both the engine and the gearbox together as described in Chapter 2 and then to separate the gearbox from the engine on the bench.*

Removal

1   The manual gearbox is removed downwards from the engine compartment after disconnecting it from the engine. Due to the weight of the unit, it will be necessary to have a suitable method of supporting the gearbox as it is lowered during removal and subsequently raised during its refitting. A trolley jack fitted with a suitable saddle to support the transmission unit as it is removed will be ideal, but failing this, an engine lift hoist and sling will suffice. The weight of the engine will also need to be supported whilst the transmission is detached from it and an engine support bar fitted in the front wing drain channel each side is ideal for this purpose, but care must be taken not to damage the wings or their paintwork. An engine support bar of the type required is shown in photo 36.34 of Chapter 2. If this type of tool is not available (or cannot be fabricated), the engine can be supported by blocks or a second jack from underneath.
2   Disconnect the battery earth lead.
3   On 1.6 litre EFi engine models, refer to Chapter 4 for details and

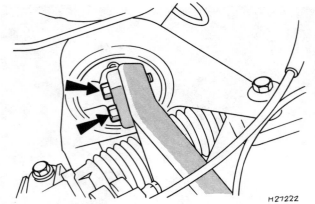

Fig. 7.10 Left-hand rear engine/transmission bolts (Sec 8)

remove the air cleaner unit. Disconnect the clutch cable from the clutch release lever as described in Chapter 6.
4   Undo the retaining nut and detach the speedometer drive cable from the transmission. Also where applicable, disconnect the speed sensor lead multi-plug. Position the cable (and where applicable, the sensor lead) out of the way.
5   Unbolt and disconnect the radio earth strap from the transmission.
6   Extract the transmission breather tube from the aperture in the chassis side member (photo).
7   On four-speed models, engage 2nd gear. On five-speed models, engage 4th gear. Positioning the selector lever in this position will ease realignment and adjustment of the gearchange linkage during the refitting procedures.
8   Unscrew and remove the three upper transmission to engine flange bolts. Note that one bolt secures the main earth strap to the battery, and one bolt retains the coolant hose locating strap (photo).
9   Unscrew and remove the two nuts securing the left-hand rear engine/transmission mounting bracket to the transmission (photo).
10   Apply the handbrake then raise the vehicle at the front and support it on axle stands at a sufficient height to allow the transmission to be withdrawn from under the front end.
11   If fitting an engine lifting bar to support the engine on HCS (OHV) engine models, unscrew and remove the number 4 spark plug to prevent it from damage.
12   Fit the engine support bar or failing this, position a jack under the engine to take its weight and lift it slightly.
13   Undo the two retaining bolts and detach the rear left-hand engine/transmission mounting bracket from the engine/transmission.
14   Undo the two retaining bolts and detach the front left-hand engine/transmission mounting bracket from the engine/transmission (photo).
15   Disconnect the lead connector from the reversing light switch.
16   Detach the wiring and then unbolt and withdraw the starter motor (photo). Refer to Chapter 12 for full details.
17   On 1.6 litre models, undo the seven engine/transmission housing bracing bolts and remove the bracing plate from each side (photos). Unbolt and remove the adaptor plate.

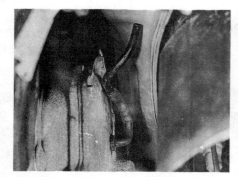

8.6 Extract the transmission breather tube from the chassis

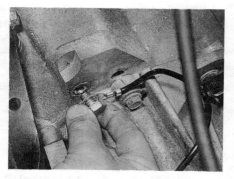

8.8 Detaching the earth strap from the transmission

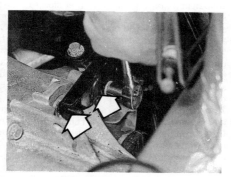

8.9 Unscrew the two engine/transmission mounting nuts arrowed

8.14 Unscrew the front left-hand mounting bolts arrowed

8.16 Unbolt and remove the starter motor

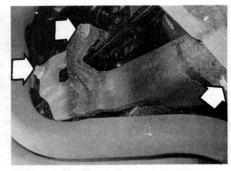

8.17A On 1.6 litre engine models, undo the retaining bolts (arrowed) ...

8.17B ... and remove the engine-to-transmission bracing plates

8.27 Supporting the weight of the transmission from above during its removal using a fabricated bracket bolted to the transmission

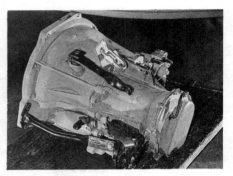

8.28 Withdrawing the transmission from underneath the front end of the vehicle

18   On 1.3 and 1.4 litre models, undo the retaining bolts and remove the engine/transmission adaptor plate.

19   Before disconnecting the gearshift rod, mark the relative fitted positions of the gearshift rod and the selector shaft as a guide for refitting and adjustment.

20   Undo the gearshift rod stabiliser to transmission retaining bolt. Separate the stabiliser from the transmission (noting the washer fitted between the stabiliser and the transmission). Tie the gearshift rod and stabiliser up out of the way.

21   Refer to Chapter 10 for details and detach the steering track rod from the steering arm on the left-hand side, and the suspension arm to spindle balljoint on the left and right-hand sides.

22   Insert a suitable lever between the driveshaft and the transmission and carefully lever the driveshaft free from the transmission. Lever against the reinforcement rib to avoid damaging the transmission housing and have an assistant pull the suspension/steering unit outwards on the side being detached to assist in the driveshaft withdrawal from the transmission.

23   When the driveshaft is detached from the transmission, tie it up out of the way but do not allow the inner CV joint to be angled more than 17° and do not force the outer CV past its stop.

24   Repeat the above procedure and detach the driveshaft on the opposite side.

25   Partially lower the engine and transmission, then unscrew the retaining nut and remove the engine/transmission mounting bracket from the transmission.

26   Unscrew and remove the remaining engine-to-transmission retaining bolts. Note that two bolts on the bulkhead side also secure the mounting bracket stay. Make a final check to ensure that all of the transmission connections have been detached and are positioned out of the way.

27   Check that the engine remains securely supported. The method of supporting the transmission during its removal is largely a matter of personal choice and/or the facilities available. It can be supported from above and lowered (using a conventional hoist) onto a trolley for withdrawal from under the vehicle, or failing this, it can be supported underneath with a suitable trolley jack and withdrawn from under the front end (photo). Whichever method is employed, engage the aid of an assistant to help guide the transmission unit down and clear of the

surrounding components in the engine compartment.

28   Withdraw the transmission from the engine taking care not to allow the weight of the transmission to rest on the input shaft at any time. Once the input shaft is clear of the clutch unit, the transmission can be lowered and manoeuvred down through the engine compartment and then withdrawn from underneath the vehicle (photo).

Refitting

29   Refitting is a reversal of removal but note the following additional points.

    (a)   *Make sure that all mating faces are clean.*

    (b)   *Apply a smear of Ford ESD-MIC220-A grease to the splines of the gearbox input shaft (no other grease will do). Do not apply too much otherwise there is the possibility of the grease contaminating the clutch friction disc.*

    (c)   *On 1.3 and 1.4 models ensure that the engine adaptor plate is correctly seated on the locating dowels on the engine.*

    (d)   *Fit new snap rings to the grooves in the inner end of each driveshaft and ensure that they are felt to snap fully into engagement as they are fitted into position in the transmission.*

    (e)   *Locate the left-hand engine/transmission mounting bracket over the three studs and fit the retaining nut from underneath.*

    (f)   *Temporarily lower the vehicle, then raise the engine/transmission unit to align the mounting brackets on the left-hand side with the threaded holes in the rubber mountings. Refit the two bolts securing the front left engine/transmission mounting bracket, then repeat this procedure and secure the rear left-hand bracket. The vehicle can then be raised and supported on axle stands at the front end again to allow the remaining refitting operations to be carried out.*

    (g)   *Refer to Chapters 8 and 10 for details on reconnecting the driveshafts to the transmission and the suspension arm/steering balljoint and track rod balljoint.*

    (h)   *Reconnect and adjust the gearchange linkage as described in Section 2.*

    (i)   *Tighten all nuts and bolts to the specified torque settings.*

    (j)   *Replenish the gearbox with oil and check the level with reference to Chapter 1.*

9 Manual gearbox overhaul – general information

Overhauling a manual gearbox is a difficult and involved job for the DIY home mechanic. In addition to dismantling and reassembling many small parts, clearances must be precisely measured and, if necessary, changed by selecting shims and spacers. Gearbox internal components are also often difficult to obtain and in many instances, extremely expensive. Because of this, if the gearbox develops a fault or becomes noisy, the best course of action is to have the unit overhauled by a specialist repairer or to obtain an exchange reconditioned unit.

Nevertheless, it is not impossible for the more experienced mechanic to overhaul a gearbox if the special tools are available and the job is done in a deliberate step-by-step manner so that nothing is overlooked.

The tools necessary for an overhaul include internal and external circlip pliers, bearing pullers, a slide-hammer, a set of pin punches, a dial test indicator and possibly an hydraulic press. In addition, a large, sturdy workbench and a vice will be required.

During dismantling of the gearbox, make careful notes of how each component is fitted to make reassembly easier and accurate.

Before dismantling the gearbox, it will help if you have some idea what area is malfunctioning. Certain problems can be closely related to specific areas in the gearbox which can make component examination and replacement easier. Refer to *Fault diagnosis* at the beginning of this Manual for more information.

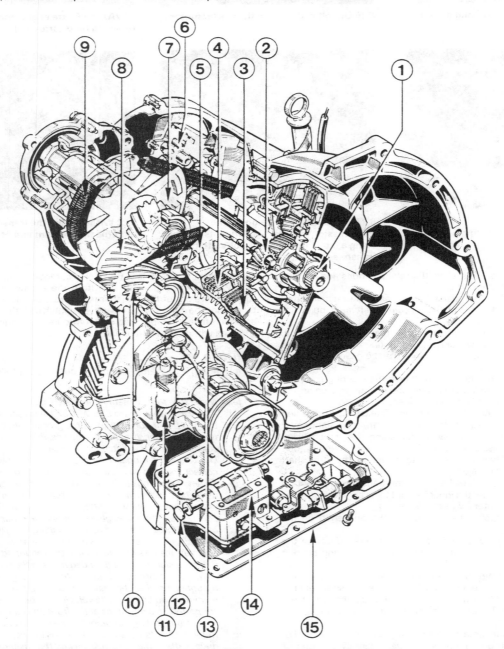

Fig. 7.11 Cutaway view showing the main components of the CTX automatic transmission (Sec 10)

1 Input shaft	5 Primary cone pulley	9 Steel thrust-link drivebelt	13 Final drive gear
2 Planetary gear train	6 Oil pump	10 Input gear	14 Hydraulic valve body
3 Reverse gear clutch	7 Secondary cone pulley	11 Speedometer drive pinion	assembly
4 Forward gear clutch	8 Reduction gear	12 Manual selector slide valve	15 Sump

Part B: Automatic transmission

10 General information

The CTX transmission is an automatic transmission providing continuously variable drive over the entire speed range. Torque from the engine is transmitted to the transmission via an input shaft and a multi-plate wet clutch (rather than a conventional torque converter employed on most automatic transmissions).

A steel thrust-link drivebelt made of disc shaped steel elements transmits the torque from the primary cone pulley (driven by the engine) to the secondary cone pulley. The secondary cone pulley is linked by a series of gears to the final drive gear which drives the differential unit and the driveshafts.

The continuous variation in ratio is produced by altering the diameter of the path followed by the drivebelt around the two cone pulleys. This alteration of the drivebelt path is produced by an hydraulic control system which moves one half of each cone pulley in an axial direction. the secondary pulley cone is also spring-loaded to keep the drivebelt at the required tension needed to transmit the torque. The hydraulic control system is governed by the position of the transmission selector lever, the accelerator and the load resistance encountered (such as up or down gradients), as well as road speed.

The selector lever is connected to the transmission selector shaft by a cable.

A gear type oil pump delivers oil (according to the input speed) to the hydraulic control system. A transmission fluid oil cooler is located in the side tank of the engine coolant radiator.

As with conventional automatic transmission systems, the CTX type has a parking mechanism. The parking pawl engages with the teeth on the outside of the secondary pulley. A starter inhibitor switch prevents the engine from being started in selector positions R, D or L.

When accelerating, the engine speed may sound higher than would normally be expected and similar to a slipping clutch on a manual transmission vehicle. The reverse is true when decelerating, with the engine speed dropping faster than the comparable drop in road speed. These are normal characteristics of the CTX transmission.

Safety note

When the vehicle is parked and left with the engine running, or when any checks and/or adjustments are being carried out, the handbrake must be applied and the selector lever moved to the P position.

Do not allow the engine speed to rise above the normal idle speed when the vehicle is stationary with the selector lever in the R, D or L position.

The engine must not run at more than 3000 rpm with the selector lever in the R, D or L position when the driving (front) roadwheels are clear of the ground.

If the vehicle is to be towed with the front wheels on the road, move the selector lever to position N. If the distance that the vehicle is to be towed is no more than 30 miles (50 km), it can be towed up to a maximum towing speed of 30 mph (50 kph). Ideally the vehicle should be towed on a trailer or dolly with the front wheels clear of the road – where the towing distance exceeds 30 miles (50 km) this is essential.

11 Selector cable – removal, refitting and adjustment

Removal

1 Unscrew and remove the selector lever knob. Unclip and detach the selector gate cover, followed by its locating frame (see Chapter 11).
2 Slide the front seats fully forward. Referring to Chapter 11, undo the two retaining screws at the rear and the four screws at the front, then lift clear of the central console, guiding it up over the handbrake lever.
3 Using a suitable screwdriver as a lever, prise free the plastic connecting eye of the selector lever from the cable, then prise free the cable retaining clip and withdraw the cable from the selector housing. If necessary, cut the carpet at the front to allow extra access.
4 Apply the handbrake, then jack up the front of the car and support it on axle stands.
5 Working underneath the vehicle, release the retaining clip and pin and detach the cable from the selector shaft lever and the transmission housing bracket.
6 Pull free the rubber gaiter from the floor and then withdraw the selector cable from the vehicle.

Refitting

7 Feed the selector cable up through the floor, refit the rubber gaiter then lower the vehicle to the ground.
8 Reconnect the selector cable to the lever and housing, ensuring that the annular bead of the cable eye faces the end of the pin. Use a suitable pair of pliers to press the pin in until it is heard to clip into engagement.
9 The selector lever must now be moved to the P position and the vehicle then raised and supported at the front end again.
10 Reconnect the cable to the transmission, then adjust the cable as follows before refitting the centre console and selector gate assembly.

Adjustment

11 The vehicle must be raised and supported on axle stands at the front end to make the cable adjustment check.

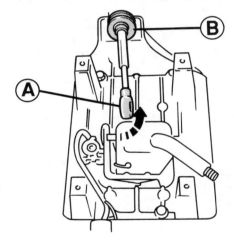

Fig. 7.12 Selector cable-to-lever connection showing connecting eye (A) and retaining clip (B) (Sec 11)

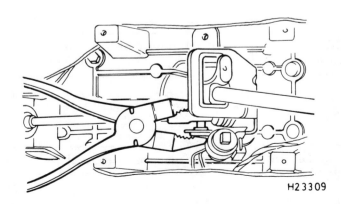

Fig. 7.13 Reconnecting the selector cable eye (Sec 11)

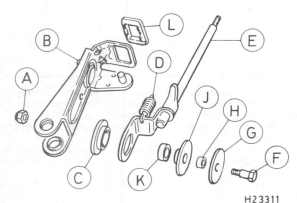

Fig. 7.14 Automatic transmission gear selector mechanism components (Sec 12)

A　Nut	G　Steel washer
B　Selector lever guide	H　Spacer bush
C　Guide bush	J　Spacer washer (plastic)
D　Spring	K　Bush
E　Selector lever	L　Plastic guide
F　Pivot pin	

12　With the selector lever set in the P position, the parking pawl engaged and the gears immobilised, check that the lever/selector shaft drilling and the cable yoke are in alignment and the connecting pin is an easy fit. If required, draw the bellows back from the yoke and screw the yoke in the appropriate direction to reposition it on the cable so that the pin fits freely. Fit the pin and retaining clip, then relocate the bellows.
13　The vehicle can now be lowered to the ground.

12　Gear selector mechanism – removal and refitting

Removal

1　Refer to Section 11 and proceed as described in paragraphs 1 to 3 inclusive to disconnect the cable from the lever housing unit.
2　Pull free the quadrant illumination light bulbholder, then undo the four retaining bolts and remove the selector lever housing unit.
3　To remove the selector lever from the housing, release the clip and extract the lever pivot pin.
4　To remove the selector lever rod from the guide, detach the spring, unscrew the retaining pin nut, withdraw the pin, nut and washer and withdraw the lever rod. The component parts of the system are shown in Fig. 7.14.

Refitting

5　Reassemble and refit in the reverse order of removal. When refitting the selector lever and bushes to the housing, ensure that the wide side of the bush guide faces up.

13　Speedometer drive pinion and/or cable – removal and refitting

　The removal and refitting details for the speedometer cable and pinion on the automatic transmission are similar to those described for the manual transmission. Refer to Section 5 and Fig. 7.15.

14　Differential output oil seal – renewal

　The removal and renewal details for the output oil seal on the automatic transmission are similar to those described for the manual transmission. Refer to Section 6 for details.

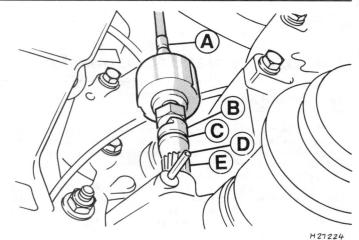

Fig. 7.15 Speedometer drive pinion and cable location in the automatic transmission (Sec 13)

A　Speedometer drive cable	D　Drive pinion
B　Drive pinion bearing	E　Roll pin
C　O-ring	

15　Automatic transmission – removal and refitting

Note: *This Section describes the removal of the automatic transmission leaving the engine in position in the car, however if an adequate hoist is available it may be easier to remove both the engine and the transmission together as described in Chapter 2, and then to separate the transmission from the engine on the bench.*

Removal

1　The automatic transmission is removed downwards from the engine compartment after disconnecting it from the engine. Due to the weight of the unit, it will be necessary to have a suitable method of supporting the transmission as it is lowered during removal and subsequently raised during its refitting. A trolley jack fitted with a suitable saddle to support the transmission unit as it is removed will be ideal, but failing this, an engine lift hoist and sling will suffice. The weight of the engine will also need to be supported whilst the transmission is detached from it. An engine support bar (similar to that shown in photo 36.34 in Chapter 2) fitted in the front wing drain channel on each side is ideal for this purpose, but care must be taken not to damage the wings or their paintwork. If this type of tool is not available (or cannot be fabricated), the engine can be supported by blocks or a second jack from underneath.
2　Disconnect the battery negative lead.
3　Remove the air cleaner unit as described in Chapter 4.
4　Disconnect the speedometer drive cable from the transmission.

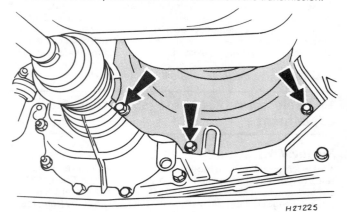

Fig. 7.16 Lower cover plate retaining bolts – arrowed (Sec 15)

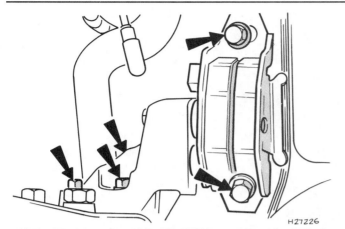

Fig. 7.17 Undo the retaining bolts indicated and remove the transmission front bracket (Sec 15)

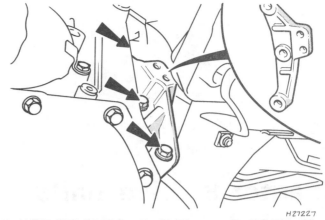

Fig. 7.18 Undo the retaining bolts indicated and remove the transmission rear bracket (Sec 15)

5   Unclip and disconnect the starter inhibitor switch wire.
6   Disconnect and separate the speed sensor connector halves (near to the brake master cylinder).
7   Release the cam plate operating cable from the carburettor linkage, then undo the retaining bolt and detach the cable support bracket from the transmission. Detach the cam plate cable link (see Fig. 2.46).
8   Unscrew and remove the upper transmission to engine flange bolts.
9   Unscrew the two retaining bolts shown in Fig. 7.10 and remove the transmission rear mounting bracket.
10 Refer to Chapter 1 for details and drain off the fluid from the automatic transmission.
11 Raise and support the vehicle at the front end on axle stands.
12 Disconnect the wiring and remove the starter motor unit as described in Chapter 12.
13 Undo the two selector cable bracket retaining bolts, disconnect the yoke from the lever and detach the selector cable from the lever on the transmission selector shaft.
14 Disconnect the starter/inhibitor and the reversing light lead from their connections at the transmission.
15 Undo the three retaining bolts shown in Fig. 7.16 and remove the lower cover plate from the lower front end face of the transmission.
16 Undo the oil cooler to transmission union nuts at the transmission end (see Fig. 2.47) and tie them up out of the way. Allow for fluid spillage as they are detached and plug the hose and transmission union connections to prevent the ingress of dirt.
17 Refer to Section 8 and proceed as described in paragraphs 21 to 24 to disconnect the driveshafts from the transmission. Note that for the automatic transmission driveshafts, the inner CV joints must not be bent by more than 20°, and the outer joints must not be bent by more than 45°.
18 The weight of the engine must now be supported independently from the mountings. This can be achieved by suspending it with a support bar (Ford tool 21-140 if available) located in the front wing drain channel each side, by using a conventional hoist and sling method, or by supporting it from the underside with a jack or blocks. Whichever method is used, raise the hoist to just take the weight of the engine (not lift it).
19 Unscrew the five retaining bolts shown in Fig. 7.17 and remove the front transmission mounting bracket.
20 Slightly release the weight of the engine from the support, then undo the three retaining bolts shown in Fig. 7.18 and detach the rear support bracket from the transmission. Take care not to damage the transmission sump pan during this operation.
21 Check that the engine remains securely supported. The method of supporting the transmission during its removal is largely a matter of personal choice and/or the facilities available. It can be supported from above and lowered (using a conventional hoist) onto a trolley for withdrawal from under the vehicle, or failing this, it can be supported underneath with a suitable trolley jack and withdrawn from under the front end. Whichever method is employed, engage the aid of an assistant to help guide the transmission unit down and clear of the surrounding components in the engine compartment.

22 Unscrew and remove the remaining engine-to-transmission retaining bolts and note the location of the earth strap.
23 Check that all of the associated fittings are disconnected and are positioned out of the way.
24 Separate the transmission from the engine. The transmission can then be lowered and simultaneously manoeuvred down through the engine compartment and withdrawn from underneath the vehicle.

Refitting

25 Refitting is a reversal of removal but note the following additional points.

   (a) *Do not apply any grease or lubricant to the input shaft splines as it could adversely effect the operation of the damper.*
   (b) *New snap rings must be fitted to the inboard end of each driveshaft before reconnecting them to the transmission. Refer to Chapter 8 for further refitting details.*
   (c) *Tighten all nuts and bolts to the specified torque wrench settings (where applicable).*
   (d) *Refer to Chapter 10 for details on reconnecting the steering track rod end and the suspension arm balljoint assemblies to the steering arm/knuckle unit.*
   (e) *If necessary adjust the selector cable with reference to 11.*
   (f) *When refitting the oil cooler, check that the plugs have been removed and that the connections are cleanly made.*
   (g) *Fill the automatic transmission with fluid (see Chapter 1).*
   (h) *Adjust the accelerator and choke cables with reference to Chapter 4.*

16 Automatic transmission overhaul – general information

In the event of a fault occurring on the transmission, it is first necessary to determine whether it is of an electrical, mechanical or hydraulic nature, and to do this special test equipment is required. It is therefore essential to have the work carried out by a Ford dealer if a transmission fault is suspected.

Do not remove the transmission from the car for possible repair before professional fault diagnosis has been carried out, since most tests require the transmission to be in the vehicle.

17 Starter inhibitor switch – removal and refitting

Refer to Chapter 12, Section 12 for details.

Chapter 8 Driveshafts

Contents

Specifications

Driveshaft type

Description .... Unequal length steel shafts, splined to the inner and outer constant velocity (CV) joints

Driveshaft designation:
  All 1.3 litre and 1.4 litre models except those fitted with automatic transmission and/or ABS .... 23 spline driveshaft
  1.4 litre models with automatic transmission and/or ABS and all 1.6 litre models. .... 25 spline driveshaft

Lubrication

Type .... Grease to Ford specification SQM-1C-9004-A (Duckhams LBM 10)
Outer joint grease quantity:
  1.3 litre (except van) .... 30 grams
  All other models .... 40 grams
Inner joint grease quantity:
  All models .... 95 grams

Torque wrench settings

	Nm	lbf ft
Track rod end to spindle carrier steering arm	25 to 30	18 to 22
Hub/driveshaft retaining nut:		
M20 x 1.5 (23 spline driveshaft)	205 to 235	151 to 173
M22 x 1.5 (25 spline driveshaft)	220 to 250	162 to 186
Lower arm balljoint to spindle carrier pinchbolt and nut	48 to 60	35 to 44
Brake caliper retaining bolts	51 to 61	37 to 45
Roadwheel nuts	70 to 100	52 to 74

1 General information

Drive is transmitted from the differential to the front wheels by means of two, unequal length, steel driveshafts. On certain models, the longer of the two driveshafts incorporates a vibration damper which is bolted in position on the shaft.

Each driveshaft unit consists of three main components, the sliding tripod type inner CV joint, the main driveshaft (which is splined at each end) and a fixed type outer CV joint. The inner end section of the tripod type joint is secured in the differential by the engagement of a snap ring, whilst the outer (ball and cage type) CV joint is secured in the front hub by the stub axle nut. The nut has a shouldered outer section which is peened over to lock it in position.

The design and construction of the driveshaft components is such that the only repairs possible are the renewal of the rubber gaiters and the renewal of the inner joint spiders. Wear or damage to the outer constant velocity joints or the driveshaft splines can only be rectified by fitting a complete new driveshaft assembly.

2 Driveshaft – removal and refitting

Removal

1 Remove the wheel trim from the front roadwheel on the side concerned, then using a small pin punch, peen back the locking portion of the front hub/driveshaft nut. Loosen off the nut about half-a-turn.
2 Loosen off the front roadwheel retaining nuts on the side concerned.
3 Check that the handbrake is fully applied, then jack up the front of the vehicle and support it on axle stands. Remove the appropriate

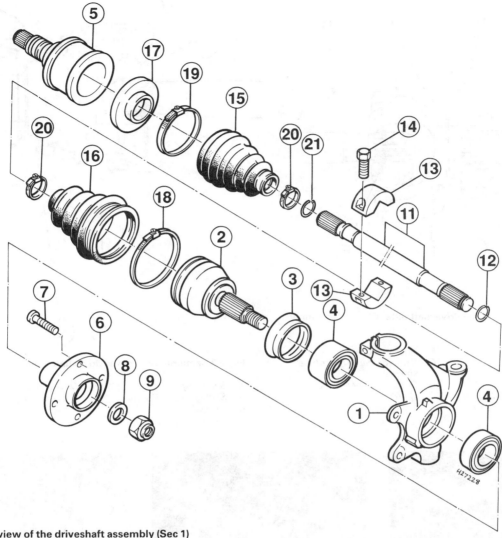

Fig. 8.1 Exploded view of the driveshaft assembly (Sec 1)

1	Hub/spindle carrier	6	Wheel hub
2	Outer CV joint unit	7	Wheel stud
3	Dust shield	8	Flat washer
4	Inner and outer hub	9	Hub/driveshaft nut
	bearings	11	Driveshaft
5	Inner CV joint		

12	Snap ring	17	Nylon washer
13	Damper (if applicable)	18	Gaiter clip
14	Bolt and lock washer	19	Gaiter clip
15	Inner CV joint gaiter	20	Gaiter clip
16	Outer CV joint gaiter	21	Snap ring

roadwheel and unscrew and remove the hub/driveshaft retaining nut and washer (photo).

4   Undo the two retaining bolts and remove the brake caliper from the spindle carrier. Support the brake unit by suspending it from above to prevent the hydraulic hose from being strained or distorted.

5   Detach the track rod balljoint from the steering arm on the side concerned as described in Chapter 10.

6   Remove the Torx head pinch bolt and nut securing the lower suspension arm balljoint to the spindle carrier. As it is withdrawn, note the fitted direction of the bolt (to ensure correct refitting). Lever the suspension arm downwards to detach it from the spindle carrier unit. Refer to Chapter 10 for the full procedure.

7   Release the driveshaft from its location in the hub by pulling the spindle carrier outwards, away from the centre of the vehicle. Do not fully withdraw the shaft from the hub at this stage, but ensure that it is free to be withdrawn when required. If it is tight in the hub, lightly tap its outer end with a soft-faced hammer or use a conventional puller and spacer as shown (photo).

8   Insert a suitable lever between the inner driveshaft joint and the

transmission case, adjacent to a reinforcing rib, then prise free the inner joint from the differential. If it proves reluctant to move, strike the lever firmly with the palm of the hand (photo). Be careful not to damage the adjacent components and be prepared for oil spillage from the transmission case through the vacated driveshaft aperture. If possible, plug the aperture or preferably and if available, insert an old driveshaft to prevent leakage and to immobilise the differential gears. Do not allow the inner tripod joint to bend more than 17° on manual transmission models or 20° on automatic transmission models. The outer joint must not be bent past its stop (more than 45°).

9   Withdraw the driveshaft from the hub and remove it as a unit from the vehicle. If the driveshaft on the opposing side is to be removed also, the differential must be immobilised by the insertion of an old CV joint or a suitable shaft before the other shaft is removed.

10   Remove the snap ring from the groove at the inner end of the splined shaft of the inboard joint (photo). *This snap ring must be renewed each time the driveshaft is withdrawn from the differential. The hub/driveshaft retaining nut as well as the track rod end balljoint split pin must also be renewed when refitting the driveshaft.*

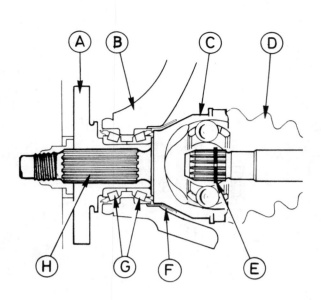

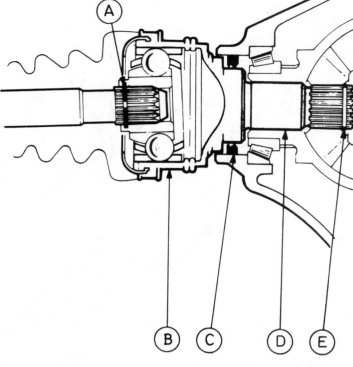

Fig. 8.2 Sectional view of the driveshaft outer CV joint assembly (Sec 1)

A   Wheel hub
B   Spindle carrier
C   Fixed outer CV joint
D   Gaiter
E   Snap ring (driveshaft-to-outer CV joint)
F   Dust shield
G   Bearings (taper roller type shown)
H   Outer CV joint splined shaft

Fig. 8.3 Sectional view of the driveshaft inner CV joint (Sec 1)

A   Snap ring
B   Sliding inner CV joint
C   Oil seal
D   Inner CV joint splined shaft
E   Snap ring

2.3 Remove the hub/driveshaft retaining nut and washer

2.7 Driveshaft separation from the front wheel hub using a conventional puller. Note the spacer location (arrowed)

2.8 Levering the driveshaft free from the transmission

2.10 Prising free the snap ring from the groove in the inner end of the driveshaft

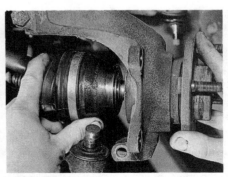

2.12 Inserting the driveshaft into the wheel hub/spindle carrier

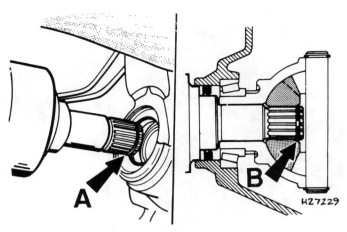

Fig. 8.4 Snap ring (A) must be renewed and fully engage in groove (B) (Sec 2)

Refitting

11   Fit a new snap ring to the groove in the splined shaft of the inner joint.

12   Smear the splines at the wheel hub end of the shaft with grease, then insert it into the spindle carrier unit (photo). Use the old nut and retaining washer to assist in drawing the shaft into position and as it is fitted, rotate the brake disc to assist in centralising the wheel bearings.

13   Remove the temporarily fitted plug (or the old driveshaft) from the differential housing, lightly smear the oil seal lips in the differential housing with grease then insert the inner driveshaft joint, aligning the splines and pushing it into position so that the snap ring is clearly felt to engage in the groove of the differential side gear.

14   Reconnect the suspension lower arm balljoint to the spindle carrier. Insert the pinch bolt (in its original direction of fitting), ensure that

the bolt is fully engaged in the groove of the ballstud, then fit and tighten the retaining nut to the specified torque wrench setting.

15   Reconnect the steering track rod to the steering arm as described in Section 28 of Chapter 10.

16   Refit the brake caliper unit to the spindle carrier and tighten the retaining bolts to the specified torque wrench setting.

17   Refit the roadwheel and lightly tighten its retaining nuts.

18   Fit a new hub nut and washer and tighten the nut as much as possible at this stage. As the nut is being tightened, rotate the roadwheel to ensure that the wheel bearings seat correctly.

19   Lower the vehicle to the ground, then tighten the hub nut to the specified torque wrench setting. Using a pin punch, stake-lock the nut in the groove in the end of the axle stub.

20   Tighten the roadwheel retaining bolts to the specified torque setting.

21   Check the level of the transmission oil and top up if necessary with the recommended lubricant.

3   Inner CV joint gaiter – renewal

1   The inner CV (tripod) joint gaiter can only be renewed once the inner CV joint has been disconnected from the transmission. This can be done with the driveshaft fully removed (as described in Section 2), or by leaving it in situ in the wheel hub. The latter method is described below. If it is wished to fully remove the driveshaft refer to the previous Section for details, then proceed as described in paragraphs 7 to 14 inclusive in this Section to renew the gaiter.

2   Loosen off the front roadwheel retaining nuts on the side concerned.

3   Check that the handbrake is fully applied, then jack up the front of the vehicle and support it on axle stands. Remove the appropriate roadwheel.

4   Detach the track rod balljoint from the steering arm as described in Chapter 10, Section 28.

5   Remove the Torx head pinch bolt and nut securing the lower suspension arm balljoint to the spindle carrier. As it is withdrawn, note

3.7 Release and withdraw the gaiter from the inner CV joint housing

3.9 Remove the snap ring from the tripod end of the driveshaft

3.11A Fit the new gaiter over the inboard end of the driveshaft ...

3.11B ... and locate the nylon washer (note orientation)

3.12 Tripod refitted onto the driveshaft with the match-marks aligned (arrowed)

3.14 Special pliers are required to securely clamp the inner gaiter clip on the driveshaft

the fitted direction of the bolt (to ensure correct refitting). Lever the suspension arm downwards to detach it from the spindle carrier.

6   Get an assistant to help pull the suspension unit outwards and detach the driveshaft and tripod from the transmission housing. Whilst it is disconnected at the inner end, do not allow the outer CV joint to be angled past its stop (see paragraph 8 in the previous Section).

7   Note the direction of fitting of the inner joint gaiter retaining clips, then release the clips from the gaiter and slide the gaiter back along the driveshaft (away from the transmission) and remove it together with the large nylon washer. Withdraw the tripod housing from the tripod (photo).

8   Wipe the grease from the tripod joint assembly.

9   Prise free the snap ring retaining the tripod on the inner end of the driveshaft. Check if the inner end face of the driveshaft and the tripod are 'match-marked' for position, then remove the tripod from the shaft and withdraw the gaiter (photo).

10   Clean the driveshaft. Note that the joint retaining snap ring, the track rod balljoint split pin and the gaiter retaining clips must be renewed on reassembly.

11   Slide the new gaiter into position on the shaft to allow sufficient access for reassembly of the tripod joint. Locate the large nylon washer over the shaft and into the gaiter (photos).

12   Refit the tripod on the driveshaft. It must be fitted with the chamfered edge leading (towards the driveshaft) and with the match-marks aligned (photo). Secure it in position using a new snap ring. Ensure that the snap ring is fully engaged in its groove.

13   Reassemble the tripod housing over the tripod and then pack it with the specified type and quantity of grease (see Specifications).

14   Move the gaiter along the driveshaft and locate it over the joint and onto its inner and outer seatings. Ensure that it is correctly seated and not twisted or distorted, then fit the new retaining clips. The fitted direction of the clips must be as noted during removal. The inner clip is a pinch-clamp type and secured using special pliers as shown (photo). In the event of such pliers not being available, the gaiter can be secured at this point by a suitable nylon cable tie.

15   Reconnect the suspension lower arm balljoint to the spindle carrier. Insert the pinch bolt (in its original direction of fitting), ensure that the bolt is fully engaged in the groove of the ballstud, then fit and tighten the retaining nut to the specified torque setting.

16   Reconnect the steering track rod to the steering arm as described in Section 28 of Chapter 10.

17   Refit the roadwheel and its retaining nuts, then lower the vehicle to the ground. Tighten the roadwheel nuts to the specified torque wrench settings.

4   Outer CV joint gaiter – renewal

1   The outer CV joint gaiter can be renewed with the driveshaft fully removed or with it in situ in the wheel hub, but with the outer CV joint disconnected. If the driveshaft has already been removed, proceed as described in paragraphs 6 to 14 inclusive to renew the outer CV joint gaiter.

2   Loosen off the front roadwheel retaining nuts on the side concerned.

3   Check that the handbrake is fully applied, then jack up the front of

4.6 Releasing the outboard CV joint gaiter retaining clip

the vehicle and support it on axle stands. Remove the roadwheel.

4   Detach the track rod balljoint from the steering arm as described in Chapter 10, Section 28.

5   Remove the Torx head pinch bolt and nut securing the lower suspension arm balljoint to the spindle carrier. As it is withdrawn, note the fitted direction of the bolt (to ensure correct refitting). Lever the suspension arm downwards to detach it from the spindle carrier.

6   Note the direction of fitting of the outer CV joint gaiter retaining clips, then release the clips from the gaiter and slide the gaiter back along the driveshaft (towards the transmission end) (photo).

7   To disconnect the driveshaft from the outer CV joint, first wipe away the grease from the joint. Using suitable circlip pliers, expand the snap ring and have an assistant simultaneously pull the CV joint outwards (or when *in situ*, the suspension unit outwards) to enable the shaft to be withdrawn. Whilst the driveshaft is detached at the outer end, do not allow the inner (tripod) joint to be angled beyond 17° on manual transmission models, or 20° on automatic transmission models (see paragraph 8 of Sec 2).

8   Withdraw the gaiter from the driveshaft.

9   Clean the driveshaft. *Note that the CV joint retaining snap ring, the track rod balljoint split pin and the gaiter retaining clips must be renewed.*

10   Slide the new gaiter along on the shaft to allow access for reassembly of the outer CV joint.

11   Locate a new snap ring into position in the outer CV joint and then lubricate the inner joint with part of the specified amount and type of grease (see Specifications) (photos).

12   Reconnect the driveshaft with the CV joint and push them together so that the circlip engages in the groove of the driveshaft (photo). If the task is being carried out with the spindle carrier attached, pull the suspension unit outwards and reconnect the driveshaft with the

4.11A Locate the new snap ring (arrowed) in the outer CV joint ...

4.11B ... partially lubricate the joint ...

4.12 ... and reassemble the shaft to the joint so that the circlip (A) engages in the groove in the shaft (B)

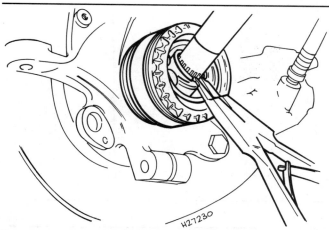

Fig. 8.5 Expand the snap ring to enable the driveshaft to be withdrawn from the outer CV joint (Sec 4)

CV joint. Guide the shaft into the joint and progressively release the suspension unit until the shaft is fully engaged with the joint and the snap ring engages in the groove in the driveshaft.

13   Pack the joint with the remainder of the specified type and quantity of grease.

14   Move the gaiter along the driveshaft and locate it over the joint and onto its inner and outer seatings. Check that it is correctly seated and not twisted or distorted, then fit new retaining clips. The fitted direction of the clips must be as noted during removal.

15   Reconnect the suspension lower arm balljoint to the spindle carrier. Insert the pinch bolt (in its original direction of fitting), ensure that the bolt is fully engaged in the groove of the ballstud, then fit and tighten the retaining nut to the specified torque wrench setting.

16   Reconnect the steering track rod to the steering arm as described in Section 28 of Chapter 10.

17   Refit the roadwheel and tighten its nuts, then lower the vehicle to the ground. Tighten the roadwheels nuts to the specified torque wrench setting.

5   Driveshaft unit – inspection and overhaul

1   Remove the driveshaft as described in Section 2.

2   Clean away all external dirt and grease from the driveshaft and gaiters.

3   Note the direction of fitting of the inner and outer CV joint gaiter retaining clips, then release the clips from the gaiters and slide the gaiters along the driveshaft towards the centre.

4   Wipe the grease from the inner and outer CV joints.

5   Prise free the snap ring retaining the inner tripod on the inboard end of the driveshaft. Withdraw the tripod, then the inboard gaiter from the shaft.

6   Using suitable circlip pliers, expand the snap ring and simultaneously have an assistant pull the outboard joint outwards to separate the shaft from the joint.

7   If removing the vibration damper from the right-hand driveshaft, mark its relative position on the shaft before unbolting it.

8   Thoroughly clean the joint components and examine them for wear or damage. A repair kit may resolve a minor problem but extensive wear or damage will necessitate renewal of the complete driveshaft unit.

9   Where the joints and possibly even the gaiters, are found to be in a serviceable condition, it will still be necessary to renew the CV joint retaining snap rings, the gaiter retaining clips and also to obtain the recommended type and quantity of CV joint grease.

10   Reassembly of the joints is as described in Section 3 (paragraphs 10 to 14) for the inner CV joint, and Section 4 (paragraphs 9 to 14) for the outer CV joint. If the vibration damper unit was removed from the right-hand driveshaft, ensure that it is refitted in the same position as noted during removal.

11   Refit the driveshaft on completion as described in Section 2.

Chapter 9 Braking system

Contents

Specifications

System type .... Servo-assisted, dual circuit hydraulic, with pressure regulation to the rear brakes. Cable-operated handbrake acting on rear brakes. Anti-lock brakes fitted according to model

Front brakes
Type.. Solid or ventilated disc, with single piston sliding calipers
Disc diameter .... 240 mm
Disc thickness:
    Solid disc.. 10 mm
    Ventilated disc....................................... 20 mm
Minimum disc thickness:
    Solid disc.. 8 mm
    Ventilated disc....................................... 18 mm
Maximum disc run-out (disc fitted)................... 0.1 mm
Maximum allowable hub run-out....................... 0.05 mm
Minimum brake pad thickness.......................... 1.5 mm
Caliper piston diameter................................... 54 mm

Rear brakes
Type.. Drum with leading and trailing shoes and automatic adjusters
Rear brake details – 1.3 litre Saloon and 1.4 litre Saloon with manual transmission:
    Drum diameter .... 180 mm (7 in)
    Minimum allowable brake lining thickness ... 1.0 mm
    Wheel cylinder diameter.......................... 20.64 mm
Rear brake details – 1.3 litre Estate, 1.4 litre Saloon with automatic transmission and all 1.6 litre models:
    Drum diameter .... 203 mm (8 in)
    Minimum allowable brake lining thickness ... 1.0 mm
    Wheel cylinder diameter – standard system ... 19.05 mm
    Wheel cylinder diameter – ABS brake system ... 22.2 mm

Rear brakes (continued)
Rear brake details – Van:

Drum diameter	229 mm
Minimum allowable brake lining thickness	1.0 mm
Wheel cylinder diameter	22.2 mm

Torque wrench settings

	Nm	lbf ft
Master cylinder unit to servo unit nuts	20 to 25	15 to 18
Servo unit to bracket/bulkhead nuts	35 to 45	26 to 33
Caliper anchor bracket to spindle carrier bolts	50 to 66	37 to 49
Caliper piston housing retaining bolts:		
Bendix caliper	45 to 55	33 to 41
Teves caliper	20 to 25	15 to 18
ABS hydraulic unit to bracket	21 to 28	15.5 to 21
Roadwheel nuts	70 to 100	50 to 74

1 General information

The braking system used is of dual-circuit hydraulic type with servo assistance to the front disc brakes and rear drum brakes. The dual-circuit system operates from a tandem master cylinder, the circuits being split diagonally on all models except the Van variant, on which it is split front-to-rear. The dual-circuit hydraulic system is a safety feature where in the event of a malfunction somewhere in one of the hydraulic circuits, the other circuit continues to operate, providing at least a reduced braking effort. Under normal circumstances, both brake circuits operate in unison to provide efficient braking.

The master cylinder (and the vacuum servo unit to which it is bolted) is located on the left-hand side of the bulkhead in the engine compartment. On all right-hand drive variants, they are jointly operated via a transverse cross link from the brake pedal.

Brake pressure control valves are fitted in-line to each rear brake circuit, their function being to regulate the braking force available at each rear wheel and reduce the possibility of the rear wheels locking up under heavy braking. Van models also have a 'light-laden' valve incorporated into the rear braking circuits for the same reason.

The front brake discs are of the ventilated type on all 1.6 litre and ABS-equipped models. Solid discs are fitted on all other models. The front brake caliper units are of single sliding piston design which ensures that equal effort is applied through each pair of brake pads to the discs. The calipers are mounted on the front spindle carriers each side.

Each rear brake drum can be simply unbolted from its rear axle flange together with the integrally fitted wheel hub unit and removed to provide unhindered access to the shoe assemblies. Each rear brake shoe assembly is operated by a single piston wheel cylinder. The leading brake shoe in each brake unit has a thicker lining than the trailing shoe so that they wear proportionally. To take up the brake adjustment as the linings wear, each rear brake shoe unit incorporates an automatic adjuster mechanism.

A cable-operated handbrake operates acts on both rear brakes to provide an independent means of brake operation.

An anti-lock braking system (ABS) is available on some models and features many of the components in common with the conventional braking system. Further details on the ABS can be found later in this Chapter.

Warning: *Dust created by the braking system may contain asbestos,*

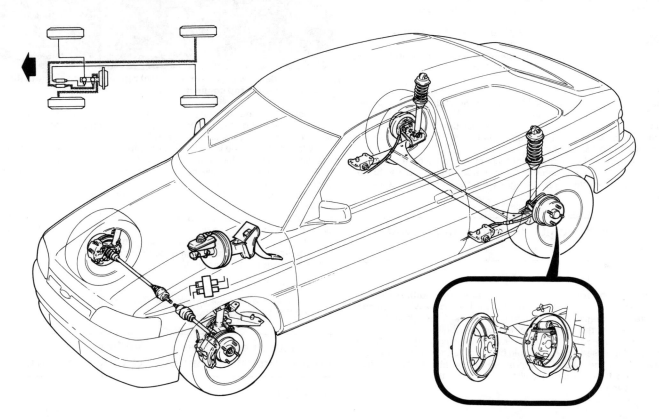

Fig. 9.1 Standard braking system layout and principle components. Note that the circuit is split front-to-rear on Van model (Sec 1)

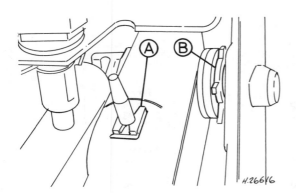

Fig. 9.2 Showing the brake pedal-to-cross link retaining clip (A) and the brake pedal cross-shaft circlip (B) (Sec 2)

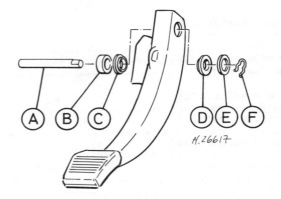

Fig. 9.3 Brake pedal components (Sec 2)

A	Pivot shaft	D	Bush
B	Spacer	E	Washer
C	Bush	F	Clip

which is a health hazard. Never blow it out with compressed air and don't inhale any of it. An approved filtering mask should be worn when working on the brakes. DO NOT use petroleum-based solvents to clean brake parts. Use brake cleaner or methylated spirit only.

2   Brake pedal – removal and refitting

Removal

1   Working inside the car, move the driver's seat fully to the rear to allow maximum working area. Access to the pedal is further improved by removing the fuse and relay unit as described in Chapter 12.
2   Disconnect the wiring connector from the brake light switch, then twist the switch and release it from the mounting bracket.
3   Using a suitable hooked tool, extract the circlip from the pedal cross-shaft.
4   Prise free and remove the retaining clip securing the pedal-to-cross link rod.
5   Press the brake pedal pivot shaft through the mounting box just far enough then release and remove the pedal and spacers.
6   Prise the bushes out from each side of the brake pedal and renew them if necessary.

Refitting

7   Prior to refitting, apply a small amount of molybdenum disulphide grease to the brake pedal pivot shaft.
8   Refit in the reverse order to removal. Ensure that the pedal bushes are correctly located and that the pedal shaft 'D' section locates in the pedal box right-hand support.
9   On completion, refit the brake light switch and adjust it if required. The pedal must have a clearance of 5 mm before it contacts the brake light switch, yet operate the brake light within 20 mm of brake pedal movement.

3   Vacuum servo unit – testing, removal and refitting

Testing

1   To test the operation of the servo unit depress the footbrake four or five times to exhaust the vacuum, then start the engine while keeping the footbrake depressed. As the engine starts there should be a noticeable 'give' in the brake pedal as vacuum builds up. Allow the engine to run for at least two minutes and then switch it off. If the brake pedal is now depressed again, it should be possible to detect a hiss from the servo when the pedal is depressed. After about four or five applications no further hissing will be heard and the pedal will feel considerably firmer.

Removal

2   Refer to Section 8 and remove the master cylinder.

3.5 Underside view of the servo unit (A) mounting bracket nuts (B) and the actuating rod connection (C)

3   Disconnect the vacuum hose at the servo non-return valve by pulling it free. If it is reluctant to move, assist it by prising it free using a screwdriver with its blade inserted under the elbow flange.
4   Working inside the vehicle, move the front passenger seat to its full rearward position, then peel back the footwell trim from the inner bulkhead on that side to gain access to the two servo unit retaining nuts. Unscrew and remove the nuts.
5   Unscrew and remove the four nuts securing the servo unit to the mounting bracket (photo).
6   Withdraw the servo unit so that its studs are clear of the bracket and pivot the inner bracket to one side. Extract the clevis pin to release the actuating rod from its shaft, then remove the servo unit.
7   Note that the servo unit cannot be dismantled for repair or overhaul and, if faulty, must be renewed.

Refitting

8   Refitting is a reversal of removal. Refer to Section 8 for details of refitting the master cylinder.

4   Vacuum servo unit vacuum hose and non-return valve – removal, testing and refitting

Removal

1   Depress the brake pedal three or four times to exhaust any remaining vacuum from the servo unit.

4.2 Detaching the vacuum hose from the servo unit

4.5 Non-return valve in the servo vacuum hose

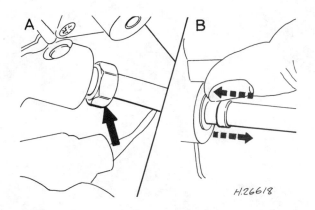

H.26618

Fig. 9.4 Servo vacuum hose detachment from the manifold (Sec 4)

A   CVH engine with
    carburettor

B   HCS engine (carburettor)
    and CVH EFi engine

2   Carefully pull free and detach the servo vacuum hose from the servo unit (photo). If the hose is reluctant to move, prise it free with the aid of a screwdriver, inserting its blade under the flange of the elbow.
3   Detach the vacuum hose from its inlet manifold connection. Depending on the fixing (see Fig. 9.4), undo the union nut and withdraw the hose or press the hose and its retaining collar inwards, then holding the collar in, withdraw the hose.
4   If the hose or the fixings are damaged or in poor condition, they must be renewed.

Non-return valve testing

5   Examine the non-return valve for damage and signs of deterioration and renew it if necessary (photo). The valve may be tested by blowing through its connecting hoses in both directions. It should only be possible to blow from the servo end to the manifold end.

Refitting

6   Refitting is a reversal of removal. If fitting a new non-return valve, ensure that it is fitted the correct way round.

5   Brake pedal-to-servo cross link – removal and refitting

Removal

1   Referring to Section 7 and 8 for details, disconnect the hydraulic fluid lines at the master cylinder and then remove it together with the servo unit (as a combined assembly).
2   On carburettor and CFi engine models, remove the air cleaner unit as described in Chapter 4 to allow increased access to the cross linkage assembly.
3   Working inside the vehicle, prise free and remove the retaining clip from the brake pedal-to-cross link pushrod.
4   Arrange for an assistant to support the weight of the cross linkage on the engine compartment side of the bulkhead. Fold down the bulkhead trim covering in the footwell on each side to allow access to the cross link support bracket securing nuts on the bulkhead. Unscrew the nuts on each side of the bulkhead and remove the link assembly from the bulkhead in the engine compartment (photo).
5   Clean the linkage components and examine the bushes for excessive wear. Renew the bushes if necessary.

Refitting

6   Refitting of the cross link assembly is a reversal of the removal

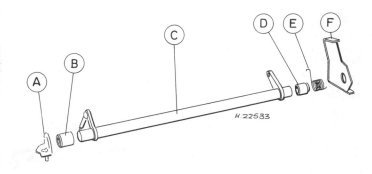

Fig. 9.5 Brake pedal cross link assembly (Sec 5)

A   Support bracket
B   Bush
C   Cross link

D   Bush
E   Return spring
F   Support bracket

procedure. Refer to Sections 7 and 8 to refit the servo unit and the master cylinder.

7 Top up the fluid level in the master cylinder reservoir and bleed the brake hydraulic system as described in Section 6.

6 Hydraulic system – bleeding

Non-ABS system

1 If the master cylinder or brake pipes/hoses have been disconnected and reconnected, then the complete system (both circuits) must be bled of air. If a component of one circuit has been disturbed then only that particular circuit need be bled. It is normal practice to bleed the brake unit furthest from the master cylinder first (in each circuit). On Van models, the circuits are split front and rear, whilst on all other models the circuits are split diagonally.

2 When bleeding the brakes on Van models, it is important to note that the vehicle must not be mounted on a 'wheel-free' hoist, it must be free standing so that the rear circuit is fully bled.

3 There are a variety of do-it-yourself brake bleeding kits available from motor accessory shops, and it is recommended that one of these kits is used wherever possible as they greatly simplify the brake hydraulic circuit bleeding operation. Follow the kit manufacturer's instructions in conjunction with the following procedure.

4 During the bleeding operation do not allow the brake fluid level in the reservoir to drop below the minimum mark, and only use new fluid for topping-up. *Never re-use fluid bled from the system.*

5 Before starting, check that all rigid pipes and flexible hoses are in good condition and that all hydraulic unions are tight. Take great care not to allow hydraulic fluid to come into contact with the vehicle paintwork, otherwise the finish will be seriously damaged. Wash off any spilt fluid immediately with cold water.

6 If a brake bleeding kit is not being used, gather together a clean jar, a suitable length of clear plastic or rubber tubing which is a tight fit over the bleed screw and a new can of the specified brake fluid (see *Lubricants, fluids and capacities* at the beginning of this manual).

7 Clean the area around the bleed nipple on the brake unit to be bled (it is important that no dirt be allowed to enter the hydraulic system) and remove the dust cap (photo). Connect one end of the tubing to the bleed nipple and immerse the other end in the jar containing sufficient brake fluid to keep the end of the tube submerged.

8 Open the bleed screw half a turn and have an assistant depress the brake pedal to the floor and then slowly release it. Tighten the bleed screw at the end of each downstroke to prevent the expelled air/fluid from being drawn back into the system. Continue this procedure until clean brake fluid, free from air bubbles, can be seen flowing into the jar, and then with the pedal in the fully-depressed position, finally tighten the bleed nipple (photo).

9 Remove the tube, refit the dust cap and repeat this procedure on the opposing brake in that circuit.

10 Repeat the procedure on the remaining circuit.

ABS system

11 When bleeding the brakes on ABS models, the vehicle must not be mounted on a 'wheel-free' hoist, it must be free standing so that the brake circuits are fully bled.

12 The procedure is otherwise similar to that described for standard system models, but the following specific differences must be noted and adhered to.

(a) When bleeding each brake unit circuit, the bleed jar must be supported a minimum of 300 mm (12 inches) above the bleed nipple throughout the procedure.

(b) The bleed nipple of the brake unit being bled in a circuit must be unscrewed by one full turn, the pedal fully depressed, then released and allowed to quickly return to its rest position.

(c) Pause briefly at the end of each pedal stroke to allow the master cylinder to fully recover before depressing the pedal to continue the bleeding process in each circuit.

(d) When the bleeding operation on each unit in a circuit is complete, hold the pedal in the fully-depressed position as the bleed nipple is tightened.

5.4 Brake system cross link mounting to the bulkhead

6.7 Rear brake bleed nipple and dust cap (arrowed)

6.8 Bleeding a front brake unit using a one-man bleed kit

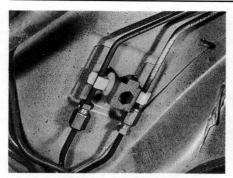

7.2 Typical rigid brake pipe connections and securing clips to the body

7.3A Typical brake hose clamp fitted to minimise fluid loss

7.3B Flexible-to rigid hydraulic brake line connection. Securing clip to location bracket is arrowed

7 Hydraulic pipes and hoses – removal and refitting

Removal

1 If any section of pipe or hose is to be removed, the loss of fluid may be reduced by removing the hydraulic fluid reservoir filler cap, placing a piece of polythene over the filler neck, then refitting and tightening the filler cap. If a section of pipe is to be removed from the master cylinder, the reservoir should be emptied by syphoning out the fluid or drawing out the fluid with a pipette. If any brake fluid is spilt onto the bodywork it must be wiped clean without delay.

2 To remove a section of pipe, secure the adjoining hose union nut with a suitable spanner to prevent it from turning, then unscrew the union nut at the end of the pipe and release it (photo). Repeat the procedure at the other end of the pipe, then release the pipe from the clips attaching it to the body. Where the union nuts are exposed to the full force of the weather, they can sometimes be quite tight. If an open-ended spanner is used, burring of the flats on the nuts is not uncommon, and for this reason it is preferable to use a split ring spanner which will engage all the flats. If such a spanner is not available self-locking grips may be used, although this is not recommended.

3 To further minimise the loss of fluid when disconnecting a flexible brake line, clamp the hose as near to the joint to be detached as is possible using a brake hose clamp or failing this, a self locking wrench fitted with protective jaws. To remove a flexible hose, first clean the ends of the hose and the surrounding area, then unscrew the union nut(s) from the hose end(s). Recover the spring clip and withdraw the hose from the serrated mounting in the support bracket. Where applicable, unscrew the hose from the caliper (photos).

4 Brake pipes with flared ends and union nuts in place can be obtained individually or in sets from Ford dealers or accessory shops. The pipe is then bent to shape, using the old pipe as a guide, and is ready for fitting to the car.

Refitting

5 Refitting the pipes and hoses is a reversal of removal. Make sure that all brake pipes are securely supported in their clips and ensure that the hoses are not kinked. Check also that the hoses are clear of all suspension components and underbody fittings and will remain clear during movement of the suspension and steering. After refitting, remove the polythene from the reservoir and bleed the brake hydraulic system as described in Section 6.

8 Master cylinder – removal and refitting

Removal

1 Disconnect the wiring multi-plug from the fluid warning indicator in the reservoir filler cap, then remove the filler cap from the reservoir. Note that the filler cap must not be inverted. The reservoir should now be emptied by syphoning or drawing out the fluid with a pipette.

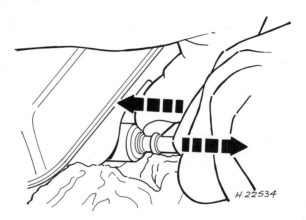

Fig. 9.6 Disconnecting the brake fluid return pipes from the master cylinder reservoir (Sec 8)

8.2 Brake master cylinder unit and hydraulic line connections

2 Identify each brake pipe and its connection to the master cylinder (photo). Unscrew the fluid line to master cylinder union nuts and disconnect the fluid lines. When disconnecting the fluid return pipes from the reservoir, press the retaining boss into the cylinder body and pull free the fluid line (see Fig. 9.6). Plug the connections and tape over the pipe ends to prevent the entry of dust and dirt.

3 Unscrew the mounting nuts and withdraw the master cylinder from the servo unit.

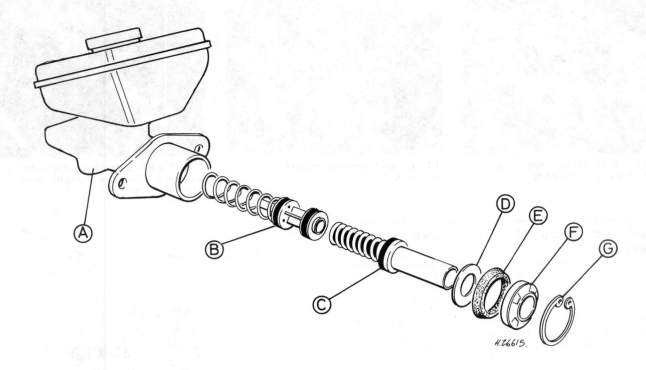

Fig. 9.7 Exploded view of the master cylinder (Sec 9)

A   Master cylinder body   C   Primary piston   E   Seal   G   Circlip
B   Secondary piston   D   Steel washer   F   Plastic spacer

4   If required, the master cylinder can be dismantled for inspection and the seals renewed as described in the following Section.

Refitting

5   Before refitting the master cylinder, clean the mounting faces.
6   Refitting is a reversal of removal. Ensure that the servo vacuum unit seal is in position and tighten the master cylinder retaining nuts to the specified torque wrench setting. Finally bleed the hydraulic system as described in Section 6.

9   Master cylinder – inspection and overhaul

1   With the master cylinder unit removed, empty any remaining fluid from it and clean it externally.
2   Secure the master cylinder in a vice fitted with soft-faced jaws to avoid damaging the cylinder.
3   Withdraw the hydraulic fluid reservoir from the top of the master cylinder by pulling and rocking it free from its retaining seals.
4   Extract the reservoir seals from the top face of the master cylinder.
5   Extract the circlip from its groove in the inner port at the rear of the master cylinder.
6   Pull free the primary piston unit from the rear end of the master cylinder bore, together with the spacer, seal and steel washer.
7   Extract the secondary piston assembly by shaking or lightly tapping it free from the cylinder.
8   To dismantle the primary piston and to remove its seal, undo the retaining screw and detach the spring from the piston. Lever the seal retainer tabs free using a suitable screwdriver as shown in Fig. 9.9 and remove the seal. As it is removed, note the fitted direction of the seal on the piston.
9   To dismantle the secondary piston unit, pull free the spring (note orientation), remove the seal retainer using the same method as that for the primary piston seal and remove the seal (noting its direction of

fitting). Prise free the seal from the other end of the secondary piston, again noting its direction of fitting.
10   Wash all components of the cylinder in methylated spirit or clean hydraulic brake fluid of the specified type. Do not use any other type of cleaning fluid.
11   Inspect the master cylinder and piston assemblies for any signs of excessive wear or damage. Deep scoring in the cylinder bore and/or on the piston surfaces will necessitate a new master cylinder unit being fitted.
12   If the cylinder is in a serviceable condition, obtain a cylinder seals/repair kit. Once removed, the seals must always be renewed.
13   Check that all components are perfectly clean before they refitted and smear them in new brake fluid of the specified type as they are assembled. *Do not allow grease, old fluid or any other lubricant to contact the components during reassembly.*

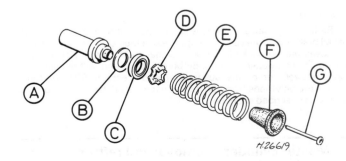

Fig. 9.8 Primary piston components (Sec 9)

A   Piston   E   Spring
B   Shim   F   Boot
C   Seal   G   Retaining screw
D   Seal retainer

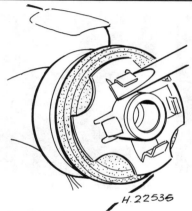

Fig. 9.9 Release the seal retainer tabs on the primary piston unit (Sec 9)

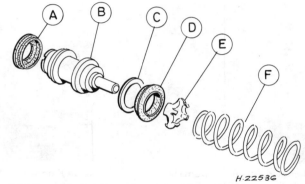

Fig. 9.10 Secondary piston components (Sec 9)

A Seal   D Seal
B Piston   E Seal retainer
C Shim   F Spring

14   Reassemble each piston in the reverse order of dismantling. Ensure that the seals are correctly orientated and the retainers are securely fitted.
15   Lubricate the pistons before refitting them to the cylinder and as they are inserted, use a twisting action to assist in pushing them into position.
16   With the secondary and primary pistons in position, fit the steel washer, a new seal, and the spacer; secure them with the circlip. Ensure that the circlip is fully engaged into its retaining groove in the rear end of the cylinder.
17   Refit the master cylinder, top up the reservoir with the specified fluid and bleed the brake hydraulic system (see Sections 7 and 6 respectively for details).

10   Front brake pads – renewal

Warning: *Disc brake pads must be renewed on both front wheels at the same time – never renew the pads on only one wheel as uneven braking may result. The front brake calipers will be of Bendix or Teves manufacture and if they or their component parts require renewal, ensure that the correct type is fitted. Dust created by wear of the pads may contain asbestos, which is a health hazard. Never blow it out with compressed air and do not inhale any of it. An approved filtering mask should be worn when working on the brakes. DO NOT use petroleum-based solvents to clean brake parts. Use brake cleaner or methylated spirit only. DO NOT allow any brake fluid, oil or grease to contact the brake pads or disc.*

1   Apply the handbrake, loosen off the front roadwheel nuts then jack up the front of the car and support it on axle stands. Remove the front roadwheels.
2   On the Bendix caliper, extract the R-clip from the cross-pin and withdraw the pin from the base of the caliper unit (photo). On the Teves caliper, prise back the support spring from the caliper housing.
3   On the Bendix caliper, prise free the blanking plug from the caliper pivot bolt (Allen type) at the top then loosen the bolt and swing the caliper unit upwards to allow access to the brake pads. To avoid straining the brake hose whilst the caliper is raised/withdrawn, detach the hose and grommet from the locating bracket. Nip the bolt tight to secure the caliper in the raised position (photos). On the Teves caliper, prise free the blanking plugs from the caliper upper and lower mounting bolts, unscrew the bolts, then withdraw the caliper unit from the anchor bracket. Suitably support the caliper to avoid straining the hydraulic hose.
4   Withdraw the inner and outer brake pads from the anchor bracket (Bendix) or caliper unit (Teves) (photo). Note that on the Teves caliper it may be necessary to prise the fixed brake pad free, but take care not to damage the caliper. If the old pads are to be refitted, ensure that they are identified so that they can be returned to their original positions.
5   Brush the dust and dirt from the caliper and piston but **do not** *inhale it as it is injurious to health*. Inspect the dust cover around the piston for

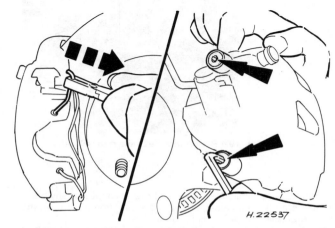

Fig. 9.11 Disengage the support spring and unscrew both brake unit retaining bolts on the Teves caliper (Sec 10)

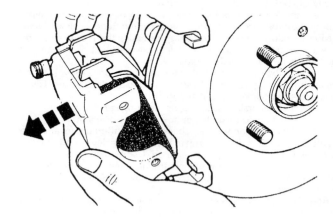

Fig. 9.12 Withdrawing the Teves caliper unit (Sec 10)

damage and for evidence of fluid leaks, which if found will necessitate caliper overhaul as described in Section 11. Inspect the anti-rattle plate for corrosion and if necessary renew it (photo).
6   If new brake pads are to be fitted, the piston in each caliper will need to be pushed back into its housing to allow for the extra pad thickness. As the piston is pressed back into the bore, it will displace the fluid in the system and cause the fluid level in the brake master cylinder reservoir to rise and possibly overflow. To avoid this possibility, a small quantity of fluid should be syphoned from the reservoir, but do allow the level of

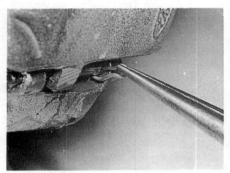

10.2 Removing the R-clip from the cross-pin (Bendix caliper)

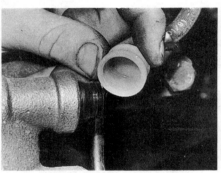

10.3A Remove the blanking plug ...

10.3B ... and unscrew the Allen bolts (Bendix caliper)

10.4 Removing the brake pads (Bendix caliper)

10.5 Removing the anti-rattle plate (Bendix caliper)

fluid to drop below the minimum mark on the reservoir wall. If any brake fluid is spilt onto the bodywork, hoses or adjacent components in the engine compartment, wipe it clean without delay.

7   Prior to refitting, check that the pads and the disc are clean and where new pads are to be installed, peel the protective backing paper from them. If the old pads are to be refitted, ensure that they are correctly located as noted during their removal.

8   Locate the inner and outer brake pad into position in the caliper anchor bracket (Bendix) or caliper (Teves). On the Bendix caliper, lower the caliper unit down, insert the retaining pin and fit the 'R' clip to secure. On the Teves caliper, relocate the caliper into position on the anchor bracket and insert the retaining bolts.

9   Tighten the pivot bolt (Bendix) or the mounting bolts (Teves) to the specified torque setting and refit the blanking plug(s). On the Teves type, relocate the caliper support spring.

10   Reconnect the brake hose in its locating bracket.

11   Repeat the procedure on the opposite front brake unit.

12   Before lowering the vehicle, check the that the fluid level in the brake master cylinder reservoir is up to the Maximum level mark and top up with the specified fluid type if required. Depress the brake pedal a few times to position the pads against the disc, then recheck the fluid level in the reservoir and further top up the fluid level to the Maximum mark if necessary.

13   Refit the roadwheels, then lower the vehicle to the ground. Tighten the roadwheel retaining nuts to the specified torque setting.

14   To allow the new brake pads to bed in and reach full efficiency, a running-in period of approximately 100 miles or so should be observed before hard use and heavy braking.

11   Front brake caliper – removal, overhaul and refitting

Removal

1   Apply the handbrake, loosen off the front roadwheel nuts on the

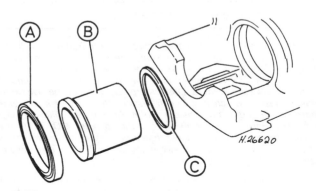

Fig. 9.13 Exploded view showing the dust cover (A) piston (B) and piston seal (C) (Sec 11)

side concerned then jack up the front of the vehicle and support it on axle stands. Remove the appropriate roadwheel.

2   Fit a brake hose clamp to the flexible brake hose leading to the front brake caliper. This will minimise brake fluid loss during subsequent operations.

3   Loosen only the union on the caliper end of the flexible brake hose.

4   On the Bendix caliper, extract the R-clip from the cross-pin at the base of the caliper unit and withdraw the pin from the base of the caliper unit. On the Teves caliper, prise back the support spring from the caliper housing.

5   On the Bendix caliper, prise free the blanking plug from the caliper Allen type pivot bolt at the top, support the caliper and unscrew the bolt. On the Teves caliper, prise free the blanking plugs from the caliper upper and lower mounting bolts then unscrew the bolts. On both caliper types, withdraw the caliper from its support bracket, support the caliper in one hand, prevent the hydraulic hose from turning and rotate the caliper to disconnect it from the hose. Do not allow the hose to be

11.7 Brake caliper anchor plate securing bolts (Bendix caliper)

11.14 Piston and dust seal in position in the Bendix caliper

strained or distorted. Once it is detached, place the caliper to one side and plug the hose.

6   Withdraw the brake pads from the anchor bracket (Bendix) or caliper (Teves). If they are likely to be re-used, mark them for identification (inner and outer, right or left-hand as applicable) to ensure that they are installed in their original locations when being refitted.

7   To remove the brake caliper anchor bracket, unscrew the two retaining bolts and withdraw it from the spindle carrier (photo).

Overhaul

8   With the caliper on the bench, wipe away all traces of dust and dirt, but *avoid inhaling the dust as it is injurious to health*.

9   Remove the piston from its bore by applying air pressure from foot pump into the caliper hydraulic fluid hose port. In the event of a high pressure air hose being used, keep the pressure as low as possible to enable the piston to be extracted but avoid the piston being ejected too quickly and being damaged. Position a suitable piece of wood between the caliper frame and the piston to prevent this possibility. Any fluid remaining in the caliper will probably be ejected with the piston.

10   Using a suitable hooked tool, carefully extract the dust cover from its groove in the piston and the seal from its groove in the caliper bore, but take care not to scratch or damage the piston and/or the bore in the caliper.

11   Clean all the parts in methylated spirit or clean brake fluid, and wipe dry using a clean lint-free cloth. Inspect the piston and caliper bore for signs of damage, scuffing or corrosion, and if these conditions are evident renew the caliper body assembly.

12   If the components are in satisfactory condition, a repair kit which includes a new seal and dust cover must be obtained.

13   Lubricate the piston bore in the caliper and the seal with clean brake fluid and carefully fit the seal in the caliper bore using the fingers only to manipulate it into position in its groove. When in position, check that it is not distorted or twisted.

14   Locate the dust cover over the piston so that its inner diameter is engaged in the piston groove. Smear the area behind the piston groove with the special lubricating grease supplied in the repair kit, then insert the piston into the caliper. Push the piston into position in the bore and simultaneously press the dust cover into the piston housing so that it is seated correctly. Take particular care not to distort or damage the seal or cover as they are fitted (photo).

Refitting

15   If the anchor bracket was removed, fit it into position on the spindle carrier and tighten the retaining bolts to the specified torque wrench setting.

16   Locate the brake pads into the anchor bracket/caliper. Where new pads are to be installed, peel the protective backing paper from them. If the old pads are to be refitted, ensure that they are correctly located in their original positions as noted during their removal.

17   Unplug the hydraulic hose, check that the unions are clean, fit a

new copper washer, then reconnect the caliper to the hose, reversing the disconnection procedure so that the hose is not twisted or strained. The hose union connection can be fully tightened when the caliper is refitted.

18   Refit the caliper unit according to type. On the Bendix type, refit the caliper to the anchor bracket, loosely locate the Allen bolt at the top, pivot the unit down and insert the cross-pin and its R-clip. On the Teves caliper, relocate the caliper unit to its mounting and insert the upper and lower retaining bolts. Tighten the bolt(s) to their specified torque wrench setting. Refit the blanking plug(s).

19   The brake hydraulic hose can now be fully tightened. When secured, turn the steering from lock-to-lock to ensure that the hose does not foul on the wheel housing or suspension components.

20   Top up the hydraulic fluid level in the reservoir and bleed the brake circuit as described in Section 6.

21   Refit the roadwheel, lower the vehicle to the ground and then tighten the wheel nuts to the specified torque setting.

12 Front brake disc – inspection, removal and refitting

Inspection

1   Apply the handbrake, loosen off the front roadwheel nuts on the side concerned, then jack up the front of the vehicle and support it on axle stands. Remove the appropriate front roadwheel.

2   Rotate the disc by hand and examine it for deep scoring, grooving or cracks. Light scoring is normal and may be removed with emery tape, but if excessive, the disc must be renewed. Any loose rust and scale around the outer edge of the disc can be removed by lightly tapping it with a small hammer while rotating the disc. Measure the disc thickness with a micrometer. Both the brake disc and the front hub run-out can be checked using a dial test gauge, although a less accurate method is to use a feeler blade together with a metal base block (photos).

Removal

3   Remove the caliper and its anchor bracket and suspend it from the front suspension coil spring (see Sec 11). Avoid straining the flexible brake hose.

4   Using a Torx type socket bit or driver, unscrew the screw securing the disc to the hub and withdraw the disc. If it is tight, lightly tap its rear face with a hide or plastic mallet.

Refitting

5   Refit the disc in a reversal of the removal sequence. If new discs are being fitted, first remove their protective coating. Ensure complete cleanliness of the hub and disc mating faces and tighten the screw to the specified torque setting. Refit the caliper/anchor bracket and tighten the

12.2A Checking the brake disc thickness using a micrometer

12.2B Checking the brake disc run-out using a dial gauge

12.2C Checking the front hub run-out using a dial gauge

retaining bolts to the specified torque wrench setting. Before refitting the brake pads, check the hub and disc run-out are as specified, then fit the brake pads into position (Section 10). Finally depress the brake pedal two or three times to bring the pads into contact with the disc.

6   Refit the roadwheel, lower the vehicle to the ground and tighten the wheel nuts to the specified torque wrench setting.

13   Rear brake drum – removal, inspection and refitting

Removal

1   Chock the front wheels, loosen off the rear roadwheel nuts on the side concerned then jack up the rear of the vehicle and support it on axle stands. Remove the appropriate rear roadwheel and release the handbrake.

2   On Saloon/Estate variants, undo the four bolts securing the hub/drum unit to the rear axle flange then withdraw the drum/hub unit from the axle (photo). If the brake drum is stuck on the shoes, remove the rubber access plug from the inside face of the brake backplate and release the automatic brake adjuster by levering the release catch on the adjuster pawl through the carrier plate.

3   On Van variants, prise free the drum retaining clip from the wheel nut stud, then withdraw the drum over the studs and remove it. Note that the retaining clip must be renewed during reassembly.

4   With the brake drum removed, brush or wipe the dust from the drum, brake shoes, wheel cylinder and backplate. *Take great care not to inhale the dust as it is injurious to health. It is recommended that an approved filtering mask be worn during this operation.*

5   If required, remove the hub from the drum as described in Chapter 10.

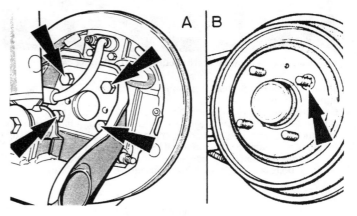

Fig. 9.14 Rear brake drum/hub securing methods (Sec 13)

A   Brake drum/hub unit   B   Brake drum retaining clip
    retaining bolts   on the Van model

Inspection

6   Clean the inside surfaces of the brake drum and hub, then examine the internal surface of the brake drum for signs of scoring or cracks (photo). If any deterioration of the surface finish is evident, renewal of the drum is necessary. To detach the hub from the drum, refer to Chapter 10.

13.2 Removing the rear brake drum/hub

13.6 Examine the inside surfaces of the brake drum for signs of excessive wear and/or cracks

14.2 General view of the rear brake assembly with the drum removed

14.3 Removing a shoe steady spring

14.4 Disengage the leading brake shoe from the bottom anchor ...

14.5A ... then from the wheel cylinder at the top

14.5B Elastic band fitted round the wheel cylinder to prevent piston ejection

14.7A Disconnecting the handbrake cable from the trailing brake shoe

Refitting

7   Check that the automatic brake adjuster is fully retracted, then according to type, refit the drum/hub unit to the stub axle. Tighten the retaining bolts securely (Saloon variants) or fit the drum over the wheel studs and press a new retaining clip over one of the studs (Van variant).

8   With the brake drum refitted, refit the roadwheel then fully depress the brake pedal several times to actuate the rear brake adjuster and take up the adjustment. Check that the rear wheels spin freely when the brakes are released then apply the handbrake, lower the vehicle and tighten the wheel nuts to the specified torque wrench setting. Remove the wheel chocks from the front wheels.

14   Rear brake shoes – renewal

Warning: *Drum brake shoes must be renewed on both rear wheels at the same time – never renew the shoes on only one wheel as uneven braking may result. Also, the dust created by wear of the shoes may contain asbestos, which is a health hazard. Never blow it out with compressed air and don't inhale any of it. An approved filtering mask should be worn when working on the brakes. DO NOT use petroleum based solvents to clean brake parts; use brake cleaner or methylated spirit only.*

1   Remove the rear brake drum with reference to Section 13.

2   Note the fitted positions of the springs and the adjuster strut (photo).

3   Remove the shoe steady springs by depressing and turning them through 90° (photo). Remove the springs and pins.

4   Pull the leading brake shoe from the bottom anchor and disconnect the lower return spring (photo).

5   Move the bottom ends of the brake shoes towards each other, then disconnect the tops of the shoes from the wheel cylinder (photo). Be careful not to damage the wheel cylinder rubber boots. To prevent the wheel cylinder pistons from being accidentally ejected, fit a suitable elastic band (or wire) lengthwise over the cylinder/pistons.

Fig. 9.15 Lubricate the points indicated before assembly – see text (Sec 14)

6   Disconnect the upper return (pull-off) spring from the brake shoes.

7   Unhook the handbrake cable from the handbrake operating lever on the trailing shoe (photos). Disconnect the support spring from the strut, twist the trailing shoe 90° and detach it from the strut.

8   Disconnect the strut from the leading shoe. As the strut is pulled from the shoe, the automatic adjuster will operate and release the pawl from the shoe (photo).

9   Clean the adjuster strut and its associated components.

10   Clean the backplate, then apply a little high melting-point grease to the shoe contact points (see Fig. 9.15) on the backplate and the lower anchor plate (photo).

11   Transfer the strut and the upper return spring onto the new leading shoe (photo).

12   Locate the other end of the upper return spring into the new trailing shoe, then twisting the shoe, engage the strut support spring

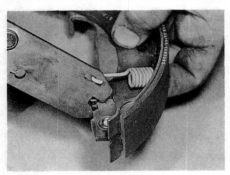

14.7B Disconnecting the support spring from the strut

14.8 Disconnecting the strut from the leading brake shoe

14.10 Lubricate the brake backplate with high melting-point grease

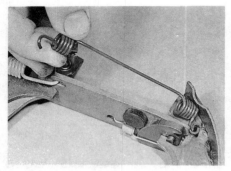

14.11 Reconnect the upper return spring to the leading ...

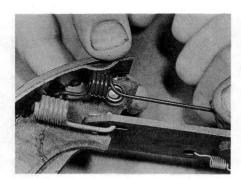

14.12A ... and trailing shoe

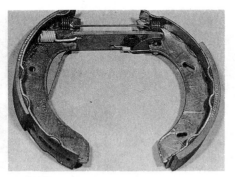

14.12B Brake shoes, strut and upper springs reconnected

and strut unit. When reconnected, check that the cam and pawl of the automatic adjuster have engaged (photos).

13   Remove the elastic band (or wire retainer) from the wheel cylinder. Reconnect the handbrake cable to the operating lever on the trailing shoe and refit the trailing shoe assembly into position on the backplate. As the shoe is engaged over the wheel cylinder, be careful not to damage the rubber dust cover.

14   Reconnect the lower return spring to the trailing shoe and, checking that the handbrake operating lever is resting on the lever stop head (not wedged against the side), locate the shoe in the bottom anchor plate. Refit the steady pin, spring and cup to secure the shoe in position.

15   Offer the leading shoe onto the backplate and insert its steady pin, spring and cup to hold it in place.

16   Reconnect the lower return spring to the leading shoe using a screwdriver to stretch the spring end into the location hole.

17   Refit the upper return spring using a screwdriver to stretch the spring end into the location hole.

18   Check that the brake shoes and their associated components are correctly refitted, then refit the brake drum with reference to Section 13.

19   Repeat the procedure on the remaining rear brake.

15 Rear wheel cylinder – removal, overhaul and refitting

Removal

1   Remove the brake drum as described in Section 13.

2   Pull the brake shoes apart at the top end so that they are just clear of the wheel cylinder. The automatic adjuster will hold the shoes in this position so that the cylinder can be withdrawn.

3   Using a brake hose clamp or self-locking wrench with protected jaws, clamp the flexible brake hose forward of the shock absorber (midway between the hose protective collar and the hose rigid connection bracket on the underside of the body). This will minimise

brake fluid loss during subsequent operations.

4   Wipe away all traces of dirt around the brake hose union at the rear of the wheel cylinder, then loosen off the hose-to-wheel cylinder union nut.

5   Unscrew the two bolts securing the wheel cylinder to the backplate.

6   Withdraw the wheel cylinder from the backplate so that it is clear of the brake shoes, then holding the brake hose steady to prevent it twisting, unscrew and detach the wheel cylinder from the hose. Plug the hose to prevent the possible ingress of dirt and to minimise further fluid loss whilst the cylinder is detached from it.

Overhaul

7   Clean the external surfaces of the cylinder, then pull free the dust cover from each end of the cylinder.

8   The pistons and seals will probably shake out, if not use a foot pump to apply air pressure through the hydraulic union and eject them.

9   Clean the pistons and the cylinder by washing in fresh hydraulic fluid or methylated spirits (not petrol, paraffin or any other mineral-based fluid). Examine the surfaces of the pistons and the cylinder bores and look for any signs of rust, scoring or metal-to-metal rubbing, which if evident, will necessitate renewal of the wheel cylinder unit.

10   Reassemble by lubricating the first piston in clean hydraulic fluid then manipulating its new seal into position so that its raised lip faces away from the brake shoe bearing face of the piston.

11   Insert the piston into the cylinder from the opposite end of the cylinder body and push it through to its normal location in the bore.

12   Insert the spring into the cylinder, then fit the second new seal into position on the second piston (as described for the first) and fit the second piston into the wheel cylinder. Take care not to damage the lip of the seal as the piston is inserted into the cylinder – additional lubrication and a slight twisting action may help. Only use fingers to manipulate the piston and seal into position.

13   Fit the new dust covers to each end of the piston.

Refitting

14   Wipe clean the backplate and remove the plug from the end of the

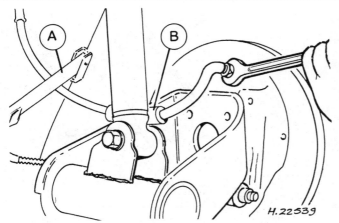

Fig. 9.16 Disconnecting the hydraulic hose from the rear brake wheel cylinder. Note the hose clamp (A) and the protective sleeve on the hose (B) (Sec 15)

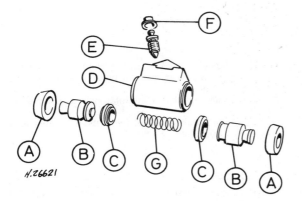

Fig. 9.17 Rear brake wheel cylinder components (Sec 15)

A   Dust cover
B   Piston
C   Piston seal
D   Wheel cylinder body
E   Bleed nipple
F   Dust cap
G   Spring

hydraulic hose. Carefully screw the cylinder onto the hose connector and then fit the cylinder onto the backplate. Tighten the retaining bolts securely, then fully tighten the hydraulic hose union.
15   Retract the automatic brake adjuster mechanism so that the brake shoes engage with the pistons of the wheel cylinder.
16   Remove the clamp from the flexible brake hose. Ensure that the protective sleeve on the hose is adjacent to the shock absorber (see Fig. 9.16).
17   Refit the brake drum with reference to Section 13.
18   Bleed the brake hydraulic system as described in Section 6. Providing suitable precautions were taken to minimise loss of fluid, it should only be necessary to bleed the relevant rear brake.

16   Rear brake backplate – removal and refitting

Removal
1   Remove the brake drum/hub assembly as described in Section 13.
2   Remove the rear brake shoes as described in Section 14.
3   Remove the wheel cylinder from the backplate as described in Section 15.
4   Compress the three retaining lugs and release the handbrake cable from the backplate by pushing it back through the plate.

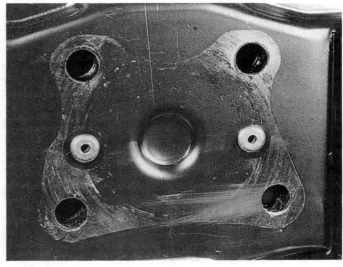

16.5 Backplate to stub axle rivets

5   Drill out the pop rivets securing the backplate to the stub axle flange and remove the backplate (photo).

Refitting
6   Refit in the reverse order of removal. Check that the plate is correctly located (with the wheel cylinder aperture at the top) before riveting it into position.
7   Refit the handbrake cable and ensure that the retaining lugs are secure.
8   Refit the wheel cylinder as described in Section 15.
9   Refit the rear brake shoes as described in Section 14.
10   Refit the brake drum/hub as described in Section 13.
11   On completion, bleed the brake hydraulic system as described in Section 6.

17   Handbrake lever – removal and refitting

Removal
1   Chock the roadwheels to secure the vehicle.
2   Remove the front seats as described in Chapter 11.
3   Where applicable, remove the centre console as described in Chapter 11.

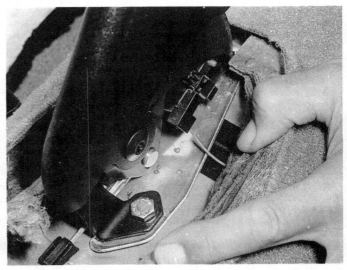

17.4 Prise back the carpet for access to the handbrake warning light switch lead connection and lever mounting bolts

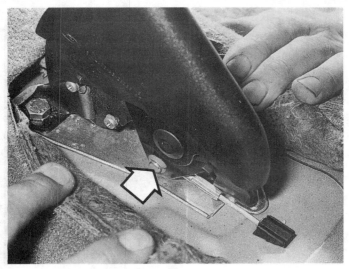

17.6 Handbrake primary cable to lever pin and retaining clip (arrowed)

4   Peel back the carpet from the area around the handbrake lever to provide suitable access to the lever and fittings (photo).
5   Detach the handbrake warning light lead from the switch.
6   Prise free the retaining clip and remove the primary cable pin (photo).
7   Undo the two retaining bolts and remove the handbrake lever and spreader plate.

Refitting

8   Refit in the reverse order of removal. Ensure that the retaining bolts are securely tightened. Check the handbrake adjustment as described in Chapter 1 to complete.

18   Handbrake primary cable – removal and refitting

Removal

1   Release the primary cable from the handbrake lever as described in the previous Section.
2   Chock the front roadwheels, then jack up the vehicle at the rear and support it on axle stands.
3   Where applicable, detach the exhaust system and remove the heat shields from the underside floor pan to allow access to the primary cable connections underneath the vehicle (Chapter 4).
4   Release the spring clip securing the pin and extract the equaliser/cable pin. Detach the equaliser from the primary cable.
5   Detach the cable guide from the floor pan, then withdraw the cable rearwards from the vehicle.

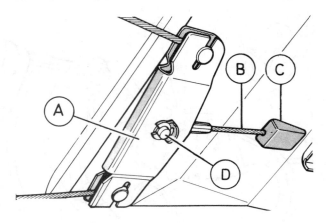

Fig. 9.18 Handbrake cable equaliser components (Sec 18)

A   Equaliser
B   Primary cable
C   Cable guide
D   Equaliser pin and spring clip

Refitting

6   Refit in the reverse order of removal. Ensure that the cable guide is secured in the floor pan and lubricate the pivot pin with a liberal amount of high melting-point grease.
7   Refit the exhaust system with reference to Chapter 4 (where applicable).
8   Refer to Chapter 1 for details and adjust the handbrake as required before lowering the vehicle to the floor.

19   Handbrake cable – removal and refitting

Removal

1   Chock the front wheels then jack up the rear of the car and support it on axle stands. Fully release the handbrake lever and remove the rear wheel(s).
2   Refer to the previous Section for details and release the handbrake primary cable from the equaliser unit.
3   Disengage the right/left-hand cable(s) from the equaliser unit (as required).
4   Remove the lock pin from the adjuster and the spring clip from the cable guides on the side concerned, then detach them from the underbody (photo).
5   Remove the rear brake drum(s) and shoes as described in Sections 13 and 14 respectively.
6   Compress the handbrake cable retainer lugs and release the cable

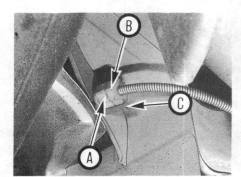

19.4 Handbrake cable adjuster nut (A) locknut (B) and lockpin (C)

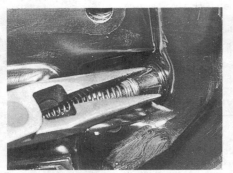

19.6A Compress the handbrake cable retaining lugs to release the cable from the brake backplate

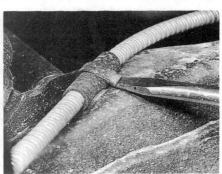

19.6B Release the handbrake cable from its locating clips

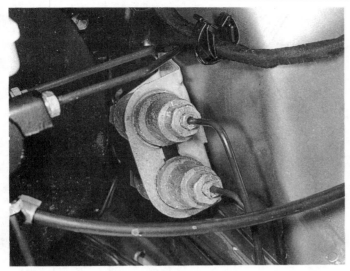

20.1 Brake pressure control valves

from the backplate and then pull the cable through. Release the cable from the underbody fixings and remove it from the vehicle (photos).

Refitting

7   Refitting is a reversal of the removal procedure. Refer to the appropriate Sections for details on the refitting of the brake shoes and drums.
8   When the cable is fully refitted (but before lowering the vehicle rear wheels to the ground) check and adjust the handbrake as described in Chapter 1.

20 Brake pressure control valves – removal and refitting

Removal

1   The pressure control valves are located in the engine compartment and are fixed to the left-hand inner wing panel (photo).
2   To remove the valve assembly, first detach the rigid brake pipes from the valves. As the pipes are disconnected, fit the exposed ends with plugs to prevent the ingress of dirt and excessive fluid loss.
3   Unscrew and remove the valve support bracket retaining nut (under the wheel arch) and then remove the valve assembly from the vehicle.
4   To remove the valves from the bracket, slide free the retaining clips and detach the valve(s).
5   Check the general condition of the insulators and if necessary, renew them before refitting.

Refitting

6   Refitting is a reversal of the removal procedure.
7   On completion of refitting, bleed the complete hydraulic system as described in Section 6.

21 Light-laden valve (Van) – removal and refitting

Removal

1   For this operation the vehicle must be raised for access underneath at the rear, but free standing. A suitable ramp (or an inspection pit) will therefore be required. If positioning the vehicle on a pair of ramps, chock the front roadwheels.
2   Detach the brake pipes from the valve and drain the fluid into a suitable container for disposal. Due to its location, care will be needed not to spill the fluid onto the hands – wear suitable protective gloves.
3   Detach the spring clip from the link rod at the axle end. Withdraw the washer and the valve link rod from the bracket on the axle, but take care not to dismantle the spacer tube from the link rod unit.

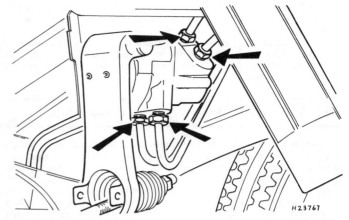

Fig. 9.19 Brake pipe connections to the light laden valve (Sec 21)

4   The axle bracket bush must be removed for renewal if it is worn or damaged.
5   Unscrew and remove the two retaining bolts, then withdraw the valve and the link rod unit from the mounting bracket.

Refitting

6   Where applicable, fit the new bush into the axle bracket.
7   Relocate the valve on the mounting bracket and fit the retaining bolts.
8   Check that the brake pipe connections are clean, then reconnect the pipes.
9   Smear the axle bush end of the link rod with a small amount of general purpose grease then fit the link rod into the bush and refit the washer and secure with the spring clip.
10   Top up the fluid level in the master cylinder reservoir and then bleed the brake hydraulic system as described in Section 6. If the original valve unit has been refitted, ensure that the valve is held fully open whilst bleeding. If a new valve unit has been fitted, the bleed clip must be left in position whilst the system is completely bled, then removed (not before) and the valve will need to be adjusted as described in the following Section.

22 Light-laden valve (Van) – adjustment

1   For this operation the vehicle must be raised for access underneath at the rear, but free standing. A suitable ramp (or an inspection pit) will therefore be required. If positioning the vehicle on a pair of ramps, chock the front roadwheels. The vehicle must be empty and the fuel tank no more than half full.
2   To adjust an original light-laden valve linkage, grip the flats on the

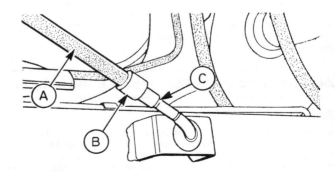

Fig. 9.20 Light laden valve linkage adjustment (Sec 22)

A   Spacer tube   C   Setting groove
B   Rubber seal

end of the rod to prevent it from rotating and turn the adjuster nut to position the end face of the rubber seal within the setting groove width (see Figs. 9.20 and 9.21).

3   To adjust a new light-laden valve, rotate the spacer tube to position the end face of the rubber seal within the setting groove width, then crimp over the end of the spacer tube against the threaded rod flats (next to the knurled section) (see Fig. 9.22).

23   Anti-lock braking system – description

An electrically driven anti-lock braking system is available on certain models in the range covered. The system only becomes operational over speeds in excess of 7 mph (4 kph). It comprises an actuation unit (servo unit and special type tandem master cylinder), an hydraulic unit, an ABS module and a sensor on each front wheel hub.

The hydraulic unit consists of a twin circuit electric pump which is controlled by a speed sensor and modulator twin valve block (one valve for each channel).

The module is located in the engine compartment and serves four main functions: to control the ABS system; to measure the vehicle speed; to monitor the electric components in the system; and to provide 'On-board' system diagnosis. The electrical functions of the ABS module are continuously monitored by two microprocessors and these also periodically check the solenoid-operated valves by means of a test pulse during the operation of the system. The module checks the signals sent by the system sensors to provide a fault diagnosis and in the event of a fault occurring in the ABS system, a warning lamp on the dashboard will light up and remain on until the ignition is switched off. A particular fault is represented by a two-digit code system stored within the module memory. A 'STAR' type tester is required to analyze the fault diagnosis system and in the event of a fault being indicated, the vehicle must be entrusted to a Ford garage for analysis.

The ABS system functions as follows. During normal braking, pressure from the brake pedal (and the servo unit) closes the master cylinder valves and hydraulic pressure is applied through the brake circuits in the conventional manner. When a front wheel starts to lock up under heavy braking, the circuit inlet valve in the hydraulic unit is closed off to prevent further pressure being applied through that circuit. In the event of this failing to prevent excessive deceleration, the outlet valve opens to reduce the pressure in that circuit thus preventing the wheel from locking up. Both valves are then momentarily and continuously opened and shut to maintain the required pressure in that circuit to provide the maximum possible hydraulic pressure (from the master cylinder) without locking up the wheel.

Slight pulsations will be felt through the brake pedal, but to reduce excessive brake pedal pulsations, a pedal travel sensor monitors any slight increase in pedal pressure and causes the pump to be switched on and off and this maintains the pedal position. When emergency braking is applied, the pedal is pressed back to a predetermined 'safety position'. When the brake pedal is released, the ABS mode is automatically cancelled.

The rear wheels are not fitted with sensors but are prevented from locking up (under all braking conditions) by means of a load apportioning valve incorporated in each rear circuit. These valves are housed in a common casting and are actuated by an arm connected to the rear axle twist-beam. The load apportioning valve is checked for adjustment and set during the vehicle pre-delivery using a special tool. Any further checks or adjustments required must therefore be entrusted to a Ford dealer.

24   Hydraulic unit (ABS) – removal and refitting

Removal

1   Disconnect the battery earth lead. Also disconnect the wiring multi-plugs from the fluid warning indicator in the reservoir filler cap and the hydraulic lines from the hydraulic unit connection (see Fig. 9.23). Remove the filler cap from the reservoir (noting that the filler cap must not be inverted). The reservoir should now be emptied by syphoning or drawing out the fluid with a pipette before disconnecting the hydraulic lines from the master cylinder. Identify each brake pipe and its connection to the master cylinder, then unscrew the union nuts and disconnect them. When disconnecting the fluid return pipes from the

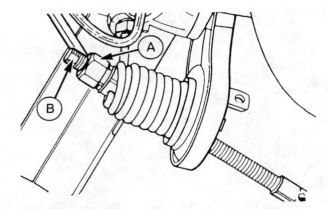

Fig. 9.21 Light laden valve linkage adjustment on a used valve, showing adjuster nut (A) and flats on the end of the rod (B) (Sec 22)

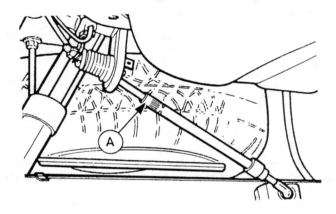

Fig. 9.22 Light laden valve adjustment on a new valve showing the crimping point (A) (Sec 22)

reservoir, press the retaining boss into the cylinder body and pull free the fluid line (see Fig. 9.6). Plug the connections and tape over the pipe ends to prevent the entry of dust and dirt.

2   Unscrew the union nuts and disconnect the fluid pipes from the hydraulic unit at the rear. Plug the connections.

3   Unscrew the retaining nut securing the multi-plug connector bracket, and the nut and bolt securing the hydraulic unit to the bracket.

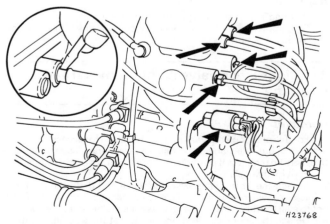

Fig. 9.23 Detach the hydraulic lines and the wiring multi-plug from the points indicated (Sec 24)

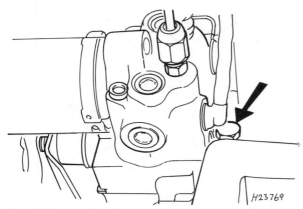

Fig. 9.24 ABS hydraulic unit-to-bracket retaining bolt location (Sec 24)

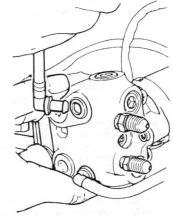

Fig. 9.25 Disconnect the fluid return lines from the ABS hydraulic unit (Sec 24)

Withdraw the hydraulic unit from the bracket and remove it from the vehicle.
4   Prise free and detach the fluid return lines from the hydraulic unit. Plug the connections and tape over the pipe ends to prevent the entry of dust and dirt.

Refitting

5   Remove the plugs from the connections as the pipes and fluid return lines are fitted. Refit in the reverse order of removal, noting the torque settings for the unit to bracket nut and bolt. Ensure that all connections are clean and secure.
6   On completion, top up the hydraulic fluid level in the reservoir and bleed the system as described in Section 6. Inspect the hydraulic line connections at the master cylinder/hydraulic unit for any sign of leaks.
7   When the battery is reconnected on EFi models, refer to Section 4 in Chapter 12 for the special restarting procedures to enable the engine management module to re-learn its values.

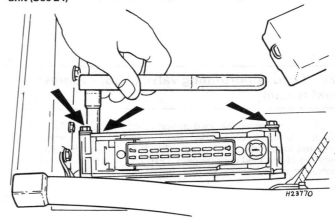

Fig. 9.26 Location of the ABS module retaining bolts (Sec 25)

25 Module (ABS) – removal and refitting

Removal

1   Disconnect the battery earth lead.
2   The module is situated opposite the battery, at the rear of the engine compartment. Swing the retaining clip out of the way and disconnect the wiring multi-plug from the module.
3   Unscrew and remove the three retaining bolts and withdraw the module from the vehicle.

Refitting

4   Refit in the reverse order of removal but take particular care when reconnecting the multi-plug. When the battery is reconnected on EFi models, refer to Section 4 in Chapter 12 for the special restarting procedures to enable the engine management module to re-learn its values.

26 Wheel sensor (ABS) – removal and refitting

Removal

1   An ABS wheel sensor is fitted in the front spindle carrier unit on each side. To remove a sensor, first raise and support the vehicle at the front end on axle stands so that the front wheels are clear of the ground.
2   Unclip and detach the sensor cable from the wiring loom. Unscrew the retaining bolt and withdraw the sensor from its location in the spindle carrier. Remove the sensor and lead from the vehicle.

3   If renewing the sensor, the replacement must have the correct lead length (on models fitted with an anti-roll bar, the lead is longer).

Refitting

4   Refit in the reverse order of removal. When inserting the sensor into position, ensure that the mating surfaces are clean and free from oil and grease. Feed the cable through the wheel arch and ensure that it is clipped in position. Secure the cable with any ties provided. When it is refitted, turn the steering from lock-to-lock and ensure that the sensor lead does not foul on any steering or suspension components before lowering the vehicle to the ground.

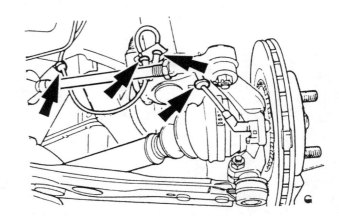

Fig. 9.27 ABS wheel sensor cable and securing clips (Sec 26)

27　Wheel sensor ring (ABS) – removal and refitting

Removal

1　Remove the brake disc from the front wheel hub on the side concerned as described in Section 12 in this Chapter.

2　Refer to Chapter 10 for details and detach the wheel hub from the spindle carrier unit.

3　Where applicable, unscrew and remove the sensor ring-to-hub retaining bolts then detach the sensor ring from the hub. In some instances, the sensor ring will be press fitted on the hub and will require a suitable withdrawal tool to remove it.

Refitting

4　Refitting is a reversal of the removal procedure. Ensure that the sensor and hub mating faces are clean. Refer to the appropriate Section in Chapter 10 for details on refitting the hub to the spindle carrier, and to Section 12 in this Chapter when fitting the brake disc to the hub.

Fig. 9.28 ABS sensor ring-to-wheel hub retaining bolts (Sec 27)

28　Load apportioning valve (ABS) – removal and refitting

The removal of the load apportioning valve on ABS equipped models is not recommended since a specialised resetting tool is required to adjust the valve unit when it is refitted. The removal and refitting of the load apportioning valve unit is therefore a task to be entrusted to a suitably-equipped Ford dealer.

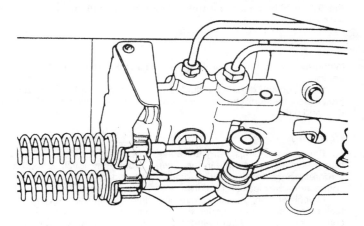

Fig. 9.29 ABS system load apportioning valve (Sec 28)

Chapter 10 Suspension and steering

Contents

Specifications

Front suspension

Type.. Independent, MacPherson struts with coil springs and integral double-acting shock absorbers. Anti-roll bar fitted to some models

Rear suspension

Type:

Saloon and Estate... Semi-independent with twist beam rear axle. Double-acting shock absorbers with coil springs and strut on Saloon models, separate shock absorbers and coil springs on Estate models

Van .... Rigid axle mounted on single leaf springs. Double-acting telescopic shock absorbers

Steering

Type.. Rack and pinion, power-assisted on some models

Turns (lock-to-lock):

Manual.. 4.6

Power-assisted.. 3.63

Steering angles and wheel alignment

Toe setting (all models):

Tolerances allowed before resetting required .... –4.5 mm toe-out to 0.5 mm toe-in, or
–0°45' toe-out to 0°05' toe-in, or
–0.78° toe-out to 0.09° toe-in

Adjustment setting (if required) .... –2.0 mm toe-out ± 1.0 mm, or
–0°20' toe-out ± 0°10', or
–0.35° toe-out ± 0.17°

Steering angles and wheel alignment (continued)

Castor angles:	
Saloon and Estate	1°15' to –1°15' (0°00' nominal), or
	1.25° to –1.25° (0.00° nominal)
Van	0°27' to –2°03' (–0°48' nominal), or
	0.45° to –2.05° (–0.80° nominal)
Maximum variation (left-to-right)	1°00' or 1.00°
Camber angles:	
Saloon and Estate	1°04' to –1°36' (–0°15' nominal), or
	1.07° to –1.60° (–0.26° nominal)
Van	0°58' to –1°42' (–0°22' nominal), or
	0.97° to –1.70° (–0.37° nominal)
Maximum variation (left-to-right)	1°15' or 1.25°
Power-assisted steering drivebelt tension	Refer to Chapter 1 for details
Maximum allowable front hub run-out..	0.05 mm

Roadwheels and tyres

Wheel types and sizes:	
Steel	13 x 5
	13 x 5 (Heavy Duty Van)
	14 x 6
Alloy	13 x 5 or 14 x 6
Tyre sizes and pressures:	
Sizes (depending on model)...	155 R 13 78T
	175/70 R 13 82T
	175/70 R 13 82H
	185/60 R 14 82H
	165 R 13-T
	165R13-REINF

	Front	Rear
Pressure (normally laden and normal use*):		
All tyres listed above	2.0 bars (29 lbf/in^2)	1.8 bars (26 lbf/in^2)
Pressure (fully laden and normal use):		
155 R 13 78T, 175/70 R 13 82T, 175/70 R 13 82H, 185/60 R 14		
82H tyres	2.3 bars (34 lbf/in^2)	2.8 bars (41 lbf/in^2)
165 R 13-T	2.3 bars (34 lbf/in^2)	3.0 bars (44 lbf/in^2)
165R13-REINF	2.3 bars (34 lbf/in^2)	3.5 bars (51 lbf/in^2)

Up to three people and 170 kg load.
Note: *For sustained high speeds above 100 mph (160 kmh) increase the tyre pressures 0.1 bar (1.5 lbf/in^2) for each 6 mph (10 km/h) above this speed.*

Torque wrench settings

	Nm	**lbf ft**
Front suspension		
Wheel hub nut:		
M20 x 1.5 (23 splines)	205 to 235	151 to 173
M22 x 1.5 (25 splines)	220 to 250	162 to 186
Lower arm balljoint to spindle carrier clamp bolt...............	48 to 60	35 to 44
Lower arm to subframe bolts (using torque-to-yield method with vehicle free standing):		
Stage 1...	50 then loosen off	37 then loosen off
Stage 2...	50 then tighten further 90°	37 then tighten further 90°
Anti-roll bar to suspension strut nut	41 to 58	30 to 43
Anti-roll bar link to roll bar nut	41 to 58	30 to 43
Anti-roll bar to subframe clamp bolts.................................	20 to 28	15 to 21
Subframe retaining bolts	80 to 90	59 to 66
Suspension top mounting nut...	40 to 62	30 to 38
Suspension strut piston rod top spring seat nut	52 to 65	38 to 48
Brake caliper anchor bracket bolts	51 to 61	37 to 45
Rear suspension (Saloon and Estate)		
Rear hub bearing nut (handed right- or left-hand thread accordingly)......	250 to 270	184 to 199
Spindle to axle nuts...	56 to 76	41 to 56
Axle front mounting bracket bolts	41 to 58	30 to 43
Axle front bush/bracket pivot nuts/bolts*...........................	102 to 138	75 to 102
Strut upper mounting nuts	28 to 40	20 to 30
Strut lower mounting	102 to 138	75 to 102
Strut upper through-bolt	41 to 58	30 to 43
Torque to be measured from the bolt head (not the nut)		
Rear suspension (Van)		
Shock absorber upper mounting..	41 to 58	30 to 43
Shock absorber lower mounting	58 to 79	43 to 58
Shock absorber mounting bracket to body	30 to 40	22 to 30
Axle/spring U-bolt nuts	33 to 41	24 to 30
Front eye bolt	70 to 85	52 to 63
Rear shackle upper bolt	40 to 49	30 to 36
Rear shackle lower bolt...	70 to 85	52 to 63

Torque wrench settings (continued)

Steering (manual)

	Nm	lbf ft
Steering wheel to column shaft bolt	45 to 55	33 to 40
Steering gear to subframe bolts	70 to 97	53 to 65
Steering column mounting nuts	10 to 14	7 to 10
Coupling to pinion spline	45 to 56	33 to 41
Track rod to spindle carrier arm	25 to 30	18 to 22
Track rod locknut	57 to 68	42 to 50
Track rod to steering rack unit	68 to 90	50 to 66
Adjustable steering through-bolt	6 to 8	4 to 6
Subframe to body retaining bolts	80 to 90	59 to 66
Lower arm to spindle carrier pinch bolts	48 to 60	35 to 44
Yoke plug	4 to 5 (then back off 60 to 70°)	3 to 4 (then back off 60 to 70°)

Steering (power-assisted)

	Nm	lbf ft
Steering coupling clamp bolts	17 to 20	12 to 15
Steering coupling pinch bolts	17 to 20	12 to 15
Steering wheel to column shaft bolt	45 to 55	33 to 40
Lower pinion nut	37 to 47	27 to 34
Track rod locknuts	57 to 68	42 to 50
Track rod to spindle carrier arm	25 to 30	18 to 22
Track rod to steering rack	72 to 80	53 to 59
Track rod inner balljoint	72 to 88	53 to 65
Lower arm to spindle carrier pinch bolts	48 to 60	35 to 44
Steering gear unit to subframe	15 plus further 90°	12 plus further 90°
PAS pump bolts	21 to 28	15 to 21
PAS pump pulley retaining bolts	21 to 28	15 to 21
Pressure hose to pump	26 to 31	19 to 22

Wheel nuts

	Nm	lbf ft
All models*	100	74

*Special nuts for alloy wheels incorporate washers

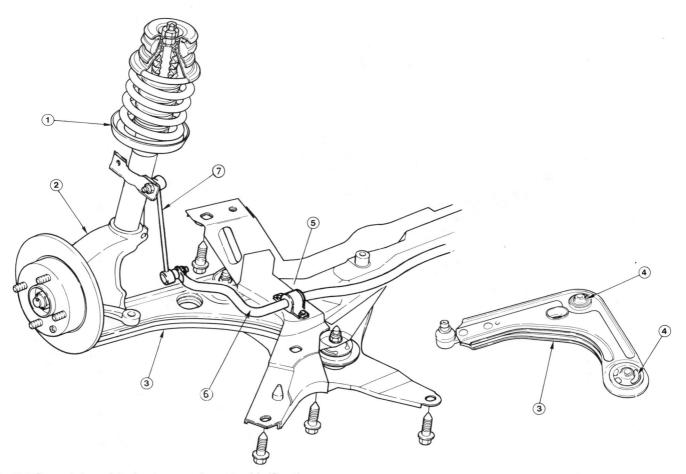

Fig. 10.1 General view of the front suspension assembly (Sec 1)

1	Strut unit	3	Lower suspension arm
2	Spindle carrier	4	Double vertical bushes
		5	Subframe
		6	Anti-roll bar (if fitted)
		7	Anti-roll bar link rod

1   General information

The independent front suspension is of the MacPherson strut type incorporating coil springs, integral telescopic shock absorbers and an anti-roll bar. The struts are attached to spindle carriers at their lower ends, and the carriers are in turn attached to the lower suspension arm by balljoints. High series models are fitted with an anti-roll bar and this is attached to the subframe and lower suspension arms by link rods with rubber bushes.

On Saloon and Estate models, the semi-independent rear suspension is of the trailing arm type incorporating a twist type axle beam. This inverted V-section beam allows a limited torsional flexibility, giving each rear wheel a certain amount of independent movement whilst at the same time maintaining the track and wheel camber control for the rear axle unit. The axle is attached to the body by rubber void bushes via brackets mounted on the underside of the body. Each bracket has a conical seating peg to ensure accurate alignment of the axle unit. It is important to note that the vehicle must **never** be jacked up at the rear under the axle beam. The axle beam itself is maintenance free but where required, the pivot bushes of the trailing arm can be renewed.

The rear suspension struts on Saloon models are similar to those used for the front suspension, the combined coil spring and shock absorber unit being mounted between the suspension turret in the luggage area at the top and the trailing arm, inboard of the stub axle unit at the bottom. The Estate model differs in that the coil spring is separate from the shock absorber and is enclosed between the underbody and the trailing suspension arm.

On Van models, the rear suspension comprises a transverse beam axle which is supported by a single leaf spring each side. Telescopic shock absorbers are used to control vertical movement.

The rear wheel hub/brake drum unit and spindle on each side form an assembly which can be unbolted from the axle without disturbing the hub bearings. The hub bearings are non-adjustable.

A variable ratio type rack and pinion steering gear is fitted together with a conventional column and two section shaft. The steering gear unit is bolted to the front sub-frame unit. A height adjustment mechanism is fitted to some variants and power-assisted steering is also available on some models.

2   Front spindle carrier – removal and refitting

Removal

1   Apply the handbrake, loosen the front roadwheel nuts on the side

Fig. 10.2 General view of the rear suspension assembly on Saloon and Estate models (Sec 1)

1   Axle beam
2   Trailing arm
3   Mounting
4   Pivot bush
5   Strut assembly (Saloon)
6   Twist axle beam, coil spring and shock absorber (Estate)

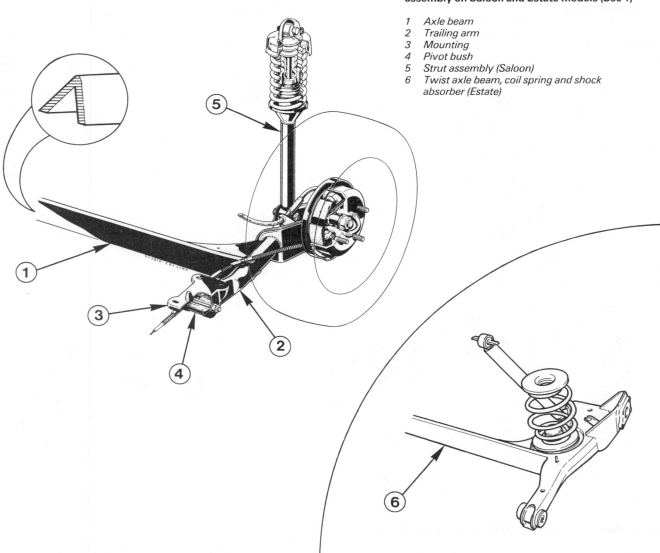

Fig. 10.3 Steering gear and column layout (left-hand drive shown) (Sec 1)

1   *Steering gear (rack and pinion) unit*
2   *Intermediate shaft and universal joints*
3   *Steering column bracket*
4   *Collapsible steering shaft*
5   *Compression spring*
6   *Convoluted shock absorbing section*
7   *Upper mounting/steering lock*
8   *Steering column height adjuster (where fitted)*

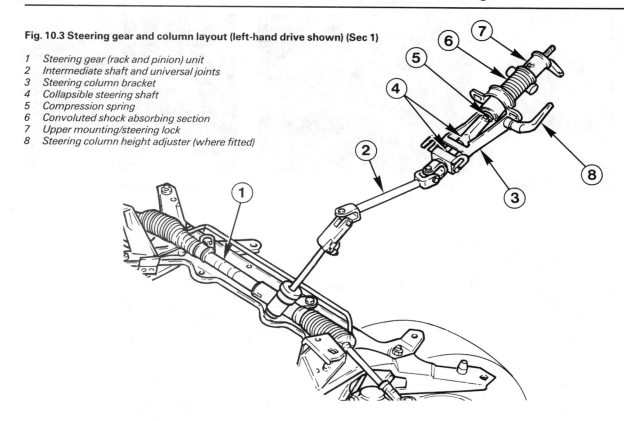

2.3 Disconnect the brake hose from the front suspension strut

2.6A Removing the lower arm to spindle clamp bolt and nut

2.6B Prise open the joint ...

concerned then jack up the front of the car and support it on axle stands. Remove the appropriate front roadwheel.
2   Using a suitable pin punch, bend back the locking tab securing the driveshaft/hub nut, then loosen off the nut.
3   Unscrew the retaining bolt and detach the brake hose and its locating bracket from the suspension strut (photo).
4   Unscrew the brake caliper unit to carrier retaining bolts, withdraw the caliper and suspend it from a suitable fixing in the inner wing to avoid straining the brake hose. Where applicable, detach the ABS sensor and its lead clip from the spindle carrier.
5   Extract the split pin from the track rod end balljoint, then unscrew the nut and detach the rod from the spindle carrier using a conventional balljoint removal tool (see photo 28.3), but take care not to damage the balljoint seal.
6   Note the direction of fitting, then unscrew and remove the lower arm balljoint to spindle clamping bolt. Prise the joint open carefully using a large flat-bladed tool and detach the balljoint from the spindle (photos). Take care not to damage the balljoint seal during the separation procedures.
7   Unscrew the brake disc retaining screw and remove the brake disc from the hub.

8   Unscrew and remove the driveshaft retaining nut and washer.
9   Note the direction of fitting, then unscrew and remove the suspension strut to spindle retaining bolt. Prise open the clamping slot using a suitable wedged tool and release the spindle from the strut. If necessary, tap the spindle carrier downwards to separate the two components (photos).
10   Connect up a universal puller to the spindle carrier and withdraw it from the driveshaft. When the driveshaft is free of the spindle, suspend it from a suitable fixing point under the wheel arch to prevent it from hanging down and its joint being pivoted beyond the maximum angle specified (see paragraph 8, Section 2 of Chapter 8).

Refitting

11   Refitting is a reversal of removal, but observe the following points.

   (a)   Ensure that all mating faces, particularly those of the disc and hub flange, are clean before refitting.
   (b)   Lubricate the hub splines with molybdenum disulphide grease and take care not to dislodge the hub bearings as the driveshaft is refitted through the hub.

2.6C ... and detach the lower arm balljoint from the spindle

2.9A Remove the suspension strut to spindle clamp bolt ...

2.9B ... and separate the spindle from the strut

(c) Tighten all nuts and bolts to the specified torque. Fit a new split pin to the track rod end balljoint nut to secure it. When reconnecting the suspension lower arm balljoint to the spindle, ensure that the joint cone is free of oil and grease. Ensure that the pinch bolt is fully engaged in the locating groove to prevent the bolt from turning as the nut is tightened.

(d) When the hub nut is tightened to its specified torque wrench setting, spin the hub to ensure that it turns freely then stake lock the nut flange into the groove in the end of the driveshaft.

3 Front hub bearings – checking

1 All models are fitted with non-adjustable front wheel bearings which are supplied pre-greased by the manufacturer.
2 To check the bearings for excessive wear, raise and support the front end of the vehicle securely on axle stands.
3 Grip the roadwheel at the top and bottom and attempt to rock it. If excessive movement is noted, or if there is any roughness or vibration felt when the wheel is spun, this indicates that the hub bearings are in need of renewal. Refer to Chapter 8 Specifications to determine whether a 23-spline or 25-spline driveshaft is fitted, then refer to Section 4 or 5 (as applicable) and proceed as described to renew the bearings.

4 Front hub bearings (23 spline type) – renewal

Note: *The front hub bearings should only be removed from the spindle carrier if they are to be renewed. The removal procedure renders the bearings unserviceable and they must not be re-used. Prior to dismantling it should be noted that Ford service tools 14-034 (installation adaptors), 15-033-01 (adaptor), 15-034 (bearing installer), 15-068 (pinion bearing cup installer), 14-038 and 14-038-01 (collet and thrust pad) 15-050 (main puller), 15-036 (hub installer), and 15-064 (adaptor), or suitable alternatives will be required. Unless these tools are available, the renewal of the spindle carrier/hub bearings will have to be entrusted to a Ford garage. Under no circumstances attempt to tap the hub bearings into position as this will render them unserviceable. On ABS-equipped models, care must be taken during the bearing removal and refitting procedures not to damage the ABS rotor.*

Removal

1 Remove the spindle carrier from the vehicle as described in Section 2.
2 Support the spindle carrier securely and using a suitable drift, tap or press the hub from the spindle carrier.
3 Use a suitable punch, tap the outer bearing race at diametrically opposed points and remove it from the spindle carrier. Do not allow the bearing to tilt during its withdrawal from the housing or it will jam and

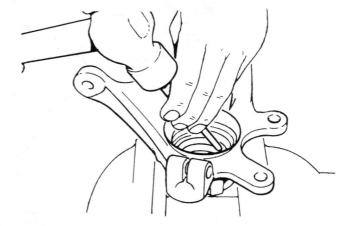

Fig. 10.4 Outer wheel bearing removal from the spindle carrier (23 spline hub type) (Sec 4)

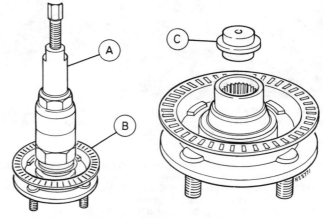

Fig. 10.5 Inner bearing removal from the spindle carrier using special tools (23 spline hub type) (Sec 4)

A Tool No 15-050   C Tool No 14-038-01
B Tool No 14-038

possibly damage the surface of the bore. Any burrs left in a bearing bore will prevent the new bearing from seating correctly.
4 Position the thrust pad (14-038-01) on the hub and the collet (14-038) on the inboard race so that it engages in the upper groove. Fit the collet to the puller (15-050), secure the retaining nut and then withdraw the inner race using the central spindle of the puller.
5 Thoroughly clean the bearing bore and hub before reassembly begins.

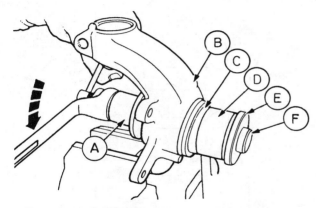

Fig. 10.6 Outer bearing installation into the spindle carrier using special tools (23 spline hub type) (Sec 4)

A	Tool No 15-033-01	D	Tool No 14-034
B	Spindle carrier	E	Tool No 15-068
C	Bearing	F	Tool No 15-034

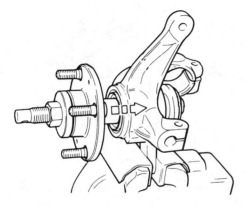

Fig. 10.8 Refitting the 23 spline hub to the spindle using Tool No 15-033-01 (Sec 4)

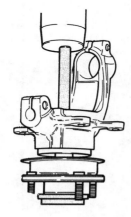

Fig. 10.9 Refitting the 23 spline hub to the spindle carrier using a press and Tool Nos 15-036 and 15-064 (Sec 4)

Refitting

6   Locate the outer bearing into position by assembling the puller bearing installer (15-034), the hub bearing installer (14-034), special tool 15-033-01 and bearing cup installer (15-068) as shown in Fig. 10.6. Once the bearing is in position, remove the special assembly tools but take care not to dislodge the inner bearing race and seal.

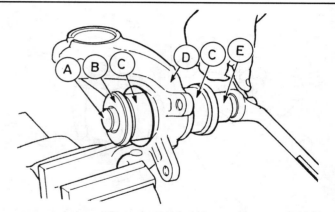

Fig. 10.7 Inner bearing installation into the spindle carrier using special tools (23 spline hub type) (Sec 4)

A	Tool No 15-034	D	Spindle carrier
B	Tool No 15-068	E	Tool no 15-033-01
C	Tool No 14-034		

7   Locate the inner bearing into position using special tools 14-034, 15-033-01, 15-068 and 15-034 assembled as shown Fig. 10.7. When the bearing is in position, remove the special assembly tools but take care not to dislodge the inner bearing race and seal.
8   The hub can be refitted to the carrier manually or using a press. Whichever method is used, care must be taken not to dislodge the bearings as the hub is reassembled to the carrier.
9   If the manual method is to be used, fit special tools 15-033-01, 15-068 and 15-034 as shown in Fig. 10.8 and tighten the nut to draw the hub through the bearings.
10   To fit the hub to the carrier using a press, fit the hub into position in the hydraulic press, then using special tool 15-064 to protect the studs, align the carrier, fit special tool 15-036 and press the carrier over the hub (see Fig. 10.9).
11   Remove the special tools and check that the hub spins freely in the carrier.

5 Front hub bearings (25 spline type) – renewal

Note: *The front hub bearings should only be removed from the spindle carrier if they are to be renewed. The removal procedure renders the bearings unserviceable and they must not be re-used. Prior to dismantling it should be noted that Ford service tools 14-040 (installation adaptor), 15-033-01 (adaptor), 15-033 (bearing installer), 14-038 and 14-038-01 (collet and thrust pad), 15-050 (main puller), 15-036 (hub installer) and 15-064 (adaptor) or suitable alternatives will be required. Unless these tools are available, the renewal of the spindle/hub bearings will have to be entrusted to a Ford garage. Under no circumstances attempt to tap the hub bearings into position as this will render them unserviceable. On ABS equipped models, care must be taken during the bearing removal and refitting procedures not to damage the ABS rotor.*

Removal

1   Proceed as described in paragraphs 1 to 5 inclusive in the previous Section.
2   Extract the bearing circlip then fit the inner race into position.
3   Pass the extractor tool through the bearing, fit a suitable puller to the extractor and withdraw the bearing outer race (see Fig. 10.10).

Refitting

4   Clean the bearing seating within the hub.
5   The new bearing can be pressed into its housing in the spindle carrier using an hydraulic press or manually according to the facilities available.
6   If using the hydraulic press method, support the spindle on the press bed, locate the bearing and press it into position using special tool

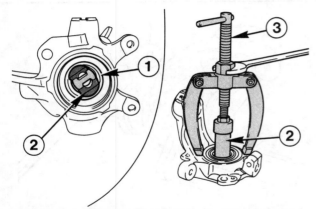

Fig. 10.10 Outer bearing race removal from the 25 spline hub type (Sec 5)

1	*Inner race*	3 *Puller*
2	*Internal extractor*	

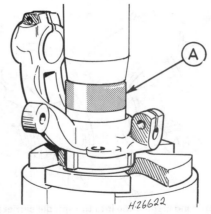

Fig. 10.11 Bearing installation to the 25 spline hub type using a press and Tool No 14-040 (A) (Sec 5)

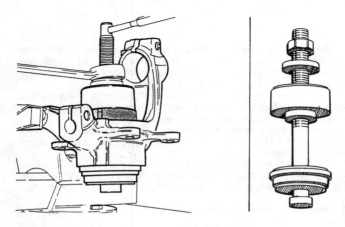

Fig. 10.12 Alterative method of bearing installation into the 25 spline hub using Tool Nos 14-040 and 15-033 (Sec 5)

14-040 (see Fig. 10.11). Check that the bearing is fully inserted and against its stops, then refit the circlip.
7   To insert the new bearing using the manual method, mount the spindle carrier in a vice fitted with protective jaws and locate special tool 15-033 (and adaptor) to the carrier. Fit the new bearing onto the tool and then fit tool 14-040 (Fig. 10.12). Tighten the nut to press the bearing into position in its housing so that it is against its stop, then refit the circlip. When pressing the bearing into position, it may also be found necessary to fit the thrust bearing to special tool 15-033.
8   Reassemble the spindle carrier to the hub. Check that the two are correctly aligned before pressing or drifting them together with the aid of special tool 15-036. To protect the studs, fit special tool 15-064 as shown.
9   Remove the special tools and check that the hub spins freely in the carrier.

6   Front suspension strut – removal and refitting

Removal

1   Apply the handbrake, then jack up the front of the vehicle and support it on axle stands. Remove the appropriate front roadwheel.
2   Open and support the bonnet. Prise free the protective cap from the strut upper retaining nut then loosen off, but do not remove, the central retaining nut (photo). As the nut is loosened off, hold the strut piston rod with an Allen key to prevent the rod from turning as the nut is loosened off as shown in Fig. 10.13.
3   Detach the front brake hose from the support bracket on the strut.

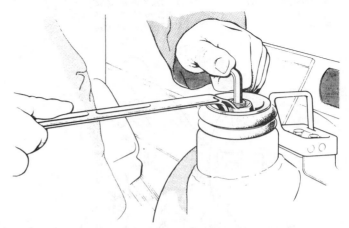

Fig. 10.13 Method to use when loosening off the strut upper mounting (Sec 6)

4   Where applicable, unbolt and detach the anti-roll bar link rod from the suspension strut.
5   Unscrew and remove the strut to spindle carrier pinch bolt shown in photo 2.9A.
6   Note the direction of fitting, then unscrew and remove the lower arm balljoint to carrier spindle clamp bolt. Prise the joint open using a

6.2 Front suspension strut upper mounting showing the protective cap over retaining nut (A) and the strut-to-body mounting nuts (B)

large flat-bladed tool and detach the balljoint from the spindle (see photos 2.6A, B and C). Take care not to damage the balljoint seal during the separation procedures.

7 Prise open the spindle carrier to strut joint and separate the carrier from the strut. Tap the carrier downwards using a soft-faced hammer to release it from the strut if necessary as shown.

8 Support the weight of the strut underneath and unscrew the two nuts securing it to the turret at the top. Lower the strut unit and remove it from the vehicle.

Refitting

9 Refitting is a reversal of removal. Ensure that the strut to spindle balljoint cone is free of oil and grease and that the carrier bolt is correctly orientated so that it engages with the location groove in the plate. Tighten all the retaining bolts to the specified torque.

Fig. 10.14 Front suspension strut coil spring compression Tool No MS-1516 and 14-023 (Sec 7)

7 Front suspension strut – dismantling, examination and reassembly

Note: *Before attempting to dismantle the front suspension strut, a tool to hold the coil spring in compression must be obtained. The Ford tool is shown in Fig. 10.14, however careful use of conventional coil spring compressors will prove satisfactory.*

Dismantling

1 With the strut removed from the vehicle, clean away all external dirt then mount it upright in a vice.

2 Fit the spring compressor tool (ensuring that it is fully engaged) and compress the coil spring until all tension is relieved from the upper mounting.

3 Hold the strut piston with an Allen key and unscrew the nut with a ring spanner.

4 Withdraw the cup, retainer (top mounting), the bearing and upper spring seat, followed by the gaiter and the bump stop.

5 The suspension strut and coil spring can now be separated. If a new coil spring or strut is to be fitted, the original coil spring must be released from the compressor. If it is to be re-used, the coil spring can be left in compression.

Examination

6 With the strut assembly now completely dismantled, examine all the components for wear, damage or deformation and check the bearing for smoothness of operation. Renew any of the components as necessary.

7 Examine the strut for signs of fluid leakage. Check the strut piston for signs of pitting along its entire length and check the strut body for signs of damage or elongation of the mounting bolt holes. Test the operation of the strut, while holding it in an upright position, by moving the piston through a full stroke and then through short strokes of 50 to 100 mm. In both cases the resistance felt should be smooth and

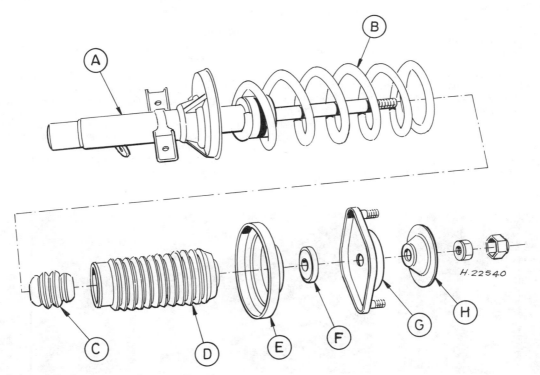

Fig. 10.15 Exploded view of the front suspension strut (Sec 7)

A	Strut	C	Bump stop
B	Spring	D	Gaiter

E	Upper spring seat	G	Top mounting retainer
F	Bearing	H	Top mounting cup

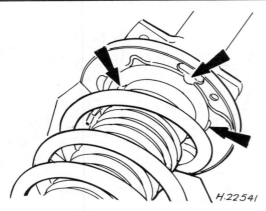

Fig. 10.16 Spring location in the lower seat (Sec 7)

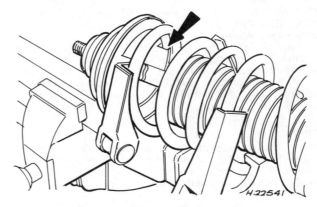

Fig. 10.17 Spring end location in the upper seat (Sec 7)

continuous. If the resistance is jerky, or uneven, or if there is any visible sign of wear or damage to the strut, renewal is necessary.

Reassembly

8   Reassembly is a reversal of dismantling, however make sure that the spring ends are correctly located in the upper and lower seats. Check that the bearing is correctly fitted to the piston rod seat. Tighten the upper nut to the specified torque.

8   Front suspension anti-roll bar – removal and refitting

Removal

1   Apply the handbrake, then jack up the front of the vehicle and support it on axle stands. Remove the front roadwheels.
2   Unscrew the retaining nut and detach the link rod from the suspension strut each side (photo).
3   Unscrew the retaining nut and detach the link rod from the anti-roll bar each side (photo).
4   Unscrew the retaining nuts and remove the anti-roll bar mounting brackets from the subframe each side, then withdraw the anti-roll bar from the side (photo).
5   Check the bar for damage and the rubber bushes for wear and deterioration. If the bushes are in need of renewal, slide them off the bar and fit new ones after lubricating them with rubber grease. If the link rod bushes are in poor or suspect condition, they will have to be renewed complete with the link rods.

Refitting

6   Refitting is a reversal of the removal procedure. Tighten the retaining nuts to the specified torque setting.

9   Front suspension lower arm – removal and refitting

Removal

1   Apply the handbrake, then jack up the front of the vehicle and support it on axle stands. Remove the appropriate roadwheel.
2   Note the direction of fitting, then unscrew and remove the lower arm balljoint to spindle clamping bolt. Prise the joint open using a large flat-bladed tool and detach the balljoint from the spindle (see photos 2.6A, B and C). Take care not to damage the balljoint seal during the separation procedures.
3   Unscrew and remove the inboard retaining bolts on the subframe unit and withdraw the suspension arm from it (photo).
4   If the balljoint and/or the inboard mounting bushes are found to be in poor condition, the complete suspension arm must be renewed. The suspension arm must also be renewed if it has suffered structural damage.

Refitting

5   Refitting is a reversal of the removal procedure, but note the following special points.

(a)   When reconnecting the arm to the subframe, the bolts must be fitted from underneath and hand tightened only.
(b)   When reassembling the suspension arm to spindle carrier balljoint, ensure that the balljoint cone is free of oil and grease.
(c)   Fully tighten the suspension arm to subframe bolts when the vehicle is lowered and is free standing. These bolts must then be tightened to the specified stage 1 torque setting, loosened off, then tightened to the stage 2 setting and further angle-tightened as specified.

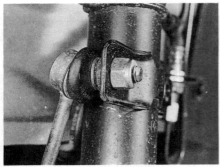

8.2 Link rod-to-strut connection

8.3 Link rod-to-bar connection

8.4 Anti-roll bar-to-subframe mounting

9.3 Suspension arm-to-subframe retaining bolts (arrowed)

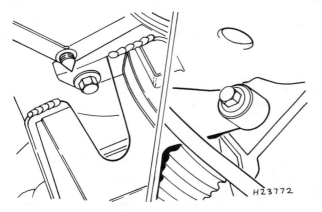

Fig. 10.18 Engine/transmission mounting bracket securing bolt locations (Sec 10)

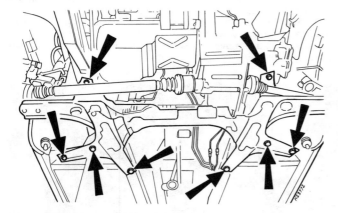

Fig. 10.19 Subframe securing bolt locations (Sec 10)

10 Subframe – removal and refitting

Removal

1   Apply the handbrake, then jack up the front of the vehicle and support it on axle stands. Remove the front roadwheels.
2   Disconnect the battery earth lead.
3   Fit an engine support bar or a sling and hoist to support the combined weights of the engine and transmission when the subframe is

detached (as during engine/transmission removal and refitting).
4   Centralise the steering so that it is in the straightahead position, then working within the vehicle, unscrew and remove the steering column-to-pinion shaft pinch bolt shown in photo 21.6.
5   Refer to Fig. 10.18 to identify its location, then undo the engine/transmission mounting bracket bolts at the subframe connection.
6   Undo the retaining nuts and detach the exhaust downpipe (Chapter 4).
7   Disconnect the gear control linkage at the transmission (Chapter 7).
8   Extract the split pin and unscrew the track rod end balljoint nut on each side, then using a conventional separator tool, detach each joint from its spindle carrier connection.
9   Note the direction of fitting, then unscrew and remove the lower arm balljoint to spindle carrier clamp bolt. Prise the joint open using a large flat-bladed tool and detach the balljoint from the spindle (see photos 2.6A, B and C). Take care not to damage the balljoint seal during the separation procedure.
10   Unscrew the retaining bolt and detach the right-hand engine support bar from the subframe unit.
11   Unscrew and remove the second engine/transmission mounting bolt illustrated in Fig. 10.18.
12   Where applicable, unscrew the retaining nuts and detach the anti-roll bar link rods from the suspension strut each side.
13   Where applicable, detach the power-assisted steering hydraulic lines from the steering gear unit (refer to Sec 25 for details).
14   Locate suitable support jacks or blocks under the subframe to support it, then unscrew and remove the eight subframe fixing bolts from the positions shown in Fig. 10.19. Lower the support jacks or blocks and withdraw the subframe. As it is lowered, disengage the steering pinion shaft from the column.
15   When the subframe is lowered from the vehicle, the steering gear unit, the suspension arms and the anti-roll bar (where applicable) can be unbolted and removed from it as necessary.
16   If the subframe and/or its associated components have suffered damage or are in poor condition, they must be renewed.

Refitting

17   Refitting is a reversal of removal, but observe the following points.

(a)   *Ensure that all mating faces are clean before refitting.*
(b)   *When raising the subframe into position ensure that the location dowels engage in the guide bores in the floor pan and carefully engage the steering pinion shaft with the column shaft. Check that the various fixing bolt holes are in alignment then loosely insert all of the retaining bolts before tightening them to the specified torque setting.*
(c)   *When reconnecting the suspension lower arm balljoint to the spindle, ensure that the joint cone is free of oil and grease. When fitted, check that the pinch bolt is fully engaged in the locating groove to prevent the bolt from turning as the nut is tightened.*
(d)   *Tighten all nuts and bolts to the specified torque. Fit a new split pin to the track rod end balljoint nut to secure it.*
(e)   *On completion, check the wheel alignment and steering angles as described in Section 29.*

11 Rear hub bearings – checking and renewal

Checking

1   All models are fitted with non-adjustable rear wheel bearings which are supplied pre-greased by the manufacturer.
2   To check the bearings for excessive wear, raise and support the rear end of the vehicle securely on axle stands and chock the front wheels. Fully release the handbrake.
3   Grip the rear roadwheel at the top and bottom and attempt to rock it. If excessive movement is noted, or if there is any roughness or vibration felt when the wheel is spun it is indicative that the hub bearings are in need of renewal.
4   Before dismantling, it should be noted that Ford service tools 14-028 (seal installer) and 15-051 (hub bearing cup installer), or suitable

11.7 Remove the outer grease cap from the centre of the rear hub ...

11.8 ... unscrew the hub nut ...

11.9 ... and remove the brake drum

Fig. 10.20 Bearing cup removal from the rear wheel hub (Sec 11)

16   To fit the grease retainer (seal), first lubricate its inner lip to ease installation, then using special tool 14-028 or a suitable equivalent, lightly tap the seal into position (ensuring that it is correctly orientated).

17   Pack the outer bearing cone with grease and fit it into position in its cup.

18   The brake drum/hub unit can now be refitted to the axle spindle. Before fitting into position, first check that the brake surface area in the drum is free of grease and oil. Locate the drum/hub into position, then fit the retaining nut and tighten it to the specified torque wrench setting whilst simultaneously rotating the drum/hub to ensure that the bearings are correctly seated.

19   Carefully tap the new hub grease cap into position in a progressive manner around its outer edge until it is fully fitted.

20   Refit the rubber blanking plug to the brake backplate and firmly apply the footbrake a few times to take up the brake adjustment. Check that the rear brakes do not bind when the brakes are released, then refit the roadwheel, lower the vehicle and then tighten the retaining nuts to the specified torque wrench setting.

alternatives, will be required to renew the hub bearings. The bearings and bearing cups **must** be from the same source as matched units.

Renewal

Bearing removal

5   To renew the bearings, unbolt and remove the roadwheel on the side concerned.

6   Check that the handbrake is still released, then remove the rubber blanking plug from the inside face of the brake backplate, reach through with a suitable screwdriver and release the automatic brake adjuster by levering the catch from the pawl.

7   Prise free the outer grease cap from the centre of the hub (photo). The cap will be deformed during its removal and will need to be renewed when the hub is refitted.

8   Unscrew and remove the hub nut but note that the hub nut threads are handed according to side, right-hand to right, left-hand to left (photo).

9   Withdraw the brake drum/hub unit from the spindle of the rear stub axle (photo).

10   Use a screwdriver or suitable lever to prise free the grease retainer (seal) from the hub bore, but take care not to damage the bore surface.

11   Remove the inner and outer bearing cones from the bore of the hub.

12   To remove the bearing cups from the hub, drive them out using a suitable punch (preferably brass). Drive each cup from its respective end by tapping it alternately at diametrically opposed points. Do not allow the cups to tilt in the bore, or the surfaces may become burred and prevent the new bearings from seating correctly as they are fitted.

13   Clean the bore and spindle thoroughly before reassembly.

Refitting

14   To reassemble, tap the new bearing cups into position in the hub using special tool 15-051 if possible to ensure that the cups are squarely inserted and abut their respective shoulders in the hub. A piece of tubing slightly smaller in its outside diameter than that of the bearing cup will suffice if the correct tool is not available.

15   Pack the inner bearing cone with grease and insert it into its cup in the hub.

12   Rear suspension strut unit (Saloon) – removal and refitting

Removal

1   Chock the front wheels then jack up the rear of the vehicle and support it on axle stands. Remove the inner wheel arch trim.

2   On ABS-equipped models, unscrew the retaining nut and detach the load apportioning valve connecting link from the axle beam.

3   Unscrew and remove the securing bolt from the strut to axle mounting (photo).

12.3 Rear strut lower mounting (Saloon)

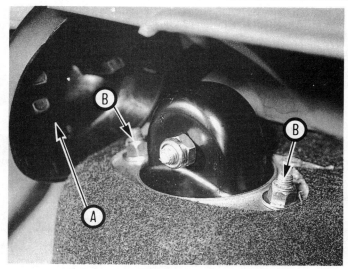

12.4 Rear strut upper mounting (Saloon) showing protective cap (A) and mounting nuts (B)

4 Prise free the protective cap from the top of the shock absorber mounting, located in the luggage compartment (photo).
5 Unscrew and remove the two retaining nuts to detach the strut unit from its upper mounting. **Do not** unscrew and remove the upper mounting bolt.
6 Withdraw the suspension unit from the vehicle.

Refitting

7 Refitting is a reversal of the removal procedure, but note the following special points.

  (a) *With the suspension strut located to its upper mounting, tighten the retaining nuts to the specified torque wrench setting.*
  (b) *When reconnecting the suspension strut to the lower mounting, hand-tighten the retaining bolt, then lower the vehicle so that it is free standing before fully tightening the bolt to its specified torque setting.*

13 Rear suspension strut (Saloon) – dismantling, examination and reassembly

Note: *Before attempting to dismantle the suspension strut, a tool to hold the coil spring in compression must be obtained. A Ford tool is available under Tool No MS-1516 (similar to that shown in Fig. 10.14), however careful use of conventional coil spring compressors will prove satisfactory.*

Dismantling

1 With the strut removed from the vehicle, clean away all external dirt then secure it in a vice.
2 Fit the spring compressor tool (ensuring that it is fully engaged) and compress the coil spring until all tension is relieved from the upper mounting.
3 Unscrew and remove the upper mounting through-bolt and nut.
4 Withdraw the upper mounting cup and the spring seat.
5 The suspension strut and coil spring can now be separated. If the coil spring or strut is to be renewed, the original coil spring must be released from the compressor. If it is to be re-used, the coil spring can be left in compression.

Examination

6 With the strut assembly now completely dismantled, examine all components for wear, damage or deformation and check the bearing for smoothness of operation. Renew any of the components as necessary.

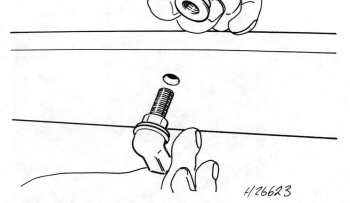

Fig. 10.21 Detaching the ABS load apportioning valve connecting link (Sec 12)

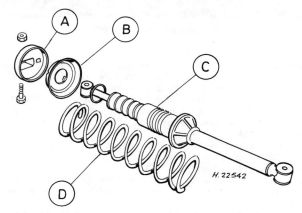

Fig. 10.22 Rear suspension strut components (Sec 13)

A   Upper mounting cup   C   Suspension strut
B   Spring seat   D   Spring

7 Examine the strut for signs of fluid leakage. Check the strut piston for signs of pitting along its entire length and check the strut body for signs of damage or elongation of the mounting bolt holes. Test the operation of the strut, while holding it in an upright position, by moving the piston through a full stroke and then through short strokes of 50 to 100 mm. In both cases the resistance felt should be smooth and continuous. If the resistance is jerky, or uneven, or if there is any visible sign of wear or damage to the strut, renewal is necessary.

Reassembly

8 Reassembly is a reversal of the dismantling procedure but note the following points.

  (a) *When the spring is located over the suspension strut, the spring seat, cup and through-bolt fitted, tighten the retaining bolt to the specified torque setting.*
  (b) *When reassembled, check that the upper and lower spring tails are correctly engaged with their spring seats before removing the spring compressor.*

14 Rear axle unit (Saloon) – removal and refitting

Removal

1 Raise and support the vehicle at the rear on axle stands. Unbolt and remove the roadwheels.

14.5 Rear axle forward mounting bolts (arrowed)

2   Refer to Chapter 9 for details and disconnect the handbrake cable equaliser from the primary cable, then detach the non-adjustable cable circlip and the cable from the underbody fastenings.
3   Disconnect the rear brake flexible hydraulic brake hoses from their rigid line connections. Clamp the hoses before disconnecting them to minimise the fluid loss and air entry into the hydraulic system (see Chapter 9 for details).
4   On ABS-equipped models, undo the retaining nut and detach the ABS load apportioning valve from the axle beam. Do not remove the load apportioning valve (see Chapter 9).
5   Locate suitable jacks or axle stands under the axle beam to support its weight (not lift it), then unscrew the mounting bracket bolts each side (photo).
6   Unscrew and remove the strut-to-axle mounting bolt each side.
7   Check that all associated fittings are clear, then lower the axle unit and remove it from under the vehicle
8   If the twist beam axle has been damaged it must be renewed. Refer

to Chapter 9 for details on removing the rear brake units from the axle. To remove the front mounting/pivot brackets from the axle, unscrew the pivot bolt.

Refitting

9   Refitting is a reversal of the removal procedure, but note the following.

(a) Reconnect the axle at the front floor mountings first, and tighten the retaining bolts to the specified torque setting.
(b) Reconnect the axle to the suspension strut but do not fully retighten the securing bolt until after the vehicle is lowered to the ground and is free standing.
(c) Ensure that all brake fluid line connections are clean before reconnecting them. Refer to the appropriate Sections in Chapter 9 for specific details on reconnecting the brake lines, bleeding the brake hydraulic system, and for reconnecting the handbrake cable and its adjustment.
(d) When the vehicle is lowered from the stands and is free standing, tighten the suspension fastenings to the specified torque wrench settings.

15   Rear axle pivot bushes (Saloon and Estate) – renewal

Note: *Before proceeding with this operation it must be noted that Ford special service tools 15-086 and 15-084 (drilled out to 12.5 mm), 30 mm dia. washer and 13 mm dia. spacers will be required to remove and install the bushes (Fig. 10.23). Unless these tools are available, it is recommended that the bush renewal be entrusted to a Ford garage.*

1   Chock the front roadwheels then raise and support the vehicle at the rear on axle stands.
2   Position a suitable support (preferably adjustable) under the axle twist beam so that it is capable of carrying the weight of the axle (**not** the weight of the vehicle).
3   Unscrew the nuts and pivot bolts, then lower the rear axle so that the bushes are clear of their mounting brackets. Take care not to allow the brake pipes to become distorted and stretched – if necessary, disconnect the hydraulic lines (see Chapter 9 for details).

Fig. 10.23 Ford Tool No 15-086 and 15-084 required to renew the rear axle pivot bushes (Sec 15)

1   *Tool No 15-086*
2   *Thrust bearing*
3   *Tool No 15-084*
4   *Washer (13 mm)*
5   *Spacer (30 mm)*

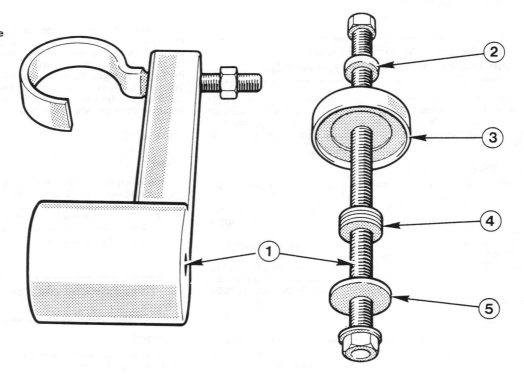

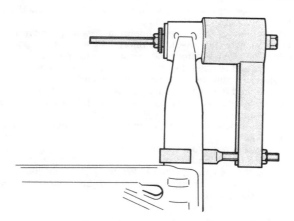

Fig. 10.24 Mounting bush withdrawal from the axle arm (Sec 15)

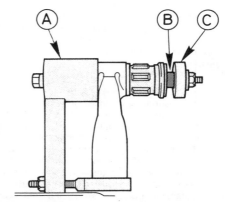

Fig. 10.25 Mounting bush installation into the axle arm using the special tools as shown (Sec 15)

A   Tool 15-086   C   Tool 15-084
B   Spacer

4   Assemble special tool 15-086 to the bush and withdraw the bush from the axle arm (see Fig. 10.24).
5   Clean the bush eye in the axle arm and lubricate it with a soapy solution before inserting the new bush.
6   Assemble the new bush together with tools 15-086, 15-084 and spacer as shown in Fig. 10.25. Ensure that the bush flange is positioned on the outside. Draw the bush fully into position so that its lip is engaged then remove the special tools.
7   Raise the axle to reposition the bush pin bores in line with the bolt holes in the mounting brackets, then insert the pivot bolts. Screw the retaining nuts into position on the pivot bolts but do not fully tighten them at this stage.
8   If necessary, reconnect the brake lines, then top up and bleed the brakes as described in Chapter 9.
9   Lower the vehicle to the ground, then tighten the rear axle pivot bolts nuts to the specified torque wrench setting to complete.

16   Rear shock absorber (Estate and Van) – removal, testing and refitting

Removal

1   Chock the front wheels, then jack up the rear of the vehicle and support it on axle stands. Remove the appropriate roadwheel.
2   On Estate models, position a jack under the coil spring area of the suspension arm (**not** under the axle beam), and raise it to just take the weight of the suspension unit.

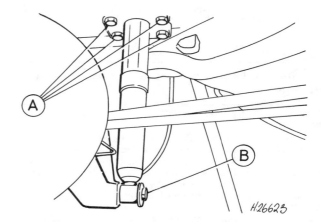

Fig. 10.26 Shock absorber upper (A) and lower (B) mountings on the Van model (Sec 16)

3   Unscrew and remove the shock absorber retaining bolt from the lower mounting (photo).
4   On Estate models, unscrew the retaining nuts securing the shock absorber top mounting on the underside of the body (from underneath) and withdraw the shock absorber unit (photo).

16.3 Rear shock absorber unit to axle mounting (Estate)

16.4 Rear shock absorber unit upper mounting (Estate)

5   On Van models, unscrew and remove the four shock absorber upper mounting bracket to body retaining bolts. Remove the shock absorber and its upper mounting bracket from the vehicle. To disconnect the shock absorber from the mounting bracket, unscrew the retaining nut, withdraw the through-bolt and remove the shock absorber from the bracket.

Testing

6   Mount the shock absorber in a vice, gripping it by the lower mounting. Check the mounting rubbers for damage and deterioration. Examine the shock absorber for signs of fluid leakage. Extend the shock absorber, then check the piston for signs of pitting along its entire length and check the body for signs of damage or elongation of the mounting bolt holes. Test the operation of the shock absorber, by moving the piston through a full stroke and then through short strokes of 50 to 100 mm. In both cases the resistance felt should be smooth and continuous. If the resistance is jerky, or uneven, or if there is any visible sign of wear or damage to the strut, renewal of the complete unit is necessary.

Refitting

7   Refitting is a reversal of removal procedure. Tighten the retaining nuts and bolts to the specified torque wrench settings (where given), then lower the vehicle to the ground.

17   Rear coil springs (Estate) – removal and refitting

Removal

1   Chock the front wheels, then jack up the rear of the vehicle and support it on axle stands. Remove the rear roadwheels.
2   Position a jack under the coil spring area of the suspension arm (**not** under the axle beam) each side, and raise them so that they just take the weight of the trailing arms beneath the suspension units.
3   Unscrew and remove the shock absorber retaining bolt from the lower attachment point to the rear axle unit each side.
4   Slowly lower the jack under the suspension arm each side and allow the trailing arms to drop and the compression in the coil springs to be released. Check that no excessive strain is imposed on the handbrake cables and/or the hydraulic hoses to the rear brake units. Disconnect them as described in Chapter 9 if necessary.
5   With the coil springs fully relaxed, withdraw them from their mounting locations between the body and the suspension arms. As they are removed, mark each for its direction of fitting and side so that they are refitted to their original locations (where applicable).

Refitting

6   Refitting is a reversal of the removal procedure but note the following special points.

(a)   When relocating the coil springs between the body and the suspension arm each side, ensure that they are correctly orientated and that their tails abut against the stops.
(b)   When the coil springs are correctly located, raise the jacks under the suspension arms and reconnect the shock absorber each side.
(c)   Tighten the retaining bolts to the specified torque setting.
(d)   If the brake cables and/or the hydraulic hoses were detached, refer to Chapter 9 for the reconnecting details and bleed the hydraulic system.

18   Rear leaf spring, shackle and bushes (Van) – removal, inspection and refitting

Removal

1   Chock the front wheels then jack up the rear of the vehicle and support it on axle stands. To allow improved access, unbolt and remove the rear roadwheel on the side concerned.
2   With the rear of the vehicle supported on stands, move the jack under the rear axle and raise it to support the weight of the axle and to take the loading from the front and rear spring mountings.
3   Unscrew and remove the shock absorber lower mounting bolt to detach the shock absorber from its mounting bracket.
4   Unscrew and remove the spring to axle U-bolt retaining nuts and remove the U-bolts. Remove the counterplate and the bump stop from the top of the spring.
5   Unscrew and remove the mounting bolt and nut from the rear spring shackle.
6   Unscrew and remove the retaining nut or bolt (as applicable) from the front mounting. Withdraw the mounting bolt (noting the flat washer fitted under the bolt head), then lower the jack under the axle just enough to allow the spring to be removed. Carefully withdraw the spring from the vehicle.

Inspection

7   If the spring mounting (shackle) pins are noticeably worn, they must be renewed. If the spring eye bushes are worn and in need of replacement, they can be withdrawn using a suitable drawbolt and spacer. New bushes can be pressed into position in the spring eye using a vice (or press).
8   If required, the rear spring shackle can be removed by unscrewing the retaining nut, removing the inboard shackle plate and withdrawing the outboard shackle plate complete with the upper shackle pin. The upper pin split type bushes must be renewed if they are worn.

Refitting

9   Refit the rear shackle and initially hand tighten the shackle pin bolt and nut.
10   Relocate the spring over the axle, align the front spring eye with the mounting and insert the bolt. Loosely secure the bolt (and where applicable, the nut) at this stage.
11   Align the rear spring eye with the shackle at the rear and loosely fit the mounting pin and nut.
12   Locate the counterplate and bump stop on the top of the spring over the axle, then refit the U-bolts and fit the retaining nuts. The jack under the axle may need to be raised to enable the U-bolt assemblies to be relocated.
13   Reconnect the shock absorber to the rear axle, then tighten the various fixings to their specified torque wrench settings.
14   Refit the roadwheel and lower the vehicle to the ground to complete.

19   Rear axle unit (Van) – removal and refitting

Removal

1   Chock the front wheels then jack up the rear of the vehicle and support it on axle stands. To allow improved access, unbolt and remove the rear roadwheels.
2   With the rear of the vehicle supported on stands, position a single jack centrally (or preferably two jacks each side of centre) under the axle beam and raise to take the weight of the axle – do not lift the vehicle.
3   Clamp the hydraulic hoses of the light laden valve to prevent excessive fluid loss and the ingress of air and dirt into the hydraulic system, then disconnect the hydraulic lines to the light laden valve and remove the clips.
4   Refer to Chapter 9 for details and remove the brake drum/hub units and then the backplate from the rear axle on each side. The backplates may be left attached to the axle, but it will still be necessary to detach the wheel cylinder brake line and also to disconnect and withdraw the handbrake cable from each rear brake backplate. As each assembly is removed, keep them separated and mark them to identify the right- and left-hand units. Note that they are handed and must not be confused or they could be incorrectly refitted later.
5   Unscrew and remove the shock absorber lower fixing bolts and

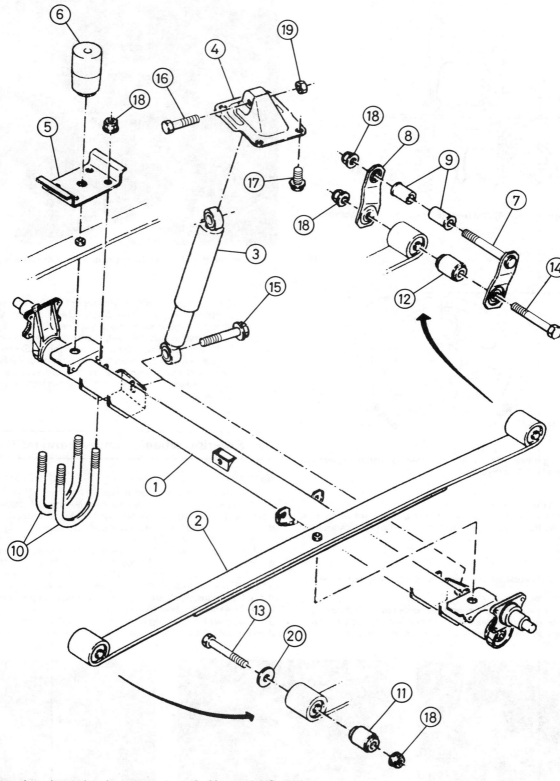

Fig. 10.27 Rear axle and associated components on the Van model (Sec 18)

1	Axle unit	6	Bump stop	11	Front spring eye bush	16	Bolt
2	Rear leaf spring	7	Shackle unit	12	Rear spring eye bush	17	Bolt
3	Shock absorber	8	Inboard shackle plate	13	Bolt	18	Nut
4	Bracket	9	Rear shackle bushes	14	Bolt	19	Nut
5	Counterplate	10	U-bolt	15	Bolt	20	Washer

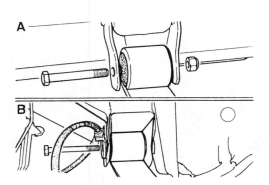

Fig. 10.28 Leaf spring rear (A) and front (B) locations and securing bolts (Sec 18)

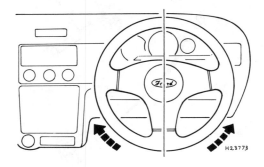

Fig. 10.29 Steering wheel alignment – centralised within a tolerance of 30° each side of vertical (Sec 20)

detach them from the rear axle.

6   Unscrew and remove the axle to leaf spring U-bolt retaining nuts, remove the U-bolts then carefully lower the axle unit and remove it from under the vehicle.

Refitting

7   Refitting is a reversal of the removal procedure, but note the following.

> (a)   *Reconnect the axle to the spring, reconnect the U-bolts and the shock absorbers to the axle on each side and then tighten the retaining bolts to the specified torque wrench settings.*

20.3 Remove the horn pad from the centre of the steering wheel

> (b)   *Refer to the appropriate Sections in Chapter 9 to refit the brake backplate and brake assemblies and ensure that they are correctly located according to the side.*
> (c)   *Ensure that all brake fluid line connections are clean before reconnecting them. Refer to the appropriate Sections in Chapter 9 for specific details on reconnecting the brake lines, bleeding the brake hydraulic system, and reconnecting the handbrake cable. Details of handbrake adjustment will be found in Chapter 1.*

20   Steering wheel – removal and refitting

Removal

1   Disconnect the battery earth lead.

2   Turn the ignition key to release the steering lock, then set the front roadwheels in the straightahead position. With the steering centralised, the steering wheel should be positioned as shown in Fig. 10.30. Move the ignition key to the OFF position.

3   Prise free the pad from the centre of the steering wheel (photo).

4   Prise free the horn pad, note their connections and detach the horn wiring at the spade connectors (these differ in size to ensure correct refitting), then withdraw the horn pad (photo). Note as it is withdrawn that it has a directional arrow mark which points up when the steering wheel is in the straightahead position.

5   Unscrew the retaining bolt from the centre of the steering wheel, then gripping the wheel each side, pull and withdraw it from the column

20.4 Prise free and detach the horn pad wires ...

20.5A ... unscrew the retaining bolt ...

20.5B ... and withdraw the steering wheel

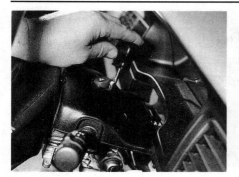

21.2A Remove the upper ...

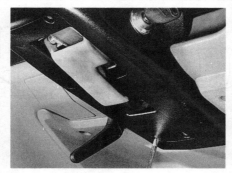

21.2B ... and lower steering column shrouds

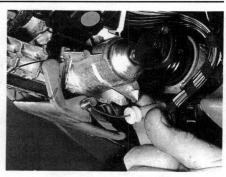

21.5 Detach the bonnet release cable from the lever

21.6 Steering column to pinion shaft coupling and pinch bolt

21.7 Steering column upper retaining nut (on the left-hand side of the column)

shaft. If the wheel is reluctant to budge, give it a sharp tap on the underside of the spoke (as near to the hub as possible) with the palm of your hand (photos).

Refitting

6   Refit in the reverse order of removal. When fitting the wheel into position centralise it as noted during removal, and also ensure that the indicator stalk is centralised to avoid damaging it with the tag of the wheel as it is pushed down the shaft. Turn the ignition key so that it is in position I (steering unlocked). Tighten the retaining bolt to the specified torque setting. When reconnecting the battery earth lead on EFi engine models, observe the special engine management relearning procedures outlined in Section 4 of Chapter 12.

21   Steering column – removal and refitting

Removal

1   Disconnect the battery earth lead, then remove the steering wheel as described in the previous Section.
2   Remove the screws and withdraw the steering column upper and lower shrouds (photos).
3   Remove the indicator switch assembly from the column with reference to Chapter 12.
4   Remove the ignition switch unit with reference to Chapter 12.
5   Detach the bonnet release cable from the lever, then remove the lever from the column (photo).
6   Unscrew and remove the pinch bolt securing the steering column to the pinion shaft (photo).
7   Loosen off the lower column retaining nuts then unscrew and remove the upper retaining nuts (photo). Remove the steering column from the vehicle.

Refitting

8   Refitting is a reversal of the removal procedure. Tighten the respective retaining bolts to their specified torque settings. Check that the steering is centralised before refitting the steering wheel (Section 20). Ensure that the wiring connections are securely made and on completion, check for satisfactory operation of the steering, the column switches and the horn.
9   When reconnecting the battery on EFi models, refer to Chapter 12, Section 4 for details of the engine management re-learning procedures.

22   Steering column – dismantling and reassembly

Dismantling

1   Remove the steering column as described in the previous Section, then securely locate it in a vice fitted with protective jaws.
2   Remove the upper thrust bearing tolerance ring from the column, then withdraw the column shaft from the column tube.
3   Insert the ignition key into the lock/switch and turn it to the I position. Now use a small screwdriver or a suitable rod to depress the plunger in the side of the barrel and simultaneously pull on the key to withdraw the lock/switch unit from the column (photo).
4   Withdraw the spring from the column shaft.
5   Prise free the lower and upper thrust bearings from the column tube and the lock/switch body.
6   To remove the steering column height adjuster (where fitted) unscrew the through-bolt and lock nut, remove the handle and lock plates, then remove the adjuster unit from the column.
7   If any part of the steering column and in particular the universal joints, are found to be excessively worn or any part of the column assembly has been damaged, it must be renewed; no repairs are possible.

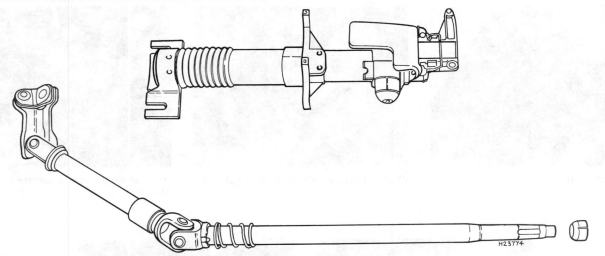

Fig. 10.30 Steering column unit removed from the column tube assembly (Sec 22)

Reassembly

8   Reassembly is a reversal of the dismantling procedure but note the following points.

  (a)   *When refitting the height adjuster unit, coat the threads of the through-bolt with Loctite and locate the handle in the locked position. Tighten the retaining bolt and nut securely.*

  (b)   *Take care when fitting the lower thrust bearing into the column tube and the upper bearing to the steering lock/ignition switch body.*

  (c)   *When fitting the steering column lock/ignition switch, ensure that the key is in the I position. As the switch/lock unit is fitted into its barrel, it may be necessary to move the key clockwise and anti-clockwise slightly to enable the housing drive to align with the barrel and fully engage.*

  (d)   *When assembling the column shaft to the tube, ensure that the upper thrust bearing tolerance ring is fitted with its tapered face towards the bearing.*

23   Steering gear rubber gaiters – renewal

1   Remove the track rod end balljoint and its locknut from the track rod as described in Section 28.
2   Release the clip(s) and slide the gaiter off the rack and pinion housing and track rod (photo).
3   Scrape off all grease from the old gaiter and apply to the track rod inner joint. Wipe clean the seating areas on the rack and pinion housing and track rod.
4   Slide the new gaiter onto the housing and track rod and tighten the clip(s).
5   Refit the track rod end balljoint as described in Section 28.

24   Steering gear (manual steering) – removal and refitting

Removal

1   Disconnect the battery earth lead.
2   Refer to Section 10 for details then disconnect and lower the subframe from the vehicle as described. Note that complete removal of the subframe may not be necessary if it is carefully lowered to allow access to the steering gear for its separation and withdrawal.
3   Unscrew and remove the two steering gear unit to subframe retaining bolts, then withdraw the unit from the vehicle (photos).

Refitting

4   Refit the steering gear to the subframe in the reverse order of removal and tighten the retaining bolts to the specified torque setting.
5   Refer to Section 10 for the relevant details on refitting the subframe assembly to the vehicle.

22.3 Releasing the steering lock

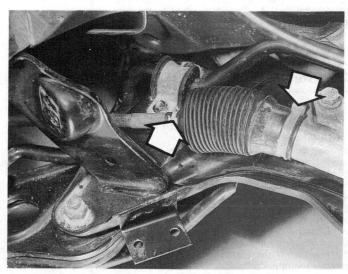

23.2 Steering gear gaiter and retaining clips (arrowed)

24.3A Steering gear retaining bolt (arrowed) to the subframe on the right-hand side

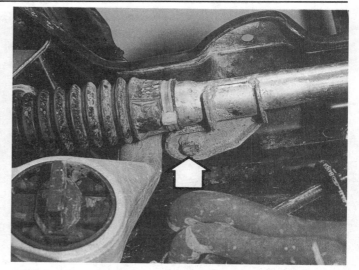

24.3B Steering gear retaining bolt (arrowed) to the subframe on the left-hand side

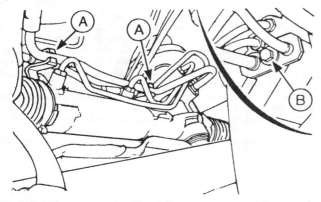

Fig. 10.31 Power steering gear and hydraulic line connections (Sec 25)

A *Hydraulic pipe locating clips*

B *Valve clamp plate bolt*

6   When reconnecting the battery on EFi models, refer to Chapter 12, Section 4 for details of the engine management relearning procedures.

25 Steering gear (power-assisted steering) – removal and refitting

Removal

1   Disconnect the battery earth lead.
2   Refer to Section 10 and proceed as described in paragraphs 1 to 12 inclusive, then proceed as follows.
3   Undo the retaining screws and detach the clips securing the power steering hydraulic pressure pipes to the steering gear unit.
4   Position a suitable container under the hydraulic pipe connections to the steering gear unit. Unscrew the bolt securing the hydraulic valve clamp plate to the valve body on the steering rack, then detach the pipes from the valve body. Withdraw the pipes from the steering gear unit and drain the hydraulic fluid into the container.
5   Plug the exposed ends of the hydraulic line connections to prevent the ingress of dirt and further fluid loss. Note that new O-ring seals will need to be obtained for fitment to the pressure and return hose connections when reconnecting.
6   Locate suitable jacks or blocks under the subframe to support it, then unscrew and remove the eight subframe fixing bolts from the positions shown in Fig. 10.19. Lower the support jacks or blocks and withdraw the subframe. As it is lowered, disengage the steering gear

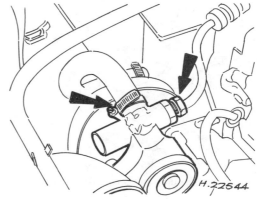

Fig. 10.32 Power steering pump unit and hose connections on the CVH engine (Sec 26)

shaft from the column. Note that complete removal of the subframe from the vehicle may not be necessary if it is carefully lowered to allow access to the steering gear for its separation and withdrawal.
7   Unscrew and remove the two steering gear unit to subframe retaining bolts, then withdraw the unit from the vehicle.

Refitting

8   Refit the steering gear to the subframe in the reverse order of removal and tighten the retaining bolts to the specified torque setting.
9   Refer to Section 10 for the relevant details on refitting the subframe assembly to the vehicle. When the subframe is in position, remove the plugs, check that the connections are clean, fit new O-ring seals to the pressure and return hoses, then reconnect the hydraulic lines to the steering gear unit. Check that the hydraulic lines and fixings are secure, then continue refitting the steering gear and subframe unit as described in Section 10.
10 On completion, top up the power steering fluid reservoir and bleed the system as described in Section 27. Check for any signs of fluid leakage from the system hoses and connections. Finally check and adjust the front wheel alignment as described in Section 29.

26 Power-assisted steering pump – removal and refitting

Removal

1   Disconnect the battery earth lead.
2   Raise and support the front of the vehicle on axle stands.
3   Undo the three retaining screws and remove the drivebelt guard

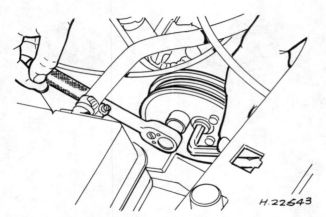

Fig. 10.33 Power steering pump pulley removal (Sec 26)

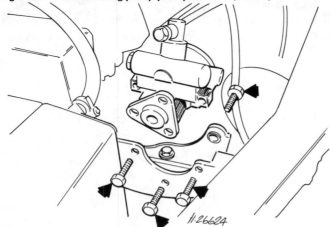

Fig. 10.34 Power steering pump and securing bolts (Sec 26)

from the underbody.
4   Loosen off the drivebelt tension by turning the tension adjustment bolt in a clockwise direction, then noting the travel of the belt around the pulleys, disengage the drivebelt from the power steering pump pulley.
5   Position a suitable container beneath the power steering pump, then unscrew and detach the fluid pressure and return hoses from the pump unit. As they are detached from the pump, allow the fluid to drain from the hoses (and the pump) into the container. Plug the exposed ends of the hydraulic hoses and the pump connections, to prevent the ingress of dirt and excessive fluid loss.
6   Insert a 9 mm Allen key into the centre of the pump drive spindle to prevent it from turning, then unscrew and remove the three pump pulley retaining bolts. Withdraw the pulley from the pump.
7   Unscrew the four retaining bolts shown in Fig. 10.34 and withdraw the pump unit from the vehicle.

Refitting

8   Refitting is a reversal of removal, but tighten all nuts and bolts to the specified torque. Remove the plugs from the pipes and ensure that the pipes are located correctly so that they do not foul any surrounding components.
9   Refit and adjust the drivebelt tension as described in Chapter 1.
10   On completion fill the power steering system with the specified fluid up to the maximum level mark, and bleed the system as described in Section 27. Check for any signs of fluid leakage from the system hoses and connections.

27   Power-assisted steering system – bleeding

1   This will normally only be required if any part of the hydraulic system has been disconnected.
2   Remove the fluid reservoir filler cap and top up the fluid level to the

'max-cold' mark using only the specified fluid. Refer to *Lubricants, fluids and capacities* at the beginning of this Manual for fluid specifications.
3   Start the engine and allow it to idle whilst slowly moving the steering from lock-to-lock several times to purge out the internal air, then top up the level in the fluid reservoir. Add the fluid slowly to prevent the possibility of aeration of the fluid in the circuit.
4   Switch the engine off, then recheck the fluid level in the reservoir and further top up if necessary. Finally check the system hoses and connections for any signs of fluid leaks, which if found, must be rectified.

28   Track rod end balljoint – removal and refitting

Removal

1   Apply the handbrake, then jack up the front of the vehicle and support it on axle stands. Remove the appropriate front roadwheel.
2   Using a suitable spanner, slacken the balljoint locknut on the track rod by a quarter of a turn (photo). Hold the track rod stationary with another spanner engaged with the flats at its inner end to prevent it from turning.
3   Extract the split pin, then loosen off the retaining nut. If the balljoint is to be renewed, the nut can be fully removed. If the existing balljoint is to be reconnected, the nut should be slackened off a couple of turns only at first and left in position to protect the joint threads as the joint is separated from the spindle carrier. To release the tapered shank of the joint from the spindle carrier, use a balljoint separator tool as shown (photo). If the joint is to be re-used, take care not to damage the seal when using a separator tool.
4   Count the number of exposed threads between the end of the balljoint and the locknut and record this figure.
5   Unscrew the balljoint from the track rod while counting the number of turns necessary to remove it.
6   If a new balljoint is to be fitted, unscrew the locknut from the old balljoint.

Refitting

7   If removed, screw the locknut onto the new balljoint and position it so that the same number of exposed threads are visible as was noted during removal.
8   Screw the balljoint into the track rod the number of turns noted during removal until the locknut just contacts the track rod. Now tighten the locknut while holding the track rod as before.
9   Engage the shank of the balljoint with the spindle carrier arm and refit the locknut. Tighten the locknut to the specified torque. If the balljoint shank turns while the locknut is being tightened, place a jack

28.2 Track rod end balljoint showing the locknut (A) retaining flats (B) and the balljoint-to spindle carrier arm retaining nut and split pin (C)

28.3 Balljoint separator tool in position. Note that the nut is left loosely in position when the thread of the joint is to be protected for re-use

under the balljoint. The tapered fit of the shank will lock it and prevent rotation as the nut is tightened.

10   Refit the roadwheel and lower the vehicle to the ground.

11   Finally check and if necessary adjust the front wheel alignment with reference to Section 29.

29   Wheel alignment and steering angles – general information

1   Accurate front wheel alignment is essential to provide positive steering and prevent excessive tyre wear. Before considering the steering/suspension geometry, check that the tyres are correctly inflated, that the front wheels are not buckled, and that the steering linkage and suspension joints are in good order, without slackness or wear.

2   Wheel alignment consists of four factors: *Camber* is the angle at which the front wheels are set from the vertical when viewed from the front of the vehicle. 'Positive camber' is the amount (in degrees) that the wheels are tilted outward at the top of the vertical. *Castor* is the angle between the steering axis and a vertical line when viewed from each side of the car. 'Positive castor' is when the steering axis is inclined rearward at the top. *Steering axis inclination* is the angle (when viewed from the front of the vehicle) between the vertical and an imaginary line drawn through the suspension strut upper mounting and the lower suspension arm balljoint. *Toe setting* is the amount by which the distance between the front inside edges of the roadwheels (measured at hub height) differs from the diametrically opposite distance measured between the rear inside edges of the front roadwheels.

3   With the exception of the toe setting, all other steering angles are set during manufacture and no adjustment is possible. It can be assumed, therefore, that unless the vehicle has suffered accident damage all the preset steering angles will be correct. Should there be some doubt about their accuracy it will be necessary to seek the help of a Ford dealer, as special gauges are needed to check the steering angles.

4   Two methods are available to the home mechanic for checking the toe setting. One method is to use a gauge to measure the distance between the front and rear inside edges of the roadwheels. The other method is to use a scuff plate, in which each front wheel is rolled across a movable plate which records any deviation, or scuff, of the tyre from the straight-ahead position as it moves across the plate. Relatively inexpensive equipment of both types is available from accessory outlets to enable these checks, and subsequent adjustments to be carried out at home.

5   If, after checking the toe setting using whichever method is preferable, it is found that adjustment is necessary, proceed as follows.

6   Turn the steering wheel onto full left lock and record the number of

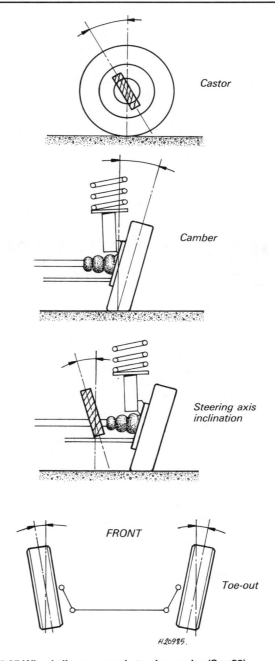

Fig. 10.35 Wheel alignment and steering angles (Sec 29)

exposed threads on the right-hand track rod end. Now turn the steering onto full right lock and record the number of threads on the left-hand side. If there are the same number of threads visible on both sides then subsequent adjustment can be made equally on both sides. If there are more threads visible on one side than the other it will be necessary to compensate for this during adjustment. *After adjustment there must be the same number of threads visible on each track rod end. This is most important.*

7   To alter the toe setting, slacken the locknut on the track rod end and turn the track rod using a self-grip wrench to achieve the desired setting. When viewed from the side of the car, turning the rod clockwise will increase the toe-in, turning it anti-clockwise will increase the toe-out. Only turn the track rods by a quarter of a turn each time and then recheck the setting using the gauges, or scuff plate.

8   After adjustment tighten the locknuts and reposition the steering gear rubber gaiter to remove any twist caused by turning the track rods.

Chapter 11 Bodywork and fittings

Contents

Specifications

Powered hood – Cabriolet
Cabriolet power hood hydraulic system fluid type...................................... Esso UNIVIS J26

Torque wrench settings

	Nm	lbf ft
Front seat slide to floor	25 to 32	19 to 24
Seat belt anchor bolts..	29 to 45	22 to 33
Seat belt lower anchorage rail securing bolt	29 to 45	22 to 33
Front seat belt height adjuster bolt..	25 to 45	19 to 33
Front seat slide to frame nuts...	25 to 45	19 to 33
Bonnet hinge bolts..	8.5 to 12	6.5 to 9
Bonnet latch bolts...	9 to 11	7 to 8
Tailgate hinge bolts..	21 to 27	16 to 20
Tailgate striker bolts	9 to 11	7 to 8
Tailgate lock bolts...	9 to 11	7 to 8
Boot lid hinge bolts	21 to 27	16 to 20
Boot lid striker bolts...	9 to 11	7 to 8
Boot lid latch bolts..	9 to 11	7 to 8

1   General information

The bodyshell and underframe on all models is of all-steel welded construction, incorporating progressive crumple zones at the front and rear and a rigid centre safety cell. The body shell range is comprehensive and includes the 3 and 5-door Escort Saloons, the 5-door Escort Estate, the 2-door Escort Cabriolet, the Escort Van and the Orion 4-door Saloon.

A multi-stage anti-corrosion process is applied to all new vehicles. This includes zinc phosphating on some panels, the injection of wax into boxed sections and a wax and PVC coating applied to the underbody for its protection.

2   Maintenance – bodywork and underframe

1   The general condition of a vehicle's bodywork is the one thing that significantly affects its value. Maintenance is easy but needs to be regular. Neglect, particularly after minor damage, can lead quickly to further deterioration and costly repair bills. It is important also to keep watch on those parts of the vehicle not immediately visible, for instance the underside, inside all the wheel arches and the lower part of the engine compartment.

2   The basic maintenance routine for the bodywork is washing – preferably with a lot of water, from a hose. This will remove all the loose solids which may have stuck to the vehicle. It is important to flush these off in such a way as to prevent grit from scratching the finish. The wheel arches and underframe need washing in the same way to remove any accumulated mud which will retain moisture and tend to encourage rust. Paradoxically enough, the best time to clean the underframe and wheel arches is in wet weather when the mud is thoroughly wet and soft. In very wet weather the underframe is usually cleaned of large accumulations automatically and this is a good time for inspection.

3   Periodically, except on vehicles with a wax-based underbody protective coating, it is a good idea to have the whole of the underframe of the vehicle steam cleaned, engine compartment included, so that a thorough inspection can be carried out to see what minor repairs and renovations are necessary. Steam cleaning is available at many garages and is necessary for the removal of the accumulation of oily grime which sometimes is allowed to become thick in certain areas. If steam cleaning facilities are not available, there are one or two excellent grease solvents available, such as Holts Engine Cleaner or Holts Foambrite, which can be brush applied. The dirt can then be simply hosed off. Note that these methods should not be used on vehicles with wax-based underbody protective coating or the coating will be removed. Such vehicles should be inspected annually, preferably just prior to winter, when the underbody should be washed down and any damage to the wax coating repaired using Holts Undershield. Ideally, a completely fresh coat should be applied. It would also be worth considering the use of such wax-based protection for injection into door panels, sills, box sections, etc, as an additional safeguard against rust damage where such protection is not provided by the vehicle manufacturer.

4   After washing paintwork, wipe off with a chamois leather to give an unspotted clear finish. A coat of clear protective wax polish, such as the many excellent Turtle Wax polishes, will give added protection against chemical pollutants in the air. If the paintwork sheen has dulled or oxidised, use a cleaner/polisher combination such as Turtle Extra to restore the brilliance of the shine. This requires a little effort, but such dulling is usually caused because regular washing has been neglected. Care needs to be taken with metallic paintwork, as special non-abrasive cleaner/polisher is required to avoid damage to the finish. Always check that the door and ventilator opening drain holes and pipes are completely clear so that water can be drained out (photo). Brightwork should be treated in the same way as paintwork. Windscreens and windows can be kept clear of the smeary film which often appears by the use of proprietary glass cleaner such as Holts Mixra. Never use any form of wax or other body or chromium polish on glass.

5   On Cabriolet models, the hood and tonneau cover can be cleaned with warm soapy water and wiped dry using a sponge or a chamois leather. Do not attempt to clean the hood or tonneau cover with an oil or petrol based liquid cleaner. Any repairs to the tonneau or hood material should be referred to a Ford dealer or a competent automotive

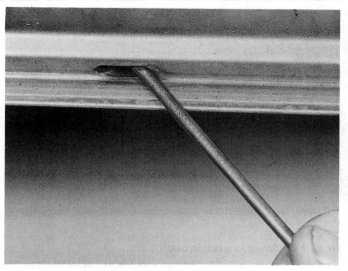

2.4 Ensure that the body drain holes are clear

upholsterer. To maintain an efficient weather seal between the hood and the windscreen frame, the joint seal should be treated once a month to a coating of suitable preservative such as cockpit spray.

3   Maintenance – upholstery and carpets

Mats and carpets should be brushed or vacuum-cleaned regularly to keep them free of grit. If they are badly stained remove them from the vehicle for scrubbing or sponging and make quite sure they are dry before refitting. Seats and interior trim panels can be kept clean by wiping with a damp cloth and Turtle Wax Carisma. If they do become stained (which can be more apparent on light coloured upholstery) use a little liquid detergent and a soft nail brush to scour the grime out of the grain of the material. Do not forget to keep the headlining clean in the same way as the upholstery. When using liquid cleaners inside the vehicle do not over-wet the surfaces being cleaned. Excessive damp could get into the seams and padded interior causing stains, offensive odours or even rot. If the inside of the vehicle gets wet accidentally it is worthwhile taking some trouble to dry it out properly, particularly where carpets are involved. *Do not leave oil or electric heaters inside the vehicle for this purpose.*

4   Minor body damage – repair

Note: *For more detailed information about bodywork repair, the Haynes Publishing Group publish a book by Lindsay Porter called The Car Bodywork Repair Manual. This incorporates information on such aspects as rust treatment, painting and glass-fibre repairs, as well as details on more ambitious repairs involving welding and panel beating.*

The colour bodywork repair photographic sequences between pages 32 and 33 illustrate the operations detailed in the following sub-sections.

Repair of minor scratches in bodywork

If the scratch is very superficial and does not penetrate to the metal of the bodywork, repair is very simple. Lightly rub the area of the scratch with a paintwork renovator, such as Turtle Wax New Color Back, or a very fine cutting paste, like Holts Body + Plus Rubbing Compound, to remove loose paint from the scratch and to clear the surrounding bodywork of wax polish. Rinse the area with clean water.

Apply touch-up paint, such as Holts Dupli-Color Color Touch, or a paint film, such as Holts Autofilm, to the scratch using a fine paint brush; continue to apply fine layers of paint until the surface of the paint in the scratch is level with the surrounding paintwork. Allow the new paint at least two weeks to harden, then blend it into the surrounding paintwork by rubbing the scratch area with a paintwork renovator, such as Turtle Wax New Color Back, or a very fine cutting paste, like Holts Body + Plus Rubbing Compound. Finally apply wax polish from one of the Turtle Wax range of wax polishes.

Where the scratch has penetrated right through to the metal of the bodywork, causing the metal to rust, a different repair technique is required. Remove any loose rust from the bottom of the scratch with a penknife, then apply rust inhibiting paint, such as Turtle Wax Rust Master, to prevent the formation of rust in the future. Using a rubber or nylon applicator fill the scratch with bodystopper paste, such as Holts Body + Plus Knifing Putty. If required, this paste can be mixed with cellulose thinners, such as Holts Body + Plus Cellulose Thinners, to provide a very thin paste which is ideal for filling narrow scratches. Before the stopper-paste in the scratch hardens, wrap a piece of smooth cotton rag around the top of a finger. Dip the finger in cellulose thinners and quickly sweep it across the surface of the stopper-paste in the scratch; this will ensure that the surface of the stopper-paste is slightly hollowed. The scratch can now be painted over as described earlier in this Section.

Repair of dents in bodywork

When deep denting of the vehicle's bodywork has taken place, the first task is to pull the dent out, until the affected bodywork almost attains its original shape. There is little point in trying to restore the original shape completely, as the metal in the damaged area will have stretched on impact and cannot be reshaped fully to its original contour. It is better to bring the level of the dent up to a point which is about 3 mm below the level of the surrounding bodywork. In cases where the dent is very shallow anyway, it is not worth trying to pull it out at all. If the underside of the dent is accessible, it can be hammered out gently from behind, using a mallet with a wooden or plastic head. Whilst doing this, hold a suitable block of wood firmly against the outside of the panel to absorb the impact from the hammer blows and thus prevent a large area of the bodywork from being 'belled-out'.

Should the dent be in a section of the bodywork which has a double skin or some other factor making it inaccessible from behind, a different technique is called for. Drill several small holes through the metal inside the area – particularly in the deeper section. Then screw long self-tapping screws into the holes just sufficiently for them to gain a good purchase in the metal. Now the dent can be pulled out by pulling on the protruding heads of the screws with a pair of pliers.

The next stage of the repair is the removal of the paint from the damaged area and from an inch or so of the surrounding 'sound' bodywork. This is accomplished most easily by using a wire brush or abrasive pad on a power drill, although it can be done just as effectively by hand using sheets of abrasive paper. To complete the preparation for filling, score the surface of the bare metal with a screwdriver or the tang of a file, or alternatively, drill small holes in the affected area. This will provide a really good 'key' for the filler paste.

To complete the repair see the Section on filling and respraying.

Repair of rust holes or gashes in bodywork

Remove all paint from the affected area and from an inch or so of the surrounding 'sound' bodywork, using an abrasive pad or a wire brush on a power drill. If these are not available a few sheets of abrasive paper will do the job most effectively. With the paint removed you will be able to judge the severity of the corrosion and therefore decide whether to renew the whole panel (if this is possible) or to repair the affected area. New body panels are not as expensive as most people think and it is often quicker and more satisfactory to fit a new panel than to attempt to repair large areas of corrosion.

Remove all fittings from the affected area except those which will act as a guide to the original shape of the damaged bodywork (eg headlamp shells etc). Then, using tin snips or a hacksaw blade, remove all loose metal and any other metal badly affected by corrosion. Hammer the edges of the hole inwards in order to create a slight depression for the filler paste.

Wire brush the affected area to remove the powdery rust from the surface of the remaining metal. Paint the affected area with rust inhibiting paint, such as Turtle Wax Rust Master; if the back of the rusted area is accessible treat this also.

Before filling can take place it will be necessary to block the hole in some way. This can be achieved by the use of aluminium or plastic mesh, or aluminium tape.

Aluminium or plastic mesh or glass-fibre matting, such as Holts

Body + Plus Glass Fibre Matting, is probably the best material to use for a large hole. Cut a piece to the approximate size and shape of the hole to be filled, then position it in the hole so that its edges are below the level of the surrounding bodywork. It can be retained in position by several blobs of filler paste around its periphery.

Aluminium tape should be used for small or very narrow holes. Pull a piece off the roll and trim it to the approximate size and shape required, then pull off the backing paper (if used) and stick the tape over the hole; it can be overlapped if the thickness of one piece is insufficient. Burnish down the edges of the tape with the handle of a screwdriver or similar, to ensure that the tape is securely attached to the metal underneath.

Bodywork repairs – filling and respraying

Before using this Section, see the Sections on dent, deep scratch, rust holes and gash repairs.

Many types of bodyfiller are available, but generally speaking those proprietary kits are best for this type of repair which contain a tin of filler paste and a tube of resin hardener, such as Holts Body + Plus, or Holts No Mix which can be used directly from the tube. A wide, flexible plastic or nylon applicator will be found invaluable for imparting a smooth and well contoured finish to the surface of the filler.

Mix up a little filler on a clean piece of card or board – measure the hardener carefully (follow the maker's instructions on the pack) otherwise the filler will set too rapidly or too slowly. Alternatively, Holts No Mix can be used straight from the tube without mixing, but daylight is required to cure it. Using the applicator apply the filler paste to the prepared area; draw the applicator across the surface of the filler to achieve the correct contour and to level the surface. As soon as a contour that approximates to the correct one is achieved, stop working the paste – if you carry on too long the paste will become sticky and begin to 'pick-up' on the applicator. Continue to add thin layers of filler paste at twenty minute intervals until the level of the filler is just proud of the surrounding bodywork.

Once the filler has hardened, excess can be removed using a metal plane or file. From then on, progressively finer grades of abrasive paper should be used, starting with a 40 grade production paper and finishing with a 400 grade wet-and-dry paper. Always wrap the abrasive paper around a flat rubber, cork, or wooden block – otherwise the surface of the filler will not be completely flat. During the smoothing of the filler surface the wet-and-dry paper should be periodically rinsed in water. This will ensure that a very smooth finish is imparted to the filler at the final stage.

At this stage the 'dent' should be surrounded by a ring of bare metal, which in turn should be encircled by the finely 'feathered' edge of the good paintwork. Rinse the repair area with clean water, until all of the dust produced by the rubbing-down operation has gone.

Spray the whole area with a light coat of primer, either Holts Body + Plus Grey or Red Oxide Primer – this will show up any imperfections in the surface of the filler. Repair these imperfections with fresh filler paste or bodystopper and once more smooth the surface with abrasive paper. If bodystopper is used, it can be mixed with cellulose thinners to form a really thin paste which is ideal for filling small holes. Repeat this spray and repair procedure until you are satisfied that the surface of the filler and the feathered edge of the paintwork are perfect. Clean the repair area with clean water and allow to dry fully.

The repair area is now ready for final spraying. Paint spraying must be carried out in a warm, dry, windless and dust free atmosphere. This condition can be created artificially if you have access to a large indoor working area, but if you are forced to work in the open, you will have to pick your day very carefully. If you are working indoors, dousing the floor in the work area with water will help to settle the dust which would otherwise be in the atmosphere. If the repair area is confined to one body panel, mask off the surrounding panels; this will help to minimise the effects of a slight mis-match in paint colours. Bodywork fittings (eg chrome strips, door handles etc) will also need to be masked off. Use genuine masking tape and several thicknesses of newspaper for the masking operations.

Before commencing to spray, agitate the aerosol can thoroughly, then spray a test area (an old tin, or similar) until the technique is mastered. Cover the repair area with a thick coat of primer; the thickness should be built up using several thin layers of paint rather than one thick one. Using 400 grade wet-and-dry paper, rub down the surface of the primer until it is really smooth. While doing this, the work area should be thoroughly doused with water and the wet-and-dry paper periodically rinsed in water. Allow to dry before spraying on more paint.

Spray on the top coat using Holts Dupli-Color Autospray, again building up the thickness by using several thin layers of paint. Start spraying in the centre of the repair area and then, with a side-to-side motion, work outwards until the whole repair area and about 2 inches of the surrounding original paintwork is covered. Remove all masking material 10 to 15 minutes after spraying on the final coat of paint.

Allow the new paint at least two weeks to harden, then, using a paintwork renovator, such as Turtle Wax New Color Back, or a very fine cutting paste, like Holts Body + Plus Rubbing Compound, blend the edges of the paint into the existing paintwork. Finally, apply wax polish.

Plastic components

With the use of more and more plastic body components by the vehicle manufacturers (eg bumpers, spoilers and in some cases major body panels), rectification of more serious damage to such items has become a matter of either entrusting repair work to a specialist in this field, or renewing complete components. Repair of such damage by the DIY owner is not really feasible owing to the cost of the equipment and materials required for effecting such repairs. The basic technique involves making a groove along the line of the crack in the plastic using a rotary burr in a power drill. The damaged part is then welded back together by using a hot air gun to heat up and fuse a plastic filler rod into the groove. Any excess plastic is then removed and the area rubbed down to a smooth finish. It is important that a filler rod of the correct plastic is used, as body components can be made of a variety of different types (eg polycarbonate, ABS, polypropylene).

Damage of a less serious nature (abrasions, minor cracks etc) can be repaired by the DIY owner using a two-part epoxy filler repair material such as Holts Body + Plus, or Holts No Mix which can be used directly from the tube. Once mixed in equal proportions (or applied direct from the tube in the case of Holts No Mix), this is used in similar fashion to the bodywork filler used on metal panels. The filler is usually cured in twenty to thirty minutes, ready for sanding and painting.

If the owner is renewing a complete component himself, or if he has repaired it with epoxy filler, he will be left with the problem of finding a suitable paint for finishing which is compatible with the type of plastic used. At one time the use of a universal paint was not possible owing to the complex range of plastics encountered in body component applications. Standard paints, generally speaking, will not bond satisfactorily to plastic or rubber, but Holts Professional Spraymatch paints to match any plastic or rubber finish can be obtained from dealers. However, it is now possible to obtain a plastic body parts finishing kit which consists of a pre-primer treatment, a primer and coloured top coat. Full instructions are normally supplied with a kit, but basically the method of use is to first apply the pre-primer to the component concerned and allow it to dry for up to 30 minutes. Then the primer is applied and left to dry for about an hour before finally applying the special coloured top coat. The result is a correctly-coloured component where the paint will flex with the plastic or rubber, a property that standard paint does not normally possess.

5 Major body damage – repair

Where serious damage has occurred, or large areas need renewal

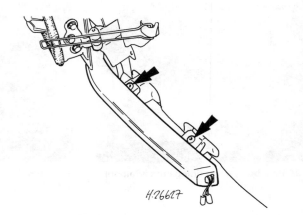

Fig. 11.1 Retaining screw locations of rear quarter bumper (Sec 6)

due to neglect, it means that complete new panels will need welding in; this is best left to professionals. If the damage is due to impact, it will also be necessary to check completely the alignment of the bodyshell; this can only be carried out accurately by a Ford dealer using special jigs. If the body is left misaligned, it is primarily dangerous as the car will not handle properly and secondly, uneven stresses will be imposed on the steering, suspension and possibly transmission, causing abnormal wear or complete failure, particularly to items such as the tyres.

6 Front and rear bumpers – removal and refitting

Removal

Front bumper

1 Raise and support the vehicle at the front end on axle stands.

2 Release the six fasteners and remove the splash shield from the underside of the vehicle at the front. The fasteners will either be clip types, in which case they can be prised free, or pop-rivets, and will need to be drilled through.

3 Undo the two bumper to wing retaining screws at the rear edge of the bumper each side (photo).

4 Unscrew and remove the four bumper retaining nuts (two each side) securing the bumper to the front end of the vehicle (photo).

5 Enlist the aid of an assistant and carefully withdraw the bumper unit forwards from the vehicle.

Rear (single-piece) bumper

6 Prise free the number plate lamp unit from the bumper, detach the wiring connectors and remove the lamp.

7 Unscrew and remove the two retaining screws securing the forward ends of the bumper to the trailing end of the wheel arch each side (photo).

6.3 Front bumper retaining screws

6.4 Front bumper retaining nuts

6.7 Rear bumper retaining screws

6.9A Rear bumper retaining nuts ((Saloon)

6.9B Rear (upper) bumper retaining nut (Estate)

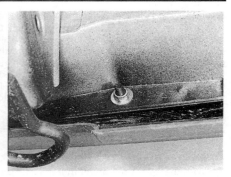

6.9C Rear (lower) bumper retaining nut (Estate)

8   Where applicable, remove the rear trim panel in the rear luggage compartment to gain access to the bumper securing nuts.
9   Unscrew and remove the bumper retaining nuts from the rear panel each side (photos). On some models access to the nuts is from underneath the vehicle whilst on others it is from within the luggage compartment after removal of the appropriate rear trim panel. Enlist the aid of an assistant, to help in pulling the bumper outwards to clear the body each side and withdraw it rearwards from the vehicle.

Rear quarter bumper

10   Reach behind the bumper, compress the rear number plate lamp retaining clips and extract the lamp from the bumper. Disconnect the wiring connectors and remove the lamp.
11   Working from above, between the bumper and the vehicle rear panel, undo the two Torx type retaining screws and then remove the quarter bumper.

Refitting

12   Refitting is a reversal of the removal procedure. Check the bumper for alignment before fully tightening the retaining nuts/screws. On rear bumpers, check the operation of the rear number plate lamp to complete.

7   Bonnet – removal, refitting and adjustment

Removal

1   Open the bonnet and support it in the open position using the stay.
2   Release the fasteners and remove the insulation panel from the underside of the bonnet.

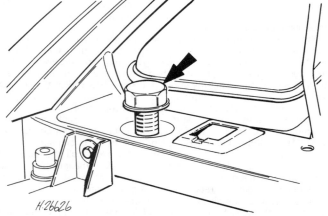

Fig. 11.2 Bonnet bump stop (Sec 7)

3   Disconnect the windscreen washer hose from its connection to the washer jet and from the locating clips to the bonnet and hinge.
4   Undo the retaining screw and detach the earth lead from its attachment to the bonnet near the left-hand hinge (photo). Also, where applicable, disconnect the heated washer multi-plug and wiring from the bonnet.
5   To assist in correctly realigning the bonnet when refitting it, mark the outline of the hinges with a soft pencil, then loosen the two hinge retaining bolts each side.
6   With the help of an assistant, remove the stay, unscrew the four bolts and lift the bonnet from the vehicle (photo).

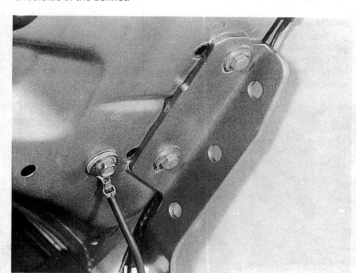

7.4 Bonnet hinge and earth lead connection

7.6 Bonnet removal

Refitting and adjustment

7   Refitting is a reversal of removal. Position the bonnet hinges within the outline marks made during removal, but alter its position as necessary to provide a uniform gap all round. Adjust the rear height of the bonnet by repositioning it on the hinges. Adjust the front height by repositioning the lock with reference to Section 9 and turning the rubber buffers on the engine compartment front crosspanel up or down to support the bonnet (see Fig. 11.2).

8   Ensure that the washer, wiring and earth lead connections are cleanly and securely made. Check the windscreen washer for satisfactory operation to complete.

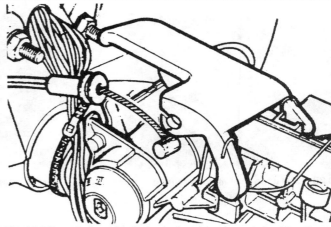

8 Bonnet release cable – removal and refitting

Removal

1   With the bonnet open, disconnect the cable from the locating slot in the lock frame then release the inner cable nipple from the lock (photo).
2   Working inside the vehicle, undo the four retaining screws and lower the bottom shroud from the steering column.
3   Detach the inner cable nipple from the release lever, then withdraw the cable through the bulkhead (noting its routing) and remove it from the engine compartment side.

Refitting

4   Refitting is a reversal of removal. On completion, check that the bonnet catch and release operate in a satisfactory manner.

9 Bonnet lock – removal and refitting

Removal

1   With the bonnet open, disconnect the cable from the locating slot in the lock frame, then release the inner cable nipple from the lock.
2   Unscrew the three retaining screws and remove the lock from the vehicle.

Refitting

3   Refitting is a reversal of removal, but adjust the lock height so that the bonnet line is flush with the front wings and shuts securely without force. If necessary, adjust the lock laterally so that the striker enters the lock recess correctly, however it may also be necessary to reposition the striker.

10 Door inner trim panel – removal and refitting

Removal

1   On models fitted with manual window regulators, fully shut the

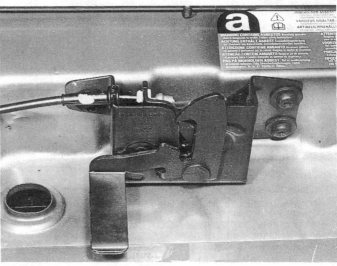

Fig. 11.3 Detach the cable from the bonnet release lever (Sec 8)

8.1 Bonnet release cable and lock

window, note the position of the regulator handle then release the spring clip and withdraw the handle (photos). The clip can be released by inserting a clean cloth between the handle and the door trim and pulling the cloth back against the open ends of the clip to release its tension whilst simultaneously pulling the handle from the regulator shaft splines.
2   Prise free the trim capping from the door pull handle taking care not to break the single retaining clip, then undo the retaining screws and remove the handle (photos).
3   Undo the retaining screw from the inner door handle bezel, slide free and remove the bezel (photos).

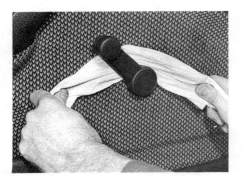

10.1A Release the regulator retaining clip as shown ...

10.1B ... and withdraw the manual window regulator handle

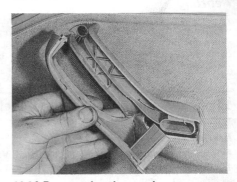

10.2A Remove the trim capping ...

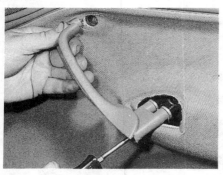

10.2B ... and undo the handle retaining screws

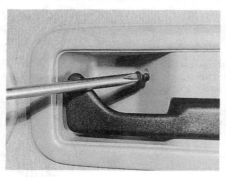

10.3A Undo the retaining screw ...

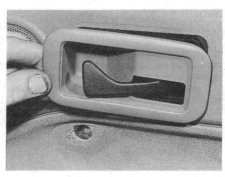

10.3B ... and remove the bezel

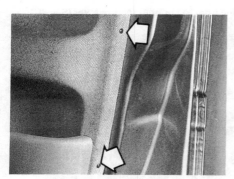

10.4 Door trim retaining screws (arrowed)

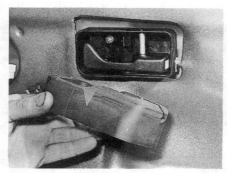

10.6A Remove the insulation surrounding the inner release handle

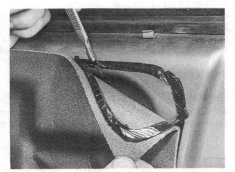

10.6B Cut through the adhesive to remove the door insulation sheet

4   Unscrew and remove the door trim panel retaining screws (photo), then lift the panel to disengage it from the top edge clips (along the window edge), then remove the panel.

5   If required (and where fitted), the door pocket can be detached from the trim panel by unscrewing the three retaining screws, one of which is fitted from the inside-out. If an ashtray is fitted to the trim, it can be removed by carefully prising it free. If the door lock inner release or other internal components of the door are to be inspected or removed, first withdraw the bezel from the inner door release unit then remove the insulation sheet from the door as follows.

6   Access to the inner door can be made by carefully extracting the insulator from the inner release then peeling back the insulation sheet. In order not to damage and distort the insulation sheet, use a suitable knife to cut through the peripheral adhesive strip whilst the sheet is progressively peeled back and away from the door. Avoid touching the strip with the hands as skin oils will adversely affect its adhesive properties (photos).

Refitting

7   Refitting is a reversal of removal, but where necessary, apply suitable mastic to the door panel before fitting the insulation sheet. When the door trim panel is refitted, check the operation of the door catch release and the window regulator (where applicable).

11   Door window glass – removal and refitting

Removal

Front door window glass (Saloon, Estate and Van)

1   Remove the inner trim panel and the insulation sheet from the door as described in Section 10.

2   Prise free the inner and outer weatherstrips from the bottom of the window aperture in the door (photo).

3   Wind the window up to close it, then have an assistant hold the

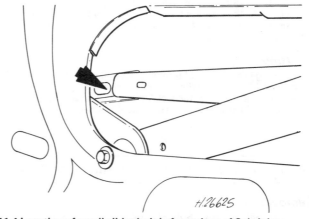

Fig. 11.4 Location of small slider bolt in front door of Cabriolet (Sec 11)

window firmly in this position whilst you unscrew the window to regulator retaining screws through the aperture in the inner door (photo).

4   Lower the window regulator, then tilting the window as required, withdraw it outwards from the door (photo).

Front door window glass (Cabriolet)

5   Remove the inner trim panel and the insulation sheet from the door as described in Section 10.

6   Wind down the window in the door, then prise free the inner and outer weatherstrips from the bottom of the window aperture in the door.

7   Undo the three retaining screws and partially withdraw the door-mounted speaker unit so that its wiring connections can be detached, then remove the speaker unit.

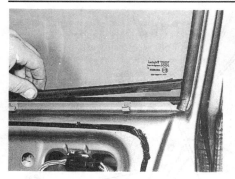

11.2 Remove the weatherstrips from the door

11.3 Undo the glass-to-regulator screws through apertures shown

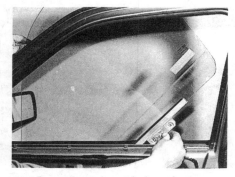

11.4 Removing a door window glass

8   Undo the door mirror trim screw, remove the trim panel and then detach the mirror adjuster wire multi-plug.
9   Lower the window in the door and then unscrew the small slider bolt shown in Fig. 11.4.
10   Raise the door glass, undo the large slider bolts, support the window regulator and unscrew the three regulator retaining bolts.
11   Lower the regulator and detach the wiring multi-plug for the regulator.
12   Move the glass rearwards to disengage it from the front guide channel, then move it carefully towards the outer panel. Carefully pull the glass upwards to disengage it from the large slider and simultaneously away from the door mirror, and remove the glass from the door.

Refitting

13   Refitting is a reversal of removal but note the following.

(a)   *When the glass is lowered into position in the door on Cabriolet models, loosely fit the retaining bolts, then close the window to ensure that the glass fits correctly before tightening the slider bolts to secure.*

(b)   *Where applicable, ensure that the wiring looms in the door are clear of the window and its regulating mechanism and that the connections are secure.*

(c)   *On refitting the window glass, check that it operates fully and freely before refitting the insulation sheet and the door trim panel.*

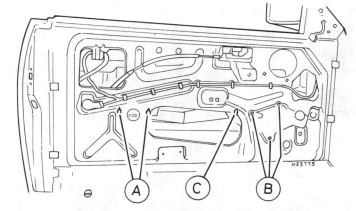

Fig. 11.5 Door window regulator retaining bolts on the front door of the Cabriolet (Sec 11)

A   Large slider bolts
B   Regulator retaining bolts
C   Small slider bolt

12   Rear quarter window glass (Cabriolet) – removal and refitting

Removal

1   Open the roof and lift the rear seat cushion.
2   Refer to Section 35 for details and remove the rear side quarter trim panel.
3   Where applicable, undo the speaker retaining screws, partially withdraw the speaker unit to detach the wiring connections and then remove the speaker unit.
4   Undo the screw, remove the cup washer and detach the roof frame main pillar bottom seal.
5   Remove the outer and inner weather strips.
6   Carefully peel back and remove the insulation sheet. In order not to damage and distort the insulation sheet, use a suitable knife to cut through the peripheral adhesive strip as the sheet is peeled progressively back and away from the door. Avoid touching the strip with the hands as skin oils will adversely affect its adhesive properties.
7   Reconnect the window regulator (handle or switch, as applicable) and with the window fully lowered, prise free and detach the window regulator arm from the channel.
8   Raise the window and then unscrew the shouldered bolt securing the regulator arm to the support channel, then tilt and lift the glass from the car.

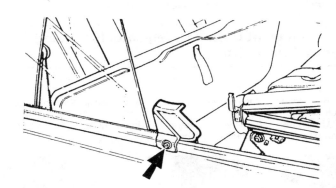

Fig. 11.6 Cabriolet roof frame main pillar bottom seal screw (Sec 12)

Refitting

9   Refitting is a reversal of removal but note the following.

(a)   *When the glass is lowered into position, and the regulator arm to support bolt is fitted, adjust the position of the glass by loosening the adjuster bolts as required and tightening them having made the necessary adjustment (see Fig. 11.8).*

(b)   *Where applicable, ensure that the wiring looms are clear of the window and its regulating mechanism and that the connections are secure.*

(c)   *On refitting the window glass, check that it operates fully and freely before refitting the insulation sheet and the quarter trim panel.*

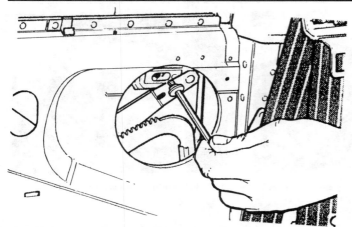

Fig. 11.7 Removing the quarter window regulator arm-to-window support channel bolt on the Cabriolet (Sec 12)

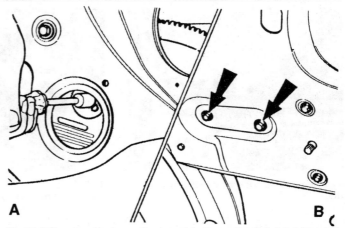

Fig. 11.8 Quarter window adjustment bolts on the Cabriolet (Sec 12)

A   Height adjustment   B   Lateral adjustment

3   Referring to Part B of Fig. 11.8, unscrew and remove the regulator arm bolts indicated.
4   Unscrew and remove the three regulator unit retaining bolts (to the right of the arm bolts), then withdraw the regulator from the side panel lower aperture.

Refitting

5   Refitting is a reversal of removal. Ensure that the wiring connections are securely made and check the operation of the regulator before refitting the window. Refer to Section 12 for details on refitting the window.

14   Door window regulator – removal and refitting

Removal

1   Remove the door trim and the insulation sheet as described in Section 10.
2   Locate the glass in the door so that the guide channel can be detached from the regulator. Disconnect the ball and socket(s) (two per front door or one per rear door), then lower the glass to the base of the door.
3   The regulator unit is secured by seven pop-rivets (front door) or four pop-rivets (rear door). Drill through the centre of each rivet, detach the regulator unit from the door and withdraw it from the lower aperture (photo).

Refitting

4   Refitting is a reversal of removal. Obtain the correct number of rivets to affix the regulator to the door. Check that the operation of the window regulator is satisfactory before refitting the door trim.

14.3 Drilling out the door window regulator rivets

13   Rear quarter window regulator (Cabriolet) – removal and refitting

Removal

1   Remove the rear quarter window as described in the previous Section.
2   On models fitted with electric windows, detach the wiring multi-plug from the regulator motor.

15.2A Remove the inner retaining clip ...

15.2B ... and withdraw the lock barrel from the door

15.5 Inner door release and retaining screw

15.6 Door lock retaining screws

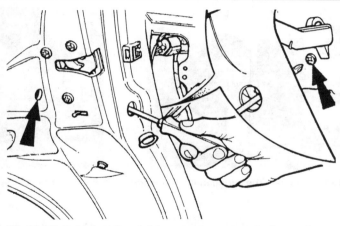

Fig. 11.9 Exterior handle retaining screw access point in rear door (Sec 15)

15 Door lock, lock cylinder and handles – removal and refitting

Removal

1 Remove the door inner trim panel and the insulation sheet as described in Section 10. Proceed as described below in the appropriate sub-Section.

Door lock barrel

2 Slide free the barrel retaining clip, detach the connecting rod and remove the lock barrel (photos).

Door lock unit

3 Remove the lock barrel as described above.
4 On models fitted with central locking, detach the wiring multi-plugs from the lock motor (attached to and removed with the lock unit).
5 Unscrew and remove the inner door release retaining screw (photo).
6 Unscrew and remove the three door lock retaining screws (photo).
7 Remove the window rear guide (rear doors only).
8 Slide free the inner release from the door, then withdraw the lock unit together with the remote control inner release and cable. If required, the connecting cable to the inner release handle can be detached from the lock by removing the cover, sliding the outer cable from its locating slot in the lock and then withdrawing the inner cable from the actuating pivot on the lock (photos).
9 On models with central locking, undo the two retaining screws to detach the lock from the actuating motor.

15.8A Remove the door release ...

15.8B ... and the door lock unit with cable

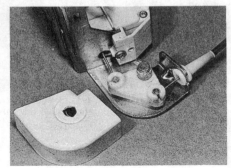

15.8C Remove cover to detach cable from the lock

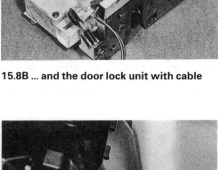

15.10A Detach the inner release handle ...

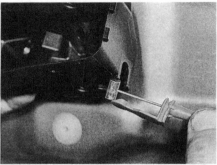

15.10B ... and disconnect the cable from the casing

15.11 Exterior handle retaining screws

16.1 Disconnect the wiring multi-connector

16.2 Door check strap screw (arrowed)

16.4 Door hinge pin bolt (arrowed)

16.5 Door striker

Inner release handle

10   Slide free the inner release unit and detach it from the door, then disconnect the release operating cable from the release handle case (photos).

Exterior release handle

11   Undo the two retaining screws, detach the link rod from the release arm of the exterior handle and remove the handle from the door (photo). Note that on the rear doors it will be necessary to remove the blanking plug in the edge of the door to gain access to one of the handle securing screws.

Refitting

12   Refitting is a reversal of removal. Check for satisfactory operation of the lock and its associated components before refitting the door trim. Check that the striker enters the lock centrally when the door is closed, and if necessary loosen it with a Torx key, re-position and re-tighten it.

16   Door – removal and refitting

Removal

1   Fully open the door, then untwist and detach the wiring multi-connector (photo).
2   Disconnect the door check link by unscrewing the Torx screw on the door pillar (photo).
3   Support the door on blocks of wood.
4   Unscrew the door hinge pin retaining screw from each hinge, then lift the door clear of the hinges (photo).

Refitting

5   Refitting is a reversal of removal. Check that the striker enters the lock centrally when the door is closed, and if necessary loosen it with a Torx key, re-position and re-tighten it (photo).

17   Exterior mirror and glass – removal and refitting

Removal

1   If the mirror glass is to removed, insert a plastic flat-bladed spatular between the glass and the housing and carefully prise it free. Where applicable, disconnect the wiring from the connectors on the rear face of the mirror (photos).

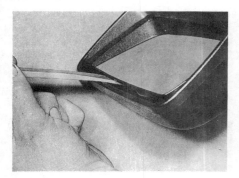

17.1A Prise free the door mirror glass ...

17.1B ... and detach the wiring connectors

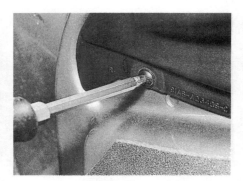

17.3 Undo the screw and remove the mirror trim

17.4 Detach the wiring multi-plug from the mirror control unit

17.5 Undo the three mirror retaining screws

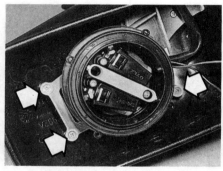

17.6 Showing mirror motor and retaining screws (arrowed)

2   To remove the mirror unit, first remove the door trim as described in Section 10.
3   Undo the door mirror trim retaining screw and remove the trim (photo).
4   Carefully prise free the control unit from the trim and where applicable, detach the wiring connector from the adjuster (photo).
5   Support the mirror, undo the three retaining screws and remove the mirror from the door (photo).
6   The motor unit can be removed if required by undoing the three retaining screws (photo).

Refitting

7   Refit in the reverse order of removal. Check that the operation of the mirror adjuster is satisfactory.

18   Interior mirror – removal and refitting

Removal

1   Using a length of strong thin cord or fishing line, break the adhesive bond between the base of the mirror and the glass. Have an assistant support and remove the mirror as it is released.
2   If the original mirror is to be refitted, thoroughly clean its base with methylated spirit and a lint-free cloth. Allow a period of one minute for the spirit to evaporate. Clean the windscreen black patch in a similar manner.

Refitting

3   During the installation of the mirror, it is important that the mirror base, windscreen black patch and the adhesive patch are not touched or contaminated in any way – poor adhesion will result.
4   Prior to fitting the mirror, the vehicle should have been in an ambient temperature of 20°C.
5   With the contact surfaces thoroughly cleaned, remove the protective tape from one side of the adhesive patch and press it firmly into contact with the mirror base.
6   If fitting the mirror to a new windscreen, the protective tape must first be removed from the windscreen black patch.
7   Warm the mirror base and the adhesive patch for about 30 seconds to a temperature of 50 to 70°C, then peel back the protective tape from the other side of the adhesive patch on the mirror base, then align the mirror base and the windscreen patch and press the mirror firmly into position. Hold the base of the mirror firmly against the windscreen for a minimum period of two minutes to ensure full adhesion.
8   Wait at least thirty minutes before adjusting the mirror position.

19   Boot lid – removal, refitting and adjustment

Removal

1   Open the boot lid and mark the position of the hinges with a pencil.

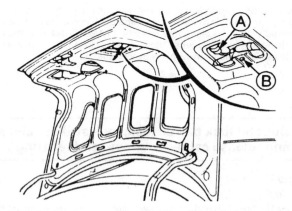

Fig. 11.10 Multi-plug (A) and earth lead (B) connection points in the boot lid (Sec 19)

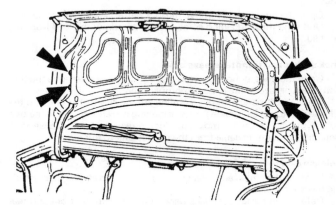

Fig. 11.11 Boot lid hinge retaining bolt locations (Sec 19)

2   Where applicable, disconnect the wiring multi-plug and the earth lead for the central locking from the boot lid. Attach a suitable length of strong cord to the end of the wire then withdraw the lead from the bootlid. Detach the cord and leave it in position in the boot. This will then act as an aid to guiding the wiring through the lid when it is refitted.
3   Place cloth rags beneath each corner of the boot lid to prevent damage to the paintwork.
4   With the help of an assistant, unscrew the mounting bolts and lift the boot lid from the car.

Refitting and adjustment

5   Refitting is a reversal of removal. Check that the boot lid is correctly

21.4 Detach the wiring connector from the tailgate

21.5 Tailgate strut and balljoint

21.6 Tailgate hinge and retaining bolts

aligned with the surrounding bodywork with an equal clearance around its edge. Adjustment is made by loosening the hinge bolts and moving the boot lid within the elongated mounting holes. Check that the lock enters the striker centrally when the boot lid is closed, and if necessary adjust the striker's position within the elongated holes.

20 Boot lid lock barrel, lock, lock striker/release unit and release cable – removal and refitting

Removal

Lock barrel

1   Open the boot and undo the screw securing the barrel retaining clip, then remove the clip.
2   Detach the barrel from the link rod and withdraw the lock from the boot lid.

Lock

3   Open the boot lid and remove the lock barrel (see above for details).
4   Undo the three retaining screws, then withdraw the lock from the boot lid.

Lock striker and remote release unit

5   Open the boot, undo the two retaining screws and remove the trim from the rear face of the luggage compartment.
6   Using a soft pencil, mark an outline around the striker unit and the release unit to act as a guide for repositioning on refitting. Undo the two Torx type screws and remove the lock striker and the release unit. Detach the operating cable from the release unit to remove it.

Release cable

7   Remove the striker and release unit as described above, then detach the release cable from it.
8   Detach and remove the kick panel trim beneath the front and rear doors on the driver's side. Fold back the carpet from around the bootlid lock release handle.
9   Withdraw the outer cable from the slot in the lever mounting plate, then detach the inner cable from the lever.
10   Remove the appropriate side trim panels from the rear of the vehicle on the side concerned to expose the cable routing. Where the cable has to pass through cavities in the body, tie a suitable length of cord to the cable end before pulling the cable through and removing it. The cord can be untied from the cable and left in situ in the vehicle. It will then act as a 'puller-guide' when the cable is being refitted.

Refitting

11   Refitting is a reversal of removal. When refitting the lock, check that the striker enters the lock centrally when the boot lid is closed, and if necessary re-position the striker by loosening the mounting screws.

21 Tailgate – removal, refitting and adjustment

Removal

1   Open the tailgate, then undo the seven retaining screws and remove the trim panel from the tailgate.
2   Using a soft pencil, mark the fitted position outline around the tailgate hinges to act as a guide for repositioning when refitting.
3   Prise free and remove the plug for access to the washer jet, then detach the hose from the jet. Attach a suitable length of strong cord to the end of the hose to assist in guiding the hose back through the aperture of the tailgate when it is being refitted. Now prise free the flexible grommet on the left-hand side and withdraw the washer jet hose from the tailgate. Undo the cord from the hose and leave it in position in the tailgate.
4   Where applicable, detach the central locking lead multi-connector and earth lead from the tailgate (photo). Attach a suitable length of strong cord to the end of the wire to assist in guiding the wiring back through the aperture of the tailgate when it is being refitted. Now prise free the flexible grommet on the right-hand side and withdraw the central locking wires from the tailgate. Undo the cord from the wire and leave it in position in the tailgate.
5   Have an assistant support the tailgate in the open position, then prise open the support strut balljoint securing clip and detach the strut each side from the tailgate (photo).
6   Unscrew and remove the hinge bolts and then lift the tailgate clear of the vehicle (photo).

Refitting and adjustment

7   Refitting is a reversal of removal, but check that the tailgate is

21.7 Tailgate bump stop

correctly aligned with the surrounding bodywork with an equal clearance around its edge. Adjustment is made by loosening the hinge bolts and moving the tailgate within the elongated mounting holes. Adjust the rear height by turning the rubber bump stop each side in the desired direction to suit (photo). Check that the striker enters the lock centrally when the tailgate is closed, and if necessary adjust the position of the striker within the elongated holes.

22 Tailgate support strut – removal and refitting

Removal

1 Support the tailgate in its open position. If both struts are to be removed, the tailgate will need to be supported by an alternative means.
2 Disconnect each end of the support strut by prising out the spring clip retainers with a small screwdriver and pulling the strut from the ball mountings.

Refitting

3 Refitting is a reversal of removal, but note that the piston end of the strut faces downwards.

23 Tailgate lock, lock barrel, striker/release unit and release cable – removal and refitting

Removal
Lock barrel

1 Open the tailgate, then remove the seven screws and remove the inner trim panel from the rear of the luggage area.

2 Depending on type, unscrew and remove the lock barrel clip retaining screw then remove the clip or undo the two retaining nuts (photo).
3 Disengage the operating rod and remove the barrel.

Lock

4 Open the tailgate and remove the lock barrel as described above.
5 Undo the three Torx type retaining screws and remove the lock unit. Where applicable, detach the wiring in-line connector from the lock (photo).

Striker and release unit

6 Using a soft pencil, mark an outline around the striker unit and the release unit to act as a guide for repositioning on refitting. Undo the two Torx type screws and where applicable, the earth lead screw, then remove the lock striker and release unit. Detach the operating cable from the release unit to remove it (photos).

Release cable

7 Remove the striker and release unit as described above, then detach the release cable from it.
8 Detach and remove the kick panel trim beneath the front and rear doors on the driver's side. Fold back the carpet from around the tailgate release handle.
9 Withdraw the outer cable from the slot in the lever mounting plate, then detach the inner cable from the lever (photo).
10 Remove the appropriate side trim panels from the rear of the vehicle on the side concerned to expose the cable routing. Where the cable has to pass through cavities in the body, tie a suitable length of cord to the cable end before pulling the cable through and removing it. The cord can be untied from the cable and left in situ in the vehicle. It will then act as a 'puller-guide' when the cable is being refitted.

Refitting

11 Refitting is a reversal of removal. When refitting the lock, check that the striker enters the lock centrally when the tailgate is closed, and if necessary re-position the striker by loosening the mounting screws.

23.2 Tailgate lock barrel, operating rod and retaining nuts

23.5A Undo the three retaining screws ...

23.5B ... and withdraw the lock from the tailgate

23.6A Undo the retaining screws ...

23.6B ... withdraw the tailgate striker plate and detach the release cable

23.9 Tailgate release handle and operating cable

24 Windscreen and fixed windows – removal and refitting

Removal

Windscreen and rear quarter and rear window/tailgate glass

1   The windscreen, rear quarter and rear window/tailgate glass are bonded in place with special mastic, and special tools are required to cut free the old units and fit replacements, together with cleaning solutions and primers. It is therefore recommended that this work is entrusted to a Ford dealer or windscreen replacement specialist.

Rear window(s) – Van

2   Working from the inner face of the door concerned, use a blunt ended instrument to push the inner lip of the weatherseal beneath the window frame starting at the top. Get an assistant to support the window on the outside during this operation.
3   With the weatherseal free, withdraw the window from the door.

Rear window – Cabriolet

4   Detach the heated rear window lead and withdraw the lead from the weatherstrip.
5   Arrange for an assistant to support the glass from the outside, then wearing protective gloves, press the window outwards and remove it from its frame. Take care not to apply undue strain to the hood material or the hood frame as the window is pressed out.
6   Remove the weatherstrip from the glass.

Refitting

7   Clean the window and aperture in the body/frame. Petrol or spirit-based solvents must not be used for this purpose as they are harmful to the weatherstrip.
8   Fit the weatherseal on the window, then insert a cord in the weatherseal groove so that the ends project from the bottom of the window and are overlapped by approximately 150 mm.
9   Locate the window on its location aperture and pass the ends of the cord inside the vehicle. Have an assistant hold the window in position.
10 Slowly pull one end of the cord (at right angles to the window frame, towards the centre of the glass) so that the lip of the weatherseal goes over the aperture. At the same time have the assistant press firmly on the outside of the window. When the cord reaches the middle top of the window, pull the remaining length of cord to position the other half of the weatherseal.
11 Reconnect the heated rear window lead and press it under the weatherstrip (Cabriolet).

25 Door and tailgate weatherstrips – removal and refitting

Removal

1   To remove a weatherstrip seal from its aperture flange, grip the strip at its joint end and progressively pull it free, working around the aperture to the other end of the strip.

Refitting

2   First check that the contact surfaces of the weatherstrip and the aperture flange are clean. Check around the aperture flange for any signs of distortion and rectify as necessary.
3   To refit the weatherstrip, start by roughly locating its ends midway along the base of the aperture concerned, but do not press them into position over the flange at this stage. Proceed as follows, according to type.

Door weatherstrip

4   In the case of a door weatherstrip, refer to Fig. 11.12 and press the strip into position at the points indicated to initially locate it. Check that the distances between each contact point are such that the strip will fit smoothly around the aperture (without distortion), then firmly press the

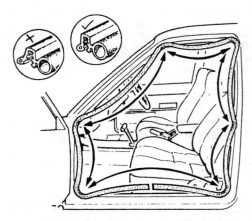

Fig. 11.12 Initial securing points when fitting a door weatherstrip (Sec 25)

strip fully into position, starting at the top edge and working down each side to finish at the bottom joint. Check that the seal is correctly located, then apply a suitable sealant to the joint to prevent the possibility of water leakage through it caused by capillary action.
5   Shut the door and check it for fit. Adjust if required by resetting the position of the striker plate to suit.

Tailgate weatherstrip

6   Position the ends of the weatherstrip so that they are centralised within 300 mm of the tailgate striker plate. A new weatherstrip will need to be measured and cut to length. Progressively fit the weatherstrip around the aperture flange, squeezing it closed over the flange by hand to secure. When fitted, check that it is not distorted, then close the tailgate and check it for fit. Adjustment of the striker plate and the tailgate bump stops may be necessary to obtain a satisfactory fit and seal.

26 Body side-trim mouldings and adhesive emblems – removal and refitting

Removal

1   Insert a length of strong cord (fishing line is ideal), between the moulding or emblem concerned and break the adhesive bond between the moulding (or emblem) and the panel.
2   Thoroughly clean all traces of adhesive from the panel using methylated spirit and allow the moulding/emblem location to dry.

Refitting

3   Peel back the protective paper from the rear face of the new moulding/emblem and then carefully fit it into position on the panel concerned, but take care not to touch the adhesive. When in position, apply a hand pressure to the moulding/emblem for a short period to ensure maximum adhesion to the panel.

27 Roof moulding (Van) – removal and refitting

Removal

1   Prise free and lift the moulding up from the roof at the front end, then pull the moulding from its location channel in the roof.
2   Clean the contact faces of the moulding and the roof channel before refitting the moulding.

Refitting

3   Locate the moulding into position over the channel, check that it is correctly realigned and then progressively press it into place using the palm of the hand.

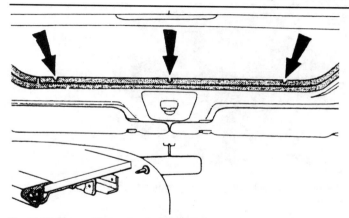

Fig. 11.13 Sunroof lower frame-to-glass frame screws (Sec 28)

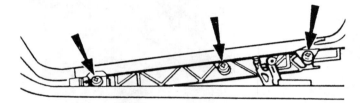

Fig. 11.14 Slacken off these screws to adjust the sunroof glass panel (Sec 28)

28 Sunroof – checking and adjustment

1   The sunroof should operate freely without sticking or binding as it is opened and closed. When in the closed position, check that the panel is flush with the surrounding roof panel, the maximum allowable gap at the front edge being 1.0 mm.
2   If adjustment is required, open the sun blind, then referring to Fig. 11.13, undo and remove the three lower frame-to-glass panel retaining screws indicated. Slide the lower frame back into the roof.
3   Loosen off the central and front securing screws, adjust the glass roof panel so that it is flush at its front edge with the roof panel, then retighten the securing screws.
4   Pull the lower frame forwards, insert and tighten its retaining screws to complete.

29 Sunroof panel – removal and refitting

Removal

1   Move the sun blind into the open position, unscrew and remove the three screws securing the lower frame and slide the frame back into the roof.
2   Undo the three roof panel-to-sliding gear screws, then push the panel up and out to remove it from the vehicle. Have an assistant lift the panel free from above as it is raised to avoid the possibility of the panel and/or the surrounding roof from being damaged.

Refitting

3   Refit in the reverse order of removal. When the panel is in position, adjust it as described in the previous Section.

30 Sunroof weatherstrip – removal and refitting

Removal

1   Wind the sunroof panel into the tilted open position, then grip the ends of the weatherstrip and pull it free from the flanged periphery of the roof panel.
2   Clean the contact faces of the panel and the weatherstrip (where the original strip is to be used) before refitting.

Refitting

3   Refit in the reverse order of removal. Ensure that the weatherstrip joint is located in the middle of the rear face of the panel.

31 Seats – removal and refitting

Removal

Front seat

1   If required, the front seat cushion can be removed on its own by undoing the two retaining screws on the underside of the seat at the front and sliding the cushion forwards. To remove the complete seat, slide the seat forward to the full extent of its travel then unscrew and remove the rear mounting bolts (one on the outer slide and two on the inner) (photos).
2   Now slide the seat fully to the rear and then unscrew the front securing bolt each side (photo). Lift the seat and remove it from the vehicle.

Rear seat cushion

3   Prise free the blanking plugs and then unscrew and remove the cushion hinge retaining screw each side (photo). Remove the cushion from the vehicle.

Rear seat backrest (Saloon and Estate)

4   Pivot the rear seat cushion forwards and then fold the backrest

31.1A Front seat/runner rear outboard retaining bolt

31.1B Front seat/runner rear inboard retaining bolts

31.2 Front seat/runner forward mounting bolt

31.3 Rear seat cushion retaining screw (Saloon)

31.4 Rear seat backrest-to-cushion hinge screws

down. Undo the two screws retaining the hinge to the backrest each side, and then remove the backrest from the vehicle (photo).

Rear seat backrest (Cabriolet)

5   Raise the seat cushion and then unscrew and remove the seat belt lower reel anchor bolts.
6   Unscrew and remove the screws (one each side) securing the backrest upper section.
7   Pivot the seat backrest down (release knob in boot), pull back the backrest cover, then unscrew and remove the two screws each side retaining the top section.
8   Detach the seat belt guide from the top of the backrest, then lift the backrest and feed the belt reel lower anchor plate through the backrest to allow the backrest to be removed from the car.
9   Unscrew the bolts securing the lower backrest to the hinges on each side and remove the backrest lower section.

Refitting

10   Refitting is a reversal of the removal procedure. Where applicable, tighten the seat belt anchor bolts to the specified torque wrench setting.

---

32 Front seat belts – removal and refitting

Removal

Front seat belt and stalk (3-door Escort and Cabriolet)

1   Prise free the upper cover, then unscrew and remove the front seat

belt upper anchor plate retaining bolt. Remove the plate and spacer.
2   Undo the lower anchor rail retaining bolt, pivot the rail towards the centre of the vehicle, pull it free from its mounting and then slide the belt from the rail.
3   Remove the rear quarter trim panel, then on the Cabriolet model, undo the two retaining screws and remove the belt guide.
4   Unscrew the bolt retaining the inertia reel unit, then remove the reel and the belt. Undo the single retaining screw and remove the front seat belt stalk from the seat frame.

Front seat belt and stalk (5-door Escort, Orion and Van)

5   Prise free the cover, then unscrew and remove the front seat belt upper anchor plate retaining bolt. Remove the plate and spacer (photo).
6   Unscrew and remove the lower anchor plate retaining bolt.
7   Remove the trim from the centre 'B' pillar by pulling free the weatherstrip, unscrewing the two retaining screws, withdrawing the trim from the panel and detaching the securing pegs (where applicable).
8   Undo the six screws retaining the scuff plate in position, extract the belt from the slotted hole and remove the scuff plate.
9   Undo the retaining bolt and detach the inertia reel unit from the central pillar (photo).
10   Undo the single retaining screw (Torx type) and detach the front seat belt stalk from the seat frame.

Refitting

11   Refitting is a reversal of the removal procedure. Tighten all fastenings to the specified torque settings and check for satisfactory operation of the seat belt(s) on completion.

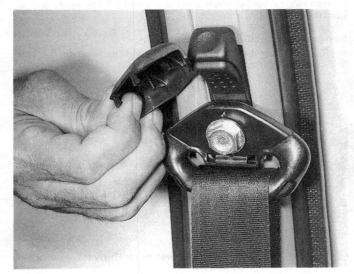

32.5 Remove the cover for access to the seat belt upper anchor bolt

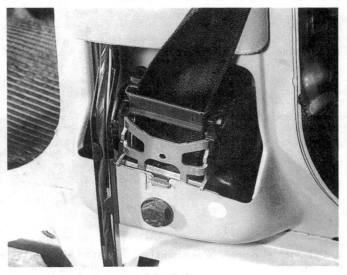

32.9 Inertia reel unit and retaining bolt

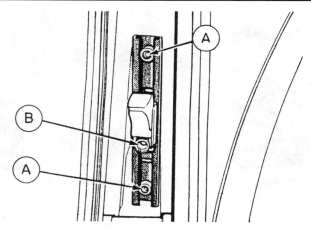

Fig. 11.15 Front seat belt height adjuster retaining bolts (A) and anchor plate bolt (B) (Sec 33)

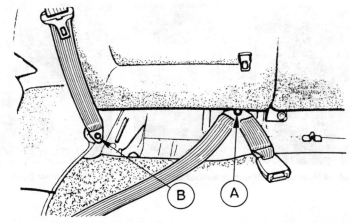

Fig. 11.16 Rear seat belt anchor plates for the central buckle/belt (A) and the reel belt (B) (Sec 34)

33 Front seat belt height adjuster – removal and refitting

Removal

1   Prise free the upper cover, then unscrew and remove the front seat belt upper anchor plate retaining bolt. Remove the plate and spacer.
2   Remove the trim from the centre 'B' pillar by pulling free the weatherstrip, unscrewing the two retaining screws, withdrawing the trim from the panel and detaching the securing pegs (where applicable).
3   Unscrew the retaining bolts and remove the height adjuster unit.

Refitting

4   Refitting is a reversal of the removal procedure. Tighten the adjuster and upper anchor plate retaining bolts to the specified torque settings and check for satisfactory operation of the seat belt on completion.

34 Rear seat belts – removal and refitting

Removal

Escort (3-door)

1   Prise free the upper cover, then unscrew and remove the front seat belt upper anchor plate retaining bolt. Remove the plate and spacer.
2   Undo the lower anchor rail retaining bolt, pivot the rail towards the centre of the vehicle, pull it free from its mounting and then slide the belt from the rail.
3   Lift the rear seat cushion for access, then unscrew the retaining bolt and remove the centre buckle/belt anchor plate.
4   Unscrew the lower reel belt anchor plate bolt.
5   Unscrew and remove the upper anchor plate bolt and detach the plate and spacer from the rear 'C' pillar.
6   Pivot the rear seat backrest down and undo the two Torx screws securing the backrest.
7   Remove the trim from the centre 'B' pillar by pulling free the weatherstrip, unscrewing the two retaining screws, withdrawing the trim from the panel and detaching the securing pegs (where applicable).
8   Remove the rear quarter trim panel (Section 35).
9   Remove the trim panel from the 'C' pillar as described in Section 35.
10   Undo the three Torx bolts and detach the rear seat backrest catch bracket.
11   Unscrew the inertia reel retaining bolt and withdraw the inertia reel unit and belt.

Escort (5-door)

12   Lift the rear seat cushion for access, then unscrew the retaining bolt and remove the centre buckle/belt anchor plate.
13   Unscrew the lower reel belt anchor plate bolt.

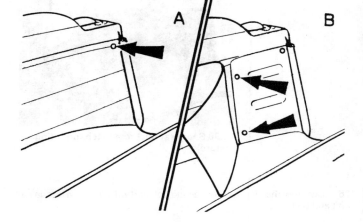

Fig. 11.17 Rear seat backrest upper section retaining screw locations on the Cabriolet (Sec 34)

A   Cover clip   B   Retaining screws

14   Detach the cover for access, then unscrew and remove the anchor plate and spacer from the 'C' pillar (photo).
15   Pivot the rear seat backrest down and undo the two Torx screws securing the backrest catch (photo).
16   Remove the trim panel from the 'C' pillar as described in Section 35.
17   Undo the three Torx bolts and detach the rear seat backrest catch bracket.
18   Unscrew the inertia reel retaining bolt and withdraw the inertia reel unit and belt.

Orion

19   Lift the rear seat cushion for access, then unscrew the retaining bolt and remove the centre buckle/belt anchor plate.
20   Unscrew the lower reel belt anchor plate bolt.
21   Detach the cover for access, then unscrew and remove the anchor plate and spacer from the 'C' pillar.
22   Pivot the rear seat backrest down and remove the trim panel from the 'C' pillar as described in Section 35.
23   Unscrew the retaining nut and remove the rear seat backrest catch pull knob from its bracket in the boot. Pull the cable from the clip on the underside of the boot.
24   Undo the two Torx screws and release the seat back catch from the mounting bracket.
25   Undo the three Torx bolts and detach the rear seat backrest catch bracket.

34.14 Rear seat belt upper anchor bolt

34.15 Rear seat backrest catch (Saloon)

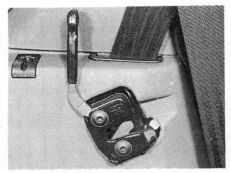

34.36 Rear seat backrest catch (Estate)

34.38 Rear seat backrest catch mounting (Estate)

34.39 Rear seat inertia reel unit (Estate)

26   Unscrew the inertia reel retaining bolt and withdraw the inertia reel unit and belt.

Cabriolet

27   Lift the rear seat cushion for access, then unscrew the retaining bolt and remove the centre buckle/belt anchor plate.
28   Unscrew the lower anchor plate bolt. To remove the static, centre lap belt, remove the lower belt buckle and twin buckle assemblies.
29   Unscrew and remove the lower reel belt anchor plate bolt.
30   Release the catch in the boot and fold down the rear seat backrest. Pull free the cover from the rear face of the backrest for access to its upper section. Undo the two retaining screws on each side (see Fig. 11.17). Remove the belt guide from the top of the backrest.
31   Raise the backrest, feed the belt anchor plate through and then remove the backrest.
32   Unscrew the retaining bolt and remove the inertia reel/belt unit.

Estate

33   Lift the rear seat cushion for access, unscrew the retaining bolt and remove the centre buckle/belt anchor plate.
34   Unscrew the lower reel belt anchor plate bolt.
35   Detach the cover for access, then unscrew and remove the anchor plate and spacer from the 'C' pillar.
36   Pivot the rear seat backrest down, undo the two Torx screws and remove the backrest catch (photo).
37   Detach and remove the 'C' and 'D' pillar trim panels followed by the rear load space trim panel as described in Section 35.
38   Undo the three Torx screws and detach the backrest catch mounting (photo).
39   Unscrew the retaining bolt and remove the inertia reel/belt unit (photo).

Refitting

40   Refit in the reverse order of removal. Tighten the retaining bolts to the specified torque settings. Check the seat belt for satisfactory operation on completion.

35   Interior trim panels – removal and refitting

Removal

Centre console (manual transmission)

1   Unscrew and remove the knob from the gear lever, then prise free the lever gaiter from the console, slide it up the lever and remove it.
2   Unscrew the four retaining screws from the positions indicated in Fig. 11.18, or on long console types, the four nuts and the two screws, then remove the console (photo). Where applicable, disconnect the wiring connections from any console-mounted switches as it is lifted clear. It may be necessary to carefully prise free the switch first in order to detach the wiring connectors from them.

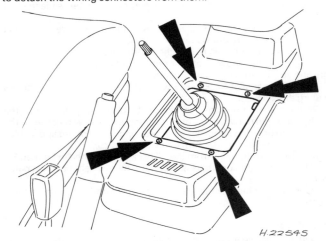

Fig. 11.18 Short-type centre console retaining screws on manual transmission models (Sec 35)

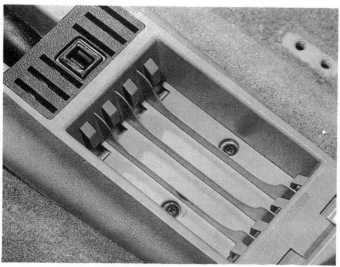

35.2 Location of two screws on long-type centre console

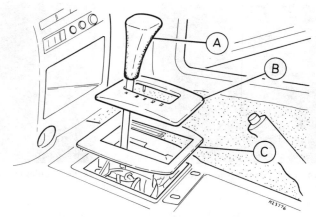

Fig. 11.19 Automatic transmission gearshift lever knob (A), lever indicator panel (B) and panel bezel (C) (Sec 35)

Centre console (automatic transmission)

3   Locate the gearshift lever in the 'P'(Park) position, unscrew and remove the knob from the lever, then prise free the lever indicator panel followed by the bezel.

4   Unscrew and remove the six retaining screws from the positions shown in Fig. 11.20 and withdraw the console. Where applicable, disconnect the wiring connections from any console-mounted switches as it is lifted clear. it may be necessary to carefully prise free the switch first in order to detach the wiring connectors from them.

Windscreen 'A' pillar trim

5   Pull free the weatherstrip from the flange on the 'A' pillar, undo the retaining screw and withdraw the trim from the pillar.

Centre 'B' pillar

6   Pull free the weatherstrip from the pillar flange. Prise free the cover, then unscrew and remove the front seat belt upper anchor plate retaining bolt. Remove the plate and spacer.

7   On five-door Escort and Orion models, undo the two screws securing the centre pillar trim.

8   Carefully prise free and detach the trim from the central pillar (to which it is attached by plastic pegs).

Rear 'C' pillar trim (Escort)

9   Hinge the rear seat cushion forwards and lower the seat backrest.

10   Where fitted, undo the three retaining screws to withdraw the speaker unit and detach the speaker wire. Do not detach the speaker from the unit.

11   Undo the two Torx type retaining screws and detach the backrest catch. Also prise free and remove the rear suspension top mounting cover (just to the rear of the catch).

12   Unscrew and remove the rear seat belt lower anchor plate bolt.

13   Prise free the seat belt upper anchor plate cover, then unscrew the retaining bolt and detach the upper anchor plate and spacer.

14   Prise free the door weatherstrip from the pillar flange.

15   On three-door Escort models, remove the rear quarter trim as described later in this Section.

16   Undo the retaining screws and withdraw the trim panel from the pillar, feeding the seat belt and anchor through the trim. Note that it is necessary to remove a cover for access to the rear retaining screw.

Rear 'C' pillar trim (Orion)

17   Hinge the rear seat cushion forwards and lower the seat backrest.

18   Detach and remove the rear parcel shelf (see paragraphs 26 to 28).

19   Unscrew and remove the rear seat belt lower anchor plate bolt.

20   Prise free the seat belt upper anchor plate cover, then unscrew the retaining bolt and detach the upper anchor plate and spacer.

21   Undo the two 'C' pillar retaining screws. Prise free the door

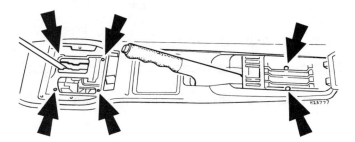

Fig. 11.20 Centre console retaining screw locations on automatic transmission models (Sec 35)

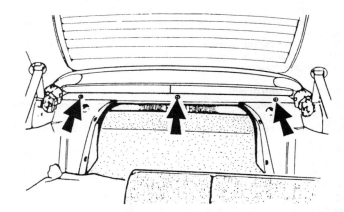

Fig. 11.21 Rear parcel shelf securing screws on the Orion (Sec 35)

weatherstrip from the 'C' pillar flange, then carefully prise free the trim panel from the pillar, feeding the seat belt through it as it is withdrawn.

'C' pillar trim (Estate)

22   Hinge the rear seat cushion forwards and lower the seat backrest.

23   Prise free the seat belt upper anchor plate cover, then unscrew the retaining bolt and detach the upper anchor plate and spacer.

24   Carefully prise free and remove the trim panel from the 'C' pillar (photo).

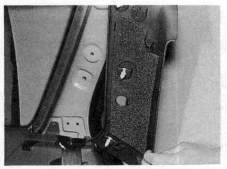

35.24 'C' pillar trim removal (Estate)

35.25 'D' pillar trim removal (Estate)

35.47 Load space side trim retaining screws removal (Estate)

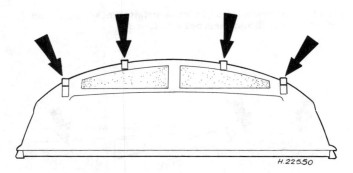

Fig. 11.22 Rear parcel shelf retaining clips on the Orion (Sec 35)

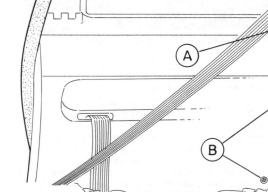

Fig. 11.23 Rear quarter panel securing screw locations (Sec 35)

A   Screw   B   Screw with washer

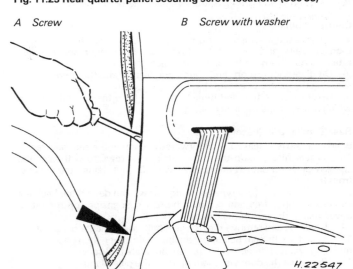

Fig. 11.24 Prise free the rear quarter panel from the 'B' pillar at the points indicated (Sec 35)

'D' pillar trim

25   Prise free the trim panel from the 'D' pillar to release it from the retaining clips and remove the trim (photo).

Rear parcel shelf (Orion)

26   Hinge down the rear seat backrest. Where fitted, detach and remove the rear speaker units from the parcel shelf.
27   Undo the retaining screw and remove the seat belt guide trim panel each side.
28   Unscrew and remove the three parcel shelf retaining screws, then lift the panel at the front edge to detach it from the four plastic retaining clips and withdraw the panel from the car.

Rear quarter trim panel

29   Detach the front seat belt at its upper and lower anchor points as described in Section 32.
30   Detach and remove the centre 'B' pillar trim as described previously in this Section.
31   Undo the two scuff plate retaining screws and ease the plate away from the quarter panel.
32   Hinge forward the rear seat cushion and backrest, then detach the belt trim guide bezel from the quarter panel.
33   Unscrew and remove the retaining screws at the rear of the panel, then prising free the quarter panel from the 'B' pillar at the points indicated, withdraw the panel (see Figs. 11.23 and 11.24). As it is withdrawn, disengage the seat belt and anchors through the panel slots.

Front footwell side cowl trim panel

34   Rotate the plastic retaining clip at the front of the panel through 90° to release the panel at the forward fixing, then ease the panel away from the three tab fasteners at the rear edge.

Scuff plate

35   Remove the front footwell side cowl trim panel as described above.
36   Prise free the door weatherstrip from the door sill flange.
37   On five-door Escorts, Van and Orion models, unscrew and remove

the screw at the lower end of the 'B' pillar trim (just above the seat belt slot in the scuff plate).
38   Unscrew and remove the six scuff plate retaining screws, then feeding the seat belt through it (where applicable), withdraw the scuff plate.

Luggage area trim (Escort Saloon and Orion)

39   Hinge down the rear seat backrest(s), and on Escort models, prise

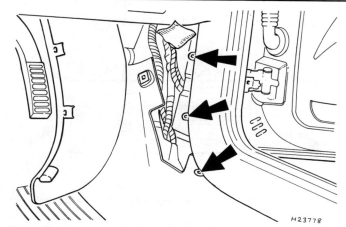

Fig. 11.25 Location of footwell side trim retaining tabs (Sec 35)

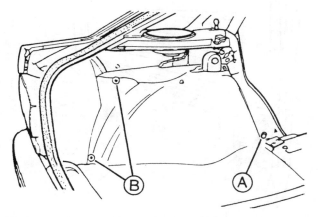

Fig. 11.26 Load space side trim retaining clip (A) and screws (B) in the Escort (Sec 35)

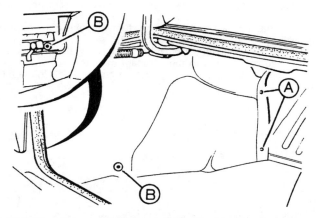

Fig. 11.27 Load space side trim retaining clip (A) and screws (B) in the Orion (Sec 35)

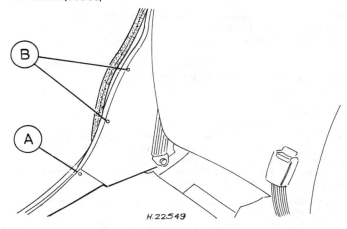

Fig. 11.28 Scuff plate screw (A) and load space side trim retaining screws at the forward end (B) on the Estate (Sec 35)

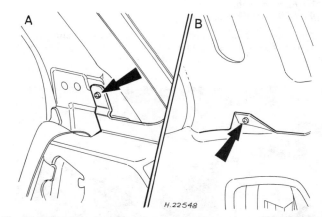

Fig. 11.29 Load space side trim retaining screw locations to the 'C' pillar (A) and 'D' pillar (B) in the Estate (Sec 35)

free and remove the trim cap from the rear suspension top mounting.
40 Prise free the trim panel retaining clips using a suitable flat-bladed tool.
41 Unscrew and remove the two trim retaining screws together with their large washers, then withdraw the trim panel.

Luggage area trim (Estate)

42 Lift the rear seat cushion and unscrew the scuff plate screw at the rear, then unscrew and remove the two load space trim screws.
43 Hinge down the rear seat backrest, then prise free the upper cover and remove the rear seat belt upper anchor plate retaining bolt. Remove the plate and spacer.
44 Undo the two Torx screws and remove the rear seat backrest catch.
45 Prise the trim panel from the 'C' pillar and remove it.
46 Prise the trim panel from the 'D' pillar and remove it.
47 Undo the screw attaching the trim panel to the 'C' pillar, then the screws securing the load space trim panel to the 'D' pillar (photo).
48 Undo the three load space trim to floor screws and the single screw securing it to the rear crossmember.
49 Lift the trim panel to release it from the inner side panel, then withdraw it from the vehicle.

Panel partition (Van)

50 Working from the front side of the panel, unscrew and remove the three panel to crossmember retaining bolts on its lower edge.
51 Working from the rear side of the panel, unscrew and remove the two bolts securing the panel to the rear face of the 'B' pillar each side, then withdraw the partition panel.

Sun visor

52 Release the visor from the retaining clip, undo the two retaining

screws at its hinge mounting and remove the visor. To remove the retaining clip, prise open the cover flap to expose the retaining screw then undo the screw and remove the clip.

Passenger grab handle

53 Prise back the trim flaps at each end of the grab handle to expose the retaining screws. Undo the screws and remove the handle.

Refitting

54 Refitting is a reversal of the removal procedure. Ensure that all

Fig. 11.30 Front-side partition securing bolts in the Van (Sec 35)

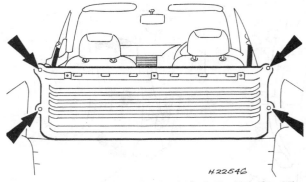

Fig. 11.31 Rear-side partition securing bolts in the Van (Sec 35)

wiring connections are securely made. Where applicable, tighten the seat belt fixings to the specified torque wrench setting and check the seat belt(s) for satisfactory operation on completion.

36 Facia – removal and refitting

Removal

1　Disconnect the battery earth lead.
2　Refer to Chapter 10 for details and remove the steering wheel.
3　Undo the two upper and four lower retaining screws and remove the upper and lower steering column shrouds.
4　Refer to the appropriate Chapters concerned for details and remove the following facia associated items.

 (a)　Lighting and indicator switches from the steering column (Chapter 12).
 (b)　Instrument panel from the facia (Chapter 12).
 (c)　Choke cable (where applicable) from the facia (Chapter 4).
 (d)　Heater controls and control panel from the facia (Chapter 3).
 (e)　Cigar lighter and ashtray (Chapter 12).
 (f)　Radio/cassette player (Chapter 12).
 (g)　LCD clock (Chapter 12).

5　Undo the two retaining screws and remove the side vent panel from the facia on the driver's side. As it is withdrawn, disconnect any wiring connections from the panel-mounted switches (photo).

6　Undo the two hinge/retaining screws securing the glovebox lid and remove it. Undo the two catch screws and remove the lock/catch unit. As the catch is withdrawn, disconnect the bulbholder/switch wiring connector.
7　Where fitted, detach and remove the footwell lights from the driver and passenger side lower facia (Chapter 12).
8　Pull free the weatherstrip from the leading edge of the door aperture each side to gain access to the outboard mounting screws (photo). Unscrew and remove the retaining screws from the points indicated in Fig. 11.32.

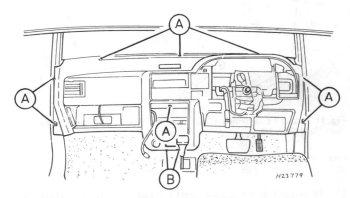

Fig. 11.32 Facia retaining screw locations 'A' (screws only) and 'B' (screws and washers) (Sec 36)

36.5 Side vent panel removal on the driver's side

36.8 Pull free the weatherstrip for access to the outboard facia screws

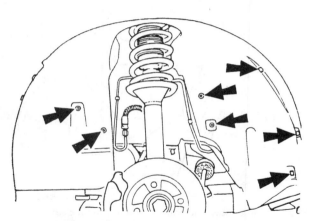

Fig. 11.33 Screw locations for wheel arch liner (Sec 37)

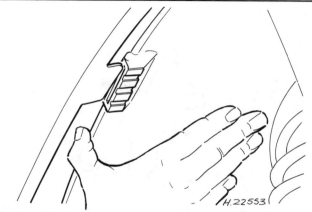

Fig. 11.34 Disengage the wheel arch liner from the retaining tang (Sec 37)

9   Withdraw the facia unit from its mounting. As it is withdrawn, note the routings of the cables attached to the facia, then detach the cable ties and remove the facia from the vehicle.

10   The associated components of the facia can (if required) be detached by undoing the appropriate retaining screws.

Refitting

11   Refitting is a reversal of the removal procedure. Ensure that all wiring and cable routings are correctly and securely made. Refer to the appropriate Chapters for details on refitting the associated fittings to the facia panel.

12   When the facia panel is completely refitted, reconnect the battery as described in Chapter 12, Section 4 (noting the special procedure for EFi models), then test the various facia and steering column switches to ensure that they operate in a satisfactory manner.

37   Wheel arch liners – removal and refitting

Removal

1   Loosen off the front roadwheel nuts on the side concerned, then raise the vehicle at the front end and support it on axle stands. Remove the roadwheel.

2   Referring to Fig. 11.33, unscrew and remove the seven Torx type retaining screws from the locations indicated.

38.1 Radiator (front) grille panel retaining screw removal

3   Press the liner inwards at the top to disengage it from the locating tang, then withdraw it from the vehicle.

Refitting

4   Refit in the reverse order of the removal procedure. Tighten the roadwheel nuts to the specified torque wrench setting.

38   Radiator grille – removal and refitting

Removal

1   Raise and support the bonnet. Unscrew and remove the four retaining screws along the top edge of the grille, then carefully lift the grille free and disengage it from the locating socket each side at the bottom (photo).

Refitting

2   Refit in the reverse order of the removal procedure.

39   Powered hood (Cabriolet) – removal and refitting

Note: *The following instructions detail the removal and refitting of the hood cover only. The removal, repair and refitting of the hood frame, insulation and headlining are specialised tasks and must be entrusted to a Ford garage or an automotive upholstery specialist.*

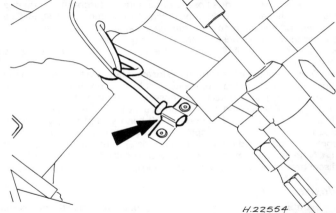

Fig. 11.35 Cabriolet powered hood spring wire rod retainers (Sec 39)

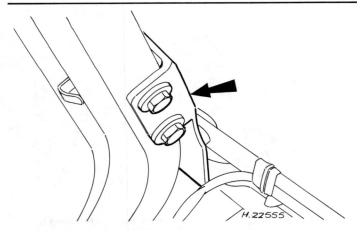

Fig. 11.36 Cabriolet powered hood hinge damper (Sec 39)

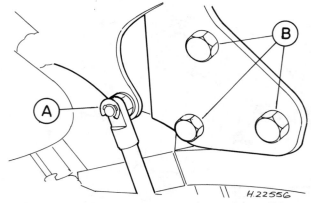

Fig. 11.37 Cabriolet powered hood hydraulic rod (Sec 39)

A   Securing clip   *B   Unit retaining bolts*

Removal

1   Open the roof, then remove the rear seat cushion by prising free the blanking plugs and unscrewing the seat hinge screw each side.
2   Remove the rear quarter trim panel as described in Section 35.
3   Raise the roof just enough the allow access to the rear parcel shelf.
4   Disconnect the spring wire rod from the retainer on each side.
5   Unscrew and remove the spring wire securing screw on each side.
6   Disconnect the spring wire from the housing at the other end on each side.
7   Detach the wiring from the heated rear window connectors.
8   Unscrew and remove the two hinge damper bolts on each side, then fully open the roof.
9   Prise free the hydraulic rod securing clip, then unscrew and remove the three retaining bolts from the brackets.
10   Enlist the aid of an assistant to help in removing the roof assembly from the car. Grip the roof and pull it towards the front to release it at the rear end, then carefully lift clear of the car.

Refitting

11   Refitting is a reversal of the removal procedure. When the roof assembly is fully reconnected, check that it operates in a satisfactory manner before refitting the rear quarter panel and seat cushion.

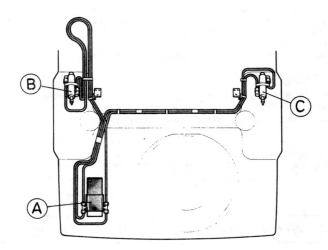

Fig. 11.38 Cabriolet powered hood operating components and hydraulic hose routings (Sec 40)

A   Hydraulic pump unit
B   Hydraulic ram (left-hand side)
C   Hydraulic ram (right-hand side)

40   Powered hood control system (Cabriolet) – hose removal, refitting and system bleeding

Hose removal

1   Open the boot lid, lower the hood and then remove the appropriate trim panels to gain access to the pump unit (in the left-hand side of the luggage area) and the hydraulic ram located behind the rear quarter panel on the side concerned.
2   Where more than one hose is to be detached from the pump, the respective hoses and their connections to the pump unit should be labelled and marked for correct identification to avoid the possibility of confusion when reconnecting them (see Fig. 11.39).
3   Loosen off the oil filler plug on the pump unit to depressurize the system.
4   Disconnect the hose(s) from the location tangs to the body and the tape securing it to the ram unit and other hoses. Loosen off the hose to pump union(s) and detach the hose(s). Note that it may well be necessary to detach and partially remove the pump unit as described in Section 42 to enable a hose on the left-hand side of the pump to be disconnected. Catch any spillage of hydraulic fluid in a suitable container and plug the hose(s)/connection(s) to prevent the ingress of dirt. Note that the hood must not be raised whilst the hydraulic lines are disconnected or hydraulic fluid remaining in the system will be ejected

Hose refitting

5   Refitting is a reversal of the removal procedure. When the hoses are reconnected, top up and bleed the hydraulic system as follows.

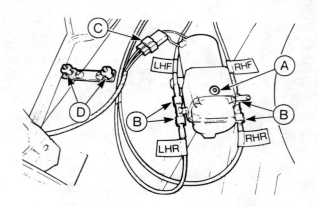

Fig. 11.39 Hydraulic hose connections to the powered hood pump unit (Sec 40)

A   Filler plug
B   Hose unions and markings
C   Pump multi-plug
D   Pump mounting

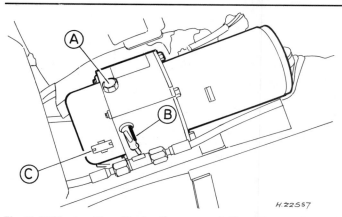

Fig. 11.40 Powered hood hydraulic pump unit (Sec 40)

A *Filler plug*
B *By-pass tap*

C *Oil level MAX mark*

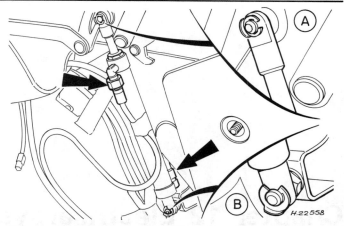

Fig. 11.41 Powered hood hydraulic ram hose connections showing the upper (A) and lower (B) mounting circlips (Sec 41)

System bleeding

6   Remove the fluid filler plug from the pump and top up the fluid level with the specified fluid type (see Specifications) to the 'MAX' mark, then loosely retighten the plug. Unscrew and open the by-pass tap 90 to 180° (maximum), then manually raise and lower the hood once. Recheck the fluid level in the pump, top up the level if required, tighten the by-pass tap and refit the filler plug.
7   Turn the ignition switch to position I (accessory), then close and open the roof five times using the roof operating switch. At the end of this cycle, the roof should operate smoothly in each direction and the pump motor should have a constant operating sound.
8   With the roof in the open position, recheck the hydraulic fluid level in the pump and top up if required to the specified level.

41 Powered hood control damper/hydraulic ram (Cabriolet) – removal and refitting

Removal

1   Lower the hood, then detach and remove the left-hand trim panel in the luggage area to gain access to the hydraulic pump unit.
2   Depressurize the hydraulic system by loosening off the pump hydraulic fluid filler plug.
3   Remove the rear quarter trim panel from the side concerned as described in Section 35.
4   Label the hoses and their connections to the hydraulic ram unit to identify them for refitting.
5   Release the circlips securing the ram unit at each end to its attachment points to the vehicle. Note that the lower securing point has the larger of the circlips.
6   Loosen off the hydraulic hose union connectors to the ram, withdraw the ram from its mounting points and position it and the hydraulic connections over a suitable container. Detach the hydraulic hoses and drain all of the fluid into the container before removing the ram unit. Use plugs to seal off the hoses and the hydraulic connections to the ram, so preventing the ingress of dirt and any further fluid leakage. Note that the hood must not be raised whilst the hydraulic lines are disconnected or hydraulic fluid remaining in the system will be ejected.

Refitting

7   Refitting is a reversal of the removal procedure. When the ram is refitted to its mountings and the hoses are reconnected to it, top up and bleed the hydraulic system as described in the previous Section, before refitting the quarter trim panel (Section 35) and the pump cover/side trim in the luggage area.

42 Powered hood operating motor and pump (Cabriolet) – removal and refitting

Removal

1   Disconnect the battery earth lead.
2   Open the boot lid, then detach and remove the left-hand side trim in the luggage area for access to the pump/motor unit.
3   Referring to Fig. 11.40, unscrew the by-pass tap 90 to 180°.
4   Lower the roof manually, then allow any residual pressure in the system to escape by loosening off the filler plug on the top of the pump unit a fraction.
5   Retighten the filler plug and tap. Detach the wiring connector to the pump motor.
6   Label the respective hoses and their connections to the pump unit for correct identification prior to detaching them to avoid any possibility of confusion when reconnecting them (see Fig. 11.39).
7   Undo the pump unit retaining nuts, then partially withdraw the pump. Locate a suitable container (or some rags) beneath it, unscrew the hydraulic hose unions and detach the hoses from the pump. Plug the exposed ends of the pump and hoses to prevent the ingress of dirt and further fluid leakage. Remove the pump unit. Note that the hood must not be raised whilst the hydraulic lines and pump are disconnected or hydraulic fluid remaining in the system will be ejected.

Refitting

8   Ensure that the hose connections are clean, then reconnect the hoses to the pump unit, hand tightening them at this stage.
9   Reconnect the pump motor wiring connection, relocate the pump into position and tighten its retaining nuts. Check that the hoses are not distorted or under undue tension, then fully tighten their unions.
10   Top up the pump with the specified hydraulic fluid and bleed the system as described in Section 40.
11   Reconnect the battery earth lead, referring to Section 4 of Chapter 12 for restarting details on EFi models.

Chapter 12 Electrical system

Contents

Specifications

System type .... 12 volt, negative earth

Battery
Type.. Maintenance-free
Capacity... 36, 50, 59 or 65 Ah (depending on model)

Alternator
Make/type:
    Bosch .... K1-55A or K1-70A
    Magneti-Marelli .... A127/55 or 127/70
    Mitsubishi .... A5T or A002T
Output (nominal at 13.5 volts with engine speed of 6000 rpm) .... 55 or 70 amps
Regulating voltage at 4000 rpm engine speed and 3 to 7 amp load .... 14 to 14.6 volts
Minimum allowable length of the slip ring end brushes:
    Bosch and Magneti-Marelli .... 5 mm
    Mitsubishi .... 3 mm
Drivebelt tension adjustment (deflection at mid-point of longest run
between pulleys) .... 4 mm

Starter motor
Make/type:
    Bosch .... DM, DW or EV
    Magneti-Marelli .... M79 or M80R
    Nippondenso .... No type numbers given

Starter motor (continued)

Output:
Bosch DM	0.8, 0.9 or 1.0 kW
Bosch DW	1.4 or 1.8 kW
Bosch EV	2.2 kW
Marelli M79	0.8 or 0.9 kW
Marelli M80R	1.8 kW
Nippondenso	0.6 or 0.8 kW

Minimum allowable brush length:
Bosch and Magneti-Marelli	8.0 mm
Nippondenso	10.0 mm

Commutator minimum allowable diameter:
Bosch (except EV type) and Nippondenso	32.8 mm
Bosch EV and Magneti-Marelli	Not available

Armature endfloat:
Bosch (except EV)	0.3 mm
Bosch EV and Magneti-Marelli M80R	Not available
Marelli M79	0.25 mm
Nippondenso	0.6 mm

Fuses (in vehicle fusebox)

Fuse identification number	Rating (amps)	Circuit(s) protected
1	25	Heated rear window, adjustable door mirrors
2	30	Anti-lock braking system
3	10	HEGO sensor (catalytic converter models)
4	15	Right-hand main beam, right-hand auxiliary light
5	20	Fuel pump
6	10	Right-hand sidelight
7	10	Left-hand sidelight
8	10	Rear foglamp
9	10/30	Instrument lights, normal/heavy duty cooling fan
10	10	Left-hand dip beam
11	15	Front foglamps
12	10	Direction indicator, reversing lights
13	20	Wiper motor, washer pump
14	20	Heater blower
15	30	Anti-lock braking system
16	3	Heated windscreen
17	3	Heated windscreen
18	15	Left-hand main beam, left-hand auxiliary light
19	20	Central locking system
20	15	Horn
21	15	Interior lights, clock, radio
22	30	Electrically operated windows
23	30	Headlamp washer system
24	10	Right-hand dip beam
25	3	EEC IV engine management system
26	5	Heated front seats
27	10	Brake stop lights
28	10	Air conditioning system

Additional fuses (in engine compartment)

Fuse identification letter	Rating (amps)	Circuit(s) protected
A	80	Supply cables to main fuse block
B	60	Supply cables to main fuse block
C	60	Supply cables to main fuse block
D	40/50	Cooling fan
E	50	Heated rear window

Relays

Relay number	Colour	Circuit
R1	Grey	Heated windscreen
R2	Red	Windscreen wiper intermittent control
R3	Grey	Heated rear windscreen
R4	Dark green	Anti-lock braking system
R5	Violet	Anti-lock braking (pump)
R6	White/Yellow	Main beam
R7	Orange	Rear wiper intermittent control
R8	Green/Red/Yellow	CFi delay relay or EFi supply relay or EEC IV supply relay
R9	Brown	Fuel pump
10	Brown	Magnetic clutch air conditioning system
11	Green	Air conditioning system
12	Brown	Engine running

Relays (continued)

13	
14	
15	
16	
17	
18	
19	
20	
21	
22	
23	
24	
25	
26	
27	

Colour	Circuit
Spare	–
Spare	–
Spare	–
Spare	–
Yellow	Interior light delay
Green	Electrically operated windows
Grey	Rear foglamp (module)
Spare	–
–/White	Busbar/ front foglamps (module)
Blue	Headlamp washer system
White	Dip beam
–/Red or Yellow	Busbar/automatic transmission. Alarm
White	Front foglamps
Black	Steering lock/starter switch
Spare	–

Bulbs

	Wattage
Headlamps – (Halogen H4)	60/65
Sidelights	5
Front indicator lights	21
Side indicator repeater lights	5
Rear lights (Saloon)	5
Brake stop lights (Saloon)	21
Brake stop/rear lights (Estate and Van)	21/5
Reversing lights	21
Rear direction indicators	21
Rear foglamps	21
Rear number plate light	10
Instrument panel warning lights	1.3
Hazard warning lamp switch bulb	1.3
Instrument panel illumination bulb	2.6
Clock illumination bulb	1.2
Cigar lighter illumination bulb	1.4
Glovebox illumination light bulb	10
Load space illumination bulb	10
Coutesy light	10

Torque wrench settings

	Nm	lbf ft
Alternator:		
Alternator adjuster bolt	11 to 13	8 to 10
Adjuster pinion central locking bolt	18 to 26	15 to 19
Mounting bolt	21 to 27	16 to 20
Pulley nut (with key)	45 to 55	33 to 40
Pulley nut (without key)	50 to 70	37 to 52
Starter motor retaining bolts	35 to 45	26 to 33
Oil pressure warning light switch (OHV engine)	13 to 15	10 to 11
Oil pressure warning light switch (OHC engine)	18 to 22	13 to 16
Reversing light switch	16 to 20	12 to 15
Wiper motor (original) to mounting bracket	8 to 12	6 to 9
Wiper motor (new) to mounting bracket	10 to 12	7.5 to 9
Wiper motor bracket to bulkhead (or tailgate)	6 to 8	4.5 to 6
Wiper motor arm to spindle nut	22 to 24	16 to 17
Wiper arm nut:		
Stage 1	17 to 18	12.5 to 13.5
Stage 2 (after operating wiper)	17 to 18	12.5 to 13.5
Washer reservoir	2.5 to 3.5	2 to 2.5
Rear lamp retaining nuts	2.7 to 3.7	2 to 3
Horn to body retaining nuts	25 to 35	19 to 26
Headlamp unit retaining screws	5.4 to 6	4 to 4.5

1 General information and precautions

Warning: *Before carrying out any work on the electrical system, read through the precautions given in Safety first! at the beginning of this manual.*

The electrical system is of the 12 volt negative earth type, and consists of a battery, alternator, starter motor and related electrical accessories, components and wiring.

The battery, charged by the alternator (which is belt-driven from the crankshaft pulley), provides a steady amount of current for the ignition, starting, lighting and other electrical circuits.

The starter motor is of the pre-engaged type incorporating an integral solenoid. On starting, the solenoid moves the drive pinion into engagement with the flywheel ring gear before the starter motor is energised. Once the engine has started, a one-way clutch prevents the motor armature being driven by the engine until the pinion disengages from the flywheel.

It is necessary to take extra care when working on the electrical system to avoid damage to semi-conductor devices (diodes and transistors), and to avoid the risk of personal injury. In addition to the precautions given in *Safety first!* at the beginning of this manual, observe the following when working on the system.

Always remove rings, watches, etc, before working on the electrical system. Even with the battery disconnected, capacitive discharge could occur if a component live terminal is earthed through a metal object. This could cause a shock or nasty burn.

Do not reverse the battery connections. Components such as the alternator, fuel and ignition control units, or any other unit having semi-conductor circuitry could be irreparably damaged.

If the engine is being started using jump leads and a slave battery, connect the batteries positive-to-positive and negative-to-negative – see *Booster battery (jump) starting* at the beginning of this manual. This also applies when connecting a battery charger.

Never disconnect the battery terminals, any electrical wiring or any test instruments, when the engine is running.

Never use an ohmmeter of the type incorporating a hand-cranked generator for circuit or continuity testing.

Always ensure that the battery negative lead is disconnected when working on the electrical system.

2 Electrical fault finding – general information

1   A typical electrical circuit consists of an electrical component, any switches, relays, motors, fuses, fusible links or circuit breakers related to that component, and the wiring and connectors that link the component to both the battery and the chassis. To help you pinpoint an electrical circuit problem, wiring diagrams are included at the end of this manual.

2   Before tackling any troublesome electrical circuit, first study the appropriate wiring diagram to get a complete understanding of what components are included in that individual circuit. Trouble spots, for instance, can be narrowed down by noting if other components related to the circuit are operating properly. In some instances, more than one component or circuit are protected by the same fuse and in such instances where the fuse is at fault, the associated components or circuits will also have failed.

3   Electrical problems usually stem from simple causes, such as loose or corroded connections, a blown fuse, a melted fusible link or a faulty relay. Visually inspect the condition of all fuses, wires and connections in a problem circuit before testing the components. Use the diagrams to note which terminal connections will need to be checked in order to pinpoint the trouble spot.

4   The basic tools needed for electrical fault finding include a circuit tester or voltmeter (a 12-volt bulb with a set of test leads can also be used), a continuity tester, a battery and set of test leads, and a jumper wire, preferably with a circuit breaker incorporated, which can be used to bypass electrical components. Before attempting to locate a problem with test instruments, use the wiring diagram to decide where to make the connections.

Voltage checks

5   Voltage checks should be performed if a circuit is not functioning properly. Connect one lead of a circuit tester to either the negative battery terminal or a known good earth. Connect the other lead to a connector in the circuit being tested, preferably nearest to the battery or fuse. If the bulb of the tester lights, voltage is present, which means that the part of the circuit between the connector and the battery is problem free. Continue checking the rest of the circuit in the same fashion. When you reach a point at which no voltage is present, the problem lies between that point and the last test point with voltage. Most problems can be traced to a loose connection.
Note: *Bear in mind that some circuits are only live when the ignition switch is switched to a particular position.*

Finding a short circuit

6   One method of finding a short circuit is to remove the fuse and connect a test light or voltmeter to the fuse terminals with all the relevant electrical components switched off. There should be no voltage present in the circuit. Move the wiring from side to side while watching the test light. If the bulb lights up, there is a short to earth somewhere in that area, probably where the insulation has rubbed through. The same test can be performed on each component in the circuit, even a switch.

Earth check

7   Perform an earth test to check whether a component is properly earthed. Disconnect the battery and connect one lead of a self-powered test light, known as a continuity tester, to a known good earth point. Connect the other lead to the wire or earth connection being tested. If the bulb lights up, the earth is good. If the bulb does not light up, the earth is not good.

Continuity check

8   A continuity check is necessary to determine if there are any breaks in a circuit. With the circuit off (ie no power in the circuit), a self-powered continuity tester can be used to check the circuit. Connect the test leads to both ends of the circuit (or to the positive end and a good earth), and if the test light comes on, the circuit is passing current properly. If the light does not come on, there is a break somewhere in the circuit. The same procedure can be used to test a switch, by connecting the continuity tester to the switch terminals. With the switch turned on, the test light should come on.

Finding an open circuit

9   When checking for possible open circuits, it is often difficult to locate them by sight because oxidation or terminal misalignment are hidden by the connectors. Merely moving a connector on a sensor or in the wiring harness may correct the open circuit condition. Remember this when an open circuit is indicated when fault finding in a circuit. Intermittent problems may also be caused by oxidized or loose connections.

General

10   Electrical fault finding is simple if you keep in mind that all electrical circuits are basically electricity flowing from the battery, through the wires, switches, relays, fuses and fusible links to each electrical component (light bulb, motor, etc.) and to earth, from where it is passed back to the battery. Any electrical problem is an interruption in the flow of electricity from the battery.

3 Battery – general checks, testing and charging

General checks – all battery types

1   Periodically disconnect and clean the battery terminals and leads. After refitting them, smear the exposed metal with petroleum jelly. Note that reference should be made to Section 4 for precautionary details when disconnecting and reconnecting the battery leads. The cautionary notes detailed in *Safety first!* should also be adhered to whenever the battery is to be inspected and serviced.

2   When the battery is removed for whatever reason, it is worthwhile checking it for cracks and leakage.

Maintenance-free battery

3   A maintenance-free battery is fitted to all models when new. The term 'maintenance-free' indicates that the electrolyte level will never need topping up during the life of the battery. In most instances, no provision is made for topping-up the electrolyte level, although some manufacturers do provide a plug through which topping up is possible where the battery has been overcharged. A maintenance-free battery will discharge in the same manner as that of a conventional battery and as such will periodically need to be tested for its voltage reading and possibly re-charged using a conventional battery charger.

Low-maintenance battery

4   Where a low-maintenance battery has been fitted (to replace the maintenance-free type), the topping-up vent plugs (or alternative system) are retained, but the need to check the electrolyte level is reduced to once a year. On some batteries the case is translucent and incorporates minimum and maximum level marks.

Regular-maintenance battery

5   Where a traditional type battery has replaced the original maintenance-free type, the electrolyte level of each cell should be checked and if necessary topped up with distilled or de-ionized water at the intervals given in Chapter 1. On some batteries the case is

translucent and incorporates minimum and maximum level marks. The check should be made more often if the vehicle is operated in high ambient temperature conditions.

6   If the need for topping up becomes excessive, and this is not due to leakage from a fractured casing, the battery is being over-charged, and the voltage regulator will have to be checked.

Testing

7   If the vehicle covers a very small annual mileage and/or is being used beyond the manufacturer's guarantee period, it is worthwhile checking the state of charge of the battery on a more regular basis (say every three months).

8   To check the condition of the maintenance-free type battery, a voltmeter will be required and ideally, the battery must be in a stabilised condition (not having been used for a minimum period of six hours) when making the check. If the engine has been run, or the battery has been charged within this period, switch the headlamps on for thirty seconds, then switch them off (also all other accessories), and leave making the check for a period of five minutes to enable the battery to stabilise. Clean the battery terminals before connecting up the voltmeter to check the reading. Typical battery condition voltage readings are as follows

Condition	Voltage reading
Poor	12.4 volts
Normal	12.6 volts
Good	12.7 volts

9   On low-maintenance and regular-maintenance type batteries, the condition of the battery can also be tested as described above for the maintenance-free type battery, or alternatively it can be tested by checking the specific gravity of the electrolyte to determine its state of charge. Use an hydrometer to make the check, and compare the results with the following table.

	Normal climates	Tropics
Discharged	1.120	1.080
Half charged	1.200	1.160
Fully charged	1.280	1.230

10   A variation of 0.040 or more between any cells indicates loss of electrolyte or deterioration of the internal plates indicating that the battery condition is suspect.

11   A further test can be made using a battery heavy discharge meter. The battery should be discharged for a maximum of 15 seconds at a load of three times the ampere-hour capacity (at the 20 hour discharge rate). Alternatively, connect a voltmeter across the battery terminals and operate the starter motor with the HT king lead from the ignition coil earthed with a suitable wire, and the headlamps, heated rear window and heater blower switched on. If the voltmeter reading remains above 9.6 volts, the battery condition is satisfactory. If the voltmeter reading drops below 9.6 volts, and the battery has already been charged, it is faulty.

12   In winter, when heavy demand is placed on the battery (starting from cold and using more electrical equipment), it is a good idea to have the battery fully charged from an external source occasionally, at a rate of 10% of the battery capacity (ie 6.5 amps for a 65 Ah battery).

Charging

13   Both battery terminal leads must be disconnected before connecting the charger leads (disconnect the negative lead first). Continue to charge the battery until no further rise in specific gravity is noted over a four-hour period.

14   Alternatively, a trickle charger, charging at a rate of 1.5 amps can safely be used overnight.

4   Battery – removal and refitting

Removal

1   The battery is located on the left-hand side of the bulkhead. First check that all electrical components are switched off in order to avoid a spark occurring as the negative lead is disconnected. Ensure that the

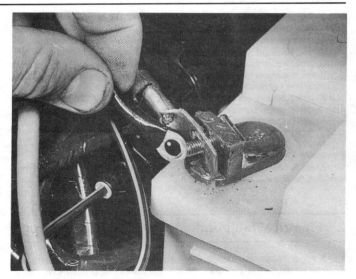

4.2 Disconnecting the earth (–) terminal leads on the battery

anti-theft alarm system is de-activated before detaching the battery. Note that if the radio has a security coding, it will be necessary to insert this code when the battery is re-connected, so ensure that it is known before disconnecting the battery.

2   Undo the retaining nut, then detach the earth leads from the stud of the battery earth terminal post (photo). This is the terminal to disconnect before working on, or disconnecting any electrical component on the vehicle.

3   Pivot up the plastic cover from the positive terminal, then unscrew the positive lead retaining nut on the terminal. Detach the positive lead from the terminal.

4   Unscrew the two battery clamp bolts and remove the clamp from the front of the battery.

5   Lift the battery from the tray keeping it upright and taking care not to touch any clothing.

6   Clean the battery terminal posts, clamps and the battery casing. If the bulkhead is rusted as a result of battery acid spilling onto it, clean it thoroughly and re-paint with reference to Chapter 1.

Refitting

7   Refitting is a reversal of removal. Smear the battery terminals with a petroleum-based jelly prior to reconnecting. Always connect the positive terminal clamp first and the negative terminal clamp last.

Note: *Vehicles fitted with the 1.6 litre EFi engine will lose the 'keep alive memory' (KAM) information stored in the module when the battery is disconnected. This includes idling and operating values, and any fault codes detected. This may cause surge, hesitation, erratic idle or a generally deteriorated standard of performance. To allow the module to 're-learn' its values on subsequent reconnection of the battery, start the engine and run it at normal idle speed for a period of three minutes so that it reaches its normal operating temperature. The engine speed should then be increased to 1200 rpm and maintained at this level for approximately two minutes. It may be necessary to drive the vehicle to allow the module to complete its 're-learning' phase – the distance required being dependent on the type of driving encountered, but is normally about 5 miles (8 km) for varied conditions.*

5   Charging system – testing

1   If the ignition warning lamp fails to illuminate when the ignition is switched on, first check the wiring connections at the rear of the alternator for security. If satisfactory, check that the warning lamp bulb has not blown and is secure in its holder. If the lamp still fails to illuminate check the continuity of the warning lamp feed wire from the alternator to the bulbholder. If all is satisfactory, the alternator is at fault and should be renewed or taken to an automobile electrician for testing and repair.

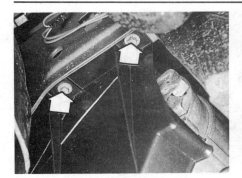

6.3 Drivebelt guard retaining bolts (arrowed)

6.6 Alternator and lower mounting/pivot bolts on an HCS (OHV) engine

6.9 Alternator removal from a CVH (OHC) engine

2   If the ignition warning lamp illuminates when the engine is running, ensure that the drivebelt is correctly tensioned (see Chapter 1), and that the connections on the rear of the alternator are secure. If all is so far satisfactory, check the alternator brushes and commutator, as described in Section 7. If the fault still persists, the alternator should be renewed, or taken to an automobile electrician for testing and repair.

3   If the alternator output is suspect even though the warning lamp functions correctly, the regulated voltage may be checked as follows.

4   Connect a voltmeter across the battery terminals and then start the engine.

5   Increase the engine speed until the reading on the voltmeter remains steady. This should be between 13.5 and 14.8 volts.

6   Switch on as many electrical accessories as possible and check that the alternator maintains the regulated voltage at between 13.5 and 14.8 volts.

7   If the regulated voltage is not as stated, the fault may be due to a faulty regulator, a faulty diode, a severed phase winding or worn brushes, springs or commutator. The brushes and commutator may be serviced as described in Section 7, but if the fault still persists the alternator should be renewed, or taken to an automobile electrician for testing and repair.

6   Alternator – removal and refitting

Removal

1   Disconnect the battery negative terminal.

2   Apply the handbrake, then jack up the front of the vehicle and support it on axle stands.

3   Where applicable, undo the two retaining bolts and remove the drivebelt guard (photo).

Alternator with V-belt drive and manual adjustment

4   On models fitted with a sliding arm type adjuster strap, unscrew and remove the top (adjuster) bolt from the strap.

5   On models fitted with a 'rack and pinion' type adjuster, unscrew and remove the pinion nut and the central bolt.

6   Loosen off the lower mounting bolts, pivot the alternator inwards towards the engine to slacken the tension of the drivebelt, then disengage the drivebelt from the pulleys and remove it (photo).

7   Where applicable, detach and remove the alternator heat shield.

8   Where applicable, detach and remove the phase terminal and the splash cover.

9   Supporting the weight of the alternator from underneath, unscrew and remove the mounting bolts. Lower the alternator and noting the connections, detach the wiring and remove the alternator from the vehicle (photo).

Alternator with flat 'polyvee' belt drive and automatic adjustment

10   Undo the retaining nuts and remove the plastic pulley guard.

11   Fit a ring spanner onto the drivebelt tensioner and rotate it clockwise to loosen off the tension from the drivebelt. Note the routing of the drivebelt, then disengage the belt from the pulleys and remove it.

12   Remove the bottom guard from the radiator. This is secured in position by clips or pop rivets. In the latter instance, it will be necessary to carefully drill the rivets out in order to remove the guard.

13   Position a jack under the radiator support bracket. The bracket must be partially lowered on the right-hand side and although the coolant hoses should be able to take the weight and strain of the radiator assembly and bracket, the jack will prevent the possibility of an older hose splitting.

14   Unscrew and remove the radiator support bracket retaining bolts on the right-hand side, then loosen off (but do not remove) the securing bolts on the left-hand side.

15   Unscrew and remove the alternator retaining bolts. Withdraw the alternator from its mounting bracket then lower the radiator/support bracket just enough to allow the alternator to be removed.

Refitting

16   Refit in the reverse order of removal. Refit the drivebelt and ensure that it is correctly re-routed around the pulleys. Adjust the tension of the drivebelt (according to type) as described in Chapter 1.

7   Alternator brushes and regulator – checking and renewal

1   Disconnect the battery negative terminal.

7.3A Undo the retaining screw and ...

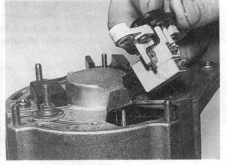

7.3B ... withdraw the brush box/regulator unit (Bosch alternator)

7.4 Measuring the brush lengths

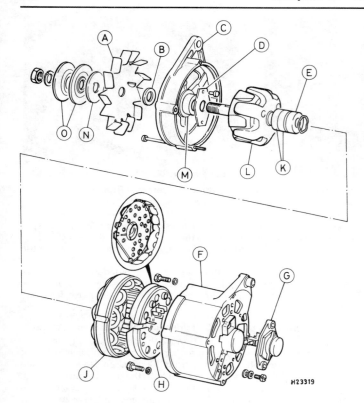

266 Chapter 12 Electrical system

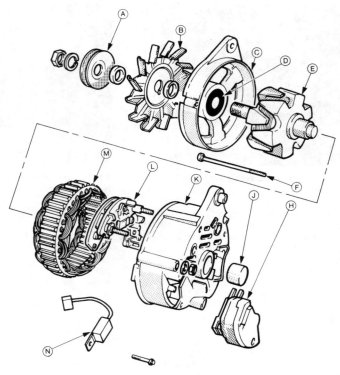

Fig. 12.2 Exploded view of the Magneti-Marelli alternator (Sec 7)

A	Pulley	H	Brushbox/regulator
B	Fan	J	Slip ring end bearing
C	Drive end housing	K	Slip ring end housing
D	Drive end bearing	L	Rectifier diode pack
E	Rotor	M	Stator
F	Through-bolt	N	Suppressor

Fig. 12.1 Exploded view of the Bosch K1-55A and K1-70A alternators (Sec 7)

A	Fan	H	Rectifier (diode) pack
B	Spacer	J	Stator
C	Drive end housing	K	Slip rings
D	Drive end bearing retaining plate	L	Rotor
E	Slip ring end bearing	M	Drive end bearing
F	Slip ring end housing	N	Spacer
G	Brushbox and regulator	O	Pulley

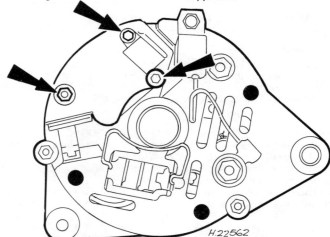

Fig. 12.3 Regulator/brush box retaining screws on the Magneti-Marelli alternator (Sec 7)

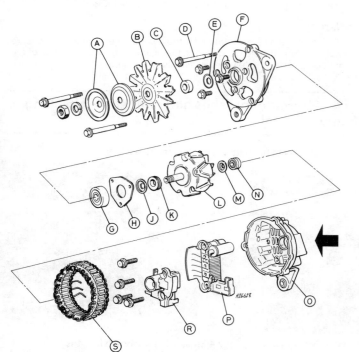

Fig. 12.4 Exploded view of the Mitsubishi A5T alternator (Sec 7)

A	Pulley	K	Thin spacer
B	Fan	L	Rotor
C	Thick spacer	M	Seal
D	Through-bolt	N	Bearing
E	Dust shield	O	Commutator end
F	Drive end unit	P	Diode pack
G	Bearing	R	Brush box
H	Bearing retainer	S	Stator
J	Dust cap		

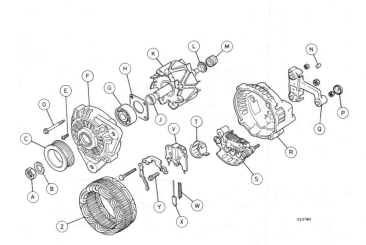

Fig. 12.5 Exploded view of the AOO2T Mitsubishi alternator (Sec 7)

A	Pulley nut
B	Spring washer
C	Pulley
D	Through-bolt
E	Retainer plate screw
F	Drive end housing
G	Bearing
H	Bearing retaining plate
J	Spacer
K	Rotor
L	Spacer
M	Slip ring end bearing

N	Plug
P	Cap
Q	Terminal insulator
R	Slip ring end housing
S	Rectifier
T	Dust cover
V	Regulator
W	Brush spring
X	Brush
Y	Regulator screw
Z	Stator

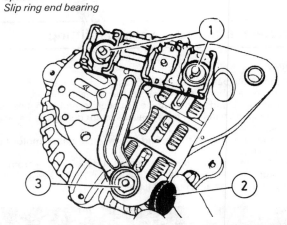

Fig. 12.8 Rectifier (1) and regulator (2) unit retaining nuts on the Mitsubishi alternator. Note that cap (3) covers the regulator nut (Sec 7)

2   Remove the alternator from the vehicle as described in the previous Section.

Bosch

3   Remove the two screws securing the combined brush box/regulator unit and withdraw the assembly from the rear of the alternator (photos).
4   Check the brush lengths (photo). If either is less than or close to the minimum specified length, renew them by unsoldering the brush wiring connectors and withdrawing the brushes and their springs.
5   Clean the slip rings with a solvent-moistened cloth, then check for signs of scoring, burning or severe pitting. If evident, the slip rings should be attended to by an automobile electrician.
6   Refit in the reverse order of removal.

Magneti-Marelli

7   Remove the three screws securing the regulator/brush box unit on

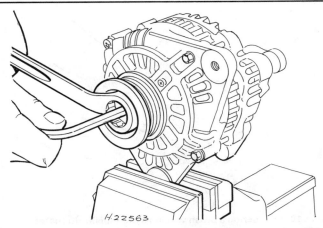

Fig. 12.6 Pulley nut removal on the Mitsubishi alternator (Sec 7)

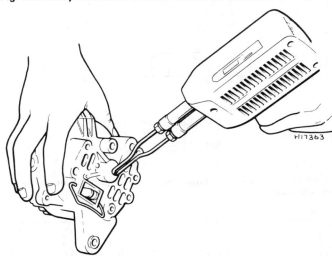

Fig. 12.7 Using a soldering iron to heat the slip ring end housing for removal of the rotor from the rear housing on the Mitsubishi alternator (Sec 7)

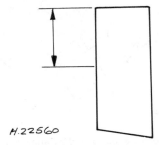

Fig. 12.9 Showing brush minimum length (wear) line on a Mitsubishi alternator (Sec 7)

the rear face of the alternator, partially withdraw the assembly, detach the field connector and remove the unit from the alternator.
8   If the brushes are worn beyond the minimum allowable length specified, a new regulator and brush box unit must be fitted; the brushes are not available separately.
9   Clean the slip rings with a solvent-moistened cloth, then check for signs of scoring, burning or severe pitting. If evident, the slip rings should be attended to by an automobile electrician.
10   Refit in the reverse order of removal.

Mitsubishi

11   Hold the pulley nut stationary using an 8 mm Allen key, unscrew the pulley nut and remove the washer.

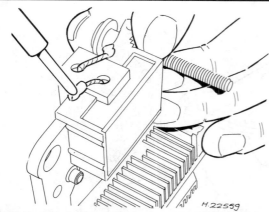

Fig. 12.10 Unsoldering a brush wire on a Mitsubishi alternator (Sec 7)

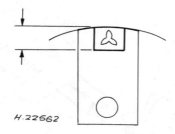

Fig. 12.11 Fitted position of new brush on a Mitsubishi alternator – see text (Sec 7)

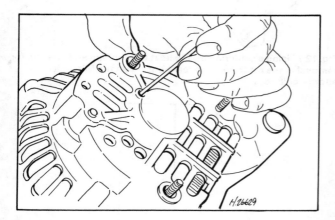

Fig. 12.12 Use a length of wire rod to hold brushes in the retracted position when reassembling the rotor to the housing on the Mitsubishi alternator (Sec 7)

12   Withdraw the pulley, cooling fan, spacer and dust shield from the rotor shaft.
13   Mark the relative fitted positions of the front housing, stator and rear housing (to ensure correct re-alignment when reassembling). Unscrew the through-bolts and remove the front housing from the rotor shaft, followed by the dust seal and the thin spacer.
14   Remove the rotor from the rear housing and the stator. If difficulty is experienced, heat the rear housing with a 200 watt soldering iron for three or four minutes as shown in Fig. 12.7.
15   Unbolt the rectifier/brush box and stator assembly from the rear housing.
16   Unsolder the stator and brush box from the rectifier using the very

minimum of heat. Use a pair of pliers as a heat sink to reduce the heat transference to the diodes (overheating may cause diode failure).
17   Renew the brushes if they are worn down to or beyond the minimum specified length. Unsolder the brush wires at the points indicated in Fig. 12.10, then solder the new brush leads so that the wear limit line projects 2 to 3 mm from the end of the holder (see Fig. 12.11).
18   Clean the slip rings with a solvent-moistened cloth, then check for signs of scoring, burning or severe pitting. If evident, the slip rings should be attended to by an automobile electrician.
19   Refit in the reverse order of removal. Insert a piece of wire through the access hole in the rear housing to hold the brushes in the retracted position as the rotor is refitted (see Fig. 12.12). **Do not** forget to release the brushes when assembled.

8   Starting system – testing

1   If the starter motor fails to operate, first check the condition of the battery as described in Section 3, or if this is not possible, by switching on the headlamps. If they glow brightly then gradually dim after a few seconds, the battery is in an uncharged condition.
2   If the battery is satisfactory, check the starter motor main terminal and the engine earth cable for security. Check the terminal connections to the solenoid, located on the starter motor.
3   If the starter still fails to turn, use a voltmeter, or 12-volt test lamp and leads, to ensure that there is battery voltage at the solenoid main terminal (ie the cable from the battery positive terminal).
4   With the ignition switched on and the ignition key in position III, check that voltage is reaching the solenoid terminal with the connector, and also the starter main terminal.
5   If there is no voltage present at the connector, then there is a wiring or ignition switch fault. If voltage is available, but the starter does not operate, then the starter or solenoid is likely to have an internal fault.

9   Starter motor – removal and refitting

Removal
1   Disconnect the battery negative terminal.
2   Apply the handbrake, then jack up the front of the vehicle and support it on axle stands. If the engine has been recently run, take care against burning the hands on the exhaust system during the following operations.
3   Undo the two retaining nuts and remove the starter motor heat shield (where fitted).
4   Unscrew the retaining nut and detach the main cable from the starter motor. Where applicable, disconnect the HEGO sensor wiring multi-plug from the locating bracket (photo).

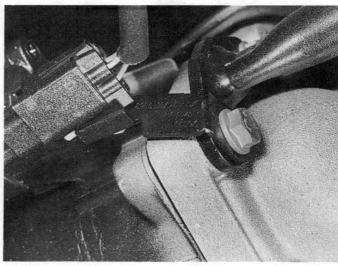

9.4 HEGO sensor wiring multi-plug connector and location bracket

9.5A Starter motor and wiring connections on an HCS (OHV) engine

9.5B Starter motor and wiring connections on a CVH (OHC) engine

9.6 Starter motor removal (CVH engine)

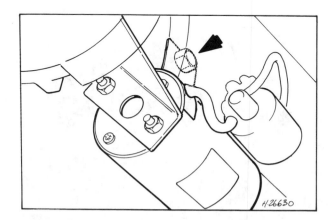

Fig. 12.13 Starter motor support bracket bolt (Sec 9)

5   Prise free the cap, undo the retaining nut and detach the wiring loom connector from the starter solenoid (photos).
6   Unscrew and remove the starter motor retaining bolts at the transmission/clutch housing and, where applicable, also unbolt and detach the support bracket. Withdraw the starter motor from its mounting and remove it from the vehicle (photo).

Refitting

7   Refitting is a reversal of removal. Tighten the retaining bolts to the specified torque. Ensure that the wiring is securely reconnected to the starter motor (and solenoid) and is routed clear of the exhaust downpipe. With the gear lever in neutral and the handbrake fully applied, check the starter motor for satisfactory operation before lowering the vehicle to the ground.

10   Starter motor brushes – checking and renewal

1   Remove the starter motor from the vehicle as described in Section 9.

Bosch starter motors

2   Undo the two retaining screws and remove the end cap (photo).
3   Wipe free the grease from the end of the armature shaft then prise free and remove the C-clip from the shaft groove. Depending on the type fitted, remove the washer/spacer(s) (photo).
4   Unscrew and remove the two through-bolts then remove the commutator end plate/housing from the starter motor (photo).
5   On the Bosch D-type starter motor, disconnect the brush link lead from its terminal stud (photo).
6   Withdraw the brush plate assembly (taking care not to damage the terminal brushes), then release the brushes from their holders in the brush plate.
7   Clean and inspect the brush assemblies. If the brushes have worn beyond (or down to) the specified minimum length they must be renewed as a set. In the case of the D-type motor, the brush plate unit complete will have to be renewed. To renew the brushes on the other types, the brush leads must be unsoldered from the brush plate terminals, then the new brush leads soldered in their place.
8   Prior to refitting the brushes, check the condition of the commutator

10.2 Remove the end cap ...

10.3 ... then remove the C-clip and any washers (Bosch starter motor)

10.4 Remove the commutator endplate

10.5 Detach the brush link lead (Bosch D-type motor)

10.9 Brush plate unit assembled over a socket with the same outside diameter as the commutator to ease assembly

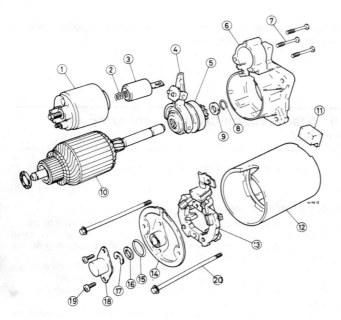

Fig. 12.14 Exploded view of the Bosch DM starter motor (Sec 10)

1	Solenoid yoke	11	Rubber block
2	Return spring	12	Yoke
3	Solenoid armature	13	Brush plate
4	Actuating arm	14	Commutator end plate
5	Drive pinion and clutch unit	15	Seal
6	Drive end housing	16	Shim
7	Solenoid retaining screws	17	C-clip
8	C-clip	18	Commutator end plate cap
9	Thrust collar	19	Securing screw
10	Armature	20	Through-bolt

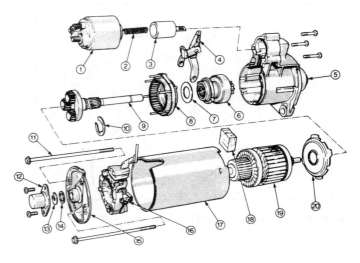

Fig. 12.15 Exploded view of the Bosch DW starter motor (Sec 10)

1	Yoke	11	Through-bolt
2	Return spring	12	Cap
3	Solenoid armature	13	C-clip
4	Actuating arm	14	Shim
5	Drive end housing	15	Commutator endplate
6	Drive pinion and clutch	16	Brush plate
7	Spacer	17	Yoke
8	Ring gear and carrier	18	Rubber block
9	Output shaft and planet gear unit	19	Armature
10	Circlip	20	Retaining plate

face on which they run. Wipe the commutator with a solvent-moistened cloth. If the commutator is dirty, it may be cleaned with fine glass paper, then wiped with the cloth.

9   Fit the new brushes using a reversal of the removal procedure. To ease fitting of the brush assembly over the end of the commutator, press them back into their holders and insert a suitable socket or tube to retain them, then align the socket with the end of the commutator and slide the brush assembly from the socket onto the commutator and into position as shown (photo). Make sure that the brushes move freely in their holders.

Magneti-Marelli starter motors
10   Undo the two retaining screws and remove the end cap and seal.

11   Wipe free the grease from the end of the armature shaft then prise free and remove the C-clip from the shaft groove. Remove the spacer(s).
12   Unscrew the retaining nut and detach the connecting link from the solenoid.
13   Undo the two retaining screws and withdraw the solenoid yoke from the drive end housing. Lift it upwards and disengage the solenoid armature from the actuation lever in the end housing.
14   Unscrew and remove the two through-bolts then remove the commutator end housing from the yoke and armature unit.
15   Detach the brush housing insulator and withdraw the brushes from the housing.
16   If the brushes have worn down to or beyond the minimum length specified, they must be renewed as a set. To renew them, cut their leads mid-point and make a secure soldered joint when connecting the new brushes.
17   Prior to refitting the brushes, check the condition of the commutator face on which they run. Wipe the commutator with a solvent-moistened cloth. If the commutator is dirty, it may be cleaned with fine glass paper, then wiped with the cloth.

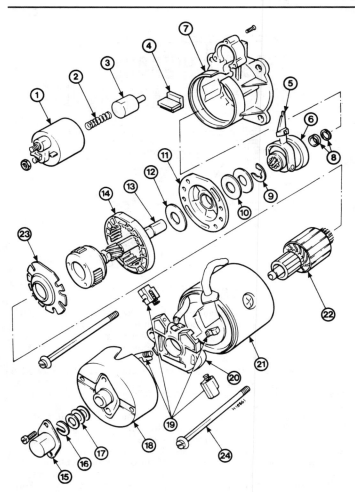

Fig. 12.16 Exploded view of the Bosch EV starter motor (Sec 10)

1 Yoke	14 Ring gear
2 Return spring	15 Commutator end housing
3 Solenoid armature	cap
4 Rubber block	16 C-clip
5 Actuating arm	17 Shims
6 Drive pinion and clutch	18 End housing
7 End housing	19 Brushes
8 C-clip and thrust collar	20 Brush plate
9 Circlip	21 Yoke
10 Spacers	22 Armature
11 Cover plate	23 Retaining plate
12 Spacer	24 Through-bolt
13 Output shaft and planet gear unit	

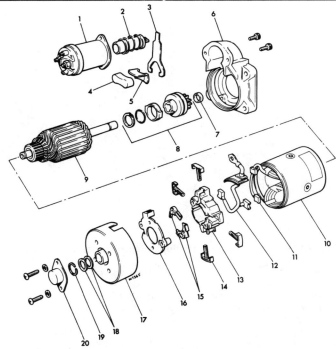

Fig. 12.17 Exploded view of the Magneti-Marelli starter motor (Sec 10)

1 Yoke	11 Brush
2 Solenoid armature	12 Brush link
3 Actuating arm	13 Brush plate
4 Rubber pad	14 Brush holder and spring
5 Plastic support block	15 Insulators
6 Drive end housing	16 Brush plate insulator
7 Thrust collar	17 Commutator end housing
8 Drive pinion and clutch	18 Shims
9 Armature	19 C-clip
10 Yoke	20 Cap

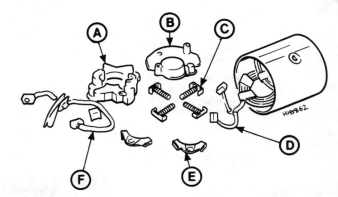

Fig. 12.18 Brush plate components – Magneti-Marelli M79 starter motor (Sec 10)

A Brush plate	D Brushes
B Brush plate insulator	E Insulators
C Brush holders and springs	F Brush link

18 Fit the new brushes and reassemble the starter motor unit using a reversal of the removal procedure. Make sure that the brushes move freely in their holders. When fitting the armature unit to the yoke, engage the actuating arm in the drive end housing together with the plastic bracket (locates in the notch in the yoke face) and rubber block. Ensure that the drive end housing is correctly aligned before fully tightening the retaining screws.

Nippondenso

19 Unscrew the two through-bolts and withdraw the commutator end plate from the main casing.
20 Remove the brush box insulator and the brush box.
21 If the brushes have worn down to or beyond the minimum length specified, they must be renewed as a set. To renew them, cut their leads

mid-point and make a secure soldered joint when connecting the new brushes.
22 Prior to refitting the brushes, check the condition of the commutator face on which they run. Wipe the commutator with a solvent-moistened cloth. If the commutator is dirty, it may be cleaned with fine glass paper, then wiped with the cloth.

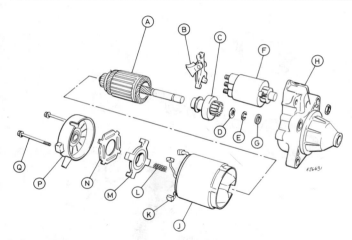

Fig. 12.19 Exploded view of the Nippondenso starter motor (Sec 10)

A	Armature
B	Actuating lever
C	Roller clutch/pinion unit
D	Lower thrust collar
E	C-clip
F	Solenoid
G	Upper thrust collar
H	Drive end housing

J	Main casing
K	Brush
L	Brush spring
M	Brush box
N	Brush box insulator
P	Commutator end plate
Q	Through-bolts

23　Make sure that the brushes move freely in their holders then reassemble the brush box, insulator and the commutator end plate. Ensure that the rubber block engages with the cut-out in the end plate, then refit the through-bolts to secure.

11　Fuses and relays – general information

Note: *It is important to note that the ignition switch and the appropriate electrical circuit must always be switched off before any of the fuses (or relays) are removed and renewed. In the event of the fuse/relay unit having to be removed, the vehicle anti-theft system must be de-activated and the battery earth lead detached. When reconnecting the battery, reference should be made to Section 4.*

1　The main fuse and relay block is located below the facia panel on the driver's side within the vehicle. The fuses can be inspected and if necessary renewed, by unclipping and removing the access cover. Each fuse location is numbered and reference to the fuse chart in the specifications at the start of this Chapter will indicate the circuits protected by each fuse. Plastic tweezers are attached to the inside face of the cover to remove and fit the fuses.
2　To remove a fuse, use the tweezers provided to pull it out of the

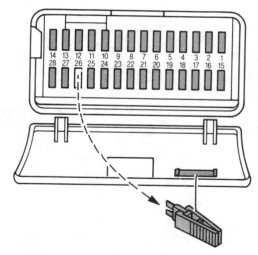

Fig. 12.20 Fuse removal using tweezers (Sec 11)

holder. Slide the fuse sideways from the tweezers. The wire within the fuse is clearly visible and it will be broken if the fuse is blown.
3　Always renew a fuse with one of an identical rating. Never renew a fuse more than once without tracing the source of the trouble. The fuse rating is stamped on top of the fuse.
4　Additional 'main' fuses are located separately in a box positioned in front of the battery and these are accessible for inspection by first raising and supporting the bonnet, then unclipping and hinging back the cover from the fusebox (photo). Each of these fuses is lettered for identification and reference to the Specifications at the start of this Chapter will indicate the circuits which they protect. To remove fuses A, B and C, it is first necessary to remove the fusebox. Fuses D and E can be removed from their locations by carefully pulling them free from the location socket in the box. In the event of one of these fuses blowing, it is essential that the circuits concerned are checked and any faults rectified before renewing the faulty fuse. If necessary, entrust this task to a Ford dealer or a competent automotive electrician.
5　With the exception of the indicator flasher relay and, where applicable, the Cabriolet powered roof relays, the remainder of the relays are fitted to the reverse side of the 'in-vehicle' fuse board. To inspect a relay mounted on the main fuse board, disconnect the battery, remove the fusebox cover and unclip the fusebox. Unscrew the six securing screws to detach and remove the lower facia panel on the driver's side. Carefully withdraw the fuse/relay block.
6　The various relays can be removed from their respective locations on the fuse board by carefully pulling them from the sockets (photo).
7　The indicator flasher relay is attached to the base of the indicator switch unit. Access to the relay is made by undoing the retaining screws and removing the steering column lower shroud. The relay unit can then be withdrawn from the base of the indicator switch (photo).
8　The Cabriolet powered roof system has four relays. Relays I and II (and a thermal cut-out) are located in the left-hand side of the luggage

11.4 Additional 'main fuses' at the front of the battery

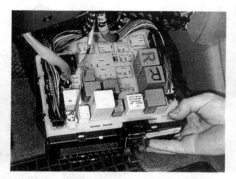

11.6 Relay locations on the underside of the fuse board

11.7 Indicator flasher relay removal

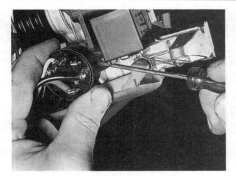

12.3A Depress the lock tabs ...

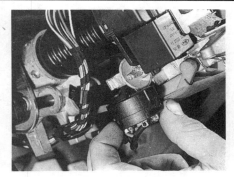

12.3B ... and remove the ignition switch

12.8A Undo the retaining screw ...

12.8B ... lift the switch clear and detach the wiring connector

12.12 Facia switch removal

area, next to the powered roof hydraulic pump, relays III and IV are located beneath the instrument cluster (together with a 15 amp fuse). Removal of the appropriate trim panel and where applicable, the associated components, gives access to the relay(s) for inspection and renewal.

9   If a system controlled by a relay becomes inoperative and the relay is suspect, listen to the relay as the circuit is operated. If the relay is functioning it should be possible to hear it click as it is energized. If the relay proves satisfactory, the fault lies with the components or wiring of the system. If the relay is not being energized, then it is not receiving a main supply voltage or a switching voltage, or the relay is faulty.

12   Switches – removal and refitting

Note: *The vehicle anti-theft system must be de-activated and battery earth lead should always be detached before disconnecting any of the switches. Ensure that the switch(es) are OFF before reconnecting the battery, and on EFi models, refer to the special restart procedures outlined in Section 4.*

Ignition switch

1   Disconnect the battery earth lead.
2   Undo the six retaining screws and remove the upper and lower shrouds from the steering column.
3   Depress the two ignition switch to lock securing tabs and withdraw the switch from the lock unit (photos).
4   Undo the six retaining screws and remove the lower facia panel on the driver's side. Unclip the fusebox panel, then detach the ignition switch wiring multi-plug connector from the fusebox. Release the switch wire from the tie clips and remove the switch.
5   Refitting is a reversal of the removal procedure. When relocating the switch to the steering lock, the barrel driveshaft must align with the switch shaft as it is pushed into position. Check the switch for satisfactory operation on completion.

Indicator switch

6   Remove the steering wheel as described in Chapter 10.
7   Undo the retaining screws and remove the upper steering column shrouds.
8   Undo the single retaining screw and withdraw the switch upwards from the steering column. Detach the wiring connector and cable tie clips from the switch (photos).
9   Separate the indicator/hazard warning relay and switch from the indicator switch unit.
10 Refit in the reverse order of removal. Refer to Section 20 in Chapter 10 for information required when refitting the steering wheel.

Facia switches

11 The facia and associated panel-mounted switches are secured in position by integral plastic or metal retaining clips. In some instances it is possible to release the switch from the panel using a suitable small screwdriver inserted between the switch and the facia to lever the switch from its aperture, but take care not to apply too much force when trying this method. Where a switch is reluctant to be released, remove the section of the facia panel or the adjoining panel/component to allow access to the rear side of the switch and compress the retaining clips to enable the switch to be withdrawn.
12 Once the switch is released and partially withdrawn from the panel, detach the wiring connector and remove the switch (photo).
13 Refitting is a reversal of removal.

Courtesy lamp switches

14 With the door open, undo the retaining screw and withdraw the switch from the door pillar. Pull out the wiring slightly and tie a piece of string to it to prevent it dropping down into the door pillar.
15 Disconnect the wiring from the switch.
16 Refitting is a reversal of removal.

Load space lamp switch

17 Open the tailgate, undo the two securing screws and remove the rear trim panel to gain access to the rear side of the switch.

12.19 Load space contact switch removal from the rear panel

12.22 Contact switch unit in the tailgate

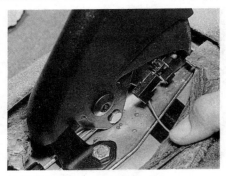

12.26 Handbrake warning switch

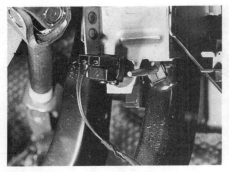

12.28 Brake stop light switch location

12.29 Brake stop light switch removal

12.35 Heater blower motor switch removal

12.38 Power-operated window control switch removal

12.41 Power-operated door mirror control switch

18   Release the switch side retaining clips using a thin-bladed screwdriver and push the switch from its location in the body.
19   Disconnect the wiring connectors and remove the switch (photo).
20   Refit in the reverse order of removal.

Rear wiper contact switch

21   Open the tailgate and remove the trim panel from it.
22   Working through the access aperture in the tailgate, use a thin-bladed screwdriver to depress the switch retaining clips and extract the switch from the panel (photo).
23   Disconnect the wiring connectors and remove the switch.
24   Refit in the reverse order of removal. On completion, check that the operation of the rear wipers, courtesy light, heated rear window and the tailgate release/central locking system.

Handbrake warning lamp switch

25   Refer to Chapter 11 for details and remove the front passenger (left-hand) seat and the centre console.

26   Detach the wiring connector from the handbrake warning switch, undo the two retaining screws and remove the switch (photo).
27   Refit in the reverse order of removal. Check that the switch operates in a satisfactory manner before refitting the seats.

Brake stop light switch

28   The brake stop light switch is attached to the brake pedal mounting bracket (photo).
29   Detach the wiring connector from the switch, then twist the switch through a quarter of a turn (90°) and withdraw it from the bracket (photo).
30   Refit in the reverse order of removal. Ensure that the neck of the switch is against the pedal before turning the switch 90° to secure it.
31   Check that the switch operates in a satisfactory manner to complete. The switch should not operate during the first 5 mm of pedal travel, but must operate within 20 mm of pedal travel. If necessary, adjustment can be made by removing the switch from the bracket and turning the adjuster nut as required.

Heater/blower motor switch

32   Pull free and remove the heater control knobs.
33   Unscrew and remove the two instrument bezel retaining screws and remove the bezel.
34   Undo the four retaining screws and remove the heater panel facia. Detach the wiring connector to the heater panel illumination bulb.
35   Compress the switch tabs to pull free the switch unit then detach the wiring multi-plug from the switch (photo).
36   Refit in the reverse order of removal.

Power-operated window switches

37   Insert a thin-bladed screwdriver between the switch and the console, then carefully prise free the switch from its location aperture. If the switch is reluctant to release, do not apply excessive force but remove the centre console (see Chapter 11 for details) and release the switch from the underside.
38   Detach the wire connector from the switch and remove it (photo).
39   Refit in the reverse order of removal then check the switch for satisfactory operation.

Power-operated door mirror switch

40   Carefully prise free the switch using a thin-bladed screwdriver as a lever, but insert a suitable protective pad between the screwdriver and the housing to avoid damage.
41   Detach the wiring multi-plug connector and remove the switch (photo).
42   Refit in the reverse order of removal, then adjust the mirror and check that the operation of the switch is satisfactory.

Power-operated roof switch (Cabriolet)

43   This switch is removed in the same manner as that described for the power-operated window switches in paragraphs 37 to 39 above.

Starter inhibitor switch (automatic transmission)

44   The starter inhibitor switch is located on the transmission housing and prevents starting of the engine with the selector lever in a drive position. Access to the switch is gained after raising and supporting the vehicle at the front end on axle stands.
45   Detach the switch multi-plug, then unscrew and remove the switch from the transmission, together with its O-ring. As the switch is removed, catch any fluid spillage in a suitable container and plug the switch aperture in the transmission to prevent any further loss.
46   Refitting is a reversal of the removal procedure. Use a new O-ring and tighten the switch securely. Ensure that the wiring connection is securely made. On completion, check that the engine only starts when the selector is in the N or P position.

13   Bulbs (exterior lamps) – renewal

Note: *Ensure that all exterior lights are switched off before disconnecting the wiring connectors to any exterior light bulbs. The headlamp and front sidelamp bulbs are removable from within the engine compartment with the bonnet raised.*

Headlamp

1   Pull free the wiring connector from the rear of the headlamp on the side concerned (photo).
2   Prise free the protector cap from the rear of the headlamp unit, then compress the retaining wire clips and pivot them out of the way (photos).
3   Withdraw the bulb from its location in the headlamp (photo). Take care not to touch the bulb glass with your fingers, but if accidentally touched, clean the bulb with methylated spirit.
4   Fit the new bulb using a reversal of the removal procedure, but make sure that the tabs on the bulb support are correctly located in the lens assembly. Check the headlamp for alignment as described in Section 16.
5   Holts Amber Lamp is useful for temporarily changing the headlamp colour to conform with the normal use when driving in France.

13.1 Detach the wiring connector ...

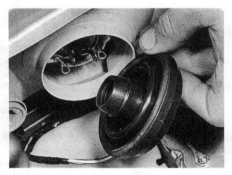

13.2A ... remove the rubber protector cap ...

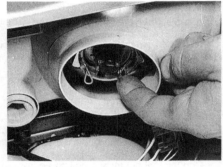

13.2B ... compress the clips ...

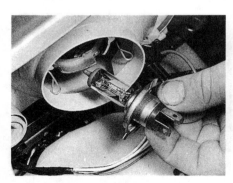

13.3 ... and withdraw the headlamp bulb

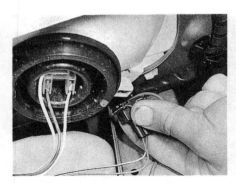

13.6 Detach the wiring connector ...

13.7 ... and withdraw the sidelamp bulbholder

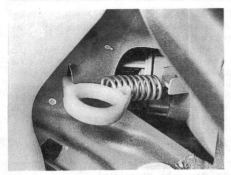

13.10 Front indicator unit retaining spring

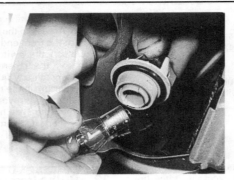

13.12 Front indicator bulb renewal

13.13 Engage the tags in their locating slots when refitting the front indicator unit

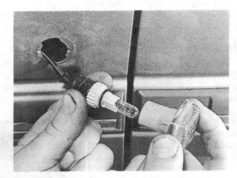

13.15 Side repeater lamp assembly

13.17 Rear lamp cluster removal (Saloon)

Front sidelamp

6   Compress the wire retaining clip and detach the wiring connector from the side lamp (photo).
7   Pull free the sidelamp bulbholder from its location in the rear of the headlamp (photo).
8   Remove the bulb from the bulbholder.
9   Fit the new bulb using a reversal of the removal procedure. Check for satisfactory operation on completion.

Front direction indicator

10   Unhook the retaining spring from the rear of the direction indicator unit and move the direction indicator unit forwards in order to release it (photo).
11   Grip the bulbholder and pull it free from the indicator unit (do not pull on the wire).
12   Depress and twist the bulb to remove it from the bulbholder (photo).
13   Fit the new bulb using a reversal of the removal procedure. As the

lamp unit is fitted into position, engage its tags in the slots of the headlamp unit (photo). Check for satisfactory operation on completion.

Front direction indicator side-repeater

14   Carefully prise the lamp from the front wing, taking care not to damage the paintwork.
15   Pull out the bulbholder and wiring, then remove the bulb (photo).
16   Fit the new bulb using a reversal of the removal procedure and check for satisfactory operation.

Rear lamp cluster

Saloon

17   Working in the rear load space, press the lock tabs (recessed in the rear face of the rear lamp unit on the side concerned) in towards the centre and pull free the lamp unit (photo).
18   Depress and twist the bulb concerned to remove it from the holder (photo).
19   Fit the new bulb using a reversal of the removal procedure.

13.18 Bulb removal from a Saloon rear lamp cluster

13.20 Rear lamp cluster removal (Estate)

13.26 Number plate lamp removal from the bumper (Estate)

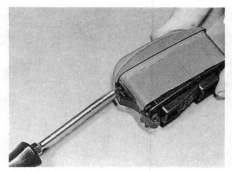

13.28A Prise open the clip ...

13.28B ... and separate the number plate lamp unit and bulbholder

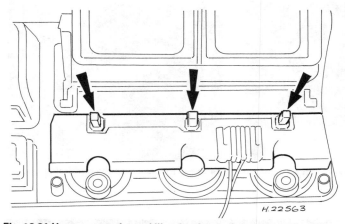

Fig. 12.21 Heater control panel illumination bulb locations (Sec 14)

Relocate the holder unit by sliding the outer end into position first, then press the inner end into position so that it clicks into place. Check that the operation of the rear lights on completion.

Estate

20   Prise back the rear trim cover on the side concerned to gain access to the light unit from within the load space. Press the lock tab down, lift the holder unit a fraction and withdraw it (photo).
21   Depress and twist free the bulb concerned from the holder.
22   Fit the new bulb using a reversal of the removal procedure. Relocate the holder unit by sliding the lower end into position first, then press the upper end into position so that it clicks into place. Check that the operation of the rear lights on completion.

Van

23   Working from within the rear of the vehicle on the side concerned, turn the appropriate bulbholder in an anti-clockwise direction and withdraw the holder.
24   Depress and untwist the bulb to release it from its holder.
25   Fit the new bulb using a reversal of the removal procedure. Check the rear lights for satisfactory operation on completion.

Number plate lamps

26   Prise the number plate lamp from the rear bumper using a small screwdriver (photo).
27   Disconnect the wiring plug and earth lead from the lamp.
28   On Saloon and Estate models, prise open the plastic retaining clip to withdraw the bulbholder from the lamp unit, then depress and untwist the bulb to remove it from the holder (photos).
29   To remove the bulb on the Van, twist the bulbholder anti-clockwise and withdraw it, then pull free the bulb.
30   Fit the new bulb using a reversal of the removal procedure. Check the operation of the lamps on completion.

14   Bulbs (interior lamps) – renewal

Courtesy lamps

1   Prise out the lamp using a small flat-bladed screwdriver (photo).
2   Release the festoon type bulb from the spring contacts.
3   Fit the new bulb using a reversal of the removal procedure, but check the tension of the spring contacts and if necessary bend them so that they firmly contact the bulb end caps.

Load space compartment lamp

4   Prise free and withdraw the lamp unit (photo).
5   Pull free the bulb from its holder and remove it.
6   Renew the new bulb and refit the lamp unit using a reversal of the removal procedure.

Instrument panel

7   Remove the instrument panel as described in Section 17.
8   Turn the bulbholder a quarter turn to align the shoulders with the slots, then remove it and pull the capless bulb from the bulbholder (photo).
9   Fit the new bulb in reverse order.

Heater control panel

10   Undo the two retaining screws from its upper edge and withdraw the instrument panel surround.
11   Pull free the heater control knobs, undo the heater control panel retaining screws and then withdraw the panel from the facia just enough to allow access to the bulbs on its rear face.
12   Twist the bulbs anti-clockwise to remove them.
13   Refit in the reverse order of removal and check for satisfactory operation on completion.

Automatic transmission selector illumination

14   Prise out the lever quadrant cover (taking care not to scratch the console), then pull the bulbholder from under the selector lever position indicator, untwist and remove the bulb from the holder.
15   Fit the new bulb in the reverse order of removal.

Glovebox lamp

16   Open the glovebox, then undo the two retaining screws and withdraw the lamp/switch unit.
17   Prise free the switch/bulbholder, then untwist and remove the bulb from the holder (photo).
18   Fit the new bulb using a reversal of the removal procedure.

Hazard warning

19   Pull free the cover from the switch, then pull free the bulb from the switch/holder.
20   Refit in the reverse order of removal and check for satisfactory operation.

Clock

21   Engage the hooked ends of a pair of circlip pliers in the two holes in

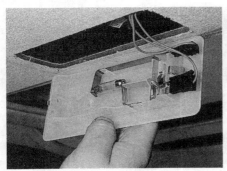

14.1 Roof-mounted courtesy lamp removal

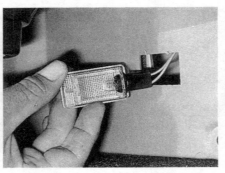

14.4 Luggage area light removed for bulb replacement

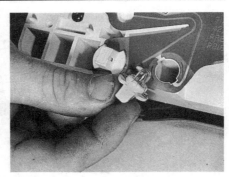

14.8 Bulbholder removal from the instrument panel

14.17 Glovebox lamp switch/bulbholder removal

14.21A Pull free the clock from the facia ...

14.21B ... for access to the bulbholder

the underside of the clock bezel as shown and carefully pull free the clock unit from its aperture in the facia. The bulbholder can then be untwisted and withdrawn from the rear face of the clock and the bulb renewed (photos).

22   Refit in the reverse order of removal.

Cigar lighter

23   Remove the lighter unit (Section 19), then withdraw the illumination ring from the facia. Remove the bulb from the illumination ring.

24   Refit in the reverse order of removal. Check for satisfactory operation on completion.

15   Exterior lamp units – removal and refitting

1   Detach the battery earth lead before disconnecting and removing any of the exterior lamp units.

Headlamp unit

2   Open and support the bonnet, then undo the four retaining screws along the top edge of the grille panel and lift it clear.

3   Remove the front indicator unit as described later in this Section.

4   Detach the wiring connections from the headlamp and side lamp in the rear of the appropriate headlamp unit.

5   Working through the cut-out of the direction indicator, unscrew the headlamp lower retaining screw, then undo the two upper securing screws from the points indicated (photo). Withdraw the headlamp unit forwards from the vehicle.

6   If the headlamp unit is to be renewed, remove the headlamp and side lamp bulbs/holders from the rear of the unit and transfer them to the replacement unit as described in Section 13. The individual parts of the headlamp unit are not otherwise renewable.

7   Refitting is a reversal of the removal procedure. When fitting the headlamp into position, ensure that the location pin sits in its recess and note the arrangement of the insulating washers on the retaining screws

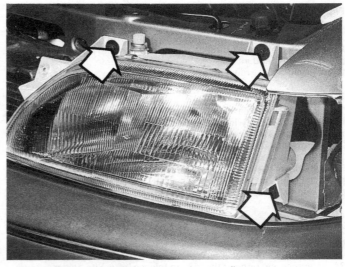

15.5 Headlamp unit retaining screws (arrowed)

(photos). Loosely locate the headlamp and temporarily fit the indicator unit to check that the gap between the headlamp and the indicator is even. Fully tighten the upper retaining screws, then remove the indicator unit to tighten the lower headlamp screw.

8   When the headlamp and indicator units are fitted and their wiring connectors attached, check the lights for satisfactory operation before fitting the front grille panel.

9   Finally adjust the headlamp aim as described in Section 16.

Front direction indicator

10   Unhook the retaining spring from the rear of the direction indicator unit (see photo 13.10).

15.7A Headlamp engagement pin

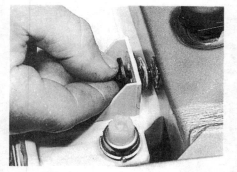
15.7B Headlamp retaining screw showing washer arrangement

15.19 Rear lamp lens showing the retaining nuts

11   Move the direction indicator unit forwards in order to release it.
12   Turn the bulbholder and release it from the rear of the direction indicator unit.
13   Remove the direction indicator unit from the vehicle.
14   Refitting is a reversal of removal. Check that the operation of the indicator is satisfactory on completion.

Direction indicator side-repeater

15   Raise and support the bonnet. Detach the indicator wiring multi-plug at the bulkhead and attach a suitable length of cord to the connector end of the wire going to the side indicator unit. This will act as a guide to feed the wire back through the body channels when refitting the lamp unit.
16   Rotate the lamp unit in a clockwise direction to release it from the body panel and withdraw it from the vehicle. When the wiring connector and cord are drawn through, they can be separated and the cord left in position.
17   Refitting is a reversal of removal. Attach the wire to the cord and draw it through the body panels, then disconnect the cord and reconnect the lamp multi-plug at the bulkhead. When the lamp is refitted, check for satisfactory operation.

Rear lamp cluster

18   Working in the rear luggage compartment, Release the rear bulbholder unit (according to type) from the side concerned as described in Section 13.
19   Unscrew the mounting nuts and withdraw the rear lamp lens from the rear of the vehicle (photo).
20   Renew the seal gasket if it is in poor condition. Refit in the reverse order to removal and check for satisfactory operation of the rear lamps on completion.

Number plate lamps

21   Prise the number plate lamp from the rear bumper using a small screwdriver, then disconnect the wiring plug (see photo 13.26).
22   Refitting is a reversal of removal.

16   Headlamp alignment – checking and adjustment

1   Accurate adjustment of the headlamp beam is only possible using optical beam setting equipment and this work should therefore be carried out by a Ford dealer or service station with the necessary facilities.
2   Temporary adjustment can be made when the headlamp unit has been removed and refitted, or to compensate for normal adjustment whenever a heavy load is being carried. Turn the adjustment screws on the top and rear of the headlamp unit to make adjustment (see Fig. 12.22 for details).
3   Before making any adjustments to the headlamp settings, it is important that the tyre pressures are correct and that the vehicle is standing on level ground. Bounce the front of the vehicle a few times to

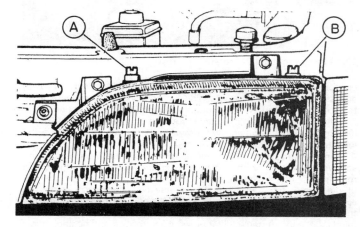
Fig. 12.22 Horizontal (A) and vertical (B) headlamp beam adjuster screws (Sec 16)

settle the suspension. Ideally somebody of normal size should sit in the driver's seat during the adjustment and the vehicle should have a full tank of fuel. Where a vehicle is fitted with an electrical headlamp levelling system, set the switch to the 'O' position before making any adjustments.
4   Whenever temporary adjustments are made, the settings must be reset as soon as possible once the vehicle is in normal use.

17   Instrument cluster – removal and refitting

Removal

1   Disconnect the battery negative terminal lead.
2   Although not strictly necessary, in order to withdraw the instrument

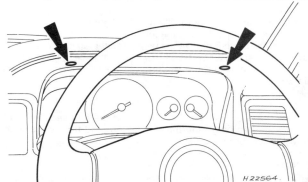
Fig. 12.23 Instrument cluster bezel retaining screw positions (Sec 17)

17.4A Instrument cluster retaining screws

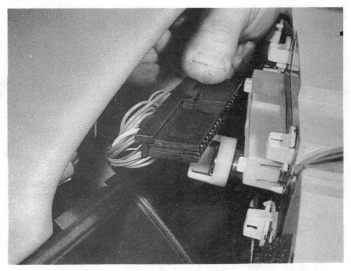

17.4B Detach the wiring multi-plugs from the instrument panel

cluster, the removal of the steering wheel will provide much improved access, particularly when detaching (and subsequently reconnecting) the speedometer and wiring multi-plugs from the rear of the unit.

3   Undo the two retaining screws from the underside top edge of the instrument panel bezel and withdraw the bezel, releasing it from the location clips each side and underneath.

4   Unscrew and remove the four instrument cluster-to-panel retaining screws and carefully withdraw the cluster to the point where the wiring multi-plugs and the speedometer cable can be detached from the rear of the cluster (photos). Note that it may be necessary to push the speedometer cable through from the engine compartment side to allow the instrument cluster to be sufficiently withdrawn. Take care when handling the instrument cluster whilst it is removed and position it in a safe place where it will not get knocked or damaged. If a tachometer is fitted, do not position the cluster unit on its face for extended periods as the silicone fluid in the tachometer may well be released.

Refitting

5   Refitting is a reversal of removal. On completion check the function of all electrical components.

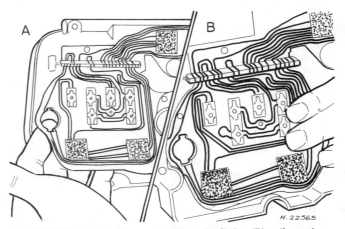

Fig. 12.24 Printed circuit removal (A) and refitting (B) to/from the rear face of the instrument panel (Sec 18)

18   Instrument cluster components – removal and refitting

Removal

1   Remove the instrument cluster as described in Section 17. As mentioned, take particular care when handling the cluster.

Printed circuit

2   Untwist and remove all of the illumination light bulbs/holders from the rear of the instrument cluster unit (photo).

3   Carefully release and remove the wiring multi-plug connector from the rear face of the cluster unit. Pull free the printed circuit releasing it from the securing pins and the air-cored gauge terminals on the rear face of the cluster.

Speedometer

4   Remove the odometer reset knob, release the four securing clips and remove the two bulbs and the cluster surround from the cluster. Withdraw the speedometer unit.

Tachometer

5   Remove the odometer reset knob, release the securing clips, remove the two bulbs and the cluster surround from the cluster.

6   Applying great care, detach the printed circuit from the air-cored gauge terminals and remove the tachometer unit from the cluster.

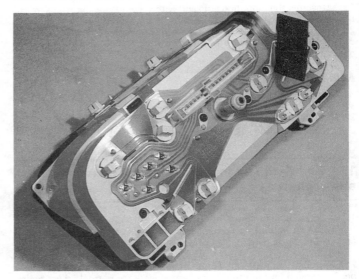

18.2 Rear face of the instrument panel

Fuel/temperature gauge

7   Remove the odometer reset knob, release the securing clips, remove the two bulbs and the cluster surround from the cluster.

8   Applying great care, detach the printed circuit from the air-cored

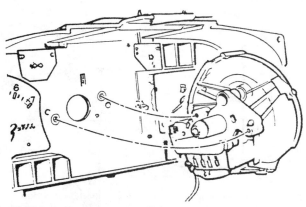

Fig. 12.25 Speedometer removal from the instrument cluster (Sec 18)

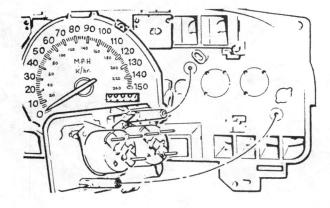

Fig. 12.26 Air-cored fuel/temperature gauge removal from the instrument cluster (Sec 18)

gauge terminals, undo the two retaining screws and remove the fuel/temperature gauge from the cluster unit.

Refitting

9   Refitting is a reversal of removal. When refitting the printed circuit, ensure that it is gently pushed back into contact with the securing pins and gauge terminals.

19 Cigar lighter – removal and refitting

Removal

1   Disconnect the battery negative terminal lead.
2   Pull out the ashtray and reaching through its aperture in the facia, disconnect the wiring from the cigar lighter.
3   Push the cigar lighter out of its location and disconnect the wiring.
4   Extract the lighter element, then reaching through with a thin-bladed screwdriver, unclip and release the lighter body from the illumination ring.
5   If required, the lighter illumination ring can be pulled free and withdrawn from the facia.

Refitting

6   Refitting is a reversal of removal.

20 Clock – removal and refitting

Removal

1   Disconnect the battery negative terminal lead.
2   Proceed as described in Section 14, paragraph 21 and carefully prise the clock from the facia. Disconnect the wiring plug from the rear face of the clock.

Refitting

3   Refitting is a reversal of removal. Reset the clock on completion.

21 Horn – removal and refitting

Removal

1   The horn(s) are located on the body front valance behind the front bumper (photo). To remove a horn, first apply the handbrake then jack up the front of the vehicle and support it on axle stands.
2   Disconnect the battery negative terminal lead then reach up and disconnect the horn supply lead.
3   Unscrew the nut securing the horn to the mounting bracket and remove the horn from the vehicle.

Refitting

4   Refitting is a reversal of removal.

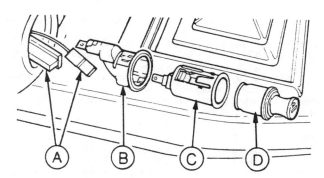

Fig. 12.27 Cigar lighter components (Sec 19)

A	Wiring connectors	C	Lighter body
B	Illuminator ring	D	Element

21.1 Horn location

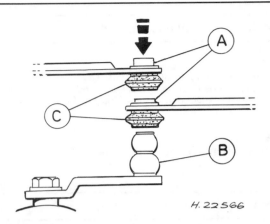

Fig. 12.28 Windscreen wiper linkage to motor balljoint connection (Sec 22)

A   Pivot bush   C   Rubber seal
B   Wiper motor arm

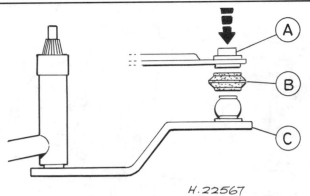

Fig. 12.29 Windscreen wiper linkage to pivot shaft connection (Sec 22)

A   Pivot bush   C   Pivot shaft
B   Rubber seal

22 Windscreen wiper motor and linkage – removal and refitting

Removal

Wiper motor

1   Operate the wiper motor then switch it off so that it returns to its rest position.
2   Disconnect the battery negative terminal lead.
3   Unscrew and remove the link arm to motor spindle retaining nut (photo). Disengage the arm from the spindle.
4   Undo the three wiper motor retaining bolts, then move the wiper motor sideways from its mounting bracket.
5   Detach the wiper motor wiring multi-plug, withdraw the wiper motor and remove its insulating cover.

Linkage

6   Remove the windscreen wiper arms (and blades) from the pivots as described in Chapter 1.
7   Disconnect the battery earth lead. Move the wiper linkage to the required position for access to the linkage balljoints, then carefully prise free the linkages from their ball pins using a suitable open-ended spanner as a lever.
8   Remove the rubber seal from the pivot bushes. Where the surfaces of the ball pins are damaged, the pivot shaft and/or motor must be renewed. The rubber seals which are located over the edge of the pivot bushes must be renewed during refitting.

Refitting

9   Refitting is a reversal of removal. Lubricate the pivot bushes and the rubber seals during reassembly. When reconnecting the link arm on the motor spindle, ensure that the arm lug engages in the slot in the taper of the motor spindle. Check for satisfactory operation on completion.

23 Windscreen wiper pivot shaft – removal and refitting

Removal

1   Operate the wiper motor then switch it off so that it returns to its rest position.
2   Disconnect the battery negative terminal lead.
3   Remove the windscreen wiper arms as described in Chapter 1.
4   Detach and remove the cowl grille. This is secured by six plastic screws and two cross-head screws (see Fig. 12.30 for location).
5   Referring to Fig. 12.31, unscrew and remove the four wiper motor

22.3 Windscreen wiper motor showing link arm-to-spindle connection (A) and two of the wiper motor-to-mounting retaining bolts (B)

bracket retaining bolts from the positions indicated, then remove the wiper motor bracket assembly. Disconnect the wiring multi-plug as the motor bracket assembly is withdrawn.
6   Prise free the wiper linkage from the pivot shaft using a suitable open-ended spanner.
7   Pull free the pivot shaft cap from the housing, release the circlip,

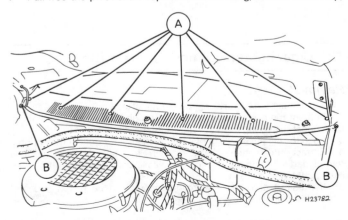

Fig. 12.30 Remove the plastic screws (A) and the cross-head screws (B) to remove the cowl grille (Sec 23)

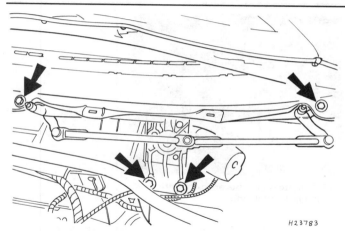

H23783

Fig. 12.31 Wiper motor bracket retaining bolt locations (Sec 23)

withdraw the two special washers and remove the pivot shaft. The special washer and spring washer can then be removed from the shaft.

Refitting

8   Refitting is a reversal of removal. Lubricate the pivot shaft, bushes and rubber seals during reassembly. When reconnecting the link arm on the motor spindle, ensure that the arm lug engages in the slot in the taper of the motor spindle. When the wiper arms are refitted, check that they are set in the correct position as shown in Fig. 12.33. Check for satisfactory operation on completion.

24 Tailgate wiper motor and linkage – removal and refitting

Removal

1   Operate the wiper then switch it off so that it returns to its rest position. Note that the wiper motor will only operate with the tailgate shut as the spring tensioned connector pins must be in contact with the contact plates.
2   Disconnect the battery negative terminal lead.
3   Remove the wiper arm with reference to Chapter 1.
4   Unscrew the nut from the spindle housing protruding through the tailgate.
5   Undo the eight plastic screws and remove the trim panel from inside the tailgate.
6   Disconnect the earth lead and the in-line wiring connector to the wiper motor (photo).
7   Unbolt and remove the wiper assembly from inside the tailgate (photos).
8   If necessary, the wiper motor can be detached from its mounting

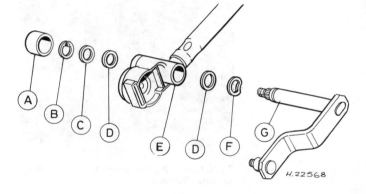

H.22568

Fig. 12.32 Wiper pivot shaft components (Sec 23)

A	Cap	E	Bush
B	Circlip	F	Wave washer
C	Special washer (1.8 mm)	G	Pivot shaft
D	Special washer (0.15 mm)		

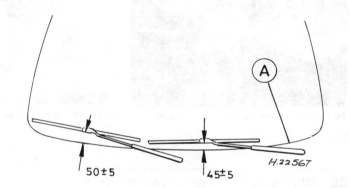

H.22567

Fig. 12.33 Parked distance (mm) of windscreen wiper arms/blade from the edge of the cowl grille (A) (Sec 23)

bracket by unscrewing the three retaining bolts (photo). As they are detached, note the location of the washers and insulators.

Refitting

9   Refitting is a reversal of removal. When the wiper arm is refitted, its park position should be set correctly. On Saloon models, the distance from the point where the arm meets the centre of the wiper blade should be 90 ± 5 mm from the bottom of the rear window. On Estate models, this distance should be 75 ± 5 mm.

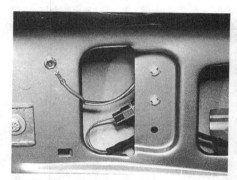

24.6 Tailgate wiper earth lead and in-line connector

24.7A Tailgate wiper motor and mounting bolts (arrowed) – Saloon

24.7B Tailgate wiper motor and mounting bolts (arrowed) – Estate

24.7C Removing the wiper motor from the tailgate (Saloon)

24.8 Tailgate wiper motor-to-mounting bracket bolts (Saloon)

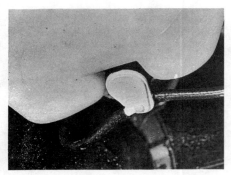

25.1 Washer pump and hose connections

25.2 Washer reservoir and retaining bolt

25.9 Remove trim for access to the tailgate washer nozzle

25   Windscreen/tailgate washer system components – removal and refitting

Removal

Washer pump

1   To remove the pump unit from the reservoir, first syphon out any remaining fluid from the reservoir, then detach the washer hoses and the wiring multi-plug to the washer pump. The pump can now be pulled (or if required), levered free from the reservoir (photo).

Reservoir and pump

2   To remove the washer reservoir and pump, first unscrew and remove the reservoir retaining bolt in the engine compartment (photo).
3   Refer to Chapter 11 for details and remove the wheel arch liner trim on the left-hand side.
4   Detach the pump multi-plug and the pump hoses and disconnect them from the reservoir. Drain any fluid remaining in the reservoir/pump into a suitable container.
5   Unscrew and remove the two reservoir retaining bolts from under the wheel arch then remove the reservoir and pump unit from the vehicle.
6   If required, pull or prise free the pump to remove it from the reservoir.

Hoses

7   The hose system to the windscreen washers is sectional with nylon connector pieces where required. This means that any section of hose can be renewed individually when required. Access to the hoses in the engine compartment is good, but it will be necessary to detach and remove the insulation panel from the underside of the bonnet to allow access to the hoses and connections to the washer nozzles.
8   The front washer reservoir also supplies the rear tailgate washer by means of a tube running along the left-hand side within the body apertures as shown.

Nozzles

9   These are secured to the body panels by retaining tabs which are an integral part of the washer nozzle stem. To remove a washer nozzle, first detach and remove the insulation from the underside of the bonnet, or the appropriate trim piece (according to type) for the tailgate washer (photo).
10   Using suitable needle-nosed pliers, squeeze together the nozzle retaining tabs, twist the nozzle a quarter of a turn and withdraw it from its aperture in the body (photo). Once withdrawn, the hose can be detached and the nozzle removed. Do not allow the hose to be retracted into the body whilst the nozzle is detached.

25.10 Washer nozzle removal

26.2 Radio/cassette removal

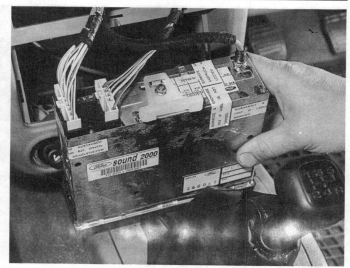

26.3 Wiring and aerial lead connections on the rear face of the radio/cassette

Refitting

11   Refitting is a reversal of removal. Always renew the pump to reservoir seal washer and ensure that all connections are securely made. When reconnecting the pump hoses, ensure that the hose marked with white tape is connected to the corresponding white connection on the pump.

12   On completion, top up the washer reservoir using a suitable washer additive, such as Turtle Wax High Tech Screen Wash, and check that the operation of the washers is satisfactory. If necessary, adjust the washer jets by inserting a pin into the centre of the jet and directing the flow at the top part of the windscreen/rear window.

26   Radio/cassette player – removal and refitting

Removal

1   Disconnect the battery earth lead. If the radio has a security code, make sure this is known before disconnecting the battery.

2   In order to release the radio retaining clips, two U-shaped rods must be inserted into the special holes on each side of the radio (photo). If possible, it is preferable to obtain purpose made rods from an audio specialist as these have cut-outs which snap firmly into the clips so that the radio can be pulled out. Pull the unit squarely from its aperture or it may jam. If the unit proves difficult to withdraw, remove the cassette tray (or where applicable, the CD player) from beneath the unit, then reach through the aperture and ease it out from behind.

3   With the radio/cassette sufficiently withdrawn, disconnect the feed, earth, aerial and speaker leads. Where applicable, also detach and remove the plastic support bracket from the rear of the unit (photo).

Refitting

4   Refitting is a reversal of removal. When the leads are reconnected to the rear of the unit press it into position to the point where the retaining clips are felt to engage. Reactivate the unit in accordance with the code and the instructions given in the Ford Audio Operating Manual supplied with the vehicle.

27   Compact disc player – removal and refitting

The removal and refitting procedures for this unit (where fitted) are similar to those described for the radio/cassette player in the previous Section, but do not remove the bezel securing screws above the CD player.

28   Speakers – removal and refitting

Removal

Door-mounted speaker

1   Remove the trim panel from the door concerned as described in Chapter 11, then undo the speaker retaining screws, withdraw the speaker unit from the door and disconnect the wiring (photos). Note that the speaker unit must not be detached from the moulding.

Rear quarter panel-mounted speaker
(Cabriolet)

2   Lower the hood. On manually-operated types, lock it in the lowered position then pull free the roof release lever knob.

3   Remove the quarter window regulator or lift switches (according to type) and remove the rear quarter trim panel as described in Chapter 11. Undo the three retaining screws and withdraw the speaker unit. Disconnect the wiring from the speaker unit. Note that the speaker unit must not be detached from the moulding.

Rear parcel shelf-mounted speaker
(Orion)

4   Detach the wiring connector from the speaker unit, then loosen off

28.1 Door-mounted speaker removal

28.5 Rear parcel shelf-mounted speaker (Escort Saloon)

28.7A Load space-mounted speaker unit (Estate)

28.7B Detach the wiring from the speaker

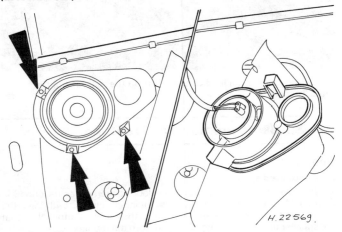

Fig. 12.34 Rear quarter panel speaker retaining screws and wiring connector on the Cabriolet model (Sec 28)

(but do not remove), the speaker retaining bolt sufficiently to allow the speaker unit to be withdrawn, leaving the bracket and bolt in position in the speaker recess.

Rear parcel tray-mounted speaker (Escort Saloon)

5   Unscrew the three retaining screws, lower the speaker unit from the parcel tray, then detach the wiring connections (photo). Note that the speaker unit and its moulding must not be separated.

Load space trim-mounting speaker (Estate)

6   Remove the appropriate luggage area side trim panel as described in Chapter 11 for access to the speaker unit.
7   Unscrew the three retaining screws, withdraw the speaker unit and detach the wiring connections (photos). Note that the speaker unit and its moulding must not be separated.

Refitting

8   Refitting is a reversal of removal.

29   Radio aerial – removal and refitting

Removal

Manual type (Saloon and Estate)

1   Remove the trim cover from the access aperture in the headlining beneath the aerial by carefully prising it free.
2   Working through the aperture in the headlining, undo the single retaining screw, withdraw the aerial and detach the cable base from the roof (photo).

Manual type (Cabriolet)

3   Open the boot lid, disconnect its support strut from the left-hand side panel then undo the two retaining screws and remove the luggage area side trim panel.

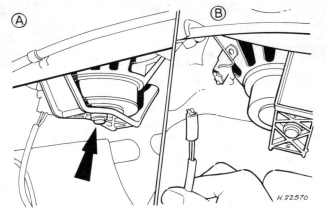

Fig. 12.35 Remove the retaining bolt (A) and detach the wiring connector (B) to remove the rear parcel shelf-mounted speaker unit on the Orion (Sec 28)

4   Unscrew and remove the aerial mast, then unscrew and remove the collar retaining nut to remove the spacer and upper seal washer.
5   Working within the luggage area side of the quarter panel, unscrew the lead and remove the aerial unit.

Electric aerial (Cabriolet)

6   Open the boot lid, disconnect its support strut from the left-hand side panel then undo the two retaining screws and remove the luggage area side trim panel.
7   Unscrew the aerial upper retaining nut, then remove the bezel and the seal washer.

29.2 Roof-mounted aerial retaining screw

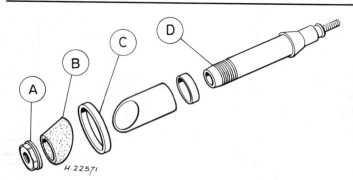

Fig. 12.36 Manual aerial components on the Cabriolet (Sec 29)

A Top collar nut
B Spacer
C Seal washer
D Lower aerial unit

8 Working from the luggage area side, unscrew and remove the self-tapping screw securing the aerial bottom bracket to the apron.
9 Unscrew the knurled type nut to detach the aerial from the base of the unit, then detach the wiring and aerial lead at their connections and withdraw the aerial unit from the vehicle.

Refitting

10 Refitting is a reversal of removal. Ensure that the contact surfaces of both the body panel and the aerial are clean before fitting the aerial into position.

30 Power amplifier – removal and refitting

Removal

1 This unit is fitted to models equipped with the Premium Sound System and is located in the area between the glovebox and the bulkhead.
2 To remove the amplifier unit, undo the retaining screw, lower the unit complete with its support bracket and detach the wiring multi-plug connectors. If required, the bracket and the amplifier unit can be separated by unscrewing the four Torx screws.

Refitting

3 Refit in the reverse order of removal.

31 Central locking system control unit – removal and refitting

Removal

1 Disconnect the battery earth lead.
2 Remove the side trim from the driver's side footwell as described in Chapter 11.
3 Withdraw the central locking control unit from its location bracket and detach the multi-plug wiring connections from it (photo).

Refitting

4 Refit in the reverse order of removal. Check the operation of the system to complete.

32 Anti-theft alarm system – general information

General

1 This system provides an added form of vehicle anti-theft security. When the system is activated, the alarm will sound if the vehicle is broken into through any one of the doors, the bonnet, boot (or tailgate). The alarm will also be triggered if the ignition system is turned on or the radio/cassette disconnected whilst the system is activated.
2 This system is activated/de-activated whenever one of the front

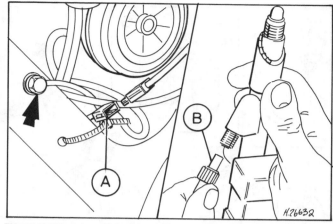

Fig. 12.37 Electric aerial wiring (A) and aerial (B) connections (Sec 29)

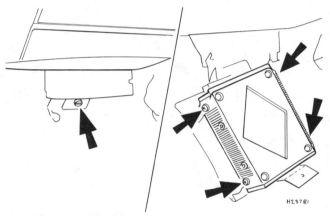

Fig. 12.38 Power amplifier securing bolts (Sec 30)

31.3 Central locking system control unit location

doors is locked/unlocked by the key. The system operates on all doors, the bonnet and boot lid (or tailgate) whenever the central locking system is activated or in the case of manual locking, when each door is individually locked. It is important to note that opening the bootlid/tailgate first when the system is activated will trigger the alarm. In addition to the alarm being sounded, the ignition/starting system is also immobilized when the system is activated.
3 A further security feature included is that even though the battery may be disconnected whilst the system is activated, the alarm

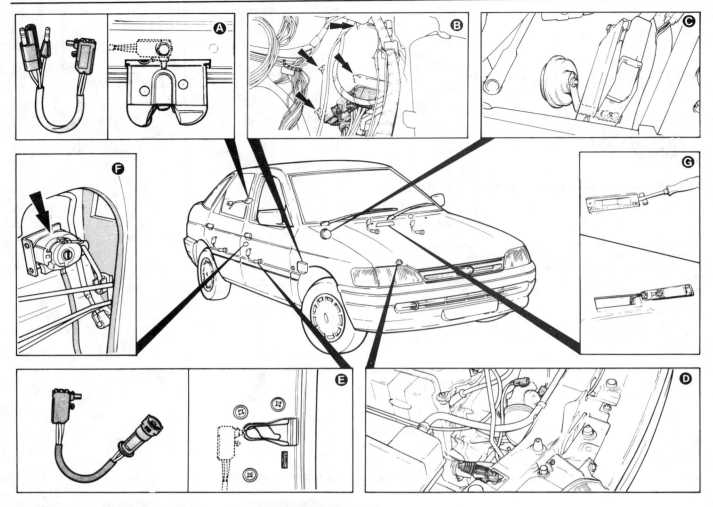

Fig. 12.39 Anti-theft alarm system components and their locations (Sec 32)

A   Trip switch (luggage   C   Alarm horn   E   Alarm switch (doors)   G   Clock
     compartment)   D   Alarm switch (bonnet) F   Activation switches
B   System module

activation continues as soon as the battery is reconnected. Because of this feature, it is important to ensure that the system is de-activated before disconnecting the battery at any time, such as when working on the vehicle.

4   The system incorporates a diagnostic mode to enable Ford mechanics to quickly identify any faults in the system.

System activation and check

5   Fully insert the door lock key into the lock of the front door (driver's or passenger side), turn the key as far as possible and hold in this position for one second. With the doors, bonnet and boot lid/tailgate all closed, a twenty second activation delay starts from this point, although access to the luggage area is still possible within the activation period without triggering off the alarm. When the bootlid/tailgate is closed, the activation period of twenty seconds restarts.

6   The initial activating period is confirmed by the control light in the clock flashing on and off in a fast sequence, then when the activation period is completed, the control light flashes are reduced to a slow (low frequency) sequence.

7   De-activation of the alarm system can only be made by unlocking either of the front doors with the key. This also applies when the alarm has been triggered. If the bootlid/tailgate is opened before one of the front doors is unlocked, the alarm will be tripped and can only be stopped by unlocking one of the front doors.

8   Any malfunctions in the system will be indicated by the action of the

control light as soon as the ignition is switched on. When the system is in good operational order, the control light will illuminate for a period of five seconds, but where a system fault exists, the light will illuminate for a period of twenty seconds.

9   As well as the above mentioned features, models fitted with central locking incorporate a double locking system, whereby the inner door handles are also locked. This system is activated by turning the door key fully to the rear (unlocked) position, then to the front (locked) position within a period of four seconds. A sound buzzer indicates that the vehicle is double locked. When this system is in operation, it can only be de-activated using the door key to unlock one of the front doors. In the event of the battery going flat or an electrical fault in the system developing whilst the system is activated, the doors can still be unlocked in the normal manner using the key.

10   The bootlid/tailgate remote release fitted to the centre console is only active when the ignition is switched off and double locking is not engaged.

11   Any malfunctions in this system are indicated by the control light in the clock in the same manner as that described for the conventional anti-theft alarm system (paragraph 8).

12   In the event of a fault in the system being indicated, first check that all doors, the bonnet and the bootlid/tailgate are fully closed. If the system switches are checked, ensure that their wiring connections are good and secure, also that the switch plungers are clean and are able to move freely.

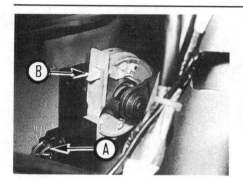

33.3 Door lock switch wiring connector (A) and retaining catch (B) – anti-theft alarm system

33.12 Bonnet alarm switch removal (anti-theft alarm system)

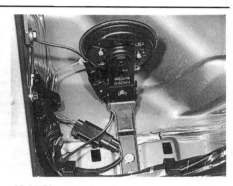

33.15 Alarm system horn

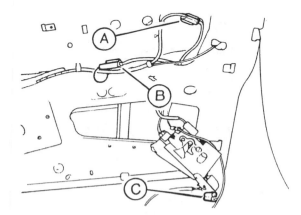

Fig. 12.40 Door locking and anti-theft alarm system wiring connections (Sec 33)

A   *Central locking multi-plug*
B   *Door lock ajar switch multi-plug*

C   *Alarm switch multi-plug*

33 Anti-theft alarm system components – removal and refitting

Removal

1   Before disconnecting any components of the anti-theft alarm system, first check that the system is de-activated, then disconnect the battery earth lead.

Door lock switch

2   Remove the trim panel and the insulation sheet from the door as described in Chapter 11.
3   Detach the wiring multi-plug connector from the alarm switch in the door (photo).
4   Release the snap lock catch, withdraw the switch from the door lock cylinder and remove it from the door.

Door lock ajar switch

5   Remove the trim panel and the insulation sheet from the door as described in Chapter 11.
6   Detach the wiring multi-plug from the door lock ajar switch.
7   Remove the door lock unit as described in Chapter 11.
8   Release the retaining clip and detach the door ajar switch from the door lock. It is probable that the retaining clip will break when releasing the switch in which case it will need to be renewed.

Bootlid/tailgate ajar switch

9   Undo the seven retaining screws and remove the trim panel from the bootlid or tailgate (as applicable).
10   Detach the wiring loom multi-plug, then referring to Chapter 11 for details, remove the lock unit from the bootlid/tailgate.
11   Release the retaining clip and detach the ajar switch from the lock unit. It is probable that the retaining clip will break when releasing the switch in which case it will need to be renewed.

Bonnet alarm switch

12   Grip the switch flange and pull the switch unit up and clear of its aperture in the front cross-panel (photo).
13   Disconnect the wiring connector and remove the switch.

Alarm horn

14   Where the vehicle is fitted with ABS, detach and remove the ABS module as described in Chapter 9.
15   Detach the wiring from the horn, undo the horn bracket retaining bolts and remove the horn together with its retaining bracket (photo).

Alarm system module

16   Detach and remove the cowl side trim panel (see Fig. 12.40 for location).
17   Detach the wiring multi-plug from the module, then release the module from the four retaining clips and remove it.

Refitting

18   The refitting of the respective components is a reversal of the removal procedure. Ensure that all component retaining clips are secure, the wiring looms are correctly routed and that the wiring connections are secure. Check for satisfactory operation of the system to complete.

NOTES:

1. All diagrams are divided into numbered circuits depending on function e.g. Diagram 2b : Interior lighting all models.
2. Items are arranged in relation to a plan view of the vehicle.
3. Items may appear on more than one diagram so are found using a grid reference e.g. 2/A1 denotes an item on diagram 2 grid location A1.
4. Complex items appear on the diagrams as blocks and are expanded on the internal connections page.
5. Feed wires are coloured red (black when switched) and all earth wires are coloured brown.
6. Brackets show how the circuit may be connected in more than one way.
7. Not all items are fitted to all models.

WIRE COLOURS

B	Blue
Bk	Black
Bn	Brown
Gn	Green
R	Red
Rs	Pink
S	Grey
V	Violet
W	White
Y	Yellow

FUSE	RATING	CIRCUIT
1	30A	Heated Rear Window And Electric Mirrors
2	30A	Anti-lock Braking System
3	10A	Lambda Sensor
4	15A	Main Beam RH
5	20A	Fuel Pump
6	10A	Side Lamp LH, Instrument Illumination
7	10A	Side Lamp RH
8	10A	Foglamp Rear
9	10A	Cooling Fan
10	30A	Dip Beam LH
11	15A	Foglamp Front
12	10A	Direction Indicator, Reversing Lamps
13	20A	Wiper Motor, Washer Pump
14	20A	Heater Blower
15	30A	Anti-lock Braking System
16	3A	Windscreen De-ice
17	3A	Windscreen De-ice Relay
18	15A	Main Beam LH
19	20A	Central Door Locking/Anti-thieft Alarm
20	15A	Horn, Hazard Flashers
21	15A	Interior Lamps, Cigar Lighter, Radio, Clock
22	30A	Electric Windows
24	10A	Dip Beam RH
25	3A	EEC IV Module
27	10A	Stop Lamps, Heated Washer Jets

KEY TO SYMBOLS

PLUG-IN CONNECTOR	
EARTH	
BULB	
DIODE	
FUSE	
SOLDERED JOINT	S1012

INTERNAL CONNECTION DETAILS

a = Alternator Warning Lamp
b = Handbrake Warning Lamp
c = Main Beam Warning Lamp
d = Instrument Illumination
e = Fuel Gauge
f = Temperature Gauge
g = Oil Pressure Lamp
h = Tachometer
i = Voltage Stabilizer
j = ABS Warning Lamp
k = Choke Warning Lamp
l = Flasher Warning Lamp LH
m = Flasher Warning Lamp RH

KEY TO INSTRUMENT CLUSTER
    (ITEM 97)

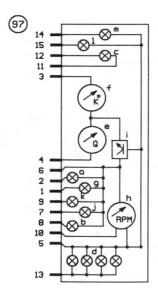

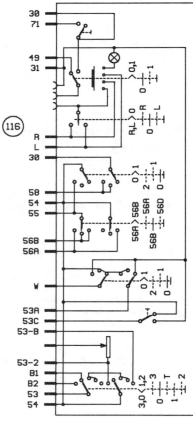

H24160

Key to wiring diagrams

ITEM	DESCRIPTION	DIAGRAM/ GRID REF.
1	ABS Hydraulic Control Unit	3b/D7
2	ABS Hydraulic Motor	3b/C7
3	ABS Module	3b/D1
4	ABS Pump Relay	3b/J1
5	ABS System Relay	3b/J3
6	Air Temp. Sensor	1a/C5, 1b/C2, 4/C2, 4a/C2
7	Alternator	1/A2, 3/B3
8	Amplifier (Audio)	5/G7
9	Anti-theft 'Alarm On' Indicator	5a/H4, 5b/H5
10	Anti-theft Bonnet Switch	5a/A2, 5b/A2
11	Anti-theft Door Lock Switch LH	5a/K7, 5b/J8
12	Anti-theft Door Lock Switch RH	5a/K2, 5b/J2
13	Anti-theft Door Switch LH Front	5a/K8, 5b/K8
14	Anti-theft Door Switch LH Rear	5a/M8, 5b/M8
15	Anti-theft Door Switch RH Front	5a/K1, 5b/K1
16	Anti-theft Door Switch RH Rear	5a/M1, 5b/M1
17	Anti-theft Horn	5a/C1, 5b/B1
18	Anti-theft Module	5a/G7, 5b/E8
19	Anti-theft Tailgate Switch	5a/M5, 5b/M4
20	Auto. Trans. Inhibitor Switch	1b/F7, 2/B6
21	Auto. Trans. Relay	1b/H4
22	Auto. Trans. Selector Illumination	2b/L4
23	Battery	1/G8, 1a/H4, 1a/H8, 1b/J8, 2/F8, 2a/F8, 2b/C8, 3/D8, 3a/D8, 3b/J8, 4/L8, 4a/L8, 5/C4, 5/C8, 5a/D8, 5b/C8
24	Canister Purge Solenoid	4/B1, 4a/B1
25	Central Locking Motor LH Front	3a/K8, 5b/J7
26	Central Locking Motor LH Rear	3a/L8, 5b/L7
27	Central Locking Motor RH Front	3a/K1, 5b/J2
28	Central Locking Motor RH Rear	3a/L1, 5b/L2
29	CFI Power Delay Relay	4/K3
30	Choke Switch	1/K3
31	Cigar Lighter	2b/J7
32	Clock	2b/E6
33	CO Adjuster Potentiometer	4a/B7
34	Coolant Temp. Gauge Sender Unit	1/B5
35	Cooling Fan Motor	1/A6
36	Cooling Fan Switch	1/B6
37	Crank Position Sensor	1a/E2, 1a/E6, 1b/D5, 4/D5, 4a/D5
38	Dim/Dip Relay (Dimmer Relay 1)	2/G3, 2a/F4
39	Dim/Dip Relay (Dimmer Relay 2)	2/F2, 2a/E3
40	Dip Beam Relay	2/E4, 2a/C5
41	Direction Indicator Flasher Relay	2a/K3
42	Direction Indicator Lamp LH	2a/A8
43	Direction Indicator Lamp RH	2a/A1
44	Direction Indicator Side Repeater LH	2a/C8
45	Direction Indicator Side Repeater RH	2a/C1
46	EDIS Module	4/C8, 4a/C8
47	EEC IV Module	4/H8, 4a/H8
48	EFI Power Delay Relay	4a/K3
49	Electric Door Mirror Control Switch	3/H3
50	Electric Door Mirror LH	3/H8
51	Electric Door Mirror RH	3/H1
52	Electric Window Control Switch LH	2b/K6, 3a/K5
53	Electric Window Control Switch RH	2b/K4, 3a/K4
54	Electric Window Motor LH	3a/J8
55	Electric Window Motor RH	3a/J1
56	Electric Window Relay	3a/D4
57	Engine Run Relay	3/C4
58	Engine Temp. Sensor	1a/A2, 1a/A6, 1b/B6, 4/B6, 4a/B5
59	ESC 2 Ignition Module	1a/B4
60	ESCP 1 Ignition Module	1a/B8
61	ESCP 2 Ignition Module	1b/C8
62	Foglamp Front LH	2a/A6
63	Foglamp Front RH	2a/A3
64	Foglamp Relay Front	2a/C4
65	Foglamp Switch Front	2a/K1, 2b/J2
66	Foglamp Switch Rear	2a/K6, 2b/J6
67	Footwell Lamp LH	2b/E8
68	Footwell Lamp RH	2b/E1
69	Fuel Gauge Sender Unit	1/M5
70	Fuel Injectors	4/E2, 4a/E4
71	Fuel Pump	4/M5, 4a/M5
72	Fuel Pump Relay	4/K1, 4a/K1
73	Fuel Shut Off Solenoid	1a/D1, 1a/D5
74	Glove Box Lamp/Switch	2b/F7
75	Handbrake Warning Switch	1/K5
76	Headlamp Unit LH	2/A7
77	Headlamp Unit RH	2/A2
78	Headlamp Washer Relay	3a/D2
79	Heated Rear Window	3/M4
80	Heated Rear Window Relay	3/C3
81	Heated Rear Window Switch	2b/J5, 3/K3
82	Heated Washer Jet LH	3/A8
83	Heated Washer Jet RH	3/A1
84	Heated Windscreen	3/H6
85	Heated Windscreen De-ice Relay	3/E4
86	Heated Windscreen Relay	3/F8
87	Heated Windscreen Switch	2b/J2, 3/L1
88	Heater Blower Motor	3/K7
89	Heater Blower Switch	3/L5
90	Heater Blower Switch Illumination	2b/F6
91	Horn	3/A2, 3/A3
92	Idle Speed Solenoid	4a/D3

H24161

Key to wiring diagrams (continued)

ITEM	DESCRIPTION	DIAGRAM/ GRID REF.
93	Ignition Coil	1a/D2, 1a/D6, 1b/C4, 4/C3, 4a/C3
94	Ignition Relay	1/E2, 1a/J1, 1a/J5, 1b/H2, 2/E1, 2a/C2, 2b/A2, 3/C1, 3a/C3, 3b/G3, 4/H1, 4a/H2, 5a/E2, 5b/D1
95	Ignition Switch	1/K2, 1a/M2, 1a/M6, 1b/M2, 2/K2, 2a/K2, 2b/K3, 3/L2, 3a/H2, 3b/M2, 4/M2, 4a/M2, 5/G1, 5/G5, 5a/H2, 5b/G2
96	Inertia Switch	4/G1, 4a/G1
97	Injector Ballast Resistor	4/F2
98	Instrument Cluster	1/J3, 1a/L2, 1a/L6, 1b/K3, 2/J3, 2a/J3, 2b/J4, 3b/L4, 4/M4, 4a/M4
99	Interior Lamp Delay Relay	2b/B4
100	Interior Lamp Door Switch LH Front	2b/F8
101	Interior Lamp Door Switch LH Rear	2b/M8
102	Interior Lamp Door Switch RH Front	2b/F1, 3a/G1
103	Interior Lamp Door Switch RH Rear	2b/M1
104	Interior Lamp/Switch	2b/L5
105	Lambda Sensor	4/E5, 4a/E5
106	Lamp Cluster LH Rear	2/M7, 2a/M7
107	Lamp Cluster RH Rear	2/M2, 2a/M2
108	Link (Fitted To Manual Models – With Alarm)	5a/E2, 5b/D2
109	Link (Fitted When Manual Trans.)	1/F3
110	Link (Fitted To Models Without Alarm)	1a/J2, 1a/J6
111	Link (Fitted To Models Without Intermittent Rear Wash/Wipe)	3a/D5
112	Low Brake Fluid Sender Unit	1/D6
113	Luggage Comp. Lamp	2b/M5
114	Luggage Comp. Lamp Switch	2b/M6
115	Main Beam Relay	2/H4, 2a/G5
116	MAP Sensor	4/D1, 4a/D1

ITEM	DESCRIPTION	DIAGRAM/ GRID REF.
117	Maxi-Fusebox	1/F7, 1a/G4, 1a/G7, 1b/H7, 2/E7, 2a/E7, 2b/B7, 3/D7, 3a/D7, 3b/H7, 4/K7, 4a/K7, 5/B3, 5/B7, 5a/C7, 5b/B7
118	Multi-Function Switch	2/K4, 2a/L4, 2b/J5, 3/M4, 3a/J4, 5/J2, 5/J6
119	Number Plate Lamp	2/M4, 2a/M4
120	Oil Pressure Switch	1/C5
121	Power Delay Relay	1b/J3
122	Radio Illumination	2b/F6
123	Radio Unit	5/H3, 5/G8
124	Reversing Lamp Switch	2/B5
125	Spark Plugs	1a/D3, 1a/D7, 1b/C4, 4/C4, 4a/C4
126	Speaker LH Front	5/E4, 5/E8
127	Speaker LH Rear	5/L4, 5/L8
128	Speaker RH Front	5/E1, 5/E5
129	Speaker RH Rear	5/L1, 5/L5
130	Speed Sensor	4/E5, 4a/E5
131	Starter Motor	1/C6
132	Stop Lamp Switch	2/C2
133	Stop Lamp Switch/ABS Pedal Sensor	3b/F3
134	Suppressor	1a/B2, 1a/B6, 1a/C4, 1a/C8, 1b/B3, 1b/F8, 4/B2, 4/D8, 4a/B2, 4a/D8
135	Tailgate Release Motor	5b/M5
136	Tailgate Release Switch	5b/J4
137	Throttle Control Motor	1b/D3, 4/D3
138	Throttle Position Sensor	1b/D4, 4/D3, 4a/D3
139	Washer Pump Front/Rear Screen	3a/A8
140	Washer Pump Headlamp	3a/B8
141	Wiper Intermittent Relay Front	3a/F5
142	Wiper Intermittent Relay Rear	3a/D5
143	Wiper Motor Front	3a/B3
144	Wiper Motor Rear	3a/M4
145	Wheel Sensor LH	3b/A8
146	Wheel Sensor RH	3b/A1

H24162

Key to wiring diagrams (continued)

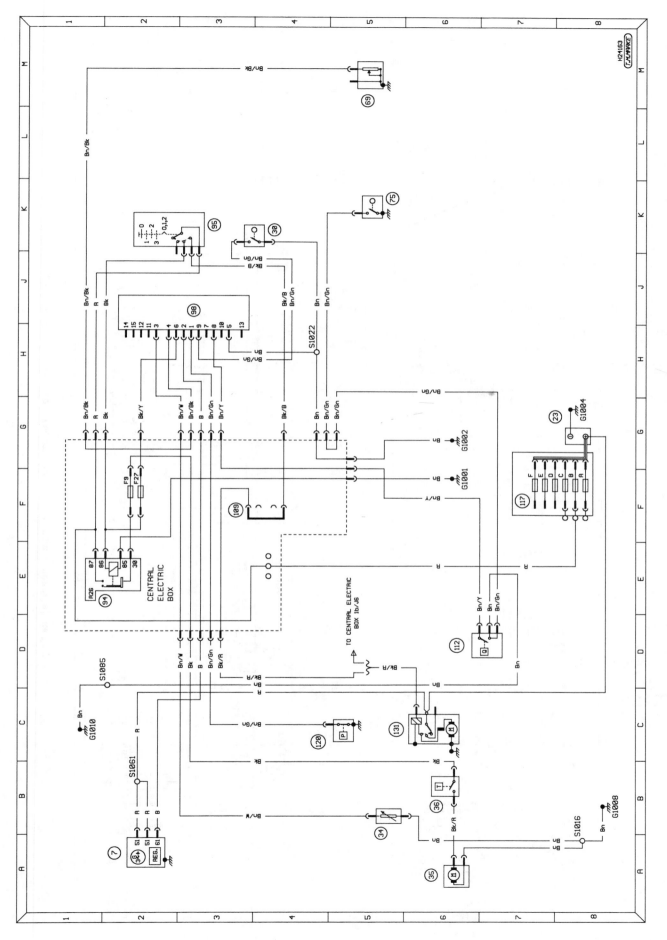

Diagram 1: Starting, charging, cooling fan, gauges and warning lamps

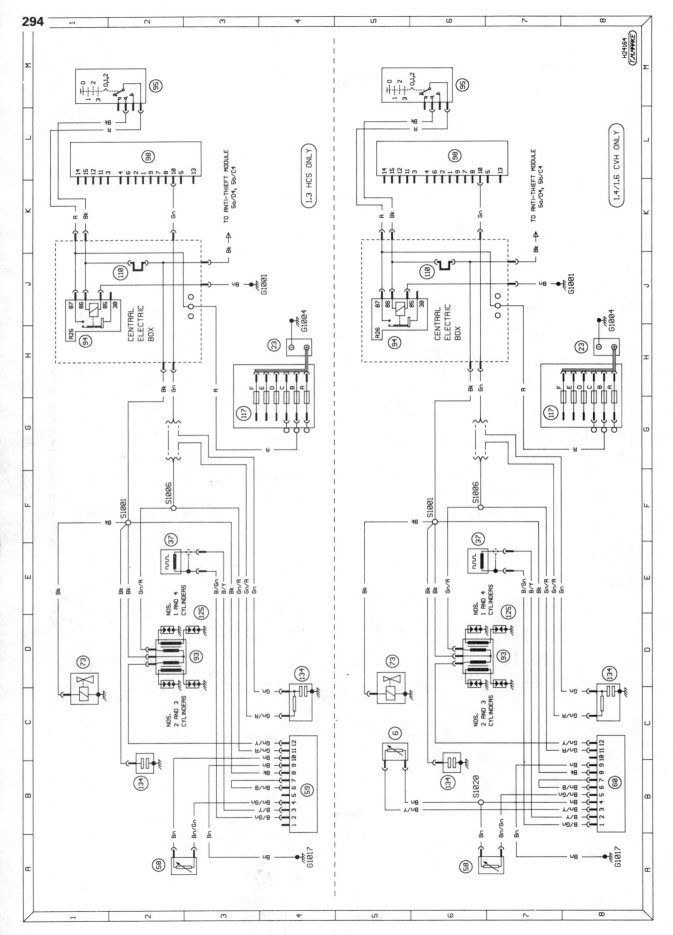

Diagram 1a: Ignition variation – all carburettor-engined models (manual gearbox)

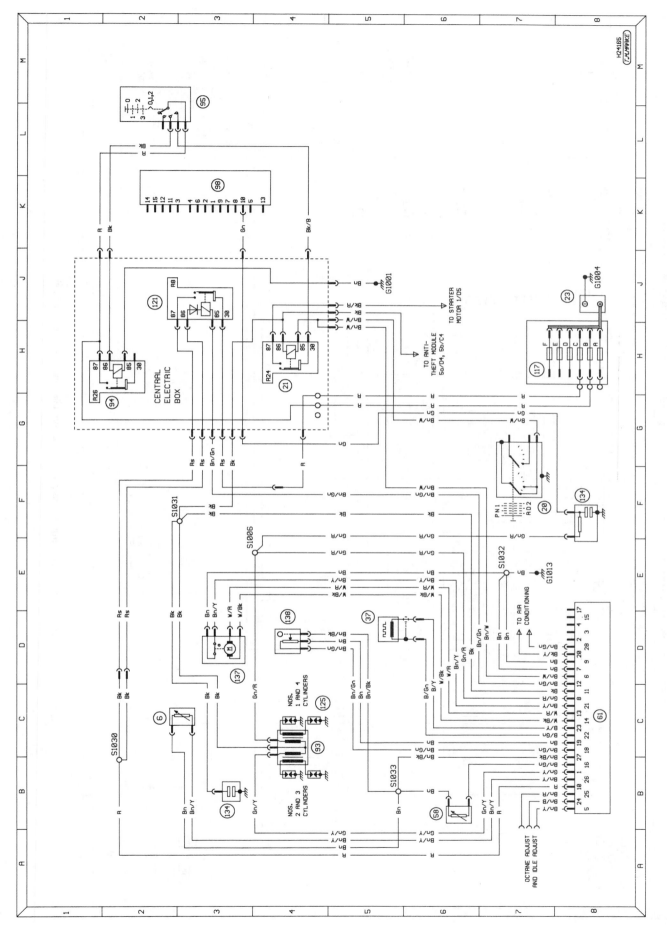

H24185

Diagram 1b: Ignition variation – 1.6 CVH-engined model (automatic transmission)

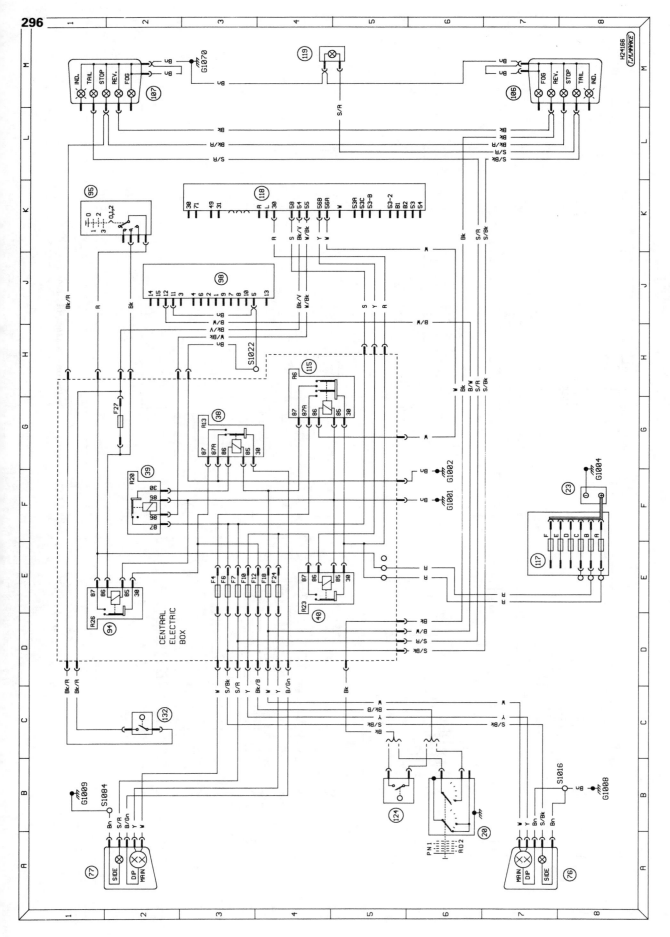

Diagram 2: Exterior lighting – head/side, stop and reversing lamps (all models)

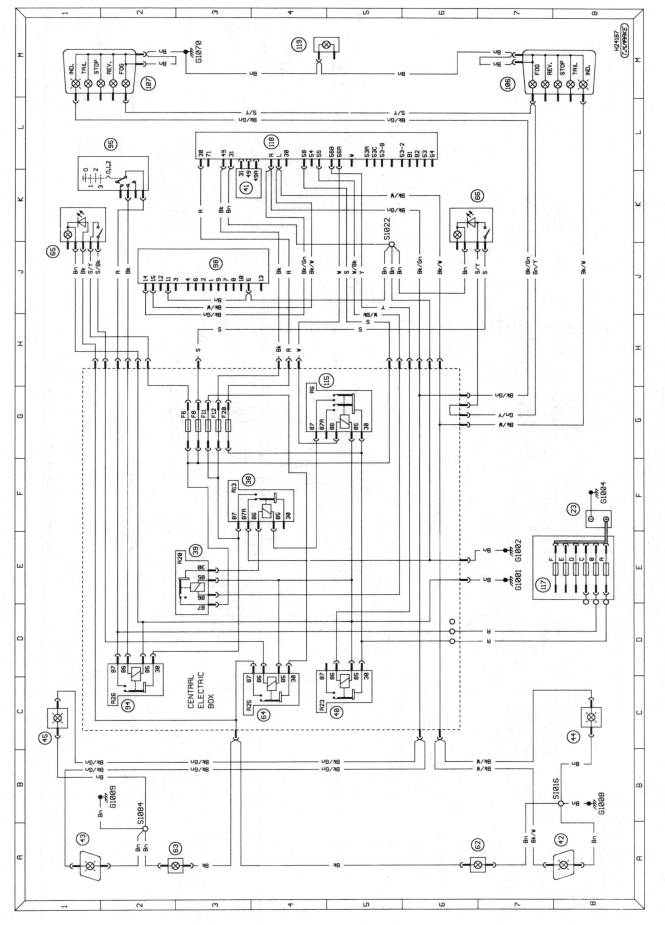

Diagram 2a: Exterior lighting – fog and direction indicator lamps (all models)

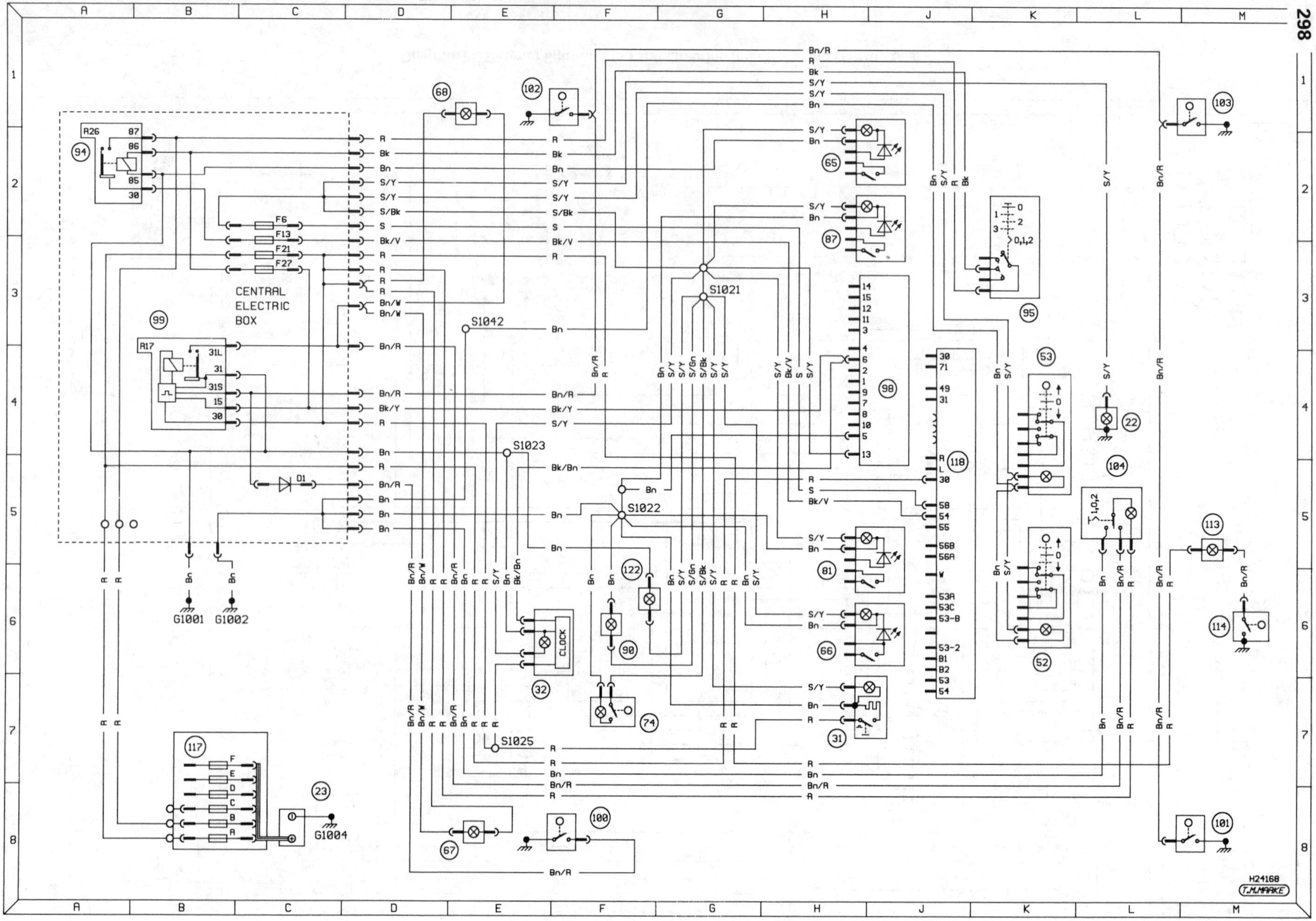

Diagram 2b: Interior lighting – all models

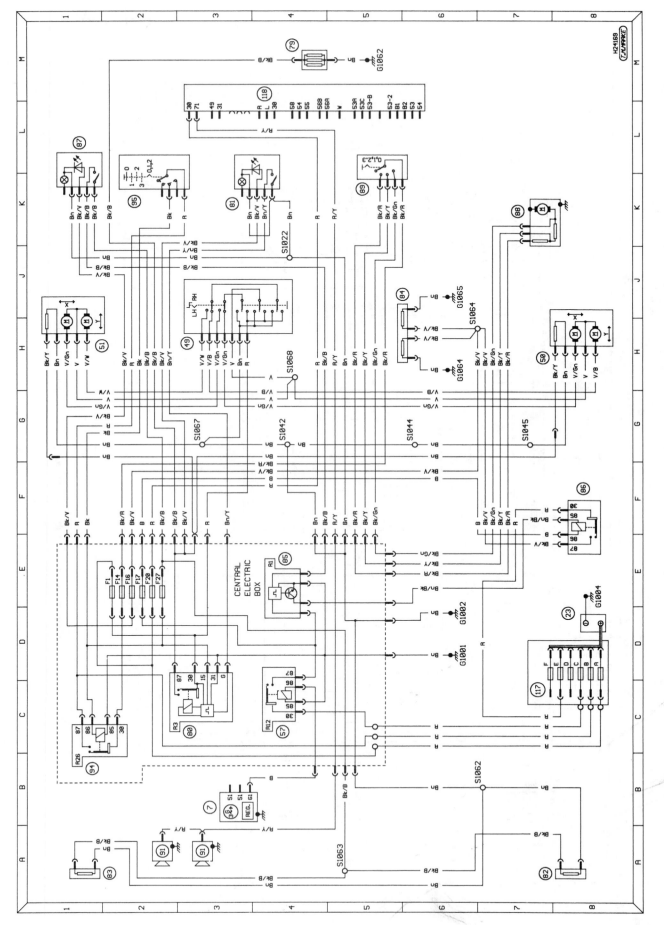

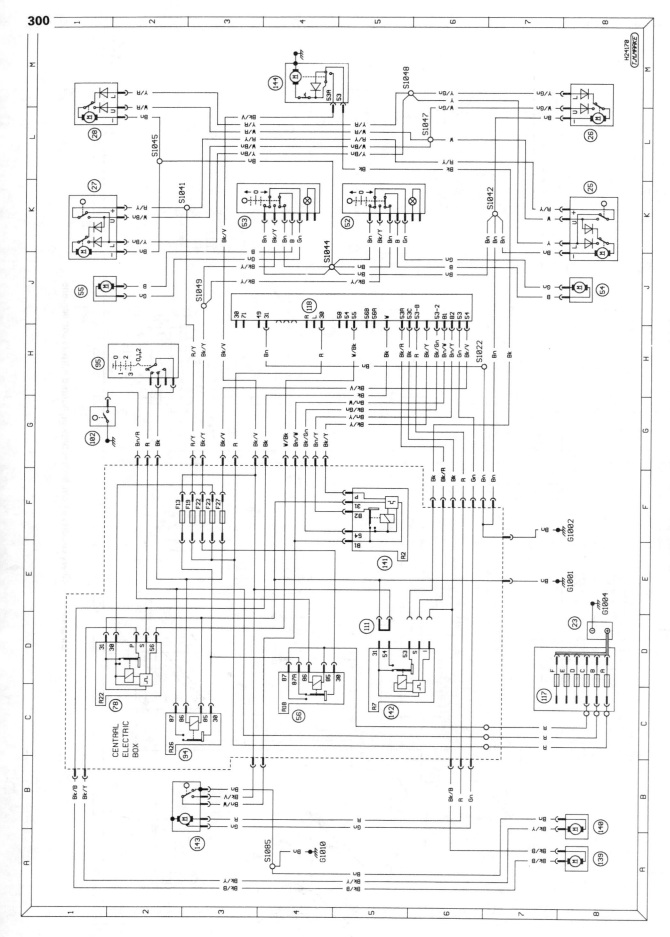

Diagram 3a: Ancillary circuits – wash/wipe, central locking and electric windows

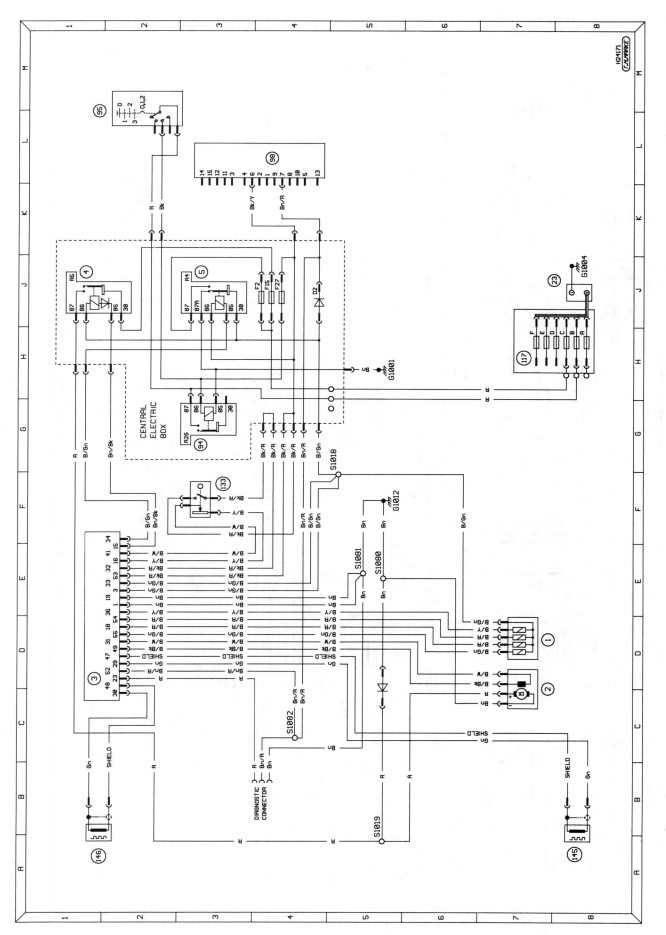

Diagram 3b: Anti-lock braking system

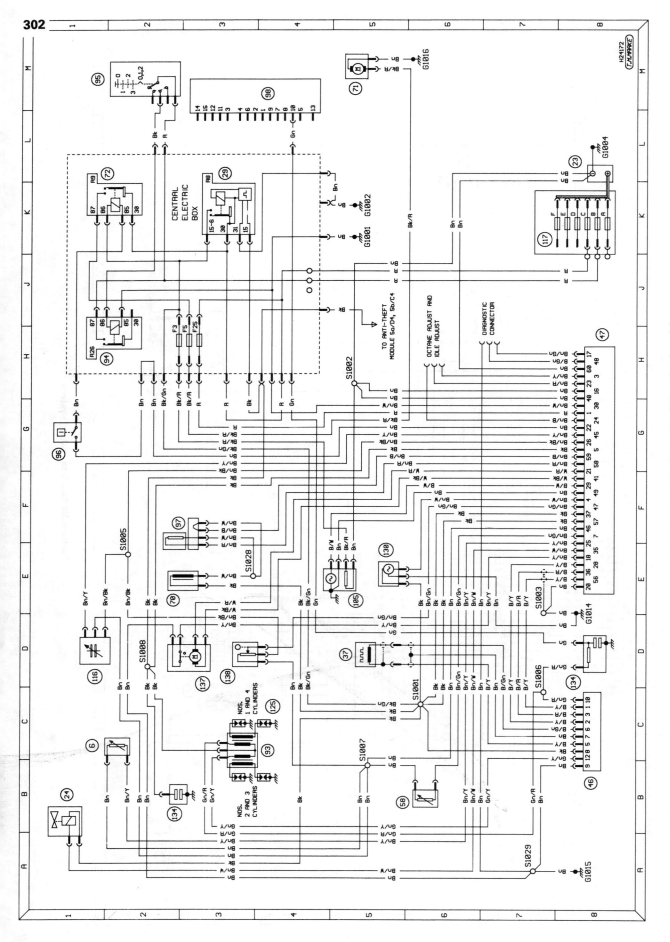

H24172

Diagram 4: Fuel injection and ignition – 1.4 CFi-engined model

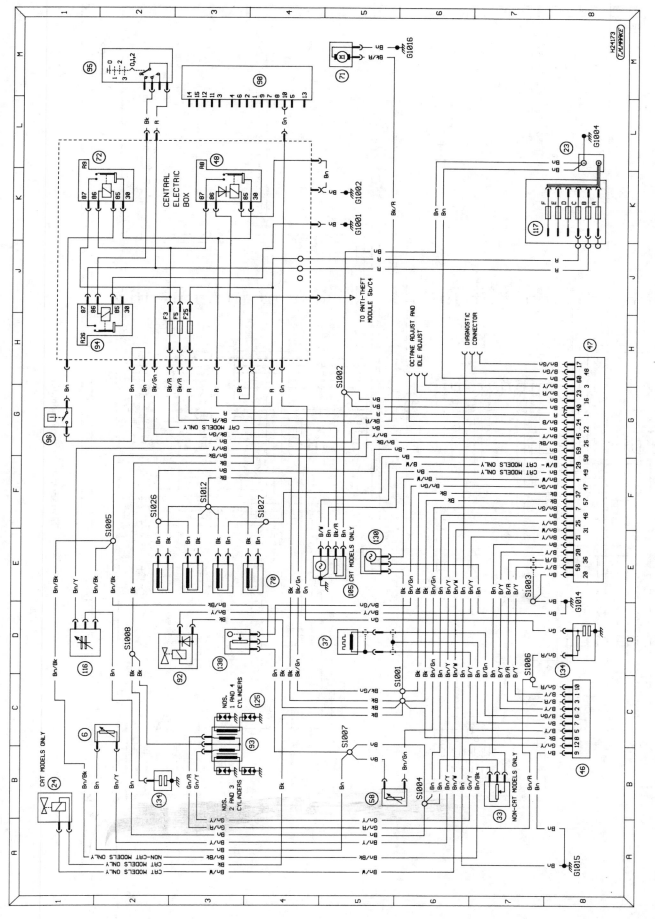

Diagram 4a: Fuel injection and ignition – 1.6 EFi-engined model

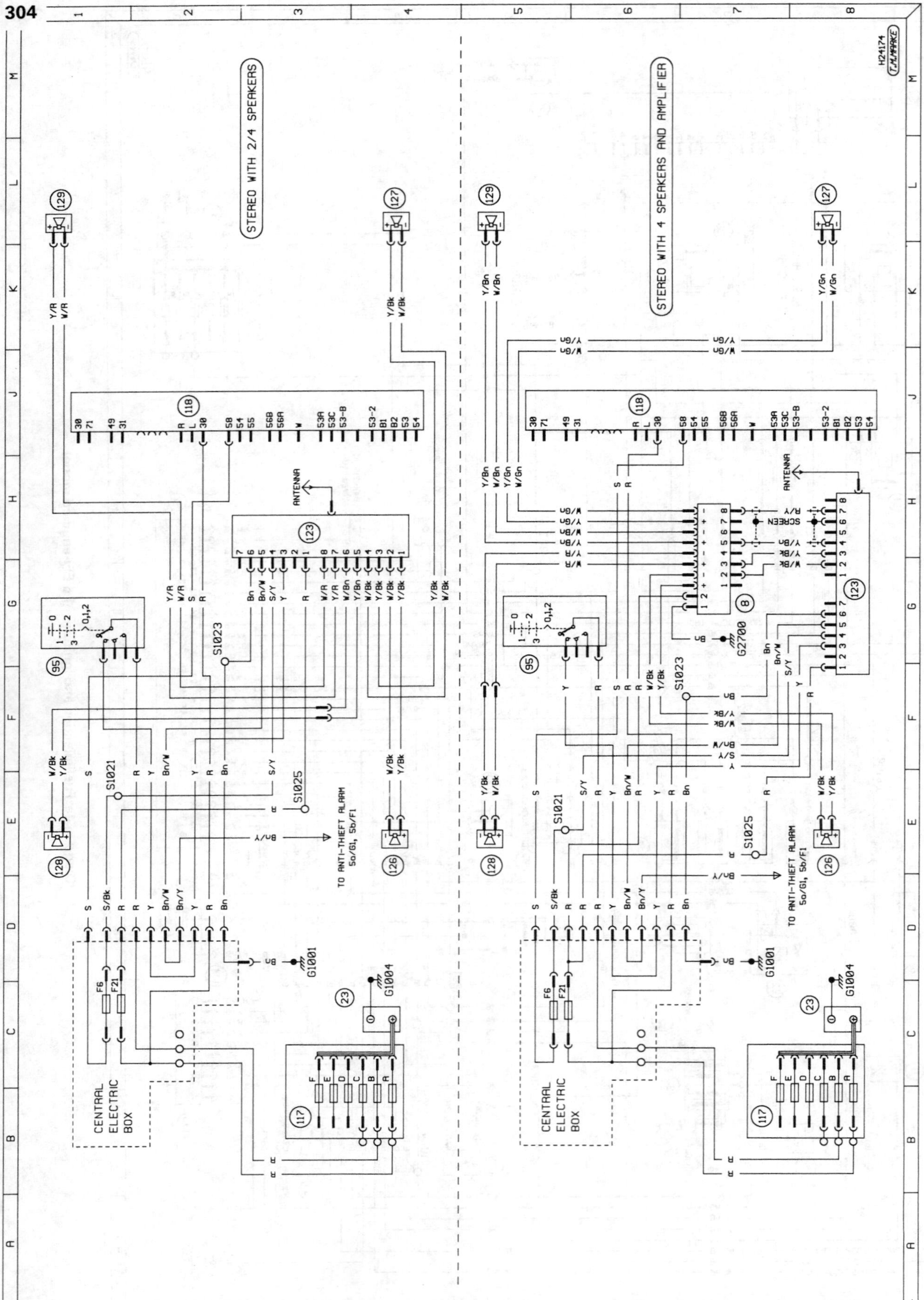

STEREO WITH 2/4 SPEAKERS

STEREO WITH 4 SPEAKERS AND AMPLIFIER

H24174

ANTENNA

CENTRAL ELECTRIC BOX

TO ANTI-THEFT ALARM 5a/G1, 5b/F1

G1001

G1004

G2700

SCREEN

S1021

S1023

S1025

Diagram 5: In-car entertainment

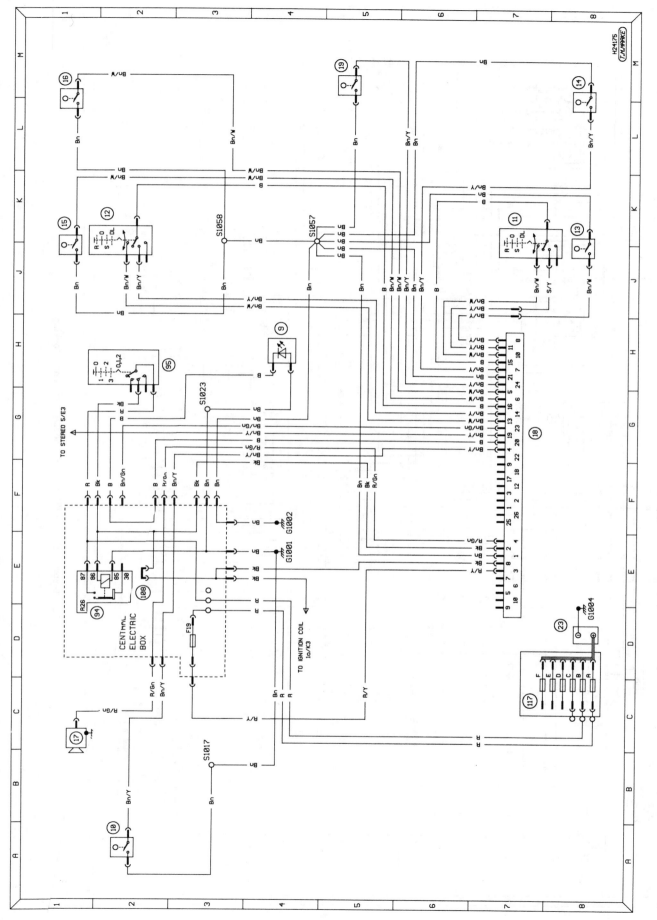

Diagram 5a: Anti-theft alarm – models without central locking

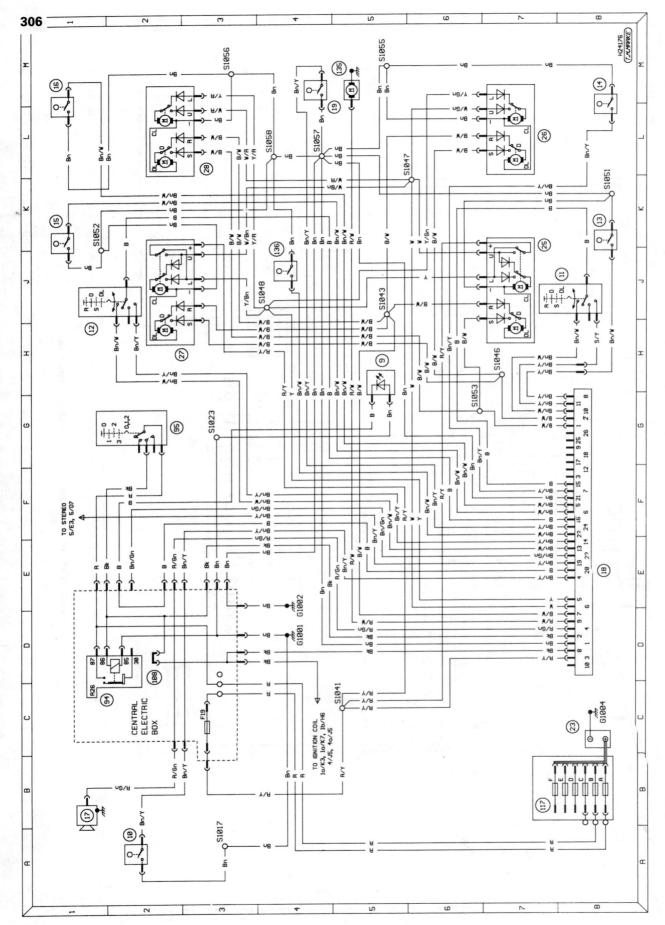

Diagram 5b: Anti-theft alarm – models with central locking

Index